DISTANT FRIENDS AND INTIMATE ENEMIES

This bold, sweeping history of the turbulent American–Russian relationship is unique in being written jointly by American and Russian authors. David Foglesong, Ivan Kurilla, and Victoria Zhuravleva together reveal how and why America and Russia shifted from being warm friends and even tacit allies to being ideological rivals, geopolitical adversaries, and demonic foils used in the construction or affirmation of their national identities. As well as examining diplomatic, economic, and military interactions between the two countries, they illuminate how filmmakers, cartoonists, writers, missionaries, and political activists have admired, disparaged, lionized, envied, satirized, loved, and hated people in the other land. The book shows how the stories they told and the images they created have shaped how the two countries have understood each other from the eighteenth century to the present. It also reveals how often their clashes have arisen from misunderstandings and misrepresentations.

David S. Foglesong is Professor of History at Rutgers University. He is the author of *The American Mission and the "Evil Empire": The Crusade for a "Free Russia" since 1881* and *America's Secret War against Bolshevism: U.S. Intervention in the Russian Civil War, 1917–1920.*

Ivan Kurilla is a professor of history at Ohio State University. He previously taught at the European University at St. Petersburg before being forced to leave Russia in 2024. He is the author of *Transoceanic Partners: America and Russia in the 1830s–1850s, Frenemies: History of Opinions, Phantasies, Contacts, Mutual (Mis)Understanding of Russia and the USA,* and *Americans and All the Rest* (all in Russian).

Victoria I. Zhuravleva is Professor of History and Chair of the Department of American Studies at the Russian State University for the Humanities, Moscow, Russia. She is the author of *Understanding Russia in the United States: Images and Myths* (in Russian) and *The Common Past of Russians and Americans* (both in Russian and in English).

DISTANT FRIENDS AND INTIMATE ENEMIES

A History of American–Russian Relations

David S. Foglesong
Rutgers University, New Jersey

Ivan Kurilla
Ohio State University

Victoria I. Zhuravleva
Russian State University for the Humanities, Moscow

CAMBRIDGE
UNIVERSITY PRESS

Shaftesbury Road, Cambridge CB2 8EA, United Kingdom

One Liberty Plaza, 20th Floor, New York, NY 10006, USA

477 Williamstown Road, Port Melbourne, VIC 3207, Australia

314–321, 3rd Floor, Plot 3, Splendor Forum, Jasola District Centre, New Delhi – 110025, India

103 Penang Road, #05–06/07, Visioncrest Commercial, Singapore 238467

Cambridge University Press is part of Cambridge University Press & Assessment, a department of the University of Cambridge.

We share the University's mission to contribute to society through the pursuit of education, learning and research at the highest international levels of excellence.

www.cambridge.org
Information on this title: www.cambridge.org/9780521111058

DOI: 10.1017/9780511844126

First published 2025

Cover image: Political Cartoon of Uncle Sam Talking to Russian Bear by William A. Rogers. Bettmann / Getty Images

Printed in the United Kingdom by CPI Group Ltd, Croydon CR0 4YY

A catalogue record for this publication is available from the British Library

A Cataloging-in-Publication data record for this book is available from the Library of Congress

ISBN 978-0-521-11105-8 Hardback

Cambridge University Press & Assessment has no responsibility for the persistence or accuracy of URLs for external or third-party internet websites referred to in this publication and does not guarantee that any content on such websites is, or will remain, accurate or appropriate.

For EU product safety concerns, contact us at Calle de José Abascal, 56, 1°, 28003 Madrid, Spain, or email eugpsr@cambridge.org

Contents

Figures

Acknowledgments

After working on this book for many, many years, we are pleased to express our deep appreciation to the people who have helped us complete this project (though we do not have space to name all of them). Above all, we are grateful to Michael Watson, Executive Publisher for History at Cambridge University Press. He first suggested that we write a new, comprehensive history of American–Russian relations after an excellent survey by John Lewis Gaddis went out of print. In the following years, Michael provided detailed comments and sound advice on our draft chapters. We thank Michael for his patience and his wise guidance. Also at Cambridge University Press, Editorial Assistant Rosa Martin has answered numerous questions as she expertly steered our completed typescript into production. Three anonymous external reviewers provided thoughtful comments on our work. We thank them for helping us to improve the book.

As we note in the Introduction, *Distant Friends and Intimate Enemies* builds upon the foundation established by historians who wrote sweeping examinations of American–Russian relations in previous decades. We are especially indebted to the outstanding work of Nikolai Bolkhovitinov, Norman Saul, and John Lewis Gaddis.

David Foglesong expresses his special gratitude to Xiaohui ("Sophie") Dang for the many ways she assisted and supported his work on this book. In addition to providing steady encouragement, she made travel arrangements, journeyed with him to distant archives, and even assisted with the photographing of many documents. He also thanks the US Embassy in Moscow, the Kennan Institute, and the Rutgers University Global Travel Grants program for financial support of travel to Russia, as well as the Rutgers Research Council for funding research at the University of Arkansas.

Ivan Kurilla extends his gratitude to Liudmila for her steadfast support of his work, both during peaceful times and amid the challenges of emigration. Despite the difficult circumstances that led to his dismissal during the war, he also wishes to acknowledge the European University at

St. Petersburg, which was an exceptional place for research in Russia. Additionally, he is grateful to Wellesley College, Bowdoin College, and Ohio State University for their assistance when it was most needed. Special thanks go to Professors Nina Tumarkin, William G. Rosenberg and Angela Brintlinger for their unwavering support, as well as to colleagues in the field of Russian–American history, both in the United States and in Russia.

Victoria Zhuravleva is deeply grateful to Alexander for his long-term support of her never-ending research projects and assistance with the preparing of cartoons for publication. She expresses her special thanks to the people at the Library of Congress, the National Archives, the Foreign Policy Archive of Imperial Russia, and the State Historical Library who helped her to collect materials. She also would like to acknowledge the Fulbright Program and the Kennan Institute, which provided financial support of her trip to the United States. Last but not least, she wishes to express her great appreciation to specialists on US–Russia relations from both sides of the Atlantic for the exchange of ideas within international conferences, including those she organized in Moscow at the Russian State University for the Humanities.

INTRODUCTION

After thousands of Poles revolted against Russian rule in January 1863 – a critical moment during the American Civil War – many in the Union faced a moral and ideological dilemma. Should they be faithful to the traditional American sympathy for brave rebels against Old World monarchies? Or should they side with Imperial Russia, which many had long seen as the only friendly power in Europe? The debate in northern newspapers centered less on factual information than on questions of identity. Was autocratic Russia, as it brutally suppressed the Polish Insurrection, a barbaric empire unlike republican America? Or was Russia, like the United States, a Christian power, whose Tsar Alexander II emancipated its serfs shortly before President Abraham Lincoln issued the Emancipation Proclamation and who suppressed secession much as the North fought the South? Southern editors' commentary also often revolved around issues of positioning, with sneering parallels drawn between "Alexander II and Abraham I" and analogies made between the struggles of Poland and the Confederacy – thus giving the same comparisons opposite meanings.[1]

When Russia sent warships from the Baltic and Pacific to New York and San Francisco in the fall of 1863, the debate in the North briefly gave way to almost unanimous and euphoric welcomes of the Russian fleets, which many believed deterred British and French intervention on the side of the Confederacy. As lavish balls feted the Russian officers, many editors rapturously explained why Americans were like Russians, citing the vast sweep of their territorial expansion and the huge growth of their populations, as well as the abolition of serfdom and slavery. Russia had its own reasons for sending the ships – to avoid having them bottled up in the Baltic by the British Navy, and to put them in position to prey upon British and French commercial shipping in the event of a clash over the rebellion in Poland. Yet the ways Americans hailed the Russian warships reflected a widespread belief in a genuine and enduring friendship between the two giant and distant countries. Many Russians, including the admiral who commanded the ships at San Francisco, shared that sentiment.[2]

1

As the episode reflects, American–Russian relations have often been a focus of contestation over national identities and destinies. For example, while some American writers in the nineteenth century depicted Russian fighting against Circassians as an advance of civilization like America's wars against Indians, others rejected the parallel and likened the peoples of the Caucasus to the heroic warriors of ancient Greece, birthplace of democracy. Although many African American leaders compared pogroms in Russia to lynching and race riots in the United States, many white Americans denied the analogy or insisted that pogroms were much, much worse. While the United States was a model of freedom to many liberal intellectuals in Russia from the late eighteenth century to the twenty-first, it exemplified a money-mad materialism and vicious racism to other Russian writers, who extolled Russia's superior spirituality and its supposed banishment of racial discrimination.

The enormous enthusiasm about the Russian fleets in the Union in 1863 also illustrates how the United States and Russia have not always been rivals, adversaries, or enemies. From the mutual diplomatic recognition at the start of the nineteenth century to the 1890s, the American republic and the Russian autocracy had very warm and friendly relations. Despite the differences between their political systems, ideologies, cultural values, and religious beliefs, Americans and Russians[3] perceived common enemies (Britain and France) and important mutual interests (particularly freedom of the seas and trade). Although commercial competition in the Far East and American public revulsion at anti-Semitism and political repression in the Russian empire strained ties in the early twentieth century, friendly relations returned during the First World War, when the United States was a vital source of munitions and loans for Russia. Even as the United States intervened against Bolshevism during the Russian Revolutions and Civil War, it upheld the principle of Russian territorial integrity (apart from the independence of Finland and Poland). While Washington refused to recognize Soviet Russia from 1917 to 1933, Bolshevik leaders greatly admired Americans' advanced technology, which played a vital role in the rapid modernization of the Five-Year Plans. During the Second World War, the United States and the Soviet Union were allies, and when the war ended most people in both countries believed in the possibility of postwar cooperation. Even during the "Cold War" between 1947 and 1989, there were important phases of reduced tensions when leaders of the two countries focused more on the common interests of avoiding nuclear war, controlling the arms race, and expanding trade. Finally, after the Cold War, US and Russian leaders repeatedly made serious efforts to develop an economic and strategic partnership.

It is therefore not true, as President Vladimir Putin and other prominent Russians have asserted, that the United States (and the West in general) have always sought to contain or break up Russia.[4] It is also not correct that "there has actually never been a period of sustained good relations between Russia and the United States," as a distinguished historian wrote in the premier journal of the American foreign policy establishment.[5]

In contrast to views of American–Russian conflict as inherent, inevitable, and perpetual, we emphasize in this book how often clashes have arisen from misunderstandings, illusions, exaggerations, and sensationalist distortions. Thus, false assertions that the tsarist government deliberately instigated a horrible pogrom at Kishinev in 1903 inflamed the rupture in American–Russian relations in the early twentieth century. Erroneous claims that the Soviet government was inciting communist revolutions in the United States and Western Europe after the Second World War figured importantly in the outbreak of what Americans called a "cold war." Unwarranted fears in this century that Washington seriously sought to spark a "color revolution" inside Russia spurred and justified internal repression by the Kremlin that appalled and alienated many Americans.

Some have argued that the problems in US–Russian relations have stemmed not from misunderstandings, but from "divergent fundamental values and state interests."[6] Yet, as many scholars have recognized, perceptions of international threats are subjective, and definitions of interests are contested. It is therefore essential to examine how international "realities" have been imagined and how foreign policy outlooks have been constructed.[7]

As we examine the many shifts from friendly to hostile or from adversarial to amicable relations, then, we focus above all on the stories Americans and Russians have told and the images they have produced. In other words, we concentrate on the discourses that have shaped how Russians and Americans have understood or misunderstood each other. As political scientist Ronald Krebs has argued, "rhetorical contests shape the course of politics," and facts or events are given meaning when woven into stories.[8] We do not merely document the manifold mutual perceptions of Russians and Americans. Instead, we investigate the motivations and consequences of the storytelling and image-making. We show how old narratives have been challenged or discarded, with new dominant narratives resetting the boundaries of debate. We also reveal how the hierarchies of images have changed, with some being featured and others being marginalized.

Our focus on how words and images have generated meanings and influenced policies does not mean that we ignore how leaders of states have pursued geopolitical interests or responded to international pressures – themes emphasized by "realist" scholars of international relations. Yet, in contrast to realists, we do not see interests as simply existing objectively due to geography or economics, and we highlight the influence of non-state as well as state actors (as many "liberal" students of international relations do). While "liberal" scholars have stressed the autocratic or democratic nature of regimes as drivers of international relations, we highlight the ups and downs in American–Russian relations within periods when the types of regimes did not change significantly.[9]

Our "constructivist" approach reveals how persistently the process of constructing national identity both in Russia (be it the Russian Empire, the USSR, or post-Soviet Russia) and in the United States has revolved around images of "the Self" and "the Other." We study how Russians and Americans created knowledge about each other in relation to their nation-building and as part of the development of their self-images. Each of the countries at any historical moment produced multiple images of itself, but it was the "watching" society that selected features of the Other for use in domestic political debates. Therefore, we analyze when and why Americans used Russia's image and Russians used America's image over centuries.[10]

To many Americans and Russians, the other country not only posed threats of aggression and subversion, but also constituted the polar opposite of their own values and national identity. American politicians and journalists often depicted bloody Russian "Oriental" or "Asiatic" despotism as the antithesis of peace-loving American or Western democracy and freedom. Russian political and media figures, in turn, condemned American arrogant universalism and hypocrisy as contrasts to Russia's defense of national sovereignty and faithfulness. In both cases, focusing on the evils of the foreign nation deflected attention from the home nation's faults and affirmed its virtues.[11] Such scapegoating, with the projection onto a foreign nation of traits people wish to downplay or disregard in their own society, has been common in the construction of images of enemies.[12] Yet it has been unusually intense and pervasive in American–Russian relations. More than any other foreign foes that the two nations had fought in the past, America and Russia became intimate enemies.

Although other pairs of countries have also been central to the shaping of each other's identities for extended periods, Russia and the United States have been imaginary twins or alter egos more persistently than any other couple.[13] Until late in the nineteenth century, Great Britain was arguably the most important Other both for the United States and for Russia.[14] Yet, after the Anglo-American rapprochement in the 1890s, Britain's place in American demonology was taken briefly by Spain and Germany, and more enduringly by Russia.[15] True, Anglophobia persisted among Irish Americans

4

and others in the United States in the first half of the twentieth century, but it largely died out with the decline and decolonization of the British empire.[16] After the Anglo-Russian entente of 1907, Britain and Russia ceased being archenemies for a time, and the revival of their enmity after 1917 was not as obsessive or widespread as in the nineteenth century.[17]

Even China and the United States have not been as mutually constitutive for as long as Russia and America have been. One distinguished historian argued that Americans have had a uniquely intense and enduring preoccupation with China.[18] Yet Americans have also had a lasting obsession with Russia, and the United States has not been as vital to Chinese dreams and hatreds as it has been to Russians'.[19] In a valuable study of persistent American stereotypes in the twentieth century, Donald Davis and Eugene Trani contrasted positive and romantic views of China to continuing negative and hostile views of Russia.[20] Yet, as we show, American attitudes toward Russia have actually swung between enthusiasm and antipathy, with the casting of Russia as alternately an object of an American mission and a demonic foil for affirmation of American moral superiority being a key reason for the special significance of the American–Russian relationship across three centuries.

Several scholars before us have written accounts of the full history of Russian–American relations, and their books were all shaped by the times in which they wrote. During the Second World War, when the United States and the Soviet Union were allies, Foster Rhea Dulles traced the relations between the two peoples in the hope of assisting efforts to find "an enduring basis for understanding and good will."[21] As postwar relations deteriorated, Vera Micheles Dean still expressed hope that the two great powers could be peacetime allies, yet she exaggerated continuities between tsarist and Soviet absolutism in a way that unintentionally foreshadowed subsequent American demonization of Russia.[22] With Soviet–American hostility peaking by 1950, Thomas Bailey claimed that tsarism had been as hostile to democracy as was Stalinism and tried to show that the idea of a historic Russian–American friendship was a myth.[23] Boldly challenging the anticommunist hysteria of the Cold War, William Appleman Williams starkly reversed the blame for that conflict, finding the birth of US "containment" strategies in America's tragically beclouded responses to the Bolshevik Revolution and in an earlier struggle between the United States and tsarist Russia over Manchuria.[24] Amid the easing of superpower tensions in the 1970s, John Lewis Gaddis highlighted how the subordination of ideological differences to the pursuit of common interests had been the key to earlier periods of friendly relations as well as the era of détente.[25] In the same period of optimism about opportunities for cooperation, Nikolai Sivachev and Nikolai Yakovlev emphasized the "objective inevitability of peaceful coexistence between countries with different socioeconomic systems," not conflict or war, and they expressed confidence that the positive developments of the early 1970s in US–Soviet relations could not be destroyed.[26] Yet US–Soviet détente soon died, and amid "the New Cold War" of the first half of the 1980s Robert Daniels focused on "the roots of confrontation" between the United States and Russia, which he predicted would "not disappear or cease to challenge the United States, regardless of the coloration of its government."[27] Having read these earlier surveys of American–Russian relations, we are cautioned against trying to forecast the future and we strive to avoid projecting the present back into the past.

Like our predecessors, we have been influenced by major developments in American–Soviet and American–Russian relations during our lives. Early in our scholarly careers, we witnessed astonishingly bold reforms in the USSR, the dramatic ending of the Soviet–American Cold War, and subsequently the disintegration of the Soviet Union. Those personal experiences contribute to our awareness as historians of the possibility of rapid changes in American–Russian relations. As we have written this book, since 2008, we have observed a drastic deterioration of relations between Russia and the United States. That degeneration has heightened our belief in the importance of scholarly collaboration that transcends disputes between the two countries.

One of the major ambitions of this history of Russian–American relations is to put the "Cold War" in perspective as only one segment in more than 200 years of interaction between the governments and peoples of the two countries. The overwhelming majority of scholarly studies of US–Russian relations have focused on the period of "the Cold War," which they have approached as an unprecedented, unique, and discrete era. In recent decades many scholars of the Cold War have recognized that ideas played central roles and argued for greater attention to ideologies. Yet, even though the ideological conflicts – capitalism vs. socialism, communism vs. liberalism, Protestantism and Catholicism vs. atheism – erupted long before 1945, that has not led many scholars to stretch their frames beyond the forty-five years following the Second World War.[28]

During the conflict between the superpowers, Soviet journalists, propagandists, and academic authors often depicted the "Cold War" as a new phase of an ideological struggle between socialism and capitalism that began in 1917.[29] With the collapse of the Soviet Union, Russian scholars developed more detached, less ideologically charged analyses of the post-1945 superpower conflict that were based on new access to previously unavailable archival records.[30] Yet few of the post-Soviet studies developed views of the "Cold War" as part of the longer history of relations between Russia and the West.[31]

A second objective of this book is to present a more expansive and inclusive view of "relations" between Russia and America than is available in previous surveys, which focused above all on political and diplomatic developments. Although this new history of American–Russian relations gives due attention to decisions by political leaders and negotiations between diplomats, it also describes and analyzes the roles of many non governmental actors – including American engineers who participated in the building of railroads in Russia, Russian revolutionaries who appealed for support of their efforts to overthrow the tsarist government, American missionaries who sought to convert Russians to Protestant faiths, Russian novelists who captivated American readers, American journalists whose reports from the Soviet Union often reinforced popular stereotypes, and Soviet filmmakers whose images of American threats shaped the Russian public's conception of living in a besieged fortress.

Our third objective is to delve more deeply into the cultural and ideological dimensions of American–Russian relations by uncovering and analyzing the ideas, assumptions, and aspirations that inspired, guided, and drove the diverse actors. We regard ideologies in a more detached and critical way than earlier overviews which promoted mytho-logical notions about Russian–American kinship[32] or perpetuated moral-istic judgments about alleged essential differences between the two nations.[33] We also take ideologies more seriously than earlier surveys that viewed them mainly as rationalizations for the pursuit of economic interests[34] or treated them primarily as cynical justifications for uses of state power.[35] In contrast, we emphasize the importance of ideologies as the systems of ideas, values, and myths that peoples inside and outside of governments used to make sense of the world. From that vantage, formal ideologies were parts of broader political cultures that were affected by ideas about foreign nations. Hence, in this book we examine public discussions in Russia and America of relations with the other nation not only to see the ways they justified or impinged upon policies but also to understand how they shaped visions of future development and drew the boundaries of nations. In each chapter we analyze the changing images of the other nation that shaped each imagined community, and we utilize a variety of images – political cartoons, propaganda posters, magazine covers, advertisements, and paintings – to illustrate how ideas, attitudes, assumptions, and emotions animated Russian–American encounters.

Political cartoons hold a special place among the visual sources used in our book. Because of their specific genre, these images have been convenient mechanisms for maintaining one-dimensional perceptions of the *Other* and for visually framing long-standing American and Russian myths about each other. Our analysis of political cartoons as historical sources includes careful attention to their language, their use of symbols, and their placement in magazines or newspapers.[36] From the late nineteenth century, when political cartoons became a regular feature in newspapers, through much of the twentieth century, editors, propagandists, and political leaders recognized the special power of cartoons. During the First World War, the US Committee on Public Information had a Bureau of Cartoons that made suggestions to cartoonists all across the country and that viewed cartoons as more weighty than pamphlets or editorials in the molding of public opinion.[37] Following the Second World War, systematic studies of the habits of newspaper readers across the United States found that editorial cartoons were extremely popular, drawing more attention from men than any other part of newspapers except the most widely read front-page news stories.[38] In the Soviet press, cartoons were often closely tied to the rhetoric of top leaders, who sometimes gave instructions directly to cartoonists.[39] Both Russian/Soviet and American cartoons therefore merit close analysis.

The fourth major goal of this work is to develop fully perspectives from both sides of the American–Russian relationship. As historian Akira Iriye has pointed out, "a uninational outlook is not adequate for understanding the complex forces that have shaped the mutual interactions between Americans and other peoples."[40] Yet the most comprehensive study of Russian–American interactions by Soviet authors was so stridently polemical that it really only presented the official Soviet outlook.[41] Earlier surveys by US historians were based almost exclusively on American sources and focused lopsidedly on American perspectives. In contrast, in this book we devote roughly equal attention to American views of Russia and Russian views of America.

This new survey takes full advantage of the recent publication of a large number of exhaustively researched monographs in Russian and English on specific periods of US–Russian relations, which are listed in the Bibliography. Especially important in the foundation for this survey are the extraordinary series of books by N. N. Bolkhovitinov and Norman Saul.[42] The Herculean work of such scholars has enabled us to present a new interpretive analysis of more than three centuries of American–Russian interaction based on much broader and deeper knowledge than was available to our predecessors.

We – two Russians and one American – write in different ways, but we have endeavored to harmonize the structures and styles of the chapters for which we are the primary authors. Ivan Kurilla wrote Chapters 1 to 3 and collaborated with Victoria Zhuravleva on Chapter 4. Zhuravleva was responsible for Chapters 5 to 8. David Foglesong wrote Chapters 9 to 18. We have revised all of the chapters in response to comments, criticism, disagreements, and suggestions from each other. Thus, *Distant Friends and Intimate Enemies* is a fully collaborative work, completed despite the drastic worsening of relations between our countries as we wrote.

1

FROM FIRST CONTACTS TO FLEDGLING DIPLOMATIC RELATIONS, 1607–1807

OVERVIEW

Captain John Smith, best known as the governor of Jamestown, the first permanent English settlement in the Americas, was also the first American whose biography included Russian pages. Before being assigned to a Virginia Company ship bound for the New World in 1607, Smith fought against the Turks in Europe. He was captured and enslaved, but managed to escape and found his way to a Russian fortress on the Don river, where he discovered "a garrison of the Muscovites." The Russian governor helped Smith to get rid of his slave's irons and gave him a letter of credence that helped the English soldier to return home. Many years later, Smith recalled that "[I]n all his life he seldom met with more respect, mirth, content, and entertainment" than on his return to England through Russian land. Smith's Russian experience may have shaped the experience of the Jamestown colonists. In his memoirs, Smith described in detail the construction of Russian fortresses made without iron nails: Muscovite towns, he wrote, "have rampiers made of that woodden walled fashion, double, and betwixt them earth and stones, but so latched with cross timber, they are very strong against any thing but fire."[1] This in-depth discussion suggests that Smith may have used his knowledge of Don fortifications to defend Jamestown.[2]

John Smith's story illustrates an important similarity between Russia and America during the first centuries of their interaction. Both countries steadily expanded into hostile territories beyond their respective frontiers, using arms, knowledge, religion, and education to subdue "uncivilized" peoples. Many cities in what is now considered the heart of Russia were founded as fortresses to protect the Muscovite state from the nomadic tribes at the same time as Englishmen were beginning to master the North American continent; thus, Tambov (1636) was a contemporary of Williamsburg (1632). Geographic discoveries, trade (including in furs), war, missionary work among local peoples, displacement, subjugation, and often destruction of the local population and the tillage of their "virgin" lands shaped both Russian and American history. In light of these common challenges and experiences, the two countries would have much to learn from each other about the best practices of colonization once communication became more frequent. During the eighteenth century, America and Russia attracted similar groups of migrants from German lands: Mennonites settled in Pennsylvania and the south of Russia alike, while Moravian Brethren founded both Bethlehem, Pennsylvania (1741), and Sarepta on the Lower Volga river (1765), building the two cities according to the same town plan.

Over the course of the first two centuries following the foundation of Jamestown, the English inhabitants of the American continent and the Russians accumulated knowledge about each other. For the first century and a half, however, Russians and Americans had virtually no direct contacts and reports from the other country were generally considered exotic stories.

In the middle of the eighteenth century, Russian explorations of the North Pacific made Russia an American power. With English settlements confined to the Atlantic seaboard, these explorations did not lead to immediate contacts, but they set the stage for future competition and rivalry. The two expansionist movements eventually met in Alaska and the Far East, changing the direction of their subsequent expansion efforts. Later, the vital role of the frontier in Russian and American history would become a subject of scholarly reflection in both countries, with peculiarities of the national development of both countries explained by reference to the influence of the "civilizing movement" of their states and societies into the vast continental spaces of Siberia and the American West.[3]

In 1763, an American ship brought cargo directly to Russia for the first time. From that moment on, mutual interest grew rapidly, stoked by the American War of Independence, which became part of the political and philosophical debate among Russian scholars of Enlightenment ideas. Americans, for their part, became acquainted with Russia first as a potential threat that could send troops to assist George III and then, suddenly, as an ally in the American quest for neutral trade. The European wars that followed the French Revolution of the late eighteenth century saw an increase in the amount of American trade to Russian ports, creating an economic incentive for the establishment of diplomatic relations between the two countries. In this chapter, we discuss how Russia and America created their first images of each other, the evolution of these images during America's War of Independence, and the subsequent increase in mutual interest that led to the establishment of diplomatic relations between the two nations.

FIRST CONTACTS

Russian Tsar Peter the Great (1682–1725) began his quest to reform his state with a long journey through Europe (1697–1698), during which time he mastered modern technologies and became acquainted with Western people. Among other encounters, he had a conversation in London with a group of Quakers, and later received a letter from William Penn, the founder of Pennsylvania.[4] Yet it was Peter's decision to introduce tobacco-smoking to his domains as a part of his Westernization campaign that would have the most profound impact on the future of the American colonies. In exchange for access to the plans of much-coveted naval innovations and the opportunity for Russian shipbuilders to develop their skills in English shipyards, Peter had signed the first contract granting English merchants the right to import tobacco to Russia in 1697. However, Russia would not become a real market for Virginia and Maryland tobacco until a decade later, when Peter began to use tobacco as a key tool to force his nobles to break with old Russian customs. Tobacco was widely used during festivities hosted by the tsar with the goal of turning his subjects into Europeans. The Westernizing efforts of a Russian tsar brought profit to Americans while proving unhealthy to those who adopted the habit.[5]

The second quarter of the eighteenth century witnessed the development of European-style science in Russia. Peter the Great founded the Academy of Sciences, comprised of educated Germans and the first Russian scientists, in 1724. By the middle of the century, researchers from Russia had joined the "republic of letters," an international community of scholars that shared the results of their research. It was within that community that Russians first learned of Benjamin Franklin, while American researchers found out about Russian polymath Mikhail Lomonosov and physicist Franz Aepinus.[6]

Benjamin Franklin was the most popular American among Russians in the second half of the eighteenth century. His *Bon Homme Richard* was published in Russian in 1784, at the peak of the Russian fascination with American society caused by American independence. Russian Enlightenment publisher Nikolay Novikov went so far as to state that Franklin "will, several centuries hence, be viewed as a god. Electricity transforms all physics, the English colonies transform all politics. Franklin was a leader in both those changes."[7] Franklin met many Russians during his time in Paris, including the founder of Russian comedy, Denis Fonvizin, and the director of the Imperial Academy of Arts and Sciences, Yekaterina Vorontsova-Dashkova, the first woman to lead a national academy. It was at Franklin's suggestion that Vorontsova-Dashkova was elected to the American Philosophical Society in 1789. Not coincidentally, Franklin himself became the first American member of the Imperial Academy of Sciences later the same year.

The only Russian to witness the American Revolution and play a role in it was Fedor Karzhavin (Figure 1.1). The son of a wealthy St. Petersburg merchant, he helped the French to arm the rebels during the American War of Independence. In the process, he established good connections in several American cities, especially in Williamsburg in the late 1770s and early 1780s. During that time, he likely became acquainted with Washington, Madison, and Jefferson. In 1777, Karzhavin even offered President of the

VELUTI IN SPECULUM.

Figure 1.1 Caricature by an unknown artist, with Karzhavin's handwritten notation in Russian: "King George sees in the devil's mirror what will happen to his colonies in America." Courtesy of Russian State Library, Moscow.

Continental Congress John Hancock his services as the American envoy to Russia, but the idea was not considered.[8]

FIRST IMAGES

In the middle of the eighteenth century, Russians portrayed America as a country of Native Americans or Indians. Among the first texts on America published in Russia were a dissertation about how Indians settled in America (1762) and "an American tale" about an Abenaki Indian who saved a young English officer; the latter was translated several times and published under different titles between 1769 and 1798.[9] The European Enlightenment, particularly the great Genevan philosopher Jean-Jacques Rousseau's idea of a "Noble Savage," informed Russians' image of the American Indian: Russians perceived Native Americans as "natural" people not spoiled by civilization. This depiction fostered a rather positive view of Indians that persists in Russian tradition.

Mikhail Lomonosov, in his "Letter on the Use of Glass" (1752), mentioned American "simpletons" that exchanged gold for beads. In his 1759 verse "On America," Alexander Sumarokov, one of the founders of Russian poetry and theater, condemned Europeans who "wanted to purify the souls of mortals but killed their bodies."[10] In the 1770s, Novikov's magazines ran translations of German and French writings about Native Americans; in 1784, he also published "An Indian's Letter about European Mores" that used this "uncivilized view" to highlight and criticize Europe's sins[11] – an obvious extension of Rousseau's ideas. For a Russian reader in the eighteenth and early nineteenth centuries, the very word "American" meant "Indian." In that period, the most famous Russian work about America was Ivan Krylov and Alexander Klushin's opera *Americans* (*Amerikantsy*, 1788), about Indians' encounter with Europeans; the piece, full of praise of liberty, was banned by Russian censors until 1800.[12]

Russian interest in America skyrocketed in the 1780s, following the news of the success of the War of Independence and the establishment of a new government of the United States.[13] Between the American revolution and the beginning of the revolution in France (which diverted educated Russians' attention from America and focused it on a new drama), events on the far shore of the Atlantic were the focal point of Russian discussions about politics. At first, most of the books and articles that appeared in the Russian press were translations from French or German sources or were based on them.[14] The first book about the English colonies in North America written by a Russian was published in 1783, when Dmitry Ladygin (or Lodygin) compiled information about America gleaned from European authors and news reports.[15]

That year, another Russian subject, Karl F. M. Snell, the rector of a church school in Riga, published a book in German about American independence and its influence on Russian commerce.[16]

The Russian literate public diligently followed events in America. Novikov, who published the semiweekly *Moskovskie vedomosti* newspaper from May 1779 to May 1789, made sure that American content was fully represented on its pages. He even introduced an "America" section to the newspaper's magazine supplement (*Pribavlenie*) and announced in its 1784 issue that "The Declaration of Independence of the United North-American states belongs among the most important adventures of our century."[17]

At that time, Russian enlightened intellectuals characterized Americans primarily as lovers of freedom. "Freedom, in its full form, is the most beloved feature of the Americans," stated Novikov's newspaper in its article "On the Form of Government among Americans," published in 1784.[18] In 1784, Novikov devoted several issues of *Pribavlenie* to describing the views of American Quakers and published an article about them in a magazine, *Pokoiashchiysia trudoliubets* (*Resting Hardworker*). He paid special attention to the Quakers' refusal to take part in state coercion and to their lack of deference to state bureaucrats. Responding to the interest of Russian educated readers in the events of the American Revolution and the creation of the United States, Novikov published a long article by the German professor Franz Dominikus Häberlin on the influence of American independence on European politics.[19] Häberlin's article was very pessimistic in its depiction of the American future, criticizing the inevitability of the United States' dependence on some European power; the low quality and high price of its goods; and its growing tendency toward aristocratic rule, which he considered the worst possible form of government. Other articles in the same magazine were much more enthusiastic about the future of the new republic. A biography of Washington, for instance, ended by envisioning that the United States "will become a refuge of freedom, driven out of Europe by luxury and debauchery."[20]

The most radical Russian thinker of the epoch, Alexander Radishchev, wrote his *Ode to Freedom* in 1783 or 1784 upon learning of the final success of the American War of Independence.[21] In his daring verses, Radishchev exclaimed, "your leader is freedom, Washington" and rhetorically addressed the "famed land": "It may not be my fate/To reach thy free and happy shores/But let my ashes rest beneath your earth."[22] The verses marked the first time that a Russian openly dreamed of America, the land of freedom. From that moment on, America became a substitute for utopia in the minds of many Russian thinkers: though America was just as unreachable as utopia because of its great distance from Russia, it was seen as a place where their hopes and dreams for the ideal social order had been fulfilled.

Radishchev had studied in Leipzig and was, at the time of writing the ode, a customs officer in St. Petersburg (by 1790 he would become the head of the St. Petersburg customs office). In his work, he met merchants and ship captains from around the globe, giving him easy access to European and American news. The *Ode* could not be published in Russia at the time of writing, but in 1790 Radishchev was able to get his book *Journey from Petersburg to Moscow* – which contained grim observations of Russia's problems, including serfdom and lack of freedom – into print. *Ode to Freedom* became part of the book, although in a heavily edited form: surprisingly, all mentions of America had disappeared from the text. Elsewhere, the book depicted America in a negative light, featuring a highly emotional condemnation of American mistreatment of the natives and the introduction of slavery on the continent: "Evil Europeans, preachers of peace in the name of the god of truth, teachers of meekness and humanity, to the root of the fierce murder of conquerors instill the cold-blooded murder of enslavement." Radishchev called on God "to empty those countries of plenty."[23] While the text still praised American freedom of the press and favorably compared Benjamin Franklin to the Russian Mikhail Lomonosov, the new republic was not painted as positively as it had been in the *Ode* some six or seven years earlier. One explanation for this might be a difference in genre between the two works: the *Ode* was aimed at celebration, while the *Journey* was meant to denounce and rebuke. Another possible explanation is that Radishchev had, over time, become disillusioned with the American republic: the Russian author saluted the promise of the new beginning embodied by the Declaration of Independence but regretted the shape that the Constitution gave to the Republic, especially the entrenchment of slavery.[24]

Empress Catherine II found Radishchev's writings most disturbing, commenting that he was "a rebel worse than Pugachev" because he "hailed Franklin, as the instigator, and dreamed himself to be similar."[25] Radishchev was sentenced to death for his writings, but then pardoned and sent to Siberian exile instead. Indeed, before the French Revolution in 1789 revived comparisons with the American War of Independence, Empress Catherine thought about affairs on the new continent within the traditional framework of colonial rebellion, like the Corsican struggle with France.[26] It was the news from France that forced her to start thinking in social and ideological terms about the American revolution and its Russian sympathizers.

Thus, the early reaction of a Russian radical to the news of the American revolution and the Empress' response to his book anticipated a pattern that would be repeated many times in Russian society: the revolutionary thinker adored American freedom, although it was spoiled in his eyes by racial oppression and other problems, while the State saw the reformist's interest in the republican model as threatening domestic turmoil and therefore insisted that the American experience was unsuitable for Russia.

Contemporaneously, Americans developed their images of Russia. They were less interested in Russia than in more familiar England and France, and indeed borrowed their initial descriptions of the eastern empire from the English and French political traditions. Eventually, however, when Russian policies started addressing America's international positions, they began to develop their own attitudes. For many, Russia was merely an exotic country or even a metaphor for remoteness: "We are as much strangers to the affairs of our own State as if we liv'd in Siberia!" exclaimed a delegate to the Continental Congress complaining of the lack of news from home.[27] Other delegates mentioned Russia as a faraway land that produced fur and sailcloth or as a great power associated with despotism and military threat that was nevertheless sometimes a friend.[28] The first American travelers to visit Russia for leisure, at a time when the Napoleonic wars made the traditional European tour to Paris and Rome dangerous, discovered that Russia included the Caucasus and added "Asiatic features" to their descriptions of the country, thus "Orientalizing" the empire.[29]

For many Americans, Russia was primarily a model despotism. Young John Quincy Adams described Russian government as "entirely despotical" and Russian society as "wholly composed of nobles and serfs, or in other words, of masters and slaves."[30] Some twenty years later, the first female historian of the American revolution, Mercy Otis Warren, described the Russian government as the "court of a despotic female at the head of a nation of machines" and her subjects as "ready by their precipitate counsels to aid their arbitrary mistress in their bold designs and despotic mandates." She added that Catherine herself, "the dictatress of Europe, determined the ruin of princes, and the annihilation of kingdoms."[31]

At the same time, Russia, like America, was a new land and a rapidly rising power. In an early instance of geopolitical fantasy, in the midst of the Revolutionary War, American envoy to France Silas Deane predicted an alliance between Great Britain, America, and Russia, which "united will command not barely Europe, but the whole world united." He explained that "Russia, like America, is a new state, and rises with the most astonishing rapidity," such that an alliance between the two states and Great Britain would be "unparalleled in the annals of Europe, or perhaps of the world. Like a colossus, with one foot on Russia and the East, and the other on America, it will bestride, as Shakespeare says, your poor European world."[32] For the contemporaries of the Napoleonic expansion, Russia was increasingly seen as the only hope of resisting French dominance. Young American Joseph Allen Smith, who traveled from St. Petersburg to the Caucasus in 1803–1804 and witnessed Russians fighting in Circassia, wrote to a prominent Federalist politician, Rufus King, that "it is the Russian soldier alone who is capable of placing a boundary to the ambition of France."[33] Such a vision of the Anglo-Saxon world allied with Russia and counterpoised against Europe would recur in many world crises.

BEGINNINGS OF RUSSIAN AMERICA

Russian explorations of the northeastern part of Eurasia eventually brought the daring pioneers to the American continent. The Great Northern Expedition of 1733–1740 (also known as the Second Kamchatka expedition) led by Vitus Bering and Alexei Chirikov discovered and mapped the

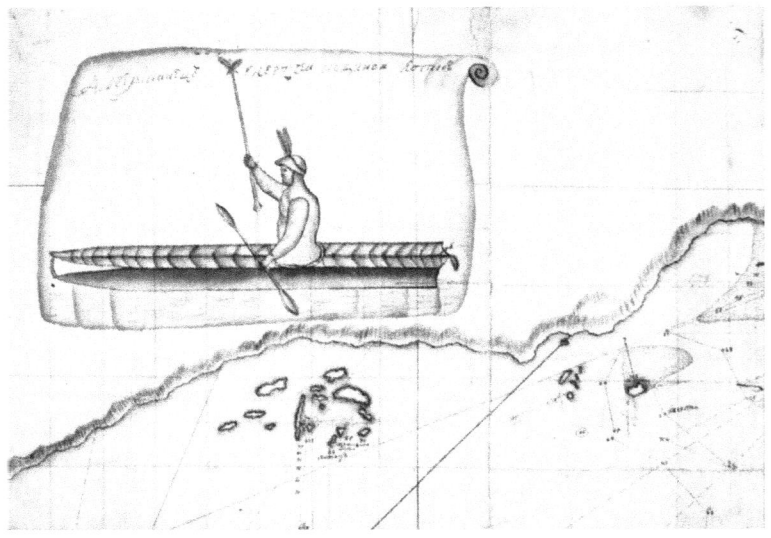

Figure 1.2 Bering's first encounter with Aleuts at Shumagin Island. Drawing by Sven Waxell, the mate of Bering's ship *St. Peter*. Inscription reads: "An American in a boat made of sealskin." Logic Images/Alamy.

northwestern part of America, including Alaska, the Aleutian Islands, the Commander Islands, and Bering Island (Figure 1.2). That exploration became the basis for Russia's claim to the lands in the north Pacific. During the second half of the century, Russian explorers, hunters, and fur traders increased their presence in the region.

Irkutsk merchant Grigorii Shelikhov founded the first permanent Russian settlements in North America between 1784 and 1786 on Kodiak Island and the Kenai Peninsula. Although the state authorities were initially reluctant to support Shelikhov's adventures, he continued petitioning Irkutsk and St. Petersburg, eventually receiving permission to construct a shipyard on the American shore and (to that end) to relocate twenty craftsmen and ten families of farmers to Alaska. This was just the beginning of Russian settlement on the American continent.[34]

Shelikhov considered Americans possible competitors in his Alaskan endeavors. In 1788, he was instrumental in the Russian government's decision to deport John Ledyard, an American traveler who, with the encouragement of Thomas Jefferson, journeyed from St. Petersburg through Siberia to as far east as Yakutsk and planned to travel on to Alaska and America. Ledyard was the first American to visit and describe Siberia, but he never stepped on the soil of Russian America.[35] Nevertheless, he saw the continuity between Siberia and America in the anthropology of the natives divided by "a small sea." Ledyard wrote to Jefferson from the Siberian city of Barnaul that the local "Tartars resemble[d] the aborigines of America: they are the same people . . ., and had not a small sea divided them, they would all have still been known by the *same name.*"[36]

In 1799, the government chartered the Russian American Company, shares of which were owned by members of the Imperial family and by Siberian merchants. Even earlier, in 1790, fur trader Alexander Baranov had signed a contract to supervise hunting activities in America; in subsequent decades, he would play a key role in establishing regular administration there.[37]

From the very beginning, American captains and fur traders crossed paths with Russian settlers on the coast of Alaska. The relationships between Russians and Americans were complex, ranging from mutual assistance to rivalry. Baranov, who was the Chief Manager (essentially the governor) of Russian America from 1799 to 1818, frequently complained that the Americans sold firearms and gunpowder to the native tribes, which used them only against Russians. In that early period, however, Alaska was a very distant geographic region for both countries and thus a very marginal concern in their relations.

EARLY DIPLOMACY

With the onset of the American War of Independence, the Russian government had two options. The first was to equate the rebels to the Russian peasants and Cossacks led by Yemelian Pugachev that had been the force behind a recent uprising in the Volga and Urals regions and were eventually suppressed, with enormous effort, only in 1774. When George III asked Catherine the Great to send Russian troops to fight George Washington's army, he certainly hoped that she would view the War of Independence in this light. Catherine, however, took the second approach, preferring to see the Revolutionary War not as a threat to monarchy as a whole, but as a development that might – by undermining the British – increase Russia's weight in the European balance of power. The Empress quickly – and correctly – predicted, in a private letter of June 30, 1775, that she would "live to see America break away from Europe."[38]

In her letter of September 23 (October 4), 1775, Catherine refused to send Cossacks to George III's aid, citing the fatigue of the Russian troops following the recent war against Turkey (1768–1774), the Swedish threat, and unsettled "Polish affairs" (meaning the first partition of Poland in 1772) as impediments to sending her army to "another hemisphere." Catherine further expressed concern about how the other European powers might react to such an expedition.[39]

The news of Catherine's refusal to assist her British relative eventually made its way to the ears of the Continental Congress. Three years after Catherine's letter, the first French minister to America, Conrad Alexandre Gérard de Rayneval, informed the Continental Congress in a secret session about Russia's attitude. However, he attributed to Catherine different reasons for this decision than she herself had given. The French diplomat claimed that, after the English king applied to the Empress of Russia "for a body of her troops for the American service," Catherine replied that "she would not send her troops against a people who asked only for justice and liberty." In Rayneval's version of events, George III went so far as to promise that "a large district in America would be assigned to the Empress," but she answered "in such a manner, as discouraged a renewal of the application."[40]

Americans desperately needed friends of their cause. For several years, they had believed English propaganda about the imminent arrival of Cossack troops that would fight against them. Now, the mere fact of Catherine's refusal to assist King George was interpreted in America as indicating the Empress' support for the colonists' liberty. In reality, however, she was not such an admirer of their cause. It was state interest, not a love of freedom, that guided the foreign policy of Catherine and her chancellor, Count Nikita Panin.[41]

Panin was the architect of a Russian foreign policy that sought to create a "Northern System" that would bring Russia, Prussia, Great Britain, Denmark, Sweden, Poland, and Saxony together against the houses of Habsburg and Bourbon. The distribution of influence within such a group was, however, subject to change. As early as 1776, Panin wrote that the American rebellion would have a huge impact on his Northern System: whether or not England[42] succeeded in suppressing the Americans, England would be weakened by the struggle and Russia would thus become the leading member of the coalition.[43] Such a view ruled out any Russian support to England in her war against the colonies.

Beyond the strategic considerations, commercial interests shifted the balance of Russian sympathies toward the Americans. Although American privateer activity in the North Sea in 1778 damaged English trade with the Russian port of Arkhangelsk and even required a squadron to be dispatched to guard the trade route, Russian public opinion was nevertheless favorable to the Americans.[44] In the summer of 1779, the Secret Committee of the College of Foreign Affairs under Nikita Panin opined that "the loss by England of her colonies on dry land would be not only unharmful but might even be advantageous to Russian commercial interests."[45]

Desperate for friends, the American rebels interpreted these calculated decisions as a sign of Russia's friendly disposition toward their cause. During many subsequent turns in Russian–American relations, commentators would vacillate between these two perspectives, framing this and similar stories of rapprochement as being grounded in shared values or in calculated interests as political needs demanded.

Russian policy toward the War of Independence culminated with the declaration of Armed Neutrality prepared by Panin and issued on February 28 (March 10), 1780. Support for the right of neutral ships to trade was rooted not only in the context of the European balance of power in the early 1780s, but also in Russia's strategic aim to significantly increase its maritime capacity and trade with recently acquired seaports on the Black Sea. The Act, issued in 1780, established Russia's support for the principle of freedom of the seas and promised that the Russian navy would defend free trade. Russia upheld the right of neutral ships to navigate between the ports of belligerent nations and their right to carry goods belonging to belligerents (with the exception of military contraband, narrowly defined). The Act also used a narrow definition of "blockaded port," limiting it to describing a port entrance that was controlled by the physical proximity of an enemy's navy.

France and Spain were quick to welcome Armed Neutrality, and between 1780 and 1783 neutral Denmark, Sweden, Prussia, Austria, Portugal, and the Kingdom of the Two Sicilies also joined the League of Armed Neutrality, thus rendering futile Britain's efforts to cut off American trade with Europe.[46] John Adams called the Russian Declaration the "great event" and underlined that, although the British highlighted the word "neutrality," it was in fact "as decisive a determination against them, as a declaration of war would have been, perhaps more so."[47] Benjamin Franklin also singled it out as "the great public event in Europe of this year."[48]

In 1780–1781, Nikita Panin was working on a European peace treaty that could not come to fruition until the end of the American war. Panin accordingly devoted significant energy to engineering a truce between England and her rebel colonies (as a temporary solution), as well as to undertaking negotiations mediated by Russia that allowed each colony to decide whether it wanted to remain loyal to England or become independent. These negotiations in fact paved the way for American independence (probably for all colonies except the two Carolinas, which were occupied by the British at that time). French ambassador to Russia Marquis de Verac reported to Paris that Panin "ha[d] displayed too much of an inclination for the Americans and too much dissatisfaction with England." The French diplomat also came to believe "that the secret view of Russia [wa]s for the independence of the Americans."[49] Despite the obvious British objections to the plan, Panin held "to his idea of consulting the Americans themselves, and making them the arbiters of their own fate."[50] England objected to the armistice until the British defeat at Yorktown in October 1781 made American independence inevitable and Russian mediation unnecessary.

It was in the midst of those diplomatic activities and partially as a response to Armed Neutrality that the Continental Congress adopted a December 15, 1780 resolution to send an envoy to Russia. The young republic sent its diplomats without prior agreement from the states to which they were sent, a practice known as "militia diplomacy." The instructions given to Francis Dana who was appointed for the mission to Russia, were issued four days later and stated as his object "to engage her Imperial Majesty to favor and support the sovereignty and independence of these United States, and to lay a foundation for good understanding and friendly intercourse" between Americans and Russians. Dana was instructed to seek formal recognition of the United States and a commercial treaty between the two countries, but his starting point was to suggest that the United States "be formally admitted as a party to the convention of the neutral maritime powers for maintaining the freedom of commerce."[51] Upon arrival in St. Petersburg in September 1781, Dana was hoping to meet with Count Panin, as everybody assured the American envoy that Panin had "the most favorable sentiments of the United States of any of Her Imperial Majesty's Ministers."[52] However, Panin was discharged from his duties before he could meet with Dana, and Russia's foreign policy took a different direction entirely.

The death of Austrian Empress Maria-Theresa in November 1780 made her son Joseph the Emperor and provided an opportunity for the pro-Austrian faction in St.Petersburg to build a new alliance against Turkey (the alliance would eventually lead to the Russian annexation of Crimea in 1783). The new expansionist plans required that European countries, especially France, that might interfere with the Russo-Austrian scheme to annex Ottoman territories be busy with the wars in Europe and on the American continent. The plans also called for better relations with England, as the latter might otherwise compromise the naval operations. As a result, those now responsible for Russian foreign policy – Grigory Potemkin, Alexander Bezborodko, and Ivan Osterman – turned their backs on the American envoy.[53]

Thus, despite spending two years in the Russian capital, Dana failed to receive any official recognition or get a response to his inquiries. Several lower-ranking officials met with the American envoy, but this was far from what he desired. After Dana's mission failed, no new diplomatic initiative emerged for almost twenty years. Yet Dana's time in the Russian capital would eventually bear fruit thanks to the experience that his thirteen-year-old private secretary gained in St. Petersburg. His name was John Quincy Adams.

DIPLOMATIC RELATIONS ESTABLISHED

Among American visitors to the Russian Empire in the decade that followed the American Revolution, we should single out John Paul Jones, the first hero of the American Navy. After the end of the Revolutionary War, he was dismissed and went to Europe looking for opportunities. In 1788, Jones was hired by Russia and assigned as a rear-admiral to the Black Sea squadron. Jones took part in several naval skirmishes, but proved unsuited to subordinate himself to the regular military chain of command of the empire and returned to St. Petersburg to write a proposal for joint Russo-American action in the Mediterranean. In a letter addressed to Osterman, Jones noted that the Algerians had seized "several merchant ships belonging to American citizens" and that Congress intended to send a force against the

Algerians. "Since the Turks govern the Regency of Algeria, and the Algerians are helping the Turks against us in the present war, is this not the right moment to propose to the United States that they take the side of Her Imperial Majesty against the Turks and Algerians?" Jones pointed out that the American navy had been discharged following the Revolutionary War, and that the United States had more good sailors than ships, whereas in Russia there were more good ships than good sailors.[54] The alliance did not work out, and Jones himself suffered from the intrigues of Englishmen in the Russian capital. In late 1789, he left St. Petersburg for Paris, where he witnessed the first years of the revolution before dying in 1792. However, Jones astutely noticed that American interests and Russian capabilities coincided in the Mediterranean vis-à-vis the Turkish vassals of the Barbary coast. The story was to be continued.

American trade to Russian ports steadily increased over the last decades of the eighteenth century. Historians estimate that 400 or 500 American ships made the voyage to Russian harbors annually in the years leading up to 1800.[55] The European continent was immersed in the constant wars that followed the French Revolution, and American merchants used the opportunity of neutral trade to vastly increase their presence in the ports of the old continent. The turns of European politics and Emperor Paul's accession to the Russian throne in 1796 moved Russia away from its alliance with Britain and into a friendship with France at the same time as the United States also turned to France. This coincidence, a true success of French diplomacy, resulted in the reaffirmation of the principles of Armed Neutrality in 1800. American trade with Russia helped increase demand for the formal representation of the interests of merchants and seamen to the Russian authorities and led to the renewal of the discussions about diplomatic recognition. Bold steps began to be taken after March 1801, when new leaders came to power in both countries: President Thomas Jefferson in the United States and Emperor Alexander I in Russia.

The son of Paul and the grandson of Catherine the Great, Alexander was educated by a Swiss Enlightenment philosopher, Frédéric-César de La Harpe. After concluding the young grand duke's course of study in 1794, La Harpe returned to Switzerland to lead the republican movement, eventually becoming the head of the Helvetic Republic in 1799. His relationship with Alexander endured throughout the Tsar's life; they corresponded on political matters and La Harpe would participate in discussions of Switzerland's future at the Congress of Vienna in 1815. The American Republic was an important subject in their correspondence: La Harpe called the United States a "republic whose institutions provide for persecuted Europeans a refuge against oppression, and material resources against poverty." In another letter, La Harpe warned Alexander against repeating the mistakes of the Black Codes in the American South while reforming the Russian legislative landscape,[56] implying that he saw a similarity between Russian serfs and American slaves.

News of the Swiss republican's influence on the Russian autocrat reached the United States soon after Alexander ascended to the throne. Thomas Jefferson had learned of the relationship by the fall of 1802, when he received a copy of English bookseller John Hurtford Stone's letter to American writer Joseph Priestly, who passed it on to the president. Stone wrote: "M. de La Harpe, a Swiss, the primary mover of the revolution in Switzerland, one of their Directors ... had been chosen by the late Empress Catherine to educate the present Emperor. ... and was chosen not only as a man of talents, but still more extraordinary, as a Republican. Alexander has, therefore, received a thorough Republican education."[57]

Jefferson read the description of the Russian tsar with a "strong spasm of the heart in his favor,"[58] later explaining, "The apparition of such a man on a throne is one of the phenomena which will distinguish the present epoch so remarkable in the history of man."[59] Jefferson's high opinion of the young Russian tsar who started his reign as an enlightened liberal continued for most of his life; he even put a bust of Alexander in his Monticello estate right opposite a bust of Napoleon, symbolically opposing tyranny (Napoleon) to liberty (Alexander).[60]

The Russian tsar likewise expressed a genuine interest in the American president. It seems to be no coincidence that the Russian historian and editor of *Vestnik Evropy* Nikolai Karamzin, whom Alexander I tasked with writing a *History of the Russian State* in 1803, published in his magazine of the same year a paean of praise to Thomas Jefferson, writing that the latter "deserves the wonder of every true patriot through the courage of his government, firmness of his system, with rare impartiality and personal love of country." Jefferson was presented to the Russian reader as "worthy of great dignity and preeminence in the mighty Republic."[61]

Jefferson probably never read that piece, but in 1810 he wrote a marvelous passage to Governor John Langdon that singled out the Russian tsar for praise above all other monarchs of Europe. Louis XVI, the kings of Spain, Naples, Sardinia, Denmark, Prussia, Sweden, and Austria, and the queen of Portugal, he wrote, were "fools," "idiots," "mere hogs in body as well as in mind," and "really crazy," not to mention "George of England," who "was in a strait-waistcoat." "So," Jefferson concluded, "will every hereditary monarch be after a few generations. Alexander, the grandson of Catharine, is as yet an exception. He is able to hold his own. But he is only of the third generation. His race is not yet worn out."[62] For American statesmen like Jefferson, Russia was a different kind of European monarchy, not as spoiled as others. The Romanov dynasty (which Jefferson dated from Catherine the Great), they felt, was young and able to keep Enlightenment ideas alive. Looking at these attitudes at several centuries' remove, we can see the sharp contrast with Americans' later view of Russia as representative of the most archaic features of European society, an embodiment of everything in Europe that Americans despised and wanted to leave behind.

During the first years of his reign, Alexander I was preparing a fundamental reform of state government that was expected to include the creation of ministers, the reform of the civil service, and the establishment of constitutional laws for the western parts of the Russian Empire (all of which were achieved), as well as the abolition of serfdom, the creation of a representative state body, and the introduction of the separation of powers (which did not come to fruition). Diplomatic relations with America meshed well with this domestic liberalization. Thus, the epoch of Jefferson and Alexander provided not only diplomatic and commercial, but also philosophical and personal incentives for the establishment of diplomatic relations.

Unsurprisingly, it was La Harpe who first addressed Thomas Jefferson, "one of the most respected members of the noble society of people pursuing enlightenment and liberty for all," on behalf of his royal pupil Alexander in October 1803. La Harpe wrote that the Russian tsar had "read and admired" Jefferson's speeches and that he had asked the author of the letter to help him "to know Jefferson more closely." The Swiss citizen expressed hope that he would "contribute to bring together two men" who could influence a "considerable portion of humankind."[63] The letter was delivered by the poet, diplomat, and proponent of world republicanism Joel Barlow, who accompanied it with his own description of La Harpe and his own advice on the essence of a possible response to the Russian Emperor.

Meanwhile, growing pressure from merchants eventually led to the appointment of the first US consul to St. Petersburg. Levett Harris of Philadelphia assumed these duties in 1803. The direct impetus for the establishment of diplomatic relations came, however, from the Mediterranean and recalled the prophecy (or analysis) of John Paul Jones some fifteen years earlier. In early 1804, the Barbary power in Tripoli seized the American frigate *Philadelphia*, and Harris asked the Russian authorities for their help. The Russian Empire was in a formal alliance with the Ottoman sultan, a suzerain of the Barbary coast, and possessed its own navy in the Mediterranean. Russian chancellor Alexander Vorontsov immediately reacted to the American request using Russian leverage in Constantinople, and soon *Philadelphia* was freed. On June 15, 1804, Thomas Jefferson addressed his first official letter to Alexander I, thanking him for interceding and stressing the importance of commerce between the two countries: "your flag will find, in our harbours, hospitality, freedom and protection."[64] In his response, the Russian tsar went so far as to praise a "free and wise Constitution which assures the happiness of all and of each."[65]

It was during that period that Alexander I also courted young traveler Joel R. Poinsett, one of the rare Americans to visit St. Petersburg. During a private audience, Poinsett reported in his letter home, the tsar "put many pertinent questions about our country & our system & after hearing my replies said emphatically well that is a glorious form of govt. & if I were not an Emperor I would be a Republican, meaning of course that if he were not an Autocrat, a sovereign per se he would be one of the sovereigns." Interestingly, contrary to Jefferson's anticipation of the Russian flag in American harbors, Alexander explained to Poinsett that Russia "cannot create a mercantile marine and [we] have been hitherto entirely dependent upon England for the transportation of our produce." The tsar hoped that the United States would relieve this dependence.[66]

The president and emperor exchanged another few polite letters, but diplomatic recognition became inevitable only with a new turn of European politics. In the first years of the Napoleonic wars, Russia was part of the English coalition against France, while the United States leaned toward France and despised Britain. However, Napoleon's victory over the anti-French coalition forced Alexander to sign a peace treaty in Tilsit in July 1807; Russia joined the Continental system against England, thus finding itself on the same side as the United States. Moreover, both Russia and the United States faced obstacles to their trade caused by the struggle for dominance between the British and the French, and the start of diplomatic contacts between the two was a natural consequence of the situation. Thomas Jefferson explained his understanding of Alexander's policy to William Duane, the editor of the Philadelphia newspaper *Aurora*: both Russia and America were supporters of neutral rights, and "although in questions of restitution he will be with England, in those of neutral rights he will be with Bonaparte and every other power in the world, except England." Jefferson also expressed his confidence "that Russia (while her present Monarch lives) is the most cordially friendly to us of any power on earth, will go further to serve us, and is most worthy of conciliation."[67]

Jefferson initiated contacts between the two countries in the summer of 1807 when he instructed the US minister in London to approach a Russian representative there. International complications and domestic political difficulties further delayed matters: the Napoleonic wars and the American embargo on England distracted attention from the diplomatic appointments. After all that, when President Jefferson in mid-1808 appointed his close friend and former secretary William Short to be the first US minister to Russia, he met with resistance from Congress. Short was on his way to Russia when Jefferson sent his nomination to the Senate; the Senate, however, unanimously rejected it. The reasons for this insult to the president were mostly domestic, relating to the enmity between Jefferson and Congress during the final months of his presidency. However, the official rejection claimed that the mission to Russia was unnecessary. This marked the first time that partisan concerns in the Senate and tensions between the executive and legislative branches of American government influenced the development of diplomatic relations between the United States and Russia.

Despite this setback, Russia appointed Andrei Dashkov to serve as chargé d'affaires and consul general in Philadelphia; the first Russian diplomat arrived at his post on July 1, 1809. The battle between the president and the Senate over the nomination of his American counterpart continued into the presidency of James Madison, who eventually (after several attempts) secured the nomination of John Quincy Adams. Adams, a son of the second president, had lived in St. Petersburg in his teens as a secretary to Francis Dana and arrived back there in October 1809. Diplomatic relations had finally been established.

CONCLUSION

During the first two centuries of contacts between Russians and Americans, the two sides developed their first images of the other country, met each other in the North Pacific, and finally established diplomatic relations.

Many of the patterns established in these early years would be repeated in the decades that followed. Russian radicals began using America as the image of a utopian land of freedom, an image that stoked fear in the heart of the imperial government, which was concerned that such an example would undermine its control over its domains. They also developed a certain ambivalence about the United States as a land of slavery and mistreatment of Native Americans. Americans, for their part, vacillated between seeing Russia as a despotic power and viewing it as a liberal one, but their attention focused primarily on what they considered the friendly attitude of the Russian government toward American aspirations in international affairs. Diplomatic relations between the two countries were established in the midst of crisis in Europe, the first of many instances of Russian–American rapprochement during European crises and wars.

Russian expansion in the northwest of the American continent created a territory named Russian America that was ruled by the Russian American Company. By the end of the eighteenth century, Russian administrators had become vigilant about the growing activity of American merchants and explorers in the North Pacific, but the low intensity of these contacts kept relations in the region rather friendly. Thus, the era of Russian–American diplomatic relations promised friendship, commerce, and the growth of interest in one another.

2

DIPLOMACY AND REBELLIONS, 1807–1841

OVERVIEW

The United States and Russia established diplomatic relations amid the Napoleonic wars in Europe. Within a few years, both countries found themselves fighting wars on their own soil, Russia against the invading French army and America against the British. The natural temptation to compare foreign and domestic circumstances laid the foundation for the first open debates in the United States about the merits of the Russian Empire, debates that were designed to promote the domestic agenda, but also constructed the image of Russia as America's Other. When the commercial interests of the two countries collided in the Northwest of the American continent, a leading Boston merchant, expressing the will of his fellow traders, readily used the negative image of Russia as an argument to convince US politicians to take a harder line in the dispute.

The decades of the 1810s–1830s were a period of "aftershocks" following the American and French revolutions. Most of the discussions in the United States about Russia and in the Russian Empire about America, as well as a significant proportion of the diplomatic efforts of both nations, were provoked by a series of rebellions and revolutions in different parts of the world. The Latin American wars of independence, the Greek rebellion against Ottoman rule, the Decembrist mutiny and Polish uprising in Russia, and the Canadian Rebellion of 1837 all led to the intensification of discussions about the roles of Russia and the United States both as states and as political models. The debates in the United States included the possibility of Russia's intervention in Latin America and Greece and Russian assistance to the Canadian rebels. They also focused on the suppression of the Decembrists and the Poles. The tsar's court and a large part of Russian society were preoccupied with maintaining the European status quo. They were also concerned about the role the American model might have played in the rebellions.

The democratic republic and the autocratic empire were forced to establish coherent policies and attitudes toward both popular uprisings and each other's reactions thereto, thus establishing the pattern for future inter-actions during international crises. Whereas scholars of the period have historically been most interested in the "Russian interference" that provided the context for the formulation of the Monroe Doctrine, emphasized the American exaggeration of Russian threats, or argued that US–Russian rela-tions in that period could have been placid were it not for the tumult of ideas and human follies,[1] this chapter demonstrates that the interplay of inter-national and domestic concerns produced a mixed outcome.

DIPLOMATS

At the beginning of the nineteenth century, Americans' knowledge of Russia was quite limited and derived mostly from European opinions. The first people to bring home first-hand accounts about this distant country were diplomats.

The position of US minister to Russia was considered an important one. Accordingly, it was entrusted to top members of the young republic's elite. Among these ministers were two future presidents of the United States: John Quincy Adams (minister in 1809–1814, president in 1825–1829) and James Buchanan (minister in 1832–1833, president in 1857–1861). In addition, George Mifflin Dallas, a son of James Madison's Secretary of the Treasury, was a junior member of a special American mission to Russia in 1813 that aimed to negotiate peace with England, served as minister to Russia in 1837–1839, and became vice president in 1845–1849. In 1818, President James Monroe considered sending one of the war heroes Andrew Jackson and William Henry Harrison to St. Petersburg.[2] Although neither man was ultim-ately appointed, both would eventually become US presidents. Foreign rela-tions were still a vital factor for the young republic, and Russia played a leading role in European affairs during and especially after the Napoleonic wars.

US diplomats found life in Russia hard, both owing to the different climate and because of the aristocratic environment in St. Petersburg. An infant daughter of the first US minister, John Quincy Adams, died in the Russian capital in 1812. George Washington Campbell, the third minister (following the brief tenure of William Pinckney in 1816–1818), lost his three children to typhus in the space of a week in 1819. Another minister, John Randolph of Roanoke, fled Russia just a month after his arrival in 1830, citing bad weather and an adverse political climate. However, at least one American experienced no personal hardship while staying in St. Petersburg. A wealthy South Carolinian slave-owner who had previously served as both governor of and congressman from that state, Henry Middleton, was appointed as US minister to Russia in 1820 and held the post until 1830, setting the all-time record for a US representative to the country.

The US government directed each of its successive representatives in Russia to convince Russia to sign a treaty on commerce and the rights of neutral parties in wartime. Russia, while reaffirming its support of the principles, politely refused to sign such an agreement, preferring to avoid conflict with the rules established by England.

The Russian government took a different approach to making appointments to diplomatic positions. The heads of the first mission – consul general, chargé d'affaires, and later minister Andrei Dashkov and the first minister, Fedor Pahlen (son of the main conspirator who assassinated Emperor Pavel in 1801) – came from less prominent noble families, a remote position in a new state not being considered an important or influential one. The lower-ranking diplomats at the mission, meanwhile, were people gifted in journalism, individuals who possessed literary and artistic skills. The Russian government, having previously experimented with influencing the British government through public opinion, was aware of the need to create a positive image of their country in the eyes of American newspaper readers. Thus, consul in Boston and later New York Alexei Evstafiev (Eustaphiev) for many years actively participated in newspaper debates and became known as a talented playwright in America. Pavel Svin'in, a secretary of the Russian Consulate General in Philadelphia who eventually became famous as an editor and painter, received direct orders ("encouragement") from Consul Nikolai Kozlov to publish "rebuttals" to French propaganda in American newspapers in order "to enlighten the American public, which eagerly reads the gazettes."[3]

Svin'in published several articles about Russia in American periodicals. In his 1813 book *Sketches of Moscow and St. Petersburg*, Svin'in stated that "no two countries bear a more striking resemblance than Russia and the United States," which had managed to build the glorious cities of St. Petersburg, Philadelphia, and New York in places that had been – until a mere few hundred years earlier – wilderness.[4] Upon returning to Russia, Svin'in published a series of articles about the United States and a book in which he heaped praise on Americans but criticized their "passion" for trade. "Money is the god of Americans," Svinin wrote, a phrase that would be repeated by Maxim Gorky a century later in his *City of a Yellow Devil.*[5] Svin'in – whose painting of Robert Fulton's steamer *Paragon* is the earliest surviving image of one of the first US steamships (Figure 2.1) – also became one of the early Russian enthusiasts of steamship-building.[6]

Figure 2.1 Pavel Svinin. *Steamboat Travel on the Hudson River*, 1811–c.1813. Courtesy of The Metropolitan Museum of Art.

Among the first important appointments was that of Petr Poletika to the position of a counselor of the Russian mission in 1809. Poletika received other appointments – to Rio de Janeiro, Madrid, and London – in quick succession, but in 1817 he returned to the United States as the third Russian minister. After concluding his tenure in 1822, Poletika became the most authoritative expert on American affairs in Russia and published his book about the United States in French (the publication of the Russian translation was halted by censors, and it never appeared in print).[7] He went on to hold many important state positions, including membership of the State Senate of the Russian Empire, and would be remembered as having, "despite great simplicity and good nature, the formality and grumpiness of a Quaker and an American."[8]

The first diplomatic engagement between Russia and the United States, in the early years of their official relations, was an offer by the Russian government to serve as mediator between the United States and England, an offer that was widely discussed in 1813 (Figure 2.2). The United States even dispatched commissioners to participate in the negotiations – incumbent minister Adams, Secretary of the Treasury Albert Gallatin, and former Federalist senator James Bayard – but the English government

Figure 2.2 "Bruin become Mediator or Negociation for Peace." American cartoon about the Russian mediation attempt. Philadelphia: William Charles, c. 1813. Courtesy of Lilly Library, Indiana University, Bloomington, Indiana.

ultimately refused to accept mediation. Nevertheless, that period made Russia the focus of American debates for the first time.

"RUSSIAN CELEBRATIONS" AND AMERICAN DEBATES ABOUT RUSSIA IN 1813

In 1812, the French Grand Army invaded Russia and even took possession of its ancient capital, Moscow. By the end of the year, however, a lack of supplies, the early onset of winter, and incessant attacks by the Russian army had forced Napoleon to retreat, and the French flight from Russia became a disaster. The following year, the Russian army began its victorious foreign campaign that led to the capture of Paris in 1814. During this period, America was at war with Great Britain, Russia's ally in the anti-Napoleonic coalition. That fact did not, however, harm diplomatic relations between the two nations. Russia and the United States were developing mutually profitable commerce, and their respective governments had no reason or inclination to criticize each other's domestic institutions. The news of Napoleon's defeat in Russia came to the United States in early

March 1813, almost simultaneously with the news of Russian Emperor Alexander I's offer to help negotiate peace between the United States and England. Those events sparked interest and even prompted the first public discussion on Russia in the United States.

Some Americans, including Thomas Jefferson, looked at Russia as a distant empire that was less corrupt than other European monarchies and that was friendly toward America. Still, when it came to public perceptions of the other nation, views on both sides continued to be rather exoticized. In Russia, the vision of America as a country of savage Indians continued to develop and proliferate, fueled by the popularity of James Fenimore Cooper's novels and George Catlin's pictures of Indian life. Similarly, in the United States, a "Russian" was often seen as a semi-civilized Cossack, wild and ignorant. The Cossacks, however, were also seen as model warriors, and indeed had the opportunity to prove their military prowess in the War of 1812.

Russia did not immediately emerge in 1812 as a country to which it was important for the United States to pay attention. Two major European powers, England and France, were significant Others for the young United States. The major political parties of the epoch had clear preferences in their foreign policy: Jeffersonian Republicans, including President Madison's administration, relied on France, while the Federalist party pushed for better relations with England. Thus, the War of 1812 alienated Federalists, but made it difficult to promote their foreign policy orientation. However, they found their way. In 1813, two American cities became the sites for huge celebrations of the victories of Russian armies over France.[9] The organizers of the celebrations obviously intended them to be demonstrations of their disapproval of President Madison's "pro-French" foreign policy. The political and newspaper battles surrounding the "banquet campaign" illustrated the process of the construction of the Other in domestic political discussion.[10] Such polemics were important to shaping the American image of Russia.

Throughout 1813, political speeches, banquet toasts, and newspaper articles used "Russia" as an argument in domestic controversies. Opponents of the Madison administration painted Russia as "a noble and gallant nation" that was successfully struggling "against a horde of ruthless and unprincipled invaders." They considered the Russian fight against Napoleon to be "an event tending to the complete emancipation of the world."[11] The Russian victories, the Federalists claimed, afforded Americans "the best if not the only hope of peace; the best if not the only chance of escape, from the toils of French alliance, and the consequent horrors of French domination."[12]

The president's supporters, for their part, turned to attack Russia. They criticized the "silly idea of celebrating the Russian Victories, or rather the rigors of a Russian winter," equating it to celebrating "the ravages of a pestilence in the East Indies."[13] The "Russian victories [. . .] had crimsoned the earth with the blood of thousands of innocent victims,"[14] they wrote. The celebration was an "anti-American" idea on the part of the Boston Federalists "because the success of Russia was thought by them to be auspicious to the cause of our enemy."[15]

During these first "Russian debates" in the United States, the image of Russia became a matter of political dispute between Federalists and Republicans. A deep split between the two parties took the form of a discussion of the merits of a distant empire. The assessment of Russia's level of civilization was constructed to meet the political needs of domestic polemics. Russian diplomats sought to engage in these discussions to create a favorable opinion of Russia among Americans. As a result, two competing images of Russia took initial shape. To one side, Russia was a barbaric country; to the other, it was a rapidly developing nation that cherished its independence and was fit to become a major player in the European concert of powers. In the two centuries that have elapsed since the Napoleonic wars, the image of Russia in the United States has transformed and developed, but these elementary building blocks remain part of its foundation.

THE NORTHWESTERN CONTROVERSIES

Within two decades after the Russian American Company (RAC) was created to govern imperial territories in the American Northwest, the first conflict between Russians and Americans emerged. For the first two decades of the nineteenth century, the RAC was dependent on Boston merchants to provide food supplies for the Russian population of Alaska, but constantly complained via diplomatic channels that the Americans sold firearms and other goods to the native people, creating a physical threat to Russians and causing commercial losses. The situation changed when the RAC founded Fort Ross (1812) in California (north of today's San Francisco), establishing agriculture and trade with the Californians as well as initiating regular shipments of food and other supplies from St. Petersburg along this almost circumglobal route.[16] These logistical improvements laid the groundwork for the introduction of restrictions against American competitors in the region. Russia's affirmation of its hold over the North Pacific was reflected in the issuance of an Imperial Decree (*Ukaz*) in 1821 that limited foreign merchants' ability to trade on the coast of Russian America. This came as a blow to the commercial interests of New Englanders, and the US government lobbied Russia to abolish the decree. Although the Russian government was reluctant to repeal its laws, it did eventually hint to American diplomats that the decree would not be strictly enforced.[17]

The political differences between the United States and Russia gradually became arguments in discussions of the trade disputes. An influential Boston merchant, William F. Sturgis, published an article in the October 1822 issue of *North American Review* in which he called Russia a country "only connected with the civilized world by an extremely limited commerce," but noted Russia's efforts "to monopolize commerce and usurp territory" on the northwestern part of the American continent. The author further expressed concern that Russia might annex California and alerted compatriots to the potential emergence on the United States' western frontier of "a formidable population, subjects of an ambitious and despotic government."[18] Thus, Sturgis juxtaposed Russian despotism against American freedom to defend US mercantile interests on the Pacific. This approach would be developed further in the debate over the Monroe Doctrine.

THE HOLY ALLIANCE AND THE MONROE DOCTRINE

With the end of the Napoleonic wars, US–Russian relations were relegated to a secondary concern for both societies. America entered a phase of relative harmony in domestic politics known as the "Era of Good Feelings," while the Russian emperor abandoned liberal reforms at home. In the second half of his rule, Alexander I turned his attention to religious and spiritual life. From 1815, he befriended Madame de Krüdener, a Lutheran mystic, and seemed to encourage Protestant influence in Russia, a reality that initially provided new opportunities for US–Russian engagement. David Ramsay, in his *Universal History Americanised* (1819), described Russia as a natural field for the Protestant mission – "the most intimate connections of Russia are with those protestant nations in which the power of godliness most prevails" – and welcomed the "great opportunities" created by the fact that "the policy of the government holds out encouragement to the settlement of foreigners, and indulges all protestants with free toleration." Indeed, during this time, Protestant missions actively collaborated with the Russian government and with the fledgling Russian Bible Society (established in 1812). After Alexander's death, however, the Russian authorities closed the Russian Bible Society, thus bringing to an end its collaboration with the American

Tract Society in translating and spreading Bibles and religious literature across Russia. The American missionaries managed to recover from this setback: in the 1830s, almost every New England ship arriving in Kronstadt carried Bibles and religious tracts. Reports indicate that, during this period, the American Tract Society printed hundreds of thousands of copies annually for distribution in Russia.[19]

In his foreign policy, Alexander I focused on building the Holy Alliance, a conservative union of European monarchs aimed at maintaining the political status quo on the continent. Any revolution or change of power could precipitate an intervention by the Holy Alliance to restore the "legitimate" monarch.

By contrast, the Americans took great interest in the early 1820s in revolutionary affairs in Spain, the successes of the Latin American wars for independence, and the Greek rebellion against the Ottoman Empire. When, in 1823, a French army acting under a mandate from the Holy Alliance suppressed the revolution in Spain, it sparked widespread fear that the Holy Alliance might intervene in the affairs of the former Spanish colonies in America.

It was former US Minister to Russia John Quincy Adams, who was by 1823 the Secretary of State, who formulated the principles of US foreign policy that would be included in President James Monroe's now-famous address of December 1823. His main idea was to distinguish American foreign policy from its European counterpart. Three paragraphs of the address became known as the "Monroe Doctrine"; they emphasized the principles of "non-colonization," "nonintervention," and "noninterference." The Monroe Doctrine was inspired by the United States' expansionism in the western hemisphere, where its interests were inevitably colliding with European ambitions, but the immediate impetus for its promulgation was fear of Russian policy and the prospect of Holy Alliance intervention in Latin America.[20] US policymakers responsible for formulating the doctrine were well aware that such intervention was impossible; their positions were functions of their desire to shape the outcome of the 1824 presidential elections.[21] Politicians formulated foreign threats in order to achieve their domestic goals, which included both personal presidential ambitions and national expansion; thus, notwithstanding Russian plans and Holy Alliance capacities, the perception and use of the threat was an important part of Washington politics in 1823.

When Russia refused to recognize a US-backed minister from Gran Colombia (a state that existed from 1819 to 1831 and included present-day Colombia, mainland Ecuador, Panama, and Venezuela, along with parts of northern Peru and northwestern Brazil), it sparked a conversation among the Monroe administration. In a draft note to Alexander I, Secretary of State John Quincy Adams responded by mentioning "a duty to independent Christian Nations to entertain with each other, the friendly relations which sentiments of humanity and their mutual interests require" and called the Colombian would-be minister a "diplomatic agent of Peace." The words "Christian" and "Peace" were subsequently stricken from the draft at the request of John Calhoun, over Adams' objection that "all the point of my note was in these two words, as my object was to put the Emperor in the wrong in the face of the world as much as possible."[22] Adams sought to highlight the disputable nature of Russia's membership in the community of civilized (Christian) nations in an attempt to manipulate Russian policies. Having spent years in St. Petersburg, he knew which themes were sensitive for the Russian tsar.

Another variation on the theme of Russia as America's Other came that year from newly elected Congressman Daniel Webster. In December 1823, when South Carolina Congressman Joel R. Poinsett linked the recognition of Latin American countries to the recognition of the Greeks, Webster suggested the appointment of a special US agent to the Greeks.[23] Aspiring to the fame that would come with being recognized as the main proponent of American nationalism, Webster prepared and delivered a speech "On the Greek Revolution," in which he insisted that the United States should promote the values of self-government and independence worldwide. Russia, Webster claimed, had betrayed Greek freedom with its anti-revolutionary Holy Alliance. The United States, he argued, must therefore demonstrate that its principles were different from Russia's by sending a commissioner to the struggling Greeks.[24] Webster's proposal did not mesh well with any presidential contender's domestic politics and was accordingly rejected, but he added to the developing use of Russia as the opposite pole to American values.

Russian minister Baron Tuyll (1822–1826) explained the imperial attitude toward the republic in the epoch of towering legitimism. He told Adams that "difference of principle did not necessarily involve hostile collision," and claimed that the Imperial Government distinguished "between a republic like that of the United States and rebellion founded on revolt against legitimate authority."[25] Alexander I perceived the United States as a conservative republic, one that did not spread revolutionary ideas and thus posed no threat to the European restoration that followed the defeat of Napoleonic France. Moreover, just as Americans had cast aspersions on Russia's level of civilization, the Russian nobility had their own reservations about Americans. Baron Pavel Krüdener, Russian minister to the United States in 1827–1837, once commented that Americans were "people still too young to be civilized."[26] Being "not civilized" in the eyes of the educated people in Russia meant staying outside of European civilization and thus posing a lesser threat to the European order. That being said, such benign neglect provided more opportunities for the rebellious part of Russian society to borrow from the American example.

AMERICAN DREAMS AND THE DECEMBRIST REBELLION

Many Russians in the first third of the nineteenth century looked to the United States as the model of a more liberal, enlightened, and democratic society. This vision animated such disparate people as Emperor Alexander, governmental reformers, and revolutionaries. The first Russian minister to Washington, Andrei Dashkov, when departing for home in 1818, confessed to Louisa Catherine Adams that he was "too much of a republican now to be happy at home," but noted that he expected changes there along American lines. Mrs. Adams responded that, judging from her experience, "in that country *they had all to do*" to develop a democracy.[27] Yet Dashkov had some reason for his optimism: Tsar Alexander I, despite having turned his back on the liberal projects of the beginning of his reign, was at that time demonstrating a desire to resume reforms. Indeed, it was in 1818 that Alexander promised, in an address to the Warsaw Sejm (parliament), to give Russia a representative body. The promise threatened some Russian nobles and offended others, but it inspired liberal Russians. However, the promise was never fulfilled, and the reaction came sooner than expected.

This oscillation of the supreme will explains to some degree the fate of the liberal press in Russia and the American theme in Russian conversations. Russian magazines of the epoch devoted significant attention to the United States. Between 1815 and 1820, *Dukh zhurnalov* (*The Spirit of Magazines*) published many articles about the US Constitution and numerous texts about the United States.[28] The first issue of 1819 featured an article, "Spirit of the Times," that openly favored a parliamentary regime over a monarchy. Such an article could have appeared in Russia only with very strong support from the highest levels of the Russian bureaucracy, and the article itself expressed views in line with the tsar's promise to give his subjects a constitution. A series of articles about America culminated with the publication of a "State Calendar of the American United States for 1819" that described the US political system in detail. Soon afterwards, the authorities closed the magazine. The conservative group around Alexander had won out over the liberals and destroyed the latter's hopes. In 1820, revolutions in Spain, Portugal, and various Italian states induced the Russian government to chart a more conservative course in its domestic affairs. *Dukh Zhurnalov* was too liberal to survive.

Young Russian nobles who returned from Alexander I's European campaign of 1813–1815 dreamed of the social and political modernization of Russia. They (and their younger friends who grew up after the Napoleonic wars) studied the European states, but many of them became attracted to the American model. As military and civil officers of the empire, they formed secret societies to discuss ways to reform Russia. Following Alexander I's death in late 1825, they tried to force his younger brother Nicholas, who inherited the throne, to adopt a constitution, and led their regiments to the central square of St. Petersburg. The rebellion was brutally suppressed with gunfire, and the participants were executed or exiled to Siberia. The group became known as the Decembrists, a reference to the month in which they made their noble attempt.

The Decembrists' constitutional projects were modeled on the US constitution (and even some state constitutions). One of the two rival constitutional projects that emerged among the circle of conspirators – the one authored by Nikita Muraviev – was an adaptation of the US Constitution to Russian soil. He translated the American terms into Russian, while keeping the basic structure of the state quite similar to that of the United States. Thus, the legislative power should belong to a "People's *Veche*" (assembly) consisting of two chambers, the Supreme Duma and the House of Representatives. Russia's territory should be organized into thirteen "powers" (*derzhavy*) and two regions (*oblasti*), Moscow and Don. The emperor was kept as the Chief Executive of Russia, but his constitutional powers were described in similar terms to those of the US president. In addition, the document stated that, upon taking office, the Russian emperor should take an oath that used similar words to the oath taken by the US president. The government of Russia, meanwhile, should consist of four departments (*prikazy*) – treasury, war, navy, and foreign affairs – just as the initial US administration did.

Certainly, there were differences from the US Constitution. Members of the emperor's court, for instance, were deprived of the rights of citizens for the duration of their "personal service" to the tsar and could not be elected to public office. Serfdom was to be abolished. One article of the document stated that "A slave, upon touching Russian soil, becomes free."

Other Decembrists criticized Muraviev's Constitution on two main grounds. First, the federal organization of the state reminded people not of the United States, but of Russia's own fragmentation during the feudal system of the Middle Ages, which had left it vulnerable to foreign invasion. Second, the high property qualification for those hoping to gain a public position was seen as merely replacing the old hereditary aristocracy with an aristocracy based on wealth.

Pavel Pestel, the author of a rival constitutional project more reminiscent of French law under the Jacobins, was more radical, but also confessed that the American example was an important source of inspiration. His project even introduced presidential power to replace the monarchy.

One small paragraph in a US newspaper did acknowledge that the Russian rebels had been inspired by the American experience. Appearing in September 1826, it read: "In the late conspiracy in Russia, the leaders adverted often to the institutions of the United States and the example of Washington. What evidence this of the influences belonging to the history of our Revolution and condition!"[29] However, this was a definite exception to the general depiction of the conspiracy as something distant. As the Decembrists did not seek independence, most Americans seemed not to recognize that this revolt had a similar purpose to their own revolution.

Indeed, even Henry Middleton, then the American minister to Russia, did not realize that the Decembrists' rebellion was inspired by the American example. He forwarded to Washington the official narrative that "the Decembrists were merely a group of selfish, cowardly, and criminal noblemen, who were jealous of the beneficent power of the government and whose only aims were personal advantage and glory."[30] We should mention here that Middleton's appointment stemmed from President Monroe's desire to have a prominent slave-owner in St. Petersburg at a time when the Russian tsar was arbitrating a dispute between England and the United States over the slaves taken by the British during and after the War of 1812. However, Middleton remained in Russia long after the arbitration had ended.[31] Louisa Catherine Adams, wife of the first American minister to St. Petersburg, knew the secret to his long tenure there: a wealthy planter, Middleton had, "independent of his Salary [as minister] fifty thousand dollars a year which ... enable[d] him to live as a Minister should live in Russia."[32] One should not expect much attention to liberal rebels from a slave-owner. While many US diplomats shared Middleton's doubts that democracy was appropriate for Russia, none of his successors "ever made the case for autocracy so baldly as he."[33]

When Alexis de Tocqueville juxtaposed American liberty to Russian despotism and servitude in his famous *Democracy in America* and stated that for the two countries "Their point of departure is different and their paths diverse; nevertheless, each seems called by some secret design of Providence one day to hold in its hands the destinies of half the world,"[34] his prediction attracted the attention of American readers. One reviewer dared to argue with the French observer, insisting that "the principle of democracy," once established firmly in America and then Western Europe, was "destined also to conquer to itself, with a certain, though slow and toilsome progress, the eastern half of that continent."[35]

In Russia, the period after the Decembrists' revolt saw the suppression of free discussions and the calming down of the American theme in Russian magazines. Nikolai Polevoy, an editor of *Moskovskii telegraf,* was the son of an Irkutsk merchant who had been one of the founders of the Russian American Company. His magazine devoted many pages to American themes, and Polevoy himself wrote on America.[36] Not coincidentally, Polevoy was also the author of the *History of the Russian People* (1829–1833), a book narrating Russian history from the point of view of the common man, in opposition to the dominant statist tradition of Nikolay Karamzin's *History of the Russian State.* A follower of French romantic historiography, Polevoy was interested in the development of people, as distinct from the development of the state, and the American experience was for him an important example of popular achievements. It was Polevoy who authored the first Russian article on American literature, publishing it anonymously in *Moskovskii telegraf* in June 1828. The article is important not only because it distinguished American literature from English writing, but also because it reflected a shift in the meaning of "American" for the Russian people: whereas before, "American" had meant "native American" or "Indian," the word was now used to refer to the literature of the new nation.[37] Polevoy's magazine was published in the epoch after the Decembrist rebellion, and his attempts to publish news from the United States were met with harsh censorship.

In 1833, Russian minister of education Sergey Uvarov formulated a famous ideological triad – "orthodoxy, autocracy, nationality" – that became the basic ideological doctrine of the empire. While Uvarov's circular letter included no direct reference to the American example, the very fact that this was the first attempt to shape an official ideology betrayed a historical awareness indicative of modernity, an understanding that the American and French revolutionary experiences posed challenges for the stability of Russian society.[38]

For a long time, discussions of the American political system were a privilege reserved for the highest stratum of Russian society. Top-level dignitaries could freely discuss the highs and lows of American democracy. At the very top of that pyramid, Emperor Nicholas showed an interest in Americans. During the 1830s, Russian readers looked at the United States through the prism of James Fenimore Cooper novels and, of course, Alexis de Tocqueville's *Democracy in America.* Cooper was read everywhere, from the imperial palaces to nobles' provincial estates. Indeed, shortly after Dallas arrived as US minister to Russia, the empress even asked him whether Cooper had written a new book, as she had enjoyed his novels *The Pioneers, The Spy,* and *The Last of the Mohicans.*[39]

Tocqueville, too, found a large audience in Russia. His famous contrasting of Russia and America first appeared in a Russian journal in 1836 as part of Alexander Turgenev's Paris correspondence, albeit with the "despotism" passage omitted.[40] Unlike their American counterparts, however, Russians could not discuss this comparison in public, as governmental censors banned discussion of Russian politics. The main conclusion that Tocqueville's Russian noble readers drew from the book was that the American experiment was interesting, but impossible in Europe. This was the time that the Russian liberal public first split into Slavophile and Westernizer camps. Russian Slavophiles, who insisted on the existence of a unique Russian Way of development, were more interested in reading Tocqueville than either the Westernizers or the democratic revolutionaries of subsequent generations.[41] The exceptionalism of the American example inspired a Russian version of exceptionalist philosophy, while universalists–Westernizers were uninterested in a model that could not be used at home. Tocqueville's writings helped Russians to reject the American example and called into doubt its status as a threat to the European status quo.

Tocqueville was frequently compared to another famous French writer, Astolphe de Custine, who traveled to Russia later in the same decade and published his caustic memoir *Russia in 1839.* This work exposed and highlighted the dark side of life under absolute monarchy. While Custine's book was immediately banned in Russia, it was widely read by the educated Russian nobility, as well as in Europe and the United States, helping to produce negative images of Russia that persist. More than a century later, Russia scholar and diplomat George F. Kennan stated in his book about Custine that "whereas a great deal of what he had seen in Russia ... really existed, a great deal also existed which he had not seen,"[42] meaning the brighter side of Russian people and society.

POLISH REBELLION AND FREEDOM OF THE PRESS

The American media returned to Russian themes in 1830, when news of rebellion in Poland revived interest in that remote part of the globe. A comparison of the American reactions to the two major rebellions of the decade, the Decembrists in 1825 and the Poles in 1830, reveals a sharp contrast: unlike the Decembrist rebellion, the Polish uprising was seen through America's own experience as a pursuit of national independence and was accordingly praised by the rising American nationalists. During the rebellion, the US press mainly reprinted the opinions of anti-Russian British newspapers, thereby developing the latter's negative image of Russia as a barbaric, oppressive, and Asiatic country. The suppression of the Poles awakened strong anti-Russian feelings in Europe. American historian Martin Malia considered that period to mark the turning point toward a darker portrayal of Russia on the part of Westerners.[43] The period also served as the pretext for a discussion between American and Russian statesmen about the important issue of freedom of the press.

In their private correspondence, Americans in Russia described with astonishment the tight Russian control over periodicals. James Buchanan, US minister to Russia in the early 1830s, wrote to his brother Edward: "The Press is under so strict a censorship, that nothing is published except what the Government pleases. Every avenue through which liberal opinions might enter this empire is carefully closed; & in fact but few even of the higher classes of society know much of our country or its institutions."[44] In another letter, he was even more critical: "They know but little of our Country, & probably desire to know still less, as they are afraid of the contamination of liberty."[45] The latter statement was not quite just; at the very least, Russian elites were fascinated by the influence of the free press on American society. How, wondered Russian statesmen and journalists alike, did the United States manage to coexist with such a mighty tool for shaping public opinion as newspapers?

However, the lack of a free press may also have caused problems for Nicholas I's government, which was – unlike that of his liberal brother Alexander I two decades earlier – not prepared to fight for foreign public opinion. In his dispatches to Secretary of State Edward Livingston, Buchanan – who proved to be more tolerant toward the Russian way of life and state institutions than many of his predecessors – pointed out the bias and one-sidedness of English and French reporting on the Polish events and lamented the refusal of the Russian government to launch counter-propaganda efforts in Europe and the United States. He wrote to the Secretary of State that, in the absence of a free press in Russia, "the representations of the injured party pass every where current, almost without contradiction."[46] In the American envoy's opinion, at least, a free press could have helped to explain and defend the Russian autocrat's policy.

FROM THE COMMERCIAL TREATY OF 1832 TO A NEW MEDIATION ATTEMPT

The foreign policy of Andrew Jackson's administration was focused on supporting American trade. The 1832 Commercial Treaty between Russia and the United States was one of the major successes of Jacksonian diplomacy.[47] Russian Emperor Nicholas I agreed to sign the treaty at a moment of increasing tensions with England,[48] thus indicating for the first time his inclination to use the United States to counterbalance his relations with Russia's major European rival. Buchanan's attempts to fulfill another request made by the Jackson administration – namely, to get Russia to sign a Treaty on Neutral Rights in the event of war – met with less success.

In July 1837, Emperor Nicholas assigned a new minister to Washington: Alexander Andreevich Bodisco, whose name would become linked to many important episodes in the two countries' cooperation. The instructions to the new minister provided a complete description of the Russian government's vision of American politics and Russian goals. The head of Russian foreign policy pointed out that relations with the United States "were based on a certain identity of our interests." The instructions stressed that Russia wished "that American Union confidently occupied its place in the World Theater. Its prosperity and internal tranquility is . . . the object of our most sincere hopes." Karl Vasilievich Nesselrode also analyzed the influence of US domestic politics on American foreign policy and ascertained that the best period was under the administration of President John Quincy Adams and his Secretary of State, Henry Clay. "However, in 1829 the Administration of Mr. Adams and Mr. Clay was overthrown by a demagogic faction that under the name of democratic party flattered to the common people." Nesselrode blamed the Democratic Party for the deterioration of US–Russian relations. However, he saw the problem as a temporary one and hoped that American politicians would "restore the old trust."[49] It was with these instructions that the Russian diplomat began his tenure in the US capital. His work started with the need to deal with the rebellion in Canada against British rule and with its American sympathizers.

The late 1830s might provide the best evidence for the argument that Russian–American friendship emerged in response to a "common foe." The Canadian Rebellion of 1837–1838 even sparked rumors of Russian interference in North American affairs to assist the anti-British uprising. Although these rumors were never borne out, Bodisco did speak to the leaders of the Canadian rebels, Louis-Joseph Papineau and Robert Nelson, at a meeting organized by Democratic Party politicians. Nicholas I's confession during his last meeting with Dallas before the latter's departure in the summer of 1839 is also revealing. After the usual mutual assurances of friendship, the minister said that "our highest interests as a nation were identified with those of Russia." "Not only are our interests alike," the tsar answered, "but (with emphasis in his tone) our enemies are the same."[50] However, the Russian government soon changed course: it began looking for a way to improve relations with Great Britain and help Washington to settle its old disputes with London.

Nesselrode's general assessment of the American party system in 1837 remained accurate throughout Bodisco's tenure. The Whigs, who represented the northeastern United States, the country's commercial heart, were interested in the development of Russian trade and were therefore considered allies by Russian diplomats. The US administration, meanwhile, largely remained under the control of the Democrats, regarded in Russia as demagogues. (Not to be outdone, Democrats referred to the Russian minister Bodisco in private correspondence as a "patronizing Whig."[51]) Alexei Evstafiev, who held the post of Russian Consul in New York for almost fifty years, also criticized the United States as if he were an American Federalist.[52] Russian diplomats' bias against Democrats was based on their preference for conservative republicanism, the political philosophy represented in American politics by the Federalists, the Whigs, and later the Republicans.

In April 1841, Vice President John Tyler acceded to the presidency upon the death of President Harrison. Observing the cabinet shakeup, Russian diplomats sought to calculate its potential impact on international relations. Nicholas I observed that the new conciliatory administration would make it possible for him to improve Russia's relations with Great Britain, so he offered the two countries his services as a mediator in their border dispute. On March 18 (March 30), 1841, Nesselrode dispatched an instruction that obliged the Russian minister to offer Nicholas' mediation. However, it was clear in London, Washington, and St. Petersburg alike that the mediation offer was merely a gesture of Nicholas' good will: no side had asked Russia for mediation, and under the circumstances it was not clear what Russian mediation would address; the new US and British administrations were ready to negotiate.

For St. Petersburg, the offer to mediate the Anglo-American conflict was, first and foremost, a way to establish greater intimacy with England. It was also an indication of Russia's desire to expand its international role beyond the European continent. For Washington, meanwhile, even such circumstantial participation by Russia in settling relations with its former mother country created an international context that made it possible to withstand diplomatic and military pressure from England.

CONCLUSION

US–Russian relations during the period between the establishment of diplomatic relations and the first Whig administration in Washington reflected the large geographic distance between the countries. The only clash of interests – which took place in the North Pacific – occurred without real conflict, while diplomacy was mostly focused on each country's relations with England. The Decembrist, Polish, Greek, and Canadian rebellions provided opportunities to discuss political models and the limits of foreign interference.

The years that followed the signing of the commercial treaty of 1832 were a period of intensive internal development for both countries, which was accompanied by the search for new allies on the international stage. The Russian emperor alternately tried to strengthen relations with Great Britain or to use American affairs as leverage in Anglo-Russian relations. US politicians, meanwhile, began to see Russia not only as a longtime trade partner, but also as a country whose interests could make it a promoter of America's rise on the world stage. However, a new epoch arrived by technology train.

3

BEGINNING OF A FRIENDSHIP: COOPERATION, CRISIS, AND TRANSFORMATION, 1841–1860

OVERVIEW

The second third of the nineteenth century was a period of intensive interaction between the Russian Empire and the United States. Neither before nor since that period have the two nations supported each other on the world stage for such a long period of time and in such diverse ways.

In the two decades before the American Civil War, Russian–American relations improved and intensified dramatically. The diplomatic rapprochement was paired with the emergence of mutual good feelings on the part of the populations of the two countries, as evidenced by journalistic accounts of public celebrations of foreign visits, political speeches, and changes in the wording of school textbooks. By the time of the Crimean War (1853–1856), American public opinion was decidedly on the Russian side, while during the American Civil War Russia was considered the major European supporter of the Union government.

Among the explanations for the Russian–American friendship in the middle of the nineteenth century, the most popular is the "common foe" hypothesis.[1] Indeed, Great Britain was the major competitor of the Russian Empire at that time and was also regarded as a traditional threat by US politicians. However, for most of the 1840s Russia was attempting to reach political concord with England, while the United States escaped serious potential conflict with Britain by signing the Webster–Ashburton Treaty in 1842, after which American–British relations never returned to the level of hostility that they had seen in previous decades. The improvement of US–Russian relations can instead be explained by a more nuanced view that takes into consideration the rapid increase in diplomatic and technological cooperation between Russia and America, which improved the two nations' knowledge of one another and led to warmer attitudes. During this time, increasing tensions over the fate of slavery and serfdom were the main reason for the growing Othering of America and Russia, respectively, in the domestic debates of the two countries. This chapter will trace cooperation and its consequences, as well as changing perceptions and their political use.

For the United States, this was a period of explosive growth: of its territory, its resources, and its geopolitical ambitions. Having begun in the modest position of a small country distant from Europe, it transformed itself into a continental power that aspired to be the model for liberal political forces across the Old World. The Russian Empire supported and promoted the rise of the United States on the international scene. During consecutive crises, Russian diplomacy steadily assisted the United States in its quest to occupy a higher place in the international hierarchy of states and to achieve its goals in the remotest corners of the world.

For the Russian Empire, which was in the 1830s at the peak of its power, but had begun to realize that its technological backwardness compared with England could prove a military weakness, the main challenge was finding a source of technological innovations. Barred from accessing the most advanced British military inventions, the Russian authorities turned to North America. Engineers and experts from the far side of the Atlantic became the foundation of Tsar Nicholas I's modernization program. It is important to note that the transportation and communications revolutions were at the core of the program. Steamships, railroads, and the telegraph were the centerpieces of Russian–American technological cooperation.

Such a complementarity of needs and capacities was a major precondition for the two countries' rapprochement during the period, although it was not the only factor that secured their greater intimacy. From the viewpoint of more ideologized historical periods, a friendship between an autocratic monarchy and a democratic republic was a paradox. In the nineteenth century, however, philosophical disagreements played a negligible role in shaping international relations. The leading Russian newspaper put it the following way in 1861: "If to maintain commercial and friendly intercourse with a foreign country one should require it to possess political and societal organization in accordance with the principles of modern philosophy, the majority of countries would live in solitude."[2] The European revolutions in the middle of the century temporarily called into doubt this approach, but it would survive the crisis.

DIPLOMATS AND THEIR ROLE IN SHAPING MUTUAL IMAGES

For most of the period, Russia was represented in the United States by an experienced career diplomat, Alexander Bodisco. He held the position of Russian minister from 1837 until his death in 1854 and became the most esteemed foreign diplomat in Washington. Bodisco occupied a large house in

Georgetown where he organized social events for American elites. The Russian government preferred to discuss all issues of Russian–American relations through its minister in Washington, leaving US ministers in St. Petersburg with little diplomatic role. Bodisco played a key role in organizing Russian engineers' visits to the United States and hiring Americans to work in Russia, and deserves credit for assisting with the Russian–American rapprochement during his tenure.

After Bodisco's death, the key role in the management of Russian–American cooperation – and especially the flow of engineers to Russia – went to the US minister who was in St. Petersburg between 1853 and 1858, former Connecticut Governor Thomas H. Seymour. He brought with him as attachés two young people who were destined to reform American university education: Daniel Coit Gilman (the future first president of Johns Hopkins University) and Andrew Dickson White (the cofounder and first president of Cornell University).

The services rendered by US diplomats in shaping Russia's image in the United States have not been sufficiently appreciated. In particular, it was their tirelessness in studying and describing Russia and their struggle against the hostile stereotypes promoted by the European press in the 1830s that helped to draw the two nations closer to one another. Several articles and books written by Americans who had experienced life in the distant country – all of them officials at the US mission to St. Petersburg – were published in the United States during the 1840s. These books and articles were not mere travelogues but something more akin to encyclopedias of Russian customs, state, and society. The texts helped to meet growing popular interest in Russia, a country that had recently turned to the United States as a source of innovations.

Churchill C. Cambreleng, US Minister to Russia in 1840–1841, was an active member of the Democratic Party, while his successor, Charles Stuart Todd (1841–1846), and his secretaries, John L. Motley and John S. Maxwell, were American Whigs, but party differences did not influence their perceptions of Russia. None of them was a professional diplomat, as there was no such profession in the United States at that time. Politicians and merchants, military officers and men of letters – all were appointed to Russia for political reasons, possessing little or no knowledge about the empire. And all, upon returning home, published texts that painted Russia in the most favorable light.[3] Thus, American diplomats in the 1840s became the main propagandists of Russia and the Russians, playing an important role in turning US public interest and sympathies toward what had been until recently merely an exotic empire.

The story of the American minister to Russia in 1850–1853, Neill Brown, offers a rather different perspective. A former Tennessee governor, Brown was appointed at a moment of Russian–American estrangement caused by Russia's role in suppressing the Hungarian revolution of 1849. He had little formal education and no prior experience of diplomacy; he did not speak Russian – or, indeed, any language other than English. His appointment to this diplomatic post stemmed solely from his role in the Whig Party, whose candidate for the presidency (Zachary Taylor) had won the 1848 election. The Russian diplomat Eduard Stoeckl, a contemporary of Brown, described him as "a person of moderate principles and talents."[4] Brown arrived in Russia without his family. His modest salary did not permit him to attend aristocratic balls and parties in St. Petersburg, and he felt lonely and frustrated. Without a diplomatic agenda, he devoted his reports to sarcastic commentaries on the Russian way of life. He concentrated on xenophobia and police surveillance, which he saw as characterizing the whole of Russian society.[5] He insisted that "secrecy and mystery characterize everything" and that "all they [Russians] have is borrowed, except their miserable climate." Brown complained that the Russian government "possesses in an exquisite degree the art of worrying a foreign representative without giving him even the consolation of an insult."[6]

These caustic descriptions of Russia were found some eighty years later by a young George F. Kennan, who compiled his own report (signed by Ambassador William C. Bullitt) that was almost a carbon copy of Brown's dispatches. The young diplomat insisted that Brown's depictions precisely described Joseph Stalin's Soviet Union.[7] Such a vision ignored the obvious differences between the tsarist monarchy and the Soviet state, though it did expose a specific problem in American judgments of Russia. For Brown, republican liberties like freedom of the press and democratic elections were the ultimate values. Unable to find any corresponding reality in Russia and blind to any Russian achievements that could not be fitted into this mental framework, his descriptions of Russia became lists of what Russia lacked, an inventory of negatives. Obviously, this list of negatives might well have looked very similar a century later, thus producing an image of "never-changing" Russia. However, one of the major changes that Russia experienced during this period, namely technological modernization, entailed internalizing an American value, which improved Russia's image in the eyes of Americans.

RUSSIAN MODERNIZATION AND AMERICAN EXPERTISE

In the second half of the 1830s, the Russian government of Nicholas I started a program of technological modernization of the country that included railroad construction, the introduction of steam engines into the transportation system, the spread of elementary education, and other innovations aimed at helping Russia catch up to her European rivals. The autocrat wanted to modernize the empire while leaving its political system untouched. Since in that era the world leader in technological innovation was England, the main international competitor of the Russian Empire, and Nicholas did not want to become in any way dependent on Great Britain, the Russian government decided to rely on US expertise to support its program.

The first sign that relations between the two countries had been taken to a new level was an official tour of the United States by Russian Navy officers, after which the Russian government ordered a new steamship, the *Kamchatka* (Figure 3.1), to be built in an American shipyard. The steamship, built in New York by 1841, became the most modern addition to the

Figure 3.1 Alexey Bogolyubov. Steamship *Kamchatka*, 1848.
Courtesy of Peter the Great Russian Naval Museum, St. Petersburg.

Imperial Navy, even if the construction cost was more than double the figure that had initially been calculated.[8]

After this first experience of engineering cooperation, the focus of US–Russian cooperation shifted away from naval projects. The reason for this was not only the difficulties that the Russian government faced in controlling construction expenses, but also that a naval force could never solve the problems of a continental, predominantly land-locked empire. Instead, it was overland transport that should play the leading role in Russia's economic and political breakthrough. The steam engine could help to solve that problem, too. The tsar's choice of American engineers and US contractors (rather than European experts) to build a railroad between St. Petersburg and Moscow was not merely a political step in his long-term game against London, but also an important move toward the United States.

In the summer of 1839, two Russian officers, engineers of the Department of Communications Lieutenant-Colonel Pavel Melnikov and Colonel Nikolai Kraft, were sent to Europe and the United States to study different railroad systems. Upon their return to Russia, the engineers suggested using the expertise of American specialists to build a railroad between St. Petersburg and Moscow. In 1842, their department's official *Journal* published a detailed report by Melnikov about US railroads, accompanied by his drawings.[9] The Russian engineer paid special attention not only to technical peculiarities, but also to organizational experience of construction.[10] Melnikov and Kraft came to believe that the American example fitted Russian conditions the best. The vastness of the American continent made overland transport just as important for America as it was for Russia. "Railroads are a requirement for Russia," Melnikov insisted. "It can be said that they are invented for her needs as well as for America, much more so than for any country in Europe."[11]

Since influential dignitaries doubted that Russia even needed railroads, Nicholas I established a committee for preliminary discussion and project preparation that was headed by Count Alexander von Benckendorff. The committee's first decision, in the spring of 1841, was to invite Kraft and Melnikov, "who had visited America," to share their opinions with the committee's members.[12] In the commission's final report, prepared within six months of its creation, references to the American experience loomed large. In response to Count Toll, the Chief Manager of the empire's communications, who argued that the canal system was adequate for St. Petersburg's transportation needs,[13] the commission analyzed the Erie Canal, pointing out that "in North America the development of railroads is going on despite the vast length of canals in that country."[14] The bureau-crats had established America's development as a model for Russia.

On January 30, 1842, the commission decided to invite Melnikov and Kraft's American acquaintance George Washington Whistler, the chief engineer of the Boston and Albany Railroad, to consult on the projected construction.[15] The Russian government also invited two Philadelphia engineers, Andrew Eastwick and Joseph Harrison, who had offered their services in building the rolling stock for the railroad during Melnikov and Kraft's American journey. On the advice of Whistler, an offer was also made to Ross Winans of Baltimore; though he refused to go himself, he sent his two sons, Thomas Decay and William Louis Winans. These Americans played a key role in equipping the railroad with rolling stock. Melnikov and Kraft were appointed the chief managers of railroad construction, which was divided into Northern and Southern parts. In May 1847, the first part of the railroad – between St. Petersburg and Kolpino – was launched, in 1849 it reached Tver, and on November 13, 1851, Nicholas I attended the grand opening of the whole railroad.[16]

The builders of the railroad used the technical practices and engineer-ing solutions that had been deployed to construct American railroads, both those that the Russian engineers had brought back with them from the United States and those introduced by the American consultant Whistler. Their machinery was either brought from the United States or built in the Russian Alexandrovskii plant using American designs and under the super-vision of US contractors. American specialists also trained the first Russian engine drivers for the railroad. This railroad project laid the foundation for the development of future railroads in the empire.[17]

The Russian engineers' voyage to America influenced other communi-cations as well. Soon after his return from the United States, Melnikov was sent by his Ministry to the Volga river to gauge the potential for steam navigation development. In his own words, Melnikov "found himself on the banks of the Volga with fresh impressions of what was seen a year before on the magnificent rivers of the United States of America." He was aston-ished by the outdated system of goods delivery, which still relied on barge haulers and horses. Melnikov was enthused by the idea of improving Volga navigation using "the most advanced system, namely American steamships, not known in Europe." Melnikov tried to convince Volga merchants to invest in steamship-building, but faced resistance and was forced to petition his own ministry.[18]

As was often the case in Russia, society was less ready for innovation than the government. The ministry formed a special committee that adopted several of Melnikov's recommendations, including funding the construction of one steamship "as a model and example," and endorsed his opinion that North American steamers were the best available.[19] Melnikov had managed to convince the Russian authorities that the United States provided the best model for the development of steam transportation. Indeed, in his last interview with US Minister Charles S. Todd before the latter left Russia early in 1846, the heir apparent to the Russian throne, Great Prince Alexander, made inquiries about Mississippi steamers and Mississippi Valley railroads.[20]

After construction began on the Petersburg–Moscow railroad, the news that the Russian emperor was favorably disposed toward American citizens spread in the United States. *Nile's National Register* informed its readers on April 22, 1843, that the Russian government had collected information about "every improvement in the armies or navies, or in mechanics or the arts which may be invented or introduced in Europe or America." If any of these innovations were considered applicable to Russia "or can be made useful or profitable," the article went on, "the inventor, or his invention, or both, are immediately transferred to Russia."[21] Many Americans headed to the empire to participate in various engineering projects, to teach in agricultural academies, and even to conduct dental work on Tsar Nicholas.[22] These Russian contracts became the first major foreign recognition of the United States' ability to provide technological leadership and assistance. This gave Americans new reason to believe in their role and destiny as a world leader – following the formulation of the religious and moral image of a "city upon a hill" in the seventeenth century and the invention of democracy in the eighteenth, Americans began in the 1840s to believe in their special mechanical skills and inventiveness as a new sign of their status as a chosen people.[23]

By the early 1850s, Russian opinion considered the United States "a huge hotbed of industry."[24] Nicholas I's epoch was full of admiration for Peter the Great and the technical breakthrough that Russia had achieved in the early eighteenth century. Nicholas and his dignitaries considered their task analogous to Peter's: they looked at the United States the same way Peter had looked at Holland. Just as the Netherlands had been the source of the most advanced technologies (namely shipbuilding) in Peter's day, so too was the United States (for steamships and railroads) in Nicholas I's era. This attitude toward the United States soon became a stereotype, one that was revived whenever the Russian or Soviet government sought a new breakthrough.

THE TECHNOLOGICAL FLOW OF THE 1850S

New orders of steamships and steam engines continued to be placed with American shipbuilders during and after the Crimean War. The new authority figure in Russian East Siberia, Governor General Nikolai Muraviev, played an active role in placing these orders. Thus, at his request, Captain of the 1st Rank Petr Kazakevich, accompanied by Captain-Lieutenant G. Kroun, was sent to America to order steamships and machinery for Nikolaevsk-on-Amur. The two Russian officers acquired the steamships *Amerika* and *Amur,* the barge *Lena,* and the supply ships *Yaponets* and *Mandzhur,* as well as various machinery to be used in Siberia.[25] Russian Polish émigré Count Adam Gurovskii, in an 1858 contribution to *Vestnik promyshlennosti,* saw a symbolic meaning in the purchase: machinery that presented "a peculiarity of the mind of American people, absent in other countries," would, when sent to Siberia, acquaint that "virgin country" with "modern results of the spirit of inventiveness, spirit of creativity" and thus "serve as sunrise of true enlightenment."[26] Not only was American machinery considered the best, but it also represented the spread of enlightenment in Eastern Russia.

After a new monarch came to the throne in 1856, the number of shipbuilding orders increased. The Russian orders came just in time to save the US shipbuilding industry from a crisis. According to Gurovskii, in 1858 the Russian-ordered frigate *General Admiral* was the only ship under construction "on the main shipyard of a New York shipbuilder, the largest in all the Union."[27] Thus was US Vice Consul George Hutton so enthusiastic when he informed the Department of State that the Russian government was going to order several ships to be built in New York,[28] advising them to send several different ships to Russia: "one of our best new steam frigates, and one of our first class [...] sloops, with their new armament – and also, when ready, one of the new steam corvettes." The American consul considered it to be in the United States' "future political interest that the Russian Navy should increase in strength and efficiency and that much of the credit thereof should be ascribed to us."[29] Russia became a vast market for American-made ships.

The Crimean War opened another Russian market to American entrepreneurs. Sam Colt, the famous inventor and gun-producer, made three trips to Russia – in 1854, 1856, and 1858 – with a view to selling his firearms. Although an attaché to the US mission, Andrew Dickson White, apparently considered Colt's voyage futile,[30] the Russian government did sign a contract with the American businessman, and in 1855 the Tula armory began producing firearms under his patent.[31] After the Crimean War, Colt delivered the modern equipment to produce rifle barrels to the Sestroretskii armory.[32] The Russian defeat in the war forced the government to reform its army, and the new models for weapons and technologies for their production again came from the United States.[33]

American businessmen and fortune-seekers soon realized that the Russian authorities were expecting new technological miracles from the Americans. Even while the war was still ongoing, Seymour complained that the Russian capital was full of annoying Americans, "one half of whom, at least, ha[d] any quantity of projectiles for the Imperial Government."[34] Immediately after the peace treaty was concluded, the diplomats of both countries faced the flow of Americans going to Russia to offer their inventions for sale.

There were plenty of inventions in Russia, both home-made and imported. However, among the domestic inventors were no "Colts" and "Singers" – managers and businessmen who were able to introduce their inventions into industrial production and everyday use. The socioeconomic structure of Russian society did not create the incentives that would have improved productivity. With a lack of private funds that could have been used to support experimentation with new inventions, state funds constituted the primary source of support for innovation. However, a state bureaucrat, unlike an American entrepreneur, was safer when he bought and adopted proven technologies from abroad rather than risking state money on untried ones at home. In 1856, Vice Consul G. M. Hutton warned the State Department: "Any tools or machinery sent here must be of well established reputation – they will adopt and use – but dislike experimenting."[35]

Lacking a public that would take the initiative to invent and adopt new technologies, the Russian state became the main agent of modernization. Progressive bureaucrats like Melnikov explained the profitability of steamships to merchants, while the state treasury paid for railroad construction. Thus, two results were achieved simultaneously: introducing steamers, railroads, and the telegraph to Russia; and giving joint-stock societies confidence that these innovations were efficient and merited private investment going forward. The fact that the state had taken on this role created an asymmetry in Russian–American cooperation in the field of technology transfer: the main contracting parties were the Russian state and American private businessmen and inventors. This difference also highlighted the two countries' divergent paths to modernization: whereas in the United States the steam engine was initially introduced to transport passengers and freight, the Russian government was motivated more by military and security concerns than by the country's economic needs. However, the technological innovations promoted by the state modernized Russian society, as the American traveler and writer Bayard Taylor observed at the end of the 1850s: "change is at last making itself felt even in Moscow – the very focus of Russian nationality. When the Locomotive once enters a city the ghosts of the Past take flight for ever."[36]

In the sphere of technology, Russia was a recipient of modern American models and experience. There were also policies that encouraged Russians and Americans to look at the Other's experience as a mirror of their home debates. The first such policy was the territorial expansion of the two countries, which culminated for the United States and was on the rise for Russia during the 1840s.

US TERRITORIAL EXPANSION AND RUSSIA'S WAR IN THE CAUCASUS

After the one-year tenure of Churchill Cambreleng as US minister to Russia, the position in St. Petersburg passed to Colonel Charles S. Todd, who stayed there from 1841 to 1846. During that period, the United States made a huge leap in its territorial expansion (including the annexation of Texas, the division of Oregon, and the start of the Mexican War). Todd's reports to Washington revealed a favorable Russian attitude toward American plans, but also demonstrated that the diplomatic corps in St. Petersburg possessed a good level of understanding of the main tendencies of American politics, astutely predicting that territorial expansion would deepen the split between states and put the Union in danger "as a consequence of the domestic slave question."[37]

The Russian government favored the possible annexation of Texas by the United States not only because it would annoy Great Britain, but also owing to its understanding that the two nations faced similar challenges. In late March 1845, former president and influential congressman John Quincy Adams noted in his diary that Russian minister Bodisco had "no objections to the annexation of Texas to the United States. He said laughing that Russia, herself in the habit of taking ten times the amount of Texas, could not object to that measure, but the main point was to do it in a genteel way."[38]

Bodisco's comment came about in the context of a discussion between himself and Adams about the possibility of the United States seizing Monterey, one of the largest harbors on the Pacific coast, from Mexico

DEFENCE OF THE CALIFORNIA BANK

Figure 3.2 Defence of the California Bank. A satire voicing American suspicions of foreign designs on California after the discovery of gold there in 1848. Among other European heads, Tsar Nicholas I of Russia, as a bear, who recites, "As something is 'Bruin' I'll put in my 'paw'/ While the Nations around me are making a 'Jaw.'"
Courtesy of Library of Congress.

(Figure 3.2). The Pacific Ocean appeared in the conversation for a reason. The activization of US foreign policy in the region begun by Daniel Webster, Secretary of State in 1841–43, meant that America joined the power struggle there. By the early 1840s, Great Britain and Russia were the leading European powers in the North Pacific. This gave the United States another chance to play on the existing tensions between the European powers. Todd reported from St. Petersburg that Russia's attitude toward American aspirations was a salutary one: "Russia does not interfere with our claim to the N. W. Coast between 42 & 49."[39] At the same time, Russia's own expansion to the east and south drew a lot of American attention.

Until the mid-1840s, US journals did not pay much attention to Russia's eastern policy. But, as US expansionism surged during that period, comparisons to Russia naturally emerged. US minister to Russia Charles S. Todd, commenting on the appointment of Count Vorontsov as the new Russian governor in the Caucasus, compared the war in that region to the "Florida affair."[40] George L. Ditson's *Circassia; or a Tour to the Caucasus,* published in 1850, became the first description of an American's journey to that disturbing region of the Russian Empire. In the Introduction, Ditson wrote that in the Caucasian war "Americans ... may recognize ... many of those shameless and cruel features which characterized our wars with the Red Men, as we drove tribe after tribe from their homes, lands, and the sacred graves of their fathers." Nor was Ditson the first to draw such a comparison: he cited Russian prince Kochubey as having told him, "These Circassians are just your American Indians – as untamable and uncivilized."[41]

American journalists and statesmen of the 1830s–1840s had very limited knowledge of the Islamic East or the peculiarities of the political, religious, military, or cultural relations of the different peoples who inhabited the Black Sea region. They lacked the terms, concepts, or notions to have these conversations. Russian policy and conflicts were therefore described by analogizing them to domestic problems, with the choice of analogy depending on the current political situation. The major points of comparison were the Indian wars as an analogue of the Caucasus war, the Mexican War as a parallel to the Russo-Turkish wars, a comparison of Turkey to Cuba in the sense that both controlled strategic waterways, and a general view of the Russian Empire's eastern policy as part of the religious wars or "progress of civilization" in the Orient. These analogues would change with the change in attitudes caused by the revolutions in Europe.

EUROPEAN REVOLUTIONS

In February 1848, when a revolution struck France and then other European countries, the United States had just concluded the war with Mexico by annexing a large portion of Mexican territory. The Democratic cabinet of President James K. Polk included two former American envoys to Russia, Vice-President George M. Dallas and Secretary of State James Buchanan. That reality notwithstanding, the American government seemed to have no special policy toward Russia during the first stage of the "Spring of Nations."

The initial reaction to European events was hope that democracies modeled after America would emerge in the Old World. The Young America Movement, which promoted expansion and domestic reforms, gained a second wind from the European news. It envisaged the quick advent of an Americanized Europe. However, Americans and Europeans were concerned about Russia's possible role in the European turmoil. Russia's political ends in the flow of events were unclear. Some Americans even began to advise the Russian emperor as to how he should use the situation in Europe. The *New York Herald* published one such letter under the title "What the Emperor of Russia Ought to Do in the Present Crisis of European Affairs." Despite its fantastical nature, the plan illustrates an important feature of the American attitude: while Russia must not interfere with democratic movements in Europe (including those in Russian-administered Poland), it could become a liberating force for Eastern peoples, from Turkey to India and China.[42]

The essence of the American concern was the problem of political supremacy in Europe and a possible shift in the balance of power. US minister to Berlin Andrew J. Donelson expressed concern that "Russia's army of a million [might pour] into the centre of Europe" in response to the revolutions.[43] For American politicians of a conservative bent, Russia was not a battleground for the struggle between liberal and authoritarian principles, as the rest of Europe was. Russia (except for Poland) and the United States were external forces vis-à-vis European affairs.

The new US minister to St. Petersburg, Ralph Isaacs Ingersoll, understood well the main headache of his superiors and was quick to inform both Secretary of State Buchanan and his Berlin colleague Donelson that "Russia will not interfere . . . in the concerns of her neighbors."[44] By the middle of April he assured President Polk that "Poland is the only point where the popular movement will press upon Russia."[45]

Reassured that Russia and Great Britain would not interfere in the "natural" course of events in Europe, American diplomacy lost most of its interest in the Russian position. Ingersoll even received permission to leave St. Petersburg, which he had been denied earlier in the spring, and the new minister, Arthur P. Bagby, arrived in the Russian capital only at the end of the summer. Contrary to Ingersoll's prediction, Russia did meddle in the European revolutions, but not in Poland: in 1849, the Austrian emperor faced the powerful Magyar uprising and asked for Russian help. Russia's assistance to Austria in suppressing the Hungarian rebellion was less an act under the mandate of the Holy Alliance than it was part of Russia's struggle for "national aims" in the Balkans and emergency aid to an ally. In no other instance did Russia interfere in the mid-century revolutions. The policy-makers of all the nations, from the republican United States to the absolute Russian monarchy, preferred to formulate foreign policy aims based upon state interest, understood in terms of alliances, territorial gains, and diplomatic statuses. For America, this meant a refusal to follow the radical philosophy of the Young Americans. For Russia, it entailed abandoning the legitimist principles of the Holy Alliance.

Whereas diplomats and government officials everywhere saw the crisis almost exclusively in terms of relations between states, public opinion both in the United States and in Europe considered the revolutions of 1848–1849 a struggle between competing sets of principles. Americans were just beginning to learn how to use public opinion in Europe to their advantage.

DEBATES ABOUT RUSSIA AND AMERICA

In the first half of the nineteenth century, Americans frequently compared the US political system, way of life, or culture to the English or French models. When they needed an example of a society that was the absolute opposite of their own, they used the Russian Empire. In the spring of 1848, as the Senate discussed the territorial acquisitions that had resulted from the Mexican War, Senator Daniel Webster cited Russia as a country whose example the United States could not emulate: "Russia may rule in the Ukraine and the provinces of the Caucasus and Kamtschatka by different codes, ordinances, or ukases. We can do no such thing." In other words, the United States could not extend its Constitution to the alien population of the new territories, which had different traditions, had never held jury trials, and had never elected their governments.[46] For the democratic United States, the Russian Empire was a political model opposed to its own, one that was gradually becoming a significant Other for American democratic identity.

The Russian intervention into the Hungarian rebellion sparked an outburst of anti-Russian sentiment on the part of the American public. The *New York Herald* now described the events in Europe as a great struggle between "the liberal cause, and Russia leading the despots." In the event that Russian despotism were to win, the article went on, it would "immediately turn towards America, to punish us, the instigators, the first to lift up before the world the standard of republicanism."[47]

Some experienced politicians used this public indignation to build political constructions for domestic use.[48] Defending the leader of the Hungarian rebels, Louis (Lajos) Kossuth, against Austrian and Russian demands that he be handed over to the Austrian authorities, the leader of American nationalism, Daniel Webster, urged his fellow citizens to "understand the position in which we stand, as the great republic of the world, at the most interesting era of its history," subsequently explaining to a friend that he wanted to "touch the national pride, and make a man feel sheepish and look silly who should speak of disunion."[49]

The early aftermath of the European revolutions of 1848–1849 provided the first opportunity for Americans to amend their self-identification to reflect the new importance of their republican model for the Old World.

This seemed to call for radical change to Russia's image in American political debates and journalists' depictions, especially those of journalists agitated by exiled Hungarian leader Kossuth's tour of the United States in 1851–1852. Thus, several magazines of the era published negative reviews of George Leighton Ditson's book about his Caucasian travels. The reviewers accused the author of being biased toward Russia and therefore failing to recognize that, as the *New Englander and Yale Review* put it, the Circassians were "fighting for their lives and their freedom." In a revealing manner, the reviewer used American analogues to explain Russian realities: "By the treaty of Adrianople in 1829 Turkey ceded to Russia all the littoral of the Black Sea; which is very much as if Mexico should cede to the United States Cuba or Porto Rico."[50] Whereas Ditson compared the Circassians to American Indians, calling the Russian advance in the Caucasus a "civilizing" move, an author writing in the *U.S. Democratic Review* doubted the Russian civilizing mission and compared the people of the Caucasus to "the followers of Leonidas at Thermopylae."[51] Thus, the use of different analogies allowed American publications to portray the very same events in completely opposite ways.

Many democratic and nationalist European revolutionaries considered the United States the model for their constitutional projects. Thus, the new generation of American politicians dreamed of revolutionizing the international order to position the model democratic republic as the leading state rather than a mere survivor within the existing world system based on legitimism and monarchical rule. As Russia was the main guarantor of the Vienna system of international relations, created after the Napoleonic wars, it could not escape becoming a major target. The polarization of views on the philosophy of international relations in the 1850s is well demonstrated by several books written and published in the United States that aimed to challenge Alexis de Tocqueville's prophecy that Russia and the United States were destined to master half the world each.

In 1854, George N. Sanders, the former editor of the *U.S. Democratic Review* and one of the Young America leaders, who was now the US consul in London, invited exiled revolutionaries to dine at his house. Russia was represented by Alexander Herzen, who perspicaciously linked the "idea of giving a diplomatic dinner to the enemies of all existing governments" to the Americans' belief that they sent ambassadors "not to kings but to peoples."[52]

The most comprehensive framework that would have revolutionized the international system in that period came in a book published by a young Whig politician, Henry Winter Davis, in 1852. Titled *The War of Ormuzd and*

Ahriman in the Nineteenth Century, it became, in a historical irony, the first book devoted to US–Russian relations and one of the first American books on international relations. The structure of the book explained the author's idea: from the history of the Holy Alliance created in Vienna, he proceeded to the sequence of "revolts against the Holy conspirators" in 1830 and 1848–1849, then continued by contrasting "American and English liberty" with "Russian Dictatorship." His last chapter was devoted to "The American Republic and the Last War of Freedom and Despotism" that would eventually erupt.[53]

This short but sharp surge in anti-Russian sentiment among Americans forced the senior Russian Consul General in New York, Alexei Evstafiev (who had proved himself an efficient propagandist forty years earlier, during the War of 1812), to write a monograph criticizing the US political system and the country's foreign policy. Evstafiev completed his book in May 1852: although it was never published and thus did not influence the public in either country, it skillfully summarized the official Russian view of American democracy, which was shared by many Russian elites.

Evstafiev presented a comparison between "one of the extremes, the popular American Republic," and "its antipodal Russian Despotism." The Russian diplomat considered the main question of his time: "whether monarchies combine against republics, or republics are sworn to destroy all monarchies." He pounced on the United States and on Americans, criticizing the attitude that would later become known as American exceptionalism, and was especially indignant about the American belief "that nothing anti-republican has any value, that no good, physical or moral, can spring from the soil of monarchy," reminding Americans of the irony of "their own doctrine that, in all respect, a negro slave is better off, much better, than the negro in a state of freedom!!"[54]

Two other books juxtaposing Russia and America published in the United States in the mid-1850s were written by emigrants from Russia. In his book *Russia as It Is* (1854), Adam Gurowski, who emigrated from the Russian Empire after participating in the 1830 Polish rebellion, challenged Tocqueville's comparison of the two countries, arguing that there were no similarities between Russia and America beyond their collective geographic vastness. Instead, Gurowski insisted that "Russia is saddled by despotism [while] America initiates history and humanity into a new era – which a century ago was looked on as an Utopia – constructing a social order on the foundations of equality and liberty."[55]

A second émigré, revolutionary activist Ivan Golovin, took the opposite approach, making a radical attack on America in his *Stars and Stripes* (1856).

He denounced European "panegyrists of American democracy" and insisted "that unlimited competition, unbounded love of material interests, are not fit to resolve the questions pending in our age." Praising America as an open field for social experiments (and describing the socialist commune Icaria and even Mormons as a kind of socialist community), Golovin caustically addressed the political principles upon which the United States was built: "democracy is developing the material instincts of man at the expense of his intellect and morality; [...] and that honour and intellect being in minority with man, the government of the majority is that of dishonesty and stupidity."[56]

The writing and publication of books in the field that we would now call comparative politics was a new phenomenon. It reflected the fact that both American society and Russian society perceived approaching crises; the books' content also foreshadowed the bipolar vision of the world. In the mid-1850s, increased domestic tensions, combined with the collapse of the post-Napoleonic world order, especially hurt the Russian Empire.

THE CRIMEAN WAR

The anti-Russian sentiments of the early 1850s proved to be short-lived. The revolutionaries were unable to mount a serious challenge to the dominant conservative attitude in American foreign policy, which soon brought US diplomacy significant rewards. This was during the time of the Crimean War (1853–1856). In December 1852, *U.S. Magazine and Democratic Review* had written a sarcastic article about diplomatic agents in Europe that included the pejorative sentence "Who knows and who cares what our representatives have done, or are doing, at the commanding points of the eastern world, St. Petersburg, and Constantinople" – a statement intended to emphasize the remoteness of the Russian and Ottoman empires from America.[57] A year later, these two capitals would capture the attention of the entire world.

Russia had plunged into war against the Ottoman Empire, which was supported by Great Britain, France, and the Kingdom of Sardinia. St. Petersburg found no allies in the battle it waged on the Crimean Peninsula in the Black Sea, and its enemy had the British press on its side. The longtime Russian Minister to Washington, Alexander Bodisco, had died in January 1854, at the very beginning of the Crimean War, complicating the diplomatic connection between Russia and the United States.

In March 1854, Secretary of State William Learned Marcy informed his friend James Buchanan, then the US minister in Great Britain, that Russia's defeat, which seemed probable, would encourage Great Britain and France to meddle in American affairs, a consideration that was "Russianizing some of our people."[58] At the same time, in an official instruction to Thomas Seymour, the US minister in St. Petersburg, Marcy insisted that the United States must "maintain existing friendly relations with each of the belligerents" and should not "in any way [...] compromise our neutrality."[59]

As the hostilities in Crimea developed, American public opinion gradually became more sympathetic to Russia and more inimical to "entente cordiale." The Allies' declaration that they wanted to use force to establish international justice was particularly ill-received in the United States. Seymour expressed an opinion widespread among his compatriots when he reported to Marcy that there was "more reason to expect interference in the affairs of our Country from those who are in alliance against Russia, than from any other source."[60]

However, US diplomacy did not confine itself to expressing its own position on the conflict. The United States took advantage of the aggravated international situation to increase its influence on the world stage. Indeed, the Russian chargé d'affaires in Washington, Eduard Stoeckl, assessed the preliminary discussions of the possibility that the United States might mediate the conflict as a manifestation of the American aspiration "to play a more active role in European affairs."[61]

In his first dispatch to Washington as a minister to Russia, Seymour advised the US government to send an American frigate to the Baltic Sea. "The presence of an American war vessel would have the effect to check any improper interference with our commerce in that sea."[62] Such a suggestion was in fact a Russian dream. An (anonymous) Englishwoman who spent the war in St. Petersburg reported that "The Russians, upon the strength of their hopes, were always threatening us with the American fleet in the Baltic, which would place the Allied fleets between two enemies. Is the old adage about extremes meeting really so near the truth?"[63] Indeed, the Crimean War accelerated the Russian–American rapprochement. While no American fleet entered the Baltic, these events paved the way for the Russian navy's visit to New York a decade later.

Even more important in this light were US attempts to use the Crimean War to amend some dispositions of international law. Throughout the previous decade, commercial treaties were almost the only form of international agreement that US diplomats signed. During the Crimean War, American diplomacy managed to introduce a novelty into the international system. The Convention on Neutral Rights, signed by the United States and Russia on July 22, 1854, would become a model; it was followed by similar conventions with the Kingdom of the Two Sicilies, Nicaragua, Peru, and

Hawai'i.[64] Such countries as Prussia, Sweden, Denmark, and the Netherlands were also invited to join the system of guarantees to neutral parties, but refused to sign the treaty out of fear of provoking a negative reaction from Great Britain and France.[65] In other corners of the world, the United States made significant advances, most importantly in Japan (where Commodore Matthew C. Perry got the first treaty signed in 1854) and in Persia (Iran), where Russia facilitated American success.[66]

Certainly, among the tasks of US diplomacy was to use the war to strengthen collaboration with Russia. US Secretary of State Marcy told Seymour that, since the war between Russia and the European powers would leave "deep wounds" from which their relations would likely take a long time to heal, American proposals of a "more intimate commercial connection" should be received with favor by the Russian government and people.[67] Marcy described American public opinion during the Crimean War as decidedly pro-Russian. Indeed, tens of American surgeons went to work in Russian hospitals in Crimea, many of them dying there.[68] While most of these surgeons sought "adventure, money, experience, or all of the above,"[69] they chose to support the Russian side because the American public was positively disposed toward Russia.

The United States gained obvious benefits from the crisis of the international system in the middle of the nineteenth century. It managed to introduce new elements of international law that strengthened its commerce and added democratic attractiveness to its international standing. For its part, Russia considered the United States the only ally that could be trusted in the challenging context of a war against a coalition of European powers.

Thus, in the critical period of 1848–1856, when the Vienna system of international relations cracked, Russia and the United States took important steps toward each other. During that period, constraints in the form of fears about the negative reaction of Great Britain were tossed aside and the United States finally signed a long-desired convention on neutral rights, inaugurating a new collaboration between the two countries.

One of the results of the Crimean War was the collapse of the legitimist doctrine and the emergence of new philosophies of international relations. Affluent South Carolina planter and influential politician Francis W. Pickens, who succeeded Thomas Seymour as US minister to St. Petersburg in 1858, attached great importance to the cooling of Russia's relations with Austria after the Crimean War and called his government's attention to the fact that "all the Sclavonic race under the Hapsburg crown look to Russia as their 'Fatherland,' and feel that she is the protector of their peculiar race."[70]

Pickens witnessed the very beginning of the Pan-Slavist ideas that would spread throughout Russia and the Slavic territories of Europe in the second half of the nineteenth century. Major battles were approaching in the domestic affairs of both nations. However, the main topic of Pickens' dispatches was Russia's preparations for the abolition of serfdom.

SLAVERY AND SERFDOM

The existence of social institutions based on forced labor and personal bondage – slavery and serfdom – in their respective countries brought antebellum America and Russia even closer together on the eve of the emancipation of the serfs. Notwithstanding the many socioeconomic differences between the two institutions, the institutions' defenders and critics alike cited the example of the other country to support their positions.[71]

Unlike American Negroes in the southern United States, serfs were not the private property of nobles. Serfs possessed some property of their own – potentially including a house, cattle, and agricultural tools – and had societal institutions of their own (the peasant community), but were attached to the soil that belonged to a noble. Slaves in America were themselves the property of a slaveholder and had neither property nor organization of their own.

There were, however, many commonalities between the two. Depending on their respective positions, Russians and Americans either emphasized the evil of both serfdom and slavery, singled out one of them as relatively beneficial, or praised both as good institutions. Thus, antebellum Southern intellectual George Fitzhugh called Russia, along with the American South, "the only conservative section of civilized christendom."[72]

Comparisons between serfdom and slavery were common for many years. However, in the 1830s, mutual interest had been rather incidental. It steadily increased with the intensification of political debates about – and public awareness of the problem of – the fate of the two "special institutions."

By the mid-1850s, this theme loomed large in diplomatic reporting and public debates. In the summer of 1859, Pickens wrote to Secretary of State Lewis Cass that the Russian government found itself in a position where "it is extremely difficult to stand still, and still more difficult to move forward on that subject [the abolition of serfdom]." The American envoy went on to predict that "the Feudal system . . . shall be finally overthrown throughout Europe."[73] By linking serfdom to feudalism, Pickens distinguished it from American slavery; he made no analogies to American Negro slavery, as the latter was by no means a feudal phenomenon. After returning home in the fall of 1860, the rich planter was elected Governor of South Carolina, and a few weeks later his State proclaimed its secession. This was the first event of the political crisis that would grow into the Civil War that ended slavery.

However, there were opponents to slavery and serfdom who considered the institutions similar. The translation of Harriett Beecher Stowe's *Uncle Tom's Cabin* into Russian, lectures about Negro slavery in Russian universities, and travelers' articles in leading journals not only presented occasions for discussing the problems of their own society, but also created a tendency to focus on American slavery in Russian perceptions of the United States.[74]

Dmitrii Kachenovsky, a professor at Kharkov University, defended his doctoral dissertation in 1855 at Moscow University, where he established close ties with a group of liberal intelligentsia. His research interests included international law, and he was among the first Russian scholars to publish a study of US history – a biographical article about Daniel Webster.[75] A student of Kachenovsky, the famous sociologist Maxim Kovalevsky, recalled that in the late 1850s his mentor "for months in a row expounded on the history of abolition of negro trading, and hundreds of his students in his allusions fairly recognized an attack on serfdom."[76] Another student of Kachenovsky, Pavel Zelenyi, remembered his lecture of November 10, 1857: "[E]very listener clearly understood and felt that in telling about slaves' suffering, Kachenovsky meant whites as well as blacks."[77]

The story of Kachenovsky lecturing Russian students about the evils of American slavery in order to criticize serfdom had a parallel in the United States. Also in the fall of 1857, young Andrew Dickson White returned from his post as attaché to the US delegation in St. Petersburg and lectured his compatriots on the evils of serfdom. White recollected in his *Autobiography* that he sketched the effects of the serf system on serfs and serf-owners. He "made it black indeed, as it deserved, and though not a word was said regarding things in America, every thoughtful man present must have felt that it was the strongest indictment against our own system of slavery which my powers enabled me to make." White explained why he choose such a method to criticize an American evil: whereas attacking slavery directly would have "at once shut the minds and hearts of a large majority of the audience," his description of the evils of Russian serfdom "set people at thinking" and let them "discover the truth for themselves."[78] The two educators used the same strategy to achieve similar aims in two different countries. Even more revealingly, they did so for similar reasons: although there was no formal censorship in the United States, mainstream public opinion played effectively the same role as the Russian state censors, creating an incentive to bypass this censorship by using the example of the other country as an analogue.

CONCLUSION

Russia's decision to base its technological modernization on American expertise became the single most important factor enabling a US–Russian rapprochement. Russian orders helped American industry and boosted American self-confidence, while public interest in the distant empire moved American diplomats and travelers to produce original accounts of Russia.

Discussions about the fates of slavery and serfdom, as well as territorial expansion, facilitated rapprochement between the two countries during the 1840s. The European revolutions of 1848–1849 caused a crisis in American views of Russia and prompted the appearance of several books that portrayed Russia and the United States as opposite poles on the political map.

The domestic agendas of both Russia and the United States changed rapidly in the antebellum decade: the problem of slavery quickly found its way to the highest level of national debate in America, while Russia became preoccupied with the problem of its own institution of unfree labor and, following its defeat in the Crimean War, began to plan for the abolition of serfdom. The similarity between the two countries' national agendas brought them closer together, a process that culminated in their friendly relations during the American Civil War.

4

THE NOONDAY OF FRIENDSHIP, 1861–1881

OVERVIEW

The American Civil War not only shattered the political system of the United States and altered the course of the Republic, but also provided an opportunity for foreign powers to engage – albeit rather symbolically – in this domestic struggle. Russia, which had just begun its own reformation, emerged as the staunchest ally of the federal government. The fundamental reforms that had begun in the two countries with the emancipation of the serfs in 1861 and the abolition of slavery in 1865 continued with Reconstruction in the American South and the "Era of Great Reforms" in Russia. In their pursuit of solutions to their domestic conflicts, the two countries turned to each other as their best allies and models, inspiring change in one another and bolstering one another's resolve.

Meanwhile, the territorial expansion of the two countries culminated in the meeting of their frontiers on the Asian coast of the Pacific Ocean. At the same time, the status of Alaska, a remote and militarily defenseless territory, also demanded some kind of solution. Following intensive debates within the Russian government, Russian America was sold to the friendly United States in 1867, in a deal that marked the zenith of Russian–American relations.

In myriad spheres, encounters between the two countries multiplied. The wartime visits of Russian squadrons inaugurated a series of friendly missions by the Russian fleet to the United States and by American naval vessels to Russian ports in the late 1860s and 1870s. Grand Duke Alexis, the son of the Russian tsar, made a triumphant tour of the United States in 1871–1872. The Centennial International Exhibition in Philadelphia in 1876 featured substantial Russian participation, helping to foster genuine interest in Russian culture among Americans for the first time, while American engineers and entrepreneurs continued to build enterprises in the Russian Empire.

For the first time, emigrants from Russia – mainly revolutionary democrats and religious minorities such as Mennonites – arrived in the United States. The anti-Semitic policies of the Russian government were just becoming a cause for concern among some American politicians, but did not yet have the potential to spoil the Russian–American friendship.

Russian and American journalists continued to compare Russian territorial acquisitions in Central Asia with America's westward expansion and Indian wars. They considered both to be civilizing missions among savage and barbarian peoples. The American public viewed the Russo–Turkish War of 1877–1878 through the sympathetic eyes of their war correspondents within the Russian army.

Scholars of early Russian–American relations produced untold volumes on the Russian Navy's visits to American harbors in 1863–1864 and the Sale of Alaska, making them the two most-studied episodes of nineteenth-century diplomacy between the two countries.[1] These studies bolstered the arguments of those who emphasized the "historical friendship" between the nations, but came in for criticism from those who read these events more cynically: as being the result of pure selfishness on the part of the Russian authorities. Our narrative resolves this apparent dichotomy, revealing how state interests intertwined with the dominant identity discourses of the two nations, thus leaving room for each to interpret the other's political decisions in the most positive light.

For many decades, politicians and politicized scholars also debated the comparative legacy of Russian and American rule of Alaska, especially in terms of governmental relations with the natives and the environmental habits of the pioneers. Russian scholars eventually formed a research tradition and took the lead on studying the early history of Russian America, while the most recent books by American historians have extended the story into the last third of the nineteenth century, when America sought to integrate the newly acquired territory culturally and politically.[2] These works make it possible to summarize the story in a balanced way, as we do in the chapter below.

RUSSIA AND THE CIVIL WAR: DIPLOMATIC AND NAVAL RESPONSE

The outbreak of the Civil War in North America divided the European countries. Great Britain announced its neutrality, thus recognizing the South as a belligerent side – the first step toward diplomatic recognition. France followed suit.

Russia, while also neutral, was set apart by its firm refusal to deal with the rebel states. Alexander II's attitude toward the conflict in North America was defined by the United States' significance for the international balance of the age. The existence of the United States, Russian chargé d'affaires in Washington Eduard Stoeckl wrote to St. Petersburg, was "more important for us than for any other state." Russia needed to secure its interests and to promote its influence in the Pacific. In that quarter, continued Stoeckl, Russia had "already met and will continue to meet obstacles created by England, so Americans' assistance will be useful for us."[3] Indeed, Russia's goal of regaining the international standing lost with its defeat in the Crimean War demanded the existence of a strong United States that could counterbalance England and France. Whatever happened in American politics, Russia's primary concern was a strategic one.

In July 1861, world newspapers published a dispatch by Russian minister of foreign affairs Alexander Gorchakov, who lamented the outbreak of a civil war and stated that "Russia has the friendliest interests in America." Gorchakov called Russian–American relations "a manifestation of natural solidarity of interests and sympathies" and stated that "the American Union may rely on the most sincere compassion on the part of our Emperor during the crisis it is going through at the present time."[4] Unlike British and French diplomacy, which encouraged the Confederacy in its attempts to gain diplomatic recognition, the Russian Empire unequivocally supported the federal Union, the only European power to do so. Gorchakov repeatedly assured Stoeckl in March 1862 that Russia recognized in the United States "only the government that is situated in Washington."[5]

The diplomats of the two countries played an important role in Russian–American rapprochement during the period. Throughout the war, the experienced diplomat Stoeckl represented the Russian tsar in Washington. Abraham Lincoln's administration was represented in St. Petersburg alternately by ministers Cassius Marcellus Clay and Simon Cameron. Unlike the Russian representative, neither of them possessed any diplomatic experience.

Cassius Clay was a rare example of a Southern abolitionist. By the time of Lincoln's election, he was a prominent figure in the Republican Party. Finding no role in Washington after the outbreak of the Civil War, he agreed to go to Russia. Very few ministers were as successful in St. Petersburg and as deeply interested in Russian society as Clay. His abolitionist views and his southern background made him very sympathetic to the peaceful Russian emancipation of the serfs, while his aristocratic upbringing enabled him to feel comfortable among the St. Petersburg nobility. Indeed, one historian has noted that "This representative of America's 19th century 'landed gentry' made Russia and America appear more similar than they actually were."[6]

In 1862, Clay – apparently concerned that he was not participating in the historic struggle going on at home – resigned from his position in Russia and returned to the United States, where he received the rank of major-general. He would soon apply to President Lincoln for permission to return to St. Petersburg. In the meantime, however, Lincoln's first Secretary of War, Simon Cameron, lost his job and went into temporary "exile" in Russia. Cameron brought with him the famous traveler and author Bayard Taylor as a secretary of legation. Since Cameron left St. Petersburg less than a month after arrival, Taylor would act as chargé d'affaires until Clay's return in 1863. A kind of celebrity in the Russian capital, Clay was not the initiator but one of the major channels of intensive bilateral relations during and immediately after the Civil War.

Taylor, a writer and poet, tried to make his creative writing part of US–Russian relations. One of his first endeavors in Russia was a poem on the one-thousandth anniversary of the Russian state, a copy of which Cameron gave to Prince Gorchakov. He in turn showed it to the emperor, who was "very much touched and delighted."[7] Taylor further informed a friend that three years in Russia would enable him "to produce such a work on Russia as has not yet been written – to do justice to this great nation of the Future."[8] Having discovered "how little is really known of" the Russian people, Taylor aimed to become "the first man to describe this great nation in her true aspects."[9] During his time in Russia, Taylor would write several books, some of them indeed inspired by Russian material, although his premature departure would preclude him from fulfilling his promise.

Preliminary information about the Emancipation Proclamation was met with enthusiasm in Russia. During the first stage of the American Civil War, the Russian government had supported Lincoln's administration on the basis of geopolitical concerns. After the United States began to follow Russia's example in abolishing slavery (starting in the rebellious states), the similarities in their domestic agendas increased Russians' sympathy for the Northern cause. As Gorchakov wrote in a dispatch, "Both countries carried out a struggle for emancipation, both had to face disagreements and foreign intrigues."[10]

The American Civil War had already left Russia isolated on the international scene, and this challenging situation became even less favorable following the Polish rebellion of 1863. For its part, the American public was too absorbed with its domestic turmoil to sympathize with the Poles; in any case, the Republican administration took a strategic view of the rebellion, seeing the Poles as allies of hostile France and England – and, as Cassius Clay suggested, Catholic conspirators rather than fighters for freedom. Yet

St. Petersburg's military suppression of this uprising in the western part of its empire provoked a harsh reaction from England, Austria, and France. With the specter of the Crimean War-era anti-Russian coalition once again looming large, and anticipating a breakdown in relations, Alexander II decided to send six of the strongest ships of the Russian Baltic fleet out of that bottle-necked sea in order "for the ships to spread in the different quarters [...] and, as soon as they learned trustworthily about the split with the Western powers, to cut commercial routes and do their best to damage the commerce of our enemies."[11] Rear-Admiral Stepan Lesovskii was appointed the commander of the Atlantic Squadron and sent "to the coast of the North-American United States" to wait for the resolution of the Polish question.[12] In the process, the Russian squadron, which consisted of relatively new ships built in 1860–1862, also sought to demonstrate the new naval capacity that Russia had acquired with its rearmament program.

By the end of September, the Atlantic Squadron had dropped anchor in New York harbor. The Americans greeted the approximately 3,000 Russian seamen enthusiastically. At the same time, another Russian squadron, under the command of Rear-Admiral Andrei Popov, entered San Francisco harbor, where it was met equally enthusiastically.

The secrecy of the naval visit provided fertile soil for rumors. Among the most popular were suspicions of a secret military alliance between Russia and America and even preparations for a joint expedition against the French in Mexico. Scholars agree that Lincoln and other US officials were well aware that fear of a European war was the main reason for the fleet visits, but chose to frame the presence of Russian ships as evidence of Russian support for the Union cause in order to improve domestic morale and help warn England and France against interfering in the American conflict.[13] And indeed, the presence of the Russian fleet in Northern harbors during the Civil War played a role in preventing the European powers from interfering diplomatically or militarily in the Civil War on behalf of the South and helped to strengthen Russian–American friendship.

THE EMANCIPATION OF THE SERFS AS A MODEL FOR THE ABOLITION OF SLAVERY

On February 19, 1861, Alexander II abolished serfdom. Some American newspapers published the text of Alexander II's emancipation decree on the day of the attack on Fort Sumter: April 12, 1861.[14] But, at first, the events of the Civil War seemed to overshadow this dispatch from a distant empire. Moreover, during the first stage of his presidency, Lincoln actively sought to avoid the theme of slavery and even promised to keep it intact in order to maintain – or, once fighting had broken out, reestablish – the Union. Consequently, no immediate comment on the emancipation of the Russian serfs can be found in the official papers of Lincoln or his Cabinet.

Unsurprisingly, Southern newspapers warned against the calamities that the abolition of serfdom would entail, including reducing "at once to beggary nearly the whole of the Russian nobility, hitherto the ruling power in the State." One Southern author argued that a Negro or Russian "will not work, when released from bondage," painting an apocalyptic picture of Alexander II's situation: "his revenues falling off, agriculture neglected, manufactures brought to a dead halt, and his whole empire threatened with ruin."[15] The Northern press, in response, ironically lamented that it was "a sore subject with our pro-slavery people, this faithlessness of Russia to the cause of human oppression."[16]

For the abolitionist press, doubt in the ability of the United States to serve as the model for the rest of mankind was a serious challenge to American identity and demanded action.[17] The abolitionist Gerrit Smith, at a meeting held in Peterboro on April 27, 1861, linked the Russian example to the American future: "Russia has declared the liberty of her twenty millions of slaves; and America must now give up her four millions."[18] The comparison gained popularity among radical speakers in the North. Senator Charles Sumner called for the government to free the slaves in order to avoid a bloody uprising, pointing out that in Russia emancipation "began from above."[19] That was certainly a call for President Lincoln to act.

In September 1862, Lincoln set his mind to abolition, issuing a Preliminary Emancipation Proclamation. Soon afterward, Andrew Dickson White developed his 1856 lecture about Russian serfdom, amended to add the emancipation of the serfs, into an article published by *Atlantic Monthly* in November 1862.[20] Throughout 1863, the Russian example was used with increased frequency. "The Czar of Russia set the noble example, and Abraham Lincoln has followed in his wake," exclaimed a writer in the *White Cloud Kansas Chief* on January 1, 1863, the day that the Emancipation Proclamation took effect.[21]

With the Civil War pushing Lincoln's government to political radicalization, the peaceful reform in Russia was even more attractive as an argument for the abolition of slavery. Lincoln made a special effort to use the Russian example as a propaganda tool. When chargé d'affaires of the US mission in St. Petersburg Bayard Taylor returned to America, he lectured about the Russians who had put an end to the institution of involuntary labor by peaceful means. When Lincoln attended Taylor's public appearance on December 17, 1863, he immediately realized the propagandistic potential of the lectures and urged Taylor to continue. The writer agreed, emphasizing that "the complete success of the scheme of emancipation in Russia has much significance for this nation at the present time."[22] Thus, the Russian Empire was recognized as a model for addressing the most profound American problem.

Although Russian society was mostly absorbed by its own problems at this time, the American Civil War and the abolition of slavery attracted the attention of conservatives and radicals alike. Russian diplomats in Washington Stoeckl and Carl Robert Osten-Saken supported Lincoln, but considered radical reformers "demagogues" and feared that the Civil War might eventually turn into a revolution that would inspire European anarchists.[23] Even more alarmed were Russian landlords, who saw the American example as a mirror of their own problems. Influential laird Nikolai Motovilov had traded in serfs before emancipation; he also claimed to have spiritual contact with Russian Orthodox elder Seraphim of Sarov (who had died in 1833 and would be canonized in 1903). During the Civil War, Motovilov equated Russian revolutionaries to American abolitionists. In a secret report addressed to Alexander II on April 15, 1866, Motovilov informed the tsar that on April 1, 1865, Seraphim's spirit had warned him about the murder of Abraham Lincoln, because God disliked Lincoln's "terrible oppression, devastation and humiliation" of Southern slaveowners. Motovilov complained that the same "injustice" had been visited on the Russian nobility by "the prevailing Decembrists, ardent abolitionists."[24] He felt himself a victim of the same revolutionary wave that was sweeping the United States.

Russian revolutionary democrats likewise claimed that the American Civil War paralleled the Russian struggle between landed nobility and democratic commoners – although, unlike Motovilov, they supported the Northern cause. Russian émigré democrat Alexander Herzen saw the Civil War as the "second American revolution." Writer and journalist Nikolai Chernyshevsky, a leading figure of his generation, avidly followed the events of the Civil War, always preferring radical solutions to any hint of compromise with the Southerners.[25] The problem of race and slavery was also part of the 'split among nihilists," a fierce polemic between the columnists of the two major democratic magazines of Russia, *Sovremennik* and *Russkoe slovo*, that took place in 1863–1866. Varfolomey Zaitsev published a favorable review of one of the first "scientific" books on racial inequality translated into Russian. In his review, naturalist ideas served as an apology for slavery.[26] In Zaitsev's view, this apology solved the biggest problem that Russian revolutionary democrats faced when studying the American model: the combination of the democratic republican government that they adored and the slavery that they despised. However, this apology came too late to spread in Russia. While most Russian democrats condemned Zaitsev's position, the story demonstrates how "scientific" support for racism found its way into the science-oriented group of Russian radicals.

In the end, slavery and serfdom both disappeared within a short period that was marked, in both countries, by huge social and political upheaval combined with a national identity crisis.[27] An analysis of American society's reaction to the abolition of serfdom helps us to understand better the evolution of "mainstream" Northern opinion, which moved during the Civil War from suppressing abolitionist propaganda to embracing the emancipation of slaves in the South. The information about the serfs' emancipation could not be ignored as easily as abolitionist propaganda, with the result that the anti-slavery cause received "powerful encouragement" from Russian news.[28] With this radical change, Russia eliminated the institution that had dominated American constructions of Russian identity. This turn of events not only required changes to the American image of Russia, but also facilitated changes in the American Self as Russian reform aided its American counterpart. Moreover, it was that rare situation in American–Russian interactions where Russia was perceived as going ahead of the United States in reforming its society; historically, America had more often served as a model for Russian reforms. US democracy and federalism proved to be obstacles to the abolition of slavery, while in autocratic Russia serfs were freed by the tsar's decision, thus giving an additional argument to the Russian monarchist liberals. For the first time in history, American progressives felt their society was lagging behind.

POSTWAR ENCOUNTERS AND THE SALE OF ALASKA

The assassination of Abraham Lincoln in April 1865 coincided for Russians with the death of Alexander II's elder son Nicholas, the heir apparent, from meningitis. During the ensuing mourning period in Russia, references were made to the American president. A year after Lincoln's death, on April 4 (16), 1866, Alexander II barely escaped an assassination attempt, news that provoked an outpouring of sympathy from Americans. The US Congress congratulated the Russian tsar in a joint resolution of its two chambers and sent a special mission to St. Petersburg under the command of deputy navy minister Gustavus Vasa Fox. Fox was authorized to use the newest monitor, USS *Miantonomoh*, to deliver the document, express gratitude for Russia's support of the federal cause in the Civil War, and deepen naval cooperation between the two countries. The tour of Russia on which members of the Fox mission embarked featured a series of festivities that took Russian–American friendship to new heights (Figure 4.1). Newspapers in both countries followed the warm welcome that these Americans received in Russia.

The visit paved the way for the decision to sell Russian America to the United States.

Russian diplomats had been discussing the possibility of selling Alaska to the United States since the Crimean War, even going so far as to draft a treaty on the topic. However, it was only after the Civil War that the decision was made and the bargain struck. The sale of Alaska should be seen as one of the liberal reforms that the Russian government implemented in the 1860s. Top government officials such as the influential Grand Duke Constantine and Finance Minister Michael Reutern considered the Russian American Company that administered Alaska to be part of an old feudal monopolist system incompatible with the free-trade requirements of the liberal age.

The tsar's government made the final decision during a secret meeting in December 1866. The reasons for sale included financial calculations (a colony on another continent was expensive to maintain, while the $7.2 million received for Alaska would help support railroad construction), the failure to reform the Russian American Company, the strategic vulnerability of the territory in the event of a new war, the perceived inevitability of Alaska's future acquisition by the United States, and the desire to maintain amicable relations with the United States.[29] Admittedly, an anti-liberal wave was already starting to temper the tsar's reformist spirit. However, territorial acquisitions in Central Asia and especially the Far East made the loss of this American possession less problematic. Certainly, a significant segment of the Russian elite was very disappointed by the sale of the "Russian land," just as they had been with the abolition of serfdom, but in an absolute monarchy the tsar's decision could not openly be called into question.

In the United States, too, the purchase ignited controversy. American newspapers ridiculed the Alaska Purchase: *Leslie's Illustrated*, for example, depicted the Russian tsar as cheating the ingenuous US Secretary of State (Figure 4.2).

However, Secretary of State William Henry Seward skillfully steered the ratification process. Seward was an ardent expansionist, so it was no coincidence that he directed the United States' last continental acquisition, the territory later nicknamed "the Last Frontier."[30] He and Russian Minister in

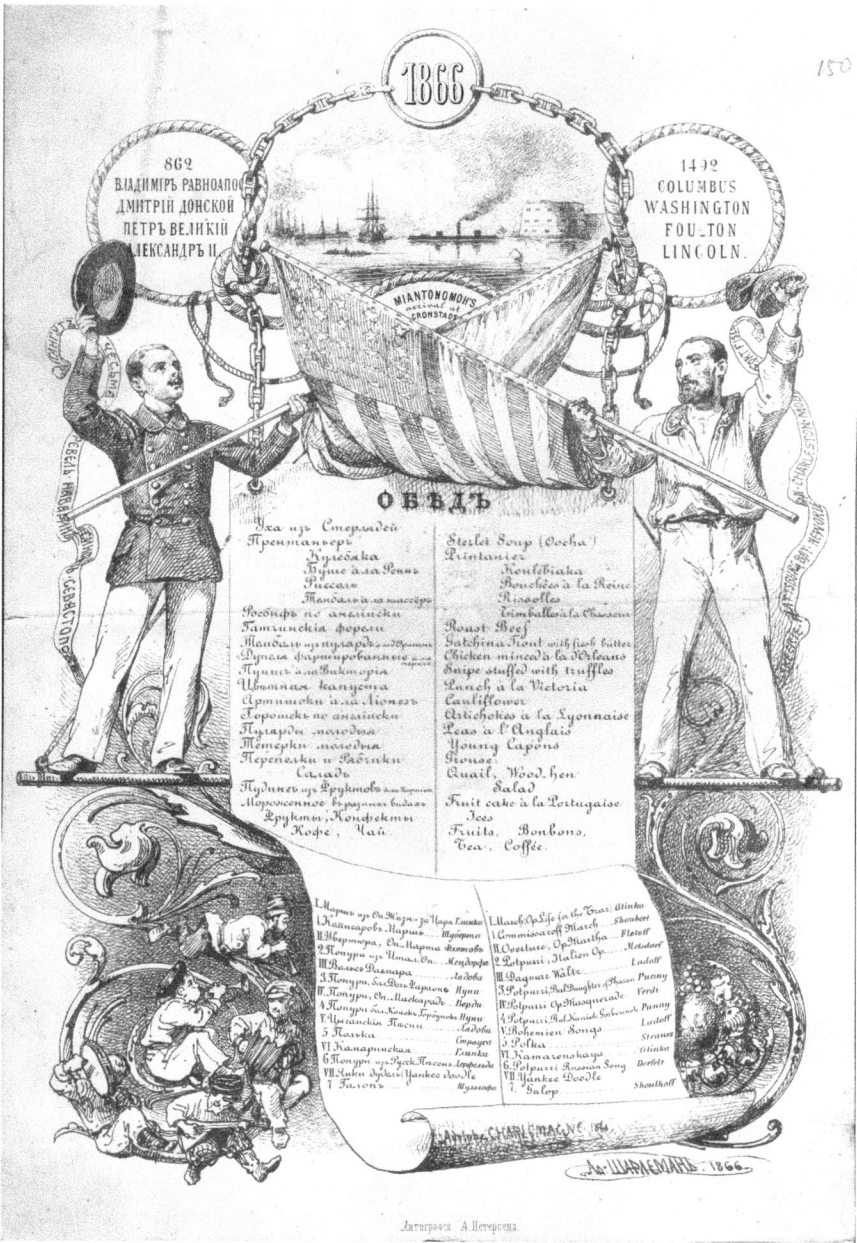

Figure 4.1 A. Sharleman. Menu of the dinner given on occasion of the USS *Miantonomoh*'s arrival in Kronstadt, 1866. Courtesy of State Historical Museum, Moscow.

THE TWO PETER FUNKS.

RUSSIAN STRANGER—"*I say, little boy, do you want to trade? I've got a fine lot of bears, seals, icebergs and Esquimaux—They're no use to me, I'll swop 'em all for those boats you've got.*"
[Billy, like other foolish boys, jumps at the idea.]

Figure 4.2 "The Two Peter Funks." *Leslie's Illustrated*, May 25, 1867.

Washington Eduard Stoeckl signed the treaty on March 30, 1867. For the Andrew Johnson administration, it provided a happy way of diverting public attention from the difficult Reconstruction process and battles against Congress.

Internationally, the Alaska purchase was seen by England and its North American possessions as a threat, and by the European powers as proof of the strong Russian–American alliance. However, the bargain was overshadowed by a series of events that would change the entire system of international relations. The Austro-Prussian War of 1866 marked the start of German unification, while 1867 brought the emergence of Austria-Hungary from the Austrian Empire and, across the Atlantic, the formation of the Dominion of Canada from the Province of Canada, Nova Scotia, and New Brunswick.

The Alaska purchase added to the United States territory that had belonged to Russia for almost a century and a half. Despite its tiny population and the relatively limited activities of the Russian American Company, that epoch left a significant impact on the local people and on perceptions of Alaska both in Russia and in America. The Russian Orthodox Church had gained a foothold among the native and creole populations, while place names still commemorate Russian pathfinders and seamen.

The sale of Russian America coincided with the rapid development of the Russian Far East, to which the Russian government reallocated its resources. It was in Alaska and Eastern Siberia that the American and Russian frontiers met in the middle of the nineteenth century. Even before the Civil War, an American businessman and commercial agent for the Amur, Perry McDonough Collins, suggested a plan to link America and Siberia through a network of steamships and railroads that would stretch inland from the Pacific toward Lake Baikal. After that plan foundered (partially because St. Petersburg feared the prospect of rapid American expansion into a region still underdeveloped by Russia), Collins started another enterprise. With the head of the Western Union telegraph company, Hiram Sibley, he obtained all the permissions and gathered funds for the construction of a Russian–American telegraph line that would connect San Francisco and Moscow via British Columbia, Russian America, and Siberia. Explorations of the future route took place in 1865–1867, until the success of the Atlantic cable made the project obsolete. However, American exploration of the continental interior along the North Pacific had a lasting impact. The American government and new settlers of Alaska benefited from a book about the natural resources and local peoples of the region published in 1868 by the English artist Frederick Whymper, a former participant in the Western Union party that had explored Russian America.[31] An even more profound long-term impact was made by an American member of another party that explored the Siberian part of the route, the young George Kennan, who would go on to become the United States' most influential authority on Russia.

US–RUSSIA MILITARY AND TECHNOLOGICAL INTERACTION IN THE 1870S

In 1870–1871, Russia's Pacific and Atlantic fleets arrived in the United States. Grand Duke Alexis traveled on board one of the vessels that dropped anchor in New York in November 1871. Alexander II had sent him to the

United States in response to a long-standing invitation from the American government, which wished to thank Russia for its aid during the Civil War.

Grand Duke Alexis attended endless receptions and balls, visited wharves and museums, theaters and universities, was received at the White House, took a trip to Niagara Falls, experienced the Mardi Gras parade in New Orleans, and went on a buffalo hunt in the West organized by Buffalo Bill (William F. Cody), in which members of the Sioux nation participated. Although President Ulysses Grant was rather reserved during his meeting with Grand Duke Alexis, the American public welcomed the Grand Duke with open hearts. His visit had long-term consequences for Russia–US relations, becoming a symbol of the two countries' unity on the international stage, their naval partnership, and popular affinities.[32]

In parallel with the Grand Duke's American tour, Russia was flirting with conflict with Great Britain over St. Petersburg's refusal to abide by the 1855 Treaty of Paris, signed after the Crimean War. The treaty, which had for more than a decade restricted Russia's room for maneuver in the Black Sea, was viewed both in the Russian Empire and in the United States as interfering with Russia's sovereign rights – as Secretary of State Hamilton Fish emphasized in his instructions to US Minister in St. Petersburg Andrew Curtin.[33] Given the timing, the Russian fleets' visit to New York was perceived by London as a new sign of a Russia–US naval rapprochement, forcing Great Britain to agree to abolish provisions of the Paris Treaty later that year. The United States, for its part, made Britain pay for the damage caused by the Confederate cruiser *Alabama*, which had been built in the British shipyards during the American Civil War.

In 1872, General William Sherman returned the Grand Duke's visit, spending extensive time in Russia as part of his European tour. He received a warm welcome from Emperor Alexander II, traveled around the Caucasus, and had a grand time in Moscow and St. Petersburg. Later, during the Russo-Turkish War, Sherman published articles that presented Russia's view of the conflict.[34]

Thus, throughout the 1870s, military and technological cooperation continued to be one of the main factors cementing US–Russia relations. The Centennial International Exhibition in Philadelphia provided another vivid demonstration of these constructive interactions. The first world's fair to be held in the United States, this 1876 exhibition was intended to showcase the technical and technological progress America had achieved in the 100 years since the Declaration of Independence. The Centennial Exhibition provoked great interest among Russian entrepreneurs, merchants, and inventors.[35] The US press admitted that the Russian exhibit "rivals in completeness and magnificence that of any other country."[36] Meanwhile, the members of the Russian delegation learned about the American scientific and technological innovations that could be useful for the development of various industrial sectors of the Russian Empire.[37] As a result, the country's contribution significantly expanded the two nations' mutual knowledge.

As the Centennial International Exhibition was being held in the United States, the Eastern Crisis (1875–1878) was unfolding in Europe. This crisis, which would devolve into the Russo-Turkish War of 1877–1878, was caused by the decline of the Ottoman Empire under pressure from the national liberation movements of the Balkan peoples and by the growing tensions between the great powers. Russia was implementing its Pan-Slavism program and expanding into Central Asia. This was perceived by Great Britain as a threat to its colonial and geopolitical interests, while Austria-Hungary saw it as a challenge to its position in the Balkans.

The American public was highly sympathetic to Russia protecting the Christian population of the Balkans from Muslim violence, behavior that meshed well with Americans' own ideas. The US diplomats in St. Petersburg believed that the Eastern Crisis was a battle over principles, not over territories.[38] Accordingly, Russian Slavophiles viewed the United States as Russia's only possible ally on the Eastern Question.[39]

In the winter of 1876–1877, Russia's Pacific and Mediterranean fleets arrived in San Francisco and New York in order to put psychological pressure on Benjamin Disraeli's government. The fleets received a warm welcome in the United States, because, among other things, Grand Duke Alexis, who was popular in American society, was on board one of those ships. The vessels would leave the United States only in May 1877, after Great Britain announced its neutrality.[40]

The American public's favorability toward Russia during the Eastern Crisis was due in no small part to the writings of the US journalist and professional foreign correspondent Januarius MacGahan, who had reported Turkish soldiers' massacre of Bulgarian civilians in July 1876.[41] In the Balkans, he worked closely with Eugene Schuyler, a diplomat, scholar, and writer who was then the US Consul General in Constantinople and had first become interested in Russia when the Russian fleets visited the United States during the Civil War.

Nor was this the first time that Schuyler and MacGahan had joined forces to influence American public opinion on Russia. During Russia's 1873 Khivan campaign – which Schuyler joined as the secretary of the US Mission in St. Petersburg, while MacGahan was a correspondent for the

New York Herald – both men connected Russia's expansion in Central Asia with spreading civilization. Of the two, however, Schuyler took the more nuanced stance: he was more critical of the methods employed by the Russian military administration and offered more pragmatic explanations of Russia's policies in Central Asia, conceptualizing them not only in terms of the civilization–barbarism binary, but also in terms of the Russian Empire's national security, commercial interests, and prestige.[42]

As so many times in the past, Russian policy and conflicts were described in the United States by analogizing them to domestic problems. Americans were interested in Central Asia because its uninhabited spaces, as well as its warlike and fierce nomadic peoples, reminded them of the American West. They were therefore inclined to believe that the Russians were implementing their "manifest destiny" in Central Asia as they absorbed territories, westernized this Oriental space, and civilized its inhabitants. MacGahan and Schuyler's reports in the US press in the years leading up to the Russo-Turkish War confirmed these perceptions and helped to frame Russia's mission in this war as a civilizational one.

Perhaps unsurprisingly, then, when MacGahan – by this time a war correspondent attached to the headquarters of the Russian Army – died of typhus fever during the Russo-Turkish War at the age of thirty-three, he had earned the respect of the Russian royal family, and of Russian officers and soldiers.[43] Schuyler, who was also among those reporting on the Russo-Turkish War, continued to promote Russia's stance, even if he criticized the horrors of war.[44] In line with MacGahan and Schuyler's reporting, American cartoonists depicted Alexander II as a Christian liberator leading a "crusade" against the barbarian Turks in pursuit of a "noble mission" (Figure 4.3).[45]

The writings of Francis Green, who had been appointed a military attaché with the US Mission in St. Petersburg and had witnessed the battles of Shipka and Pleven, were in much the same vein. He presented the Russo-Turkish War as akin to the emancipation of the serfs and the freeing of the slaves, although he did criticize the unhygienic conditions in the Russian army and Russia's backward sociopolitical system.[46] Both Green and General Sherman were convinced that "a Russian victory was in the interests of Civilization."[47] On the whole, despite the military setbacks Russia faced, the Russo-Turkish War shattered Americans' long-held belief that the Russian Empire was entirely dependent on foreigners and unable to wage a war alone.[48]

Americans backed up their rhetorical support for the Russian cause by supplying Russia with weapons and collecting money for the Red Cross. The

Figure 4.3 "The Present Crusade. The Attitude of the Tsar in Declaring War against the Turks." *Harper's Weekly*, May 26, 1877. Courtesy of ProQuest LLC.

Russian Army widely used American Smith & Wesson revolvers and Gatling guns. In addition, the three firearms plants in Izhevsk, Tula, and Sestroretsk manufactured a total of 1,000 *Berdankas*, the rifle invented by the American engineer and Union Army colonel Hiram Berdan, per day. By the end of the war, the Russian Army had over a million *Berdankas* – although in the process the Russian military engineers Alexander Gorlov and Konstantin Gunius so thoroughly modified the design that it became known even in the United States as "the Russian rifle."[49]

By 1878, Russian–American military cooperation was strong enough to support a secret operation in which the United States built cruisers for the Russian fleet. Captain Leonid Pavlovich Semechkin was in charge of the operation. A veteran of the Atlantic Squadron expedition to New York in 1863, he had also represented the Russian Naval Department at the Centennial International Exhibition in Philadelphia. Wharton Barker, a Quaker banker and entrepreneur from Philadelphia, acted as the Russian government's agent. He established a straw steamer company, ostensibly to set up a steamer service between Alaska and San Francisco, and acquired three fast vessels that had been modified by Cramp & Sons, a shipbuilding company. A fourth ship was purpose-built from a Russian design. All the ships were taken out to open sea, where Barker transferred them to Semechkin in neutral waters as regular notarized transactions. Russian crews boarded the ships and sailed to Kronstadt, where the "American" cruisers were fitted with weapons and assigned to Russia's Pacific Fleet.[50]

The success of this secret operation testifies to the strength of US–Russian military cooperation, which continued to intensify as the 1870s progressed. Indeed, when Admiral Thomas Selfridge, Jr., during his 1879 visit, wanted to see the Russian Navy's torpedoes, Admiral Petr Kazakevich, the military governor of Kronstadt, responded, "With pleasure, we have no secrets from Americans."[51] At that time, the Americans likewise kept no military and technological secrets from the Russians.

THE OUTLINES OF FUTURE CONTRADICTIONS

Starting in the late 1860s, the Russian Empire gradually began to abandon its liberal reforms. In their place, a conservative nationalistic discourse developed within the tsarist government. The resulting Russian intolerance stimulated ethnic and religious emigration from Russia to the United States. Its victims made their own significant contribution to the conflictual area of bilateral relations.

In the 1870s, the "Jewish question" took center stage in this context. Previously, the American public had not been particularly interested in this issue, since the United States had its own internal "aliens": the Black population. It was only after the Civil War, as the country grappled with the problem of integrating Black citizens into American society, that the Jewish question gained increasing resonance. Accordingly, the first massive anti-Jewish pogrom in Odessa in April 1871 attracted the attention of the US press.

Schuyler, who was then Consul in Reval, became the first American diplomat to compile an overview of the condition of Russian Jews. Schuyler's report described legal restrictions on their movement and choice of occupation and pointed out that discrimination against Jews was mostly economic rather than religious. Although Schuyler drew parallels between Russia's and the United States' amalgamation policies, the "pale of settlement" that prevented the Jewish minority from being integrated into Russian society more broadly troubled him as much as the spread of ultranationalist ideas.[52] At that time, however, cases of discrimination against American Jews in Russia were isolated incidents and Jewish emigration from the Russian Empire to the United States was small. These issues were not yet creating any official or public problems. That would happen only later in the nineteenth century.

Russian Jews were part of a wave of religious emigration from Russia to the United States that began with the ethnically German Mennonites in 1874. That year, a military reform threatened to eliminate the exemption from recruitment into the Russian army that Mennonites, as committed pacifists, had been granted by Catherine II. Following pressure exerted by Great Britain and the United States, Mennonites were given permission to legally emigrate to other countries. Between 1873 and 1880, as many as 10,000 Mennonites crossed the ocean, settling in the Midwest. The Volga Germans followed in 1875, for religious and ethnic reasons. Both groups were welcomed to the United States, where they painted a picture of Russia as a country of intolerance.

As they adapted to their new homeland, Mennonites opened colleges and became actively involved in charity and missionary activities. They directed their efforts initially toward Native Americans and African Americans, and later toward Russian emigrants. Mennonites from Ukraine and Crimea helped spread Russian wheat cultivars such as red winter and spring wheat (Turkey Red and Durum), which would result in the United States becoming the world's leading producer of wheat and thus a competitor of Russia on the world grain market.[53]

There were also certain tensions in the Far East, where American poachers were plying their illegal trade along Russian shores. Overall, however, these frictions were minor. Both countries continued to demonstrate an interest in mutually advantageous cooperation. Gorchakov stressed that Russia's relations with the United States needed to retain their "traditional cordial sincerity," since "this country has a great value for us on the grounds of general policy, where we must desire to have it more for us than against us, and even more so, where we are forced to have contact with it in the Far East."[54] This was a stance held by both states.

AMERICANS AND RUSSIANS LEARNING ABOUT EACH OTHER

In the 1870s, Americans and Russians each gained substantial knowledge of the other owing to the transport and communication revolutions, the increased number and circulation of newspapers and journals, similarities in the two countries' development trajectories, and the climate of bilateral relations. The Russian Empire and the United States exchanged delegations, top-level state visits, and exhibitions. Diplomats, entrepreneurs, correspondents, scholars, scientists, and ordinary tourists from both sides crossed the ocean. All these tendencies, along with the evolving international agenda, laid the foundation for increased mutual interest and for using one's own national experience to conceptualize that of the other nation. Generally speaking, this decade served as a kind of a prologue to the two nations' subsequent large-scale and variegated "discovery" of each other. Ironically, while America's knowledge of Russia mostly focused on the life of the latter's upper classes, exotic descriptions, and stories of major cities, Russia's knowledge of the United States was far more diverse and colorful, yet it had a limited distribution because of the low literacy level of the Russian population.

It was during this period that the American public began to engage with the multifaceted world of Russian culture. In 1867, Schuyler published the first English-language edition of Ivan Turgenev's novel *Fathers and Sons*. This marked the start of Schuyler's career in Russian Studies that he continued during his diplomatic service in Russia. Later, he translated Leo Tolstoy, published a two-volume biography of Peter I based on materials from Russian archives, and played a special role in introducing Americans to various aspects of life in the Russian Empire.[55] Jeremiah Curtin, the Secretary of Legation in St. Petersburg (1865–1869), likewise popularized knowledge of Russia in the United States by, among other things, translating Russian literature.

American translations of Turgenev's novels and stories transformed the Russian writer into a cult figure among the New England literati and also made him popular with the reading public, particularly young people. In Russian literary circles, Turgenev was nicknamed "the American," a moniker he embraced. He corresponded with William Dean Howells and William James and influenced both these authors, as well as American literature in general.[56] Their love for Turgenev led Americans to discover more of Russian literature. Following the 1869 tour of Dmitri Agrenev-Slavinskii's folk choir and the virtuoso pianist Anton Rubinstein's triumphant concert tour in 1872–1873, they also discovered Russian music.[57]

For all this knowledge, Americans remained mostly optimistic and fairly naïve in their image of Russia. This country was treated as a historical enigma for the modern era, and as a civilization characterized by a harmonious relationship between the monarchy and society. It was imagined as a mostly Asian country, making Russians good intermediaries between the East and the West. But it was also portrayed in the US media as a country ready to be gradually westernized thanks to Alexander II's reforms.[58]

Even though American innocents abroad did criticize the gap between rich and poor, ordinary people and the aristocracy, they also stressed certain similarities between Russians and Americans, such as authenticity and a "natural democratic streak."[59] Those opinions stemmed from the belief that the two nations, which were relatively young compared with Western Europe, were taking gigantic strides toward greatness, even though they were traveling their own distinct paths.[60] Correspondents of the US periodicals traveled primarily to the more "exotic" Russian regions, such as Siberia. After their journey to this cold and snowy Russian area, Thomas Knox and George Kennan wrote books that enjoyed great popularity among American readers.[61] Kennan's striking text, which described the history, geography, and ethnic culture of Siberia, was a particular favorite. At that time, the future critic of tsarism had a rather favorable impression of the Russian monarchy and its suppression of the opposition through, among other things, Siberian exile.

More pessimistic evaluations of Russia's development prospects began to spring up in the American press following the terrorist activities of the People's Will organization, created in 1879. From that time, the term "nihilism," borrowed from Turgenev's works, was used as a negative descriptor of the Russian revolutionary movement as a whole. American writings associated it with terrorism and the destruction of the foundations of society: *The New York Times* stressed that "Nihilism is the present of Socialism, without the future."[62]

In parallel, American public discourse of the late 1870s largely ceased to emphasize the similarity between Americans and Russians as two "young nations." An editorial in the *St. Louis Missouri Republican* emphasized that the Russian Empire "is far behind her European neighbors, not because she is too young, but because she is too old."[63] Along similar lines, Schuyler opined that Russia's problems had "arisen from the fact of her being an Empire of the nineteenth century under a government of the fifteenth."[64]

In Russia, the "American topic" was deeply entrenched in literature. Nikolai Chernyshevsky and Fyodor Dostoevsky proposed mutually exclusive concepts of the human being and thus created a cultural dichotomy in the Russian literary and public consciousness. The American Other played a special role in their imagined worlds. Chernyshevsky's characters traveled to the United States to study advanced sociopolitical practices that they could use in resolving Russia's principal problems. America therefore revived them instead of depersonalizing them. Dostoevsky's characters, in contrast, were impelled by despair and hopelessness to flee across the ocean. America served as a metaphor for a failed life, existential impasse, death; it was the place where Dostoevsky's characters irrevocably lost themselves. Seen through Dostoevsky's Slavophile lens, escape to the United States was a liberal myth, and the American Idea was a mirage and a cruel mystification.[65] However, despite this ideological division, the United States retained its charm in the representations of Russian liberals, radicals, and even some conservatives. Magazines in Russia regularly covered the political and socioeconomic life of the American Other as seen through Russian eyes.[66]

At the turn of the 1870s, the ideas of Alexander Herzen and Nikolai Chernyshevsky and the works of European utopian socialists contributed to Romantic notions of a real-life journey to the United States. These ideas spread among the *narodniki*, or populists, as the American West had enough vacant land for implementing commune projects. Ivan Debogorii-Mokrievich, a Ukrainian populist and columnist, became one of the principal promoters of settlements in America. He traveled to the United States in 1869 and spent a year at the Oneida Community of Bible communists. Dreaming of "dotting the globe with agricultural communes," he then took part in establishing a radical group in Kiev that sought to cross the ocean.[67] In 1872, three members of the Kiev group went to the United States to establish a commune, among them the future terrorist and writer Grigorii Machtet. Upon his return to Russia, Machtet published a series of sketches in the *Nedelia* weekly describing everyday life in the American heartland. Machtet focused particular attention on the "Progressive community" of Vladimir Geins (William Frey), where he had spent eight months.[68] Geins was a Russian nobleman who had changed his last name to Frey (derived from the English word "free") and in 1871 established a commune in Kansas that was based on the principles of communal property ownership and complete rejection of private life. In 1875, he and his family joined the group of the socialist revolutionary Nikolai Chaikovsky and the Christian pacifist Alexander Malikov. Ideological conflicts and problems with daily life resulted in the commune's collapse within four years. In 1883, Frey himself aided a group of Jewish refugees from Russia in establishing a communist commune in Oregon. In the end, he abandoned communism in favor of philosophical positivism.[69]

Trips to the United States and direct participation in American life became a sobering experience for many Russian revolutionaries and dreamers. Some became Americanized; some went back home.[70] Ultimately, by the late 1870s, the palette of ideas that the Russian revolutionary intelligentsia entertained about America had been generously sprayed with dark colors. Mikhail Vladimirov, who had traveled around the United States, wrote, "We are used to seeing the United States as perfection. . . . To get at least an approximate idea of the scale of American outrages, one needs to live here for a long time and to experience them firsthand."[71] Nonetheless, Nikolai Slavinskii, the brother of William Frey's wife Mary, stressed that the Russian emigrants had gone through a very useful "practical school" in America, even though many of them had ultimately failed to fulfill their abstract projects.[72]

Despite being somewhat disillusioned by the realities of the United States' development, Russian observers uniformly described the country as a new and bustling young world. Their travelogues abound with such information about the American political and socioeconomic system as could prove useful for the development of Russia itself. Of course, these presentations of the United States as a land of opportunity did not prevent them from denouncing "commercialism," lynchings, political corruption, and sweatshop practices.[73]

On the one hand, people like Eduard Tsimmermann, who made two American journeys ten years apart, presented a highly positive collective image of Americans as creative doers, democrats, and optimistic people. Tsimmermann rejected the charges of materialism and praised Americans' versatile minds. This nation, he believed, had been entrusted with the mission of sharing its prosperity with humankind.[74] He stressed the similarities between the two nations, which made him certain that Russia should follow the American path to agricultural progress by developing the lands along the Amur River and in the Russian South.[75]

Others, among them former military officer Pavel Ogorodnikov, who traveled across the American continent by train in 1869, were interested in the differences between Russians and Americans and also in the drawbacks of the US system as such.[76] Yet, despite being critical of certain realities of the United States, Ogorodnikov showed the variety of American life and painted a picture of this country as a place with sufficient freedom and resources to create a new social order.[77]

Russian travelers and journalists closely followed the situation of Native Americans and African Americans. They were prompted to do so by the enduring popularity of James Fenimore Cooper's novels in Russia.[78] Historical parallels such as the two countries' expansion policies and the emancipations of the slaves and serfs also played an important role in the perception of the American Other. This contributed to creating among Russians the image of America as a nation both "civilized" and "barbarian." Intrigued by Native Americans, Russian first-hand observers lamented their harsh exploitation in the United States and admired their dignity, cultural uniqueness, and striving for a life independent of the dictates of white civilization.[79] At the same time, descriptions of the former slaves' condition were dominated by compliments for the North's victory over the South and for the country's successes at integrating African Americans into society during Reconstruction. Generally, Russian travelers exoticized their descriptions of former slaves, just as Americans did in their depictions of former serfs.

CONCLUSION

In the 1860s and 1870s, US–Russian relations largely took the form of a mutually advantageous partnership, as evidenced by interactions during the Civil War, the sale of Alaska, and the Eastern Crisis. These bonds were strengthened by military and technological cooperation, cultural exchanges, and Russians' and Americans' increased interest in each other. In later periods, historians and politicians in both countries would turn to this era in search of a blueprint for "Russian–American friendship" that could transcend the two countries' different political systems.

In both countries, images of the Other were used to look for similarities, not to seek out differences. The aim was not to emphasize one's own advantages, but to use comparisons to buttress the argument that Russians and Americans had always been friends. Public discourses in the United States and the Russian Empire were full of parallels: the liberator tsar and the emancipator president; the peoples of the Caucasus and Native Americans; the civilizational missions of Russians in Central Asia and of Americans in the West; Russia's stance during the American Civil War and the US stance on the Polish question (since in both cases the other's territorial integrity was at stake). Moreover, not only did Russia see the United States as a model for

handling its domestic political problems, but also the peaceful abolition of serfdom in the Russian Empire was acknowledged in the Unites
States as a model for constructively handling America's own urgent
problems.

At that time, the two nations met on the Pacific coast. The sale of Alaska
had delayed their competition for commercial dominance and military
control of the region while simultaneously laying the foundations for this
competition. In a short time, domestic and international changes would
result in the accumulation of bilateral tensions and negative mutual
perceptions.

5

ROMANCE AND REVULSION, 1881–1901

OVERVIEW

Over the last two decades of the nineteenth century, relations between Russia and the United States were mostly characterized by a friendly status quo. Their policy of mutual favors in various regions of the world largely stemmed from the absence of major geopolitical conflicts or contradictions in trade and economy. Those would accumulate only at the turn of the twentieth century. Another factor bolstering interstate interactions was a shared desire to counter the designs of Great Britain in Europe and in the Western Hemisphere in the era of Pax Britannica. This latter element of the Russia–US friendship lost its former significance after the Spanish–American War of 1898. However, cooperation prevailed in official bilateral relations until the early twentieth century. An emerging geopolitical clash of interests in the Far East and competition on the world grain and oil markets were softened by the active development of trade, economic, and technological collaboration, as well as by the alluring prospect of Americans gaining access to Russia's Asian market. Thus, the widespread contention that this period marked the end of the friendly relationship between Russia and the United States is unfounded.[1] In fact, it marked just the start of its gradual erosion.

This erosion was stimulated by the American reaction to anti-Jewish pogroms in the Russian Empire, repression against the fighters for Russian freedom there, and the mass emigration of ethnic (Jews, Poles, Finns, Russian Germans, and Lithuanians) and religious (Dukhobors, Shtundists, Catholics, and Lutherans) minorities from the Russian Empire to the United States. Yet the period was also marked by two of the most obvious manifestations of the Russia–US "historical friendship": America's philanthropic movement during the Russian famine of 1891–1892 and the Russian Empire's participation in the Chicago World's Fair of 1893. The last two decades of the nineteenth century further saw an expansion of people-to-people contacts thanks to the transportation and communications revolutions, which made travel and connections quicker and cheaper. The two peoples' continued mutual fascination also led to an explosion of fiction and non-fiction books about the other on both countries' book markets, as well as of articles in their respective presses.

In the United States, competing images of Russia were inserted into the ideological context of late Victorian culture, with its notions of a hierarchy of races and the US messianic idea. The perception of Russia correlated with Americans' understanding of progress and of true Americanism, while the comparison with the Russian Empire allowed them to conceptualize their own achievements and failings. Russia, for its part, actively discussed the American experience of socioeconomic development. These discussions were prompted by the need to modernize the country, by developing new technologies and ways of structuring labor and capital. The US political system had long attracted Russian revolutionaries and reformers, for whom conceptualization of the American experience helped to illuminate the reasons for Russia's backwardness and mechanisms for overcoming it. The Russian Nativists, by contrast, used the negative characteristics of the US reality to protect Russia's "specific way" of national development.

Ultimately, the hierarchy of Russian images of the United States and US images of Russia was determined by domestic sociocultural and political features: both Russians and Americans constructed their self-perceptions by comparison with the imagined Other. Recent studies have explored this approach to mutual image construction.[2]

This chapter provides a comprehensive description of Russia–US relations during the period 1881–1901.[3] It will cover areas of predominant cooperation and the nascent conflict. It will focus both on Russians and Americans discovering each other on a large scale and on contradictions in the mutual perceptions stemming from the domestic developments in each country as well as from the overall alterations in the international relations system.

RUSSIAN–AMERICAN RELATIONS, 1881–1901: DIPLOMATIC STATUS QUO

The reign of Alexander III (1881–1894) was marked by national consolidation around the Throne and the Church, Russification, and counter-reforms. These measures emphasized Russia's unique path of development and presented the new tsar "as the most Russian of Russians."[4]

Yet this politics of reaction had only limited influence on official Russia–US relations, which retained their fundamentally cooperative character. In 1881, on behalf of the American people, the US government expressed its sincere condolences on the assassination of Alexander II, comparing it to the assassination of Abraham Lincoln. Later the same year, on behalf of the Russian people, the government of the Russian Empire expressed its condolences on the assassination of President James Garfield, comparing it, in turn, to the assassination of Alexander II. Russia also made every effort to assist in the search for the US expedition of the polar explorer George DeLong, whose ship sank off the coast of Siberia in June 1881.

Its friendship with Washington was important for St. Petersburg as it sought to implement its foreign policy program in Central Asia and the Far East, where Russia's interests clashed with Great Britain's. Consequently, Russia was willing to support the Monroe Doctrine when Secretary of State Richard Olney expanded its meaning during a border dispute between British Guiana and Venezuela in 1895 (the so-called Olney Corollary). In addition, Russia was one of the first to recognize the Hawaiian Republic established by the United States and did not raise any objections when the United States annexed the Hawaiian Islands in 1898.[5]

In the 1880s and 1890s, the two countries' diplomats focused on three issues: the "Jewish question," mutual extradition of criminals, and seal conservation in the northern Pacific. The United States was primarily interested in the first question, Russia was most interested in the second, and both countries were equally interested in the third.

On the "Jewish question," the principal difference between the two governments stemmed from differing interpretations of Article 1 of the Russia–US Treaty on Commerce and Navigation of 1832.[6] Washington insisted that the principle of equal rights of all American citizens visiting Russia be observed, while St. Petersburg stressed that American Jews could not enjoy greater privileges than Russian Jews and must abide by Russian laws in this area. Friendly relations between the two countries made it possible to compromise and to reach gentlemen's agreements of sorts on individual cases, but not to resolve the problem as a whole.

The mass migration of Russian Jews during the reign of Alexander III added a further dimension to the "Jewish question" in bilateral relations. This influx to American shores was a result of the pogroms and increased discrimination against the Jewish minority in the Russian Empire in the early 1880s.[7] More than 130,000 Jews immigrated to the United States in 1881–1889, and a further 300,000 in 1890–1898.[8] Many of these Jews sought to naturalize and obtained American citizenship. Since the Russian Empire had a law on the books criminalizing unauthorized adoption of foreign citizenship, however, St. Petersburg did not recognize the passports of naturalized Jewish Americans who did not obtain permission to renounce their Russian citizenship – an approach the Russian Empire shared with its Ottoman counterpart.[9] In response, the State Department started another round of naturalization negotiations, but these came to nothing. As a result, on February 18, 1891, Secretary of State James Blaine proposed that governments should be held responsible for the international consequences of their domestic policies. In the context of Russia–US relations, this would have made the tsarist government responsible to the United States for the mass emigration of Russian Jews caused by its policy on the "Jewish question."[10] In 1901, however, the State Department admitted that it was powerless and warned American Jews of the possible negative consequences of traveling to the Russian Empire.[11]

For its part, the Russian Empire was interested in discussing the issue of mutual extradition of criminals, as it sought to return to Russia those revolutionaries who had fled to the United States. The State Department – which hoped for a reciprocal gesture from Russia on the naturalization issue and sought to implement the US government's new policy of protecting the country from an influx of "undesirable immigrants" – was amenable.

On March 28, 1887, the convention between the United States and the Russian Empire for the extradition of criminals (the Extradition Treaty) was signed. Two days prior, the text of the convention, obtained by bribing a State Department employee, had been published in the American press.[12] It prompted a wave of public protest, as the treaty allowed the tsarist government to demand the extradition of all Russian political émigrés in the United States on the pretext that they had participated in a plot to assassinate the tsar. A campaign launched against the treaty prevented its ratification in the Senate for six years, since the considerations of governmental expediency clashed with Americans' lofty idealism and their belief in the United States' special mission to provide asylum for religious and political dissidents.

The problem of protecting fur seals in the northern Pacific was of no concern to the public, but was a major headache for diplomats. In the early 1880s, uncontrolled seal hunting, or sealing, had brought the animals to the brink of extinction both in Russian and in American territorial waters. In that respect, Russia and the United States had the same goal. Yet, in the early 1890s, the governments of the two countries failed to establish real cooperation on the issue of conserving seals. Preserving the species would require a multilateral treaty between Russia, the United States, Great Britain, and Japan that would prohibit all seal-hunting at sea and impose at least a temporary prohibition on land sealing. In the meantime, in the late nineteenth century, both Canadian and American poachers continued illegally hunting seals in Russian waters in the Far East and smuggling goods to sell to the region's indigenous populations, thus doing damage to Russia's fisheries and fur trappers there.

As the (First) Sino-Japanese War in East Asia ended in 1895, the first major geopolitical contradictions made themselves felt between Russia and the United States. The Russian Empire protected the territorial integrity of the Chinese Empire and enshrined their alliance in the Defense Treaty of 1896. Minister of Finance Sergei Witte gained the consent of the Chinese government to extend the Trans-Siberian Railway across Manchuria to Vladivostok. This southern branch was named the Chinese Eastern Railway. Its ownership was transferred to the Russo-Chinese bank established by the Russian government. In 1898, by leasing the Kwantung Peninsula with Port Arthur (Lushun), Russia finally gained an ice-free port in the Pacific. Soon thereafter, St. Petersburg demonstrated its readiness to someday switch from the policy of "peaceful economic expansion" proclaimed by Witte to territorial acquisitions. Following the Spanish–American War, the United States was also pulled into the international conflict in the Far East and began a rapprochement with Great Britain. At the same time, the US concerns about Russia's economic and diplomatic course in the Far East were balanced by the alluring prospect of promoting American goods and capital on the Asian markets of the Russian Empire thanks to the construction of the Trans-Siberian Railway. The government of Nicholas II, in its turn, did not intend to pursue broad territorial expansion in the Far East for some time.[13] After the Spanish–American War, Russia recognized the annexation of the Philippines and agreed, if with reservations, to John Hay's Open Door Note of 1899, which called for guaranteeing the territorial integrity of China, as well as equal trade and investment opportunities for all foreign countries.

COUNTRY OF POGROMS AND EXILE: RUSSIA IN AMERICAN MESSIANIC PROJECTS

Despite the predominance of positive developments in bilateral relations, the last two decades of the nineteenth century were marked by the first large-scale anti-Russian campaign in American society in response to the "Jewish question" in Russia. In the minds of the overwhelming majority of observers in the United States, anti-Semitism was a symbol of the government's policy of religious intolerance, a policy typical of insufficiently civilized countries such as the Ottoman Empire. Consequently, when the "Jewish question" was used to build an image of Russia, the "barbarity–civilization" and "medievalism–modernity" binaries loomed large, while the Russian Empire itself was positioned as part of Asia – and thus on the periphery of global development.[14]

American newspapers and magazines were flooded with articles and cartoons about the discrimination that those Russian Jews who thronged the shores of America had faced in their homeland (Figure 5.1). Russian diplomats decried this "ink crusade," attributing it to "London's intrigues" and

Figure 5.1 "The Shadow of the Cross." *Philadelphia Press*, May 17, 1891.

"Jewish campaigning." Yet the reasons for this flood of articles went far deeper: they were rooted in Americans' sincere compassion for victims of religious intolerance and in developments within the United States.

First, Russian Jewish immigrants joined the New Immigration. This wave was made up of low-income Italians, Greeks, and religious and ethnic minorities from the Russian Empire, Austria-Hungary, and the Ottoman Empire. Of these, the largest groups were Italians, Slavs, and Jews. Debates about these "new immigrants" thus became part of an ongoing conversation among the public and politicians alike regarding national identity and immigration policy. In Gilded Age America, this discussion was tinged with the racial fears and biases typical of Victorian ideology that had a class derivation, as well as an ethno-religious (Anglo-Saxon Protestant) one.[15] Concerns about this influx of Jewish immigrants became an additional argument in the arsenal of those Americans who condemned Russia's anti-Semitic policies and contributed to demonizing Russia as a whole.[16]

Second, many American Jews feared a rise in anti-Semitism arising from the arrival of their Eastern European coreligionists who spoke Yiddish, settled in ghettos in large cities (primarily in New York, which became home to 70 percent of Russian Jewish emigrants), and tended to embrace socialist and anarchist ideas.[17]

Third, American Jews who traveled to Russia were discriminated against. This sparked protests that the civil rights of American citizens – both natural-born and naturalized – had been violated.

Fourth, having been subjected to the politics of Russification and religious intolerance, Jews brought with them an openly negative image of the Russian Empire.[18] Criticizing Russia's repressive policies toward Jews and other religious and ethnic minorities allowed the American public to demonstrate its commitment to the principle of freedom of conscience and its readiness to take international steps to defend it. At protest rallies and in the public speeches of those who had witnessed the despotism of the tsarist regime, as well as in the press and in Congress, there developed a certain messianic rhetoric: Russia was transformed into an object of America's mission to bring freedom to the world.[19]

Fifth, interest in the "Jewish question" was reinforced by analogies between Russia's anti-Semitic policy and racial discrimination in the United States (be it against Black Americans, Chinese immigrants, or Native Americans). Observers in the United States used such analogies for various purposes. Some (including African Americans) drew these parallels to highlight problems at home and attract attention to the hypocrisy of those who criticized anti-Semitism in Russia.[20] Others tried to overcome doubts about America's right to be a "lighthouse for all mankind" and Americans' obligation to fight injustice abroad, highlighting the differences between discriminatory policies in the United States and those in the Russian Empire .

Starting in the late 1880s, protests against anti-Semitic policies became an important addition to America's first "crusade" to bring democracy to the Russian Empire. However, the Jewish question did not lose its independent significance for Russia–US relations. Closer collaboration between members of the American Jewish community and "friends of Russian freedom" in the United States would be established in the early twentieth century, following the Kishinev pogrom. But the latter would make every effort to show Americans that Russia did not oppress only Jews – that the Russian Empire was a giant prison for all fighters for its political renewal.

The nature of the Russian revolutionary movement drew Americans' attention after Alexander II was assassinated by members of the Narodnaya Volya (People's Will) on March 1, 1881. Debates around this issue were closely tied to describing Siberia as a place of exile. For the reading public, both matters were tinged with a certain exoticism and sensationalism. The liberal journalist George Kennan joined the discussion after making another trip to the Russian Empire following a debate with William Armstrong, a businessman and a consulate employee who had accused Kennan of being unwilling to see the "horrors of Tsarism."[21] In Siberia, deeply impressed by his meetings with political exiles, Kennan found his new religion – humanism – and converted to the "anti-tsarist" faith.

On returning to the United States, Kennan embarked on a personal crusade. Between November 1887 and the mid-1890s, he published dozens of articles in leading American journals and gave hundreds of dramatic lectures, often appearing in shackles like a convict. In October 1891, his book *Siberia and the Exile System* was published in New York and London. Kennan downplayed the differences between liberals and radicals when it came to their methods of struggle, gave Russian revolutionaries a more Western image, and presented Russia as a "huge prison," where any opposition was punished with exile to Siberia. While he sincerely believed his conclusions to be objective, Kennan in fact crossed the line between an observer and a preacher: his "new religion" was accompanied with the typical spiritual rebirth, exalted faith, and messianic impulse.[22]

Meanwhile, Russian political emigrants in New York initiated a campaign of their own: against ratifying the Extradition Treaty, which allowed the tsarist government to demand the extradition of all Russian political émigrés in the

United States. Indiana Senator William Dudley Foulke, an abolitionist and a member of the movement to reform the civil service, joined their campaign, as the treaty called into question Americans' faith that the United States was a safe haven for freedom fighters.[23] Foulke viewed Russian history as moving backward: the freedom-loving Slavs who had established such forms of self-governance as the *mir* (commune) and the *veche* (folk assembly) had been subjugated first to the Tartar Mongols and then to the tsars of Muscovy. An Asian form of governance had ultimately been established in Russia, Foulke argued, linking the foreign expansionism of the Russian Empire to its domestic despotism.[24]

Thus, the first crusade for Russian freedom was born in the United States in 1887–1894 as a joint project of Kennan and the opponents to the Extradition Treaty. The attendant comparisons of Russia and the United States were structured around such dichotomies as "progress–regress," "civilization–barbarism," and "light–darkness." Criticism of religious oppression in Russia was an important mechanism for constructing the country's image as an "Empire of Darkness." As the first Protestant missionaries trickled into the Russian Empire, members of the movement for Russia's renewal educated the American public into the belief that Russian modernization would be impossible without religious reform.[25]

In Philadelphia and Denver, organizations sprang up to provide financial support for political exiles and to collect signatures on a petition against their oppression to be submitted to Alexander III. In April 1891, in Boston, through the efforts of the revolutionary Sergei Stepniak-Kravchinskii, a terrorist and member of People's Will, the Society of American Friends of Russian Freedom (SAFRF) was established to legally assist Russian patriots in their struggle to liberalize the Russian Empire.[26] Starting in 1891, the American edition of the *Free Russia* magazine was published under the editorship of Edmund Noble, a Boston journalist of Scottish origins. He played one of the key roles in the first "crusade" for a "Free Russia," always stressing that the seeds of democracy had already been sown in Russia; that, despite Russians' many differences from Americans, national character was not an obstacle to Russia's progress; and that the Russian people were capable of borrowing from the Western experience.[27]

The society's founders and first members were mostly public and religious figures who advocated progressive reforms in the United States. Former abolitionists and their children imbued the movement with the crusading spirit typical of their era. They contributed to transforming Russians enslaved by despotism into one of the objects of the American mission to bring freedom and democracy to the world. Comparing the slave-owning South and the Russian Empire was an important rhetorical device: Russian revolutionaries were transformed into John Brown's generation and the Extradition Treaty into the "new fugitive slave law." At the same time, comparing peasants to Black Americans engendered doubt as to the capability of Russian "dark people" to modernize quickly.[28] Supporters of Russian freedom had to overcome this clash of ideas, which they did partly with the aid of liberals and radicals from Russia who toured the United States giving lectures, as well as of political emigrants.

As the 1880s gave way to the 1890s, the American movement for a "Free Russia" was very energetic, yet it remained small and largely limited geographically to the Northeast. It also suffered from organizational and financial difficulties and was opposed by US diplomats as well as by some ordinary US citizens, who recommended that their compatriots focus on solving problems at home, from discrimination against Native Americans and Black Americans to cruel punishments inflicted on women and children.[29] (Figure 5.2). But the most consistent opponents of the Free Russia campaign were to be found among the American Russophiles.

The "new Russophilia" of the turn of the twentieth century was a complex and multifaceted phenomenon. One of its leading figures was Isabel Hapgood, a conservative translator and journalist. She criticized Kennan for artfully concealing facts and called upon people to look at Russian life "with the eyes of the heart." Such an approach, she argued, would enable observers to see an organic connection between the tsar and the people, to understand the special role of the Orthodox church in Russia's harmonious development, and to recognize the profound spirituality of the Russian people.[30] Another prominent Russophile was the liberal Charles Crane, a businessman and philanthropist from Chicago who spared no money or effort to promote Russian music in the United States and to create the conditions for Americans to seriously study Russia, resulting in the establishment of a center for Slavic Studies at the University of Chicago.[31] America's Russophiles were united by their desire to understand the uniqueness of Russian civilization and to comprehend the scale of Russia's cultural legacy, including its music and literature. Unlike the Slavophiles in Russia, American Russophiles did not oppose the Russian Empire to the West. They recognized Russians' right to a special path of revival conducive to gradual "top-down" reform that would enable them to preserve such national characteristics as spirituality, psychological depth, and collectivism.[32]

Figure 5.2 "Is Russian Cruelty Worse than American Dishonor?" *Life*, February 26, 1891.

Ultimately, despite a six-year delay in ratification, the Extradition Treaty went into force in 1893. A subsequent movement to denounce the treaty likewise failed, and the "crusade" began to fizzle out. Officially, the United States was interested in maintaining a friendly status quo with Russia; the 1887 treaty also appealed to those social groups in the United States that, driven by nativist sentiments, linked the spread of anarchism to the baleful influence of "nihilists" arriving from across the ocean.

The American movement for Russia's political renewal provoked a negative reaction from the court of Alexander III. Tsarist diplomats in the United States unfailingly reproached the State Department for the various "sore spots" of US sociopolitical development – including lynchings of Black Americans, discrimination against Native Americans and Chinese immigrants, corrupt politicians, hypocritical lawmakers, and discontent among farmers and workers – at the slightest attempt to criticize the domestic policies of the Russian Empire.[33] Alexander III himself regularly perused diplomatic reports from Washington, adding sarcastic marginalia concerning American ways.

Despite this first serious ideological challenge, however, in the 1880s and 1890s, the two states' relations continued to be dominated by pragmatism, cooperation, and the idea of historical friendship.

DEMONSTRATION OF SYMPATHIES AND MUTUAL INTEREST: AMERICANS IN "STARVING RUSSIA," RUSSIANS IN THE COLUMBIAN EXPOSITION

America's philanthropic movement during the 1891–1892 famine in Russia holds a special place in the history of bilateral relations. It was the first example of people-to-people diplomacy in action, since aid came from private groups and individual states, and it was also the first international humanitarian act of such large scope both for the American Red Cross and for the United States in general.[34] Within that movement, old and new images of Russia were superimposed on each other, and markers of its backwardness became clear. This philanthropic movement was in part responsible for the connection that began to emerge in the American consciousness between the idea of searching for "free markets" and the sense of a national mission to liberate the world.[35] Idealism and pragmatism intertwined in the motivations of participants in the relief campaign, who were driven both by profit-seeking and by altruism. Such mixed motivations were typical of the American nation in general, an idea that Herman Melville crystallized in his novel *The White Jacket* (1850): "And let us always remember that with ourselves, almost for the first time in the history of earth, national selfishness is unbounded philanthropy; for we cannot do a good to America but we give alms to the world."[36]

One center of the philanthropic movement took shape in December 1891 on the initiative of William Edgar, the editor of the *Northwestern Miller* magazine, published in Minneapolis. The first Russian Famine Relief Committee was established here, and it would work together with its counterpart from Nebraska. The *Northwestern Miller* became a mouthpiece of sorts for the movement, calling on Americans to be humane and generous, reminding them of the help Russia had provided during the American Civil War of 1861–1865, and never failing to tell its audience that by sending cargoes of flour and corn abroad they were tapping into new markets for their products.[37] A second major philanthropic center emerged that same month in Iowa through the cooperative efforts of Benjamin Tillinghast, the editor of *The Davenport Democrat* newspaper, and Clara Barton, the president of the American Red Cross. American women played a special role in the Iowa movement.[38] It was people from Iowa and Nebraska who introduced Russia to American corn.[39]

While western states collected foodstuffs, eastern states collected money to purchase and ship them. In early 1892, the major centers on the East Coast were Philadelphia and New York. In Philadelphia, the effort was driven by Rudolf Blankenburg, a well-known Quaker reformer who would go on to serve as the city's mayor.[40] In New York, the Philanthropic Committee of the Chamber of Commerce managed the collection of financial donations and the *Christian Herald* bought wheat and other food for sending to Russia on a separate ship.[41] The Russian Famine Relief Committee of the United States, under the direction of John Hoyt, the former editor of the *Wisconsin Farmer and Northern Cultivator* magazine and the third Governor of Wyoming Territory, began operating in January 1892 in Washington, D.C., and – working in close collaboration with the American Red Cross – became the coordination center for the entire campaign.

Despite the launch of the American "friends of Russian freedom" campaign, which promoted the idea that the republic of freedom and democracy should not aid the empire of despotism, and the refusal of Congress to allocate funds to cover the shipping expenses,[42] the philanthropic movement succeeded in sending to Russia five ships filled with food and medications. In the United States, these became known as the "Famine Fleet." As Hoyt stressed in his report, the social and political differences between the countries did not stop Americans from realizing their special debt to the Russian people for Russia's contribution to the Union cause during the American Civil War.[43]

In total, considering the cost of freight; money collected by the American Red Cross; and funds sent via the US Embassy, through various committees, and personally to Leo Tolstoy, the American people's aid to Russia during the famine was worth approximately 1 million dollars (or 2 million rubles). It was enough to feed 800,000 people for a month.[44]

The "Famine Fleet" safely reached Russia. There, the tsarist government, which had rejected offers of famine aid from other countries, made an exception for the US ships. The fleet was met by crowds of people, an orchestra played the American anthem, the American "Stars and Stripes" flag flew everywhere, and newspapers were filled with pieces on the mutual aid of the two countries and the idea of historical friendship.

With the help of US diplomats, the shipments were unloaded and distributed to those provinces hit by famine. On the Russian side, the railway shipments were monitored by Count Andrei A. Bobrinskii, a prominent Americanophile who was a member of the Russian Red Cross and a representative of the special Russian famine commission created by Alexander III.[45] Those American visitors who accompanied the shipments were heartily welcomed in the royal palace, in aristocratic mansions, and in peasant homes.[46]

The Russian painter Ivan Aivazovsky, who was then in the United States, painted two pictures, *The Relief Ship* and *Distributing Supplies* (Figure 5.3).

Figure 5.3 Ivan Aivazovsky. *Razdacha prodovol'stviia* (*Distributing Supplies*),1892.

Wishing to stress the unity of the two peoples, Aivazovsky unintentionally emphasized Americans' messianism. In the latter painting, peasants pray while looking at the American flag, just as peasants in famine-stricken provinces prayed to members of American philanthropic committees and, during the famine of 1921–1922, peasants in Soviet Russia would pray to members of the American Relief Administration.

Those members of the US philanthropic committees who visited the starving provinces made a major contribution to shaping nineteenth-century Americans' ideas about the Russian Empire. In their representations, famine was certainly a marker of the country's backwardness. The main conclusion drawn by the majority of observers was that the famine stemmed from exhausted soil, extensive agriculture, and the peasant commune. Americans further noted passivity, fatalism, and ignorance to be traits of Russian peasants. They did not think these features of the national character to be permanent – peasants could change, should their circumstances change, but, thus far, they needed a paternalistic system that included the aid of their former owners, *zemstvos* (local administrative assemblies), and the government, just as freed slaves in the South required the patronage of their former owners.[47] Despite this rather limited view of the peasantry, those philanthropists who traveled to starving Russia disseminated more nuanced perspectives on its ruler and government, the program to fight the famine, and the Russian nobility than had previously been available to Americans.[48] They spread the image of Russia as a historical friend to whom prosperous America extended a helping hand in gratitude for the favors Russia had rendered the American people during the American Civil War. Russia's return gesture of good will was its extensive participation in the Chicago World's Fair, where the Russian exposition was the largest the imperial government had ever mounted abroad.

The World's Columbian Exposition, held in Chicago in 1893, occupies a special place in nineteenth-century Russian–American relations. Never before had such a large group of Russians traveled across the ocean, either to present their country's technological and cultural achievements or just as tourists. Various ministries had prepared special reviews of their achievements that had been translated into English and were intended to overcome the idea of Russia's "eternal backwardness." In Chicago, Russia wanted to showcase its entrance into the era of industrialization, symbolized by the Trans-Siberian Railway, and to see the new American technologies needed for the successful modernization of Russia's economy. Among the Russian exhibits, Americans were attracted by those things that were exported from Russia, promised opportunities for Americans in the Russian market, and emphasized Russians' creative genius.

Tourists were unfailingly attracted to the exhibition of Russian paintings, which featured works by Ilia Repin, Ivan Aivazovsky, and Vasily Vereshchagin. A very successful 1888 exhibition of Vereshchagin's art in the United States had already introduced the American public to his works condemning the horrors of war.[49] Audiences also flocked to the performances of Evgeniia Lineva's Russian folk choir organized by Charles Crane.[50] The concerts of Russian classical music performed by the American Symphony Orchestra, conducted by Voitek Glavach, a composer and conductor from the Mariinsky opera theater, likewise aroused great enthusiasm.[51] Petr Tchaikovsky's popularity in the United States eclipsed that of all other Russian composers as a result of his triumphant concert tour of 1891.[52]

The World's Fair also featured diverse lectures on Russia. A prominent role therein was played by Prince Sergei Volkonsky, grandson of the Decembrist Volkonsky. He had received an excellent education, and traveled to the United States at the behest of the Ministry of Education. A gifted speaker fluent in English, Volkonsky strove to destroy American stereotypes of Russia, which he claimed boiled down to the "usual clichés of snow, wolves, secret police." He lectured to invariable acclaim on education, religion, and philosophy, and made many acquaintances among those members of the American intellectual elite and businessmen who were also patrons of art. After the exhibition, he spoke at the leading US universities, and in 1896, the Lowell Institute in Boston invited him for another lecture tour.[53]

The Columbian exhibition became a true forum of Russia–US affinities. Just a short while earlier, the American "Famine Fleet" had docked in Russia, and now a Russian fleet commanded by Vice Admiral Nikolai Kaznakov arrived on American shores to take part in a naval parade as a part of the Columbian exhibition. Alexander III charged his cousin, Grand Duke Alexander Mikhailovich, with expressing official thanks to President Grover Cleveland for the American people's aid to Russians struck by the 1891–1892 famine, and, on behalf of the emperor, Minister Grigori Kantakuzen presented valuable gifts to the heads of the various philanthropic committees that had supported this effort.[54]

No other nation showed such a profound interest in the Chicago World's Fair as the people of the Russian Empire, who were going through something of an "American craze." Never before had Russia published so much about the United States.[55] Chicago and America in general came to occupy a prominent place in Russian newspapers and magazines. Reports on business trips, articles, and books testified to Russians' particular interest in US technical and technological innovations and the secrets of the country's economic success. They uniformly wrote about Americans' skill at developing human potential through education, the press, civil equality, and political activity.[56] As the author of an article in *Vestnik Evropy* magazine stressed, using McCormick reapers and creating a system of grain elevators would not be enough to enable Russia to compete with the United States on the grain market. Instead, it was necessary to change the land-use system and to foster the personal entrepreneurship that worked wonders in the United States.[57] Such arguments were invariably followed by such oppositions as American energy vs. Russian inertia and American "cultivation of the mind" vs. Russian ignorance and the illiteracy of the masses. In this context, the typical American was seen as a *politician* skilled at gauging public demand, an *agent* embodying the Yankee industrial spirit, or a *reporter*, the public eye and public tongue of the American nation.[58]

The economist Ivan Ianzhul, a Moscow University professor whom the Ministry of Finance sent to America to describe the latter's crucial economic achievements, stressed the United States' importance for Russia as a development model. For him, Americans' economic success was rooted in their ability to manage space and time, in their energy and willingness to experiment, and, of course, in the continued development of their education system. Upon his return from across the ocean, Ianzhul gave public lectures across Russia, the most popular of which – "Millions and What to Do with Them" – promoted Andrew Carnegie's ideas.[59]

Among those who wrote about the World's Fair for different Russian magazines was Peter Tverskoi (Petr Dement'ev). His sketches, later compiled into a book, presented an extremely comprehensive and diverse image of the United States.[60] It was a "look from the inside" by a person who had moved to the United States in 1881 and adapted to life there, becoming a successful entrepreneur and a mayor. Tverskoi wrote about all aspects of American life, not hiding his criticism of racial discrimination or political corruption. However, his narrative focused on the youth and incredible flexibility of the American nation, which was conquering nature and domesticating a new world, turning deserts into orchards. He admired the vibrancy of American business and public life, the dynamic development of American civilization, and Americans' forward-looking optimism. These things, he felt, were what Russians should learn from Americans.

Overall, the Chicago World's Fair made a major contribution to shaping Russians' and Americans' knowledge of one another; promoted business, technical, and academic contacts; and stimulated the development of trade and economic relations.

THE TRANS-SIBERIAN RAILWAY, RUSSIAN ECONOMIC REVIVAL, AND THE AMERICAN "COMMERCIAL INVASION"

In 1891, Russia began building the Trans-Siberian Railway, with the goal of connecting Russia's industrial centers with Eastern Siberia. In 1892, Sergei Witte, following his appointment as Minister of Finance, turned the railway into the centerpiece of Russia's industrialization program, a mechanism for consolidating the monarchy while boosting the country's international status.

The monumental railway project stunned contemporaries. It attracted the attention of US diplomats and politicians, public and religious figures, entrepreneurs and journalists, who traveled to Siberia and the Far East. They pondered Russia's economic awakening and the new prospects it created for American trade; they discoursed on the frontier's regenerating role and Russians' right to implement their version of "Manifest Destiny" in Asia; and they drew parallels between the colonization of the American West and that of the Russian East.[61]

Some, like James Wilson, a railway entrepreneur, and John McCook, a successful New York lawyer who worked for railway corporations, saw the construction of the Trans-Siberian Railway as an opportunity for Americans to develop cooperation with Russia in the Far East and ultimately move into the Chinese market.[62] Others, like Alexander Ford, a famous American engineer who traveled through Manchuria, Eastern Siberia, and Japan, stressed that the success of the Trans-Siberian Railway rested on Anglo-Saxon technological achievements, noting that the government of Nicholas II intended to purchase in the United States three-quarters of the materials and equipment needed to complete its southern branch, the Chinese Eastern Railway.[63] Some, like Washington Vanderlip, an engineer, geologist, and gold-miner, were attracted by Siberia's gold deposits and natural resources.[64] Others, like Wharton Barker, a banker and political figure, advocated the broadest economic cooperation between Russia and the United States in exploring Siberia and in industrialization as a whole, "fueling" their involvement in Russia's economic revival.[65] Enoch Emery, an energetic and successful entrepreneur from Massachusetts who built a true "commercial empire" in Eastern Siberia, saw himself as part of a special group of people meant to bring the "Gospel of capitalism" to Russia.[66]

On the whole, the "Siberian" direction of American social and political journalism in the late nineteenth century balanced out the "demonic" image of official Russia that had emerged from the movement of the "friends of Russian freedom" and gave new hues to the picture of Siberia painted by George Kennan.[67] The accession of Nicholas II to the throne in 1894 was seen in America as having put an end of the reactionary policies of Alexander III and as making possible the alluring prospect of promoting American goods, capital, and technologies in Russia.

In Russia in the reign of Nicholas II (just as in the reign of Nicholas I), Russian interest in the realities of American development stemmed primarily from the demands of economic modernization, which accelerated in the 1890s, as well as from growing Russian competition with the United States on global grain and oil markets.

Taking the United States as a development model was popular among those Russians who advocated pursuing Russia's economic renewal by borrowing from abroad the technical innovations and cutting-edge technologies required for transportation, industrial, and agricultural revolutions. An iconic figure in this regard was Minister of Communications Mikhail Khilkov (1895–1905), who had gained experience in railway construction in the United States. It was he who spearheaded the purchase of American dredging engines and ice-breakers, as well as equipment for constructing the Chinese Eastern Railway, and led the effort to equip passenger trains on Russian railways with air-brakes made in the United States. Other active proponents of developing American business in the Russian Empire and of borrowing American technological innovations included Witte and Grand

Duke Alexis, the Russian Navy commander who had visited the United States in the 1870s.

As Russia's economic modernization accelerated from the mid-1890s, the Russian Empire needed American engineering products – from machine tools and Baldwin locomotives to Lindon Bates dredges, McCormick harvesting machines, Singer sewing machines, and refrigeration units. Russians used American techniques for combating ice cover, dredging rivers and harbors, laying rail tracks, and building bridges and tunnels. American technical experts worked in Russia, and Russian engineers traveled constantly to the United States. In 1898, Westinghouse Electric Corporation opened a plant in St. Petersburg for manufacturing air-brakes; a competing New York company built a plant in 1901 in Liubertsy, outside Moscow. In Sormovo, near Nizhny Novgorod, an American plant was built to manufacture locomotives and train cars, while the Singer Manufacturing Company opened a branch in Podolsk to produce sewing machines. From the mid-1890s, Russia also became the largest buyer of American agricultural equipment.[68] By investing in industrial manufacturing and railway construction, supplying machines and equipment, building a sewage system in Odessa and laying phone cables in Russia's major cities, Americans made a real contribution to the economic progress of the Russian Empire, expanded cooperation between the two countries, and contributed to harmonizing bilateral relations at both governmental and public levels.

This does not, of course, mean that the two countries' trade and economic relations were entirely smooth. The conflicts between them stemmed primarily from their growing competition on the world grain market. In the 1880s, Russia produced more grain than the United States. However, the United States produced twice as much wheat as Russia, a fact that – combined with its mechanized agriculture and state-of-the-art grain elevators, as well as the advantages conferred by its transportation revolution – meant that it was rapidly gaining on Russia in the world grain market. Multiple pieces published in Russia in the 1880s and 1890s reflected the growing concerns of Russian grain producers.[69] A similar clash came on the international oil market, where the Nobels, known as "the Rothschilds of Baku," competed with J. D. Rockefeller, America's main oil tycoon.[70] Tariff disputes generated frictions, too. Washington used the Dingley Tariff of 1897, a piece of legislation that represented the peak of American protectionism, to impose levies on Russian sugar. Talks failed to get this additional tariff removed, so Russia responded by raising levies on imported goods and machines manufactured from American cast iron and steel. But all these tensions could not prevent the further development of the two countries' mutually beneficial interactions, as the Russian government was highly interested in trade and economic cooperation with the United States, while American industrial goods found an excellent market in European Russia and had even more alluring prospects in Siberia.[71]

RUSSIANS "DISCOVER" AMERICA, AMERICANS "DISCOVER" RUSSIA

On the one hand, the last two decades of the nineteenth century saw a major expansion in opportunities for mutual awareness, due both to in-person experiences like business trips and mass migration from the Russian Empire to the United States, and to publications ranging from travelogues and articles in the press to translations of the other country's literature and fiction. On the other hand, both in America and in Russia, real images of the other state coexisted with imaginary ones. This was true not only because the reading public generally relied on "second-hand" impressions borrowed from literature and journalism, but also because the image of the Other was used to expand public recognition of the advantages and faults of domestic development.

American readers eagerly immersed themselves in the world of Russian literature, which introduced them to the realities of Russia's development and to the enigmatic world of the tortured Russian soul – to suffering, struggles, searching, thoughts, and feelings. This complex world left an aftertaste of sadness and melancholy, pessimism and glumness, that sometimes repelled those who wanted lighter reading, but literature nevertheless remained a stable source of ideas about specific features of the Russian national character. For their part, American realist writers found in the works of Turgenev, Tolstoy, and Dostoevsky what the US national literature required as it embarked down the path of realism after the Civil War.[72]

Leo Tolstoy was the most popular Russian writer in the late nineteenth-century United States. He piqued Americans' interest through his novels; on account of his religious beliefs, ethics, and social philosophy, which both inspired and shocked readers; and because of his view of life. He both influenced US literary figures, philosophers, and social reformers and was influenced by them. To wit, as a young man, Tolstoy had tried to follow Benjamin Franklin's thirteen virtues; later, he came to revere Henry George, the author of *Progress and Poverty*, and translated Henry David Thoreau's essay "Civil Disobedience" for publication in Russian. A never-ending stream of American visitors flocked to Yasnaya Polyana, while Tolstoy himself corresponded with public and religious figures, politicians, scholars, and journalists in the United States as American society grappled with the question of its own renewal.[73]

In Russia, too, images of the United States largely came from literary sources. America was associated with things mysterious and heroic, a perception informed by the popularity of adventure novels by the American writers Bret Harte and Fenimore Cooper. To Russians, the United States seemed like an alien and even otherworldly place. During this period, the notion of America as an underworld solidified in the minds of the Russian reading public due to the spread of the cult of Edgar Allan Poe. Poe, who influenced the Russian symbolists, found a mass readership, since his tales of horror were available very cheaply. Together with adventure novels and detective stories, these publications created a mythologized image of America. In addition, Russian readers of various classes fell in love with the realist Mark Twain, while critics and a more refined reading public favored the works of Nathaniel Hawthorne, Henry Wadsworth Longfellow, Ralph Waldo Emerson, Walt Whitman, and William Dean Howells.[74]

A more realistic and nuanced image of the United States was added to the Russian-language literature via descriptions of the lives of Russian emigrants. These were primarily the fruit of the writer Vladimir Korolenko's trips to America.[75] After visiting Chicago in 1893, Korolenko published his story "Bez iazyka" ("Without the Language") in *Russkoe bogatstvo* magazine. He stressed Russian emigrants' difficulties in adapting to this alien linguistic and socio-cultural milieu, yet duly praised the opportunities America offered. Korolenko's works frequently criticized America for its soulless society hungry for high-profile sensations, but his condemnation of American customs was far from absolute.

The journeys Russians and Americans made across the ocean could have allowed them to test the notions they had established about the other country through their reading. All too often, however, travelers to both states emphasized those elements that made it possible to draw comparisons with their own culture.

By the early twentieth century, many American travelers' pieces about the Russian Empire fitted into one of two above-mentioned narratives: the liberalist and universalist ("crusading") or the Russophilic. A third, Russophobic, narrative also existed: its hallmarks were a focus on the Russian Orthodox religiosity cultivated by the church, the overall state of inertia in the country, and the metaphor of cold/winter. The image of "snowy Russia shackled by cold" stressed the Russian Empire's Oriental nature and the lethargic state of the Russian people, focusing readers' attention on the fundamental political and sociocultural differences between the West/United States and Russia.

This discourse generated a certain Russophobic pessimism concerning the economic revival and political renewal of the Russian nation.[76] American observers' choice of narrative was determined by their ideology, their "pre-knowledge" of Russia (often borrowed from British sources or European travel guides), and the degree of their desire to be objective. The choice was also determined by which Russia they were interested in: a modern, urban one characterized by economic renewal and the colonization of Siberia, or a politically and socially backward one with an agrarian economy and a starving population beset by epidemics.

A similar binary was visible among Russian observers of the United States. They were primarily interested in those issues that correlated with the problems of Russia's national development. The United States remained a model for those who supported national economic and political modernization. However, while liberal westernizers (intellectuals and members of the bourgeoisie) tended to idealize America in their representations, revolutionaries were becoming disappointed. Their unsuccessful 1870s experiments with establishing agricultural communes in America, their knowledge of the political corruption and racial antagonism of the Gilded Age, and their engagement with the works of Henry George and Edward Bellamy led many members of the Russian revolutionary intelligentsia to abandon their Romantic and utopian ideas. However, this process was equivocal and would find its starkest manifestations only later. For instance, even as the Marxist Vladimir Ulyanov (Lenin) criticized the US political system, he stressed that America's progressive farming model provided an example for modernizing the agrarian system in the Russian Empire. He insisted that Russia had to choose "the American way," abandon the peasant commune, and develop intensive farming methods.[77]

In their turn, Slavophiles, Russian Nativists, courtiers, and conservative monarchists represented America as the antipode of Russia, emphasizing that the latter had to travel its own, "unique path." They perceived the US development model as "anomalous" and "unnatural," characterized by a multitude of faults, and fraught with possible collapse. Americans' radical acquisitive individualism and self-interested violence were counterposed to Russians' religiosity, communal spirit, and unique spirituality. By demonizing America's Protestant industrial civilization, they romanticized Russian Orthodox agrarian civilization. In this narrative, Americans were depicted as hypocrites, expansionists, and soulless dealers motivated by greed alone.[78]

In the 1880s and 1890s, Russian and American societies were dominated by a multiplicity of images. Both peoples wanted to know and understand each other better. As a result, the field of American Studies emerged in Russia through the efforts of the sociologists and historians Pavel Mizhuev, Stepan Fortunatov, and Maxim Kovalevsky, while the field of Russian studies emerged in the United States thanks to the intellectual and educator Archibald Coolidge, the philologist Leo Wiener, and such Russophiles as Isabel Hapgood and Charles Crane.

CONCLUSION

Over the last two decades of the nineteenth century, the factors that had underpinned Russia–US collaboration in earlier periods continued to buoy official relations: the absence of major geopolitical and economic conflicts; a pragmatic partnership within the Vienna system of international relations; and an unwillingness to boost the ideological aspect of the interstate dialogue.

The nascent transformation of mutual perceptions in this period related to the declining role of Europe, as a civilizational entity, in both America's and Russia's constructions of their respective national identities. The changes taking place both in the Russian Empire and in the United States, as well as in international relations, resulted in the two states becoming mutual constitutive Others to the increasing exclusion of Europe.

The notion of Russia as an object of America's mission to liberalize the world began to emerge in the United States during the first "crusade" for a "Free Russia" and the campaign against discrimination against Russian Jews. This notion led to the internationalization of American reformism. But, with the exception of this brief period in the late 1880s and early 1890s, a Russophilic image of Russia generally dominated. Americans believed in Russia's gradual transformation, took an interest in its culture and spirituality, saw Russia as a valuable international and economic partner and a "historical friend of the United States," and considered its foreign political expansion analogous to that of all the other great powers.

In the Russian Empire, discussions of the United States and assessments of the American experience of development were directly connected to different visions of Russia's own future. But, up until the early twentieth century, these discussions and assessments were dominated by perceptions conducive to harmonious bilateral relations. A kind of watershed would come in 1901, when several negative trends observed at the end of the nineteenth century (in ideology, geopolitics, and economy) would begin to sour Russia–US relations and mutual perceptions.

6

COLLISION AND REVOLUTION, 1901–1905

OVERVIEW

In the early twentieth century, the mounting tensions in Russia–US relations spilled over into crisis in 1903–1905. This crisis had four major dimensions.

First, the Russian Empire and the United States found themselves in geopolitical conflict in the Far East because of a clash between the two countries' expansionist ambitions. The crisis peaked during the Russo-Japanese War of 1904–1905. The United States sided with Japan and completed its rapprochement with Great Britain, which in turn sought to defend the principle of maritime neutrality during the war when Nicholas II's government refused to do so.

Second, economic contradictions between the two countries had sharpened. Although American manufacturers continued to be keenly interested in the Russian market, the two countries' growing competition on the world grain and oil markets, as well as the "tariff war" that broke out between the two countries in 1901, fueled tensions. In the "tariff war," the government of Nicholas II responded to additional US duties on Russian sugar by introducing duties on US-made machines and iron and steel goods. It would continue until the Portsmouth Conference of 1905, ultimately causing more damage to American exporters than to Russian sugar manufacturers.

Third, ideology came to impact official Russia–US relations for the first time. As the Russian government faced first a war with Japan and then a revolution, it slotted the United States into its black-and-white matrix of internal and external enemies. In turn, US government officials viewed both Russia's foreign policy and its domestic situation through their own ideological lens, which was framed by the ideas of Progressivism. This ideology coexisted with President Theodore Roosevelt's concern over the balance of power and interests in East Asia.

Fourth, large numbers of Americans mobilized in an anti-Russian campaign following anti-Semitic discrimination and violence there, particularly a brutal pogrom (riot) in 1903 in Kishinev, in the southwestern part of the

Russian Empire. This event, as well as the American "crusade" for a free Russia that peaked during the Russian revolution of 1905–1907, stoked the existing geopolitical and ideological crisis. The spread of pro-Japanese sentiments among Americans and their eager welcome of the revolution gave rise to diverse reactions in the Russian Empire. Nationalistic and conservative pro-monarchic outlets gave a boost to anti-American sentiments and sought to emphasize the drawbacks of the US political system. The liberal intelligentsia, by contrast, hoped for moral support from Americans and turned to the US experience of development as a model for Russia's renewal. On the far left, radicals expected financial aid and were dissatisfied with Roosevelt's peacemaking efforts, which helped the tsarist regime to survive the revolutionary crisis.

The conflict in the Far East, the Russian revolution, and the first large-scale "war of images" have been addressed by many scholars. Historians unanimously agree that the United States' and Russia's interests clashed because of their expansionist ambitions. However, they diverge on how to classify the two states' imperialism, as well as on which type had a greater impact on the escalation of the conflict in the Far East.[1] Additionally, classic American works on Russia–US relations have often discussed the conflict in the Far East in isolation from the events of the Russian revolution.[2] This chapter presents a more inclusive and comprehensive perspective on this era of crisis in bilateral relations. It demonstrates that the explanation for both the Russian Empire's and the United States' ambitions in the Far East can be found in the interaction of their foreign and domestic policies. It focuses on the connection between the Russo-Japanese War and the 1905 revolution. It also explores the new frame of mutual perceptions established when, under conditions of conflict, both countries' earlier multiplicities of images of the other came to be replaced by dichotomous visions of processes across the Atlantic.

RUSSIA AND THE UNITED STATES ON THE WAY TO CRISIS IN THE FAR EAST

In 1898, the diplomatic missions in Washington and St. Petersburg were transformed into embassies, testifying to the growing significance of bilateral relations.[3] In the years that followed, the diplomats of both countries would focus on two problems: competition among great powers in the Far East and the growing contradictions of economic relations.

In Russia, between the second half of the 1890s and the end of the Russo-Japanese War, the government, public, and press turned their attention away from the empire's western borders and toward its southeastern ones. A range of approaches to – and rationales for – this "turn to the East" were suggested. Supporters of the first one, such as Nikolay Przhevalsky, a famous Russian explorer of Central and East Asia, advocated territorial expansion – a kind of "conquistador imperialism." A second approach was propagated by the so-called "*vostochniki*" (Orientalists), among them Prince Esper Ukhtomsky, the publisher of the *Sankt-Peterburgskie Vedomosti* newspaper, Chairman of the Board of the Russo-Chinese Bank, and Head of the Board of the South Manchuria Railway. They claimed that Russia was advancing into "yellow" Asia not as a conqueror, but as a protector seeking to save Asians from Western exploitation. The "*vostochniki*" shared their critique of Western materialism and democracy with the author of a third approach, the philosopher and poet Vladimir Soloviev, a "liberal imperialist" who saw Russia as defending Christian Europe from the "yellow peril." Alexey Kuropatkin, Russia's War Minister (1898–1904) and subsequently Commander of the Manchuria Army and Commander-in-Chief of the Far Eastern Army, voiced a similar concern about the "influx of the yellow race." Finally, the leading proponent of a fourth approach, Russian Finance Minister Sergey Witte, advocated a program of "peaceful penetration" into China, centered on the construction of the Trans-Siberian Railway. Witte shared the Orientalists' open dislike of military aggression, but he did not think that the Russian Empire was an Asian country.[4]

Until the spring of 1903, Russia generally pursued Witte's program for "peaceful economic penetration" into China, simultaneously opening up additional opportunities for those American manufacturers who exported goods and materials for this Russian advance. Foreign Minister Vladimir Lamzdorf (1900–1906) supported Witte. However, the first blow to Witte's program had been dealt by Lamzdorf's predecessor, Mikhail Muraviev (1897–1900), as early as 1898, when he approved Russia's occupation of Port Arthur. Moreover, even Witte's peaceful policy contributed to bringing the war closer to home, as it prompted contradictions with Great Britain and Japan and pulled Russia into an international conflict in the Far East. At the same time, a group headed by Captain Alexander Bezobrazov, an influential coterie that had the ear of Emperor Nicholas II, geared Russia's Far Eastern policy toward more active land grabs. This group included Grand Duke Alexander Mikhailovich, Rear Admiral Alexey Abaza, Admiral Evgeny Alexeyev (until 1903), Prince Felix Yusupov, and reactionary Interior Minister Vyacheslav von Plehve (from April 1902).

Meanwhile, following the Spanish–American War in 1898, the United States made the Far East a higher priority of its foreign policy. Two men, Admiral Alfred Mahan and the intellectual Brooks Adams, directly influenced the political course of the William McKinley and Theodore Roosevelt administrations in Asia. Both stressed that the United States needed to gain access to China's market and viewed Russia as the principal obstacle to carrying out these plans. For Mahan, Russians combined the ruthless barbaric energy of Slavs with the mendacity of Asians.[5] To Adams, they were the heirs to Byzantine tradition and were on the periphery of the new world order created by industrialization.[6]

One instrument by which America sought to implement its "Far Eastern" program was the Open Door Policy, proposed by Secretary of State John Hay in his September 1899 note addressed to Great Britain, Germany, and Russia. The note was authored by William Rockhill, a diplomat and specialist in Oriental studies who was an advisor to Hay and the "godfather" of the United States' Far Eastern policy. He considered the Open Door Policy, which appealed for the territorial integrity of China and equal trade and investment opportunities for all foreign countries, to have both commercial and political contents. American Protestant missionaries who had expended significant funds and efforts on evangelizing the Chinese had also appealed to the McKinley administration, requesting that "China's doors be kept open." They had influence on Edwin Conger, the US minister to China (1898–1905).[7] American entrepreneurs eyeing China's markets were no less persistent.

As Washington sought new allies in London and Tokyo, American columnists and journalists endeavored to popularize the country's altered foreign policy priorities by framing the conflicts in the Far East as confrontations between civilized Anglo-Saxons and barbaric Slavs. This ideological and geopolitical tension began to grow following the suppression of the Boxer Rebellion (1898–1901) by a multilateral intervention that included both US and Russian forces.

Nevertheless, before 1903, there was no clear opposition between the Far Eastern strategies of St. Petersburg and Washington. Although the Boxer Rebellion had given the Russian Empire an argument for maintaining its presence in Manchuria – namely, to protect its railway and investments there – the Russian government did not object to the Open Door Policy, signed an agreement on withdrawing troops from Manchuria, and implemented the first stage of that agreement in the fall of 1902.[8] In Washington, Secretary of War Elihu Root was an active proponent of cooperation with Russia, while Theodore Roosevelt, who became president in 1901, believed through the end of that year that "Russia's march over barbarous Asia does represent a real and great advance for civilization," as he wrote in 1899.[9] Thus, while there were major frictions between Washington and St. Petersburg, and mistrust was building, a desire for compromise persisted. In particular, those in both countries who were interested in trade and economic cooperation sought to smooth over any contradictions.

"CIVILIZATION" VS. "BARBARISM"

By 1903, the growing mistrust and frictions between Russia and the United States could no longer be tamed. The ensuing crisis of bilateral relations was sparked by Russia's 1903 transition to an aggressive "new course" in the Far East, the United States' growing expansionist ambitions there, and an anti-Russian campaign in American society in the wake of the 1903 Kishinev pogrom.

In May 1903, the Russian Empire announced its "new course" in the Far East. Banking on its military presence in Manchuria, St. Petersburg sought to incorporate Korea into the Russian Empire. Russia's expansionist plans thus came into conflict with Japan's imperial ambitions. Japan had been carrying out a program of "peaceful penetration" into Korea and other strategically important neighboring areas: China, Indo-China, and the Russian Far East. Both the White House and the Department of State considered Japan's demands (unlike those of Russia) to be legitimate, as they stemmed from the need to ensure continued development.

By this time, as April 1903 correspondence between John Hay and Theodore Roosevelt demonstrates, anti-Russian sentiments were already on the rise in Washington.[10] In June, Hay published a memorandum in which he openly accused St. Petersburg of derailing Russia–US cooperation in the Far East and of violating its promises to comply with the Open Door Policy.[11]

Certainly, the activities of the Bezobrazov Group were an open provocation. However, Russia was not alone in conducting an expansionist policy in the Far East; the United States was doing likewise. Additionally, Washington had decided in favor of Japan's influence in Manchuria and Korea before Russia even adopted its "new course." As early as April 1903, the pages of US newspapers and magazines were filled with articles on Russia's annexationist policies in Manchuria, which were framed as a threat to the interests of the United States. Leading American cartoonists depicted the hypocrisy of Russian rulers.[12] In Russia, too, cartoonists demonstrated their wit on the topic of expansionism, depicting Uncle Sam's insatiable appetite for territory.[13]

The Kishinev pogrom in Bessarabia, in April 1903, also made a particular contribution to this "war of images" between Russia and the United States. There, 2,750 Jewish families were affected by the mob violence, in which 49 people were killed, 400 were injured, 600 women were raped, and an estimated 2.5 million rubles in property damage was perpetrated. Contrary to the claims put forward in American newspapers and magazines, the Kishinev tragedy occurred not on the direct orders of St. Petersburg, but due to the rampant anti-Semitism of the local press, local authorities' delay in taking action to protect the Jewish population, and the Russian Empire's long-standing discrimination against Jews as the domestic Other. Those involved in the Easter pogrom accused Jews of "having crucified Christ," of committing ritual murders of Christian children, and of disseminating revolutionary radicalism. They also relied on the idea (widespread among peasants) that the tsar had personally sanctioned anti-Jewish violence.[14]

In the United States, humanitarian motives and messianic idealism, combined with pragmatic concern that dispossessed Russian Jewish emigrants might flood the country, powered a large-scale protest movement against anti-Semitism in Russia. At protest rallies, in clubs, at church services, and in magazines and newspapers, the "civilization–barbarism" binary was used to characterize the events in Russia.[15] American cartoonists ingeniously visualized this opposition using the "Kishinev" verbal code to "barbarize" Russia's domestic and foreign policies.[16] They likened Russia to the Ottoman Empire by drawing parallels between anti-Jewish violence and the Turks' atrocities against Armenians, contributing to the "Orientalizing" of American's image of the Russian government in general.[17] Participants in protest rallies calling upon Washington to intervene drew analogies with the supposed liberating mission of the United States in Cuba.[18] Thus, the pogrom gave a new impetus to the American messianic idea as the crucial component of the "crusade" to create a renewed Russia.

Russian Ambassador Artur Cassini expressed his government's stance on the US protests when he pointed out participants' hypocrisy – after all, they lived in a country that oppressed Native Americans and lynched Black Americans.[19] The authors and cartoonists of *Novoe Vremia*, a semi-official newspaper published by Alexey Suvorin, an anti-Semite, actively pursued this topic,[20] focusing on the United States' policy of racial discrimination. They had first homed in on this during the Spanish–American War, creating an image of Americans as imperialists and hypocritical racists who fought to free dark-skinned people and Asians far beyond their borders while (in the Jim Crow era) discriminating against them domestically.[21] In this respect,

Russian diplomats in the United States and the Russian official press took the same stance as many American anti-imperialists.

In the wake of the Kishinev pogrom, one *Novoe Vremia* cartoon decried US "double standards" by depicting Uncle Sam driving down the road of progress holding a flag that read "Freedom and Equality" as he ran down Black Americans (Figure 6.1).[22]

While American cartoonists likened the Russian Empire to the Ottoman Empire to barbarize the former, *Novoe Vremia* cartoonists used the image of the Ottoman Empire to demonstrate that lynchings of Black Americans were no different from massacres of Christians by Turks.[23] That same year indeed saw an upsurge in racial strife in the United States. The American press published articles on the horrors of the Kishinev pogrom

Figure 6.1 "Forward, Uncle Sam!" *Novoe Vremia. Illustrirovannoe prilozhenie,* June 12/25, 1903. The inscription on the road sign reads: "The road of progress." The inscription on the flag reads: "Freedom and Equality." Courtesy of the State Public Historical Library, Moscow, Russia.

next to reports on lynchings and anti-Black riots and discussions of the plight of the Chinese in California and Native Americans across the country. Yet American public figures, rabbis, journalists, and former abolitionists alike denied that there were any similarities between pogroms and lynchings. American "friends of Russian freedom" strove to shift the focus from criticizing problems of racial discrimination within the United States itself to denouncing the evil of national and religious oppression in the Russian Empire.[24] Contrasting discrimination against Jews to racial discrimination in the United States helped Americans to overcome their doubts about their country's special advantages in a period of racial troubles.

CZAR—"EXCUSE ME, I'M TOO BUSY WEEPING OVER THIS DELAWARE AFFAIR."

Figure 6.2 "Czar – 'Excuse Me, I'm Too Busy Weeping over This Delaware Affair.'" *Brooklyn Daily Eagle,* July 2, 1903. Courtesy of the Brooklyn Public Library, Center for Brooklyn History.

There were some, however, who saw Russian and US discrimination as parallel developments. Since the late nineteenth century, Black Americans had drawn analogies between American racism and Russian anti-Semitism, accusing critics of anti-Jewish violence in the Russian Empire of hypocrisy and of being willing to close their eyes to problems with the United States' own political development.[25] A number of American cartoons also reflected this idea. For instance, a cartoon in the *Brooklyn Daily Eagle* depicted the tsar waving away a petition to protect Russian Jews, as he was busy mourning the victim of a lynching in Delaware (Figure 6.2).[26]

Facing public pressure to intervene, aware that a crisis in Russia–US relations was already brewing on account of the contradictions between the two countries' policies in the Far East, and in light of the possible influence of the Jewish community on the upcoming presidential elections, Roosevelt decided to present Nicholas II with a petition protesting against the perse-cution of Russian Jews that had been signed by thousands of Americans, including eminent politicians and public figures. Having been warned by St. Petersburg that such a diplomatic démarche had no prospect of success, Roosevelt gave the text of the petition to the press, stating that the tsarist government had officially refused to accept it.[27] In the United States, the president's action significantly bolstered the public's messianic enthusiasm, while in Russia it prompted accusations of American meddling in the domestic affairs of the Russian Empire.[28]

THE RUSSIAN EMPIRE AND THE UNITED STATES DURING THE RUSSO-JAPANESE WAR: POLITICS AND IMAGES

On the night of January 27/February 9, 1904, the Japanese Navy, com-manded by Admiral Togo Heihachiro, attacked Russian naval ships in the open harbor of Port Arthur. In response, Russia declared war on Japan. On both sides, the war was an unjust war of conquest, and there was opposition to war both in Russia and in Japan.[29]

The United States said it would remain strictly neutral and proposed the neutralization of China. In January 1905, the Department of State addressed other powers with the third Open Door note.[30] The Russian government supported the Washington administration's initiative to neu-tralize China, but with two qualifications: first, that St. Petersburg did not accept that neutrality applied to Manchuria; and second, that Russia would not consider itself bound by this agreement in the event that another power violated it.[31]

Despite Washington's proclaimed neutrality, no one had any doubt whose side the Roosevelt administration's and the public's sympathies were on. This was obvious from cartoons and editorials in the press, from the collection of money to support Japan's army, from the US syndication of Japan's loans, and from private parties at which state officials (including the president and the Secretary of State) did not shy away from expressing pro-Japanese sentiments. Since official relations between Russia and Japan had been severed, the United States – via its diplomatic and consular representatives – protected the interests of Japanese citizens in Russia, including POWs and detained civilians.

During the war, Russia abolished the principle of Maritime Neutrality, putting foods, coal, and cotton on the list of contraband goods. Russian authorities arrested neutral steamers carrying these contraband goods, among them American ships. Naturally, this provoked a negative response from the US government.[32] The United States accordingly became an active ally of Japan: it expanded exports of foods, medicines, and army uniforms to Japan; stepped up interaction between the two countries' intelligence agencies; and sided with the Japanese government in opposing Russia's attempts to use ports in neutral China to dock and repair its naval ships.[33]

By the start of the Russo-Japanese War, a negative attitude toward the Russian Empire had come to dominate both official and public discourses in the United States. These anti-Russian sentiments were skillfully fueled by the Japanese, who acted as consummate image-makers. They promoted among the American public the idea of a commonality between Japanese and European cultures, cultivating an image of Japan as a disciple of the West and a protector of the American Open Door Policy. Russia's decisive loss in this "war of images" contributed to its military defeat.[34]

There were various reasons for the American "fascination with Japan" in the early twentieth century. Proponents of moving into the Chinese market believed that Japan helped protect American interests and advanced the eastward spread of Western principles. President Roosevelt personally admired the Japanese, writing in 1904 that "The Japs have played our game because they have played the game of civilized mankind."[35] Such American "friends of Russian freedom" as George Kennan, who was in Japan from March 1904 as a military correspondent for *Outlook* magazine, believed that the defeat of medieval, semi-barbaric Russia at the hands of civilized, modern Japan would bring a revolution in Russia closer. Kennan started circulating the liberal *Osvobozhdenie* (*Liberation*) magazine among Russian POWs in Japan.[36] Members of the American Jewish community wished for Russian defeat, as they wanted to weaken the tsarist regime that oppressed their coreligionists and thereby precipitate a revolutionary transformation of Russia's political system. Jacob Schiff, head of the major banking house Kuhn, Loeb & Co, syndicated Japan's four war loans in the United States, the last of which floated on the eve of the Portsmouth Conference.[37]

Oscar Straus, another leader of the American Jewish community, contributed significantly to revising the history of the Russia–US friendship on the pages of American newspapers, journals, and magazines in 1903–1905. He explained that Americans were on the side of Japan because Tokyo was fighting on the side of enlightenment and civilization against the despotism and expansionism of the Muscovites.[38] Straus and all those who sought to destroy the idea of the Russia–US friendship stressed the latter's selfishness at every stage, from Catherine II's Declaration of Armed Neutrality to sending Russian naval ships to US shores in 1863–1864. They insisted that the United States owed no debt to Russia: money had changed hands during the Sale of Alaska, while Russia's support for the Union cause during the Civil War had been repaid during the philanthropic movement of 1891–1892.[39]

Japanophilia and Russophobia were not universal sentiments in the United States.[40] Wharton Barker, a Russophile from Philadelphia, and Charles Smith, former US Minister to Russia, engaged in a polemic with Oscar Straus. Both appealed to the idea of mutually advantageous bilateral economic cooperation and insisted that there was incontrovertible proof of Russia's friendly conduct during the most critical periods of American history.[41] In 1904, Senator Albert Beveridge published a book that created an image of the Russian Empire as a valuable partner for advancing American interests in China. The book became a bestseller, selling 20,000 copies in its first 6 weeks on the market. In his opinion, the United States should seek a rapprochement with Russia, not Japan, since the Russian Empire would provide American goods with access to Northeast China and Siberia once the Trans-Siberian Railroad was completed.[42]

However, American society was clearly dominated by supporters of Japan, who wished it a speedy victory over the Russian Empire and construed the war as a fight between civilization and barbarism, progress and regression.[43] Accordingly, the American media's "war of images" against Russia was unprecedented in its scale (though it had been foreshadowed by a smaller campaign in the early 1890s). Talented cartoonists "fought" on its "frontlines." They savored the endless string of crushing Russian defeats, played upon drunkenness and corruption in the Russian army, and derided its commanders' lack of talent.[44] Within the "civilization–barbarism" binary, a demonic image of official Russia was contrasted with a romantic image of Japan.[45]

Figure 6.3 "He Is One of Us. Changing His Food Made a Powerful Boy of Him."
Judge, April 8, 1905.

Japan, as the "Yankee of the East," was made a member of the "civilized powers" club (Figure 6.3), while Russia was removed from the club – becoming, like the Ottoman Empire before it, the "sick man of Europe."[46] Following the Battle of Tsushima, the Russian Navy's final, crushing defeat in the war, Japan's Vice Admiral Togo was depicted as "Dewey of the East," while Japan's military and economic supremacy was likened to that of the United States during the Spanish–American War.[47] The Russians, for their part, were analogized to the Spanish.[48] A favorite metaphor in this period was that of the "Japanese David vs. the Russian Goliath":[49] the Japanese were superior to Russians not in courage and bravery (which Russian soldiers constantly demonstrated, as Americans observed), but in mastering advanced military strategy and tactics and in modernizing their economy.

Cartoonists visualized opinions voiced in the press, at club meetings, and at receptions, as well as in the reports of American military correspondents and military observers of the Russian army.[50] While editorials were decidedly more nuanced and reserved,[51] it was these cartoons that flooded leading press outlets in the United States, kicking the anti-Russian campaign into overdrive. This "war of images" gave Japan powerful moral support.

Americans' pro-Japanese stance and the "war of images" against Russia provoked a negative response from St. Petersburg. The Russian pro-government press was filled with articles arguing that Washington was spearheading the destruction of traditionally friendly bilateral relations, that the United States wished to take Russia's place in Manchuria, and that there existed a secret US–Japan alliance. These articles posited that American Jews were behind the anti-Russian propaganda, claiming that the American people as a whole still had friendly sentiments toward Russia despite Washington's actions and the anti-Russian hysteria in the press.[52]

Given the anti-Russian campaign, Cassini repeatedly wrote articles for the US press calling upon Americans to see the Russo-Japanese military conflict as a war between the white and yellow races, between Christianity and heathenry.[53] To contribute to Cassini's efforts, Prince Esper Ukhtomsky arrived in the United States in the spring of 1904 on a lecture tour. Although he spoke in four states, nowhere did he attract a large audience.[54] In an article for *Harper's Weekly*, Ukhtomsky wrote that Russian society was deeply shocked by the pro-Japanese sentiments that prevailed in the United States and warned of Japan's intention to dominate the Far East.[55] American periodicals regularly reported that Russian satirical *lubki* depicted the United States and England as open allies of Japan, and thousands of Russians believed it to be true.[56]

Satirical *lubki*, popular among the Russian peasantry, from whose ranks soldiers were recruited, became the primary weapon of Russia's visual propaganda during the Russo-Japanese War. American military observers of the Russian army testified to how widespread was the stereotypical perception of the Japanese enemy as "yellow-faced heathens" among soldiers, officers, and Russian society as a whole.[57] Some *lubki* depicted Uncle Sam as a "sly well-wisher" of Japan, who, together with John Bull, was pushing the Japanese Emperor toward an abyss.[58] However, the dominant image of Uncle Sam was that of a banker giving money to Japan. He was depicted as holding a gigantic purse on which the Japanese relied. Pesky, insect-like Japanese soldiers attacked him for his bounty, which the owner of the capital was in no hurry to share (Figure 6.4).[59]

It should, of course, be kept in mind that the *lubki* and cartoons were not the only representations of the Japanese in Russia. The Russian "non-partisan" press, as well as those Russian officers and soldiers who met directly with the Japanese, offered the reading public images of the Japanese "with a human face." Meanwhile, the liberal and radical proponents of Russian modernization counted on Japan's victory to discredit the ruling regime and were, in that sense, "defeatist." They were accordingly not

Figure 6.4 Russian *lubok* "V pogoniu za den'gami (Pesnia iapontsev)" ("In Pursuit of Money [Japanese Song]"), 1904. Courtesy of the State Public Historical Library, Moscow, Russia.

hostile toward Americans on the grounds of their pro-Japanese sentiments, since they shared Americans' view that Russia's defeat would create the conditions for revamping its political system. That being said, liberals and radicals (from social democrats to anarchists) imagined different futures as a result of this process.[60]

On the whole, war propaganda paradoxically served to increase revolutionary sentiments. Russia's defeat at the hands of such an unworthy and "uncivilized" non-white enemy dealt a powerful blow to the prestige of the Russian Empire and became the key catalyst of the revolution. Following the outbreak of revolution at home and the crushing naval defeat at Tsushima in May 1905, Nicholas II was forced to agree to peace negotiations with

Japan. For its part, Japan had virtually exhausted its resources following the protracted and bloody Battle of Mukden in February–March 1905 and was also ready for peace. President Roosevelt acted as an intermediary in setting up the talks. In June, the emperors of Russia and Japan agreed to negotiate in Portsmouth, New Hampshire.

THE PORTSMOUTH CONFERENCE

President Roosevelt's peacemaking initiative brought him a Nobel Peace Prize and enhanced the United States' international prestige. Prior to the Portsmouth Conference, Roosevelt had dispatched his friend and fellow Harvard graduate George von Lengerke Meyer to St. Petersburg as the new US Ambassador to Russia. Meyer, having hastily abandoned his diplomatic post in Rome, was granted his first audience with the emperor in April 1905, and would liaise with him in the following months of the war and then throughout the Portsmouth Conference.

The peace conference began on July 27/August 9, 1905. Japan's delegation in Portsmouth was headed by Foreign Minister Jutaro Komura, assisted by Baron Kogoro Takahira, Japan's Ambassador to Washington. The Russian delegation was headed by Sergey Witte (with Ivan Korostovets as his personal secretary), assisted by Russia's new Ambassador to the United States, Baron Roman Rosen. An outstanding diplomat, Rosen had superb political acumen and insight, spoke flawless English, and was a man of the world.[61] More than 100 journalists covered the peace conference, including correspondents of *Novoe Vremia* and *Russkoe Slovo*. When the negotiations opened, American society was still dominated by pro-Japanese sentiments; these gave way to more critical assessments only as the conference was drawing to a close.[62]

Russia being flexible, the two delegations rather quickly arrived at agreements on eight of the twelve items for discussion. The Japanese then agreed not to demand that Russian ships in neutral ports be turned over to them or that Russia restrict its naval forces in the Far East. Thereafter, the conference stalled, as Russia flatly refused both to pay indemnities and to cede the island of Sakhalin to Japan. It took Roosevelt's intervention in the negotiations (initially on the side of the Japanese) to achieve progress. Mindful of his peacemaker status and desirous of maintaining a balance of power in the Far East, he sought to "make peace" by writing letters both to the Russian emperor and to the Japanese emperor. Roosevelt urged the former to cede the southern part of Sakhalin to Japan and pressed the latter to forgo indemnities. Witte, meanwhile, actively engaged the press and explained Russia's stance, an approach that compared favorably in the eyes of the American public with the haughty behavior of the Japanese delegation. In the end, the Russian Empire ceded the southern part of Sakhalin and Japan forwent the indemnities. The peace treaty was signed on August 23/September 5, 1905.[63]

All the Russian participants in the conference claimed that it was Witte who succeeded in turning the tide of American public opinion in Russia's favor and securing an honorable peace for the empire.[64] Researchers, however, continue to debate the scale and depth of changes in public preferences, the hierarchy of key figures, and their motivations. American scholars emphasized the role of President Roosevelt as the key figure, while giving Witte due credit; some expanded the gallery of "Portsmouth heroes" by inducting Meyer into it.[65] Soviet historian Boris Romanov recognized the roles of both Roosevelt and Witte, although he doubted the latter's version of his exclusive diplomatic success.[66] In general, however, the Soviet Cold War historiography preferred to emphasize the domestic reasons that prompted the two countries' governments to seek peace, chief among them a resource crisis in Japan and a revolutionary crisis in Russia.[67]

If we consider the evolution of public sentiments by examining not only diplomatic correspondence, personal accounts, and press reports, but also cartoons that indicate the shift in public opinion, certain nuances can be added to the long-standing historiographical debate. Roosevelt's stance remained unwaveringly pro-Japanese throughout the conference, his concerns about a possible imbalance of power in the Far East notwithstanding. During the conference, American journalists and cartoonists sang praises to Japan's victory. The US press was dominated by a demonic image of the defeated Russian Empire and a romantic image of the victorious Japan.

By September, three factors had weakened these pro-Japanese views. The first was the shift in the balance of power in the Far East and the shaping of the so-called "Eastern Monroe Doctrine" that Japan intended to implement in alliance with China. The second was the growing popularity of Witte, who certainly won the final round of talks and on whom Americans came to pin their hopes of Russian reform. The third was the activities of American Russophiles, who reminded their fellow Americans about the history of Russian–American friendship and drew their attention to the ambiguous situation in the Far East and to the United States' own imperialist policies.[68]

Americans were generally inspired by the Portsmouth peace treaty, although some voices criticized the fruits of Roosevelt's efforts.[69] In Russia, officers who had fought in the war wanted peace, while the "war party" and top-level bureaucrats accused Roosevelt of having robbed Russia of victory. Social democrats and Marxists were also critical of the outcome, as they had hoped that the revolution would transform from a political movement into social change. Meanwhile, liberal periodicals such as *Sankt-Peterburgskie Vedomosti, Vestnik Evropy,* and *Russkie Vedomosti* gave Roosevelt special credit for putting an end to a war that had been both meaningless and disastrous for Russia.[70] Ultimately, their assessments of the activities of Roosevelt and Witte, as well as of the results of the Portsmouth Conference, depended on how people on both sides of the Atlantic viewed the prospects of the Russian revolution.

THE REVOLUTION OF 1905–1907 AND AMERICANS' "CRUSADE" FOR RUSSIA'S FREEDOM

Watching the first Russian revolution play out, American society went through its first peculiar "cycle of hopes and disappointments" concerning the prospects of Russia's modernization, finally transforming the Russian Empire into an object of the American mission to bring freedom and democracy to the world.

The American public began to discuss the forthcoming Russian revolution in earnest and with great enthusiasm in the second half of 1904. In October 1904, the Society of American Friends of Russian Freedom (SAFRF), relaunched in Boston, started working at full tilt. Russian liberals and radicals, who traveled across the ocean in hopes of winning the American people's support for their struggle for Russian freedom, encouraged Americans in their belief that the Russian revolution would become a constructive Western-style movement. Two primary figures were the historian Pavel Miliukov, future leader of the Constitutional Democrats, and Ekaterina Breshko-Breshkovskaya, one of the leaders of the Socialist Revolutionary Party.[71] The latter's visit was instrumental in establishing the New York branch of SAFRF, which, together with the Boston branch, became a leading center of Americans' accelerating "crusade" for a "Free Russia."[72]

After Russian soldiers opened fire on a peaceful demonstration in St. Petersburg in January 1905, the overwhelming majority of American periodicals sharply condemned the massacre as a manifestation of medieval cruelty. The image of Nicholas II was "barbarized" through comparing him to Ivan the Terrible.[73] In parallel with the extant demonic image of official Russia, a romantic image of the Russian people was constructed. Influenced by the universalist euphoria, American liberals pushed aside their doubts as to whether the ignorant Russian people were ready to take part in governing their state. American conservatives' image of the "eternal Rus" was likewise sidelined. These ideas were replaced with a romantic image of Russia as a country moving toward its own 1776 – a country willing, under liberals' guidance, to enact a political revolution and religious modernization and follow the Western development model. The press was full of parallels with the events of the American revolution, and the authors of these articles searched for "founding fathers" among the main characters of the Russian revolutionary drama.[74] Various observers in the United States viewed the American revolution as the reference model, while the French Revolution was taken as a cautionary tale about the dangers of the social chaos, anarchy, and terror typical of the large-scale destruction of an "old regime." In this context, the image of the French King Louis XVI was intended to discourage the Russian emperor from making the mistakes that had cost the French monarch his head.[75]

In the first half of 1905, a "crusading spirit" was in the air in the United States. Russians were grouped together with Cubans in the messianic plans of American political and public figures, priests and philanthropists, journalists and columnists. In their view, Americans had to help Russians in their movement toward freedom by enlightening them through publications, by supporting them morally and financially, and by bringing diplomatic pressure to bear. Cartoons illustrated this messianic enthusiasm, ideological zeal, and political idealism.[76] The Freedom of Religion Manifesto, issued by Nicholas II in April 1905, garnered special approval among members of various Protestant denominations in the United States, who hoped that the spread of Protestantism would be an element of Russia's national revival. They took the manifesto as a signal to step up their efforts to spread the "true faith" in the Russian Empire.[77]

On the wave of infatuation with the Russian revolution, political assassination was justified, even if indirectly and for a short while, as a means of accelerating political modernization in such backward countries as the Russian Empire.[78] The writer Mark Twain, a longtime participant in Americans' "crusade" for a "Free Russia," called for open resistance to tyrants in a piece he wrote for the *North American Review*.[79] Certainly, the denizens of the Lower East Side in New York and socialists such as Jack London welcomed political assassinations as a way of fighting for freedom in Russia. London enthusiastically stressed the differences between the Russian revolution, on the one hand, and the American and French Revolutions, on the other hand.[80] In 1908, he published *The Iron Heel*, a novel born of his acute interest in the Russian revolution, which had inspired him to dream of a revolution against oligarchic capitalism in the United States.

In general, Americans supported the Russian revolution until late 1905, when it seemed to diverge from a liberal model. Thereafter, it caused concern and disappointment owing to its "dangerous trends": growing social tensions, uprisings in the army and in the navy, strikes and industrial protests, the establishment of Workers' Councils (Soviets), and continued Jewish pogroms. These metamorphoses in the fight for freedom led it to become known as a "Révolution à la Russe."

The end of the Russo-Japanese War also contributed to the change in American public opinion. Following the Portsmouth Conference, US investment in Russia increased, Tokyo–Washington relations cooled, and pro-Japanese sentiments in the United States consequently declined. These developments, in turn, promoted the spread of more nuanced ideas of official Russia, including through the romantic image of Witte, who had played a key role in brokering peace in Portsmouth. He had also been the person to prepare Nicholas II's October Manifesto of 1905, which granted certain new freedoms to Russian citizens – a move met with great enthusiasm on the other side of the Atlantic. American observers saw Witte as the "Russian Lincoln" liberating the Russian people from the chains of political and civil slavery, a strong figure who could save Russia from being plunged into revolutionary chaos and anarchy.[81] Witte's image began to lose its romantic aura in early 1906, however, when it became clear that he had failed to adequately address the situation and thus lost the confidence both of the pro-government camp and of the liberals.

The last major upsurge in US interest in the Russian revolution occurred when the First State Duma was convened in April 1906. While for many Russians the real revolution was just beginning, for most Americans it was over, as it had transformed into a general popular uprising against the government – an uprising fraught with political and social chaos, total anarchy, bombs, and Browning guns. Events in Russia demonstrated for Americans that the Russian people's path toward freedom lay through enlightenment, since ignorance turns into "freedom Russian style."

Such members of the conservative establishment as US Ambassador to Russia Meyer arrived at a pessimistic conclusion: "Russia is entering upon a great experiment, ill-prepared and really uneducated . . . . The great mass of the Russian people are not much superior to animals with brutal instincts . . . . They do not know what they want, except that they want everything at once – what has taken other nations generations to acquire."[82] American universalist liberals, meanwhile, believed that the principal outcome of the Russian revolution would be the development of the foundations of parliamentarism. Consequently, they kept an eye on those Russian political visitors who traveled across the ocean for moral and financial support.[83]

As the Russian revolution transformed from a political movement to a social one, only America's radicals (both socialist and non-socialist) remained inspired. For them, the Russian revolution was an unprecedented event that would inspire social reformism in the United States itself. "Gentlemen socialists" such as William English Walling, Arthur Bullard, Ernest Poole, and Durland Kellogg made a particular contribution to shaping the American radical discourse on Russia. Like the Marxists, they saw the social component as the essence of the Russian revolution; unlike the Marxists, they banked on peasants as the agents of social democracy. They believed that the road to socialism lay not through industrial capitalism, but through a "peasant revolution." Like George Kennan and his fellow liberal "crusaders," they saw the negative aspects of the national character as resulting from the despotic regime and believed Russians to be capable of democracy. Meanwhile, for the "gentlemen socialists," the significance of the Russian revolution lay in its unique social message for the whole of humankind, and not in moving down the road of establishing the "United States of Russia."[84]

On the whole, however, the American public's initial universalist euphoria soon gave way to profound disappointment in the results of Russia's first revolutionary experiment.[85] Liberals and socialists in Russia thus experienced a reciprocal disappointment, as they had not realized how fickle public opinion in the United States was and that the "crusading spirit" of the progressivist era would not necessarily translate into real action.

CONCLUSION

The period between 1901 and 1905 saw the emergence of four trends that would influence Russia–US relations for some time to come.

First, the period put a definitive end to the Russian–American "distant friendship," which gave way to outright rivalry. Great Britain was no longer seen as a common adversary of Russia and the United States, and the latter backed Japan over Russia in the Russo-Japanese War. Russia, defeated in that war by a non-white race, blamed both England and the United States.

Second, the Russo-Japanese War gave rise to the United States' first large-scale "war of images" against Russia. In that "war," the Russian Empire lost decisively: all the laurels went to the "Japanese David" who had faced down the "Russian Goliath." Henceforth, the "David vs. Goliath" metaphor would become a staple trope used in the United States to demonstrate the imperial ambitions of authoritarian Russia, which was prepared, in pursuit of those ambitions, to attack small but more progressive states. The "war of images" further served to make Nicholas II the embodiment of Russia in American eyes; he was claimed to be responsible for everything, both good and bad, happening in the country. This approach would be replicated throughout Soviet and post-Soviet history.

Third, in 1903–1905, both countries began to use the image of the Other for their political purposes on a far greater scale, on different levels and in different contexts. In the United States, while it was still sometimes used to criticize the domestic political situation, the image of the Russian Empire was primarily deployed to demonstrate that, even though the United States had drawbacks and social conflicts, it remained the country of freedom and democracy by comparison. Russia, in turn, engaged in massive criticism of the double standards that led Americans to condemn the Kishinev pogrom at the same time as racial violence proliferated across the United States. It was during this period that the image of Americans as hypocritical racists, sneaky imperialists, and dishonorable capitalists obsessed with making profits – an image that would become a staple of Soviet propaganda – took definitive shape.

Fourth, during the Russian revolution of 1905–1907, Americans' "crusade" for Russian freedom peaked and their notion of being part of Russia's renewal was shaped. American society's response to the Russian revolution demonstrated how easily universalist euphoria and a romantic myth of Russia could give way to disappointment, Russophobic pessimism, and the image of a "Révolution à la Russe." It happened then and it would happen in the future, because Americans' vision of the prospects of Russian modernization was shaped not only by events in Russia, but also by Americans' own messianic enthusiasm, ideological zeal, and religious impulses.

7

INTERACTIONS AND CONTRADICTIONS, 1906–1914

OVERVIEW

In December 1907, Secretary of War William Howard Taft, who had held pro-Japan views before and during the Russo-Japanese War, visited St. Petersburg as part of his round-the-globe trip. In Russia, his visit was perceived as a sign that Washington wanted to restore the two countries' mutual understanding, which had been destroyed by the crisis of 1903–1905. It was no accident that *Novoe Vremia* compared Taft's visit to Gustavus Fox's special mission in 1866, at the zenith of the Russian–American friendship. Taft traveled to St. Petersburg on the Trans-Siberian railway, was impressed by the Russian Empire's economic progress, and joined the advocates of Russia–US cooperation in the Far East.[1]

As Taft's journey indicates, between the Russo-Japanese War and the outbreak of the First World War in Europe in 1914, the governments of both the Russian Empire and the United States demonstrated a desire for more harmonious relations. Even in 1911, at the height of a conflict over Russia's refusal to accept the passports of American Jews, the two governments collaborated on the protection of fur seals, and the Russian government gave a most friendly welcome to a squadron of American battleships that was sent to Europe to demonstrate the growing naval power of the United States.[2] This trend toward renewed cooperation was also bolstered by mutual interest in expanding the export of American goods, capital, and technologies to the Russian Empire, as well as by cultural exchanges.

Nonetheless, conflicts arose in some areas. In the Far East, US "dollar diplomacy" clashed with a Russian "sphere of influence" arrangement with Japan. In Persia, where Russia had long had interests, American businessman-adventurer Morgan Shuster's efforts to reorganize the financial system triggered tension with St. Petersburg. Within the United States, two large-scale public campaigns – against extraditing Russian revolutionaries who had fled to the United States and in favor of abrogating the 1832 commercial treaty in order to protest Russia's anti-Semitic policies – demonstrated that many

Americans valued ideals more highly than trade and pragmatic cooperation. Meanwhile, liberals and radicals arriving from the Russian Empire reinforced American images of the Russian people as waiting for help from overseas. In response, the official and semi-official press in the Russian Empire, as well as conservative and nationalist party publications, criticized the American policy of "double standards" and the "defects" of American democracy.

Because of their focus on the Far Eastern situation and the abrogation of the 1832 Treaty,[3] historians traditionally depicted the period between the end of the Russo-Japanese War and the start of the First World War as a continuation of the crisis in bilateral relations. Recent studies, however, have proposed a more balanced assessment of the era.[4] This chapter demonstrates that the period displayed in equal measure a trend toward conflict and a trend toward cooperation. On the whole, official Russia–US relations emerged from a state of crisis during this period because of both governments' desire to find compromises. The promotion of economic cooperation, academic study of the other country and its people, and the expansion of people-to-people contacts further helped ease tensions by the end of this period.

THE FAR EAST: WHY RUSSIA–US RAPPROCHEMENT DID NOT HAPPEN

Following the Japanese victory over Russia in 1905, the changing balance of power in the Far East and the growing tension in US–Japan relations created the conditions for a possible rapprochement between the Russian Empire and the United States. There were proponents of this course in St. Petersburg and in Washington at both governmental and public levels. However, Russia's progress in that direction was circumscribed by Russia–Japan interaction in the region, as enshrined in the 1907 Russo-Japanese Agreement. Russia's Foreign Minister, Alexander Izvolsky, believed the gradual elimination of tensions there through fair political and economic settlement of relations with Japan and Great Britain to be one of the crucial components of the Russian Empire's policy.[5]

The United States, for its part, continued to be guided by the Open Door concept in structuring its Far Eastern policy. Accordingly, in both the 1905 Taft–Katsura Agreement and the 1908 Root–Takahira Agreement, the United States and Japan pledged mutual respect of each other's territorial possessions and spheres of influence in the Pacific. The latter agreement brought temporary stability to US–Japan relations following the damaging immigration crisis of 1906–1909. This crisis had been stimulated by Californian nativists, who supported the exclusion of Japanese immigrants from the country and the establishment of segregated schools for those Japanese children already there. They organized riots in San Francisco and sought to influence the government in Washington.[6]

St. Petersburg considered joining the Root–Takahira Agreement. However, Roman Rosen, Russia's Ambassador to the United States, suggested that a trilateral Russia–US–China agreement would be more acceptable.[7] Yet this plan never materialized, and the struggle for railway concessions in China – initiated by American entrepreneurs and supported by the US government – only aggravated Russia–US contradictions in the Far East.

From 1909, President Taft and his Secretary of State, Philander Knox, sought to contain Japanese expansionism in Asia. Acting in the spirit of "dollar diplomacy," they attempted to use American financiers' and entrepreneurs' economic projects for political purposes. Willard Straight, a representative for a US banking group, assisted them in the elaboration and execution of this policy. In 1909, Knox proposed a plan to neutralize all railways in Manchuria, including the Chinese Eastern Railway and the South Manchuria Railway.[8] He intended to either bring the railways under the ownership of China's government while retaining international control or else transfer them to the ownership of an international bank syndicate. Since Knox's plan threatened both Russia's and Japan's positions, it spurred a Russia–Japan rapprochement, enshrined in a 1910 Russo-Japanese Agreement. The agreement reflected Russia's desire to secure its Far Eastern flank and Japan's intention to prepare for land grabs from Korea (which would be annexed later in 1910) and China. In response, Washington established the fourth consortium (comprised of the United States, Great Britain, France, and Germany), which in April 1911 concluded a loan agreement with China that gave the states of the consortium the right to implement monetary reform in China and to develop industrial production in Manchuria. The agreement also stipulated that the consortium enjoyed a monopoly on financing any subsequent projects related to those objectives.

Despite Washington's dissatisfaction, Japan and the Russian Empire (the latter with the support of England and France, its Entente allies) joined the consortium in June 1912 as full members. As a condition of its membership, St. Petersburg – which had hoped to reconcile the warring parties by recognizing the nominal sovereignty of the Qing Dynasty and had opposed Washington's attempts to gain international support for the Republic of China – was forced to recognize Yuan Shikai's government. In the Unites States, cartoonists portrayed the "Russian bear" as the main obstacle in China's path to a republican form of government.[9] Russia's official press, in turn, accused the United States of using anti-Russian sentiments in revolutionary China to build its own commercial empire.[10] Meanwhile, the attitude to the Chinese revolution in the United States had unequivocal consequences. With time, Washington's failure to support the genuine enthusiasm in China for a republican revolution resulted in the entrenchment of both radical Chinese ambitions and anti-revolutionary thought in American society.[11]

In building its Far Eastern strategy after the Russo-Japanese War, Washington failed to account for Russia consequently becoming interested in building stable relations with Japan in East Asia. The tsarist government was willing to cede ground in Korea for the sake of its more important interests in Northern China and then to split its sphere of interests in Inner Mongolia with Japan (the 1912 Sazonov–Motono agreement). This was the final move in the joint Russia–Japan game played in response to the Taft–Knox program in the Far East. As a result, the Japanese Empire continued its territorial expansion (although Washington aimed to contain Japanese expansionism in the Far East) and moved to the foreground in Russia–US relations in the Far East. On the whole, the failure of the Taft–Knox "dollar diplomacy" testified to the United States' limited opportunities in East Asia and was "a classic case of projecting interests beyond capabilities."[12]

Despite this friction, Russia and the United States cooperated effectively on at least one issue in the region. Concerted actions on the part of the Russian and American delegations at the 1911 Washington Conference on preservation and protection of fur seals resulted in a fifteen-year convention signed on June 24/July 7, 1911. Unfortunately, this agreement came only after over "10,000,000 seals had been killed and the herds reduced to a fraction of their original numbers, to fewer than 200,000."[13] However, the fact that St. Petersburg and Washington succeeded in achieving this consensus in the same year that the American Jewish Committee and "friends of Russian freedom" launched an anti-Russian campaign provides an important indication of the extent to which official relations could be insulated from public pressures.

AMERICANS JUDGE OFFICIAL RUSSIA: ANTI-TSARIST CAMPAIGNS IN THE UNITED STATES AND THE ABROGATION OF THE 1832 TREATY

In 1907, Russia's first revolution ended, and while the "gentleman socialists" retained their interest in the cause of Russian freedom, they shifted their attention to reforming American society. William English Walling, the author of *Russia's Message* (1908), stressed that years would have to pass before Russians would arrive at the final stage of their revolution.[14] In addition, after Walling joined the US Socialist Party in 1910, he began to lose faith in peasants as the principal driver of a Russian revolution.

Meanwhile, George Kennan continued to submit the problems of lawlessness in Russia to the court of American public opinion while ignoring many of the developments occurring there, from industrialization to the changing composition of the revolutionary movement.[15] Kennan educated Americans to believe that the Russian Empire remained a prison for political dissidents, as well as ethnic and religious minorities, and was still far from establishing a westernized political system.[16] However, similar to William Foulke, the former president of the Society of American Friends of Russian Freedom (SAFRF), who had visited Russia in 1907,[17] Kennan believed that the seeds of democracy, having finally been planted in her soil, would sprout in the future.

Russian radicals and liberals who came to the United States also fanned the flames of American liberal universalism. These visitors ranged from Nikolai Tchaikovsky, a veteran of the Russian revolutionary movement, to Alexey Aladin, the leader of the Trudovik (Labor Group) faction in the First Duma, to the leader of the Constitutional Democrats Party (Kadets), Pavel Miliukov, who was already well known in the United States.

Tchaikovsky and Aladin traveled across the ocean in 1907 to oppose loans to the tsarist government and to collect funds for the Socialist Revolutionary Party. Having arrived on US shores, they said what Americans wanted to hear, drawing parallels with the American revolution and talking about the fight for the constitutional system in Russia. Writing to Kennan before his trip, Tchaikovsky stressed, "Even though repressions are carried out in many places, they fail to achieve their goal of suppressing the revolutionary sentiments and instead deepen the revolutionary unrest among the masses."[18] Tchaikovsky and Aladin succeeded in raising $50,000 for the revolutionary cause and helped such influential people as Jacob Schiff oppose American loans to the tsarist government. Pleased with the results of his efforts, Aladin wrote from the United States: "[The] Russian progressive movement has never before had such brilliant opportunities in the U.S. as it has now. America knows me, America believes me, America loves me."[19]

Their propaganda tour garnered great publicity, thanks in part to the national SAFRF, which had been reestablished in March 1907, with its headquarters in New York. In addition to long-standing "friends of Russian freedom," the society gained such new members as Herbert Parsons, a Republican and a close friend of Roosevelt; Seth Low, a municipal reformer and president of the National Civic Federation; Jane Addams and Lillian Wald, well-known humanitarians; and the American Jewish leaders Jacob Schiff and Isaac Seligman.[20] *Novoe Vremia* reacted harshly to the reestablishment of the SAFRF, going so far as to suggest cutting diplomatic ties with the United States, since the two countries had been developing independently of each other and did not need each other.[21]

Pavel Miliukov, the leader of the Kadets, presented Americans with his own vision of Russia's destination. Charles Crane had the Civic Forum, a non-political organization, invite Miliukov to the United States. His three-day visit was a triumph. He addressed an audience of 4,000 at Carnegie Hall on "Constitutional Government for Russia" and declared that America should extend moral aid to Russian liberals. Unless they won the political struggle, he declared, the peasant masses would smite down the monarchy and also bury any hope of a liberal and democratic regime in Russia. Miliukov truly believed that it was the evolutionary liberal program, and not the revolutionary one, that would triumph. However, both he and his more radical compatriots unfailingly appealed to Americans' messianic sentiments, encouraging them to believe that they would play an important role in Russia's modernization.[22]

Both American activists and political propagandists from the Russian Empire opposed the extraditions of Latvians Jan Pouren and Christian (Krišjānis) Rudowitz, who had participated in the 1905–1907 revolution and then fled to the United States. A public campaign organized in 1908 by the SAFRF together with Jewish community leaders reminded Americans that their republic had to remain a safe haven for everyone fighting against political and religious tyranny.[23] This campaign served as a preparatory step for a national movement in support of abrogating the 1832 commercial treaty.[24]

The American Jewish Committee (AJC) planned, when it initiated the campaign, to use the abrogation of the treaty and the signing of a new one as an instrument for gaining for American Jews the same rights that other US citizens traveling to Russia enjoyed. The Taft administration, however, did not wish to further strain relations with Nicholas II's government over an effort that not only had no hope of success, but also carried the potential to harm American business and bilateral relations in general.[25] The AJC, having lost hope of a diplomatic settlement of the "passport question" that would have ensured passport rights for American Jews equal to those of other Americans in Russia, launched a national movement in January 1911. The American Jewish lobby emphasized that the 1832 treaty was as insulting to the United States as the extradition treaty, a move that made it possible to pool their efforts with those of the "friends of Russian freedom."[26] The latter likewise criticized Russia's domestic policies, although they made no demands for the abrogation of the treaty.[27]

In the United States, both universalist liberals and conservatives appealed to Americans' national pride. New Jersey Governor and future president Woodrow Wilson, addressing a massive rally at Carnegie Hall in New York, expounded on this idea: "America is not a mere body of traders; it is a body of free men. Our greatness is built upon our freedom – is moral, not material. We have a great ardor for gain; but we have a deep passion for the rights of man. Principles lie back of our actions."[28] Cartoonists, joining the campaign to protect American citizenship, deployed the "darkness–light" dichotomy, framing Russia as an object of the US mission to reform the world.[29]

Americans' idealism trampled pragmatic considerations. The treaty was abrogated in 1911, despite warnings from American diplomats such as William Rockhill, who had just left the post of US Ambassador to Russia, and Curtis Guild, who replaced Rockhill in that position. The cancellation of the treaty also disregarded protests from American Russophiles and entrepreneurs interested in developing trade and economic relations with Russia. The White House and the Department of State did everything they could to mediate between the advocates and opponents of abrogation. Ultimately, instead of the resolution that the House of Representatives had been considering, which was offensive to Russia, the Senate adopted, with minor amendments, an address by President Taft instructing the ambassador in St. Petersburg to inform Nicholas II's government that the United States wished to terminate the treaty and start negotiating a new one.[30] This approach observed international legal decorum.

Russian officials and diplomats were inclined to explain the success of the American campaign by reference to "Jewish scheming." Russia's nationalists accordingly launched an anti-Semitic campaign. Their ideologue was the journalist Vasily von Egert, who published several pamphlets full of anti-Semitic and anti-American rhetoric. Egert, who formulated his principal ideas in the book *We Must Defend Ourselves* (1912), called upon the Russian government to transform the country into the last bulwark of the fight against global Jewry and to do everything to relocate all Jews to other countries, chief among them the United States. Responding to his American critics in a brochure translated into English, Egert drew a parallel between pogroms and lynchings.[31] Nationalist brochures and pamphlets emphasized Americans' "double standards": they lectured Russians on the "Jewish question," yet the United States restricted the numbers of Asian immigrants it admitted and had failed to address other types of racial discrimination at home.[32]

Octobrists, the extreme right wing of Russian liberalism, also opposed granting Jews equal rights. They therefore joined forces with the nationalists and far-right reactionaries to submit to the Duma a bill on declaring a trade war on the United States.[33]

Miliukov's Kadets, meanwhile, took the abrogation of the treaty as an opportunity to criticize nationalist ideology in general and anti-Semitism in particular. They believed that the tsarist government's policies concerning the "Jewish question" were the root cause of the abrogation of the treaty.[34] Russian left-wing and centrist publications (*Vestnik Evropy, Russkie Vedomosti, Rech*) demanded a new treaty that would align with the interests of both countries.[35]

In the end, the Ministry of Trade and members of the business community insisted that general restrictive measures against "Made in USA" goods be abandoned and that talks on concluding a new agreement be launched. However, it would become clear that a new treaty could not be concluded without resolving the "passport question." Despite its efforts, the Taft administration failed to achieve this goal: the tsarist government could not be moved on the "passport question," as it was tied to the domestic legislation on Jews, which had not been liberalized. As a result, there was no prospect of reaching an agreement that the US Senate would ratify, especially since the press and the AJC remained vigilant.

In the wake of the failed negotiations, bilateral trade continued, as a result of the mutual interest of both American manufacturers and Russian consumers. However, its volume was much reduced: a special memorandum prepared by the State Department's Bureau of Foreign Commerce in the summer of 1912 stressed that exports of American agricultural equipment to Russia had declined by 25 percent during the first five months of 1912, while overall exports to Russia had fallen by 18 percent.[36] In addition, growing anti-American sentiments dealt a blow to Americans' investment projects in Russia and deprived them of profitable long-term contracts.[37]

The movement in support of abrogating the 1832 treaty had long-term consequences for US foreign policy, as well as for bilateral relations. Historians have rightly stressed that "as in East Asia, American concern was projected into an area beyond the influence of American power" and that "the passport treaty abrogation debacle demonstrated on both sides how moralistic and ethnic passion was gaining over inept and lackadaisical government actions."[38] This movement simultaneously advanced the internationalization of the "Jewish question" in Russia, allowed pressure groups to demonstrate their ability to influence US foreign policy, and painted the United States as a country of tolerance and religious freedom in contrast to a Russian Empire filled with superstitious bigotry.[39]

In 1911, the year that the treaty was abrogated, relations between the Russian Empire and the United States were also roiled by developments in Persia. A group of American advisors led by the financier Morgan Shuster arrived in Persia in May 1911 on an unofficial mission to reorganize the country's financial system. However, Persia had long been a sphere of Russian interests, and Russian diplomatic and military pressure forced Shuster to leave the country in December 1911. Attempting to smooth over the ensuing conflict, the US government declared it had nothing to do with Shuster's mission and refused to protest his deportation. Yet Shuster launched an anti-Russian campaign in the American press and in Persia, criticizing the tsarist government's foreign policy and its cynical expansionist methods. These efforts had a detrimental effect on the image of official Russia in American public discourse.[40]

THE PROSPECTS OF RUSSIA–US COOPERATION IN TRADE AND TECHNOLOGIES

Despite the geopolitical and ideological contradictions between the two countries, their mutual interest in expanding exports of American goods, capital, and technologies to Russia helped balance bilateral relations. In the years before the First World War, the Russian Empire steadily modernized its economy. Many people on both sides of the Atlantic attributed Russia's successes in building an efficient economy to Russians' having learned the "lessons" of American entrepreneurship and gained the latter's competitive edge. Americans viewed themselves as mentors revealing to Russians the secrets of capitalism, technological progress, mass production, and the culture of mass consumption.

The most popular brands in Russia included McCormick harvesting machines and Singer sewing machines.[41] Before the First World War, American enterprises began manufacturing their goods in Russia for Russian customers. The International Harvester Company plant produced McCormick reapers in Lubertzy, the Singer Sewing Company (Figure 7.1) opened a plant in Podolsk, and the Westinghouse Air Brake Company conducted operations in St. Petersburg. The latter joint-stock company received a large order for street cars for Moscow, where the Westinghouse

Figure 7.1 Vladimir Tabourine's advertising poster of the Singer Sewing Company in Russia.

Electric Company had a plant.[42] In 1909, Russia also started importing Henry Ford's mass-produced Model T automobile.[43]

In the 1900s and 1910s, the flow of American investment grew, to the approval of the tsarist government and members of Russia's business community. Americans were major investors in the insurance business, as well as leaders in using US technologies to develop natural-resource deposits in Russia: gold in Eastern Siberia; copper, gold, quartz, and iron in the Urals; and oil in the Caucasus.[44]

A special place in bilateral relations was held by a large-scale investment project developed by the American mining engineer and promoter John Hays Hammond, a longtime friend of Sergey Witte who was also a close friend of President Taft. He arrived in Russia on the invitation of the tsarist government in December 1910 and met with Prime Minister Pyotr Stolypin and other high-ranking governmental officials. Through the efforts of US Ambassador William Rockhill, who believed Hammond's arrival to be a highly auspicious event for US–Russia relations, the entrepreneur was granted an audience with Nicholas II. In anticipation of Hammond's visit, Grigorii Vilenkin, the Russian financial agent in Washington, wrote an article in *Novoe Vremia* in which he emphasized American entrepreneurs' interest in modernizing the Russian economy.[45]

Hammond's project envisioned investing $300 million in building an irrigation system in Turkestan, where the tsarist government planned to expand cotton-growing to help relieve domestic industry's dependence on American cotton. He also planned to construct grain elevators, build railroads, and obtain coal-mining concessions. Hammond was warmly received in Russia both by the government and in business circles, and he was greatly inspired by his trip.[46] Despite these auspicious beginnings, however, Hammond's project was ultimately derailed by the anti-Russian campaign in the United States advocating the abrogation of the 1832 treaty and by the retaliatory anti-American campaign in Russia. He did not want to quarrel with influential members of the Jewish lobby. Representatives of Southern states were also displeased with a project that might have a detrimental impact on American cotton exporters.[47] Nevertheless, such failures could not prevent America's economic expansion into the Russian Empire.[48]

American authors paid close attention to Prime Minister Pyotr Stolypin's reforms intended to eliminate the peasant commune and give peasants private ownership of land, in some cases by moving them to Siberia. Observers in the United States viewed the reforms not only as an important step toward the rebirth of the Russian countryside, but also as an opportunity to increase the sales of American agricultural equipment and to teach Russians how to make their agriculture profitable. For their part, economists, columnists, and public figures in Russia, as well as Russian emigrants in America, proposed opening offices of Russian agricultural companies in the United States to collect information, study agricultural practices, purchase seeds, and advertise "Made in Russia" products across the Atlantic.[49] The similar climates of Russia's steppes and the Great Plains of the United States facilitated this effort, encouraging American agricultural specialists to study Russian methods for growing frost- and drought-resistant crops and to be more interested in working with their Russian counterparts. Russian emigrants who moved to the United States – primarily

Russian Germans, including Mennonites – also improved knowledge of Russia's agricultural practices.[50]

The two countries' burgeoning trade and technology cooperation was supported by the establishment, in May 1913, of the Russian–American Chamber of Commerce, a body that reported to the Russian Ministry of Trade and Industry.[51] In July 1913, the columnist Michael Imkhanitsky traveled to the United States as a representative of the Chamber on a special propaganda mission. He visited New York, Chicago, and Washington, informing Americans about Russia's special interest in deliveries of American-made goods, be they tractors or cars, refrigerators or typewriters, shoes or pens, telephones or machine tools. In an interview given to the *New York Times*, he said, "We have never fought against each other, and have been friends on several occasions, so I should say American and Russian commercial men ought to find much for their common interests …. It is no exaggeration to say that Russia is ready to be Americanized."[52]

RUSSIA LOOKS AT AMERICA

During the pre-war period, America indeed remained a land of inspiration for different strata of Russian society. It was a "promised land" for those who were searching for a better life. Members of ethnic and religious minorities fled discrimination; Jews sought to escape the pogroms that accompanied the 1905–1907 revolution. Peasants and workers went to America in search of land and better earnings. Between 1901 and 1910, 1.6 million people emigrated to the United States from the Russian Empire; a further 868,000 emigrated in 1911–1914. Of these, 43.8% were Jews, 27% Poles, 9.6% Lithuanians, 8.5% Finns, 5.8% Germans, 4.4% Russians, and 1% representatives of other ethnicities. The share of ethnic Russians grew to 12% in 1909–1913, owing primarily to labor migration.[53]

For proponents of Russia's economic modernization, both in the government and among the public, the United States remained a place from which to borrow technologies and technical innovations. For liberals, it was also a source of political inspiration. Miliukov's Kadets, who represented the left wing of Russian liberalism, perceived the United States as a political ideal that provided an alternative to the European model of sociopolitical development. They were primarily interested in constitutionalism, federalism, and Americans' approach to the process of organizing elections, all of which they considered important for modernizing Russia's political system. This interest did not preclude the Kadets from criticizing US racial discrimination, political corruption, and other shortcomings of American development, yet nor did these flaws render the American political model irrelevant – just as their condemnation of US imperialism did not prevent the Kadets from advocating a strong Russia–US alliance in the global arena in general and the Far East in particular.[54]

Progressives, who represented the center of the liberal movement and the interests of Russian industrialists and agriculturalists, displayed special interest in the secrets of American economic success, new forms of industrial and agrarian development, technological progress, and labor culture. While they took a more critical view of US political life, this did not prevent them from giving due credit to the democratic system, which enabled the country to use reforms to overcome its emerging problems. Progressives believed that the American culture of reforms was something Russians would do well to learn.[55]

The Octobrists, for their part, took an equivocal position on the American development model. As Russian liberals with conservative leanings that inclined them toward moderate reforms in Russia and a patriotic vision of its foreign policy, they viewed the United States as a country of contrasts. Economic and technological innovations and the establishment of corporations were admirable and should be imitated. However, these features were combined with the triumph of luxury, political depravity and plutocracy, a "war of whites against blacks," and crude materialism – all of which should be condemned.[56]

The professoriate, which largely represented the left and centrist wings of Liberalism, was behind the development of academic American studies (*Amerikanistika*) in Russia at the turn of the twentieth century, making it a decidedly applied discipline. Westernizing liberals perceived the American development model as a point of reference for Russia. It was no accident that the St. Petersburg sociologist Pavel Mizhuev published several books on the principles of American democracy in 1906–1907,[57] just as Russians were going through revolution and determining their prospects of modernizing their political system. While Stepan Fortunatov, a Moscow-based historian, focused on the American experience of federalism and the principles that underpinned the operations of the US legislature, the sociologist and historian Maxim Kovalevsky discussed American local institutions, stressing to his students these institutions' truly democratic nature.[58] In 1907, Kovalevsky, as a university representative, became a member of the State Duma and the State Council. Whether he spoke about the constitution, civil rights and freedoms, principles of self-governance, agrarian reforms, tariffs, railroad construction, academic and religious freedoms, the future of Finland, or developing Siberia, Kovalevsky's speeches before these bodies were full of American references. Another First State Duma deputy and member of the constitutional movement, the historian, sociologist, and political scientist Moisey Ostrogorsky, attempted to import to Russia the best of critically evaluated US democratic practices. His comprehensive two-volume work *Democracy and Political Parties* was the *pièce de résistance* of pre-revolutionary American studies.

The economist Ivan Ozerov, Professor of Law at Moscow University and at the Commercial Institute in Moscow, similarly assessed "American lessons" for Russians. In his opinion, the United States served as a model for how not to starve, how to provide jobs for the population, and how to tread the path of progress, but its crucial lesson for Russia related to building up human capital by developing education, the press, civil equality, and political activity. That was, in Ozerov's opinion, the principal thing Russia should learn from the United States, together with innovative agriculture, new forms and principles of production and sales, and the skills of managing space and time.[59] Ozerov promoted his ideas in the liberal newspapers *Rech* and *Russkoe ekonomicheskoe obozrenie*, as well as in the US press. He believed that Russia–US economic rapprochement would increase American influences on the Russian people and would be conducive to instituting fair governance.[60]

Among these founders of academic *Amerikanistika* in Russia was one exception to the rule: Alexis Babine, a conservative and a trailblazer of both Russian American Studies and American Slavistics. Babine's ideological credo made his attitude toward the American experience a sober one. In his two-volume work on US history, he duly gave credit to the "phenomenal economic progress" and "historically unprecedented growth of people's prosperity" in the United States. He also, however, pointed out the profiteering that was pervasive in American society, as well as the corrupt influence of capitalism on the government and the justice system.[61]

But it would be the writer Maxim Gorky who would make the most significant contribution to the creation of this Russian image of America as a kingdom of gain and crude materialism – a country of capitalism that strips people of their individuality. Accompanied by his common-law wife, the actress Maria Andreeva, Gorky arrived in the United States in the spring of 1906 on a mission from the Bolshevik faction of the Social Democratic Party to raise funds for the revolutionary cause and to fight against a planned loan to the tsarist government. Gorky was already famous in America, where his books had been translated into English. During his visit, newspapers featured cartoons where the Statue of Liberty offered her torch to the writer so that he could light his own torch of freedom.[62] Gorky himself made speeches that bolstered Americans' messianic sentiments: he claimed to have arrived to ask for freedom for Russians who were ready to follow the American example. At first, he was ecstatic about the United States and said so in his many interviews.[63] However, the Russian Embassy made it public knowledge that Gorky had a lawful wife and children back in Russia. Overnight, he was transformed in the eyes of the American public from "the revolution's stormy petrel" into an immoral anarchist who "may be deported from the country on charge of bigamy."[64]

This reversal, combined with the failure of his "Bolshevik mission" (although he did raise $10,000), turned Gorky decidedly against the United States. Upon his return home, the writer accordingly produced numerous anti-American pamphlets and sketches: "The City of the Yellow Devil,"[65] "The Mob," "The Kingdom of Boredom," etc. These were subsequently compiled into a collection titled *In America* that would become a Soviet propaganda classic by virtue of the criticisms it leveled at capitalism. "The City of the Yellow Devil" was not so much anti-American as it was anti-capitalist and anti-urbanist. It concerned the tragedy of a human being in a city, and as such carried a universal message. However, Gorky's sketch was dominated by the metaphor of soullessness, of terrible and filthy materialism which became a staple of anti-American discourse in the Russian Empire and then in the USSR.

This image of the United States as a hostile Other was solidly entrenched in the representations favored by court members, high-ranking officials, politicians, and public figures of conservative, nationalistic, and monarchist persuasions. The US stance during the Russo-Japanese War and Washington's abrogation of the 1832 treaty unquestionably contributed to its dissemination. The United States was seen as a country of "double standards," where Jewish profiteers and financiers called the shots, where politicians courting voters were ready to sacrifice the interests of business and the country's international prestige. "Intrigues" of American Jews were mentioned regularly in the reports of Russia's Ambassador to the United States, George Bakhmetev (1911–1917), who – like many in Russian diplomatic and governmental circles at the time – was an open anti-Semite.[66] Such comments also featured prominently in the anti-Semitic campaign launched by the Russian nationalist faction in the State Duma following the abrogation of the 1832 treaty. In the *Zemshchina* newspaper, as in *Novoe Vremia*, criticism of American racism served to justify anti-Semitism in Russia.[67]

At the same time, there was a "pro-American" group in the Russian government and diplomatic corps whose members saw the United States as a pragmatic partner, believed that relations with the United States were in Russia's national interest, and advocated mutually advantageous cooperation between the two countries. Among them were Minister of Finance Vladimir Kokovtsov (1904–1905, 1906–1914) and Ambassador to the United States Roman Rosen (1905–1911).

Meanwhile, ordinary Russians discovered America through popular culture, from variety shows to music to the serial detective stories about Nat Pinkerton, who was twice as popular in Russia as Sherlock Holmes. The Pinkerton craze began in Russia in 1907, and 6,200,000 books priced under 15 kopecks had been sold by 1915.[68] In Russian mass culture, the concept of America was largely based on light entertainment, and a special place in this pantheon belonged to Black Americans. For example, the owner of the Aquarium and Maxim, the largest and most popular clubs and restaurants in Moscow, was Frederick Thomas. Thomas, who transformed these venues with vaudeville acts and American minstrel-style music, had been born into a family of former slaves, worked as a waiter in Chicago and Brooklyn, and toured Europe before finally settling in Moscow, where he adopted the name Fyodor Fyodorovich.[69] Americans who visited Russia further reported that their Black compatriots were successfully touring various cities and introducing Russians to the charms of ragtime.[70]

AMERICA LOOKS AT RUSSIA

In the pre-war years, a growing number of American visitors reached the shores of the Russian Empire. They often traveled on the Trans-Siberian Railway and saw the sights of Moscow and St. Petersburg. Attendees of various congresses, scholars, scientists, writers, artists, and performers also visited the Russian Empire. These trips were conducive to restoring American images of Russia to their earlier multiplicity.

For members of the "friends of Russian freedom" movement and for all sympathizers of anti-tsarist campaigns, Russia remained an object of the US mission to reform the world, a country waiting for aid from across the Atlantic. Representatives of the business community, Congressmen, and journalists interested in expanding economic cooperation, meanwhile, disseminated the image of Russia as a trade partner. They focused on the economic modernization of the vast empire, which promised profit to Americans themselves, and on the points of convergence in the two countries' development. In parallel, American Russophiles of all kinds called for studying Russia to better understand it and continued to popularize

Russia's multifaceted culture. For them, Russia was both a source of inspiration and an object of study.

It is hard to overestimate the impact of Russian literature on American perceptions of Russia.[71] As in Europe, Leo Tolstoy's eightieth birthday was widely celebrated in the United States. Most Americans knew him as the great writer who had revealed to the world the image of contemporary Russia and the character of its people. For a sizable subset of the public, he was also something more: a prophet and a tireless fighter for the peaceful modernization of Russian society.[72] Tolstoy's social and religious views remained a topic of heated debate in the United States, since they had implications for American reformers of all stripes.[73] Even Roosevelt, who believed that Tolstoy's "moral and philosophical teachings . . . tended to be both foolish and fantastic," not to mention directly opposed to the ideas of "those who made our Constitution," could not deny Tolstoy's influence on his contemporaries.[74]

The American public was further introduced to the great achievements of Russian culture through the performances of Russian theaters that toured the United States. In 1905–1906, the troupe of the famous Russian tragic actor Pavel Orlenev (Orlov) and his common-law wife, Alla Nazimova, an actress with the Moscow Art Theater, performed across the United States to great success. Their repertoire included the works of classic Russian and European authors, although the tour opened with Evgeni Chirikov's play *The Chosen People* (*The Jews*), performed in a Lower East Side theater in New York at a moment when Russia was in the midst of its first revolution.[75] Following the tour, Alla Nazimova remained in the United States, where she made a successful career for herself in the theater before becoming a star of American silent movies.

Americans also continued to discover the world of Russia's classical and folk music – which, unlike drama, spoke a universal language. The tours of the great Russian bass Feodor Chaliapin in 1907 and the outstanding dancers Anna Pavlova and Mikhail Mordkin for six months in 1910 contributed significantly to this process.[76] American Russophiles supported this effort to promote Russian music in their country. The philanthropist and entrepreneur Charles Crane helped to organize a church choir conducted by Ivan Gorokhov at the Russian Orthodox St. Nicholas Cathedral in New York. The choir gave its first performance in 1912. Crane financially supported the choir, took it to various American universities (including Harvard), and even arranged for the choir to give a concert at the White House for President Wilson in February 1914.[77] The translator Isabel Hapgood aided in establishing the Russian Symphony Orchestra Society in New York in 1903 and served for three years as its secretary and director. In that period, the society organized four Russian music seasons and, with a powerful concert of Russian music at Carnegie Hall in 1907, laid the groundwork for Sergei Rachmaninoff's triumphant first tour in 1909 (Figure 7.2).[78]

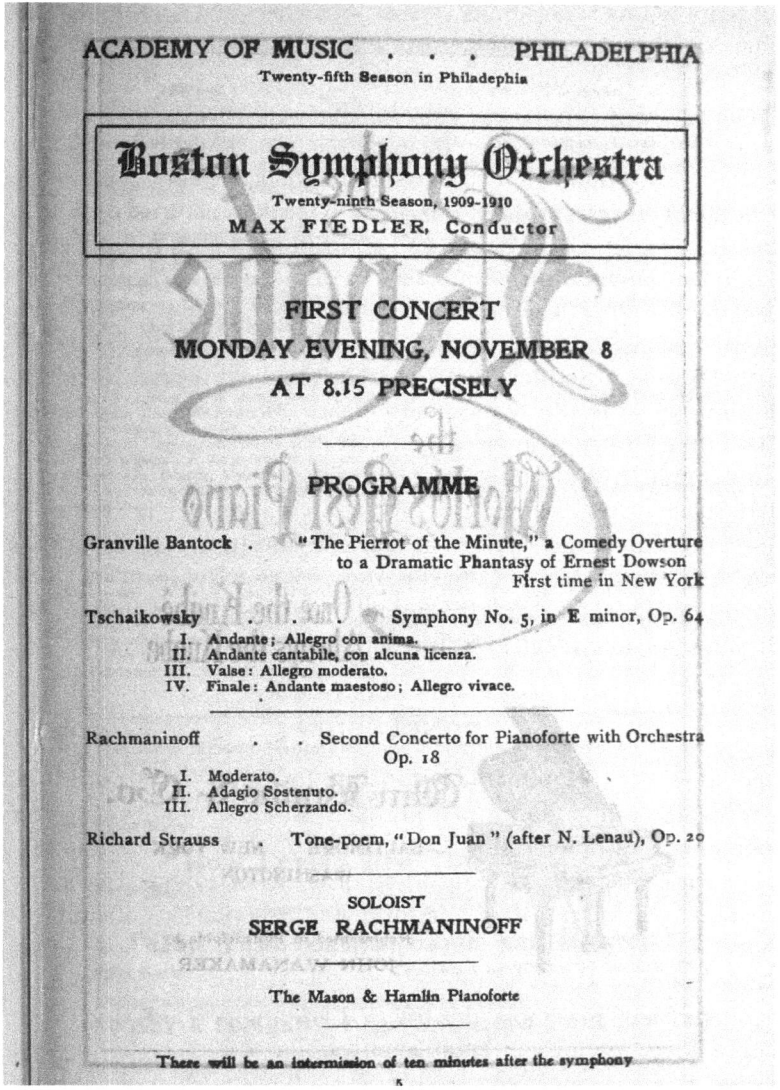

Figure 7.2 Program of Sergei Rachmaninoff's concert in the United States, November 8, 1909. Courtesy of the Boston Symphony Orchestra Archives.

The activities of American Russophiles and these expanding cultural ties advanced the development of Russian Studies in the United States. The Slavic Lecture Center at the University of Chicago was closed in 1905, as – owing to disappointment with the outcomes of the Russian revolution – Crane failed to find new lecturers. However, Crane continued to finance the annual trips to Russia of Samuel Harper Jr., who lectured at the University of Chicago on Russia's political institutions and taught Russian to a small group of students.[79] Another significant contribution to the development of Russian Studies was made by Archibald Coolidge. He published works both on Russian history and on bilateral relations, stressing the similarities between the two countries' histories despite their fundamental differences; gave public lectures; reviewed dozens of books about Russia for scholarly journals and various periodicals; and contributed to educating future specialists in Russian Studies.[80] Frank Golder, a student of Coolidge, defended in 1909 the first PhD thesis in Russian Studies, on Russia's expansion in the northern Pacific. Golder would go on to become the first Professor of Russian History at Stanford and the first library director of the Hoover Institution on War, Revolution and Peace, thereby advancing Russian Studies in the United States to a qualitatively new level.[81]

In general, growing interest in studying Russia was manifested in the United States in the founding of "Russian collections" and the establishment of Russian/Slavic sections in national and university libraries, chief among them the Library of Congress, the New York Public Library, and the Harvard University Library. However, during the pre-war period, Russian Studies in the United States was very modest in scale.[82]

CONCLUSION

Between the early 1880s and the outbreak of the First World War, Russia–US relations came full circle: from a mutually advantageous partnership and the perception of one another as distant friends, through their first crisis and a "war of images," to the diffusion of tensions, followed by pragmatic interactions and the restoration to mutual representations of a multiplicity of images. Henceforth, such cycles – impelled by changes in both global and domestic politics – would become a distinctive feature of bilateral relations.

The period between 1906 and 1914 demonstrated the continued potential for cooperation in different spheres, although the areas of geopolitical, economic, and ideological conflict that had been the legacy of the earlier crisis did not disappear. Indeed, this conflict was exacerbated by the abrogation of the 1832 treaty. Throughout this process, however, governments, diplomats, and entrepreneurs from both countries made herculean efforts to mitigate the negative consequences of abrogation for Russia–US relations.

The abrogation movement became a crucial episode in the American "crusade" for Russian freedom. It demonstrated the influence that consolidated public pressure groups could have on US foreign policy and set a precedent for future American human rights campaigns abroad in general and in Russia in particular. Specifically, by demonstrating that economic sanctions could be used in response to breaches of human rights, the abrogation movement paved the way for the Jackson–Vanik amendment to the Trade Act of 1974, which restricted trade with those states deemed to have violated freedom of emigration and other human rights.

Beyond the abrogation movement, which reflected an unwelcome effort by Americans to "educate" Russians about the "Jewish question," the peoples of the two countries had much to teach each other. In Russia, proponents of the country's modernization drew inspiration from the economic and political development of the United States, while ordinary Russians were inspired by America's mass-produced goods and mass culture. Americans, for their part, only grew more enchanted by the richness of Russian culture in its various forms – a culture that inspired them and strengthened their faith in Russia's great future. The Russian Empire and the United States were moving toward a new stage of close collaboration and affinity that would start during the First World War, peak after the February Revolution, and come to an end following the October Revolution.

8

WARTIME HONEYMOON, 1914–1917

OVERVIEW

In August 1914, the First World War broke out, marking a turning point in twentieth-century history that would cost millions of people in many countries their lives. During the first three years of this global conflict, the United States remained neutral, while Imperial Russia fought the German, Austro-Hungarian, and Ottoman empires. Russian–American relations in this period were complicated by discrimination against Jews and other ethnic minorities in Russia, by ideological differences between American democracy and Russian autocracy, and by geopolitical disagreements. Yet these elements of conflict did not hamper the two states' rapprochement, which began at the end of 1914, two years before the February Revolution, and at times resembled the euphoria of a honeymoon. However, even as new studies on Russia–US relations during the First World War regularly appear,[1] historians continue to debate the exact degree of this rapprochement.[2]

This chapter demonstrates that, contrary to what many historians have written, the surprising thaw in Russia–US relations cannot be explained only by the convergence of the two governments' interests: namely, that the Russian Empire desperately needed to buy American supplies for its armed forces, while Americans were eager to sell their surplus products.[3] Nor can it be explained solely by official relations and diplomats' activities.[4] Interactions between Imperial Russia and the United States in the years before Russia entered her second revolution in February 1917 and the United States joined the war in April 1917 call for more comprehensive consideration, with a particular focus on the often-neglected issues of the changes in the two nations' images of each other and the intensified process of Russians and Americans studying each other. This is precisely what this chapter sets out to provide.

AREAS OF CONFLICT IN BILATERAL RELATIONS

The First World War (1914–1918) was caused by clashing geopolitical and economic interests, unresolved colonial disputes, and nationalistic ambitions.[5] The emergence of two military blocs, the Entente and the Central Powers, as well as the arms race between them, propelled the world into conflict.[6] Despite its strong dynastic and economic ties with Germany, the Russian Empire found itself in the same camp as the liberal Western states of Great Britain and France, both of which viewed the German Empire as their principal adversary. This was because of Russia's contradictions with the Austro-Hungarian Empire in the Balkans, its alliance with France, and its 1907 settlement of colonial disputes with Great Britain in Persia and Afghanistan.[7]

On the eve of the war, US President Woodrow Wilson's views of Russia centered on the tension between American humanitarian ideals and economic interests. In 1911, he had supported the campaign for abrogation of the Russia–US commercial treaty of 1832, proclaiming that abrogation would uphold America's commitments to religious freedom and civil equality.[8] After Wilson was elected president in 1912, it became clear that Russia was not among the foreign policy priorities of the Washington administration. Indeed, it took sixteen months for a new US Ambassador to Russia to be appointed, much to the displeasure of Nicholas II's government.[9] Ultimately, the position went to George Marye, a businessman from San Francisco. Marye would arrive in Russia only in October 1914, by which time the First World War was already under way.

Following the outbreak of military hostilities in Europe, the United States proclaimed its neutrality and initially interacted with both blocs. Wilson, who took control of America's foreign policy, and Edward House, his personal advisor and political consultant (usually called Colonel House), were wary both of Germany emerging victorious and of Russia gaining hegemony in Europe. Later, they became concerned about the possibility of a separate Russian–German peace treaty and the potential emergence of an anti-democratic Germany–Russia–Japan alliance.[10]

St. Petersburg, renamed to the less German-sounding Petrograd in August 1914, viewed the United States' neutrality as reflecting Germanophilia and a desire to profit from the war. This perception of America's German sympathies was only bolstered when the United States agreed to represent German and Austro-Hungarian interests in the Russian Empire and to handle the issue of their POWs.[11]

In Russia, the wave of anti-German sentiment resulted in the persecution and public ostracism of the Singer Sewing Machine Company. The latter was accused of espionage on the grounds that it was falsely perceived as a German company and associated with Germany. Its offices and shops were attacked and the government temporarily took control of its factory in Podolsk, which was charged with harboring German spies. The company suffered serious losses and, in order to improve its corporate image, switched some of its facilities to military production.[12]

The Imperial Court and the government were particularly displeased with Wilson's mediation policy, which he viewed from the start of the war as the United States' special mission.[13] Indeed, the State Department's first attempts at mediation, undertaken in September 1914 on direct instructions from the president, prompted both confusion and annoyance in the capitals of all the warring states. But, although Colonel House's European tours of 1915–1916 produced no results, they did help him to monitor the ideas of Europe's most astute politicians concerning a new world order – ideas that Wilson would take into account when proposing a new system of international relations. That being said, House never got as far as the Russian Empire, due not only to his ill health, but also to the fact that neither the president nor his advisor viewed Russia as a partner in shaping that system. Moreover, House found it difficult to shed his view of Germany as a buffer protecting Europe from the Russian threat.[14]

By 1916, Wilson was confident that international relations had to be based on a "new diplomacy" that would be open and respectful of the sovereign rights of all nations. Hence his note to the warring states on December 18, 1916, suggesting that they proclaim their goals in the war; and hence his address to the US Congress on January 22, 1917, suggesting "peace without victory." Wilson thereby transitioned from secret mediation to public diplomacy.

Russian Ambassador George Bakhmetev, who called Wilson the "Self-Proclaimed President of the Universe" and a "new Don Quixote" meddling in others' affairs, nonetheless asked Petrograd to give a sympathetic response, since Russia was interested in American loans and military supplies.[15] For their part, the Ministry of Foreign Affairs, the Imperial Court, and the government press viewed Wilson's messianic peacemaking as an insult and as reflecting Germanophilia. Even the liberal Russian press condemned Wilson's attempts to stop the war before the Entente's victory. Pavel Miliukov, the leader of the Constitutional Democrats (Kadets), stressed that, while the principles laid down by the US president could serve as a foundation for future peace negotiations, "peace without victory" was out of the question. The progressive nationalist Vasily Shulgin welcomed the US desire for democratic peace without annexations and contributions yet said that talks "[could] only begin after the Allies' decisive victory."[16] The Kadets did not criticize Wilson for the United States' neutral stance, interested though they were in seeing the Americans on the side of the Entente, while progressivists explained the US policy as a desire to profit as much as possible by selling military supplies while weakening both Germany and Great Britain, America's principal economic competitors.[17]

Further impetus to this conflict in Russia–US relations was given by three ethnic questions: the "Slavic," "Polish," and "Jewish" ones.[18] The first two proved to be directly related to Wilson's vision of a postwar world order based on the principle of national self-determination. The latter was linked to the long-standing ideological conflict between the two countries over Russian anti-Semitism.

From the first years of the war, the tsarist government, pursuing its Pan-Slavic program, strove to counteract German and Austro-Hungarian propaganda among the Slavic population in the United States. Russian diplomats stressed Slavs' contribution to unmasking the actions of Austrian Ambassador Konstantin Theodor von Dumba and German Ambassador Johann Heinrich von Bernstorff.[19] Ultimately, however, the Russian Empire failed to establish control over Czechoslovak organizations across the Atlantic.

Meanwhile, Washington attempted to stimulate democratic reforms in Austria-Hungary, following Wilson's idea that every people had a right to choose the form of sovereignty that best suited it. This stance on the issue of Austrian Slavs created a precedent of interfering with other states' domestic ethnic policies and delivered a blow to the Pan-Slavic geopolitical programs both of the tsarist government and later of the Provisional Government.[20]

The war also expanded the international context of the "Polish question." This process had four principal stages. The creation of a united, free, autonomous Poland was proclaimed to be one of the goals of the war in Grand Duke Nikolay Nikolaevich's Manifesto of August 2/15, 1915. Then, on November 5, 1916, the Central Powers' Manifesto announced the establishment of an independent Poland in those Russian lands occupied by Austro-Hungary and Germany. Next, on March 15, 1917, the Provisional Government recognized the independence of Poland as a state in a "free military alliance with Russia." Finally, in November 1918, the Western allies proclaimed a united and independent Poland. Wilson's January 22, 1917, address to the Senate calling for "peace without victory" and his subsequent Fourteen Points speech played a special role in this process, as they raised the "Polish question" to the level of high diplomacy.[21]

While the government of Nicholas II conceived of the "Polish question" as part of the ethnic and religious problem of Russia's political development, for Wilson it became a way of implementing the idea that the United States had a special mission to protect smaller European nations' rights to national self-determination.[22] The leaders of the Polish community had real influence on Wilson and House's stance on the "Polish question," while the four-million-strong Polish diaspora contributed to shaping American public opinion.[23] That is why, in a memo written in early 1917, Ivan Korostovets, a member of the Ministry of Foreign Affairs' Council and an experienced diplomat who had accompanied Sergei Witte to Portsmouth in 1905, highlighted the differences between Petrograd and Washington in interpreting the "Polish question" as one of the principal obstacles to their rapprochement.[24]

US policy on the "Polish," "South Slavic," and "Czechoslovakian" questions was transformed into a mechanism for implementing the principles of Wilsonian diplomacy. This produced a clash between two messianisms: the Russian one, based on ethnic and religious principles and the ideas of pan-Slavism; and the American one, geared toward disseminating democratic ideals. This clash did nothing to improve bilateral relations.

The "Jewish question" likewise remained a stumbling block. German propaganda in the United States used stories of the "horrors of Jewish pogroms and rioting" in war-ravaged Poland as its trump card. The tone was set by *The Day,* a newspaper published in New York and edited by Herman Bernstein, an Austrian Jew who was a former secretary of the American Jewish Committee. He worked closely with Germany's Ambassador von Bernstorff and expressed the interests of German Americans, particularly Jews.[25] In January–February 1915, the media disseminated a letter that von Bernstorff had written to Bernstein. The letter reported major pogroms in 215 towns and cities across Russian Poland, as well as the perpetration of outrages by Russian soldiers. This information was accompanied by letters from victims of violence in Warsaw, Kibarty (in present-day Lithuania), and Brody (in present-day Ukraine).[26]

At the start of the war, there were indeed anti-Jewish riots in Poland, and anti-Semitic sentiments were on the rise among Russians as well, although the claim of large-scale pogroms was an open provocation. The Jewish population, having been forcibly evacuated from war-torn areas, moved *en masse* to Warsaw and other Polish cities. This kindled resentment on the part of Russians and Poles that spilled over into violence. The overcrowded Jewish ghetto in Warsaw also became a temporary refuge for those American Jews who had traveled to Russia in the summer of 1914 before the war broke out to visit their relatives. (They were subsequently allowed to return home.[27])

Differences between Russia and the United States made it impossible for them to conclude a new bilateral commercial treaty to replace the one that had been abrogated in 1911. Although they made concluding a new agreement a priority, both US Ambassador Marye and his successor, David Francis, failed in this task.[28] There were two main reasons for this. First, the Russian government held fast to its position in the "passport conflict" that had precipitated the abrogation of the previous treaty. Unable to protect the passports of Jewish American citizens, the State Department rather quickly abandoned its attempts to negotiate a commercial treaty, being justifiably concerned that a treaty that failed to resolve this question would not be ratified by the Senate. Second, in the context of war, this issue was no longer quite so acute. Russia–US trade relations were able to develop successfully without a treaty as soon as American imports came under the exclusive purview of Russian governmental agencies in the United States. *Modi vivendi* and short-term agreements served as alternatives to a new treaty.[29]

During the First World War, Jewish activists and like-minded non-Jews in the United States succeeded in retaining a certain degree of influence over public opinion. However, with the two states' rapprochement and the restructuring of mutual perceptions, there emerged a real opposition to the Jewish lobby in the United States. Additionally, the war gave some Americans reason to hope that Russia's discriminatory policies would be liberalized. This hope was fueled by Russian symbolic gestures: Nicholas II accorded a delegation of Russian Jews a favorable reception; the most egregious trials against Jews doing business beyond the Pale of Settlement were aborted; Russian generals visited synagogues; and Russian Jews were given state awards. However, the hopes for more substantial changes were never fulfilled. Thus, on the whole, the "Jewish question" maintained its negative influence on bilateral relations.

COOPERATION BETWEEN THE RUSSIAN EMPIRE AND THE UNITED STATES IN WARTIME

Despite tensions over the treatment of ethnic minorities and geopolitical and ideological issues, Russia and the United States developed unprecedented economic interaction and financial contacts. In the Russian Empire, these developments were supported by Minister of Foreign Affairs Sergei Sazonov, who pointed out to Chargé d'Affaires Charles Wilson in 1914 that the United States could take Germany's place on the Russian market. Another supporter was Finance Minister Petr Bark, who started looking for American loans in the very first months of the war. As early as October 1914, Witte, acting on Bark's instructions, visited the US Embassy in Petrograd, where he said "in strictest confidence" that the Russian government was interested in his traveling to the United States to negotiate a large loan for Russia. Although Washington saw this as an opening for concluding a new commercial treaty, Robert Lansing (at that time still a counselor to the Department of State) stressed that, given the United States' neutrality, it could not issue loans to parties at war. Witte soon passed away, but Bark continued, throughout 1915 and 1916, to actively negotiate loans with J. P. Morgan's Guaranty Trust and the National City Bank in New York. Their representatives traveled to Petrograd and fought each other for control of the "Russian business."[30]

In 1915, the Kadets in the Fourth State Duma, joined by Octobrists and centrist Progressives, formed the Progressive Bloc. Its members advocated forming a responsible government that would be able to extricate Russia from a series of military failures, welcomed American investments and railroad construction, and banked on an alliance with (and aid from) the United States. Among the proponents of an active Russia–US rapprochement that would support trade and the modernization of the Russian economy were the Octobrist Alexander Guchkov, the Chairperson of the Central War Industry Committee; the Kadet Pavel Miliukov; the Progressive Maxim Kovalevsky; and the statesman Vasily Timiryazev, who had served as Minister of Trade and Industry in 1905–1906 and 1909.[31]

For their part, American diplomats and journalists called upon their fellow citizens to step up the export of goods and capital across the Atlantic. Germany had withdrawn from the Russian market following the outbreak of war, and they hoped that the United States could take it over – not only for the duration of the war, but for good.[32] American entrepreneurs enthusiastically engaged in talks with emissaries of the tsarist government, discussing possible sales of train cars, weapons, gunpowder, military uniforms, sugar, and medical products.

In the first months of the war, various ministries started sending their agents to the United States to sign contracts. Accordingly, a commission was formed at the Russian Embassy in the spring of 1915 with a view to coordinating their activities. As the volume of orders from various ministries increased, the commission expanded its membership. It acted as an intermediary for the placement of orders worth $450 million, for which Russia would pay without recourse to loans.[33] In October, the Russian Procurement Committee, led by Maj. Gen. Alexey Sapozhnikov, was finally established in New York to make direct purchases in the United States. Initially, its activities were sharply criticized on both sides of the Atlantic. Russia's military procurement efforts essentially broke down, not least owing to the absence of a developed military industry in the United States and to Russia's own financial problems. In addition, the inexperienced Sapozhnikov established ties with American suppliers who proved to be swindlers, while other members of the committee used the situation to their own benefit.[34]

In July 1916, Sapozhnikov was replaced by Lt. Gen. Anatoly Zaliubovsky. He believed that the problems on the Russian side were the membership of the committee and a shortage of available ships, while the fact that competing British and French orders were given priority over Russian ones caused problems on the American side.[35] Zaliubovsky therefore poured significant effort into reorganizing the activities of the Russian Procurement Committee. The situation also improved because, in November 1916, the committee was granted the right to place orders without Morgan's intermediary services.[36]

The intensification of Russia–US relations during the war required that the staff of the US Embassy in Petrograd be renewed and expanded. In January 1916, Wilson decided to replace Ambassador Marye. He was well liked at the Imperial Court, but the president thought him to be too pro-Entente. For his replacement, Wilson sought a more energetic person capable of taking bilateral relations to a new level.[37] Wilson chose the sixty-five-year-old David Francis, a St. Louis newspaper publisher, former mayor of that city, former governor of Missouri, and former United States Secretary of the Interior, who was equally unfamiliar with the art of diplomacy and with Russia. However, Wilson liked his extensive experience of both politics and life, his energy and business acumen, and, most importantly, his firm conviction that the United States had a special mission in the world.[38]

In the spring of 1916, Ambassador Francis encouraged Samuel McRoberts, the vice president of the National City Bank of New York, to come to Russia to discuss a loan and the opening of a branch of the bank there. In Russia, this plan was promoted by Korostovets, who was certain that only American capital was capable of relieving Russia's wartime financial burden and acting as a counterbalance to its financial and economic dependence on Russia's allies.[39]

Following the talks, this syndicate of New York banks extended to the tsarist government a credit of $50 million against 150 million rubles deposited in the Imperial Russian Bank. At the same time, an arrangement was achieved on opening in January 1917 in Petrograd a branch of the National City Bank with $50 million of capital. In November 1916, the syndicate sold on the American market Russian state treasury obligations up to the amount of $25 million.[40] In their publications and public speeches, McRoberts and new commercial attaché William Huntington stressed that exports of American goods would go hand in hand with building factories and investing in various economic sectors. Following his return to the United States,

McRoberts launched a media campaign for a "commercial crusade" to the Russian Empire.[41]

Despite all the obstacles and Russia's financial dependence on Great Britain, the United States succeeded in setting up deliveries of war supplies to Russia as well as railroad equipment, medicines, machine tools, and metals. The Singer Sewing Machine Company made an important contribution, too, organizing large-scale production of uniforms and shells at its Podolsk factory. Several production facilities at the International Harvester plant in Liubertsy were also converted for military needs, starting to manufacture grenades.[42] Between 1914 and 1916, American exports increased from $27 million to an unprecedented $500 million. Compared with pre-war figures, Russia–US trade grew by 1,157 percent and continued to grow after the February Revolution. Absolute figures show that while Russia lagged behind Great Britain and France in terms of the volume of its trade with the United States, Russia was certainly the leader in terms of the rate at which this trade grew.[43]

The activities of the Russian–American Chamber of Commerce, established in Moscow back in 1913, made an important contribution to developing trade and economic relations and deepening mutual understanding between the two states.[44] During the war, the chamber opened offices in Petrograd, Kiev, and Tashkent, operated with support from the Ministry of Finance as well as the Ministry of Trade and Industry, and advocated for a Russia–US business partnership. In January 1915, it launched its *Bulletin*, which often published articles by a Deputy Chairperson of the Chamber, Ivan Ozerov, an economist who was a staunch promoter of American-style capitalist development and Russia–US economic rapprochement. *Russkoe Slovo*, a popular uncensored progressive newspaper, advanced the same ideas.[45]

In August 1915, Alexander Behr, another deputy chairperson of the chamber, arrived in the United States. He held talks on opening a counterpart chamber in the United States and on establishing a Russian–American bank. Speaking in New York at the International Trade Conference, Behr said, "Russia stands before you not as a petitioner, but as a welcoming hostess opening a door to her innumerable riches."[46] Upon his return, he reported that American industrialists, merchants, and financiers had tremendous interest in a trade partnership with Russia. Although the bank was never opened, Behr's visit certainly furthered the two countries' trade and economic rapprochement.

The American–Russian Chamber of Commerce, under the leadership of Charles Boynton, was opened in New York in February 1916. Boynton was married to a Russian and maintained close ties with the Russophile Melville Stone, director of the Associated Press. The chamber's membership included representatives of the largest American banks and corporations. Konstantin Medzykhovskii, the agent of Russia's Ministry of Trade and Industry, became an honorary member. The two chambers maintained close contacts.[47]

Meanwhile, the Society for Promoting Mutual Friendly Relations between Russia and the United States was founded in Petrograd in 1915.[48] The society was led by Roman Rosen, a former Russian Ambassador to the United States. Its establishment was spearheaded by Nikolay Borodin, a statistician, economist, and ichthyologist, and a Kadet in his political views. Borodin, who would go on to become the society's vice chairperson, had been an active proponent of applying the American experience to Russia since he first visited the United States during the 1893 World's Fair in Chicago. Between December 1915 and February 1918, the society, whose founders included many well-known Russian left-wing and centrist liberals, published *Izvestiia* (*Bulletin*, Figure 8.1) on the prospects of cooperation.

An additional item on the agenda of Russia–US interaction during the First World War was humanitarian issues. Americans participated in philanthropic fundraising for Russian refugees fleeing areas near the front, as well as for Russian POWs in Germany, Austro-Hungary, and Turkey. The money collected through Orthodox Church organizations and at various events, as well as the goods purchased, were sent to the Russian Empire, to charities working under the patronage of Empress Dowager Maria Fedorovna, and to the Russian Red Cross. For its part, the American Red Cross played an important part in raising funds and organizing medical aid.

Members of the Young Men's Christian Association (YMCA), acting in close collaboration with the evangelical youth organization Mayak (Lighthouse), also aided the wounded. Mayak had been established in St. Petersburg before the war and was led by Franklin Gaylord, a founder and longtime advisor of this organization. John Mott, a proponent of a rapprochement between the Russian and American branches of Christianity, also had ideological and organizational influence on the development of the evangelical youth movement in Russia and its humanitarian activities during the First World War.[49]

In the winter of 1915–1916, the United States started aiding German and Austro-Hungarian POWs in Russian camps located around Kiev and to the east of Moscow, along the Trans-Siberian Railroad. Nicholas II consented to this assistance in personal correspondence with Wilson. Since Russia further insisted on "full reciprocity," the United States made an

ИЗВѢСТІЯ
ОБЩЕСТВА СБЛИЖЕНІЯ МЕЖДУ РОССІЕЙ И АМЕРИКОЙ.

BULLETIN
OF THE SOCIETY FOR PROMOTING MUTUAL FRIENDLY RELATIONS BETWEEN RUSSIA AND AMERICA.

Вып. 1.

Петроградъ.　　　**Декабрь (December) 1915 г.**　　　**Petrograd.**

Содержаніе: Пути и способы сближенія между Россіей и Америкой. *Н. А. Бородина.*—Впечатлѣнія американскаго корреспондента отъ посѣщенія фронта русской дѣйствующей арміи (англ.) *В. Виффена.* — Русско-американскія взаимоотношенія на почвѣ религіи и благотворительности. Д-ра *Г. А. Саймонса* (англ.).—Россія съ точки зрѣнія американскаго инженера и дѣлового человѣка (перев. съ англ.). Кап. *Хофа* —Краткій отчетъ о дѣятельности Общества Сближенія между Россіей и Америкой за 1915 г.; организація лекцій и публичныхъ докладовъ; первое публичное собраніе Общества 21 окт. 1915 г. — Мелкія извѣстія. — Библіографія. — Предложенія и запросы. — Личный составъ Общества.

Contents: Ways and means orf promoting friendly relations between Russia and America by. *N. A. Borodin.*—Impressions of an American Correspondent after a visit to the front of the Russian Army by. *W. Whiffen.*—Russian-American Relations on the Ground of Religious and Charitable Matters by. Dr. *O. A. Simons.*—Russia from the Point of View of an American Engineer and Business Man. (Transl. from engl.) by Cap. *Hough.* — Brief Account on the Activity of the Society for Promoting Mutual Friendly Relations between Russia and America for 1915. — Organization of Lectures and Public Reports. — The First Public Meeting of the Society on the 21-st October 1915. — Miscellaneous. — Bibliography. — Offers and Inquiries. — Administration and Members of the Society.

Пути и способы сближенія между Россіей и Америкой.

Съ тѣхъ поръ какъ наше Общество приступило къ дѣятельности (апрѣль 1915 г.) событія, связанныя съ войной, властно повліяли на самое тѣсное сближеніе Россіи съ Соединенными Штатами на почвѣ крупныхъ заказовъ, сдѣланныхъ Россіей въ Америкѣ по снабженію арміи необходимыми предметами промышленности, включая даже такіе громоздкіе предметы, какъ вагоны. Въ связи съ этими заказами на многіе милліоны рублей съ одной стороны—направились въ Соединенные Штаты наши инженеры всѣхъ родовъ, а вмѣстѣ съ ними сотни студентовъ техниковъ, съ другой стороны—къ намъ стали пріѣзжать изъ Америки значительными партіями дѣловые люди. Никогда еще не было у насъ такъ много американскихъ гостей, и никогда Америка не встрѣчала столько русскихъ гостей. Все это естественно способствуетъ сближенію на дѣловой почвѣ къ взаимной выгодѣ обѣихъ сторонъ.

Но, кромѣ этого сближенія на дѣловой почвѣ, замѣчается паралельно идущее, не менѣе важное сближеніе культурное, начинающееся прежде

1

Figure 8.1 The first issue of the Society for Promoting Mutual Friendly Relations' *Izvestiia* (*Bulletin*).

arrangement with Spain, which represented the interests of Russian POWs in Germany and Austro-Hungary, for American organizations to provide those POWs with aid identical to that provided to the Central Powers' POWs in Russia.

Americans inspected camps and supplied prisoners with money, medications, and other aid paid for primarily by the prisoners' own governments. In the spring of 1916, the Second Division of the Embassy was formed to distribute aid among German and Austrian POWs. It was initially headed by Edward Devine, a Columbia University professor of social welfare and an expert on philanthropy. In the fall, he was replaced by Basil Miles, who had been on the US Embassy staff during the Russo-Japanese War and consequently had valuable expertise.

The American Red Cross and the YMCA played an active role in handling humanitarian issues. Since the Second Division's jurisdiction was limited to European Russia and Western Siberia, a special American Red Cross Unit assisted by the YMCA provided medications and clothes to camps in Central and Eastern Siberia. These camps – left over from the Russo-Japanese War – were notorious for their harsh conditions. The YMCA also aided in distributing governmental charity sent from the United States, while its War Prisoners' Aid section regularly provided organizational and informational assistance to the Second Division.

Aiding Austrian and German POWs in the Russian Empire was a complicated and delicate activity, especially since the fact that many of the aid workers necessarily spoke German caused local authorities to suspect them of being spies. The Americans were helped by the fact that since 1915 they had been providing similar aid to Russian POWs in Germany, Austria, and the Ottoman Empire. The tsarist government, however, allocated substantially less money to supporting POWs, which resulted in higher mortality rates.[50]

EVOLUTION OF IMAGES ON BOTH SIDES OF THE ATLANTIC

The Russia–US rapprochement during the First World War created favorable conditions for destroying mutual stereotypes and myths. In 1916, Richard Child, a military correspondent, lawyer, and subsequently a diplomat, wrote that Americans' knowledge about Russia was not only "little and distorted," but also predominantly created by adventurous American journalists and commercial agents who could not speak the Russian language. Child called upon Americans to broaden their understanding of real Russian life and upon Russians to abandon their simplified notions of the United States as a country of smokestacks and of its citizens as a people obsessed with money-making.[51]

In June 1915, Alexander Kokhanovsky, the management officer of the Russian consulate in San Francisco, had bemoaned the fact that Americans had become accustomed to "saying negative things" about Russia.[52] As soon as 1916, however, Iosef Loris-Melikov, the First Secretary of Russia's Embassy in the United States, would draw the opposite conclusion after traveling around the country. In his substantial memorandum "On a Russia–U.S. Rapprochement," he wrote that Americans, who had previously been affected by stories of cruel anti-Jewish pogroms, the horrors of exile to Siberia, and the persecution of Finns, "now are willing to listen to real-life descriptions of Russian valor, our Motherland's spiritual and economic power."[53] Concurring with Loris-Melikov, Bakhmetev stated in July 1916 that Russians "have become the focus of Americans' admiration and hopes."[54]

Russophiles with ties to the circle of Charles Crane, a businessman and philanthropist from Chicago, were expanding their ranks and were very active in constructing positive perceptions of the Russian Empire. They included, among others, Samuel Harper Jr., who regularly traveled to Russia and studied it with financial support from Crane; Isabel Hapgood, a renowned translator and popularizer of Russian culture; Norman Hapgood, an adherent of Wilsonian internationalism who was the editor of *Collier's* and *Harper's Weekly* (which Crane owned from May 1913); and Elizabeth Reynolds, the first Russian instructor at Columbia University and the future founder of the Russian Department at Dartmouth.

These people had different personalities, views, and talents, but they were united in their belief in the great future of the Russian people, in their desire to introduce Americans to the culture and history of Russia, and in their negative attitudes toward the anti-Russia propaganda of the Jewish community in the United States. They published many articles in the press and gave public lectures at universities and clubs. The liberals Harper and Crane believed in Russia's renewal and welcomed the Russian Empire's participation in the First World War. The more conservative Isabel Hapgood, meanwhile, applauded Russia's adoption of the Gregorian calendar as a symbol of American influence.[55]

Crane was the most influential of the American Russophiles, being well acquainted with both the president and Colonel House. Indeed, it was Crane who played the key role in Wilson's decision to replace Marye with Francis. The latter went to Russia in April 1916 accompanied by Harper, whose Russophile friend Frederick Corse, the head of the New York Life Insurance Company in Russia and president of the American club in St. Petersburg, became one of the new ambassador's key advisors. Additionally, Crane's son Richard was appointed personal secretary to Robert Lansing.[56]

The emphases in American perceptions of Russian were clearly shifting in 1914–1916, for several reasons. First, the public and political discourse was constructing a new demonic Other – a German one – that would come to replace the Russian Other. Instead of the Russian Tsar Nicholas II, American cartoons now featured Emperor Wilhelm II in the role of a barbaric soldier with a bloodied saber. Among the American public, anti-German sentiments began rising as soon as the war broke out – except among the anti-Entente groups of ethnic Germans, Irish, Poles, and Jews. Two factors influenced the spread of Germanophobia: Germany's methods of warfare, which were regularly characterized by the press as barbaric ones; and Germany's attitude toward the seafaring rights of neutral states, which became clear after the sinking of the *Lusitania* on May 7, 1915.[57]

Second, a growing number of articles were appearing on Russia's fidelity to its allies despite its military defeats in the first year of the war and on its ability to rise from its knees and deliver crushing blows to the enemy, as it did in the Brusilov Offensive in June–September 1916.[58] American war correspondents – including Stanley Washburn, who had ties to the Crane circle, Robert R. McCormick of the *Chicago Daily Tribune* (Figure 8.2), William Simms of the United Press, Montgomery Schuyler of *The New York Times*, and many others – made a major contribution to the shaping of this assessment. Their articles and reports, which were accompanied with photographs and illustrations, contributed to creating a positive image of Russia in the United States and to bolstering mutual good feelings. The journalists painted such positive images of Russia not only for professional purposes – in order to maintain good relations with the Russian authorities and thereby supply diverse information to their publications – but also due to their sincere impulses and belief in the renewal of the Russian Empire.[59]

Third, the American public was increasingly convinced that the war would spur Russia's liberalization, helping to transform it into a worthy partner of the Western powers fighting against "German barbarity." From the fall of 1914, George Kennan was inspired by the prospect of the war bringing about the Russian Empire's renewal. He believed that the war had consolidated all of Russia's progressive forces and objected to the opinion voiced by New York Mayor George McClellan Jr. that Russians' "civilizational code" did not allow them to be counted as a European people. Telling Americans about the internal democracy of the Russian peasants, with their common sense and capacity for self-governance, Kennan assured his fellow citizens that the war would end in a revolution in the Russian Empire. The

Figure 8.2 An advertisement published in the *Chicago Daily Tribune* for a documentary made under the personal supervision of the American war correspondent Robert R. McCormick, *Chicago Daily Tribune*, August 22, 1915.

only question was whether it could be political and non-violent. Kennan's enthusiasm wilted somewhat by the fall of 1915, following the news that the convocation of the Duma had been postponed, but he would not so easily abandon his revived faith in the creation of a free Russia.[60]

In the fall of 1916, Columbia University President Nicholas Murray Butler, writing under the penname Cosmos, published a series of articles in the *New York Times*. He depicted Russia as a kind of bridge between the old East and the new West, a country that was steadily traveling the path of westernization.[61] Indeed, as early as 1914, some American observers heard the "murmuring sound of the building of a new democracy."[62]

Americans' belief in Russia's rapid transformation was further buttressed by Nicholas II's August 1914 decree banning sales of alcohol. In the United States, the decree was perceived as a symbol of Russians' awakening from "the spell of alcoholism," since drinking had been seen as one of the main causes of the backwardness of the Russian Empire.[63] The American press dubbed the decree "a true miracle," placing it on a par with the reforms of Peter I and Alexander II. Isabel Hapgood stressed that this reform had been inspired by the United States with its temperance movement. Characteristically, in Russia itself, the reform's supporters among westernizers appealed to the American approach, while its supporters among Slavophiles referred to teetotalers within the empire, among them Old Believers and Muslims.[64] The fact that some Russian women (Maria Bochkareva and her female Battalion of Death, for instance), with the tsar's permission, participated in the war along with men further confirmed among Americans the positive nature of the transformations in Russia.

These imagological changes in the United States stimulated a search for large-scale parallels between the two countries' development, reflecting the desire of politicians, journalists, public figures, and preachers to exaggerate both the scale of Russia's reforms and the degree of American influence thereon.[65] Additionally, Russians were expected not to radically demolish their past in a revolution, but to gradually refurbish their state.[66]

The tsarist government took its own steps to shape Russia's image in the United States by sending Sergei Syromiatnikov, a well-known conservative writer and public figure, to America in early 1915. Being fluent in English, he published a series of articles explaining the stance of the imperial government on war matters and on Russia's domestic policies. US newspapers widely circulated Syromiatnikov's appeals to perceive Russia through its history, soul, and thoughts, which accorded with the discourse of American conservative Russophiles.[67] Both Syromiatnikov and Loris-Melikov further advocated that Americans and Russians should be educated about each other not only through the printed word and cinema, but also by setting up academic exchanges involving university professors and students.[68]

In 1915–1916, the Russian press published increasing numbers of articles calling for the creation of a diverse image of the United States that would transcend the stereotypes perpetrated, for instance, by pulp fiction like the Nat Pinkerton crime stories. A *Literary Digest* review of the Russian press focused on the many articles that postulated a need to expand knowledge of various aspects of American life. For instance, the *Novoe Vremia* newspaper called for establishing closer business ties between the two states and stated that Russians did not have much knowledge of America, while America had even less knowledge of Russia. The *Russkoe Slovo* newspaper stressed that those who cherished Russia's interests and wanted to contribute to the development of its productive forces should spare no effort to promote ties between the Russian Empire and the United States on the basis of mutual concessions and understanding.[69]

In February 1917, Boris Shatsky, an adjunct professor at Petrograd University, was sent to New York to establish a Russian information bureau that would educate Americans about Russia and Russians about America. He arrived after the February Revolution and, together with Arkady Zak, who worked for the Ministry of Finance, succeeded in carrying out the work entrusted to him, switching gears to protect the interests of the young Russian democracy.[70]

MUTUAL STUDIES: A NEW DIRECTION
IN RUSSIA–US INTERACTION

The Russia–US rapprochement and the two peoples' growing mutual interest gave a new impetus to the development of Russian Studies in the United States and American Studies in Russia. This interest led to the creation of specialized university departments, the development of new courses, and the publication of articles and books.[71]

Harvard professor Leo Wiener, one of the pioneers of Russian Studies in the United States, published a book in 1915 calling for unbiased study of Russia. He recommended that Russia be perceived through the lens of its fine arts, music, and religion; its public, political, and philosophical thought; and its poetry and literature. Wiener also traced the influence of the American drive for democracy both on Russian sociopolitical ideals and on the country's music culture, while nevertheless stressing the dominance of native origins in Russian cultural traditions.[72]

The development of Russian Studies in wartime could be seen in the growing numbers of students in Slavistics classes in Berkeley and Harvard and in the establishment, in 1915, of the Slavic Department at Columbia University.

John Dyneley Prince, Columbia University's Professor of Semitic and Slavic Languages, became one of the principal proponents of developing Russian Studies. He was close with the Crane circle, gave lectures on Russia, and participated in the effort to raise funds for the Russian Red Cross.[73] Together with his colleagues Mihajlo Pupin, a well-known Serbian-American physicist, and Elizabeth Reynolds, Prince enthusiastically supported the idea of establishing a Russian Studies Center at Columbia University. Crane, who promised financial support to this center, also continued to promote Russian Studies at the University of Chicago by granting Harper a four-year contract to visit Russia, teach Russian, and give lectures on Russian history.[74]

In 1914, the young American Slavist Frank Golder traveled to Russia to work in its archives. In 1917, he published a unique and still relevant *Guide* to Moscow's and Petrograd's archives.[75] Golder himself viewed the publication of this edition as the first step in establishing professional ties between Russian and American scholars – as the start of the process of exchanging ideas, materials, and people between Russian Studies in the United States and American Studies in Russia.[76] In addition to the universities of Berkeley, Harvard, Chicago, and Columbia, Russian language, history, and culture were also taught in Michigan and Missouri. In 1916, a Russian Department was opened at Seattle University. Nikolay Bogoyavlensky, the consul for Nome and Seattle, saw it as "Russia's peaceful victory" and important for developing bilateral relations, since Seattle was the gateway of America's trade with Eastern Siberia.[77]

In Russia, meanwhile, the Moscow historian Stepan Fortunatov increased the number of students in his American Studies courses by adding those from Moscow Higher Women's Courses. Addressing them, he stressed that "if we speak of the interests of the masses, and not individual persons, the United States has reached the highest level of material wealth, mental development, and happiness, one that no nation in Europe has achieved."[78]

However, it was Borodin who made the most energetic contribution to developing American Studies during this period. He incessantly emphasized the importance of US achievements for developing Russia's productive forces and for its revival. In particular, he wrote:

> It is our profound conviction that we have no other road to travel in our development than the road of North America. We need to study it, use its experience, and strive to attract its tremendous capital and technical means so that Americans would work together with Russians on exploring Russia's untapped natural resources and on developing Russia's weak industry on a large scale.[79]

In 1915, Borodin published two books on the United States in which he identified similarities between the two states' development. Although Borodin, like many Russian liberal westernizers, idealized the United States, he criticized American political corruption, the country's venal press, and sundry negative features of economic and social life. Nevertheless, he believed that the reformist nature of the US model would allow Americans to regenerate their society and address these issues. This, he felt, was something else Russians should learn from them.[80]

CONCLUSION

During the First World War, the United States was willing to engage in wide-ranging cooperation with the Russian Empire regardless of their ideological differences. In that sense, the "honeymoon" between the two countries began long before the 1917 February Revolution.

This Russia–US rapprochement – which centered around trade, the economy, and finance – was unprecedented in its scale, and only grew as the war dragged on. Russia needed deliveries of military supplies from across the ocean, as well as American capital and experience, to continue the war and modernize its economic system. The United States, meanwhile, was rising up the ranks of the global powers, was building up its industrial and financial might, and was interested in large-scale economic expansion into the Russian market. The complementary interests of the two states created the conditions for pragmatic cooperation between them. This was supported by the two peoples' mutual interest in studying each other and destroying stereotypes about each other.

These direct business contacts and this mutual inspiration would be given a new impetus by the February Revolution, as well as the United States' entrance into the war in April 1917. However, in an echo of the approach that had been taken during the crisis of bilateral relations in 1903–1905, Wilson strove to turn Russia not so much into an object of American "dollar diplomacy" as into a destination of its "crusade" for democracy. This ideological (value-based) approach would ultimately emerge as a stable trend structuring the US attitude toward Russia. As the Russian Empire moved toward her second revolution, American society was on its way toward another cycle of hopes for Russia's modernization and disappointment over its results.

9

REVOLUTION AND INTERVENTION, 1917–1920

OVERVIEW

Early in 1917, when workers, soldiers, and Duma politicians toppled the Romanov monarchy, the revolution seemed to open the way to a close political and military partnership between Russia and the United States. Americans rapturously hailed the overthrow of the autocracy, which made it possible for the United States to enter the war against Germany in April under the banner of a crusade to make the world safe for democracy. Yet, within weeks, Americans became deeply disturbed by the rising antiwar sentiment and the growing popularity of radical socialists in Russia. Despite moral and financial support from the United States, the new Russian Provisional Government, which had vowed to continue the war, became increasingly unpopular in the summer and fall. On October 25 (November 7 in America), militant socialists seized power, called for peace, and urged peoples around the world to rise up against the imperialist powers they blamed for the slaughter of the First World War. The United States refused to recognize the new Soviet government, took covert steps to support its opponents, and eventually sent small military expeditions to assist anti-Bolshevik Russians. Although anti-Bolshevik ("White") armies for a time appeared certain to crush the encircled Soviet regime, by the end of 1920 the Red Army defeated all of the Whites. Dismayed by the survival of the ruthless Bolshevik dictatorship, US officials formalized their refusal to have anything to do with Soviet Russia.

The turbulent events of those four years – the most tumultuous era in the entire history of American–Russian relations – have sparked many controversies. Could Americans have done more to support the Provisional Government and prevent the Bolsheviks from taking power? Was a German–Bolshevik conspiracy crucial to the Bolsheviks' ability to take and retain power? Were there opportunities for cooperation between early Soviet Russia and the United States or did ideological antipathies preclude any collaboration? Could America have intervened more vigorously to extinguish the fire of communism?

This chapter addresses those issues and explains why they have often been misunderstood. It also analyzes how the astonishing events of the Russian Revolutions and Civil War affected the ways Americans and Russians thought about themselves and their nations' places in the world. While the revolution against the tsarist autocracy appeared to many Americans to affirm their identity as a "redeemer nation,"[1] the Bolshevik revolution seemed to repudiate American ideals and Bolshevism came to be seen as the antithesis of Americanism. On the other hand, the communist commitment to world revolution stirred messianic fervor in some Russians while the experience of being surrounded by enemies during the civil war entrenched a notion of Soviet Russia as a "besieged fortress." To illustrate the development of those lasting ways of thinking, this chapter will highlight how Americans and Russians expressed their political visions in speeches, articles, books, political cartoons, and propaganda posters.

WAR AND REVOLUTION: FEBRUARY–MARCH 1917

Late in the harsh winter of 1916–1917, masses of common people in Petrograd rebelled against the conditions of their lives. Women took action first. Angry at having to stand in line for hours in the cold to get bread for their families, thousands of female textile workers and housewives protested in the streets on February 23, International Women's Day (early March by the calendar in the United States). The next day, hundreds of thousands of workers, outraged by shortages of food and fuel, went on strike and marched to the center of the capital. On February 25, students and middle-class citizens joined the crowds, which carried banners calling for an end to the war and the overthrow of the bungling tsarist government. After soldiers fired on the crowds, killing hundreds, on February 26, regiments mutinied and joined the revolt. At the end of February, socialist activists formed a Soviet (Council) of Workers' and Soldiers' Deputies. Meanwhile, a committee of politicians from the Duma persuaded military leaders to support the revolution and urged them to get Nicholas II to abdicate. The tsar's renunciation of the throne on March 3 led to a condition of "dual power": Duma politicians organized a Provisional Government that depended on support from the Soviet, which had much greater popular authority. For a brief period after the fall of the hated autocracy, Petrograd residents shared a widespread euphoria at their new freedom.[2]

American diplomats in Petrograd saw first-hand how the revolution erupted from below, with young conscripts rejecting orders from officers and workers seizing control of factories from their owners.[3] At first, the diplomats worried about the menace of "lawless demonstrations" and "a socialistic outbreak." They were therefore relieved by the formation of the Provisional Government and its efforts to restore order. Heartened, Ambassador David Francis reported to Washington that the revolution represented the realization of the American principle of "consent by the governed." Believing that the revolution had yielded a democratic government that would wage war more vigorously than the incompetent autocracy had, President Woodrow Wilson and his advisors quickly recognized the Provisional Government.[4]

Political cartoons in American newspapers illustrated the widely held assumption that the Russian people had embraced the shining example of the United States, just as journalist George Kennan had long predicted they would once they were freed from the shackles of the monarchy.[5] (See Figure 9.1.) Headlines made the point explicit. "RUSSIA LIKELY TO FOLLOW AMERICAN FORM OF GOVERNMENT," one paper proclaimed.[6] Much as they had in the fall of 1905, many Americans believed that Russia had suddenly and miraculously been transformed as American light dispelled Russian darkness. After years of intensifying antagonism in the United States between labor and capital, pacifists and militarists, and

"Welcome, Russia!"

Figure 9.1 "Welcome, Russia!" *Life*, May 10, 1917.

reformers and conservatives, Americans universally shared enthusiasm about a revolution that affirmed their visions of historical progress toward democracy.[7]

The misleading notion that the autocracy had been toppled in a political (not social) revolution led by patriotic liberals fundamentally distorted American responses to the Russian Revolution. From the outset the revolution actually involved a broadly based challenge to the authority of elites – not only tsarist officials, but also army officers, factory owners, and other privileged members of society tagged as "bourgeois."[8] Yet most Americans viewed developments in Russia through the eyes of a small minority of educated, westernized liberals who encouraged American illusions by telling Americans what they wanted to hear (a dynamic that would persist into the twenty-first century).[9] From the start, the socialist leaders of the Soviet sharply criticized the "monstrous war," blamed it on the aggressive ambitions of "ruling classes," and called for the peoples of the world to take the question of war or peace into their own hands.[10] Yet US policymakers and opinion leaders viewed such socialists as unrepresentative of the aspirations of the Russian people, at best foolishly naïve, and at worst tools of Germany.[11] Thus, America and revolutionary Russia had started on a collision course even as liberal leaders in both countries proclaimed harmony between their basic objectives.

WAR AND DEMOCRACY: APRIL–JULY 1917

The revolution in Russia made it possible for the United States to enter the war against Germany not on the side of one group of empires against another but on the side of democracy against autocracy. On April 2, in calling upon Congress to declare war, President Woodrow Wilson hailed the "wonderful and heartening" events in Russia, declared that the 300-year-old autocracy "was not in fact Russian in origin, character, or purpose," proclaimed that Russia actually had always been "democratic at heart," and portrayed the war as an unselfish crusade to make the world "safe for democracy."[12] Newspaper editors shared Wilson's enthusiasm. With the nightmarish Romanov despotism removed from the picture, they wrote, Americans could believe wholeheartedly that in joining the war they were not repudiating their traditional separation from Europe but fulfilling their historical mission to spread democracy throughout the world.[13]

Liberal leaders of the Provisional Government nourished Western faith in the new Russia and echoed Wilsonian rhetoric. Foreign Minister Paul Miliukov, a professor and leader of the Kadet (Constitutional Democratic)

Party, vowed that the government would strictly observe its international obligations and "devote all its energy to the achievement of victory." Endorsing Wilson's idealistic statements about the principle of self-determination, Miliukov sought to use them to support Russian war aims. Thus, the break-up of the Austro-Hungarian empire and the unification of Ukrainians from Austrian regions with Russia's Ukraine would be "in complete harmony" with Wilson's ideals, while freeing the Turkish Straits from Ottoman control and transferring them to Russia would "in no way contradict the principles advanced by Woodrow Wilson."[14] Seeking US financial and political support, the Provisional Government sent another professor, Boris Bakhmeteff, to Washington as its ambassador. After reaching America in June, Bakhmeteff repeatedly assured Americans that Russians were united in their eagerness to continue the war and that the new Russia was guided by the same democratic principles as the United States.[15]

Such statements were deeply misleading. To many Russians, "the democracy" meant workers, peasants, and soldiers – not privileged elites. Although the Soviet affirmed the need to maintain an armed defense against Germany, it expressed skepticism about Wilson's "vague, high-flown phrases" and it adamantly rejected the expansionist goals of Russian monarchists, conservatives, and many liberals. Miliukov's championing of the tsarist war aim of taking Constantinople and the Dardanelles sparked protests that led to his resignation at the beginning of May. The Soviet then called for an international conference of socialist parties to work for peace.[16]

By the end of April, American newspaper editors and cartoonists expressed worries about the unsteadiness of the Provisional Government. In the following weeks they reflected rising dismay about the intoxication of Russia from "anarchy" and "German influence." Although editors clung to wishful thinking about Russian determination to fight, they could not hide their alarm about "German intrigue," which they blamed for the wide circulation of "peace propaganda" in Russia.[17]

US officials lacked the flexibility, patience, and knowledge needed to respond sympathetically and intelligently to the complex situation in Russia. The United States was unprepared for war against Germany in the spring of 1917. American leaders feared that peace on the eastern front would enable Germany to transfer enough soldiers to win the war on the western front before US troops arrived in large numbers. The Wilson administration therefore rejected the Soviet appeal for a peace conference and urged the Provisional Government to suppress socialist agitation for peace. They extended large loans to Russia (ultimately totaling more than

$300 million) in order to enable the purchase of war supplies in the United States, but they made it clear that the financial assistance would cease if Russia left the war.[18] Thus, America's war to make the world "safe for democracy" was at cross purposes with the hopes of "the democracy" in Russia for peace.

In an effort to bolster the weak Provisional Government and the faltering Russian determination to wage war, the Wilson administration dispatched a special diplomatic mission to Russia. It was headed by Elihu Root, a corporate lawyer who had served as Secretary of War and then Secretary of State under William McKinley and Theodore Roosevelt. The selection of the prominent Republican made some sense in terms of American domestic politics: it might placate partisan critics of the Wilson administration's management of the war. But it made no sense at all in terms of Russian internal politics. As a champion of capitalist interests and an architect of American empire, Root represented the opposite of many Russians' socialist and anti-imperialist values. After sailing across the Pacific and traveling by train from Vladivostok to Petrograd, the Root mission lectured Russians about democracy, met with Provisional Government leaders, and recommended that Washington expand pro-war publicity in Russia. Since the sole socialist member of the delegation, Charles Edward Russell, was criticized and expelled by the Socialist Party because of his support for the war, even he had difficulty establishing rapport with many Russians.[19]

The Root mission also had difficulty getting its message across because hundreds of immigrants to the United States who returned to Russia in 1917 sought to discredit the mission and contradict the story it told about America. While the members of the delegation portrayed America as an advanced, productive democracy, the returned emigrants, many of them Jewish, mounted soapboxes and characterized the United States as a land of anti-Semitism, racism, capitalist exploitation, and employer violence against labor organizers. As Russell noted, the "trouble-makers" did a great deal of "mischief." One of the orators, who had returned from a brief stay in New York, was Leon Trotsky, whom Russell described as a "dreamy, hot-headed Utopian Jew" and who in return called Russell a tool of the J. P Morgan banking interests.[20]

Despite his keen awareness that "the real power" in Russia was in the Soviet and his realization that "Russia was sick of the war," Russell claimed that the United States could have kept Russia in the war through a massive $5 million publicity campaign that would have convinced Russians that Germany was the main foe of the revolution.[21] In a similar vein, some historians have argued that the United States missed a major opportunity by not launching a more extensive propaganda campaign and by not being receptive to the desires of Russian moderate socialists for a strictly defensive position in the war and a renegotiation of war aims.[22] Yet President Wilson did not see those options as viable at the time. While Wilson applauded a $1 million publicity campaign privately financed by William Boyce Thompson, the head of the American Red Cross mission in Russia, he believed that Congress and the American people would not approve of an overt propaganda campaign paid for with taxpayer money.[23] Wilson and his aides, who harshly repressed socialist criticism of the war in the United States, also were not inclined to open a discussion of war aims that might raise embarrassing questions about the expansionist designs of America's allies and diminish public enthusiasm for all-out war.

Even if Wilson had promptly approved a massive propaganda campaign, it is highly doubtful that it could have stemmed the growing support for the Bolsheviks and other radical socialists by Russians who yearned for an end to the war and had lost patience with the Provisional Government's failure to resolve issues such as increasing the supply of food to cities and redistributing land in the countryside. Criticism of Wilson's limited action reflected a persistent tendency of Americans to exaggerate their potential influence on developments in Russia.[24]

THE FALL OF THE PROVISIONAL GOVERNMENT, JULY–NOVEMBER 1917

At the end of June the head of the revamped Provisional Government, Alexander Kerensky, and his military commanders launched an offensive that they hoped would shift soldiers' attention away from politics and rumors about land redistribution. However, after initial successes, the offensive collapsed. By the middle of July, almost all regiments refused orders to advance. In the following months, military morale further deteriorated and desertion increased. Although the revolution against the autocracy at first inspired a wave of self-sacrificing voluntarism, by the summer that spirit had dissipated. A Committee on Social–Political Enlightenment formed in association with Kerensky's cabinet and funded by Thompson reached many Russians with lectures and pamphlets that attacked the Bolsheviks and presented positive images of America as an enormously productive ally. Yet even American supporters of the propaganda committee reckoned that it only delayed the Bolsheviks' coming to power by a month or so.[25]

The most important development was that an attempt to establish a military dictatorship backfired. Already in late March, some Americans began to think force would have to be used to suppress radical socialist agitation. By August, US diplomats and experts like George Kennan believed that a military dictator was the solution to Russia's troubles.[26] But, in late August, when General Lavr Kornilov sent soldiers to Petrograd to disband the Soviet and arrest Bolshevik leaders, Kerensky turned to the Soviet for support against what he suspected was a military coup. After railway workers halted Kornilov's troops, Kornilov himself was arrested. In the aftermath of the Kornilov affair, Kerensky's authority withered, in part because of suspicions that he had connived with Kornilov before turning against the general. As the Provisional Government's power evaporated, Bolsheviks won increasing support in the cities for their slogans, "Bread, peace, and land" and "All power to the soviets."[27]

Bolshevik leader Vladimir Lenin concluded that radical socialists now had a window of opportunity to seize power before counterrevolutionary forces could regroup. Although other prominent Bolsheviks argued that conditions in Russia were not ripe for a socialist revolution, Lenin insisted that a revolution in Germany was imminent, and that foreign socialists would then come to the aid of a socialist Russia. When Kerensky found that only young cadets and members of a women's battalion were ready to defend the Provisional Government, he fled Petrograd with a car loaned by the US Embassy and ineffectually tried to rally loyal regular troops outside the city. Although the Bolshevik-led seizure of power in Petrograd involved only small-scale skirmishes, it provoked bloodier fighting in Moscow, where moderate socialists strenuously resisted for a week. Small groups of conservative officers, Cossacks, and cadets then traveled south to the Don region, where they began to organize an anti-Bolshevik Volunteer Army. A civil war that had been developing for months entered a new stage.[28]

THE SOVIET PURSUIT OF PEACE AND THE BEGINNING OF FOREIGN INTERVENTION

In one of its first acts, the new Soviet government issued a Decree on Peace on October 26 (November 8 by the calendar in the United States). It proposed an immediate armistice and called for the governments of warring nations to begin negotiations toward a general peace without annexations or indemnities. However, the decree also urged workers in Britain, France, and Germany to take vigorous action to promote peace and to free the laboring masses from exploitation – a barely veiled call for revolution.

Trotsky took charge of the Foreign Ministry, renamed the People's Commissariat for Foreign Affairs (Narkomindel), and published the texts of secret treaties between Russia and the Allies that revealed their annexationist plans. Thus, the Soviet government's first steps in foreign relations were stridently provocative.[29]

The dominant American response to the Bolsheviks' seizure of power was to disdain them as foolish dupes of Germany or sinister, German-financed conspirators. In his first public comments on the revolution, Wilson expressed his "contempt" for the "fatuous" dreamers in Russia who were "compounding" with Germany. Newspapers shared his scorn. Editors called the Bolsheviks "traitors" and "agents of Germany." Cartoonists depicted them as marionettes manipulated by the German Kaiser or captives of Wilhelm II.[30]

Echoing such contemporary assertions, some scholars have depicted German financial support for the Bolsheviks as the decisive factor in their ability to take and keep power. They also have portrayed Lenin as doing Germany's bidding.[31] That perspective is distorted and one-sided. Germany spent 30 million marks for antiwar propaganda in Russia in 1917.[32] Since the exchange rate between the German mark and the US dollar in 1917 was between 5:1 and 6:1, Germany spent roughly $5 million to $6 million – several times what Thompson contributed, but about the same amount that Russell and the Root mission proposed that the United States spend on a publicity campaign. German expenditures on pushing Russia out of the war were much smaller than the $325 million in loans the United States extended to keep Russia in the war.[33] Moreover, as thoughtful Americans in Russia in 1917 understood, the Bolsheviks were devoted to their revolutionary cause, not to serving Germany.[34] Lenin was willing to take funds from any source in order to advance toward his goal of world revolution and the first foreign nation Bolshevik leaders hoped would emulate the Soviet example was Germany.

The ideological clash between Lenin's Russia and Wilson's America was thus much more important than the German–Bolshevik collusion.[35] Both radical socialists and conservative officials in the United States focused on the Bolsheviks' revolutionary objectives. To many socialists, including Socialist Party presidential candidate Eugene Debs, the Bolshevik revolution was such an inspiration that they even came to call themselves Bolsheviks.[36] To men like George Kennan and Secretary of State Robert Lansing, the fact that there were many people similar to the Bolsheviks in the United States was precisely what made Bolshevism such a menace to the "social order."[37]

While Lansing and other conservatives urged forthright condemnation of the Bolsheviks, Wilson for two years refrained from candid public expression of his ideological antipathy to Bolshevism, which would have alienated some leftists who voted for him in 1916 and would have limited his flexibility in foreign policy. Some of Wilson's statements, particularly his Fourteen Points address in January 1918, also appeared to express sympathy with the Russian quest for peace through open diplomacy.[38] As a result, historians who have read Wilson's words uncritically have concluded that he was a friend of the Soviet government and a steadfast opponent of all foreign intervention in Russia.[39]

In reality, Wilson agreed with Lansing that the United States should not recognize the Soviet government, which he regarded as illegitimate and unrepresentative of the Russian people. Within five weeks of the Bolshevik seizure of power, he approved a proposal from Lansing to launch the first form of intervention in the Russian Civil War: financial support for anti-Bolshevik forces gathering in southern Russia to be passed covertly through the British. Wilson's aides assured Ambassador Bakhmeteff that he would continue to be recognized. They also arranged to use the Russian Embassy in Washington as a channel for shipments of supplies to anti-Bolshevik forces, paid from the unexpended remainder of the loans advanced to the Provisional Government in 1917.[40]

Bolshevik leaders expected capitalist countries to be hostile to the world's first socialist state, but they did not simply lump the United States together with the other capitalist powers, as some writers asserted.[41] Instead, recognizing that the United States was a democracy, Lenin and other Bolsheviks thought public opinion would restrain US antipathy. In addition, seeing the United States as the most advanced capitalist country, Lenin considered it the most desirable source of technology for socialist modernization.[42] He and Trotsky believed that offers of trade and investment opportunities might induce American capitalists to pressure Washington for better relations with Soviet Russia as well as pit the United States against Japan, which had more rapacious ambitions in the Far East. Soviet leaders were not fooled by Wilson's expressions of sympathy with the Russian people, whom he differentiated from "their present leaders" and their "autocratic government."[43] However, in the first months of 1918 they developed a plan for Soviet–American economic relations that an American Red Cross representative carried to Washington (where it was ignored).[44]

Meanwhile, a revolution in Germany did not materialize as quickly as the Bolsheviks hoped. After tolerating Trotsky's stalling negotiating tactic of "no war, no peace" for weeks, in February the German army resumed its advance, met virtually no resistance from the weak, disorganized Russian forces, and threatened to capture Petrograd. Even as the Soviet government relocated to Moscow, many Bolshevik leaders opposed acceptance of German demands that Russia cede Finland, Poland, the Baltic states, and Ukraine. Nikolai Bukharin and others urged guerrilla warfare instead of staining the honor of the revolution by agreeing to a humiliating peace. Trotsky seriously explored the possibilities for military aid from the Allies and the United States – an expedient option Wilson and Lansing ruled out on principle. In contrast to many of his comrades, Lenin emphasized the hopelessness of fighting the powerful Germans and prioritized the preservation of the infant Soviet state. After he threatened to resign, he prevailed in a close vote.[45]

MILITARY INTERVENTION

With the Bolshevik signing of the Treaty of Brest-Litovsk on March 3, 1918, the Soviet regime became a partner of Germany in the eyes of Allied leaders and many Americans. Fearing that Germany would now be able to move forces from Russia to the western front, British and French representatives appealed to Wilson more urgently than before to send military expeditions to northern Russia and eastern Siberia to try to reestablish an eastern front against Germany. Wilson still rejected the requests. His military advisors insisted that the war would be won on the western front (where a million US doughboys arrived in the spring of 1918) and that any diversion of forces to the periphery of Russia would be unwise and ineffective. In addition, overt military intervention might appear to many to contradict the principles of non-intervention and self-determination that Wilson had espoused in relation to Mexico as well as Russia.

Finally, in June and July of 1918 Wilson agreed to send about 5,000 soldiers to Archangel (Arkhangel'sk) and roughly 8,000 troops to Vladivostok. Three main factors influenced Wilson's change of mind. First, Wilson knew he would need British and French cooperation with his plans for the postwar world after the defeat of Germany and he feared that if he continued to reject their appeals they would feel he was not a good ally. Second, in June, Wilson received a resolution by the Kadet Party and a petition from former officials of the Provisional Government that called for foreign intervention against the Bolsheviks and on behalf of Russian democracy.[46] Third, a legion of pro-Allies Czechoslovakian soldiers who had been in transit from the eastern front to Vladivostok clashed with Red forces in May 1918 and by July gained control of most of the Trans-Siberian

Railway. Wilson believed that as fellow Slavs the Czechoslovakians would get along well with non-Bolshevik Russians and could therefore serve as a nucleus around which patriotic Russians could organize. After "sweating blood" over the issue, on July 16, Wilson crafted a formal explanation of his decision. US forces could be used, he wrote, "to guard military stores which may subsequently be needed by Russian forces and to render such aid as may be acceptable to the Russians in the organization of their own self-defence."[47] Although Wilson refrained from specifying which Russians he meant, Soviet leaders had no doubts. In August, after the State Department released a modified form of Wilson's statement, Lenin attacked Wilson for having given his approval to intervention, "whether direct or indirect, open or hypocritically concealed."[48]

US intervention in the Russian Civil War has been misunderstood by historians who have focused narrowly on the expedition to Siberia.[49] In that region, US soldiers guarded military stockpiles at Vladivostok and patrolled the railway as far west as Lake Baikal, thereby assisting the shipment of supplies to anti-Bolshevik armies at the front in western Siberia. Although US troops thus avoided direct fighting against the Red Army, they did engage in small-scale battles with local Red partisans that continued through 1919 and killed scores of Americans. In northern Russia, soldiers of the 339th Infantry Regiment served on the front lines in direct combat with the Red Army and suffered much heavier casualties. The fighting was especially fierce along the rivers south of Archangel in the first months after the November 1918 Armistice on the western front. That led many relatives of the US soldiers to ask why they were still fighting there and to demand their return to America.[50] Doubts about the purpose of the expedition also provoked a brief mutiny by one company. In both Siberia and North Russia, US soldiers received support from the Young Men's Christian Association (YMCA) and the American Red Cross (ARC), which also provided food, clothing, and medical care to Russian civilians. In the Baltic region, the YMCA, the ARC, and the American Relief Administration (ARA) delivered humanitarian aid to the Russian Northwestern Army, which came close to capturing Petrograd in the fall of 1919. In parts of southern Russia controlled by General Anton Denikin, the Red Cross sought to assist refugees and strengthen morale. Herbert Hoover and other leaders of the ARA, who considered food a vital weapon against Bolshevism, withheld US aid from Bolshevik-controlled territory. Soviet leaders, not unreasonably, viewed the American humanitarian organizations in the several theaters of the civil war as appendages to foreign intervention.[51] Thus, while focusing solely on the expedition to Siberia can make US intervention in Russia seem almost neutral or benign, that expedition must be seen as only one of many locations and forms of intervention.

During the Cold War, Americans repeatedly denied Soviet charges that the United States had sought to overthrow the young Soviet government.[52] However, since the end of the Cold War, American scholars have generally recognized the anti-Bolshevik thrust of US policies.[53] Some, instead of being embarrassed by the record of US hostility to the Bolsheviks, have argued that the Wilson administration could and should have intervened more aggressively to ensure their downfall.[54] That view disregards the constraints on US policymakers, including the preoccupation with defeating Germany until November 1918 and the rising public and congressional criticism of the expeditions to Russia after the end of the First World War.[55] Although the foremost US expert on Russia, George Kennan, urged more direct action against the Bolsheviks and others, including Ambassador David Francis, called for sending larger expeditions to Russia, Wilson felt unable to accept those recommendations. Since he had declined to present a fully candid explanation of the purposes of the small expeditions, the president was vulnerable to charges by critics that they were parts of an undeclared war waged without approval from Congress. Although Wilson finally expressed his loathing of Bolshevism in public speeches in 1919, he justified the lack of more vigorous intervention by asserting that Bolshevism would burn itself out.[56]

The Bolsheviks struggled against the foreign-supported White armies both on the battlefields in Russia and inside western nations. Although the encircled Soviet regime at one point in 1919 controlled only the heartland of European Russia, the mobile Red Army defeated the uncoordinated offensives by White forces from the east, west, and south one by one. Soviet representatives and Bolshevik sympathizers in the United States organized numerous protest meetings and published leaflets or magazines to stimulate opposition to armed intervention in Russia. In August 1918, for example, several Russian American socialists and anarchists were arrested in New York after they distributed thousands of pamphlets that denounced President Wilson for his concealed intervention in Russia and called on workers to rise up to prevent the Russian Revolution from being crushed. Ludwig Martens, who established a Soviet Russian Information Bureau in New York in 1919, claimed that his staff succeeded in mobilizing sympathetic immigrant workers and in fostering an anti-intervention mood in labor unions. More generally, Lenin asserted at the end of the year that the Soviet government survived to a significant extent because of the solidarity of the working people in foreign nations.[57]

Although Bolshevik leaders increasingly valued the survival of the Soviet state over the promotion of revolution in foreign countries, they did not abandon their international dreams. Their hopes rekindled with the revolutions that ensued from the defeat of Germany and Austria-Hungary in the fall of 1918, the proclamation of a short-lived communist state in Bavaria that November, and the creation of a slightly longer-lived Soviet regime in Hungary in March 1919. In that context, Bolshevik leaders summoned a small number of foreign radicals to Moscow, where in early March they participated in the formation of a Communist International (Comintern). Though the Comintern was nominally separate from the Soviet state, Bolshevik leaders controlled it from the outset and demanded loyalty and obedience from foreign communists, including Americans. Headed by Grigory Zinoviev, the Comintern sought to reach out from isolated Soviet Russia, use the image of the Russian Revolution to inspire foreign emulation, and provide what limited support it could to communists in distant lands.[58]

That international activity would be one of the main reasons why the United States maintained its non-recognition policy toward Soviet Russia long after it withdrew its forces from Archangel in June 1919 and from Vladivostok in April 1920. As Bainbridge Colby, who replaced Lansing as Secretary of State, explained in a diplomatic note in August 1920: "The existing regime in Russia is based upon the negation of every principle of honor and good faith" underlying relations between nations. Washington thus expressed its continuing belief that the Bolshevik regime, unrepresentative of the Russian people, would soon be replaced by a government that would not incite subversion in America and would respect its international obligations – such as paying its debts and compensating the foreign owners of assets nationalized by the Bolsheviks.[59]

LEGACIES

The experience of fighting and prevailing in the civil war had a deep impact on Soviet attitudes.[60] It inclined Soviet leaders in subsequent decades to attach high priority to propaganda to counter anti-Soviet agitation and promote sympathy for Soviet Russia in foreign countries. Using both foreign communist parties and friendly non-communist groups, the Soviet government thus sought to avert the worst danger – a united front of capitalist countries coordinating a new intervention or war. Surviving the hostile encirclement also intensified a pre-existing tendency to view Russia as a besieged fortress. Long before 1917, tsarist officials and propagandists had portrayed Russia as beset by foreign enemies – Swedes, Poles, Germans, Japanese, and others in different eras.[61] During the civil war and for many subsequent decades, Soviet artists repeatedly depicted their country as a factory fortress facing assault by foreigners in cartoons and posters that warned the Soviet people of the need to be perpetually on guard.[62] Some posters during the civil war portrayed Uncle Sam as the biggest backer of the Whites or one of the deadliest capitalist foes.[63] (See Figure 9.2.) However, in later years and different international environments, the United States was omitted from depictions of foreign interventionists or drawn as a reluctant accomplice of the main British enemy.[64] Thus, memories of US interventions could be set aside by Soviet leaders when that seemed more expedient. The interventions also could be invoked by them when that served their purposes – as when Nikita Khrushchev reminded Americans in Hollywood in 1959 that US troops had once "landed on Soviet soil to help the White Guards fight our Soviet system."[65]

Figure 9.2 "Antanta" ("Entente"). The dogs are the White leaders Denikin, Kolchak, and Yudenich. Poster collection, RU/SU 1257, Hoover Institution Library & Archives.

In the United States, as later surveys showed, the overwhelming majority of Americans either forgot or never learned about US intervention in Russia.[66] However, the perceived menace of Bolshevism made a deep impression on American political culture and national identity. Charges by American politicians and editors during the Red Scare of 1919–1920 that Soviet agents poured millions of dollars into subversive agitation in the United States vastly exaggerated the meager thousands they actually managed to smuggle into the country.[67] In later decades, however, it would be an article of faith among American anticommunists that Soviet Russia from the beginning waged a determined effort to overthrow the US government. Equally important was that the dread fear of Bolshevism greatly inflamed the existing tendency to view Russia as the opposite of the United States. While tsarist Russia's despotism and anti-Semitism had long been cast as the opposites of American freedom and tolerance, Bolshevik tyranny, atheism, and alleged immorality came to be seen more pervasively as the antitheses of American liberty, religious faith, and morality. As Woodrow Wilson put it in September 1919, Bolshevism represented "the negation of everything that is American."[68] Stories about Bolsheviks "nationalizing women" or promoting free love scandalized Americans, who would long associate progressive feminism with Bolshevism.[69] Images of lazy, bearded, bomb-throwing Bolsheviks posed them as the ethnic Other to hard-working, clean-shaven, law-abiding, native-born Americans.[70] Although the government dramatically deported 246 immigrant radicals to Soviet Russia on the troopship *Buford* in December 1919, such stereotypes of un-American radicalism persisted for decades.[71]

CONCLUSION

Thus, the American encounter with revolutionary Russia that had begun with a euphoric belief in the triumphant spread of the light of American democracy to the darkest autocracy in Europe closed with terrible fears that Bolshevism threatened everything Americans held sacred and challenged their visions of the future progress of the world. During the turbulent years from 1917 to 1920, many Americans exaggerated US ability to guide developments in Russia (a tendency that would recur in later decades). Although the United States tried to shape the course of events through loans, propaganda, covert aid, and small military expeditions, it was constrained first by preoccupation with the war against Germany and then by postwar disillusionment with the Wilsonian crusade. On the other side, the Bolsheviks seized power in 1917 with the illusion that they could spark a global revolution, but then had to defeat both White armies and foreign interventionists – an experience that left a lasting fear of being surrounded by enemies. The era ended with a rigidification of the Wilson administration's refusal to recognize the Bolshevik regime, a freeze on American–Soviet diplomatic relations that would last for another thirteen years, and the beginning of Soviet efforts to break out of international isolation.

10

FROM ESTRANGEMENT TO ENGAGEMENT, 1921–1933

OVERVIEW

At the start of 1921, the United States and Soviet Russia were utterly estranged. As President Woodrow Wilson left office, he passed on to his Republican successor Warren Harding a policy of stubbornly refusing to have diplomatic relations with the Bolshevik regime. Although Washington formally ended its participation in an economic blockade of Soviet Russia by July 1920, virtually no goods were exchanged between the two countries in the following year. Only a handful of Americans traveled to Soviet Russia in the first months of 1921, and even fewer Soviet citizens came to America then. To most Americans, the atheist Soviet socialist dictatorship seemed the polar opposite of their Christianity, democracy, and capitalism. While Soviet leaders and intellectuals admired modern America's high productivity and hoped to benefit from its advanced technology, they also condemned American racism, materialism, and plutocracy as the antithesis of Soviet equality and idealism. Closer relations between the two countries appeared extremely unlikely.

Yet, by 1933, America and Soviet Russia were enmeshed in cultural, economic, and diplomatic exchanges. In the 1920s and early 1930s, hundreds of American intellectuals traveled to the Soviet Union, eager to see the new ways of life being created in the socialist experiment. While a smaller number of Soviet poets and trade representatives journeyed to America to see the land of skyscrapers and develop economic contacts, thousands of immigrants came from Russia, and many of them deeply influenced American culture, from Hollywood movies to Broadway musicals. Engineers who could not find work in the United States after the onset of the Great Depression in 1929 ventured to the Soviet Union to help build steel mills and dams modeled on American examples, making enormous contributions to the rapid Soviet industrialization under the Five-Year Plans. Once President Franklin Roosevelt launched a New Deal in 1933 to try to overcome the depression, American capitalism and Soviet socialism seemed to many Americans to be converging – irrespective of whether they welcomed or abhorred that.

Following agreements between Roosevelt and Soviet Foreign Minister Maxim Litvinov in November 1933, American diplomats sailed to Russia to reopen the US Embassy and Soviet diplomats came to Washington – breakthroughs that were widely featured in the mass media.

Explanations of this dramatic shift in American–Soviet relations have often centered on economic and strategic interests. Soviet officials consistently showed strong desires to expand trade with America and they expressed keener interest in strategic cooperation as tensions with Japan rose in the early 1930s. Meanwhile, the Great Depression led many American business leaders to be more interested in recognition as a way to facilitate commerce with the Soviet Union, and Roosevelt realized that Russia's growing military power, as well as its Eurasian geographic position, made it a valuable potential ally.[1]

Although government decision-makers, diplomats, and businessmen focused above all on such interests, they were not the only significant actors in American–Soviet relations. Journalists, novelists, filmmakers, cartoonists, relief workers, and many others also played important roles, especially by depicting the other nation (negatively or positively) and thereby helping to affirm or redefine their own nation's identity. By examining the writing, drawing, and movie-making of that larger cast of characters, this chapter shows how Soviet–American relations in the era of non-recognition centered not only on interests but also on ideas and identities. Through the construction and revision of images of the other nation, Soviets and Americans defined and redefined the boundaries of what was permissible or desirable in their political cultures. Even more than in earlier eras, by describing the other nation and engaging in debates over its sins or virtues, Americans and Soviets articulated their visions of paths they hoped their nations would take in the future.

Contrary to the misleading notions that after the First World War the United States reverted to "isolationism" and that a self-isolating Soviet Russia developed autonomously according to ideological blueprints,[2] the two countries had intense and extensive intellectual, cultural, and economic interchanges between 1920 and 1933 that significantly affected the further development of the two nations. It is therefore essential to integrate discussion of the external policies of the United States and Soviet Russia with analysis of internal dynamics in the two societies.[3] Despite the vast gulf between the two countries at the beginning of the 1920s, they came to play vital roles in shaping each other's trajectories at pivotal moments in their histories, especially by serving as examples of evils to be avoided or models to be emulated.

FEEDING THE STARVING: A FIRST STEP TOWARD ENGAGEMENT

Strangely enough, the first move beyond the complete estrangement during the Russian Civil War involved American hopes to cure Russia of the blight of Bolshevism and provoked Soviet fears that it would undermine Communist power. After fighting between Red and White forces ended in 1921, millions in Russia faced the danger of starvation as a result of a severe drought and the effects of grain confiscation by armies. In July 1921, the famous writer Maxim Gorky issued an appeal to "all honest European and American people" to send bread and medicine to the Russian people. The most ambitious response to the appeal came from the American Relief Administration (ARA), a private organization headed by Secretary of Commerce Herbert Hoover. The ARA drew on a $20 million appropriation from Congress for purchasing food in the United States (where there was a price-depressing agricultural surplus) and transporting it to Russia on American ships. From the fall of 1921 into 1923, some 300 ARA officers and 120,000 Soviet employees distributed huge amounts of flour, condensed milk, and other food that saved the lives of millions of Russians.[4]

Hoover and some of his aides thought that, by demonstrating America's awesome productivity and efficiency, the sweeping humanitarian operation would discredit the weak Soviet regime that had been unable to cope with the famine. Hoover and his advisors also believed that sustaining and empowering educated Russians who worked for the ARA might create a foundation for a new Russian government after the impractical ideologues in Moscow lost power.[5] Thus, the United States did not simply provide aid "in a spirit of sweetness and light."[6] Fearing that there must be ulterior motives for the aid from capitalists, Lenin ordered the dissolution of a famine relief committee that included prominent non-Bolshevik figures and directed Soviet security forces to maintain close surveillance of ARA operations.

Neither the Americans' dream nor the Bolsheviks' nightmare came to pass. As Bertrand Patenaude has shown, Russian popular responses to the ARA were complex. While children expressed the most uninhibited enthusiasm, many adults also became ardent admirers of everything American, which they assumed must be the best. Although many in Russia spoke of the ARA aid as a divine miracle, others criticized American officers as arrogant or expressed suspicion that they really came to grab control of Russian natural resources. Ultimately, the ARA heightened the pre-existing esteem for American energy and effectiveness but could not stimulate a movement against the Bolsheviks by the shattered society.[7]

On the other side, the ARA mission and other American-supported relief efforts led to the moderating of some Americans' hostility to the Soviet regime and inspired some influential Americans to advocate diplomatic recognition. The American Friends Service Committee sponsored relief operations alongside the ARA, and some volunteers in the Quaker effort, especially Anna Louise Strong, became passionate pro-Soviet publicists. The American Jewish Joint Distribution Committee (JDC) sought to improve the lives of Jews in Soviet Russia by supporting the construction of hundreds of agricultural settlements in Crimea and Ukraine (which gave Soviet economic planners a prototype for modern farming techniques they would attempt to develop later). Top JDC leaders, including the prominent banker Felix Warburg, who had vehemently loathed anti-Semitic tsarist Russia, urged diplomatic recognition of the Soviet government.[8]

Perhaps most important was that James Goodrich, a wealthy businessman who had been Republican Governor of Indiana, became a champion of recognition after Hoover sent him to Russia to investigate conditions and inspect ARA operations. Although Goodrich agreed with Hoover that the Soviet socialist vision was foolish and unrealizable, after returning to America he repeatedly urged recognition in meetings with US leaders and in interviews or articles for the American press. Establishing diplomatic relations, Goodrich argued, would help American manufacturers gain a major share of the Russian market. He also claimed that recognition would accelerate the transition from communism back to capitalism that he believed was already under way with Lenin's 1921 adoption of the New Economic Policy (NEP), which allowed small-scale private commerce while retaining state control of major industries. Although Communists Goodrich met in Russia told him that the NEP was only a temporary retreat before resumption of the Soviet march toward communism, Goodrich persisted in believing that the permission of limited trade by peasants and entrepreneurs was the beginning of an inevitable evolution to capitalism. The well-meaning Goodrich thus embodied a mirror-imaging that would distort American views of Russia for many years to come.[9]

THE POLITICS AND DIPLOMACY OF RECOGNITION AND NON-RECOGNITION

A year before the relief operations began, Lenin had announced a reorientation of Soviet foreign policy. Revolutions in Germany and Hungary had not established lasting socialist states, and the Red Army had failed to carry Bolshevism to Poland when it counterattacked in the Russo-Polish War of 1920. However, Lenin declared, through the defeat of the

Whites and their foreign backers, Soviet Russia had won conditions enabling it to coexist with capitalist powers and establish commercial relations with them. Since world revolution no longer appeared imminent, Lenin envisioned a long period of Soviet development in a world of capitalist states. Subsequent stirrings of revolt in foreign countries, especially in Germany in 1923, would briefly reignite some Soviet leaders' revolutionary enthusiasm and the activity of the Communist International (Comintern) would maintain Soviet Russia's revolutionary image. Yet, throughout the 1920s, Lenin's idea of "peaceful coexistence" would guide the Comintern's rival, the People's Commissariat for Foreign Affairs (Narkomindel), which was responsible for diplomacy with foreign states.[10]

In line with Lenin's ideas, Soviet leaders persistently sought diplomatic recognition from capitalist countries. Establishing formal relations with Western countries would, they hoped, increase the prestige of the Soviet government, enhance Soviet security, facilitate the expansion of trade, and induce greater foreign investment in Soviet economic development. Soviet officials expressed particular interest in diplomatic relations with the United States, the most technologically advanced and financially powerful industrialized nation. They tried three approaches: (1) offering special opportunities to develop Soviet resources to American capitalists, who would use their presumed influence in Washington to promote recognition; (2) making large purchases of American products that they hoped would lead American producers to urge recognition; and (3) expressing willingness to engage in negotiations to resolve financial disputes.

While Lenin still actively participated in Soviet policymaking, in late 1920 the Soviet government granted Los Angeles engineer Washington Vanderlip rights to develop oil and other resources on the Kamchatka peninsula. Then, in 1922, Moscow gave oil tycoon Harry Sinclair a contract to exploit oil reserves in the northern half of the island of Sakhalin. Both areas were then under Japanese control. Lenin appears to have hoped that the concessions would lead not only to diplomatic recognition, but also to US pressure on Japan to withdraw. However, neither Vanderlip (whom Soviet leaders confused with the more powerful financier Frank Vanderlip) nor Sinclair was able to take advantage of the opportunities or to exert significant influence in Washington.[11] In the following years, Soviet trade representatives in the United States bought large quantities of American goods, starting with a major purchase of cotton in 1924, yet the demonstration of Soviet buying power did not prod Washington toward diplomatic recognition.[12]

The United States thus diverged from West European countries. Already in March 1921, Britain signed an agreement to spur trade with Soviet Russia.

A year later, British and French leaders invited Soviet and German representatives to an international economic conference at Genoa, Italy. Washington declined to participate formally in the conference. Secretary of State Charles Evans Hughes earlier had been an attorney for Standard Oil, one of the US companies whose assets had been seized by the Soviet state. He still expected the Soviet regime to fall and saw no need to engage in discussions with the weak, despicable Bolsheviks.[13] Soviet diplomats, though, stunned the organizers of the Genoa conference by signing a treaty on trade and recognition with German delegates in nearby Rapallo. It showed the West Europeans that Germany and Russia had an alternative to simply submitting to their demands for reparations, debt repayment, and compensation of property owners. The Treaty of Rapallo also reflected the Soviet tactic of playing the capitalist countries against each other, and it was a first sign that the US nonrecognition policy would become an outlier. By 1924, most West European states recognized the USSR.[14]

Despite the firm US stance, Georgi Chicherin, the People's Commissar for Foreign Affairs until 1930, and his deputy, Maxim Litvinov, repeatedly offered to open discussions with US representatives about resolving disputes. The closest the two nations came to starting such negotiations was when James Goodrich held semi-formal discussions with Soviet leaders in 1922 and 1925. Joseph Stalin, who gradually consolidated his position as the most powerful Soviet leader after Lenin died in January 1924, approved of Litvinov's meetings with Goodrich. However, the two sides remained far apart. In October 1925, the Politburo rejected Goodrich's proposal that the Soviet government annul its repudiation of responsibility for the debts of the Provisional Government of 1917. Addressing Goodrich's concern about Soviet revolutionary propaganda, Litvinov disingenuously claimed that the Soviet government did not finance or control the Comintern. Yet, as Goodrich noted, that seemed implausible to Americans, since Grigory Zinoviev was both the head of the Comintern and a member of the Politburo.[15]

Even as they eagerly sought recognition from America, Soviet leaders were unwilling to take the steps that would have removed the major concrete US objections to diplomatic relations. They feared that accepting responsibility for the American debts of previous Russian governments would embolden claims from other creditor states. They knew they could not afford to compensate American firms for assets nationalized in 1918 (which they valued at $400 to $500 million, a very large amount).[16] And they could not disband the Comintern, which remained central to the projection of their revolutionary identity and which they valued as a tool for exerting influence in foreign countries long after hopes for revolution in Europe faded.

Outrage at revolutionary agitation by the Comintern stoked persistent American opposition to opening diplomatic relations with Soviet Russia. Although fears of a Bolshevik-inspired revolution in the United States faded somewhat after the Red Scare of 1919–1920 and the adoption of immigration restrictions in 1924, conservatives still worried that recognition of the Soviet regime would embolden radicals in America. Throughout the 1920s, State Department officials cited documents that showed Comintern-supported subversive activity in labor unions and among African Americans to justify the perpetuation of the non-recognition policy. While exaggerated State Department claims about Bolshevik subversion in Mexico and Central America were less credible, officials' concerns about Communist intrigue in the United States seem to have been more genuine.[17]

Advocates of recognition did not share those fears of subversion. The two most influential champions of recognition were progressive Republican activist Raymond Robins and Senator William Borah, an Idaho Republican who became chair of the Foreign Relations Committee in 1924. They argued that diplomatic relations with the vast and growing Soviet Russia would aid American businesses and promote world peace. Robins succeeded at some moments in getting presidents to waver. In 1920, he won Senator Warren Harding's promise to consider recognition in exchange for his campaign support. When Robins sought to redeem the pledge after Harding's election, though, Hughes and Hoover squelched the idea. In November 1923, after Harding's death, Robins met with President Calvin Coolidge and prodded him to issue a statement that seemed to offer an opening. However, the new effort to midwife a diplomatic breakthrough was quickly scotched by Hughes.[18]

As the unsuccessful campaigns by Robins, Borah, and others showed, the issue of recognizing Soviet Russia was highly controversial. The debate hinged in part on practical arguments about tangible interests. Proponents of recognition argued, for example, that having US consuls and commercial attaches in Russia would provide much needed support for American businesses in that growing market.[19] Opponents countered that American exports to Russia were increasing without diplomatic relations and that recognition should not be considered until the Soviet regime recognized national debts and assured the security of foreign investments.[20]

Yet, what is more striking in numerous speeches by politicians and hundreds of editorials published in the 1920s and early 1930s is how the question of recognizing Bolshevik Russia provoked highly charged, polarized descriptions of the Soviet Union. In taking positions on Soviet Russia and American–Soviet relations, Americans passionately defined and affirmed their identities.

Long after the end of the Red Terror and the Russian Civil War, anti-communist editors repeatedly denounced Soviet Communists as criminals, maniacs, barbarians, and savages. The Bolshevik regime, they declared, was not merely impudent and brutal, but abominable and devilish. It represented the opposite of the United States. Thus, to the *Chicago Tribune* and other papers, the antagonism between American virtue and Soviet iniquity was inherent and irreconcilable. As the *Washington Post* explained in 1932, the main issue was not debts, but the fundamental nature and purpose of the Soviet regime. Hence, "the objections of the United States to recognition of the Soviet [Union] could not be overcome without the destruction of communism as it is now known throughout the world."[21]

To anti-Soviet journalists in the 1920s, as to anti-tsarist Americans in earlier decades, opposing the Russian government and sympathizing with the Russian people affirmed the special idealism and unselfish emotion of Americans.[22] While "European ears hear only the 'jingling of the guinea,'" the *Washington Post* declared, "American ears should not be deaf to the voice of Russia" and should "stand for the Russian people rather than with their despoilers."[23]

The handful of progressive politicians who championed recognition of Russia asserted, in contrast, that the Soviet Union was not so different from the United States and that extending diplomatic recognition would promote the democratization of Russia. Senator Burton Wheeler of Montana, for example, claimed that Soviet adoption of the NEP meant the abandonment of communist theory and stressed that Russian entrepreneurs were copying American methods. In a similar vein, Borah repeatedly likened Soviet institutions to American institutions and argued that "the best way to get rid of the Bolshevik rulers is for the great governments to get in touch with the Russian people."[24] Thus, the debate over recognition reflected a contest about whether engagement or ostracism was the best way to promote desired changes in Russia that would be rejoined in later decades.

During the 1924 presidential election, conservative Republicans tried another tactic that would become a recurring part of American politics: they sought to associate their opponents, especially the Progressive third-party candidate, Robert La Follette, with the danger of radicalism and the evil of Soviet Russia. In September, for example, Charles Dawes, the Republican nominee for vice president, warned voters not to be deceived by La Follette, a "master demagogue endeavoring to amalgamate them with the Socialists, flying the red flag."[25]

After La Follette and his wife, Belle, visited the Soviet Union in September 1923, she, a suffragist and peace activist, had in fact written enthusiastically about the Soviet drive for a just social order. She also wrote credulously about religious freedom and a supposed decentralization of power in the USSR. Yet La Follette himself had been disturbed by the lack of a free press or free speech in Soviet Russia. After returning to America he criticized the Communist promotion of world revolution and he did not include a plank for recognition in his 1924 platform. Conservative attacks on him as a Red were therefore unfounded smears.[26]

Some liberals who had earlier shared the general revulsion at Bolshevik despotism reacted against the cynical conservative efforts to use the specter of Bolshevism for domestic political purposes. Most dramatically, the cartoonist Rollin Kirby, who had depicted the incendiary menace of Trotsky and the heartless exploitation of peasants by Lenin in 1921, now attacked Dawes and other Republican operatives for dishonestly holding up the scarecrow of Bolshevism to try to frighten voters. (See Figure 10.1.) Kirby's paper, the Democratic Party-affiliated *New York World*, would continue later in the 1920s to criticize unwarranted fear of the Soviet Union. Thus, while antipathy to Soviet Russia had fired a broad anti-radical consensus in the early 1920s, later in the decade it increasingly became a wedge issue, widening the divisions between conservatives and progressive reformers.[27]

THE COMINTERN, COMMUNISM, AND AMERICAN INTERNAL DIVISIONS

Throughout the 1920s, while Soviet diplomats and trade representatives pursued normalization of relations with the United States, Comintern officials provided thousands of dollars in financial support to American radicals and urged them to struggle for power in labor, political, ethnic, and racial organizations. Comintern support enabled American leftists to do things they otherwise could not have done (such as establishing newspapers), and many radicals were drawn to the Comintern and Communist Party as organizations that genuinely served their ambitions. Yet Comintern aid and advice generally did not lead to increased power for leftist radicals. It also had severely negative side-effects: it undermined the attainment of diplomatic recognition by inflaming US officials' anger at Soviet subversion, antagonized the Communists' rivals in labor and leftist movements, and handed ammunition to conservatives for attacks on progressive activists as tools of Soviet Russia.

Figure 10.1 "Trotting It Out Again." Cartoon by Rollin Kirby in *New York World*, September 13, 1924.

In line with a 1920 directive from Lenin, Communists joined non-Communist unions, fought against leaders of the unions, and tried to take control of some of them. While Samuel Gompers, head of the American Federation of Labor (AFL), had vehemently opposed Soviet communism ever since the Bolshevik seizure of power in Russia, the Comintern-inspired drive to discredit the AFL leadership spurred the AFL to remain one of the fiercest opponents of the USSR after Gompers' death in 1924. When dissenting labor leaders, notably in the Chicago Federation of Labor, favored diplomatic relations and trade with Soviet Russia, Gompers smeared them as pro-Bolshevik. When non-communist leaders of AFL member unions discussed plans for a trip to the Soviet Union in 1927, AFL leaders attacked the idea as a "communistic scheme" and deterred some union heads from joining the mission. A small delegation still traveled to Moscow, met with Chicherin and Stalin, and issued a report that recommended recognition. However, AFL leaders persisted in opposing recognition as a step that would legitimize the Communist Party in the United States and embolden challengers to their power.[28]

Jewish leftists, including leaders of clothing workers' unions, were among the most ardent proponents of recognition of the Soviet Union, which outlawed anti-Semitism and included many Jews in top government positions. Yet Comintern tactics alienated many Jewish socialists and contributed to their harsh criticism of American Communists. Although the Comintern provided crucial financial support for the creation of a Yiddish socialist paper in New York, the Communist drive for control of organizations antagonized and undermined non-Communist radicals.[29]

Since 1917, many American feminists had seen inspiration in Soviet Russia, where women had the right to vote before they won it in the United States, where women gained opportunities for better education and professional careers, and where progressive family legislation eased access to abortion, facilitated divorce, and equalized power within marriages (at least in theory). Scores of young American women visited Soviet Russia in the 1920s, with some staying to help build a new society. Female activists in the United States also enthusiastically promoted diplomatic recognition of the Soviet Union, which they saw as a step toward world peace. Yet, in the 1920s, conservative American women successfully used the specter of alleged Bolshevik policies on sex and the family (including tales of the supposed "nationalization of women" and stories of abandoned, destitute women) to attack feminist reformers. In addition, patriotic women and their allies in the US military relentlessly attacked peace activists as pinks or Reds. Under the impact of this conservative offensive, many moderate women felt pushed to express their abhorrence of Reds and to disassociate themselves from controversial individuals or groups.[30]

Black Americans responded in three very different ways to the Comintern and Soviet Russia. Many religious and business leaders viewed the atheism and anti-capitalism of Communists as anathema. Non-Communist radicals born in the United States, such as the labor leader A. Philip Randolph, tended to see the Russian revolutions as inspirations, but blamed Communists for splitting Black Socialists and strongly opposed receiving directions from a foreign entity. Other radicals, many of them immigrants from the West Indies, were strongly attracted to the Comintern after it in 1920 adopted positions on race and colonialism that harmonized with their ideas. Although such radicals felt less affinity for the US

Communist Party, which in the early 1920s seemed indifferent or even hostile to Black activists, they benefited from Communist financial support for their travel, education, and publishing. Later in the 1920s and in the early 1930s, several important Black women radicals came to see the Communist Party as a powerful anti-racist movement and they greatly valued their travel to the Soviet Union, where they studied and became more sophisticated activists.[31]

Many Black radicals carried enthusiasm about communism and the Soviet Union into the 1930s, which would see a peak of activism against lynching and racial injustice. Comintern leaders contributed to that success by pushing the Communist Party to address racial oppression. Communists gained reputations as defenders of oppressed African Americans, especially in the long defense of the Scottsboro Boys, Black youths falsely accused of raping two white women in Alabama (1931–1937).[32] Yet the Comintern also prodded the Communist Party to maintain after 1928 that Black Americans had a right of self-determination, that "the Black Belt" in the South had a right to secede from the United States – a position opposed by almost all Black Communists and attacked by anticommunists.[33]

The Comintern exerted some positive influence on American communism, especially in the early 1920s when it allowed US Communists flexibility about tactics for applying Bolshevik principles. It also spurred the Communist Party to reach beyond the foreign-language federations of immigrants and enlist more native-born Americans. However, especially after Joseph Stalin (General Secretary of the Communist Party) and his supporters came to control the Comintern line, it became more rigid. On the whole, Comintern policies undermined more than they advanced progressive social reform in the United States.

The relationship between the Communist Party in the Soviet Union and the international communist movement became a key issue in the power struggle between Stalin and his allies, on one side, and Trotsky and Zinoviev on the other. In December 1924, Stalin began using the phrase "socialism in one country" to express confidence that socialism could be built in the USSR even without aid from the world proletariat and to attack the alleged lack of faith of his rivals, who supposedly viewed Soviet Russia as an appendage of revolution in the West. Stalin's use of the concept to outmaneuver his opponents in the following years did not mean an abandonment of commitment to eventual world revolution. Instead, it declared the primacy of the Soviet state in the global struggle against capitalism and imperialism. Yet, in part because of the reporting of *New York Times* correspondent Walter Duranty, many Americans came to regard Stalin as ideologically "moderate" in contrast to "the firebrand Trotsky."[34] Especially after the defeat and exile of Trotsky in the late 1920s, that perception eased some Americans' opposition to relations with the USSR.

SOVIET IMAGES OF AMERICA

The divergence of official and popular views of America in early Soviet Russia has often been emphasized. While the Soviet government and Communist Party harshly criticized US imperialism, racism, and economic exploitation, historians have stressed, ordinary Russians loved Hollywood movies, enjoyed listening to American jazz, and read adventure novels set in the United States.[35] However, official and popular attitudes were more complicated than that suggests. While many ordinary Russians had idealized views of America as a land of abundance, some non-Communist workers and managers resisted Bolshevik efforts to impose an American tempo or techniques in factories. In addition, many Orthodox priests and believers resented American Protestants for supporting Russian Protestant churches and condoning Bolshevik religious persecution.[36]

The official Soviet press certainly did propagate some extremely negative images of the United States, for example with stories of the poverty or exploitation of workers that sought to debunk myths of America as a country where ordinary people could easily become wealthy. However, *Pravda* and other papers also published glowing accounts of aspects of American life, such as the excellence of roads, the millions of cars, and the wide use of radios.[37]

In an era when the Soviet state was still working hard to overcome widespread illiteracy, one of the most powerful ways the Soviet press shaped popular attitudes was through political cartoons that extolled Soviet achievements and depicted communism's internal and external enemies. Communist leaders closely supervised the publication of caricatures, which they viewed as important weapons in their political struggles. Many of the most vivid images appeared in the popular illustrated magazine *Krokodil*, which had a print run that ranged between 100,000 and 500,000 copies. The full-color covers of *Krokodil* often depicted British and French imperialist violence, from Africa and India to Syria and Indochina, yet no cover focused on US military interventions in Haiti or Nicaragua. Cartoonists frequently portrayed the brutal killing of workers in European countries, but not in America. *Krokodil* envisioned military threats to the USSR from Britain, Germany, and other European powers, but hardly ever pictured the United States as a prime instigator of aggression against Soviet Russia. America, then, had a special place, apart from other capitalist countries, in the political imagination of *Krokodil*'s artists.[38]

True, cartoonists sometimes depicted America as greedy or domineering, for instance with an image of Uncle Sam gathering the biggest pile of chips in a poker game with European nations.[39] They also portrayed the United States as a competitor. In 1929, to take one of the most striking examples, a magazine cover featured an elderly, straining Uncle Sam leading in a race while a much younger Soviet runner at the back of the pack looked ahead confidently to the finish – an early illustration of the Soviet aspiration to catch and surpass the most advanced capitalist country, which would spur Soviet policies for decades.[40] (See Figure 10.2.)

Yet, on the whole, Soviet cartoonists depicted America more positively than they did any other Western nation. *Krokodil* virtually never portrayed

Figure 10.2 *Krokodil*, May 1929. "A Long-Distance Race." Courtesy of *Novaia Gazeta*.

foreign politicians or capitalists favorably, yet Americans were the exceptions. In 1929, for example, a cover displayed a handsome Henry Ford behind the steering wheel of a shiny red car, ready to drive a Soviet worker to Nizhny Novgorod (where Ford had agreed to help build a huge automobile factory).[41] This was a striking celebration of the fulfillment of a Soviet dream of utilizing American technological expertise to aid Communist modernization.

Thus, early Soviet images of the United States were more complex than a simple dichotomy between official and popular views suggests. The contradictory and ambivalent feelings about America also can be seen in three prominent writers' accounts of trips to the United States.

In the fall of 1922, the scandalously dissolute poet Sergei Esenin sailed to New York with his older American wife, the famed dancer Isidora Duncan. Esenin was not a fanatical Bolshevik: rural and religious themes in his poetry distinguished him from the officially promoted proletarian culture. However, US authorities suspected that he planned to disseminate Red propaganda and briefly detained him. After being released, Esenin found his breath taken away by the scale of New York's industrial dynamism and felt his head spin after seeing the dazzling energy and electricity of Broadway. On the other hand, like Maxim Gorky earlier in the century, Esenin decried "the rule of the dollar" and portrayed Americans as "a very primitive people when it comes to their own inner culture." "In its heart America doesn't believe in God," Esenin wrote in one of two articles published in *Izvestiia*, the Soviet government newspaper, in 1923.[42]

Spurred in part by Esenin's writing, the poet Vladimir Mayakovsky journeyed to the United States in 1925. Even more than Esenin, Mayakovsky was amazed by New York's massive buildings and loved its streetlights. He walked onto Brooklyn Bridge one evening like a "deranged believer" going "to his church." Yet, in greater detail than Esenin, Mayakovsky deplored Americans' racism, their calculating materialism, and their pornographic entertainment.[43] The passionately romantic Mayakovsky also criticized what he saw as excessive Soviet enthusiasm for the regimented mass production techniques of Henry Ford. After returning to the Soviet Union, Mayakovsky published his observations in periodicals and delivered many public lectures about his trip. According to a *New York Times* correspondent who attended one of the lectures in Moscow, the crowd of long-haired, wild-eyed bohemians eagerly approved the poet's raving about America's boorish materialism. Thus, Mayakovsky significantly shaped Soviet public views of the United States.[44]

While Mayakovsky toured America at the height of the "roaring twenties" prosperity, the modernist writer Boris Pilniak visited at the depth of the capitalist slump in 1931. Since the anarchist-oriented Pilniak had been attacked in the preceding years for ideological non-conformity, he needed to be careful with how he depicted America in *O'kei: Amerikanskii roman* (*OK: An American Novel*), published in 1933. Like Esenin and Mayakovsky, Pilniak admired the technological advancement of "the most Western West," yet he went further than his predecessors in depicting New York as an urban Hell. Criticizing the monotony and shallowness of life in America, where advertising everywhere obscured views, Pilniak contrasted it to the USSR, where "one can spot the Polar Star whenever one looks at the sky." Thus, Pilniak left no doubt about which country offered the world a brighter guiding light to the future.[45]

In claiming a Russian cultural and spiritual superiority to the crassly materialistic United States, Soviet writers drew on and perpetuated ideas that had roots in the writing of Slavophiles in the nineteenth century.[46] Thus, critical views of America were neither peculiar to the Soviet era nor simply artificially manufactured by government officials and foisted on the public.

Top Soviet leaders' views of America were almost as complex as those of Pilniak, Mayakovsky, and Esenin. Lenin loved stories by Jack London, whose tales of strong-willed heroes overcoming desperate challenges helped to make him the most popular foreign author in early Soviet Russia.[47] Stalin bought American cars for Soviet officials, rode in a Packard himself, and cited a vast, mechanized farm in Montana as a model for Soviet agriculture. Yet he also declared that the USSR could not follow the American example of privately owned farms and had an exaggerated view of the intensity of Anglo-American rivalry for resources and markets. Stalin's rival Trotsky proclaimed in 1926 that "Bolshevism has no enemy more fundamental and irreconcilable than American capitalism," yet his prophecy that "Americanized Bolshevism will defeat and crush imperialist Americanism" presumed that Soviet Russia would learn from the United States and utilize advanced American technology.[48] Lenin, Trotsky, Stalin, and other Soviet leaders enthusiastically promoted *Amerikanizm* as a model of the high-tech productivity and energetic, efficient spirit they hoped to see in the Soviet Union.

Even more than leaders' statements and writers' reports, films played vital roles in Soviet–American cultural exchange. In part because Lenin and other Soviet leaders saw an opportunity to raise much needed revenue, the Soviet government allowed Hollywood movies to be screened widely in the 1920s. American films were shown much more often than films from any other foreign nation, and American stars (especially Mary Pickford and Douglas Fairbanks) were extremely popular with Russian audiences. In order to contain the ideological impact of the movies, the Soviet press published articles that criticized their consumerist themes and the Communist Youth League (Komsomol) held meetings to counter the movies' possible subversive impact. However, the characters in many American films also exhibited traits Soviet leaders sought to instill in Russians, including athletic fitness, strength, optimism, joyfulness, and willpower. Thus, American popular culture could be useful in molding new Soviet men and new Soviet women.[49]

Hollywood movies strongly influenced Soviet directors, who adopted American techniques such as montage (juxtaposition of images or sequences). In one hilarious film, *The Extraordinary Adventures of Mr. West in the Land of the Bolsheviks* (1924), director Lev Kuleshov used American-style acrobatic stunts and slapstick comedy as he mocked American stereotypes of barbarous, bearded, menacing Bolsheviks. Mr. West, a wealthy, bespectacled YMCA leader, comes to see the true Bolshevik character when a heroic Soviet police officer rescues him from a Moscow gang that held him captive. By portraying the American capitalist as misguided by anticommunist magazines rather than malicious and by suggesting the possibility of overcoming negative stereotypes, the movie harmonized with the Soviet policy of seeking positive relations with the United States.[50]

IMAGES OF SOVIET RUSSIA IN AMERICAN MOVIES, NEWSPAPERS, AND BOOKS

Movies were by far the most powerful means of shaping American mass attitudes between 1920 and 1933, with half of the US population seeing at least one movie each week. The largest movie companies increasingly resembled major corporations, and they cooperated with conservative government officials and censors. Under such influences, Hollywood producers, directors, and actors – many of them from the former Russian empire – propagated sharply negative images of Bolshevism and Soviet Russia. Films about workers and strikes depicted labor union activists as frenzied Bolsheviks.[51] On the other hand, movies typically portrayed tsarist Russian elites sympathetically – even films from studios founded by Jewish immigrants. In *The Last Command* (Paramount, 1928), "the most dangerous revolutionist in Russia," a pretty young woman, is unable to go through with shooting a general and Grand Duke because she sees that he is an honorable patriot. In *Rasputin and the Empress* (MGM, 1932), a great box office success, Nicholas II is shown to be kind, well-meaning, and devout. The loving Romanov family is first preyed upon by the sinister mystic Rasputin and then shot by ruthless Bolsheviks.[52]

Leftist groups, especially the International Workers' Aid founded in 1921, sought to contest Hollywood depictions of Bolshevik villains and romantic Russian royalty by producing a number of documentaries about life in Soviet Russia. But their films, usually shown in ethnic neighborhoods and union halls rather than movie palaces, reached only a small fraction of the audience that saw Hollywood productions.[53]

Written accounts of visits to the Soviet Union contributed much more strongly to a rethinking of ideas about the country. In the late 1920s and especially in the early 1930s, American interest in Russia surged. Thousands of Americans traveled to Russia, and after they returned many of them reported on what they saw. Most of them were not naïve "political pilgrims" predisposed to worship at the shrine of Soviet socialism.[54] Instead, they tended to be thoughtful observers who suspected that the extremely negative earlier images of Bolshevik Russia were exaggerated or at least outdated. As journalists, ministers, professors, engineers, and others published articles and an unprecedented number of books, many Americans reconsidered notions of Russia as the diabolical opposite of the United States that had prevailed at the beginning of the 1920s.[55]

On the other hand, in some ways anti-Soviet sentiment grew more intense. When the Soviet anti-religious campaign widened after 1929 to target Protestant denominations as well as Catholic and Orthodox priests, it spurred broader indignation at the religious persecution.[56] In addition, as membership in the small Communist Party slowly increased during the Great Depression, conservatives grew more alarmed. Their denunciations became even more vehement and were often tinged by anti-Semitism. In December 1931, for example, the national editor of the Methodist press decried a march on Washington as "a demonstration harking over from Russia" that was "led by Jewish communistic agitators" and unclean, godless foreigners who called for the overthrow of the US government.[57]

Yet the same Methodist paper also printed letters from Russia by another Methodist editor, who discounted any danger from communism. Dr. Dan Brummitt, who toured Russia in the summer of 1931, reported that, instead of continuing to be the demonic opposite of the United States, the country was rapidly becoming more like America: "Russia is trying to do in one generation what industrial America has done in three or four." Since Russians had been freed from "the grip of a greedy state-plus-church autocracy," Brummitt found, much had improved. Reminding readers of the negative images of brutal tsarist Russia propagated by George Kennan and others decades earlier, Brummitt declared in an eye-opening passage: "Every road to Siberia, which once was red from the bleeding feet of exiles, is now rutted from the wheels of tractors going to make bread." Instead of casting stones at Russian sins and having them point in response to American abuses such as lynching and racial discrimination, Brummitt argued, Americans should ask: "How shall two great social ideals live together in the same world?"[58]

Some Americans who traveled to Russia used their experiences to support traditional notions of American superiority. For example, in *Seeing Red* (1931), Eve Garrette Grady, the wife of an engineer who worked in Russia, asserted that the standard of living was so low there that "the unemployed in the breadlines of New York City are better off than the working man of Soviet Russia." In addition, "the terrors of underworld warfare in our gangster ridden cities pale in comparison with the gang rule of Red Russia." Yet such figures no longer dominated public discussion. When the prominent writer and Soviet sympathizer Louis Fischer challenged Grady at a meeting of the Foreign Policy Association, she was thrown on the defensive. After Grady resorted to a personal attack on Fischer, she was rebuked by the chair of the meeting (to loud applause by the audience), and then left the room.[59]

While anticommunists stressed differences between America and Russia, in the early 1930s more writers emphasized similarities. In contrast to the old stereotype of Bolsheviks as bums who did not want to work, journalist Ella Winter highlighted in *Red Virtue* (1933) how Russians were developing a new, disciplined work ethic. Photographer Margaret Bourke-White, author of the widely read *Eyes on Russia* (1931), featured how Russian women were becoming more like American women: they were just as eager to wear the latest fashion and, at least in the cities, they were even beginning to imitate "American slimness."[60]

While some historians have emphasized how American intellectuals looked to Western Europe for solutions to problems in the United States and have downplayed the influence of the USSR,[61] many Americans who visited the country in the early 1930s reported that they saw much to emulate. With the United States mired in a deep depression, the industrializing USSR seemed a land of hope, energy, and enthusiasm. Theater director Hallie Flanagan, who traveled to Moscow in 1926 and 1930, found state-supported, didactic, experimental theater thrilling, and back in the United States she staged Soviet-style plays.[62] Novelist Waldo Frank recorded in *Dawn in Russia* (1932) how exhilarated he was by the wholesome spirit he encountered in a land freed from the foul "cult of money." More down-to-earth writers such as economist Rexford Tugwell (later a key advisor for President Roosevelt's New Deal programs) expressed hopes that the laissez-faire United States could learn from the Soviet example of rational economic planning.[63]

Even some of the harshest critics of the Soviet Union now recommended the establishment of diplomatic relations. Most notably, philosopher Will Durant, who briefly visited Russia in 1932, depicted it as a land of "slavery, barbarism and desolation" in *The Tragedy of Russia* (1933). But Durant nonetheless urged recognition in order to (1) open "a vast market" by making it easier to extend long-term credits for Soviet purchases, (2) strengthen the US strategic position in the Far East, where Russia opposed Japanese expansion, and (3) encourage the moderation of the Soviet regime.[64]

THE ROAD TO RECOGNITION

Unlike the democratic US government, the Stalinist dictatorship did not need to consider possible public opposition to the establishment of diplomatic relations. On the contrary, the Kremlin worried that increased contacts with Americans might stimulate excessive admiration of America. While top Soviet officials valued American engineers as models of discipline and competence, the well-clothed and well-fed Americans embodied implicit challenges to notions of Soviet superiority.[65] After the peak of enthusiasm for Ford and Americanization at the start of the First Five-Year Plan, stories in the Soviet press about American technology became less glowing, more practical, and more confident about Soviet industrial progress. More importantly, Soviet pictorial propaganda became more sharply critical of American religious bigotry, racial violence, economic woes, and gangland crime in the early 1930s – at precisely the same time as the number of American tourists and engineers in the Soviet Union surged.[66]

While Soviet anti-Americanism intensified, American anticommunism faltered. Some conservatives discredited anticommunist fears by making false accusations. Most notoriously, Ralph Easley, head of the pro-business National Civic Federation, and Representative Hamilton Fish (Republican, New York) cited documents that turned out to be forgeries when they claimed that prominent advocates of recognition received Soviet funds and that the Soviet trade organization Amtorg had plotted a revolt in the United States for May Day 1930.[67]

In contrast to the National Civic Federation, many American manufacturers grew more sympathetic to recognition of the USSR as exports to the rapidly industrializing Soviet Union increased to around $100 million (roughly 3 percent of total exports) by 1930, and as markets in other countries shrank owing to a worsening global depression. Alexander Gumberg, a businessman, publicist, and "fixer" who had emigrated to America from Ukraine in the early twentieth century, played a key role in the expansion of commerce and the development of a more favorable view of Russia. He drew on connections to Soviet officials facilitated by having a brother who was an ardent Bolshevik, while also cultivating wide contacts among American bankers and industrialists. In the summer of 1929, Gumberg arranged for a huge delegation of ninety-five executives to tour the Soviet Union on a luxurious train. After returning to America, they expressed support for recognition of the USSR.[68]

Despite such growing sentiment, business groups remained divided over diplomatic recognition.[69] On one side were companies that remained bitter about Soviet nationalization of their assets in 1918 or feared competition from Soviet exports of grain. Especially in 1930, government officials, some business leaders, and anticommunist journalists heatedly accused the Soviet Union of "dumping" products on the American market at low prices in a deliberate effort to depress American prices and hurt American producers.[70] (In reality, Soviet leaders desperately sought to earn as much hard currency as possible in order to buy equipment for new factories, and low agricultural prices hampered their efforts.[71]) On the other side were corporations eager to export to the USSR and encouraged by the United States getting one-quarter of Soviet foreign purchases in 1930. Although US–Soviet trade even at that peak accounted for only a small part of total US commerce, some US industrialists hoped that they would gain more of the Soviet market in the future and were sharply disappointed by a cutback in Soviet purchases in 1931.[72] As a result of the division, businesses did not apply strong, unified pressure on the Roosevelt administration for or against recognizing the USSR.

From late 1932 through much of 1933, a terrible famine caused primarily by ruthless Soviet policies to seize grain led to the deaths of millions of people along the Volga River, in the North Caucasus, and particularly in Ukraine. Joseph Stalin blamed Ukrainian nationalists for resistance to grain requisitions and sent top Soviet officials to Ukraine to insist on harsh fulfillment of extreme quotas.[73] While some foreign journalists in the Soviet Union, particularly Walter Duranty of the *New York Times*, infamously claimed that there were only "food shortages," others courageously declared that there was widespread famine.[74] Ukrainian American leaders who wrote to President Roosevelt to oppose recognition of the Soviet Union argued that the famine was "a result of the political and cultural conflict between Ukrainian nationalistic aspirations and Moscow's imperialistic and centralizing designs," as well as opposition to the brutally imposed collectivization of agriculture.[75] Yet Roosevelt did not see that letter or similar appeals; they were not part of the correspondence his aides selected for him.[76]

Having heard conflicting reports about conditions inside the USSR, Roosevelt focused mainly on Soviet external relations. He hoped that the establishment of diplomatic relations between the two enormous countries would help to deter aggression by Japan (which had invaded Manchuria in 1931) and Germany (led by Nazi Adolf Hitler after January 1933). Although Roosevelt typically avoided clear public statements about his private thinking, he seems to have had a farsighted notion of how the United States and the Soviet Union might become strategic partners.[77]

Statements by Litvinov and other Soviet leaders indicated that they, too, viewed mutual diplomatic recognition as most important for its relation to the preservation of world peace and the deterrence of aggressors. Cartoons in *Krokodil* also suggested to Soviet readers that the Japanese naval threat to the United States had been the prime stimulus of the US decision to recognize the Soviet Union.[78]

To reduce Catholic opposition to recognition of the atheist Soviet Union, FDR shrewdly invited Father Edmund Walsh, the most prominent Catholic anticommunist, to meet with him at the White House, and he secured from Foreign Minister Litvinov a pledge that Americans in the USSR would be able to worship freely.[79] To allay conservative fears of Soviet-financed subversion, Roosevelt extracted a pledge from Litvinov that the Soviet Union would not support revolutionary propaganda against the United States (though it did not specifically mention the Comintern). Finally, the two leaders agreed that future diplomatic negotiations would seek to resolve financial issues between the two countries, with the Soviet Union pledging to pay somewhere between $75 and $150 million in compensation for seized assets and repudiated debts. Thus, Roosevelt and Litvinov agreed to establish diplomatic relations on the foundation of some vague compromises and concessions that helped to make the agreements popular in both countries in the short term. Yet they also promoted some unrealistic expectations and created the potential for future bickering.[80]

On November 18, 1933, one day after Roosevelt announced the agreements, thousands of Ukrainian Americans who marched in New York and Chicago to protest Soviet atrocities in their homeland were attacked by

Communists seeking to break up the demonstrations. One month later, Communists and protesters clashed again. Although newspapers featured the protests on their front pages, the demonstrations did not slow the US move to open an embassy in Moscow.[81]

CONCLUSION

By the end of 1933, then, the Soviet leaders and their American well-wishers had finally achieved the long-sought goal of diplomatic relations with the United States. That achievement created a foundation for potential strategic cooperation that would be hugely important less than ten years later, when the two countries became military allies in the Second World War. Yet from the vantage of the twenty-first century, other developments in the 1921–1933 period seem equally important. Especially through the export of movies, tractors, and engineering expertise, Americans made crucial contributions to the forging of new Soviet personalities and the building of new Soviet industries. After being seen for years as the negation of American mainstream values, Soviet Russia came to be regarded more often as an inspiration for overcoming racism, an example of effective economic planning by government officials, and a model for an unselfish spirit of dedication to the public welfare. Thus, Americans and Soviets significantly shaped each other's societies, but the positive achievements would prove fragile as international turmoil worsened in the following years.

11

HOPES AND HORROR, 1934–1941

OVERVIEW

When excited US diplomats arrived in Moscow in December 1933 to open an embassy in Russia for the first time since 1918, many in the United States and the Soviet Union had high hopes for relations between the two huge countries. Soviet leaders, increasingly concerned about the danger of Japanese and German aggression, believed the establishment of diplomatic relations with the United States had great international significance. They eagerly sought a security pact with Washington and they expected to use American loans to expand their purchases of both military and consumer products. Top US leaders had vaguer aspirations for eventual strategic cooperation, but American diplomats had lofty ambitions for expanding US influence in the USSR, and some American business executives talked about dramatically raising trade so that the United States would again be the prime exporter to the Soviet Union.

The hopes soon gave way to disappointment, bitter accusations, and then a near rupture of relations. Although trade rose from the trough of 1931–1932, the modest growth in US exports did little to lift the American economy. The White House was unable to pursue a security agreement because of public and congressional aversion to foreign entanglements. American anticommunists charged that Moscow violated its promise to halt subversive agitation in the United States and portrayed Russia as still determined to incite revolution all around the world. After a lull in 1934, Soviet propagandists returned to harshly caricaturing American poverty, inequality, and joblessness, which were implicitly contrasted to the full employment and supposedly stronger economy in the USSR. When the Kremlin staged treason trials of former top Soviet leaders and shot many of them between 1936 and 1938, American conservatives spotlighted the differences between the savage Soviet purges and US law and order. Even many liberals who had supported cooperation with the USSR were horrified by how the bloody Soviet dictatorship seemed akin to fascist totalitarianism.

After the Soviet Union signed a non-aggression pact with Nazi Germany in 1939 and then seized eastern Poland, the Baltic states, and part of Finland, outraged Americans demanded the breaking of diplomatic relations with the USSR.

To many writers, the descent of Soviet–American relations from the honeymoon of 1933 to the horrors of the following years revealed the profound iniquity of Joseph Stalin and the essential evil of the Soviet system, which "was never a fit partner for the West," as diplomat and historian George F. Kennan put it.[1] From that perspective, it was naïve folly for Roosevelt to embrace the Soviet Union. The president should have recognized instead, one scholar argued, that "Stalin's regime was an abomination that had to be checked and ultimately changed."[2]

Such interpretations exaggerate Roosevelt's naïveté and disregard the complexity of the menacing international situation in the years before the Second World War. From 1933 to 1939, Soviet leaders genuinely sought to develop collective security arrangements with more peace-loving capitalist countries against fascist aggressors. However, British leaders, haunted by the specter of communist revolution and in some cases sympathetic to fascist ideology, tried to appease Germany and Italy instead.[3] Although Roosevelt's public speeches bowed to the dominant "isolationist" sentiment in the United States, privately he had a farsighted, realistic vision that Japanese and German expansionism made a new world war likely, that the United States probably would be drawn into the war, and that the Soviet Union could be a valuable partner against both aggressors. He therefore wisely set aside ideological differences with Soviet communism, refrained from overreacting to dismaying Soviet actions, and preserved a foundation for future cooperation even as many politicians and editors fulminated about Soviet duplicity and brutality.[4]

Although US–Soviet relations were not marked by major achievements between 1933 and 1941, the impressions produced in this era had deep and lasting impacts. The widespread American notion that the Soviet and Nazi dictatorships were twin totalitarianisms would strongly influence US attitudes and policies toward the Soviet Union in later decades.[5] On the other side, the long depression would influence Soviet leaders' expectations of a new depression in America after the Second World War. Despite the general postwar prosperity, images of American unemployment, hunger, and homelessness would continue to be featured prominently in Soviet propaganda until the late 1980s. Since the two nations' images of each other figured so importantly in their

definition of their identities, mutual representations in political cartoons, magazine covers, and movies will receive extended attention in
this chapter on the troubled era when the United States and USSR went
from potential partners to virtual enemies.

DELUSION AND DISCORD: US DIPLOMATS IN THE USSR

In December 1933, Soviet leaders honored William Christian Bullitt, the
newly arrived US ambassador, with a lush party in the Kremlin. After
drinking and eating for hours, Bullitt and Stalin sat down to talk. When
Stalin inquired whether there was "anything at all in the Soviet Union" that
Bullitt desired, the ambassador boldly asked for fifteen acres of prime land
on a hillside where he wanted to build an embassy that would resemble
Monticello, Thomas Jefferson's estate in Virginia. He would thus create
a highly visible symbol of American democracy. Stalin immediately agreed
to Bullitt's request and promised that Bullitt would be able to see him "any
time, day or night," as soon as he requested a meeting. Before parting, the
two men kissed.[6]

The night in the Kremlin went to the head of the ambassador, who
now believed that he and other Americans could have immense influence in the Soviet Union. Thinking that Soviet leaders desperately
needed close cooperation with the United States to ward off Japanese
aggression in the Far East, Bullitt (along with the State Department)
took a very hard line in negotiations over the terms for repayment of the
debts of the Provisional Government from 1917.[7] In November 1933,
Roosevelt and Litvinov had agreed that the Soviet Union would pay the
United States an amount between $75 and $150 million for "the
Kerensky debt" as a percentage above the ordinary rate of interest on
a "loan" to be granted by the US government or American bankers.[8]
Since the Bolsheviks opposed the Provisional Government's continuation of the war against the Central Powers that US loans financed,
and since Washington had used at least $50 million from the unex-
pended part of the loans to support anti-Bolshevik forces in the
Russian Civil War, Soviet leaders did not feel a moral responsibility for
the Kerensky debt. Stalin wanted to give Washington the minimum
necessary to secure a loan.[9] Litvinov pledged to Roosevelt that he
would recommend payment of $100 million. However, Bullitt insisted
that the Soviet Union could only have a more restricted "credit" toward
purchases in the United States and he demanded that Moscow repay

$15C million – the maximum in the range Roosevelt had discussed with Litvinov.

Having overplayed his hand, Bullitt quickly became embittered. When the negotiations stalled, Bullitt blamed "the slippery Jews" who dominated the Soviet Foreign Ministry.[10] Then, in the summer of 1935, he reacted very emotionally when American Communist leaders participated in a meeting of the Comintern in Moscow. Although the main purpose of the meeting was to announce a shift to a popular front policy that curtailed radicalism and prioritized cooperation with friendly capitalist states, Bullitt decried the alleged violation of Litvinov's 1933 promise not to promote revolutionary propaganda against America. Bullitt urged FDR to revoke the recognition of Soviet consuls in America, restrict visas granted to Russians, and publicly condemn Moscow. Although the president authorized a formal State Department protest, he rejected the punitive steps Bullitt proposed. In 1936, Bullitt resigned and became ambassador to France, where he continued to vent anti-Soviet sentiment, but had little impact on Roosevelt's thinking.

Loy Henderson, the second-ranking diplomat in the US embassy for much of the period from 1934 through 1938, shared Bullitt's anger about the Comintern and believed that Litvinov was dishonest in the debt negotiations.[11] While Henderson recognized by 1936 that the Kremlin was *not* pushing foreign communists to incite immediate revolution, he was still convinced that the Kremlin eventually planned to promote the overthrow of all capitalist governments. Only a complete change of the Soviet system and its ideology would bring an end to Soviet "interference in American internal affairs," he reported.[12]

Among the other diplomats in the embassy, George F. Kennan stood out. During his training as one of the State Department's first experts on Soviet Russia in the late 1920s, Kennan absorbed from Russian émigré tutors a romantic view of the high culture of Russia before the Bolshevik revolution. He also adopted the official Washington view in the era of non-recognition that the American and Soviet systems were inherently incompatible. In a private letter in January 1931, he explained that "there can be no possible middle ground or compromise between the two" systems and predicted that "within twenty or thirty years either Russia will be capitalist or we shall be communist." A year and a half later, when asked whether the Soviet people were content with their government, Kennan recognized the enthusiasm of young communists, but forecast that communism would falter – either by not keeping its promises of material abundance or by having consumerist pleasures sap ideological zeal. As a result of such disaffection, he anticipated, Russia could go overnight from being "the most morally unified country in the world" to having "the worst moral chaos."[13] Thus, before he ever set foot on Russian soil, Kennan had formed two views that would have lasting influence in his diplomatic career: a deep pessimism about the possibility of cooperation between the United States and the Soviet Union; and a fascination with the possible demise of Soviet communism.

As Bullitt's interpreter and a secretary in the US embassy in 1934, Kennan developed respect for the idealism of some Communist leaders, enjoyed a very lively social life, and savored the raw passion with which Russians lived – a bracing contrast to his own more fragile and neurotic spirit. Yet the assassination of the Leningrad leader Sergei Kirov near the end of 1934 marked the beginning of a series of purges, show trials, and mass executions that would shut down contacts between American diplomats and Soviet citizens. The Stalinist terror caused Kennan to feel an intense revulsion at the brutal Communist system that put him "at odds with official thinking in Washington for at least a decade thereafter."[14]

In later years, Bullitt and Kennan would be praised as realists who clearly saw the essential evil of the Stalinist system and as prophets who foresaw an inevitable Soviet–American clash.[15] Yet the record of their years in Moscow in the 1930s shows that the highly emotional and ideological men swung wildly from being infatuated with Soviet leaders to being intensely hostile to the Kremlin. As Kennan's close friend and fellow diplomat Charles Bohlen later recalled, Kennan always found it difficult to "divorce his visceral feelings from his knowledge of facts."[16] Both Kennan and Bullitt confused Soviet internal and external policies and lost sight of the important strategic and economic interests that the United States and the Soviet Union shared in a very dangerous world.

A MADMAN'S REALISM: STALIN AND SOVIET REPRESENTATIVES IN AMERICA

Joseph Stalin has often been viewed as a murderous madman. Between 1934 and 1939, he relentlessly pushed the Soviet secret police to hunt for spies, saboteurs, and subversives that he suspected were hidden in Soviet institutions and to execute hundreds of thousands of loyal Soviet citizens. The mass arrests and executions decimated the Communist Party leadership, the Soviet foreign intelligence services, the USSR's diplomatic corps, and the generals of the Red Army on the eve of the outbreak of the Second World War. Surely, many have thought, such a psychotic tyrant cannot have been capable of directing an intelligent and rational foreign policy.[17]

Yet, in these same years, Stalin's international vision was typically clear, his forecasts about the future often proved correct, and his foreign policy decisions were generally cautious responses to the security predicaments the Soviet Union faced. Throughout the 1930s, Stalin repeatedly warned that a new world war was approaching, and he ordered massive investment in heavy industry and the military so that the USSR would be able to beat back foreign invaders. Japan posed the most immediate threat to Soviet borders, with clashes between the two countries' armed forces in 1937 and 1938. But Stalin also worried about threats from Romania, Poland, and especially rapidly rearming Nazi Germany, which became the main enemy identified in Soviet war plans in 1935. Fearing above all a united anti-Soviet coalition of imperialist powers, Stalin approved Foreign Minister Litvinov's efforts to enhance Soviet security by securing recognition from the United States (which Stalin felt had "the most serious significance"), by entering the League of Nations in 1934, and by negotiating mutual assistance agreements with capitalist countries – a course celebrated by the Soviet press.[18]

As the Soviet Union faced dangers both in the east and in the west, the United States seemed a rare friend. The numerous intelligence reports that Stalin read alerted him to real, exaggerated, and imaginary plots by Japanese, Polish, German, British, and French spies and saboteurs, but rarely identified American suspects.[19] After Soviet talks with Roosevelt and Bullitt in late 1933 and early 1934 made it clear that the United States would not agree to a security pact against Japan, Stalin and his aides reduced their expectations, sought to tamp down American fears of communist subversion, and focused on acquiring American machinery that would improve Soviet living standards and defense capabilities. In 1936, Stalin dispatched trade commissar Anastas Mikoyan to the United States to study the food industry and purchase related machines. During the following years, Stalin and the Politburo repeatedly approved major purchases of American products, including airplanes, naval artillery, automobiles, tanks, and warships. Thanks to such purchases, by 1938 the United States became the leading exporter to the Soviet Union (with a total value of $70 million).[20] Thus, although Communist ideology shaped the wider worldviews of Soviet leaders,[21] it had virtually no influence on Stalin's policy toward the United States, which centered consistently on Soviet economic and strategic interests.

Contrary to assertions that Stalin lost interest in relations with the United States after 1934,[22] Stalin closely monitored Soviet purchasing commissions in America through the end of the decade. Moreover, he read reports specially prepared for him by the Soviet embassy in Washington on political developments in the United States, including a public campaign in defense of Stalin's exiled rival Trotsky.[23]

The Soviet ambassador to Washington from 1934 to 1938, Alexander Troyanovsky, was less volatile and more effective than Bullitt. Having served as the Soviet envoy to Japan before coming to America, Troyanovsky had a keen awareness of the potential value of Soviet–American cooperation against aggressor nations that he regularly expressed in public speeches in the United States.[24] American "isolationism" – reflected in a series of Neutrality Acts passed by Congress and in strong public sentiment against involvement in a new war in Europe – did not alter his belief. In a report to Litvinov on the eve of the US presidential election in the fall of 1936, for example, Troyanovsky held that the foreign policy orientation of the United States was "extremely important" and that, even if it avoided being drawn into war, its support for one side could have a decisive impact on the outcome. Troyanovsky therefore argued that the Soviet Union needed to cultivate friendly relations with the United States to encourage the Americans to be on the side of the USSR if war came.[25]

In pursuit of that objective, Troyanovsky met with a wide variety of Americans – politicians, journalists, businessmen, doctors, engineers, and farmers more than workers. As a former officer in Imperial Russia who conducted himself with dignity and charm, Troyanovsky was popular in America. When the confrontation between Stalin and Trotsky reached a peak between 1936 and 1938, Troyanovsky worked hard to counter the influence of American sympathizers with Trotsky. Although there were fewer than 1,000 Trotskyists, Troyanovsky worried for a time about the influence of those intellectuals through the larger Socialist Party and the left-wing press. By 1938, he claimed to have peeled away some prominent supporters of Trotsky, and he reported that their influence had waned.[26] The Soviet government also sought to influence American public opinion by approving visits to the USSR by figures who were regarded as sympathetic (such as United Mine Workers leader John L. Lewis) and rejecting requests for interviews with Stalin by Americans who were viewed unfavorably.[27] Thus, top Soviet leaders and diplomats saw relations with the United States as not merely a matter of interacting with Washington policymakers and powerful businessmen, but also as involving significant efforts to reach and influence American public opinion.

MODEL OR MENACE? US PUBLIC VIEWS
OF THE USSR, 1933–1936

As the United States struggled through the depression and the world drifted toward a new war, Americans diverged sharply in their views of the Soviet Union. Their conflicting attitudes can be associated with three main groups: conservative anticommunists, liberal anticommunists, and Communists and their sympathizers. The ways members of these groups thought about change inside the United States significantly influenced how they saw the USSR.

Alarmed by how New Deal reforms and rising labor militancy challenged their interests and values, conservative anticommunists vehemently attacked the infiltration of communism across America, especially in unions, universities, and government bureaucracies. Editors of conservative newspapers claimed that "Communism in the guise of liberalism" was advancing rapidly, with government advisors trying to remake America according to a "dangerous foreign pattern."[28] Such conservatives, especially the press magnates William Randolph Hearst and Robert McCormick, depicted both the New Deal and communism as opposed to "real Americanism" and envisioned Moscow as the ultimate source of the socialist menace to "the American Way."[29] Striving to prevent the re-election of FDR in 1936, Hearst charged that the "Bolshevist tyranny in Russia has ordered all its Bolshevists, Communists, and revolutionists in the United States to support Mr. Roosevelt."[30] McCormick's *Chicago Tribune* similarly alleged that the Comintern had ordered US Reds to stop Roosevelt's Republican opponent, Alf Landon.[31] (While Comintern leaders did want to back FDR, the head of the US Communist Party persuaded them that endorsing the president would be counterproductive, and he criticized Roosevelt in his own campaign.[32]) After Roosevelt won a landslide victory, the Hearst press railed less often about the New Deal and communism, but the *Chicago Tribune* continued to impugn both Roosevelt's domestic policies and his foreign policy as Red-inspired.

While liberal anticommunists supported the New Deal, they agreed with conservatives that Soviet communism was antithetical to American individualism and democracy. Influential liberals such as the columnist Walter Lippmann and the philosopher John Dewey argued that collectivism and totalitarianism threatened traditional liberal values, whether they emanated from the communist left or the fascist right.[33]

Yet, in the troubled 1930s, when the persistent depression seemed to have discredited capitalism and fascist militarism posed the greatest threat of a new world war, other liberals persisted in seeing the Soviet Union as a positive model of economic progress. To left-leaning liberals like the editors of *The Nation* and *The New Republic*, economic advances were more important than political liberties, and, at least in less developed countries like Russia, dictatorship appeared a necessary means to positive ends. Non-communists such as the Methodist minister Harry F. Ward therefore remained sympathetic to the Soviet Union even as its repressiveness became more glaring.[34]

Communists, of course, viewed the Soviet Union with even more enthusiasm, and their numbers increased dramatically across the decade. Membership in the Communist Party of the United States (CPUSA) rose from 19,000 when Roosevelt became President to more than 70,000 on the eve of the Second World War. Many Jewish Americans who saw the Soviet Union as the most powerful antifascist force in the world were drawn to the Communist Party. By 1936, a majority of its members were American-born for the first time. Under the leadership of Kansas-born Earl Browder, the CPUSA adopted the slogan "Communism Is Twentieth-Century Americanism" and prominently displayed American flags at its rallies. Despite the small size of the CPUSA, its disciplined, energetic members exerted a disproportionate influence on American attitudes toward the Soviet Union – both by promoting sympathy for its policies and by provoking negative reactions to their fealty to Moscow.[35]

AMERICAN REACTIONS TO THE SOVIET SHOW TRIALS, 1936–1938

Nothing riveted American attention on the Soviet Union more than the sensational trials of top Communist officials and Red Army officers in August 1936, January 1937, June 1937, and March 1938. The Old Bolshevik leaders and Soviet generals were accused of participating in conspiracies with the exiled Trotsky and foreign powers to assassinate Stalin and overthrow the Soviet government. There was a particle of truth in some of the accusations: in the early 1930s, a number of high officials had become critical of Stalin's policies of collectivization of agriculture and forced-pace industrialization, with some secretly discussing the removal of Stalin. Yet most of the accusations were groundless, and the confessions presented in court were extracted through torture or threats.[36]

Especially at the outset of the show trials in 1936, many Americans believed the defendants were guilty. On the right, especially, antipathy to Trotsky as a fervent champion of world revolution spurred acceptance of the accusations that he and his followers inside the Soviet Union had plotted against Stalin. Thus, the *Chicago Tribune*, a Republican paper, imagined that the "plot to do away with Stalin" was an effort to forestall the adoption of a new constitution that "would dispose of the worst rigors of the Bolshevik system and lay the foundations of a more democratic system."[37] Democratic papers were divided over the trials, with some believing Trotsky's assertion that the confessions were forced, while others found it probable that Trotsky, the "disciple of unrest," had schemed to promote an uprising against Stalin.[38]

Given the uncertainty of the information available at the time, what is most striking about the early reactions on both sides is the way they reflected a recurring penchant for projecting American hopes and prejudices onto the Soviet screen. In response to the trials, many editors made categorical judgments that emphasized differences between Russia and the West. Both liberal and conservative papers declared that the trials revealed how Russians were "Asiatic" or "Oriental": "Oriental fatalism" led to the abject confessions; the trials were "inexplicable except as examples of Oriental tyranny and cruelty"; Stalin's yearning for vengeance stemmed from his being "an Asiatic."[39] Editors also repeatedly cited the show trials to affirm the superiority of American institutions and values. The *Philadelphia Inquirer*, for example, highlighted how the trials accentuated "the contrast between the dictated slavery of Russian Communism and the freedom of American democracy."[40]

Anti-Stalinist intellectuals such as Max Eastman and John Dewey generally argued that the charges at the trials were cynical inventions by a bloody despot and that the Soviet terror resembled an earlier purge among Nazis in Germany.[41] That line of thinking contributed to a widespread tendency among Americans to equate "Red Fascism" and "Brown Bolshevism," to see them as "twin totalitarianisms."[42] On the other hand, intellectuals such as political scientist Frederick Schuman, who prioritized the maintenance of an antifascist Popular Front, with the Soviet Union the spearhead of collective security against fascist aggressors, tended to conclude that Trotsky and the defendants were guilty.[43] The debate over the show trials generated a ferocious controversy that led to the severing of old friendships and connections.

The trials in Moscow also sparked intense friction between career diplomats and the wealthy lawyer Joseph E. Davies, a loyal Democrat whom Roosevelt sent to replace Bullitt in January 1937. Appalled by what they saw as Davies' credulousness about the cynical charges of conspiracies, Kennan and other diplomats scorned Davies as hopelessly ignorant and naïve. Yet, as Davies' private correspondence showed, he was actually not so obtuse. In April 1938, for example, he reported to Washington that the "alleged trials" were "not trials at all," called the Terror "horrifying," and depicted the communist regime as "a terrible tyranny." His efforts to maintain a public appearance of cordial relations between Washington and Moscow were in line with the wishes of Roosevelt, who asked him to focus on assessing the political, economic, and military power of the USSR. In contrast to many European and American anticommunists, Davies emphasized that the Soviet Union was spending vast sums – around a quarter of national revenue – on preparation for war and that, despite the negative impact of the slaughter of top Red Army officers, the country's vast size and resources would make it a formidable force. Davies continued to promote that opinion after leaving Moscow in June 1938 to become ambassador to Belgium. During the Second World War his judgment would be vindicated as more accurate than the views of those who underestimated Soviet resilience.[44]

HEROISM AND BETRAYAL: THE SPANISH CIVIL WAR, 1936–1939

In the same years when the show trials fascinated and appalled Americans, both Soviet and American newspapers were filled with gripping stories of civil war and foreign intervention in Spain. The conflict from the summer of 1936 to March 1939 pitted right-wing military rebels, wealthy landowners, and the Catholic clergy, supported by fascist Italy and Germany, against the left-leaning Spanish Republic, aided by sympathizers from many foreign nations but by only one state, the Soviet Union. The Soviet press immediately dramatized the menace of fascism and called for donations of food and medicine to the Republic.[45] Stalin at first refrained from military intervention that would alienate Britain and France, potential partners in collective security against the fascist powers. However, after Italy and Germany sent guns, planes, and troops to help the Nationalist forces under General Francisco Franco, and Britain and France did nothing to thwart the fascist intervention, Stalin decided at the end of August 1936 to begin massive covert shipments of arms to prevent the fall of the Republic.[46] The United States, on the other hand, joined the British and French in an arms embargo aga_nst both sides in the civil war that hurt the democratic government mo_e than it did the abundantly armed fascist rebels.[47]

Seeking to sustain a broad Popular Front coalition, the CPUSA, the Comintern, and the Kremlin discouraged and suppressed radicalism. Stalin urg=d the Spanish government not to nationalize the property of foreigners or middle-class Spaniards. CPUSA leader Earl Browder named a contingent of American volunteers the Abraham Lincoln Brigade in order to emphasize tha_ the goal was to defend the republic, not to launch a socialist revolution. Soviet security agents killed many anti-Stalinist revolutionaries.[48]

Nonetheless, alarmed American conservatives claimed that Russia was promoting communist revolution in Spain and that a Red Spain would lead

Figure 11.1 "Beginning to Bear Fruit." © *Chicago Tribune*, August 12, 1936. Licensed by Tribune Content Agency.

to a Red Latin America, perhaps even communist revolution in the United States. (See Figure 11.1.) Seeing Spain as one front in a global struggle against radicalism, many American anticommunists sympathized with Franco and the fascists. Some raised relief funds for the Nationalists. The head of Texaco, an admirer of Hitler, provided much more important aid: he shipped oil on credit to fuel the fascist armies, while refusing to honor his company's contract with the Republic's oil company.[49]

On the other side of the American political spectrum, left-leaning liberals and Communists saw the Spanish Civil War as a crucial test of resistance to fascist aggression and viewed the Soviet Union as heroic for being the only country that provided effective aid to the Republic. Almost 3,000 Americans traveled to Spain to fight in the international brigades that helped defend the Republic. Roughly 70 percent of them were Communists. At least a third were Jewish. While anticommunist writers derided them as pawns in the cynical global maneuvers of the Kremlin, the volunteers were courageous idealists. Spearheading offensives by Republic forces, several hundred of the Americans were killed. After fascist advances split the Republic's territory in 1938, members of the Abraham Lincoln Brigade left Spain, but most continued to believe passionately in the antifascist cause.[50]

Memories and stories of the Spanish Civil War have had pronounced political and ideological meaning ever since the fascist victory in March 1939. Anticommunist writers have argued that the Soviet restraint of a social revolution damaged authentic popular antifascist enthusiasm. Combined with the Soviet taking of Spain's gold supply as payment for arms shipments, that allegedly meant the USSR "betrayed" Spain.[51] That perspective is unrealistic. The defense of the Republic against modern German and Italian warplanes required equivalent military equipment, not merely mass enthusiasm. Pursuit of an immediate social revolution in Spain, including the confiscation of foreign property, would have made the acquisition of advanced aircraft and other arms from capitalist countries, including the United States, even more difficult. Since the Soviet Union was straining to pay for its own armaments and for anti-Japanese forces in China, it is unreasonable to think that it could have altruistically given its best aircraft and tanks to Spain. In 1938, FDR belatedly and surreptitiously tried to assist the Republic by allowing the confidential purchase of American aircraft that could be shipped through France, but he did not offer to donate the planes. It is therefore unfair to single out the Soviet Union as uniquely "duplicitous" or to hold the USSR to a lofty standard of unselfishness that no other state met.[52] Even in late 1938, when the Republic's situation was desperate, the

Soviet Union sold enormous amounts of war matériel to Spain, some on credit. The worse betrayal of Spain was by its fellow democracies, which were dedicated to appeasing the fascist aggressors or were paralyzed by anti-communist and "isolationist" public sentiment.

RED SPIES AND THE AMERICAN COUNTERSUBVERSIVE IMAGINATION

During the New Deal, conservative anticommunists in America often asserted that the Roosevelt administration had been penetrated by a vast, sinister network of communist agents who passed to their Soviet handlers enormous troves of important secrets and gained control of government agencies that were turning American capitalism toward Soviet-style socialism. Elizabeth Dilling's book *The Red Network* (1934) was an extreme example of the broader countersubversive nightmare.[53] Since then, the charges about enormous and effective espionage operations by disloyal Americans have been made in subtler and more sophisticated ways.[54] Such accusations sometimes obscured how Americans who agreed to spy for the Soviet Union in the interwar era typically did so for idealistic reasons, usually did not believe that their actions were harming the United States, and generally failed to provide much valuable confidential information. Although Elizabeth Bentley, the lover of Soviet spymaster Jacob Golos, was a non-ideological opportunist, the American contacts she handled generally were idealists who were not motivated by financial rewards.[55]

Cy (Isaiah) Oggins, the son of Russian Jewish immigrants, was, as his biographer wrote, "a man of astonishing faith and innocence," who "imagined himself an American Robin Hood among the Bolsheviks." As a student at Columbia University, Oggins was radicalized by seeing the repression of the Red Scare. He joined the Workers Party of America in 1924, began working for the Comintern later in the 1920s, and then served the Soviet intelligence organization OGPU in China and Europe, which were much more important targets than the United States in the 1930s. Oggins was arrested in Moscow in February 1939 as an alleged Trotskyite, imprisoned, and finally killed in 1947.[56]

Harry Gold, the son of Jewish immigrants from Ukraine, faced anti-Semitic insults and bullying growing up in Philadelphia, lost faith in American capitalism during the Great Depression, and came to view the Soviet Union as the staunchest opponent of fascism. As a socialist who wanted to help the Russian people to live better, Gold agreed to obtain secrets about mundane chemical processes in factories where he worked and convey them to his Soviet handlers, starting in 1935. (During the Second World War, he would play a much more important role as a courier for atomic secrets.[57])

Harry Dexter White, whose Jewish parents fled pogroms in Lithuania and came to America in 1885, became an economist and a key adviser to Secretary of the Treasury Henry Morgenthau. Although he was not a Marxist and did not believe in communism as a political ideology, he had a strong interest in the Soviet planning system and he felt that strategic cooperation with the Soviet Union was important. From 1935 to 1938, White provided documents about routine Treasury Department discussions to his handler, Whittaker Chambers, but he was more enthusiastic about writing memoranda to guide Soviet monetary policy. Colonel Boris Bykov of Soviet military intelligence (GRU) complained that White was the least productive of Chambers' sources.[58]

Chambers, a Columbia graduate with a yearning for an all-embracing faith, became a Communist in 1925 and by the early 1930s was attempting to gather intelligence for the GRU. However, Chambers' most ambitious schemes, such as trying to photograph blueprints for new submarines, all failed. His superior, Bykov, repeatedly objected that the information gathered was worthless or at best second-rate. In 1938, disillusioned by the violent Soviet purges, Chambers broke with the GRU and communism.[59]

Soviet espionage in America in the 1930s did yield some valuable information that would have been expensive or impossible to purchase, for example about industrial solvents and a formula for making a steel alloy. Yet, during the decade, Soviet representatives probably gained much more information through open visits to manufacturing plants from which they were making purchases. A thorough investigation by the FBI in 1941 found that there had been very little successful espionage.[60] Notions about diabolically clever and pervasive Soviet spying in America thus have been overblown.

ROADS TO WAR, 1936–1941

In the late 1930s, the threat of a new world war loomed ever more ominously. Japan greatly expanded its atrocious war in China in the summer of 1937, then launched probing attacks on Soviet positions in the Far East from its puppet state in Manchuria. Germany reoccupied the Rhineland in 1936, then invaded and annexed Austria in March 1938. Britain and France did nothing. Six months later, British and French leaders accepted Adolf

Hitler's demands for the Sudetenland in Czechoslovakia at the Munich Conference, from which the USSR was excluded. The appeasement failed to satiate German expansionism, and in March 1939 Nazi forces occupied the rest of the Czech lands, with Slovakia established as a German satellite state. Japanese and German aggression posed more and more urgently the question of whether the United States and the Soviet Union could cooperate in the Pacific and European theaters.

Roosevelt strongly approved of the Soviet Union's desire to purchase warships built in the United States, first expressed in the fall of 1936. New Soviet ships based at Vladivostok might deter a Japanese attack. However, the Navy Department viewed the USSR as a potential enemy, and it stubbornly resisted the idea, even threatening American companies with the loss of Navy contracts if they built ships for the Soviets. In June 1938, FDR finally overcame the foot-dragging and secured Navy approval for the construction of a Soviet battleship, but by then American shipyards were fully committed to fulfilling the Navy's orders for itself. Although Roosevelt failed to provide vigorous leadership in this, as in other cases, the episode reflected his persistent interest in developing a tacit strategic partnership with the Soviet Union.[61]

Despite Stalin's justified suspicions that British and French leaders hoped to turn Nazi aggression against the Soviet Union, in April 1939 he offered Britain and France a formal, unequivocal alliance against Nazi Germany.[62] However, they evaded giving direct answers, and negotiations dragged on for months. Joseph Davies starkly warned FDR that, if the USSR did not get a firm alliance with the hesitant British and French, it would "get a nonaggression pact with Hitler."[63] Roosevelt was therefore saddened but not shocked when, in August 1939, Stalin finally agreed to a nonaggression pact with Hitler that ensured Soviet security at least for a time. It also secured access to German manufactured goods, allowed the USSR to expand in 1939–1940 at the expense of Finland, the Baltic states, and Romania, and permitted the USSR to incorporate lands in eastern Poland after Germany invaded that country on September 1, 1939.[64]

FDR grew angrier in the following months. In November, after Finnish leaders resisted Soviet demands to move the border between the two countries further from Leningrad, the Red Army attacked. While the overmatched but determined Finns fought back, Washington announced a moral embargo on the export of war matériel to the USSR, and Roosevelt denounced the Soviet Union as a dictatorship "as absolute as any other dictatorship in the world."[65] Outraged by Soviet conduct, many Americans urged the expulsion of Soviet ambassador Konstantin Oumansky, who replaced Troyanovsky in

June 1939. They also demanded the withdrawal of Davies' replacement, Laurence Steinhardt, from Moscow.[66] But FDR still declined to break diplomatic relations. After Stalin refrained from a military occupation of Finland and concluded a treaty that ended the war in March 1940, Roosevelt's diplomatic aide Sumner Welles started negotiations with Oumansky to explore possibilities for luring the Soviet Union away from the embrace of Nazi Germany. Although the United States refused to accept the Soviet annexation of the Baltic states in the summer of 1940, Roosevelt and Welles emphasized the mutual American and Soviet interest on the other side of Eurasia, where both nations sought to contain Japan and aid China. In January 1941, as tensions with Japan and Germany mounted, Washington lifted the embargo on sales to the USSR.[67]

The Roosevelt administration's pragmatic policies made it vulnerable to attacks. The *Chicago Tribune*, for example, insinuated that the president's military build-up in order to present a "challenge to Hitler" had been "made in Moscow."[68] To many conservative anticommunists, Hitler and Mussolini were lesser dangers than Stalin and Soviet communism. That perspective and the more widely shared view that communism and fascism were equally repugnant significantly constrained the Roosevelt administration as it sought to keep open the possibility of a Soviet–American strategic alignment.

INSPIRATION, VILIFICATION, AND SEDUCTION: IMAGES OF THE OTHER

In contrast to the contestation in America, Soviet media unanimously followed the Kremlin line. After the Roosevelt–Litvinov agreements, Soviet cartoonists abruptly stopped drawing negative caricatures of America for a year. During the second half of the 1930s, they never depicted the United States as an enemy or a threat. Even when *Krokodil* marked the twentieth anniversary of the October Revolution by pictorially reminding its readers of how Soviet Russia had faced foreign interventionists all around its periphery during the Civil War, Uncle Sam was not among the depicted invaders (Britain, Japan, and Poland).[69]

One of the most influential Soviet depictions of America ever published presented both high praise and stinging criticism. After traveling across the United States by car in 1935, Ilya Ilf and Evgeny Petrov portrayed Americans as energetic, friendly, helpful, and hard-working in a series of articles and a widely read book. Like Esenin, Mayakovsky, and Pilniak earlier, Ilf and Petrov admired America's advanced technology. For instance, they glowed about the astonishing Golden Gate Bridge at San Francisco. On the other hand, the two correspondents characterized Americans as incurious and unthinking, complained about obnoxious advertising, and derided Hollywood movies as tasteless and stupid – vastly inferior to uplifting Soviet films.[70] As Lisa Kirschenbaum has shown in a meticulous analysis, their extravagant criticism of "idiotic" and "fascist" Hollywood films concealed their respect for the technical quality of the productions and their contented writing of a screenplay while in sunny California, yet Soviet critics still felt their work underplayed the failures of American capitalism.[71]

Claims about the superiority of the Soviet Union's culture and way of life were the most important role for images of America. Crime, hunger, and unemployment figured most frequently in Soviet cartoonists' images of America, sometimes accompanied by explicit assertions that those problems were absent or banned in the Soviet Union.[72] More impudently, *Krokodil* echoed a statement by Stalin and implicitly claimed that Soviet elections were better than elections in America (where politicians betrayed those who voted for them).[73]

After the Nazi–Soviet Pact in August 1939, when the Soviet Union became a tacit ally of Germany and the United States indirectly supported Britain and France against Nazi aggression, Soviet representations of America became more starkly negative. Cartoonists regularly vilified the heartless greed of American capitalists and the rapacity of American imperialism, which, they suggested, were leading to clashes with Britain and Japan.[74] Although Stalin and his aides had eagerly made massive purchases of American arms, Soviet cartoonists now had the gall to repeatedly attack American weapons sales as betraying US pretensions to be a liberty-loving and humane society.[75] (See Figure 11.2.) Perhaps most important was that Soviet artists expressed increased confidence that the young socialist Soviet Union would catch and surpass the aged capitalist United States.[76]

While Soviet writers, filmmakers, and cartoonists followed the turns of Kremlin policy, their counterparts in the United States painted much more varied images of the Soviet Union. At one extreme, some African Americans, such as the writer Langston Hughes and the actor and singer Paul Robeson, depicted the Soviet Union as an inspiring example of a nation freed from racism. At the other pole, liberal and conservative anticommunists portrayed the bloodstained Soviet dictatorship as the antithesis of American liberty and democracy.

Although many African Americans were disillusioned by the Soviet sale of oil to Italy after Mussolini attacked Ethiopia in 1935, prominent journalists, writers, and actors persisted in their admiration of the Soviet Union's

Figure 11.2 "American Enterprise." *Krokodil*, No. 31, 1939. The sign above the torch reads: "The best weapons in the world." Courtesy of *Novaia Gazeta.*

commitment to racial equality.[77] In the mid-1930s African American newspapers repeatedly printed stories and photographs of Blacks who were treated as equals and had successful careers in the Soviet Union, thereby using images of life in the USSR to give Blacks in the United States hope that they could one day be free from racial prejudice and discrimination.[78] Militant sharecroppers and labor organizers in Alabama gained inspiration and confidence from fancifully envisioning Russians as "new Yankees" and Stalin as a "new Lincoln" who would aid them in their struggles.[79] As late as July 1939, a cartoonist for one of the leading African American newspapers, *The Chicago Defender*, contrasted lynching in the United States, which made a mockery of its claim to be a democracy, to the Soviet Union's commitment to racial emancipation, which made it a true democracy.[80]

While cartoonists significantly influenced American and Soviet political imaginations, films reached even wider audiences. By far the most important depiction of America in a Soviet film in the 1930s was in the extremely popular *Circus* (1936). The plot centered on a white woman who fled a Kansas mob with her Black baby and found safety, acceptance, and love in the Soviet Union. Although, in general, Soviet indictments of American racism became less frequent and vehement after 1933, *Circus* illustrated how America continued to be used as a foil for claims that racial hatred had been transcended in the loving Soviet family of nations.[81]

The most striking theme in American movies about the Soviet Union in the pre-war era was consumerist seduction as an antidote to communist revolution. In *Ninotchka*, released in the fall of 1939, a highly disciplined, self-sacrificing Soviet trade official travels to Paris, where she succumbs to frivolous fashion, champagne, and the sparkle of a capitalist city. The comedy won rave reviews from critics, who loved the impious ribbing of the USSR.[82] In *Comrade X*, screened the following year, a pretty trolley driver in Moscow who initially spouts propaganda about millions of unemployed Americans is won over by a handsome American reporter who explains that revolution is impossible in a country where people enjoy the pleasures of baseball, hot dogs, and boogie-woogie. Critics' enjoyment of the "spoofing of Soviet Russia's philosophy of life, love, and government" and the "digs at ways other than our democratic freedom" reflected the ideological significance of the celluloid concoction.[83] Both movies ended with the attractive Soviet women escaping from the grim, gray life in the USSR and joining their foreign lovers abroad – a scenario that foreshadowed later American dreams of liberating Soviets from communism.

Notions about the seductive appeal of capitalist consumer goods were disseminated not only by Hollywood scriptwriters, but also by American academics. In November 1939, for example, Arthur May, a professor of history at the University of Rochester who had visited the USSR the previous summer, emphasized to hundreds of members of a club the contrast between the ignorant anti-capitalist ideas of his official guides and the longing of ordinary Russians for jazz and American lipsticks.[84] Many Russians did indeed yearn for such commodities, and Soviet officials sought to provide champagne, ketchup, and other symbols of the coming of plenty after years of hardship.[85] Yet, as the reception of *Ninotchka* and *Comrade X* showed, many Americans found in stories of Russian commodity cravings the comforting illusions that Soviet communism no longer offered a viable alternative to capitalism and that it might soon be displaced by, rather than synthesized with, consumerism.

CONCLUSION

The story of American–Soviet interaction in the first seven years after the establishment of diplomatic relations has often been presented as a tale of how a trusting America was deceived by the false promises of cynical Soviet leaders and how naïve, pro-Soviet US leaders failed to confront the depravity of the Stalinist system. Others have portrayed the inability to fulfill the initial hopes for economic and strategic cooperation as an inevitable result of the inherent conflict between liberal democracies and immoral Soviet totalitarianism. This chapter presented a more complicated and contingent narrative. Roosevelt's and Stalin's genuine and pragmatic pursuit of cooperation was hampered by William Bullitt's intemperate diplomacy and by the Navy's persistent obstruction of shipbuilding for the USSR. The tensions that followed the brief honeymoon in the winter of 1933–1934 were also inflamed by conservative Americans' exaggeration of communist threats, the shocking descent of the Soviet Union into the Great Terror of 1936–1938, and each country's use of negative images of the other to affirm its own superiority. Despite those sources of enmity, the United States and the Soviet Union avoided a complete rupture in relations and preserved the possibility of partnership as they neared involvement in the Second World War.

12

ALLIES, 1941–1945

OVERVIEW

On June 22, 1941, German armies smashed into the Soviet Union across an enormous front, igniting the largest and bloodiest war in human history. In response, British Prime Minister Winston Churchill, whose empire had been at war with Nazi Germany since September 1939, set aside his ardent, long-held anticommunism and immediately proclaimed British support for the Soviet Union. Kremlin dictator Joseph Stalin also rapidly and pragmatically reoriented the Soviet line from attacking the imperialism of Britain and America to hailing those countries as allies against fascist aggression. Despite predictions by US military experts that Germany would crush the Red Army within six weeks, President Franklin Roosevelt ordered an urgent effort to deliver military supplies to the Soviet Union. In October, as Soviet forces desperately defended Moscow against being captured, Roosevelt defeated congressional efforts to bar Lend–Lease assistance to the USSR. Two months later, after Japan attacked Pearl Harbor and Germany declared war on the United States, America and the Soviet Union became formal allies.

During the next three and a half years, the United States provided more than $11 billion worth of Lend–Lease aid to the USSR that greatly assisted Soviet forces as they did most of the work of defeating Nazi Germany. Despite mutual suspicions and fears that their partners might conclude a separate peace with Germany, the Soviet–British–American alliance held together through the final defeat of Germany in the spring of 1945. The alliance thereby demonstrated that differences in ideologies, values, and political systems did not prevent effective cooperation.

Ever since 1945, the Grand Alliance has sparked conflicting interpretations. To some Americans, the wartime partnership showed again what had been evident during the nineteenth century and the First World War: that, on the most important international issues, American and Russian interests converged rather than conflicted.[1] More commonly in the United States, the strange alliance between Christian, capitalist, democratic America and atheist, communist, totalitarian Russia has been viewed as at best a regrettably necessary temporary arrangement – one that should never have been celebrated and that inevitably gave way to renewed antipathy once the German threat was eliminated.[2] In contrast, to many Soviet citizens, as well as to many Russians in the early twenty-first century, the successful alliance showed the possibility of cooperation with the West on terms that recognized Soviet/Russian vital interests and accepted the USSR/Russia as a leading force in the world.[3]

Controversy has continued also over the allies' relative contributions to the victory. In the Soviet Union and in post-Soviet Russia, the idea that the USSR at terrible cost saved the world from Nazism has been central to the affirmation of exceptionalist national identities: while all the other nations Germany invaded were conquered, only the Soviet people were able to withstand the fascist onslaught.[4] In the West, on the other hand, many have complained that the Soviets ungratefully discounted Allied contributions to the defeat of fascism.[5] One author has gone so far as to argue that British and American air and sea power, not the Red Army's destruction of German armies, played the decisive role.[6] Straining to counter Soviet statements that minimized the importance of Lend–Lease aid, some Americans have sought to inflate the significance of that assistance.[7] More balanced assessments, in contrast, have concluded that the limited Western aid in 1941–1942 was not crucial to Soviet survival, though it boosted Soviet morale, and the greatly expanded deliveries in 1943–1944 significantly improved Red Army mobility and communications, thereby speeding the defeat of Germany.[8]

Often American politicians, journalists, and historians have gone beyond downplaying to actually forgetting the Soviet role in the defeat of Germany: they have claimed that the victory in the Second World War was a triumph of the democracies and commemorated the June 1944 cross-channel invasion of Nazi-occupied France as the climactic battle of the war – even though it came long after the key Soviet victories at Stalingrad and Kursk in 1943.[9] Thus, in America, as in the Soviet Union and post-Soviet Russia, stories about the Second World War have been so bound up with nationalist mythmaking that they have tended to obscure the real historical experience of the Grand Alliance by the American and Soviet peoples.

While presenting a concise narrative of American–Soviet political and diplomatic relations during the Second World War, this chapter focuses above all on the conflicting stories Americans and Soviets told about the war and the complex meanings they found in a partnership marked by suspicion, gratitude, anger, and admiration. As Americans and Soviets imagined and described each other, they affirmed or redefined their own identities. That storytelling and identity construction has continued for decades since the war, making it arguably the most important legacy of the wartime alliance.

STALIN, ROOSEVELT, AND WARTIME DIPLOMACY

Eleven days after German armies attacked the Soviet Union, on July 3, 1941, Joseph Stalin addressed the Soviet peoples by radio to explain why the Red Army had retreated from many western districts, to inspire Soviet citizens to fight in defense of their native land, and to encourage his "brothers and sisters" to be confident of victory in their "war of liberation." They would not be fighting alone against the Nazi war machine, he assured them: he repeatedly emphasized that they would have "loyal allies in the peoples of Europe and America" as part of "a united front of peoples standing for freedom and against enslavement." The readiness of Britain and the United States to aid the USSR, he added, "can only evoke a feeling of gratitude in the hearts of the people of the Soviet Union."[10]

Stalin's speech initiated a major ideological shift. Less than three months earlier he had approved a Comintern directive that ordered Communist parties around the world to blame the Second World War on "the national bourgeoisie" and praised the struggle against the "imperialist war" in England and the United States.[11] Yet now he launched a dramatic reinterpretation of the war that downplayed communist ideology and cast Britain and America as valuable allies in the struggle of the freedom-loving peoples against the fascist aggressors.

Contrary to assertions that Soviet propaganda insistently sought to hide or denigrate the contributions of Western nations and that Soviet elites never expressed gratitude to their American allies,[12] numerous Soviet propaganda posters, magazine covers, and political cartoons acclaimed the American–British–Soviet alliance and featured images of American and British flags and soldiers.[13] (See Figure 12.1.) The pictorial association of the Soviet Union with America and Britain boosted morale and lent prestige to the Soviet government. It is true that Stalin and the Soviet press sometimes complained about the British and American delay in opening a second front in Western Europe or about the small scale of their military operations (which engaged at most a third of the number of Axis divisions engaged by Soviet forces).[14] Yet Stalin also repeatedly and warmly acknowledged the aid of the Western Allies. For example, he declared on May Day in 1944 that Soviet successes had been "assisted to a significant degree by our great Allies, the USA and Great Britain." Under

242

Figure 12.1 "Then Be It So! Then Beat Him So!" *Krokodil,* No. 22, June 1942, celebrating agreement between the USSR, the UK, and the United States. Courtesy of *Novaia Gazeta.*

Stalin's guidance, leading Soviet newspapers often celebrated the destruction of the Nazi menace by the Grand Alliance, which they depicted more favorably than many Soviet citizens viewed it.[15]

In wartime meetings with Western officials, Stalin and his key aides stressed their priority objectives: to have German forces drawn away from the eastern front by the creation of a major front in Western Europe; to secure the borders the USSR had during the period of the Nazi–Soviet pact (after the annexation of the Baltic states); to prevent Germany from attacking the Soviet Union again after the war by working with the Western Allies to control Germany; and to obtain massive reparations from Germany and major financial assistance from Washington to rebuild what Axis forces had destroyed. While Stalin still envisioned a slow, gradual transition of Europe and the world toward communism, he did not favor Soviet incitement of revolution to hasten achievement of that long-term goal. Since British and American leaders did not vigorously oppose Soviet territorial ambitions during the war and on some occasions approved of a Soviet sphere of influence in Eastern Europe, Stalin and his top foreign policy advisers believed that Soviet objectives were compatible with postwar cooperation with Britain and the United States.[16] Even if British and American leaders had reservations about Soviet actions, Stalin believed, it would not matter because the advance of the Red Army across Eastern Europe would put the USSR in a position to achieve its political and territorial goals there. Having observed how the British and Americans largely excluded Soviet representatives from decision-making on the composition of governments in Italy when the Allies occupied much of the southern part of that country in 1943, Stalin concluded that he would be able to follow that precedent in Eastern Europe.[17]

Like Stalin, Roosevelt focused primarily on concrete strategic interests, not abstract ideals like self-determination.[18] Roosevelt's wartime policy toward the Soviet Union proceeded from six major assumptions: (1) that it would be extremely difficult for America to defeat both Germany and Japan if the Soviet Union were conquered; (2) that it was therefore vital to deliver extensive aid to the USSR; (3) that America did not have important economic or strategic interests in Eastern Europe; (4) that Central and Eastern Europe should not be allowed to become the flash point for a third world war; (5) that in the course of defeating Germany the Soviet Union would assume a dominant position in Eastern Europe; and (6) that mutual respect for each other's spheres of influence would provide a foundation for postwar cooperation between the United States and the Soviet Union. While FDR occasionally intimated these assumptions to trusted journalists and advisers, he never fully and candidly articulated his foreign policy vision. Twenty years earlier, while serving as Assistant Secretary of the Navy, Roosevelt had seen how President Woodrow Wilson first succeeded in mobilizing America to enter the war against Germany as a crusade to make the world "safe for democracy," but then failed to win approval of his plans for the postwar world, in part because of revelations about compromises Wilson had made that contradicted his principles. That experience led FDR to think that Americans needed idealistic public statements in order to be fully motivated to wage war and that US leaders needed to conceal the details of their diplomatic negotiations that could undermine faith in their leadership.[19]

Roosevelt thus embodied a tragic contradiction: he felt compelled to foster expectations that he would not be able to fulfill. Seven weeks after the German invasion of the Soviet Union, the president met with Churchill off the coast of Newfoundland. The two leaders then jointly issued the Atlantic Charter, which proclaimed the principles they hoped to see realized in the future, starting with a prohibition of territorial aggrandizement and a commitment to "the right of all peoples to choose the form of government under which they will live."

The diplomacy of the Grand Alliance during the next three and a half years repeatedly violated those Wilsonian principles. In November 1943, when Roosevelt traveled to Tehran for a conference with Churchill and Stalin, the president explained to Stalin his idea that the postwar peace would be secured by four policemen (the United States, the UK, USSR, and China), assured Stalin that he understood the Soviet Union's need for friendly governments on its borders, and accepted the Soviet demand to move Poland's borders to the west. In October 1944, as Roosevelt knew, Churchill flew to Moscow, where he agreed with Stalin to divide Eastern Europe into spheres of influence, with the Soviet Union predominant in Romania and Bulgaria while Britain would have predominant influence in Greece. In February 1945, Roosevelt made an arduous journey to Yalta, where he accepted the Soviet demand for territory in eastern Poland. He also agreed with Stalin and Churchill that the Soviet-imposed, Communist-dominated government in Poland would be reorganized with the addition of some democratic leaders. To mollify members of Congress and the American public, FDR got Stalin and Churchill to approve a lofty sounding Declaration on Liberated Europe that pledged that free elections would be held in occupied territories. Yet he signaled that he did not intend to fight Stalin over democracy in Eastern Europe when he remarked that Poland had been a source of trouble for more than 500 years. Two weeks later, when Roosevelt reported to Congress about the Yalta conference, he misleadingly suggested that the Yalta agreements were founded on Atlantic Charter principles and would spell the end of spheres-of-influence arrangements.[20]

The president's approach to the Soviet Union also was marred by another major contradiction. Although Roosevelt sought to cultivate friendly, trusting relations with Stalin, he decided not to inform the Soviet leader about the American–British project to develop an atomic bomb, even though Stalin knew about the Manhattan Project from espionage.[21] Roosevelt appears to have believed that postponing sharing of information about the super weapon would put him in a stronger negotiating position after the war. Thus, while FDR tried to build a foundation for postwar cooperation, he undermined that foundation with his atomic secrecy as well as with the way he managed American public opinion.[22]

FROM ENMITY TO ENTHUSIASM: THE PRESS AND POPULAR ATTITUDES

From the start of the Soviet war against fascist invaders, Roosevelt and his aides had faced a complex challenge of handling popular attitudes. The day after the invasion, Under Secretary of State Sumner Welles explained that, although the atheist Soviet regime was as repugnant to Americans as the Nazi dictatorship, Washington viewed Germany as the primary immediate threat and would therefore aid the USSR. Welles' statement won approval from some editors, particularly liberals who saw Hitler as the greater of two evils and recognized that a quick German conquest of the vast resources of Russia would jeopardize both America and Britain.[23] However, many more editors argued that Communist Russia and Nazi Germany were equally evil – a perspective that disregarded the much greater scope of German expansionism, the Nazi belief in Aryan racial supremacy, and the fascist glorification of war.[24] Some conservatives went further, insisting that communism represented the worst enemy of the American way of life and declaring that they hated Russian totalitarianism more than German totalitarianism.[25] Both moderate and conservative newspapers opposed US aid to the USSR, expressed horror at the idea of democratic America being an ally of undemocratic Russia, and emphasized that the United States had nothing in common with the despotism of Stalin.[26] Although 72 percent of Americans surveyed in July hoped Russia would win the war,[27] there were also many, especially in the Midwest, who wished Germany and Russia would destroy each other.[28]

Yet, by March 1945, when the Red Army neared Berlin, 55 percent of Americans surveyed believed that Russia could be trusted to cooperate with the United States after the war. More Americans then expected postwar conflict with British imperialism than with Soviet communism.[29] In April, as

Americans increasingly anticipated that Russia would join the war against Japan, a plurality of Americans (49 percent) even favored a permanent military alliance with Russia.[30] When victorious Soviet and American soldiers embraced at the Elbe River, most Americans had dramatically changed their views of Soviet Russia. *The Philadelphia Inquirer*, which had portrayed Soviet Russia as a totalitarian beast just like Nazi Germany in June 1941, now showed G.I. Joe and G.I. Ivan marching arm-in-arm.[31] Editors who had stressed the differences between Soviets and Americans in 1941 now highlighted their similarities and counted Russians among the "free men" of the world.[32] Cartoonists often depicted Russian and Allied hands shaking as a symbol of the successful military collaboration, which inspired optimism about friendly relations in the future.[33]

According to some historians, the growth of trust and favorable attitudes were based on knowledge, while the persistence of suspicion and hostility to the Soviet Union among a minority of Americans stemmed from ignorance and prejudice.[34] By contrast, other scholars have argued that support for Russia hinged on "denial of the truth," while the minority who remained hostile were "more often right than not."[35] Neither of these perspectives is satisfactory: both pro-Soviet and anti-Soviet Americans had accurate knowledge and both succumbed to illusions. Anticommunists correctly saw the Stalinist system as a brutal, totalitarian dictatorship, but many also indulged in wishful thinking that the system would collapse during the war or be replaced by a Christian state after the war.[36] Americans who sympathized with Soviet Russia rightly perceived that the Soviet Union changed in some important ways during the war – for example, with an end to persecution of the Orthodox Church – but many also underestimated the potential for American–Soviet friction after the war.

A more satisfactory understanding requires a focus not on simple ignorance or knowledge but on choices about what to emphasize. More than previous scholars recognized, those choices were influenced by attitudes toward the New Deal.[37] To conservative anticommunists, people who thought in terms of class and favored government redistribution of wealth were equally misguided, regardless of whether they were in America or in Russia.[38] The *Chicago Tribune*, one of the fiercest critics of both FDR and Stalin, regularly linked the New Deal's alleged assault on "free American enterprise" both to domestic Communists and to the Soviet planned economy. "Reds" were the enemy, whether they were American radicals infiltrating the government in Washington or Soviets spreading the poison of communism in Europe.[39] On the other hand, liberal Democrats who championed reforms to make life better for the "little people" criticized reactionary financiers and big businessmen whether they were Americans or Polish exiles. Thus, Ralph McGill, editor of the *Atlanta Constitution*, denounced men "high in business and political circles, who think that once the war is done we ought to break off with Russia."[40]

Most Americans recognized at the time that Nazi Germany, which had conquered almost all of Europe, was the most powerful enemy of the United States and that the Red Army would be crucial to the defeat of Germany.[41] As a result, they tended not only to set aside their negative views of the Stalinist regime, but also to demand that others cease criticizing the Soviet Union. Thus, in the spring of 1942, James Reston, a young, but increasingly influential, *New York Times* correspondent, argued that there was no point in "carping" at the Russians, asserted that it was actually a good thing Russia was just as totalitarian as Germany, since that enabled it to match the German war machine, and called anti-Russian remarks "un-American."[42] The minority who nevertheless continued to express criticism of the Soviet Union exposed themselves to charges that their comments resembled Nazi propaganda.[43]

The astonishingly tenacious Soviet stand against the German invaders at Stalingrad in late 1942 and early 1943 – a story regularly featured on the front pages of American newspapers – spurred a shift in American public views. Many Americans came to think that Stalin and the communist system played vital roles in Soviet military successes and deserved respect. *Time* magazine, which had vilified Stalin after the Nazi–Soviet pact, lionized him as a hero in January 1943.[44] Political cartoons depicted the hammer and sickle – formerly symbols of the cruel communist regime – as vital weapons against Hitler.[45] Even some of the most vehemently anticommunist editors glowed about "the amazing Red Army" and called its victory at Stalingrad the decisive turning point of the war, one that doomed Hitler's power.[46]

While communism remained the antithesis of Americanism to conservative anticommunists,[47] Communists gained greater acceptance in the United States during the war. As they volunteered to serve in the military, supported a no-strike pledge by unions, and transformed the Communist Party from a revolutionary organization into a political association, Communists became as numerous as they had been before the Nazi–Soviet pact.[48]

Between the poles of pro-Soviet and anticommunist sentiment, most Americans focused on the need to maintain Soviet–American cooperation for the sake of victory in the war and the preservation of peace in the postwar world. Those priorities led to overwhelming enthusiasm about the Yalta Conference in February 1945. Across the country, editors and columnists expressed relief that Roosevelt, Churchill, and Stalin had met to affirm their unity against Germany and to work out necessary compromises on difficult questions (Figure 12.2).[49]

Later, especially after Germany surrendered, journalists, politicians, and some scholars would criticize the Yalta agreements, especially for FDR's alleged betrayal or "sell-out" of Poland.[50] Such critics tended to forget what most Americans keenly recognized in February 1945: that the Red Army already had occupied all of Poland, that Soviet armies were within thirty miles of Berlin while American and British forces were much further away, and that the agreement to modify the composition of the

BRIGHT DAWN ON THE BLACK SEA

TUESDAY, FEBRUARY 13, 1945.

Figure 12.2 Daniel Fitzpatrick, "Bright Dawn on the Black Sea," *St. Louis Post-Dispatch*, February 13, 1945. Digital Collection, The State Historical Society of Missouri.

Communist-dominated Polish government was the best that Roosevelt and Churchill could obtain, given the facts on the ground.

Despite dismay at some Soviet actions, particularly the arrest of sixteen non-Communist Polish leaders, most editors continued through the battle for Berlin to prioritize global collaboration between the great powers over localized political disputes.[51] Belief in the necessity and possibility of post-war cooperation with Russia was not based mainly on euphoria and illusions, as some influential historians suggested.[52] Instead, it stemmed primarily from knowledge of the huge Soviet role in the crushing of Nazi Germany, expectations that the Soviet Union would enter the war against Japan, and a deep desire to avoid a third world war.[53] In addition, the liberation of German concentration camps in the spring of 1945 revealed the full horror of the Holocaust and stimulated greater support of Soviet demands for harsh treatment of Germany.[54]

Soviet popular attitudes toward America during the war are more difficult to gauge because of the absence of public opinion polls and the strict government control of the press. US diplomats in Moscow believed that Russians became so enthusiastic about American culture and so eager to have good relations with the United States after the war that the Stalinist regime would not dare to risk a rupture in relations with Washington.[55] Many Soviet citizens did enjoy Hollywood movies (which returned to theaters for the first time in years) and loved listening to jazz musicians, who could tour again with official approval.[56] In addition, Lend–Lease shipments of food made deep impressions on millions of Soviets, some of whom went on to become lifelong and influential friends of America.[57] Even Ilya Ehrenburg, the most widely read Soviet journalist, who scorned America's lowbrow culture, highlighted US shipments of war matériel in an effort to bolster Soviet morale.[58]

Yet Soviet attitudes were more complex than US diplomats realized as they starkly contrasted a xenophobic government to a pro-American public. While Soviets highly praised some Lend–Lease deliveries, especially Studebaker trucks, they disdained other American products, particularly tanks that were regarded as inferior to Soviet tanks. Many Soviet citizens expressed anger at the long delay in the opening of a second front in Western Europe.[59] Rumors even circulated that the United States and Britain deliberately postponed their invasion in order to bleed and weaken the USSR. Some Soviet citizens fantasized that the British and Americans would compel the Communist regime to do away with the hated collective farms. Yet others, proud of Soviet military achievements and suspicious of the capitalist powers, privately urged the Kremlin to prepare for an inevitable future conflict with the perfidious Western Allies.[60]

The complicated nature of Soviet views can be seen in the Soviet–American interaction at air bases in Ukraine in the last year of the war. Following Stalin's approval of a request by Roosevelt, from April 1944 to the spring of 1945 more than 1,000 US airmen were based near Poltava and flew shuttle bombing missions against Nazi Germany. While Soviet officers envied how well equipped the Americans were, they also criticized American racism, insubordination, and messiness. Some Soviets were shaken by the evidence of American material abundance, but others continued to believe in their ideological superiority and the preeminence of the Soviet system.[61] The friction that developed between Soviets and Americans has sometimes been depicted as a reflection of a fundamental and unique conflict between Soviet and American political cultures.[62] Yet the sharpest clashes broke out when drunken Americans picked fights and when US servicemen sought sexual relationships with Soviet women – behavior that caused conflict in other allied countries, such as China, as well as in the USSR.[63]

KINDRED ALLIES OR ALIEN COMRADES?

The four years of the wartime alliance formed one of the most intense phases in the long history of Russians (or Soviets) and Americans using images of each other to define their identities. The alliance prompted the Soviet media to dramatically alter their relatively simple portrayals of America. It also spurred filmmakers, correspondents, and intellectuals in the United States to wrestle in more complicated ways with the similarities and differences between the two countries.

In the totalitarian Soviet Union, there was little open dissent from the official media's depiction of America as an ally who shared the core values of freedom, justice, and civilization, in contrast to the barbarous fascist enemies.[64] Although Soviet officials worried that exposure to Western goods and influences could stimulate doubts about the superiority of Soviet socialism, they did not believe it necessary to emphasize differences from the United States in order to present the USSR as a moral beacon to the world and a liberator of enslaved nations. During the wartime alliance, even a wealthy American capitalist – a villain in earlier and later periods – could be depicted positively. Thus, in Aleksandr Korneichuk's play *Mr. Perkins' Mission to the Land of the Bolsheviks* (1944), an American millionaire travels to the Soviet Union and discovers that, in contrast to his preconceptions, it is not an oppressed land. As long as Americans discarded their prejudices, the play suggested, the two great countries should be able to continue working together.[65] Preoccupied with inspiring people to fight the vicious German invaders, Soviet filmmakers concentrated on the real war on their territory and made no effort to glorify the uncontroversial alliance with distant America.[66]

In the democratic United States, in contrast, there was some sharp public contestation of images of the USSR. Major controversies erupted over heavy-handed attempts by filmmakers to laud the Soviet regime and harsh caricatures of Russia by anticommunist journalists.

US government officials and Hollywood studios cooperated in several efforts to sell Americans on the virtues of their Soviet allies. Most notoriously, FDR and former Ambassador Joseph Davies hoped that *Mission to Moscow* (1943), a clumsy film that portrayed Stalin as a kindly genius, would foster pro-Soviet sentiment and demonstrate American goodwill to Moscow. Stalin's approval of the showing of the movie in the USSR opened the door to a much wider distribution of American movies, which Soviet officials valued in part because they showed Soviet citizens that they were not alone in the war against fascist aggressors. However, *Mission to Moscow* provoked protests by anti-Stalinists outside American theaters, received harsh reviews from critics who blasted its whitewashing of recent Soviet history, and flopped at the box office.[67]

Yet other wartime pictures won more critical acclaim, were more popular with audiences, and are noteworthy for the ways they likened Russians to Americans. *North Star* (1943), which *Life* named the movie of the year, explicitly identified Russians as "free men" or "free people." Films also featured the role of religion in Russian life. Thus, in *Song of Russia* (1944), which earned a rave review from the *New York Times*, an American orchestra conductor marries a Russian girl in an Orthodox ceremony in her native village.[68] Such depictions of Russian religiosity were not unrealistic fantasies. In the most famous of the Soviet wartime films, *She Defends the Motherland*, shown in America as *No Greater Love*, one of the lead female characters observes Lent, a dying partisan's last words are "May the Lord forgive you," and his comrades place a cross over his grave – a reflection of the Soviet wartime shift away from earlier anti-religious policies.[69] These movies thus contributed to the wider public valorization of Russians as spiritually akin to Americans.

Even more than movie-makers, newspaper and magazine correspondents were at the center of controversies over representations of America's ally. During the war, the number of American journalists in the Soviet Union greatly increased. Many of them wrote books that not only recounted their experiences, but also described the character of the Russian people and the nature of the Soviet system, which they implicitly or explicitly compared with the United States.

The famous photographer Margaret Bourke-White and her husband, the left-leaning writer Erskine Caldwell, arrived in Moscow first, six weeks before the German invasion. Caldwell's radio broadcasts during German air raids, Bourke-White's striking photographs, and the articles and widely praised books they wrote after they returned to America in November 1941 fascinated Americans, encouraged them to sympathize with the Soviets, and urged them to see similarities with those hard-working, patriotic people. In one article, for example, Caldwell pointed out that both countries were "treacherously attacked" by enemies and emphasized how much Russians liked and respected Americans. Bourke-White's remarkable photographs had even more impact. A photo essay showing Russians crowded into one of the few open churches in Moscow, spread across twelve pages in *Life* magazine, offered powerful support for the idea FDR promoted that Russians, like Americans, worshipped God.[70]

Time gave that idea an anticommunist twist at Christmas 1943. After Stalin allowed the Russian Orthodox Church to elect a new patriarch, Henry Luce's magazine put the elderly patriarch on its cover with the portentous caption "God sits in the corner – but waits." It thereby implied that after the war Russia's religious masses might challenge the (supposedly) weak Soviet government.[71]

A more explicitly anti-Soviet account provoked controversy a year later. After traveling to the USSR in the summer of 1944, William L. White, one of the editors of the strongly anticommunist *Reader's Digest*, produced the best-selling *Report on the Russians* (1945). Although White observed that Russians were like Americans in some ways (for example, they were young, fresh, and unspoiled), on the whole he stressed the differences between the shoddily dressed, underfed Russians and Americans. Poor, shabby, hierarchical Russia, he asserted, resembled Mexico more than the United States. Implicitly contrasting American freedom to Soviet un-freedom, White wrote that Soviet factories resembled the Atlanta Penitentiary and that Russians were conditioned to living as if in prison. Equally importantly, White suggested that "oriental" Russians belonged to a different racial category: they had "an even stronger tradition from the Mongolian Emperor Genghis Khan than they do from Karl Marx."[72]

White's account, which reviewers and other correspondents harshly criticized, was an outlier among the wartime books by American journalists, who tended to portray America's allies in a glowing rather than glaring light.[73] Yet the stereotypes he invoked of Russians as slovenly, bearish, and "oriental" were typical among the relatively few Russophobic journalists and diplomats who vented their ill-tempered views of the Soviet Union during the war. As the Red Army drove German forces out of Eastern Europe, for example, former Ambassador to Russia William Bullitt conjured the specter of Attila the Hun and warned that Western civilization was "threatened by hordes of invaders from the East." Like White, Bullitt faced sharp rebukes from readers.[74]

While the minority of Russophobes defined Soviet Russia as morally, temperamentally, and racially different from the United States, champions of cooperation with the USSR emphasized parallels between the clean-shaven, square-shooting peoples. "The Americans and the Russians are both frontier peoples," declared liberal Vice President Henry Wallace. Even more influential than Wallace's speeches and articles was a best-selling book by Wendell Willkie, the Republican presidential candidate in 1940, who spent two weeks in Russia in September 1942. Urging Americans to discard cartoon images of uncouth, wild Bolsheviks, Willkie repeatedly highlighted how the Soviet Union resembled the United States. For example, the "calm, quiet, confident pride and patriotism" he saw in Siberia was a quality he had often known in America, "especially in the West." Such descriptions supported Willkie's central message: "we must work with Russia after the war" and "there can be no continued peace unless we learn to do so."[75]

Neither the advocates of collaboration with the valiant Russians nor the foes of Soviet communism presented objective observations. In the long run, what was most important in their conflicting accounts was not the details of their descriptions but the cultural and ideological work they were doing. As so often in Russian–American relations, the public debate revolved not only around facts, but also around the subjective placement of Russia as either akin to America or the opposite of the United States.

CONCLUSION

As Soviet, American, British, and Canadian soldiers completed the defeat of Nazi Germany, hopes for postwar collaboration were still very much alive. Although the percentage of Americans who trusted the Soviet Union to cooperate with the United States in the future fell from 55 percent in March 1945 to 45 percent in May, the lower figure was still a plurality (since

17 percent were undecided).[76] After the Yalta Conference, Roosevelt had been disturbed by wrangling over the reorganization of the Polish government and by Stalin's suspicions that US agents were negotiating a separate peace with German generals, but, before Roosevelt died on April 12, he decided to downplay the difficulties and preserve faith in working together on the biggest issues of international security.[77] Among Soviet officials, a strong consensus prevailed about both the desirability and the possibility of postwar cooperation.[78] A week after Roosevelt's death, Stalin signaled the importance he attached to unity with the Allies in dealing with Germany by having *Pravda* publish a rebuke to star correspondent Ilya Ehrenburg, who had complained that the allies advanced easily into Germany from the west while the Red Army faced stiffened resistance in the east.[79] To many Soviet citizens, the joint victory over fascism seemed to create a precious opportunity for Soviet society to develop as part of the civilized world instead of in isolation. Some prominent intellectuals even dared to hope that cooperative relations with the Western powers would allow for a gradual democratization of the Soviet system.[80]

In hindsight, many Western writers have seen a postwar confrontation between the United States and the Soviet Union as inevitable.[81] Yet that was not how most Americans and Soviets viewed the relations between their countries in the spring of 1945, when Yanks and Red Army soldiers embraced at the Elbe River. As most Soviets and Americans celebrated the triumph over Nazi Germany, they did not anticipate that their countries' foreign policies and identities would be dramatically transformed in the months and years ahead.

13

FROM ALLIANCE TO ENMITY, 1945–1953

OVERVIEW

Between the death of Franklin Roosevelt in April 1945 and the death of Joseph Stalin in March 1953, American–Soviet relations deteriorated dramatically. In the spring of 1945, US and Soviet soldiers warmly celebrated their joint defeat of Nazi Germany, but three years later they confronted each other in a tense standoff over Berlin. During the first two years after the Second World War, Soviet and US diplomats met repeatedly to discuss their countries' interests, but, after the summer of 1947, top officials, especially in Washington, felt it would be pointless to talk further with leaders of the other country. At the end of the Second World War, many American business leaders envisioned Russia as a vast postwar market for their products, and Soviet leaders hoped that US loans would help rebuild the USSR, yet by 1950 the economic exchange between the two countries shrank almost to nothing. Most importantly, in the aftermath of the victory over Germany, most people in the United States and the Soviet Union still viewed the other nation as a partner, but within three years Americans and Soviets overwhelmingly viewed each other as dangerous enemies.

This chapter describes and explains that drastic degeneration of relations by focusing on four dimensions: the personalities and emotions of top leaders; the postwar structure of international power; the ideologies of Soviet and American societies; and especially the influence of the media in both countries.

The acute paranoia of Joseph Stalin was a key factor: it led him to conjure foreign threats that helped him to keep control of his top aides and the general Soviet population.[1] On the other side, President Harry Truman's ignorance, parochialism, and impatience meant that he lacked a sympathetic understanding of Soviet needs after the devastating war against Germany and was intolerant of Soviet demands for respect of their country's interests.[2] Truman's inclination to confront Soviet leaders was encouraged by US diplomatic and military representatives, who had become frustrated and angry over their personal treatment by Soviet officials.[3]

Although the unique personalities and strong feelings of top policy-makers fueled the dramatic shift in Soviet–American relations, they do not provide a sufficient explanation for the development of a conflict that neither Stalin nor Truman desired in 1945 and that would persist long after the two leaders left the scene. While Stalin showed a pathological suspicion even of close advisers, most of his foreign policy decisions were pragmatic and based on rational calculations about the correlation of forces, as Norman Naimark has demonstrated.[4] The emotions of top officials also do not explain why so many people in the two countries came to accept depictions of a fundamental conflict between two ways of life that most had not seen as irreconcilable in 1945. A full understanding of the broad deterioration of relations requires examination of how leaders of the two countries reflected widely shared assumptions and embodied deeply rooted political cultures.[5]

The "bipolar" structure of international relations after the Second World War stemmed not only from the defeat of Italy, Germany, and Japan, but also from the weakening of two other nations that had been great powers before the war, namely Britain and France. In the new situation after 1945, the United States and the Soviet Union possessed much greater power relative to other countries. There were also new elements in the balance of power, particularly the Red Army's occupation of Eastern Europe and the development of nuclear weapons, first by the United States and then by the Soviet Union. These unprecedented conditions created new dangers and opportunities. Some of the weakened nations, most notably Britain, appealed to the United States to defend their interests against encroachments by the empowered Soviet Union. US officials feared that Soviet leaders would exploit economic difficulties in Western Europe to extend their influence beyond their sphere in Eastern Europe. Soviet leaders feared that Britain and the United States would try to shake Soviet control of Eastern Europe through covert action and economic seduction.[6]

Changes in the structure of power help to explain some important postwar dynamics. With the United States having by far the most prosperous economy in the world and a monopoly of nuclear weapons until late in 1949, many American leaders felt almost omnipotent and expected that the postwar world naturally should be shaped in accordance with their visions. Meanwhile, Soviet leaders, conscious of how much stronger their country had become with the development of heavy industries and modern weaponry, were less inclined to compromise where they felt their country's vital interests and prestige were involved.[7]

Such feelings and assumptions about the balance of power, combined with the divergence of American and Soviet economic and strategic interests, made some friction between the two countries inevitable. Yet those factors do not by themselves explain the development of highly charged antipathies on both sides.

Understanding that passionate animosity requires analysis of the roles of ideologies, which have often been treated in one-sided ways. For many years, Soviet journalists, propagandists, and scholars stressed the way anti-Soviet ideologues in the United States incited hostility toward Soviet communism after the Second World War.[8] Meanwhile, prominent American historians have blamed Soviet leaders' communist ideology for making "the cold war" inevitable while disregarding the influence of American beliefs.[9] This chapter develops a more balanced analysis of how ideological outlooks in *both* countries spurred the deterioration of Soviet–American relations after 1945.

After the victories over Germany and Japan, a revived American sense of a mission to reorder the world collided with a Soviet sense of entitlement, because of the USSR's enormous sacrifices in the war, to enhanced positions around the perimeter of the Soviet Union. As tensions between Washington and Moscow escalated in the late 1940s, more and more Americans came to share ideas that had first become prevalent thirty years earlier: that Communists in Russia sought to exploit social conflicts in the West to advance the cause of world revolution; that America could not reach a diplomatic accommodation with such an immoral regime, and that the United States could hasten the collapse of the Communist dictatorship. Soviet officials and writers also increasingly emphasized ideas that had emerged three decades earlier: that the capitalist West was inherently hostile to Soviet socialism; that Soviet Russia was encircled by imperialist forces; and that it needed to mobilize ideological allies abroad to ward off the menace of a united anti-Soviet crusade.

Such ideological antagonism did not erupt spontaneously. Instead, journalists, propagandists, and politicians deliberately fomented changes in how Americans and Soviets thought about the other country. By concentrating on that agitation, this chapter shows how what Americans began to call the "Cold War" was not an objective reality but a subjective creation.[10] From that vantage, the "early Cold War" can be seen as a crucial phase in the longer-term construction of difference between Russia and America.

VICTORIES, VACILLATION, AND VILIFICATION:
MAY–DECEMBER, 1945

Early in the morning on May 9, 1945, the people of Moscow received news of the formal end of their motherland's long war against Germany. As Muscovites poured into the streets, loudspeakers blared the Soviet anthem, "The Star Spangled Banner," and "God Save the King." After someone began to shout "Glory to our Allies," thousands gathered outside the US Embassy. When American diplomats and officers came and went, the crowd grabbed them and joyfully tossed them in the air. "Long live Truman!" the Muscovites shouted. "Long live Roosevelt's Memory! Long live the great Americans!" To George Kennan, the chargé d'affaires, who made a brief speech to the cheering crowd, the demonstration of "almost delirious friendship" for Americans suggested that Russian popular enthusiasm about the United States was so great that it might be a threat to the Soviet government's control of its population.[11]

After almost four years of terrible hardship and bitter sacrifice, most Soviet citizens hoped for better, easier lives and a lasting peace. They believed their country had risen to become a great power with a right to a strong voice in world affairs, especially concerning developments near its borders, and they expected that hard-earned right to be respected by their wartime allies. Some young intellectuals hoped that the wartime alliance with the Western democracies would lead to political and cultural liberalization. In the warm postwar climate, they hoped, there would be more space for individual expression, and it would be easier to socialize with Americans. On the western edges of the Soviet empire, Ukrainian nationalists spread rumors of American and British support for a war of liberation from Soviet rule. Yet, for the vast majority of the people of the Soviet Union, dreams of freer and more comfortable lives did not conflict with faith in their great leader, which had been raised to a new height by victory in the Great Patriotic War.[12]

As the war ended, the aging master of the Kremlin did not have a fixed plan for Soviet postwar foreign policy. Remembering how Roosevelt had assured him at Tehran and Yalta that he understood the Soviet Union's need for friendly governments on its borders, Stalin believed that it would be possible to maintain both a sphere of influence in Eastern Europe and generally friendly relations with the United States. Soviet diplomatic experts on Britain and the United States had advised Stalin that the United States would be interested in continued cooperation with the Soviet Union and would not vigorously or persistently express concern with the periphery of the USSR. Proud of what Soviet armies had achieved at great cost, Stalin and his top aides believed Soviet security requirements were as legitimate as those of America and Britain, whose interests in Southern and Western Europe he recognized. Although they had not abandoned the old Communist vision that capitalism eventually would be replaced by socialism throughout the world, Stalin and most other Soviet leaders thought that the process could be so gradual that it would not trigger direct clashes between the Soviet Union and the leading capitalist countries. In the postwar years, Stalin showed no interest in inciting socialist revolutions in Europe and repeatedly opposed armed seizures of power by Communists, in part because he did not want to antagonize the United States or the United Kingdom.[13]

Soviet expectations that cooperative relations with the United States and United Kingdom would be maintained were reflected in propaganda posters that repeatedly hailed the three allies' crushing of the Hitlerite foe and depicted the victory in the war as a shared achievement. Long after the victory over Germany and even after the defeat of Japan, Soviet artists depicted the Soviet, American, and British flags side by side against the Japanese, German, and Italian aggressors. As late as December 1945, Soviet posters continued to feature images of American and British generals and diplomats as allies, accepting the German surrender and judging the German war criminals.[14]

American images of and attitudes toward the Soviet Union were much more varied. Proud of the enormous economic productivity and military power of the United States, many Americans believed that they should be able to steer the postwar world in accordance with US ideals and interests. Right-wing nationalists, especially, felt that the Soviet Union should be compelled to go along with US plans. As early as May 1945, for example, Robert McCormick's *Chicago Tribune* urged the United States to insist that the Soviet Union and other foreign countries follow the US lead and to cut off lend–lease assistance to those who did not comply.[15]

Yet a larger group of Americans viewed such bumptious unilateralism as dangerous and urged further efforts to reach agreements with the Soviet government, especially concerning the control of nuclear energy and the treatment of Germany. Liberal supporters of the New Deal, including labor union leaders and the editors of *The Nation* and *The New Republic*, believed that cooperation with the Soviet Union was essential to fulfill their hopes for an effective United Nations and to avoid a third world war. The most prominent advocate of such views was Henry Wallace, who had been Vice President under FDR and served as Secretary of Commerce until September 1946. In numerous speeches, Wallace urged a sympathetic understanding of how wartime destruction had left the Soviet Union with dire economic needs and how a history of foreign invasions had instilled a sense of insecurity in

Russia that the United States could ease by accepting a Soviet sphere of influence in Eastern Europe.[16]

After the Soviet Union entered the war against Japan in August 1945, a solid majority of Americans (54 percent) thought Russia would cooperate with the United States after the war. The Gallup poll did not ask whether the United States and Russia would be able to compromise and cooperate with each other. Both the phrasing of the poll question and the prevailing responses indicated crucial assumptions of the primacy of US interests and the supreme legitimacy of American visions for the postwar world.[17]

While most expected the wartime alliance to translate into postwar cooperation, a vocal and adamant minority did not. Freed from the wartime need to be circumspect about the Soviet ally, newspapers and magazines that had been vehemently anticommunist before 1941 – often edited by Catholics or fundamentalist Protestants – returned to expressing their suspicion and hostility openly. By mid-summer 1945, the hatred of Russia vented by conservative columnists and editors seemed, to moderate and liberal journalists, to amount to a disturbing campaign to spark a war against the Soviet Union (Figure 13.1).[18]

Trying to Fan a Spark Into a Conflagration

Figure 13.1 "Trying to Fan a Spark Into a Conflagration." *Atlanta Constitution*, August 6, 1945.

Most importantly, the Hearst, McCormick, and Scripps Howard newspaper chains, which together reached a large share of American readers, launched intense campaigns to replace views of the USSR as an ally with images of an evil enemy.[19] William Randolph Hearst was especially strident. Motivated by his long-running clashes with New Deal officials and left-leaning labor unions, he directed harsh attacks on his domestic foes as Red infiltrators, thereby linking them to the alleged Soviet menace. His flagship paper, the *San Francisco Examiner,* relied heavily on two major rhetorical tactics to demonize the USSR: (1) to cast Stalin and the Soviet Union as Asiatic or Mongol, rather than white; and (2) to categorize the USSR with Nazi Germany by tirelessly applying the label of "Red Fascism."[20]

However, such indignant and zealous anticommunism was counterbalanced by a consciousness, especially among liberal Protestants, of America's own faults and by calls for self-restraint in the interest of international cooperation.[21] With public opinion divided, domestic political considerations did not compel top leaders in Washington to pursue one course or another in 1945.

When Vice President Harry Truman suddenly became president upon Franklin Roosevelt's death on April 12, 1945, he felt unsure of himself and uncertain about how to conduct relations with the Soviet Union. Although Truman pledged to carry out FDR's policies, he did not know the details of Roosevelt's discussions with Stalin. Truman wanted to reach agreements with Soviet leaders and he believed that this should be possible because the Soviet government was motivated by traditional and limited geopolitical aims. Yet, like many Americans, he felt increasingly impressed by US power and expected that agreements would be largely in line with US proposals. Truman brusquely told Molotov on April 23 that the Soviet Union must carry out its agreements, particularly in Poland. But the next month he dispatched Roosevelt's troubleshooter Harry Hopkins to Moscow on a successful mission to resolve the dispute with only a minor reorganization of the Communist-dominated Polish government.[22]

Truman veered back toward toughness when he met Stalin at a conference in Potsdam (near Berlin) in July 1945. After receiving reports of the successful test of an atomic bomb in New Mexico on July 16, Truman seemed "tremendously pepped up," with a heightened confidence that he could protect US interests and promote American principles through assertive diplomacy. The news that the atomic bomb worked buttressed Truman's belief that he could safeguard the US interest in an Open Door in the Far East from Russian expansionism and refuse to recognize Soviet-dominated governments in Romania and Bulgaria until they were reorganized. Truman and Secretary of State James Byrnes also insisted on a complicated approach to reparations from Germany that would limit what the USSR would get. Stalin and Molotov resented the high-handed way the United States abandoned the much more generous Yalta Conference pledge to consider a total of $10 billion in reparations to the USSR. While American, British, and Soviet leaders reached agreements on some key issues at Potsdam, the conference began to erode the good will between the allies. Stalin and Molotov believed the major Soviet contribution to the defeat of Germany justified their demands, yet Truman saw them as "pig-headed." The combination of self-righteous American assertiveness and grudging Soviet acquiescence was ominous.[23]

As the US development of atomic bombs increased America's military power and US diplomacy grew more insistent, Stalin resolved to match US capabilities and resist coercion. When Truman informed him at Potsdam that the United States had a new, powerful weapon, Stalin told his top advisers that the Soviet Union needed to accelerate its own work on atomic weapons. After a US plane dropped an atomic bomb on Hiroshima on August 6, Stalin ordered Soviet officials and scientists: "Provide us with atomic weapons in the shortest possible time!"[24] At an unproductive conference of foreign ministers in London in September 1945, Secretary of State Byrnes jokingly threatened that, if Molotov did not quit stalling, he would pull an atomic bomb out of his hip pocket and blast him.[25] Seeing Allied pressure for concessions, Stalin instructed Molotov to be unbending. Later in the fall, Stalin emphasized to his top lieutenants that it was essential not "to give in to intimidation." Instead, Soviet leaders needed to arm themselves with a "policy of tenacity and steadfastness."[26]

In the fall of 1945, Truman grew increasingly frustrated by what he regarded as Soviet intransigence, unwarranted demands, and bullying. Soviet leaders, he complained, seemed to understand only the language of force and to respect only military power. While British officials recognized that US "atomic diplomacy" had aggravated Soviet insecurity and led Soviet leaders to be more defiantly stubborn, Truman seemed baffled by Russian bitterness.[27]

Yet Truman was not ready to abandon diplomacy. He vowed in late October that he would not compromise with "evil," but he did not prevent Byrnes from traveling to Moscow in December. There, in give-and-take negotiations reminiscent of the Yalta Conference, Byrnes obtained Soviet acquiescence to US primacy in the occupation of Japan and the presence of

US troops in China, while he agreed to recognize the governments of Romania and Bulgaria after each of them added two non-Communist members. Thus, eight months of alternation between tough talk and conciliation culminated in an accommodation over spheres of influence.[28]

While the Truman administration seemed to vacillate, conservative anticommunists excoriated Truman's alleged "appeasement" of Stalin.[29] By the fall of 1945, conservative publications depicted Russia as the land of darkness, vilified Stalin as a brutal violator of cardinal American principles, and depicted the Bear on a rampage to communize the world.[30]

In response, Soviet media portrayals of the United States became much more negative. As Vladimir Pechatnov has shown, in late 1945 and early 1946, Soviet officials saw themselves as being on the defensive against an Anglo-American propaganda offensive, with press attacks on the Soviet Union that they believed (wrongly) were instigated by the UK and US governments.[31] Soviet propagandists singled out the Hearst press, especially, as a disseminator of vile lies and slander.[32] Counterattacking, Soviet publications lampooned the US–British monopolization of atomic weapons and reverted to the stock emphasis on widespread unemployment in the United States.[33] Thus, while top US and Soviet leaders still sought accommodation, a war of words and images had erupted between the Soviet official media and the American conservative anticommunist press.

FROM CONCILIATION TO CONFRONTATION: JANUARY–SEPTEMBER 1946

When Byrnes returned from Moscow to Washington, he encountered an irritated Truman. Annoyed that Byrnes had not kept him fully informed, Truman angrily complained on January 5, 1946 that he was "tired [of] babying the Soviets" and declared that he would not "play compromise" any longer.[34]

By January 1946, public approval of Truman's handling of the presidency had declined from almost 90 percent in July 1945 to barely over 60 percent, with fewer than half of Republicans favoring Truman's conduct. Disagreements over domestic policies furnished the primary reason for Republican disaffection, but Truman was concerned about criticism of US policy toward Russia from Republican leaders, especially Senator Arthur Vandenberg of Michigan.[35] The increasing polarization between parties in the United States helped to set the stage for a polarization of relations between the United States and the Soviet Union.

Through the first weeks of 1946, the friction between the United States and the Soviet Union had not led to any armed confrontations or even serious diplomatic showdowns. Yet, amid the rising tension, political leaders, diplomats, and journalists in both countries increasingly turned to ideological explanations for the differences between them.

On February 9, 1946, Stalin came to the Bolshoi Theater in Moscow to deliver a major speech. Near the end of the address, Stalin announced ambitious plans for a new surge in Soviet industrial development that would allow the "motherland" to be "insured against all contingencies" and to "outstrip the achievements of science beyond the borders of our country." That passage, along with Stalin's reiteration of the Marxist belief that the global capitalist system contained the seeds of crises and wars, led many Americans to interpret Stalin's speech as a call for confrontation with the West. US Supreme Court Justice William O. Douglas even called it "The Declaration of World War III." Yet more central to Stalin's speech was his effort to refute assertions in the foreign press that the Soviet social system was weak, unpopular, and destined to collapse when given even "a slight shock from without." To the contrary, Stalin insisted that the Soviet Union's victory in the Second World War proved that the Soviet system enjoyed the powerful support of the people, and he asserted that it was more viable than the capitalist system. Stalin's speech thus reflected how sensitive Soviet leaders were to foreign depictions of their country and how their boasts about the strengths of the USSR concealed an underlying anxiety that it could not withstand close comparison with conditions abroad.[36]

Uncertain about how to interpret Stalin's speech as well as a recent Soviet refusal to join the International Monetary Fund and World Bank, the State Department sought guidance from the US Embassy in Moscow. The chargé d'affaires there, George F. Kennan, responded on February 22 with a long telegram that conveyed little new information, but offered a perspective and a prescription that leaders in Washington welcomed. Since the Kremlin rulers' insecurity was "traditional and instinctive" rather than based on any real conditions outside the country, Kennan suggested, US leaders did not need to be anxious about how their policies would affect the Soviet government. Since Soviet power was "impervious to logic of reason," it would be pointless for US officials to try to reason with Soviet leaders. And since the Kremlin was "highly sensitive to logic of force," US leaders could expect that confronting Russia with demonstrations of US resolve would be effective. Kennan thus provided top policymakers in Washington with a validation of their impatience with negotiation and their inclination toward confrontation.[37]

While Kennan's famous telegram has conventionally been seen as a call for "containment" of Soviet expansionism, he actually went further than that by suggesting that the United States could challenge the Soviet government's grip on its own peoples. Highlighting how the "mass of Russian people" were emotionally removed from Communist Party doctrines, Kennan encouraged policymakers to doubt the "internal soundness" of the Soviet dictatorship. He thereby foreshadowed his later initiation of a drive for the "liberation" of the Soviet bloc from communism.

In addition, Kennan made a significant contribution to the redefinition of America's former ally as fundamentally unlike the United States. Russians were "instinctive" and "neurotic," he wrote, while Americans were rational and objective. Soviet Marxists were unethical; Americans were moral. In contrast to the openness of the United States, an "oriental secretiveness" pervaded the Soviet government. Thus, Kennan's cable promoted stereotypical notions of national character that justified disengagement from negotiation.[38]

Washington officials quickly embraced Kennan's views. Secretary of the Navy James Forrestal, who had long argued that "oriental" Russians could not be trusted, sent Kennan's message to officials throughout the government and to diplomats around the world. Byrnes praised Kennan's analysis and in a speech on February 28, announced a new policy of firmness and patience that accorded with Kennan's recommendations. Truman adamantly endorsed Byrnes' vow that the United States would not "allow aggression to be accomplished by coercion or pressure or subterfuge such as political infiltration." The tougher stand reflected not only worries about Soviet expansionism, but also an assumption that the United States had the right and the duty to be the world's sheriff.[39]

The first opportunity to apply the new uncompromising and confrontational approach came in a crisis over Iran. In a 1942 treaty, Britain and the Soviet Union had agreed to withdraw forces they deployed in Iran six months after the defeat of Germany and its allies (including Japan, which surrendered on September 2, 1945). However, as the March 2, 1946 deadline for withdrawal approached, Soviet leaders decided to keep some troops in northern Iran while they attempted to extract from Iran an oil concession comparable to the concessions obtained by Britain earlier. In addition to the economic value of access to Iranian oil resources, Soviet leaders seem to have been influenced by a desire for status equal to Britain's in a country where tsarist Russia and Britain had competed for influence for decades before 1917. After Iranian Prime Minister Ahmad Qavam offered on

March 4 to present a proposal for a joint Soviet–Iranian oil venture to the Iranian parliament, the Soviet Union decided to withdraw its forces.[40]

As Soviet–Iranian negotiations proceeded, a furor erupted in the United States. Editorials proclaimed "that the Russian Bear is again on the march," and indicted Russia for "aggression," "rape," and a determination to "paralyze" the work of the United Nations, which placed the matter on its agenda. Like the prolonged Russian occupation of Manchuria in 1903, the more briefly extended occupation of northern Iran greatly increased distrust of Russia in the United States.[41]

When the Soviet government announced an agreement with Iran for the withdrawal of Soviet troops, influential journalists and politicians hailed a victory for the new US policy of "patience with firmness."[42] Actually, as the historian Natalia Yegorova has shown, the Iranian prime minister's hedged concession influenced the Soviet withdrawal more than US pressure at the United Nations.[43] Yet many Americans decided that standing up to Russia had worked, and leading newspapers praised a shift to more resolute global leadership based on American principles. Some liberal journals that had been critical of the Truman administration's unilateralism now reluctantly supported the tougher policy. The confrontation over Iran thus led to a broader consensus for vigorous US leadership in the world with less concern for Soviet sensitivities.[44]

The Soviet Union's violation of its promise to withdraw from Iran and perceptions that its conduct was dishonest, crude, and belligerent severely damaged its image in the United States. A Gallup poll in the middle of March found that more than 70 percent of Americans disapproved of Russia's policy in the world.[45]

Yet that did not mean that all Americans were now united in antipathy to Moscow and opposition to any further concessions to Soviet interests, as Byrnes claimed.[46] Influential liberal editors of important regional newspapers such as the *Atlanta Constitution* and *Louisville Courier-Journal* sharply criticized the "jingoism" and "hysteria" of American radio commentators and columnists.[47] The editors also continued to express sympathetic understanding of Soviet views of the world, including reasons for suspicion of the West, desires for security, and dread of a new war. Most importantly, they still insisted on the need for America, Britain, and the Soviet Union to work together to preserve peace and avoid a new war.[48]

One of the underlying differences between such liberals and many anti-Soviet figures was a vigorous rejection of analogies between the Soviet Union and Nazi Germany, founded in part on persistent memories of how "the valiant Russians" had fought the German aggressors.[49] Another crucial difference was a greater capacity for self-critical reflection and an aversion to self-righteous hypocrisy. Thus, the *Louisville Courier-Journal* observed that "American prejudice and xenophobia" had helped to build the rising wall between Americans and Russians, while columnist Samuel Grafton perceptively commented that one of the dangerous attractions of "melodramatic formulations" about Russia was the way they induced Americans to forget "our own problems."[50]

Near the beginning of the confrontation over Iran, in early March, former British Prime Minister Winston Churchill delivered a major address in Truman's home state that the president tacitly approved. More than six months earlier, in August 1945, Churchill had deployed the metaphor of an "iron curtain" to attack the Soviet Union's alleged division of Europe between east and west. Now he wielded the image again as he called for an Anglo-American "fraternal association" to deter further Soviet expansion.[51] Churchill's misleading speech, which belied the reality of extensive interchange between eastern and western Europe at that time, eventually would be a powerful example of how imaginative rhetoric can profoundly shape outlooks.[52] But it elicited mixed reactions in the United States at the time. While most Americans agreed with Churchill's criticisms of Soviet actions, a strong majority opposed the idea of an Anglo-American alliance.

Some scholars have argued that this simply meant that the American people were "not yet fully prepared to accept the responsibilities" that came with getting tough on Russia.[53] Yet the views of Americans, especially liberals, were more complicated than that. The influential columnist Walter Lippmann argued, for example, that joining Britain in an anti-Soviet coalition would mean forsaking the possibility of a negotiated settlement between the Soviet Union and the Western powers.[54] Others, including Ralph McGill of the *Atlanta Constitution*, opposed siding with the British Empire, which they saw as equally oppressive as the Soviet empire. African American internationalists viewed Churchill's alarmist cry about Russia as "a smoke screen" to cover his solicitation of US backing for British colonialism. Most importantly, wise commentators presciently warned that an Anglo-American alliance would provoke "a retaliatory alliance by the Soviet Union."[55] Thus, many liberals still recognized the interactive nature of relations between Russia and the West instead of seeing a fixed confrontation rooted in essential traits. Alternatives to perpetual enmity were still conceivable.

Although *Pravda* noted that Churchill's speech "met a reserved reception" in America, Soviet leaders still angrily denounced it. Stalin compared Churchill's claim of Anglo-Saxon moral superiority to Hitler's racial theories, asserted that the British leader sought to incite war against the Soviet Union, recalled how Churchill had called for aggressive foreign intervention in the Russian Civil War, and vowed that the Soviet Union would defeat any new crusade that might be launched.[56]

Churchill's address contributed to rising expectations in the USSR of a clash between the former members of the Grand Alliance. In the western borderlands, many saw Churchill's speech as a signal of an impending Anglo-American war against the Soviet Union. Ukrainian nationalist rebels dramatically increased their activity in anticipation of a war of liberation. A war scare spread among the general Soviet population, with people rushing to stockpile food and other necessities. The Kremlin ordered Soviet propagandists to sharply increase their exposure of the "anti-Soviet schemes of the Anglo-Americans."[57]

The most prominent Soviet propagandist, Ilya Ehrenburg, both reflected and exacerbated the escalating tensions when he toured the United States along with two other Soviet correspondents from April to June 1946. From the start of his visit, Ehrenburg observed a rising tendency in the American press to vent hostility toward the USSR that he later called the "onset of the cold war." After sparring with editors at press conferences and traveling through the South, Ehrenburg wrote a long article for the United Press at the end of his trip. In it, he praised America as a "great country" with a high standard of life, but dwelled on criticisms of American inequality, platitude-filled movies, and journalistic slanderers of the Soviet Union who were "preparing the Third World War." Although Ehrenburg complained that newspapers were "always opposing the freedom prevailing in America to the lack of freedom in Russia," after he returned to the USSR he wrote a series of articles for *Izvestiia* that caustically contrasted vulgar American culture to the more sophisticated arts and culture in the Soviet Union. Many American journalists indignantly rejected Ehrenburg's "sneers" and re-emphasized the difference between Soviet government control and American freedom of speech and movement.[58] Thus, a visit originally intended to promote mutual understanding expanded and intensified the war of words.

The reorientation of Soviet propaganda against the "new enemy" in the spring and summer of 1946 coincided with a shift in Soviet officials' threat perceptions. Earlier, Soviet intelligence officers had downplayed reports of foreign support for Ukrainian insurgents as rumors spread by the insurgents to bolster their reputation and morale. But, by the fall of 1946, mounting evidence of Western support led Soviet officials to take it much more seriously. Diplomats also pointed to dangers. The Soviet Ambassador to Washington reported in September that the United States sought to displace the Soviet Union's influence on its periphery, that not only extreme right-wing newspapers, but also respectable conservative publications, were advocating war against the Soviet Union, and that "the most warlike circles of American imperialism" were planning a new war, with possible strikes from bases being created near Soviet territory. Assertions that Hearst and other reactionaries were beating the drums for a new war, featured also by Soviet cartoonists, were exaggerated. But they were not simply the product of "paranoia" and the internal ideological needs of the Soviet system, as some have argued.[59]

Amid the growing sense of dangers from the West, Soviet leaders sought to tighten controls on the circulation of information about the outside world and to isolate their population from external influences. Two magazines produced by the British and American governments – *Britanskii Soiuznik* and *Amerika* – caused particular concern. As a Soviet security official informed Stalin in November 1946, *Britanskii Soiuznik* aimed to create the impression that life in the British Commonwealth, with a new social security system and high material living standards, was better than life in the Soviet Union. Since teachers, professors, and writers subscribed to the magazine, they might infect wider groups of Soviet citizens with information or ideas it disseminated. In response, security and propaganda officials urged drastically cutting the circulation of both *Britanskii Soiuznik* and *Amerika*.[60]

The widening polarization between the USSR and the United States also stemmed from developments in US domestic politics. Truman and the chairman of the Democratic Party had wanted to keep Henry Wallace in the cabinet in order to use him to mobilize the party's constituencies on the left for the midterm congressional elections. Yet, after Wallace in September 1946 made another speech urging tolerance and empathy rather than toughness toward Russia, Secretary of State Byrnes threatened to resign. With key senators and most of the media condemning Wallace, Truman fired Wallace. As a result, there were no longer any high-level US officials advocating the FDR policy of conciliation and cooperation with the USSR.[61]

GERMANY: FROM DENAZIFICATION TOWARD DIVISION

Even before Wallace's departure, friction between the former allies mounted over Germany, where US and Soviet policies increasingly diverged. Already by the spring of 1946, the US emphasis on denazification, decartelization, and democratization had given way to a growing stress on the rehabilitation of German industries and a rising fear of Communist subversion. Although Communists won only 3 percent of the vote in local elections in the US occupation zone in February, Kennan and other State Department officials feared that the Soviet Union would strive to penetrate the western zones in the pursuit of an ultimate goal of a unified socialist Germany. Believing that the revival of the German economy was crucial to the recovery of Western Europe as a whole and therefore vital to US prosperity, US policymakers put German needs and US interests ahead of Soviet demands. Fearing Soviet obstruction, but also feeling that the weak Soviet Union would be compelled to acquiesce to US plans, US decision-makers increasingly disregarded Soviet objections. In May, the head of the US military occupation, General Lucius Clay, halted the dismantling of German industries for reparations. In July, Secretary of State Byrnes became irate when Molotov insisted on the full implementation of the Yalta and Potsdam agreements about Germany. In September, Byrnes announced in Stuttgart that the United States would proceed with the economic and political unification of its zone of occupation with the zones controlled by other powers (starting with the British zone), despite Soviet resistance.[62]

Soviet leaders had dreamed of a socialist Germany since 1917, and after the defeat of Nazi Germany they hoped that eventually all of Germany would be socialist. However, their immediate priorities were to get massive reparations and to prevent Germany from being the launching pad for a new war against the Soviet Union. Almost all key Soviet officials believed that a unified capitalist Germany could not be peaceful forever. They feared that US and British leaders would be too easy on the Germans and that, after Germany recovered, it would attack the Soviet Union again. By the end of 1946, Soviet officials grew disappointed and disturbed by the policies of the United States, including the failure to fulfill its commitment to denazification of Germany. Yet Stalin still hoped to obtain more reparations and, if Germany were to be divided, he wanted the West to be blamed for that. Consequently, he remained open to further diplomatic discussions as he awaited further steps by the United States and its allies.[63]

THE WAR OF WORDS ESCALATES: 1947

In the first half of 1947, US and Soviet officials continued to explore possibilities for accommodation at negotiating tables, yet at the same time leaders and propagandists intensified the mutual vilification. The most important rhetorical blast was sparked less by Soviet actions than by a British strategic predicament. When British officials informed the

United States in February 1947 that financial constraints would compel Britain to stop subsidizing conservative forces in Greece and Turkey, the Truman administration decided it must respond. Although Stalin, abiding by his October 1944 deal with Churchill, persistently declined to support the Greek Communists, they received aid and sanctuary from neighboring Yugoslavia and Albania. Fearing that Communist guerrillas could take power in Greece and that Turkey might be intimidated by Soviet forces, Truman asked Congress on March 12, 1947 to provide $400 million in aid to the two countries. In order to justify the request to penny-pinching members of Congress, Truman melodramatically cast the local problem as part of a global struggle between two "ways of life," one distinguished by freedom and the other based on "terror and oppression."[64]

Although most African American commentators sharply criticized the hypocrisy of buttressing the racist British Empire in the name of freedom, the Truman Doctrine speech succeeded in rousing congressional and public support for a more confrontational approach to the Soviet Union and world communism. The request for aid easily passed in the Senate, by 67–23, and in the House of Representatives, by 281–107.[65] Columnist Barnet Nover approvingly concluded: "Between Russia and the United States the chips are now down." Cartoonist Herbert Block captured the spirit of standing up to Russia by depicting Uncle Sam facing Stalin atop a globe and saying, "I'm Here to Stay, Too." Thus, the idea of a Soviet and Communist threat in the eastern Mediterranean catalyzed a shift in the way many Americans thought about the role of the United States in the world.[66]

The growing tendency to depict US–Soviet relations in stark ideological terms was spurred by Secretary of Defense James Forrestal, who had long argued that capitalism and communism could not coexist. Prodded by Forrestal, Kennan wrote an article under the pseudonym "X" that captured much attention when it was published in July 1947 in the premier establishment magazine *Foreign Affairs*.[67] Kennan reiterated central points he had made earlier in his confidential "Long Telegram": that the Kremlin's stress on a menacing outside world derived not from any real foreign hostility, but from the need to justify its dictatorship; that there was little use in negotiating with Soviet leaders, who were "unamenable to argument or reason"; and that, if the United States maintained for ten to fifteen years a policy of "patient but firm and vigilant containment" of Russian expansionism, it could lead to the break-up or mellowing of Soviet power.

The article typically has been seen as significant for the way it publicized the concept of "containment," yet Kennan also promoted notions about the "liberation" of Russia. Kennan assumed that the United States could influence internal developments within Russia, particularly through propaganda campaigns ("informational activity"). Although the United States could not by itself "bring about the early fall of Soviet power," it could take encouragement from the fact that the mass of the Russian people were "disillusioned" with the Soviet regime. Hence Washington could exploit "a growing divergence ... between the great mass of Party members ... and the little self-perpetuating clique of men at the top."[68]

The broad and lasting resonance of Kennan's article stemmed not from its discussion of complex policy issues, but from the ways it defined the character of Americans and their enemy. "The issue of Soviet–American relations," Kennan concluded, was "in essence a test of the over-all worth of the United States as a nation among nations." If Americans pulled themselves together and measured up to their best traditions, they would eventually prevail over the semi-Asiatic leaders of the Soviet Union. Whereas many Americans had been uncertain about whether Russia was a friend or foe in the preceding years, Kennan firmly asserted that the United States "must continue to regard the Soviet Union as a rival, not a partner."[69]

The "X" article provoked a series of critical responses from leading columnist Walter Lippmann, who collected his articles in a book, *The Cold War* (1947). Lippmann criticized Kennan's strategy of containment for many flaws, including: yielding the initiative to Moscow, which would choose locations for conflict; making no distinction between vital (Western Europe) and less important areas; and ignoring the possibility of achieving a settlement with the Soviet Union through diplomacy backed by power. Lippmann also expressed skepticism about changing the Soviet Union: "The communists will continue to be communists. The Russians will continue to be Russians."[70]

Half of Americans did not know then what "the cold war" meant, but in the next year and a half other journalists rushed to explain it and to blame it on the Soviet Union.[71] The "cold war," numerous reporters declared, involved a "war of nerves," a "war of ideologies," and, above all, a "war of words" that the USSR was waging against the United States.[72] The hugely popular radio commentator and columnist Walter Winchell, who closely collaborated with Secretary of Defense Forrestal, had a major impact on public opinion with claims that America was losing the cold war and calls for Americans to wake up to the menace from Moscow.[73] In a widely reprinted article, syndicated columnist George Sokolsky insisted that "we did not start the Cold War," which had been "a one-way war" by Soviet Russia against America.[74] By pinning responsibility for the deterioration of US–Soviet relations squarely on disruption, non-cooperation, and aggression by the USSR, journalists repeatedly justified the US rejection of further negotiation with Moscow, which could only mean "appeasement."[75] They also conjured nightmare images of a Red tide sweeping from Eastern Europe to the English Channel and even across the Atlantic Ocean.[76]

While US reporters and policymakers portrayed the Soviet Union as an obstructionist adversary and bully, in 1947 Soviet correspondents and artists depicted the United States as a threat mainly because of the attractions of the American way of life and American journalists' allegedly slanderous depictions of the Soviet Union. The image of the United States as a land of abundance was an illusion, Soviet propagandists proclaimed with increasing shrillness. Political cartoons in Soviet magazines repeatedly sought to show that wealth and luxury in the United States were actually restricted to the few millionaires, while the millions of ordinary citizens faced poverty and unemployment.[77] Instead of longing to live as people did in the racist and materialist United States, cartoons instructed, patriotic Soviet citizens should take pride in the construction of a new way of life in their own country, where big modern buildings replaced old churches and a dignified equality replaced humiliating subordination to arrogant capitalists.[78] The real achievements and advantages of life in the Soviet Union were not reflected in the US press, Soviet media explained, because American journalists published deliberate and cynical misrepresentations.

The Stalinist leadership's determination to stress this theme is evidenced by the play *The Russian Question*, which premiered in Moscow in April 1947. Written by journalist Konstantin Simonov, who had visited America with Ehrenburg in 1946, the play won Stalin's personal approval and was performed in numerous theaters across the Soviet Union. It sought to show that the tycoons who owned US newspapers demanded negative depictions of the Soviet Union because they favored a war against Soviet communism or wanted to force the Soviet government to give trade concessions to Western corporations.[79] A subsequent film based on *The Russian Question* hyped the danger of the atomic obliteration of the Soviet Union: it opened with a publisher declaring that it was the job of his newspaper to make atomic war popular.[80] Thus, in the USSR as well as in the United States, the mass media inflamed fear and hostility with exaggerated and distorted depictions of the intentions of the other country.

CONSOLIDATION

By the fall of 1947, relations between the Soviet Union and the United States had deteriorated to the point that the former wartime allies had largely abandoned efforts to cooperate in the reconstruction of Europe and decided to focus primarily on consolidation of their influence in separate parts of the continent. The United States worked to revive economies and stabilize governments from Greece to France through Marshall Plan aid, first announced in June 1947. The Soviet Union initially hoped to partici-pate in the Marshall Plan and sent a large delegation headed by Molotov to Paris to discuss the reconstruction program. However, the Kremlin then learned that US officials had imposed conditions for disclosure of informa-tion and coordination with European integration that they knew would be difficult for the USSR to accept.[81]

Eight months later, when US officials feared that the authentically popular Communist Party of Italy might win an election, they threatened to cut off Italy from Marshall Plan aid if that happened. They also provided massive covert financial assistance to the Christian Democratic Party, which then prevailed. While the USSR gave more limited funds to the Communist Party, Stalin urged Italian radicals to be patient and not try to seize power. Nonetheless, American newspapers repeatedly depicted Stalin or a menacing Soviet bear trying to invade and dominate Italy. Such distorted images of Soviet aggression had been propagated for years by right-wing anticommunists, but now the mainstream press joined in the conflation of internal political challenges with an alleged external Soviet threat.[82]

Soviet policies often emerged in reaction to moves by the United States and its allies. In response to the Marshall Plan, the Soviet Union established the Cominform (Communist Information Bureau) in September 1947 to impose tighter discipline on Communist parties, and in January 1949 it created Comecon (the Council for Mutual Economic Assistance) to coordinate the economic development of the Soviet bloc countries. When US officials pushed ahead with the development of a capitalist western Germany by introducing a currency reform in June 1948, Soviet forces blockaded Berlin in an effort to force a reopening of discussion of a unified Germany. After the Soviet Union lifted the ineffective blockade in May 1949, the division of Germany pro-ceeded: the Federal Republic of Germany formally came into existence in September, and Stalin responded with the creation of the German Democratic Republic in October. Earlier that year, in April, the United States spearheaded the founding of the North Atlantic Treaty Organization (NATO) to coordinate defenses against Soviet aggression. The Soviet Union moved more slowly on that front, forming the Warsaw Pact in 1955.

While the US and Soviet governments worked to strengthen their respective spheres of influence in Europe, they encouraged filmmakers to promote the ideological cohesion of their own societies. Soviet leaders' supervision of film production was direct and overt, with Stalin and the Ministry of Cinematography closely reviewing scripts. US leaders played less direct roles, but they did spur a shift away from the wartime romance with Russia to the production of strident anticommunist films, particularly after the House Un-American Activities Committee went to Hollywood in October 1947 to investigate Red influence on the movie industry.[83]

Between the spy thriller *Iron Curtain*, released in May 1948, and the drama of escape from the prison of communism in *Man on a Tightrope* (1953), Hollywood produced seventy starkly anticommunist movies. Most of these films flopped at the box office, and critics derided movies like *The Red Menace* (1949) as inept and lurid. However, the sheer number of films suggests that, in an era when 60 million Americans went to a movie each week, the depictions of communist infiltration and sabotage intensified fears of subversion by the Soviet Union and its evil minions. The nightmare of Soviet atomic attack and conquest in *Invasion USA* (1952) represented a heavy-handed effort to bludgeon apathetic Americans into supporting massive defense spending, but it also foreshadowed many other dramatizations of Russian take-overs. Although many of the movies were crude, the repeated contrasts of innocent, brave, honest American individuals to immoral, cowardly, heartless Communist automatons likely contributed significantly to the habitual definition of communism as the evil antithesis of Americanism and the identification of the Soviet Union as the dark opposite of the United States.[84]

In part because of the need to invest scarce funds in rebuilding after the war, the Soviet film industry produced far fewer movies than Hollywood did in the last years of Stalin's rule. However, many of the Soviet films about the postwar conflict between East and West were well made and extremely popular. More than 24 million Soviet citizens, for example, saw *Vstrecha na El'be* (*Meeting on the Elbe*, 1949), which depicted American generals and diplomats sheltering Nazis and plotting to mobilize German anticommunism for a new war against the Soviet Union. Millions also saw films such as *Zagovor obrechennykh* (*Conspiracy of the Doomed*, 1950) which showed Americans using the cover of the Marshall Plan to try to overthrow East European governments. The popularity of the films did not necessarily mean that they made Soviet citizens loathe and fear Americans. Many moviegoers may have been drawn less by the plots about US-led threats than by opportunities to see their favorite stars dressed in furs and jewels or to gape at the luxurious, sparkling homes of American characters. It is difficult to ascertain how Soviet audiences responded to the repeated depiction of American corruption, materialism, racism, and decadence.[85] Yet the films' insistent contrasts of peace-loving, upright Soviets to devious, aggressive, war-mongering Americans probably had a cumulative impact as part of the construction of a postwar Soviet identity in opposition to its former wartime ally.

Although the Soviet government curtailed purchases of American films after 1946, and Soviet filmmakers denounced Hollywood's efforts to turn viewers into tools for imperialist military adventures, the Kremlin allowed a large number of American films (many obtained as war trophies) to be shown to the Soviet public. In part to provide diversions from the bleakness of everyday life and in part to gain revenue from the entertainment, the Soviet government permitted more foreign films (including many glamorous Hollywood pictures from the 1930s) to be screened than the small number of domestic films that were released. As a result, the Kremlin undermined efforts to instill confidence in the superiority of the Soviet way of life, thereby provoking objections from propaganda supervisors.[86]

That made it all the more important to attack the American way of life in the press. Top Soviet officials, who took caricatures seriously as weapons of satire, declared the illustrated magazine *Krokodil* to be ineffective in September 1948, called for the publication of more political cartoons, and demanded more vigorous criticism of degenerate Western bourgeois culture. Soviet ideologists were so desperate that they published hundreds of thousands of copies of old criticisms of America by writers such as Mayakovsky and even Mark Twain.[87]

The Soviet government was more successful in propagating a widespread sense of threats from the United States and its allies. One propaganda poster distributed in 1948, for example, showed a ghoulish Uncle Sam, clutching a torch in one hand and an atomic bomb in the other, facing a Red Army soldier who leans out of a window of the USSR and warns, "Don't Mess Around!" (see Figure 13.2).[88] Such frightening images helped to make the idea of hostile encirclement a major feature of the thinking of the Soviet people. The belief that the Soviet Union faced dangerous and insidious external enemies – reflected in popular novels such as *Podzhigateli* (*The Warmongers*, 1949) and *Zagovorshchiki* (*The Plotters*, 1951) – tended to unify the people and the government in a spirit of warlike resistance.[89]

Figure 13.2 "Ne balui!" ("Don't Mess Around!"), 1948. From Sergo Grigorian's collection, "Soviet Political Posters" (https://redavantgarde.com). Courtesy of Sergo Grigorian.

OFFENSIVES

Soviet propaganda images of Western ambitions to penetrate the Soviet bloc were not paranoid delusions. Even as the United States worked with its European allies to stabilize a non-communist sphere, American officials launched efforts to destabilize Communist control of Eastern Europe and the Soviet Union through covert action and propaganda. The United States provided financial support to anti-Soviet exile organizations in Germany, gave military aid to nationalist insurgents in the Baltic region and Ukraine, toughened Voice of America broadcasts to Soviet bloc countries, established Radio Free Europe to keep dreams of liberation alive in Eastern Europe, and created Radio Liberation to target the Soviet population. US officials persisted in their efforts despite doubts about the possibility of success. As George Kennan, the key figure in the launching of the campaigns, noted in his diary in 1949, the State Department concluded that it was futile "at this stage to encourage popular resistance to the Communist stooge governments."[90] However, Soviet officials were so alarmed by the expanded propaganda from the West that they made hugely expensive (though only spottily effective) efforts to jam US radio broadcasts.[91]

Although US "psychological warfare" did not shatter Communist control of the Soviet bloc, it had significant effects inside the United States. The "Crusade for Freedom," a public fundraising campaign that covered the fact of covert CIA financing of Radio Free Europe, enlisted American citizens in the drive to liberate Eastern Europe. As they made their contributions, Americans were encouraged to reflect on the blessings of freedom in the United States and envision American principles, including religious liberty, inspiring the captive peoples. These themes were also conveyed by movies such as *The Red Danube* (1949) and *Red Planet Mars* (1952). US officials' contrasts of American truth to Soviet lies and democratic "information" to totalitarian "propaganda" contributed to the broader use of the USSR as a foil for the affirmation of the American way. The government also supported scholarly studies of vulnerabilities that could be exploited to induce the dissolution of the Soviet system. Although the academics tended to emphasize the stability of the Soviet system and exerted little influence on actual US policy, the early studies helped to found the burgeoning field of Sovietology.[92]

While the United States moved beyond defensive containment of communism to offensive efforts to roll back Communist power in the late 1940s and early 1950s, the Soviet Union shifted from its cautious, gradualist postwar policies to endorse risky military adventures by Communist allies. After the Soviet Union successfully tested an atomic weapon in August 1949 and Chinese Communists established the People's Republic of China (PRC) in October, Stalin became more willing to support bolder moves. In February 1950, after extracting major Chinese concessions to Soviet economic and security interests, he agreed to an alliance with Mao Zedong, who was eager to promote revolution in Asia and to conquer the Nationalist bastion of Taiwan. Although Stalin earlier had resisted North Korean leader Kim Il Sung's ardent desire to forcefully unify Korea, now he gave his consent. Stalin had come to believe that the United States would not intervene in Korea and he wanted to eliminate the US ability to use South Korea as a launchpad for military aggression in the Far East. To minimize the risk of direct Soviet confrontations with American forces, Stalin imposed restrictions on Soviet advisers and pilots in North Korea and he maneuvered Communist China into a commitment that it, not the Soviet Union, would come to the aid of North Korea with ground forces if that proved necessary.[93]

When North Korean armies lunged south on June 25, 1950, many Americans, including President Truman, assumed that the invasion had been initiated and masterminded by Stalin. Political cartoons depicted a Soviet blow torch igniting the fire in Korea, labeled the Communist attack Stalin's "sole responsibility," and portrayed "satellite troops" as extensions of the Soviet hand reaching across Asia.[94] In contrast to the angry public vilification of Stalin, Truman and Secretary of State Dean Acheson initially pursued a restrained and cautious strategy, striving to avoid actions that might provoke Stalin into committing Soviet forces and turning the Korean war into a US–USSR conflict. However, many in Congress and the public expressed intense frustration with a limited war, called for aggressive action to achieve decisive victory, and even urged strikes against the Soviet Union. With congressional elections looming in November 1950, the Truman administration allowed US forces to cross the thirty-eighth parallel that divided Korea and drive north to the borders of the PRC and USSR. Amid the near euphoria of rolling back the North Korean armies, US officials hoped that reunifying Korea would be a resounding blow to Soviet global expansionism.[95]

Chinese Communist forces dashed those hopes when they entered the war in November, and by 1951 the war had settled into a bloody stalemate. Yet many Americans continued to view Stalin and the Soviet Union as the primary villains the United States faced in Asia and around the world. To Truman and many others, the Korean War confirmed suspicions that Stalin and the Soviet Union, like Hitler and Nazi Germany, were set on a campaign of global aggression that could be halted only through the vigorous use of US military forces around the globe. That misleading analogy, rooted in memories of German military conquests, Western European efforts at appeasement in the 1930s, and the Nazi–Soviet Pact, contributed to alarmist exaggeration of the scope of Soviet expansionism.[96] It also helped to solidify the shift from alliance to enmity which had already been completed by the outbreak of the Korean War.

Two developments in 1952 symbolized how far American–Soviet relations had deteriorated since 1945. First, George Kennan, who had observed the boisterous celebration of victory over Germany in Moscow in May 1945, returned to the USSR in 1952 as US Ambassador with some hopes for Soviet–American accommodation, but only a few months later made an ill-considered statement that cut short his tenure. Interviewed by American reporters during a stop in Berlin in September, Kennan unwisely declared that his sense of isolation in Moscow was worse than his experience of being interned in Nazi Germany in 1941. Outraged, the Kremlin declared Kennan *persona non grata.*[97]

Second, the Soviet government brought to a head a long-developing campaign against prominent Jews with alleged ties to the United States. In the spring and summer of 1952, fourteen Jewish intellectuals, all of whom had been members of a Jewish Anti-Fascist Committee that helped mobilize US public support for the USSR during the Second World War, were tried in a closed court and all but one were shot. Then, in January 1953, the Soviet press announced the discovery of a plot by leading doctors, most of them Jews, to murder Soviet officials at the behest of "imperialist intelligence services." Only Stalin's death from a cerebral hemorrhage on March 5 saved the doctors from execution and averted a new series of purges that probably would have included some of the dictator's closest aides.[98]

CONCLUSION

US–Soviet interactions in the eight years after the Second World War were marked by counterproductive policies with unintended consequences. When US officials increased their pressure on Soviet leaders to accept American plans for the postwar world, they expected that the awesome power of the United States, with its new atomic bombs and its enormously productive economy, combined with the devastated Soviet Union's desperate need for assistance in reconstruction, would lead Stalin and Molotov to bend. But Soviet leaders actually became more obdurate and defiant in the face of what they regarded as atomic blackmail and economic coercion. As Soviet leaders insisted on their right to install governments to their liking in Eastern Europe and pressed for strategic and economic gains in Turkey and Iran, they did not realize how they were eroding the American sympathy for the Soviet Union that had been fostered by the valiant Soviet fight against Nazi Germany. As the United States attempted to break the Communist grip on the Soviet bloc through covert action and hard-hitting propaganda, it prompted alarmed Communist leaders to tighten their control through terror and intensified repression.[99]

By the first months of 1953, there were very few direct contacts between Soviets and Americans. Stalin and Truman had not met after the Potsdam conference. The Soviet Foreign Minister and the US Secretary of State had not seen each other since 1947. US diplomats and journalists in the Soviet Union were almost completely isolated from the Soviet public. Even pro-Soviet journalists who had enjoyed friendly relations with Russian elites in earlier years felt the walls closing in upon them: the Soviet press denounced them as spies, their frightened neighbors avoided contact with them, and the press department of the Foreign Ministry largely ignored them.[100]

Hardly any ordinary citizens traveled from one country to the other. Trade between the two nations was minuscule. Soviet–American encounters thus consisted primarily of media representations and propaganda barrages.

Paradoxically, as live interaction between Americans and Soviets almost ceased, the two nations became more important to each other than ever in the definition of their identities. Soviet tyranny, atheism, and collectivism were never more central to the affirmation of American freedom, faith, and individualism. American militarism, corruption, and selfishness were never more vital to the valorization of Soviet dedication to peace, purity, and self-sacrifice. With relations between the two countries frozen in a grim stalemate, it sometimes seemed that the definition of the two countries as absolute opposites was eternal.

14

CRISES AND COEXISTENCE, 1953–1963

OVERVIEW

In the first decade after Stalin died, top leaders of both the Soviet Union and the United States earnestly wanted to ease tensions and reduce spending on armed forces. Dwight Eisenhower, Georgy Malenkov, Nikita Khrushchev, and John Kennedy succeeded at some moments in thawing the frosty hostility between their countries. Yet they did not halt the escalating arms race or reduce friction in a sustained way. Turning momentary thaws into an end of the Cold War was impossible, many have argued, because of the fundamental irreconcilability of the two nations' universalist ideologies.[1] However, such interpretations tend to obscure four significant breakthroughs when ideological differences were downplayed or transcended: a summit meeting at Geneva in 1955, an agreement for cultural exchanges in 1958, a visit to America by Khrushchev in 1959, and a partial test ban treaty in 1963.

Reaching and sustaining those achievements was difficult because of both domestic and international politics. Ambitious politicians exaggerated the menace of the enemy and clamored for tough, confrontational policies. European colonies that gained or fought for their independence in this peak period of decolonization drew American and Soviet officials into competition for the admiration and allegiance of peoples in the "Third World." Alliance politics also hampered a shift from confrontation to cooperation: Chinese Communists hectored Soviet leaders to be more aggressive against American imperialism, while US leaders utilized the idea of a Soviet threat to strengthen NATO.

Yet, other Americans and Soviets seized opportunities to bridge the polarized hostility between their countries. Scientists exchanged ideas about the dangers of radioactive fallout and ways to monitor or even halt nuclear weapons testing. Musicians and dancers performed in the cities of the other superpower and dramatized their humanity in contrast to demonic images of their nation. American tourists traveled to the Soviet Union in growing numbers, and their reports on what they saw often clashed with stereotypical representations of the USSR. Soviet students traveled to the United States in new educational exchange programs, and their visits made deep, lasting impressions. While some filmmakers and journalists reinforced negative stereotypes about the rival country, others challenged conventional notions and urged friendly relations between the two peoples. Thus, even as the two states developed much greater capacities to destroy each other, American and Soviet citizens learned about each other in ways that often strengthened belief in the possibility of living together on the same planet.

Soviet and US officials keenly recognized the importance of public attitudes both at home and abroad. They expended significant sums to sustain domestic morale, deflect foreign criticisms, and encourage faith around the world that their countries charted the most promising paths to the future. Soviet attacks on American racism, militarism, and imperialism complemented the presentation of the USSR as a peace-loving multi-national country that had banished racial prejudice and that championed anti-imperialism across the planet. American depictions of Moscow as the locus of an aggressive world communist conspiracy provided crucial justification for US military deployments in defense of "the free world." Meanwhile, contrasts of American religious faith and freedom to Soviet atheism and religious persecution buttressed Americans' sense of virtue and appealed to religious believers across the globe. Americans and Soviets thus continued, as in previous decades, to use each other as foils for the affirmation of their national identities.

Nonetheless, in the turbulent years from Stalin's death to Kennedy's assassination, advocates of dialogue and conciliation gradually eclipsed champions of isolation and confrontation. This chapter describes that shift, not as a manifestation of an abstract "discourse" in one country,[2] but as an interactive evolution. It shows how the United States and Russia haltingly moved from bitter enmity toward coexistence and cooperation despite crises in Germany, Hungary, Cuba, and other parts of the world.

NEW LEADERS, NEW IDEAS, AND OLD THINKING

Stalin's successors were scared. The old tyrant had told them the country would perish without him because they were "blind like young kittens" and could not recognize enemies. Now, in March 1953, he was gone. The enormous empire had industrialized and developed massive military power during his reign, but its economy was still dwarfed by US productivity and it was nearly surrounded by adversaries' military bases. The new leaders in the Kremlin feared that foreign powers might be emboldened by Stalin's death to foment a new war or to stir trouble inside the Soviet Union.

The new Soviet leaders' worries did not leave them paralyzed. Instead, their anxieties spurred them to launch a peace offensive to enlist foreign sympathizers, reduce international tensions, and raise their standing at home. Four days after Stalin's death, Vyacheslav Molotov, who regained the post of Foreign Minister, declared that the Kremlin's chief concern in foreign policy was "not to permit a new war, to live in peace with all peoples." A week later Premier Georgy Malenkov proclaimed Soviet interest in negotiations with the West, announcing that "there is no dispute or unresolved question that cannot be settled peacefully by mutual agreement."[3]

Many in the West immediately dismissed such statements as propaganda ploys. Yet the Soviet government also initiated important policy changes. It urged its North Korean and Chinese allies to make concessions that facilitated an armistice in the Korean War (signed in July). It moved to reduce military spending. It floated the idea of a meeting between Eisenhower and Malenkov to discuss issues such as disarmament and the control of atomic energy. And it halted the extreme propaganda vilification of America. For example, the leading illustrated magazine *Krokodil* published virtually no anti-American cartoons for three months – a shift that suggested many of the top Soviet leaders did not believe demonization of the United States was necessary to maintain their grip on power.[4]

On the other side, many Americans' antipathy to the Soviet Union had come to focus on the "evil" Joseph Stalin. When he died, American newspaper editors declared that he was "sure of a monstrous place in history" and compared him to Genghis Khan and Hitler.[5]

Yet few American commentators saw the burial of Stalin as an opportunity to begin a new era in relations with Soviet Russia. As the *Washington Post* explained, Stalin's heirs were products of his political machine and, if they deviated from his line, they could be "even worse." The few journalists who saw opportunities from Stalin's passing tended to focus on how "the free world" could exploit Communist weaknesses, especially through propaganda appeals to the Russian people and the "enslaved nations."[6] The ideas of "rollback" and "liberation," championed in three widely read books in 1953, were more popular than dialogue and negotiation.[7]

Thus, many Americans hoped when Stalin died that Soviet subjects would rise up in rebellion against their oppressive rulers. Yet, at least among ethnic Russians, millions somberly and often tearfully mourned the longtime leader, whom they venerated as a paternal, even godlike figure. That response did not lead many American commentators to reconsider their assumptions. Instead, journalists tended to explain away the mass mourning. The *Washington Post* attributed it to the highly emotional character of Great Russians. A veteran Moscow correspondent asserted that Russians waited in long lines to see Stalin's body in order "to make damn sure he was dead."[8]

Thus, in the aftermath of Stalin's death, there was a wide gulf between American public expectations and realities in Russia. The overwhelming majority of intellectuals were devoted to the Soviet system. Even the *stiliagi*, privileged youth who aped American dress and dances, did not dream of political revolt.[9]

Like American journalists, US policymakers doubted the possibility of meaningful change from within the Soviet system and hoped to stir rebellion against it. Secretary of State John Foster Dulles repeatedly emphasized that Soviet leaders' expressions of interest in peaceful coexistence meant at most a change in tactics, not a repudiation of their aggressive ambitions or a basic alteration of their "total dictatorship." He also strongly opposed engaging in serious negotiations with the Soviets, because that might weaken the anti-Soviet sentiment needed to unify the West and justify arms spending. President Eisenhower's special adviser on psychological warfare, C. D. Jackson, stressed the unique opportunity he saw "to overload the enemy" at a moment of weakness and spur the "disintegration of the empire." Like Jackson, Eisenhower wanted to make a bold move to capitalize on the extraordinary situation and, like Dulles, he was wary of being deceived by a Soviet propaganda line. With State Department Soviet expert Charles Bohlen warning that a direct assault on the Kremlin would help the new Communist regime to consolidate its position, US planning turned toward a subtler approach. Eisenhower called for a "psychological plan" that would call attention to the Soviet government's costly expenditures on armaments, appeal to the desire of ordinary people in Russia for a better standard of living, and suggest that they could attain that if their government cooperated with the West.[10]

That idea became a central feature of a major address, "The Chance for Peace," that Eisenhower gave on April 16. While acknowledging encouraging statements by Stalin's successors, the president declared: "We care nothing for mere rhetoric." He demanded actions to prove the sincerity of Soviet interest in peace, such as signing a treaty to end the occupation of Austria, concluding an armistice in Korea, allowing the reunification of Germany, and granting East European nations full independence. Such steps, he continued, would allow Washington to work with Moscow to limit military spending and to contribute a percentage of the savings to an international fund for economic development. Since US officials knew Soviet leaders were unlikely to take some of those actions, particularly freeing Eastern Europe, Eisenhower's speech must be seen primarily as an effort to gain advantage in the global propaganda struggle.[11]

In an unprecedented move, the Soviet press published Eisenhower's speech on April 25 and welcomed it in front-page editorials that expressed a desire for negotiations. Yet privately Soviet officials considered the president's address "irritating and provocative," and their belated response seemed disappointing or propagandistic to American observers. US diplomats discounted the possibility that the Kremlin had a sincere interest in a dramatic improvement in relations, arguing that the "totalitarian" nature of the Soviet state limited its ability to shift toward détente. As a result, the prospect for warmer relations dimmed.[12]

The partially opened door slammed shut in June, when East Germans revolted against the Communist regime. Stalin's successors had encouraged a softening of the harsh policies of the East German regime and some even thought Soviet security would not be jeopardized by allowing a reunified bourgeois-democratic Germany. But violent demonstrations by underpaid, hard-driven workers in East Berlin and other cities on June 17 provoked Soviet repression and a revival of suspicion of the West. Soviet officials privately assumed that Western agents had instigated the demonstrations, and Soviet propagandists returned to emphasizing the menace of US collusion with "fascist" and "revanchist" elements in Germany. A US-supported radio station in Berlin (RIAS) had encouraged non-violent challenges to the East German government and cheered the protesters when they rebelled. But Eisenhower rejected US military aid to East German rebels as too risky. In the aftermath of the revolt, he approved C. D. Jackson's plan "to nourish resistance to communist oppression," encourage defections by East European leaders, and create underground organizations that would be ready to fight against Communist rule in the future.[13]

While the East German rising initially inspired excitement among American newspaper editors about the sprouting of seeds of freedom, the crushing of the rebellion triggered revulsion at Russian imperialism. In the summer of 1953, Americans remained as suspicious of Soviet global ambitions as they had been at the height of the Korean War in the fall of 1950. Despite the Soviet peace overtures since Stalin's death, four out of five Americans surveyed in August 1953 believed that Russia was "trying to build herself up to be the ruling power of the world." Thus, few in either country felt optimistic about the prospect of a breakthrough as the superpowers prepared to test hydrogen bombs for the first time.[14]

Domestic political dynamics in the Soviet Union and the United States also obstructed progress in Soviet–American relations. A vicious Red scare in America, spearheaded by Senator Joseph McCarthy, intimidated and stifled peace activists and civil rights leaders.[15] In Moscow, Nikita Khrushchev, First Secretary of the Communist Party, worked to undermine Malenkov by alleging that he had shown weakness in relation to US imperialism and sown ideological confusion with a declaration that nuclear war would destroy all of civilization.[16]

FROM VILIFICATION TO CIVILITY, 1954–1955

As McCarthyism climaxed and Khrushchev outmaneuvered Malenkov, leaders and propagandists often emphasized the stark differences between two ways of life. One key theme in the construction of difference concerned religion. Beginning with his inaugural address, Eisenhower often contrasted the light of American religious faith to the darkness of Soviet atheism. Congress affirmed the religious foundation of the United States by inserting "under God" into the Pledge of Allegiance in 1954 and designating "In God We Trust" as the national motto the next year. Meanwhile, a Soviet journalist's derision of the Wall Street connections of Cardinal Francis Spellman was one part of a much broader attack on the hypocrisy of a corrupt and unjust capitalist society.[17]

Yet a countervailing trend developed. American and Soviet journalists contributed to increasingly complex representations of the other country with richly detailed accounts of their experiences.

After Stalin's death, American news organizations found it easier to obtain Soviet visas and sent more correspondents to Russia. Among the journalists who capitalized on heightened public interest in the USSR by writing books about their time there, the most influential was Harrison Salisbury, the *New York Times*' correspondent in Moscow from 1949 to 1954. In part because readers of his dispatches sometimes had accused him of being pro-Soviet, Salisbury made it plain from the outset of *American in Russia* (1955), that he "detested" the Soviet system, with its obstructionist bureaucrats and its oppressive, omnipresent police. Following in the footsteps of the late nineteenth-century journalist and crusader George Kennan, Salisbury used an investigation of conditions in Siberia as a springboard for depicting the whole country as a prison. Yet the independent-minded Minnesota native broke with conventional thinking in other ways, especially by challenging the notion that Russians yearned to revolt against their oppressive Communist rulers. Ordinary Russians turned to vodka rather than thoughts of revolution, Salisbury reported, and the educated middle class was more interested in televisions than in politics.[18]

Salisbury's widely lauded book contributed to a broader moderation of American attitudes toward Russia. As Yale professor Frederick Barghoorn commented, Salisbury provided "a corrective to exaggerated hopes that the people could ... overthrow the regime." With dreams of liberating Russia fading, hopes for gradual liberalization rose. Polls showed that most Americans, especially the college-educated, were optimistic about exerting a positive influence on Russians through diplomacy, travel, and peaceful interaction.[19]

A few months after the publication of Salisbury's book, a delegation of seven Soviet journalists came to the United States – the first such tour since 1946. Visiting newspaper offices, seeing the homes of middle-class Americans, and attending a party in Hollywood enabled the journalists to write vivid articles about America after they returned to the USSR. The delegation's report stressed the need to rethink stale Soviet propaganda formulas about the United States, noted that constant emphasis on the dark sides of American life hampered the pursuit of better relations, and urged more flexible, cooperative treatment of American correspondents in the future.[20]

Khrushchev helped create the climate for the Soviet journalists' trip.[21] Seeking to break out of international isolation and reduce the cost of the arms race, he made a series of concessions, most importantly by approving a treaty to end the Soviet and Western occupations of Austria. Eisenhower and Foster Dulles had long resisted calls for a meeting with Stalin's successors, because they feared a summit would make the Soviet government seem less menacing and hence make it more difficult to secure appropriations for defense from Western parliaments. Yet Western European worries about American militarism and bellicosity, aggravated by Dulles' talk of "massive retaliation" against communist aggression, put increasing pressure on Washington. In response, Eisenhower agreed to meet with Soviet leaders at Geneva in July 1955.

In preparation for the meeting, US psychological warfare experts developed a proposal for mutual aerial inspection of each country that was designed to contrast US openness to Soviet secrecy and make the United States appear sincerely interested in resolving the Cold War.[22] The "Open Skies" proposal achieved the objective of throwing Soviet leaders onto the defensive when Khrushchev rejected it as a plan for spying. Yet Soviet officials also succeeded in improving European and American images of them simply by appearing at Geneva in suits and engaging in polite diplomatic discussions.

Conservative newspapers in the United States, which opposed any compromise with godless communists, shrilly warned from the start of the conference that well-intentioned Americans were in danger of being fooled by smiling Soviet faces.[23] Some anticommunists, such as syndicated columnist David Lawrence, also insisted that peace could come only with the liberation of Soviet bloc peoples from evil dictatorships, not from diplomacy.[24]

Yet even some of the conservative papers agreed by the end of the conference that talking was better than shooting.[25] Liberal papers tended to go much further. The *Atlanta Constitution* welcomed the opening of a way to real coexistence. Cartoonist Daniel Fitzpatrick conveyed liberal optimism most vividly with a picture of Cold War ice melting next to a flower of hope (Figure 14.1).[26]

GENEVA WEATHER REPORT

Sun., July 24, 1955   ST. LOUIS POST-DISPATCH

Figure 14.1 Daniel Fitzpatrick, "Geneva Weather Report," *St. Louis Post-Dispatch*, July 24, 1955. Digital Collection, The State Historical Society of Missouri.

One of the reasons the *Des Moines Register* was especially enthusiastic about the Geneva summit was that at the same time twelve Soviet agricultural officials visited Iowa in an exchange that a *Register* editor helped to launch. Overall, the Soviet delegation received an extremely warm welcome and extensive, positive media coverage (which the press in Moscow noted). The Soviets' sense of humor, friendliness, and acceptance of an invitation to a church service helped to win the hearts of many Iowans. At the grassroots, as at Geneva, Russians appeared human. "They don't have horns and hooves," the *Register* observed.[27]

Across the United States, the Geneva conference seemed to improve the spirit of American–Soviet interaction. "East and West Linked by New Civility," proclaimed one front-page headline. Fifty-two percent of Americans surveyed expected relations with Russia to be better from then on.[28]

The Soviet press, which vigorously promoted the Kremlin line, showed even greater enthusiasm. An editorial in *Izvestiia* heralded "the beginning of a new stage in international relations." Political cartoons persistently portrayed the Geneva summit as a major blow to the anti-Soviet press and arms manufacturers who profited from Cold War tensions. From August to December, *Krokodil* repeatedly depicted the meeting at Geneva dispelling dark clouds of distrust or crushing barriers, both of which were labelled "Cold War." In October *Pravda* expressed confidence that, in spite of the propaganda of reactionary circles in the West, "the peoples of the world will not permit the return of the cold war."[29]

To Soviet leaders, the Western demonization of the Soviet Union had been an alarming and central feature of "the Cold War." As Minister of Defense Georgy Zhukov explained to Eisenhower at Geneva, the Soviet people were "fed up to the teeth" with war and "no one in the Soviet Government" had any intention of launching an aggressive war against the United States. False Western pictures of Soviet threats, Zhukov complained, were being manufactured by "dark forces" that sought to undermine Soviet–American relations. The meetings at Geneva reduced such vilification of the Soviet Union and lessened Soviet fears of a new military intervention from the West. That helped some of them – especially Khrushchev – to feel that they could take the risk of making dramatic changes.[30]

THE CONVULSIONS OF 1956

In February 1956, Khrushchev stunned Soviet citizens by making two major speeches that linked an emerging détente and domestic liberalization. In the first address, which focused on Soviet foreign policy, Khrushchev declared, in contrast to Marxist-Leninist-Stalinist doctrine, that war was not inevitable, because Soviet thermonuclear weapons would prevent imperialists from unleashing war. Owing to the peaceable foreign policy of the socialist countries, he asserted, perilous tensions in international relations had yielded to a certain détente. During the peaceful coexistence of capitalism and socialism, Khrushchev urged, socialists should closely study science and technology in the capitalist world and he called for more trade between the two camps. Khrushchev particularly emphasized the "tremendous importance" to the Soviet Union of establishing friendly relations with the United States (though American newspapers discounted the changes his speech entailed and stressed the continuing menace of international communism).[31]

While Khrushchev envisioned trade with the United States as central to Soviet economic development, he saw a bold denunciation of Stalin as essential to building a political system in which disagreements would not be punished by death and major policies would not be distorted by the whims of individual rulers. On February 25, in a second address, Khrushchev detailed the abuses of power by Stalin dating back to the last years of Lenin. In contrast to Stalin's arbitrariness, Khrushchev proposed a return to Leninist principles, including a collective leadership and acceptance of criticism within a revitalized Communist Party.

US policymakers had mixed reactions to Khrushchev's de-Stalinization. By May 1956, Secretary of State Dulles concluded (and Eisenhower agreed) that some of the liberalizing changes were genuine and that the Soviet Union should be induced to continue moving toward being "a decent member of the society of nations." On the other hand, US officials sought to exploit the anti-Stalin campaign to loosen the ties that bound East European states to Moscow and to encourage agitation for freedom within those satellites. Informed of a riot in Poland in June, Dulles remarked: "When they begin to crack, they can crack fast. We have to keep the pressure on."[32]

Khrushchev hoped that by proving the peaceable nature of the Soviet Union he would make it hard to justify NATO before Western public opinion and thereby shake NATO unity. He did not anticipate that lowering the level of tension with the West and reducing fears of the Kremlin in the East would shake the Soviet bloc.

By May, newspapers around the world had published Khrushchev's speech, which undermined the authority of Stalinist leaders in Eastern Europe and emboldened their critics. In June a demonstration for "Bread and Freedom" in Poznań triggered a violent overreaction by the insecure

Polish regime. By October, Khrushchev had come to the verge of ordering Soviet troops to occupy Warsaw, before deciding to be satisfied with assurances from the nationalist and Communist leader Władysław Gomułka that Poland would remain within the Warsaw Pact.

Almost simultaneously, tensions exploded in Hungary. After demonstrators demanded a reconsideration of the Soviet–Hungarian relationship and withdrawal of all Soviet troops, Soviet leaders decided to suppress the widening rebellion with a military intervention that caused thousands of casualties. Appalled by the bloodshed, Soviet leaders decided to withdraw Soviet forces to allow the reformist Communist leader Imre Nagy a chance to stabilize the situation. Mindful of the global propaganda struggle, Khrushchev explained to his colleagues that it would be politically advantageous to the Soviet Union to appear more restrained than the British and French, who attacked Egypt at the end of October after it had nationalized the Suez Canal. However, when Nagy announced on October 31 that Hungary would withdraw from the Warsaw Pact, Khrushchev, prodded by the Chinese Communists, decided to send Soviet forces back into Budapest. If the Soviet Union accepted the loss of Hungary, Khrushchev explained, the Americans, British, and French would perceive it as a sign of weakness and would be emboldened to go further on the offensive.[33]

While Khrushchev weighed the implications of Soviet decisions for perceptions of the USSR, US leaders worried about the image of the United States, especially in the eyes of American voters. As the presidential election campaign of 1956 entered its final months, Democratic candidate Adlai Stevenson put Eisenhower and Dulles on the defensive by charging that their silence about the Poznań rising showed that the Republican pledge of "liberation" of the captive nations had been merely a cynical ploy. Two weeks before the election, Eisenhower affirmed the US "mission as the champion of freedom." Dulles similarly insisted on October 27 that the United States "continues its historic role" of inspiring subject peoples to demand liberty and independence.[34]

In part because of such rhetoric, Soviet leaders suspected and alleged that the United States had incited the demonstrations and rebellions in Poland and Hungary. Yet Eisenhower and Dulles restrained US policy toward both countries. Dulles ruled out the use of US force to aid Poland in a television appearance on October 21. Eisenhower barred US military aid to Hungarian rebels that he believed would risk war between the nuclear-armed superpowers.[35]

Such caution at the moment of crisis did not erase the impressions fostered by years of speeches and radio broadcasts. On October 25, thousands of Hungarians who gathered in front of the US legation in Budapest shouted for help. And as they battled Soviet forces, some Radio Free Europe broadcasters went beyond their authorization to offer tactical advice, including how to make "Molotov cocktails" and destroy tanks.[36]

Shocked and angered by the Soviet assault, US leaders sought to make the Kremlin pay a price. The US ambassador at the United Nations vehemently condemned Moscow's "cynical and wanton acts of aggression." Eisenhower approved the worldwide distribution of films of Soviet tanks killing Hungarians.[37]

Yet other considerations constrained US leaders' expression of their indignation. Dulles thought the Soviet action was "not quite as bad" as the British and French bombing of Egypt. Perhaps most importantly, top US officials did not want to "reverse the spirit of Geneva," jeopardize the small gains from that conference (such as distribution of *Amerika* magazine in the USSR), or "revive the cold war on the scale of intensity of the late Stalin period," as diplomat Jacob Beam noted.[38]

In the short term, the violent repression of the Hungarian revolution severely damaged images of the Soviet Union in the United States. Editorials scathingly denounced "Communist barbarism" and accused the Soviet government of "the foulest treachery." Cartoonists again drew images of the bloodthirsty Russian bear. The *New York Times* asserted that Soviet bullets killed "the picture of a reformed, penitent Russia seeking to repudiate Stalinism and practice coexistence."[39]

Yet the damage would have been much greater if news of events in Hungary had not been eclipsed by attention to the US presidential election and by the imperialist attack on Egypt. Although some conservatives urged breaking diplomatic relations with Moscow, by the summer of 1957 more Americans favored Soviet–American tourist exchanges than had two years earlier. To many Americans, Khrushchev became the butcher of Budapest, yet within three years the same percentage of Americans (roughly 50 percent) favored inviting him to the United States as had approved of that idea before the crises in Poland and Hungary. Thus, American public anger did not lead to a lasting increase in the number of Americans who wanted to shun the Kremlin rulers.[40]

COMPETING FOR INFLUENCE IN THE MIDDLE EAST AND AFRICA

While US–Soviet tension over Eastern Europe subsided after 1956, the superpower competition for influence in Asia and Africa expanded and intensified. Clashes between movements for independence and weakening

European colonial powers sparked especially sharp Soviet–American confrontations in the Middle East and central Africa.

After resolving to crush the Hungarian revolt, Khrushchev turned his attention to the crisis over the Suez Canal, where British and French forces seized positions on November 5. In response, Khrushchev made two threats. First, he proposed a joint intervention, along with the United States and United Nations, to halt the fighting, but indicated that the USSR was ready to act alone. Second, he directed Soviet ambassadors to warn London and Paris that they would be attacked by Soviet missiles if they did not halt their aggression. Unlike the United States, which actually had the air power to back up its warnings of "massive retaliation" against Communist aggression, Moscow did not have enough nuclear-armed missiles and long-range planes to carry out Khrushchev's threats. Yet some US officials took Khrushchev's statements quite seriously and believed that they affected British and French leaders. In reality, tough oil and currency embargoes imposed by Eisenhower did more to push London and Paris to accept a ceasefire. However, Khrushchev believed that his bluffs had worked, and that led him to resort to similar tactics later. In October 1957, for example, Soviet forces mobilized on Turkey's border to deter that US ally from attacking Syria, and in July 1958 Moscow warned of war if the United States or Britain used force to try to reverse a revolution in Iraq.[41]

Earlier, Washington had generally supported its British and French allies, yet Eisenhower's fear of antagonizing the Arab world and opening the oil-rich Middle East to wider Soviet influence led him to vigorously oppose the British–French–Israeli war against Egypt. Trying to overcome the effects of that debacle, in January 1957 Eisenhower asked Congress to authorize him to provide economic and military aid to the region, as well as to use force to protect nations menaced by "international communism." To justify his request, Eisenhower asserted that both under the tsars and under the Bolsheviks Russia had "long sought to dominate the Middle East." Like Truman in 1947, Eisenhower greatly exaggerated the Soviet threat; atheistic communism had little appeal to Muslim believers. Yet many newspapers followed the president's lead in the following years, printing editorials about the ancient Russian dream of penetrating to the Persian Gulf and political cartoons that showed the hammer and sickle on the banner of Arab nationalism or a terrifying bear moving into the region.[42] When Eisenhower sent thousands of marines to Lebanon in July 1958, he pushed Arab nationalists closer to the Soviet Union. Thus, Moscow's prestige in the Middle East rose not because of any special appeal of the Soviet system, but in reaction to US policies.[43]

The dynamics of a "zero-sum" competition, with a Soviet gain seen as a US defeat and vice versa, were evident in Africa as well as in the Middle East. The large and centrally located Congo, which gained its independence from Belgium in June 1960, became the site of a particularly heated struggle. Although Congolese prime minister Patrice Lumumba was a nationalist inclined to non-alignment in the Cold War, US officials suspected that he was under communist influence. The suspicion seemed to be confirmed when he turned to Khrushchev for planes and trucks to help him take back the mineral-rich secessionist province of Katanga. In August 1960, Eisenhower authorized the CIA to assassinate Lumumba, who was ousted by a coup in September and then killed by Belgian and Congolese soldiers in January 1961. While Khrushchev's vehement denunciations of colonialism fostered an impression of an idealistic Soviet commitment to aid national liberation struggles, his actual policies toward the Congo (as well as other new African states) were cautious and hesitant. After Lumumba's death, Khrushchev provided only limited aid to Lumumbist forces. Instead of an aggressive strategy for backing anticolonial movements, Soviet policy in Africa tended to be improvised and reactive.[44] Thus, US leaders tended to overplay Soviet and communist threats in Africa as well as the Middle East.

CULTURAL INTERACTIONS AND CHANGING REPRESENTATIONS, 1955–1961

While the United States and the Soviet Union vied for influence in less developed countries, they widened the peaceful interaction between their own societies. The late 1950s brought a significant expansion of travel, tourism, and cultural exchanges, which spurred significant changes in media representations.

After Stalin's death, the Soviet government sought to broaden its influence in the West and undermine images of it as alien and hostile by opening the doors of the country to foreign visitors and by dispatching musicians, writers, and dancers on tours of Western nations. In one early move, the Kremlin decided in March 1954 to permit tourism to the USSR.[45]

Some of the most influential American visitors were journalists who wrote books about their trips that encouraged Americans to set aside old images of a static society silently suffering under Stalinist rule. On the contrary, the journalists depicted the Soviet Union as a dynamic, powerful nation that Americans would have to coexist with for the foreseeable future.

Late in 1956, veteran correspondent John Gunther flew to Moscow and spent many weeks touring Khrushchev's land. By the fall of 1957, when the successful orbiting of the first Soviet satellite ignited public fascination with the rival superpower, Gunther managed to get a book into print. Excerpted in *Reader's Digest* and *Time, Inside Russia Today* became one of the most widely read books ever written by an American about Russia.[46]

Although the Soviet news agency TASS immediately denounced Gunther's book for containing "lies" and "gossip,"[47] the main thrust of *Inside Russia Today* was to challenge negative preconceptions about the Soviet Union. While there were indeed "frightful evils, cruelties, and suppressions," Gunther argued, there were also "some astonishing accomplishments," especially in education, science, and technology. Contesting assumptions that Russians yearned to break out of their totalitarian jail, Gunther emphasized that they were intensely patriotic, believing that Russia was *their* country. That nationalist pride, together with the upward mobility of many children of illiterate peasants, tended to make the Soviet regime "stable." Hence, the idea of "pious wishful thinkers in the State Department and elsewhere" that the Soviet Union would crumble was unrealistic. Gunther therefore stressed that it was time for Americans to adjust themselves "to the necessity of having to live in a world side by side with them."[48]

Less than a year after Gunther's book appeared, NBC correspondent Irving Levine published *Main Street, U.S.S.R.*, a thick description of everyday life in the Soviet Union. Like Gunther, Levine stressed that "the Russians are a patriotic people." He also warned that he had "never heard a Russian suggest that he would like the American army to liberate him." Many Russians had become cynical about Communist rhetoric, Levine noted, yet he cautioned that it was "naïve to think that the West simply could wait for Communist Russia to crumple from within." Instead, the West should expand commerce to help shape "a Russia that is more moderate, more reasonable, more amenable to living and letting live." While reviewers found Levine's account more superficial than Gunther's weightier work, some praised it for helping to "build a bridge between Main Street, U.S.A., and its counterpart" in the east. The idea of mellowing the Soviet Union through peaceful engagement gained further support when former ambassador Averell Harriman echoed Levine and Gunther in a book published a year later.[49]

By 1958, the number of Americans traveling to the Soviet Union increased dramatically, with 3,000 tourists going that summer. What tourists said about the country after returning to the United States troubled some American anticommunists. Journalist Eugene Lyons, for example, expressed dismay that tourists reported the Russian people loved the Soviet regime.[50]

One of the Kremlin's most ambitious efforts to promote foreign under-standing and affection was a massive festival for world youth in Moscow in the summer of 1957. By welcoming more than 30,000 young people from around the world (including about 160 Americans), the Kremlin sought to challenge the notion that it was hiding behind an "iron curtain" and promote an image of the Soviet Union as a friendly country dedicated to peace. However, the impact on American images of the USSR was slight in comparison with the effect on Soviet youth who encountered Americans in the flesh or saw televised images of American-style dancing.[51] Since young Soviets could wear jeans and boogie-woogie without losing their faith in socialism, the youth festival should not be seen as the beginning of the end of the USSR.[52] Yet it subtly undermined Soviet exceptionalism by highlight-ing the common humanity of peoples in East and West and promoted the development of a more cosmopolitan Soviet internationalism.[53]

Soviet officials divided over how to respond to the challenges posed by the infiltration of American and other Western culture via tourists, radio broadcasts, and exhibitions. While reformist Soviet officials relaxed earlier restrictions on Western fashion, music, and dancing as part of an effort to appeal to Soviet youth, more orthodox Soviet officials continued to be alarmed by the subversive potential of such influences and sought to control them.[54]

One way to tarnish the image and appeal of America was to emphasize racism in the United States. The upsurge of the civil rights movement after 1954 and heightened media attention to events such as the Montgomery bus boycott in 1955–1956 and the Little Rock, Arkansas school desegregation in 1957 gave Soviet propagandists large targets.[55] Although Soviet cartoonists attacked American racial discrimination much less often than they fired at US militarism and imperialism, US leaders' belief that Soviet propaganda about American race relations was severely damaging US prestige in the "Third World" ultimately led to much greater White House support for civil rights progress, particularly key legislation in the 1960s.[56]

While the United States and the Soviet Union vied for influence around the world, they widened the cultural interaction between their countries. In January 1958, they signed an agreement for reciprocal exchanges of radio and television broadcasts, films, students, professors, and exhibitions. Three months later, a music competition in Moscow suggested the potentially far-reaching implications of cultural encounters. Although Texan pianist Van Cliburn won rapturous applause for his passionate playing from Soviet audiences and unanimous support from the Tchaikovsky Competition jurors, some hardline ideologues opposed awarding him the top prize. Yet one of the judges argued that giving the prize to Cliburn "could end the Cold War" and Khrushchev agreed that having an American win would be good for the Soviet image in the world, so Cliburn received the award.[57]

The next year, a Soviet exhibition featuring machinery, science, and technology (including models of satellites) opened in New York and, more dramatically, an American exhibition opened in Moscow. It soon became famous as the site of the "kitchen debate" between Khrushchev and Vice President Richard Nixon, who extolled the way a model kitchen reflected the superior comfort and convenience of the American way of life. The notion that Russians could be seduced by American consumer goods was common then: it had been central to the movies *Silk Stockings* and *Jet Pilot* in 1957.[58] Paralleling the films, the organizers of the US exhibition hoped it would excite such keen Russian desire for American products that it would delegitimize Soviet claims about the superiority of socialism and engender destabilizing dissatisfaction with Soviet shortages. Despite his awareness of those American expectations, Khrushchev allowed the exhibition to open. He believed the Soviet people were proud of their country's recent technological triumphs and convinced that their rapidly modernizing nation soon would have many of the goods Americans displayed.

Khrushchev's confidence appears to have been justified. At a time when Soviet citizens generally believed what the Soviet press reported, many Soviet visitors to the exhibition expressed optimism that the USSR soon would overtake the United States. They also accepted assertions that ordinary workers in the United States could not afford the goods displayed and expressed faith that a socialist way of life, with general equality, free education, free medical care, and old age pensions, was superior to American individualistic materialism. Thus, the misleading reports by American journalists that many of the almost 3 million Soviet visitors to the exhibition had been so excited by its irresistible allure that they lost self-control may have been most important for the way they reaffirmed US public faith in the superiority of the American way of life.[59]

While Washington sent exhibitions to influence Russian views of America, the Kremlin dispatched tourists, musicians, and dancers to try to affect American images of the Soviet Union. The Soviet government authorized only a couple of hundred Soviet tourists to go to the United States each year. It expected the tourists, overwhelmingly from the educated elite, to be effective envoys for peaceful coexistence who would correct misconceptions about the country. Although the Soviet government also hoped that returned visitors' accounts would strengthen faith in the advantages of socialism, their published reports and private conversations actually contributed to continuing contestation over images of America. Two of the Soviet students sent to New York City in 1958, Alexander Yakovlev and Oleg Kalugin, who would play prominent roles in the 1980s, exemplified the ambivalence. Admiration of a land of abundance, with skyscrapers and mass-produced cars, clashed with negative views of America's racial inequality, calculating selfishness, shallow friendliness, and sexual promiscuity.[60]

Dancers achieved Soviet goals much more effectively. The Moiseyev Folk Dance Ensemble and the Bolshoi and Kirov Ballets won rapturous reviews for their performances in the United States.[61] The large Moiseyev company performed high-spirited adaptations of traditional folk dances from different parts of the Soviet Union in an effort to display the diversity of the multinational country and to reveal "the soul of the people." The company sparked keen interest and generated unprecedented ticket sales in cities across the United States in the spring of 1958. As one editorial explained, much of the excitement came from "seeing Russians – real people – laughing, dancing, waving," after having "known Soviet citizens only by hearsay" for decades. Journalists repeatedly exclaimed that the female dancers were just like American girls and women: they enjoyed dating boys and they loved to shop. While the dancers thus fulfilled Kremlin hopes to counter negative stereotypes and promote warmer feelings among Americans, depictions of the dancers in Soviet newspapers and magazines also heightened readers' pride in their country. For decades Soviets had admired America's advanced technology and vibrant popular culture; now, the Soviet press suggested, Russians were winning the admiration of Americans and matching or surpassing their cultural achievements. Thus, Soviet dancers and the representations of them influenced the reshaping of images and identities in both countries.[62]

The most important Soviet visitor to the United States, Khrushchev himself, set off in the middle of September in a gigantic new jet plane. While eager to assert Soviet technological prowess, enhance Soviet prestige, and win respect from Americans, he also longed to establish closer, more friendly relations. As he toured America, the bumptious Khrushchev occasionally vented frustrations at what he saw as insults or provocations, and his meetings with Eisenhower brought no major agreements. Yet Soviet journalists and officials hailed Khrushchev's trip for delivering a "blow to the Cold War" and causing the majority of Americans to change their minds about the USSR.[63]

Such assertions were as overblown as the fears of anticommunists and Russophobes that America was in danger of being carried away by a wave of pro-Soviet sympathy. A majority of Americans concluded that Khrushchev's visit had been "a good thing," but most remained skeptical about his propagandistic proposal for complete disarmament. Khrushchev succeeded in showing Americans that he did not "wear horns," but most still regarded him as a tough and potentially dangerous competitor.[64]

Yet Khrushchev's trip to the United States and his anticipation of a return visit by Eisenhower ushered in euphoria in Moscow. Immediately after returning to the USSR, Khrushchev voiced his hope not merely to thaw the Cold War, but to end it. Although there were "evil forces" in America that wanted to continue the Cold War and the arms race, Khrushchev reported, Eisenhower "sincerely wishes to see the end of the cold war." That, combined with the warm reception he received in many cities and the generally "objective coverage" of his visit by the press, led Khrushchev to cheer the prospect of "Soviet–American friendship."[65]

This quickly became a major theme in the Soviet press. The peaceful competition between socialism and capitalism would continue, but expanding contacts between the two countries, combined with disarmament and test ban negotiations, would make it more difficult for American politicians to propagate the alarming images of the Soviet Union that justified enormous military expenditures. Famed cartoonist Boris Efimov captured the Soviet optimism at the end of 1959 by depicting a handsome, smiling young Russian pointing to a bottle of champagne on ice and saying to a handsome, smiling young American: "Let that be the only ice remaining between us!"[66] (Figure 14.2.)

Figure 14.2 "Let That Be the Only Ice Remaining between Us!" *Krokočil,* No. 36, 30 December 1959. Courtesy of the *Novaia Gazeta.*

According to Khrushchev's foremost biographer, such enthusiasm about Eisenhower and the hollowing out of the enemy image of the United States alarmed Soviet ideological watchdogs and led to "a massive spontaneous ideological defection." Yet the dramatic reduction in attacks on US militarism and imperialism did not necessarily entail a loss of faith in the Soviet Union, which continued to vaunt its achievements with rockets as proof of the validity of Lenin's dream of a superior socialist modernity. Such faith would culminate in April 1961 when cosmonaut Yuri Gagarin became the first human in space.[67]

THE ARMS RACE AND PEACE MOVEMENTS, 1957–1960

While the United States and USSR vied in the space race, scientists and peace activists urged halts to the testing of nuclear weapons and protested against the costly, dangerous military competition. On the other hand, weapons manufacturers, military bureaucrats, and nationalistic politicians pushed for increases in spending in order to catch up or stay ahead in the arms race. Eisenhower and Khrushchev both resisted pressures to escalate arms spending and sought to appeal to the growing peace movements. However, despite their recognition of the rising power of world opinion against the arms race, both leaders ultimately responded more strongly to concerns about maintaining the global prestige of their countries.

Two events in the summer of 1957 reflected these contradictory dynamics in Soviet–American relations. In July, scientists from the United States, the Soviet Union, and several other countries met in Pugwash, Nova Scotia to discuss the dangers of nuclear weapons and ways to control them. Although the scientists did not reach complete consensus, they generally agreed on the need to break the momentum of the arms race. Moreover, the sheer fact that leading scientists from different sides of the "iron curtain" could talk face to face with respect and good will marked a breakthrough. On the other hand, in August the Soviet Union conducted its first successful test of an intercontinental ballistic missile (ICBM), which appeared to indicate that Khrushchev soon would have the ability to launch nuclear weapons on rockets aimed at the United States.[68]

American fears of Soviet capabilities became frenzied in October, when the Soviet Union launched a small satellite, Sputnik I, into orbit. To many Americans, Sputnik's harmless beeps signaled Soviet domination of space and a shameful US inferiority. The sense of national humiliation worsened in December when a Navy rocket with a tiny satellite (quickly dubbed "Flopnik") failed to lift off its launch pad. For decades Americans had been confident of their technological superiority over supposedly inept Slavs, yet now the Soviet Union seemed to have surged ahead on the road to the future.[69]

With his authority and confidence hugely boosted by Soviet rocketry, Khrushchev ventured a bold move to mobilize world opinion against the arms race. On March 31, 1958, Moscow announced a unilateral halt to nuclear tests, thereby putting Washington in a difficult position. Along with the head of the Atomic Energy Commission and the Joint Chiefs of Staff, Secretary of State Dulles had long opposed stopping US nuclear testing. Yet Dulles recognized that Soviet propagandists were succeeding in creating an image of the United States as militaristic. World opinion was so important, Dulles believed, that Washington could "lose the whole struggle with the Soviets" if it failed to take it into account. The president agreed about the power of popular attitudes. "[W]e were going to be forced by public opinion in the United States to stop tests unilaterally," he told his advisers in May. Three months later, after the United States had completed a new series of tests, Eisenhower announced that the United States would stop testing for a year, starting October 1, provided that the Soviet Union did not resume testing.[70]

Bowing to pressure from Soviet scientists and generals, Khrushchev allowed a month of tests, including the detonation of a warhead fifty times more powerful than the atomic bomb dropped on Hiroshima in 1945. But then both sides stopped. Throughout 1959, the United States, USSR, and United Kingdom all ceased nuclear explosions. That helped to create the climate for Khrushchev's visit to America (described above) and a potential breakthrough in US–Soviet relations.[71]

THE U-2 INCIDENT

In the first four months of 1960, Khrushchev continued to be ebullient about the prospects for agreements with the Western allies on Berlin and with the United States on banning nuclear weapons tests. In January, he pushed forward a massive reduction in the number of Soviet troops that displeased military leaders but was central to his plans to reduce expenditures on armed forces, increase spending on civilian needs, and fulfill the promise of communist abundance. Through the end of April, Soviet magazines reflected high hopes for a summit meeting in Paris in the middle of May and a subsequent visit to Moscow by the US president, whom the Soviets planned to give a warm and lavish welcome.[72]

Eisenhower also hoped to reach agreements that would curb the "mad race" in arms and establish a positive legacy for his presidency. Overriding opposition from the Pentagon and disregarding inflammatory hearings chaired by Democrats in Congress, Eisenhower pushed ahead toward a test ban treaty. An exchange of notes and statements between Washington and Moscow in February and March created a promising opportunity for an accord. Contrary to notions that ideological differences simply made continuation of the Cold War inevitable, Eisenhower and Khrushchev were on the verge of a major breakthrough. The president's staff drafted speeches he would give in Moscow that recalled the alliance in the Second World War and accepted mutual responsibility for the Cold War. Soviet officials agreed to almost all US requests, including for the bringing of Bibles to distribute in the USSR.[73]

Despite his hopes, in April Eisenhower twice authorized the CIA to send U-2 spy planes to fly over Soviet territory and photograph possible missile testing ranges and launch sites. On May 1 – a Soviet national holiday for celebration of the international workers' movement and therefore a day of special sensitivity for Soviet leaders – the Soviet military finally succeeded in shooting down a U-2. Khrushchev initially hoped to pin the blame for the espionage overflight on the Pentagon and CIA rather than on his friend Eisenhower. Washington first dishonestly claimed that the plane was merely gathering weather data near Turkey. Khrushchev exposed that lie by announcing the capture of the pilot deep inside the USSR. Eisenhower then took personal responsibility for approving the flight and justified it by the need to gather intelligence on Soviet capabilities in order to avoid a surprise attack.

The overflight, US statements and Eisenhower's refusal to apologize drove Khrushchev into a frenzy of indignation. The U-2 flights, he declared, were "a gross insult to the Soviet Union," which was a great power, not a small nation like Guatemala or Cuba. His friend Eisenhower had betrayed him. Soviet pride and dignity would have been damaged, he felt, if he had proceeded with the summit as if nothing had happened. Facing criticism from Chinese leaders and Soviet hardliners for having been too soft on the United States, Khrushchev denounced the United States at the first meeting in Paris. He then withdrew his invitation to Eisenhower, stormed out of the summit, and froze relations with Washington through the end of the election year. Even so, the incident undermined Khrushchev's authority and empowered neo-Stalinist champions of building military strength.[74]

The U-2 incident had major implications for Soviet and American images of each other. The Soviet press returned to vilifying American militarism, espionage, and imperialism while demonstrations in Soviet cities indignantly denounced US "reactionary circles."[75] On the other side, some American journalists and politicians sought to deflect blame for the spy mission onto the secretive Soviet Union, whose rejection of Eisenhower's 1955 Open Skies proposal made US overflights necessary. Yet the risky intrusion's violation of international law and the blatant lying about the episode shook many other Americans' faith that the United States was uniquely virtuous and the USSR was supremely sinful.[76] Thus, after many months of mounting hopes for peace, the Eisenhower–Khrushchev era ended with bitterness and recriminations on both sides.

KENNEDY, KHRUSHCHEV, AND CRISES IN GERMANY AND CUBA, 1961–1962

When Senator John F. Kennedy narrowly defeated Vice President Nixon in the presidential election of November 1960, both Khrushchev and Kennedy saw opportunities for improvements in relations between Moscow and Washington. Yet, their communication in the next two years did not lead to mutual understanding and an easing of tensions. Instead, what they thought they had learned about each other contributed to major miscalculations and two of the most dangerous crises of the Cold War.

Images significantly influenced both leaders' decisions and actions. Although Khrushchev still tried to project an image of the Soviet Union as dedicated to peace, he felt increasing pressure to appear resolute to counter criticism, especially from East German and Chinese Communists, that he had gone soft on American imperialism. Kennedy worried not only that Khrushchev saw him as young and inexperienced, but also that right-wing Americans could depict him as weak or cowardly and thereby jeopardize his re-election in 1964.[77]

Khrushchev's optimism about Kennedy stemmed in part from misinterpretations. In an effort to influence US politics, he delayed the release of the two US airmen who had been shot down when they strayed into Soviet air space until after Kennedy's election. He then expected a payoff for his supposed assistance to Kennedy's victory. Neglecting how Kennedy had often presented himself as a more vigorous Cold Warrior than Nixon or Eisenhower, Khrushchev said that Americans who voted for Kennedy disapproved of the policy of Cold War. Congratulating Kennedy on his victory, Khrushchev expressed a desire to return Soviet–American relations to the warm cooperation of Franklin Roosevelt's time.[78]

Although Kennedy did not share Khrushchev's most expansive hopes, he sought a thaw in the Cold War, particularly through agreements to curb competition in the arms race and space exploration. Underestimating Khrushchev's ideological commitment to supporting anti-imperialist and socialist movements in less developed countries, Kennedy thought deals on arms control and cooperation in outer space might lead the Soviet Union to be more restrained in the Global South. He even thought Khrushchev would accept the overthrow of the left-leaning nationalist Fidel Castro, who had come to power in a popular revolution in Cuba in January 1959. Kennedy also discounted the likelihood that Khrushchev would alter the situation in Berlin, in part because he believed Eisenhower had paid no price for having ignored an ultimatum from Khrushchev in 1958.[79]

The first eruption in relations between Kennedy and Khrushchev came in April 1961, when the new president gave his approval to a CIA plan, developed under Eisenhower, for an invasion of Cuba by about 1,500 Cuban exiles. Anxious to hide the US hand in the invasion, Kennedy reduced the US air support for the invaders, who were quickly defeated by Castro's forces. The fiasco prompted Republicans to denounce Kennedy's timidity and led him to worry that Khrushchev thought he "had no guts." US camouflage efforts did not conceal US involvement from the Soviet press, which repeatedly depicted the invasion as a blatant contradiction of American claims to stand for high ideals. The fiasco also led Khrushchev to see Kennedy as an astonishingly "indecisive" leader who could be coerced and intimidated.[80]

Six weeks after the Bay of Pigs invasion, Khrushchev used meetings in Vienna to try to bully Kennedy into acquiescing to the Soviet desire to push the Western powers out of Berlin, where educated Germans were fleeing from the Communist east to the western part of the city. While Khrushchev blustered, Kennedy patiently sought to persuade the Communist leader to subscribe to rules for superpower relations that would avert a catastrophic confrontation. Implicitly repudiating the idea of liberating Eastern Europe, Kennedy proposed that communism could remain where it had been established, but it should not seek to spread further. If each superpower stayed in its own area, he explained, dangerous collisions could be avoided. Frustrated by Kennedy's desire to maintain the global status quo, Khrushchev exploded. Apart from an agreement for the neutralization of Laos, the two leaders accomplished little at the Vienna summit, which exacerbated rather than eased the mounting tensions between the two countries.[81]

Both leaders left Vienna believing that they needed to strengthen their public stances. Khrushchev ordered his aides to distribute minutes of the summit, showing how tough he had been, more widely than usual, at home and abroad. A month after the summit Khrushchev announced that he would cancel plans to cut the size of the Soviet Army and instead increase defense spending by a third. After privately stressing to journalists how Khrushchev had beaten him up in Vienna, Kennedy delivered a major televised address in July that depicted the Soviet threat as an almost apocalyptic test of courage and will. Responding to pressure from hard-line advisers and the US media, Kennedy sought to demonstrate his readiness for a showdown by calling up reserves and increasing spending on the military and civil defense.[82]

Determined to act unilaterally to staunch the bleeding of his East German ally, Khrushchev authorized the building of a wall to separate East and West Berlin in the middle of August. Kennedy responded by reinforcing US troops in West Berlin and sending General Lucius Clay, hero of the Berlin Blockade thirteen years earlier, to the city as a symbol of US commitment to its defense. Yet, relieved that Soviet forces did not obstruct access to West Berlin, Kennedy told an aide: "a wall is a hell of a lot better than a war." Both Kennedy and Khrushchev resisted pressures for more provocative actions. US forces did not attempt to knock down the wall and Khrushchev deferred his threat to sign a separate peace treaty with East Germany.[83]

Even as the Berlin crisis subsided, though, tension mounted toward an even more dangerous confrontation. In an effort to project an image of US strength that would silence American critics of his alleged weakness, ward off calls in Congress for more missiles, and deter Communist aggression, Kennedy directed the Pentagon to reveal that the "missile gap" alleged to exist in previous years actually favored the United States. On October 21, Deputy Secretary of Defense Roswell Gilpatric announced that the United States had such overwhelming superiority in its nuclear arsenal that it could retaliate against any Soviet use of nuclear weapons by destroying the Soviet Union. Nine days later, the Soviet Union stressed the sheer size of its destructive capability by exploding a fifty-megaton bomb. Although Khrushchev was proud of that feat, it did nothing to ease the problem posed by the United States exposing that his rocket-rattling had been a bluff to hide the Soviet bloc's inferiority.[84]

Over the next six months, the pressure on Khrushchev grew even more acute. Chinese Communists disparaged his alleged timidity in the struggle against imperialism. Washington's rejection of any vow not to use nuclear weapons first aggravated the worries of Soviet military leaders. US military exercises in the Caribbean and covert sabotage operations in Cuba raised the danger that Khrushchev's authority would be further undermined by the loss of Cuba.

With his power and prestige on the line, Khrushchev gambled that by sending nuclear missiles to Cuba he could deter a US invasion of the island, partially redress the gross imbalance in nuclear forces, and give American leaders a sense of how he felt threatened by US forces near Soviet borders, particularly the Jupiter missiles which had recently been installed in Turkey. Impelled by his emotional yearning for equality and reciprocity, Khrushchev did not carefully think through the risky and expensive operation. Disregarding the domestic political pressures on Kennedy, Khrushchev expected the president to accept the missiles in Cuba, especially if they could be made operational before the United States detected them. By the middle of October, when US aircraft photographed missile installations in Cuba, the Soviet Union had sent more than 40,000 troops and scores of missiles with nuclear warheads.[85]

Kennedy's immediate reaction was to feel he had to secure the removal of the missiles or he would be impeached. Yet he wisely put off calls for US air strikes and an invasion of Cuba. Instead, he imposed a quarantine to halt further Soviet deliveries of arms to Cuba and opened negotiations. Rightly concluding that the threat of imminent US military action was necessary to impress upon Khrushchev the urgency of concessions in negotiations, Kennedy allowed preparations for an invasion to go forward. At the same time, he used his brother, Bobby, to negotiate with a Kremlin representative for the removal of the Soviet missiles in exchange for a US pledge not to invade Cuba and a confidential promise that US missiles would be withdrawn from Turkey within six months. On the morning of Sunday, October 28, believing the United States would begin bombing Cuba within twenty-four or at most forty-eight hours, Khrushchev ordered the withdrawal of the missiles he had dispatched to Cuba at great cost.[86]

As the two countries stepped back from the brink of war, people around the world breathed easier. Yet in each country leaders drew lessons that would cause new tensions in the future. In the United States, some top officials and academic analysts concluded that the United States could use calibrated applications of threats and force to compel adversaries to back down in future crises – a conclusion that exaggerated a president's control of military forces and disregarded how close the crisis came to escaping Kennedy's control. In Moscow, key military and political leaders concluded that at all costs they needed to build up their strategic nuclear forces to match the United States so that they would never again be compelled to retreat from a confrontation.

PUBLIC ANXIETIES AND PRESSURE FOR PEACE, 1961–1963

As the US–Soviet competition led to dangerous crises in Berlin and Cuba, peace activists expanded their protests and pressure. Pacifist marchers who set off from San Francisco in December 1960 received permission from Khrushchev to hike across part of the Soviet Union, distributed 100,000 leaflets to Soviet citizens (who often responded positively), demonstrated outside Soviet military installations, and walked into Moscow in the fall of 1961. On November 1, roughly 50,000 women in 60 US cities participated in protests against nuclear weapons tests organized by Women Strike for Peace. Such pressure for peace and mounting anxiety about the nuclear arms race increasingly eclipsed demands for confrontation of Communist enemies by hard-line ideologues in the United States.[87]

Filmmakers, too, expressed desires for peace and anxieties about the superpowers' growing nuclear arsenals. *Romanoff and Juliet* (1961), directed by Russian immigrant Peter Ustinov, offered a hopeful message about coexistence. When the son of the Soviet ambassador and the daughter of the American ambassador to the country of Concordia fall in love, their parents overcome their ideological differences and accept the marriage.[88] In the Soviet film *Nine Days in One Year* (1962), self-sacrificing, heroic scientists brood about how a handful of men on the other side of the planet decide whether Soviets live or die, justify work on a Soviet bomb as a way to deter annihilation by the United States, and are killed or gravely sickened by exposure to radiation. *Dr. Strangelove*, released in the United States the following year, lampooned anticommunist generals and scientists who were eager for nuclear war against the Soviet Union as deranged fanatics.[89]

The changing political and cultural climate created an opening for a breakthrough in US–Soviet relations in the year after the Cuban missile crisis. More ardently than before, Khrushchev hoped to curtail wasteful spending on a massive military establishment. In conversations with American visitors and in letters to Kennedy, Khrushchev expressed his desires for a nonaggression agreement between NATO and the Warsaw Pact, a freeze on military budgets, and an end to the Cold War. Suspicious of Khrushchev in the wake of his deceptive deployment of missiles to Cuba and fearful of Republican criticism of concessions to Communists, Kennedy responded slowly and guardedly to Khrushchev's overtures. Norman Cousins, a magazine editor and founder of the National Committee for a Sane Nuclear Policy (SANE), seized the opportunity to play an important role as intermediary. After meeting with Khrushchev in December 1962 and April 1963, Cousins helped to draft a major speech that Kennedy delivered at American University in Washington in June 1963. Boldly rejecting the vilification of the Soviet Union, Kennedy declared that "no government or social system is so evil that its people must be considered as lacking in virtue." Creating political space for a nuclear test ban, he emphasized that the American and Soviet peoples breathed the same air and drank the same water.

Six weeks later, US and Soviet representatives signed a treaty that banned atmospheric and underwater testing of nuclear weapons. In a nationwide address, Kennedy hailed the partial test ban as "a step toward peace."[90] Conservative politicians, generals, and editors vehemently opposed the treaty. They preferred to base US security on unconstrained nuclear superiority, feared Communist cheating, and objected to accepting the USSR as a partner.[91] But most editors approved of it as a first step on a long road toward ending the arms race.[92] Some liberals who believed a capitalist democracy could share the planet with a communist dictatorship optimistically saw the test ban as a promising beginning "toward ending the Cold War."[93]

By September, 80 percent of Americans approved of the treaty, which the Senate ratified 80–19. Eager to maintain the momentum, Kennedy addressed the United Nations, proposed a joint US–Soviet mission to the moon, and expressed the hope that "this pause in the Cold War" could lead to "its end." On a speechmaking tour of Western states, Kennedy repeatedly won applause for statements about moving to end the danger of nuclear incineration and for criticism of Republican rival Barry Goldwater's simplistic view of a global battle between good and evil. Khrushchev, too, grew optimistic that he and Kennedy could transcend ideological differences and build a partnership between their countries. Expecting Kennedy to be re-elected in 1964, Khrushchev thought he would have six years to work with the president to solve problems.[94]

The developing relationship between the two leaders was suddenly cut off on November 22, when Kennedy was assassinated in Texas. A shocked Khrushchev suspected that US reactionaries had killed the president in order to disrupt the emerging superpower détente. Despite his gloom, Khrushchev sent a series of messages to Kennedy's successor, Lyndon Johnson, about the need for the two countries to "learn to live without quarrels and confrontations."[95]

CONCLUSION

The Cold War did not end in the early 1960s.[96] To many conservative anticommunists in the United States, for whom opposition to Soviet communism had become central to their identities, the Cold War could not end until the Soviet Union collapsed or at least ceased supporting communists in foreign countries. To American liberal universalists, the Cold War had to continue until the Soviet Union stopped upholding a rival universalist ideology or at least allowed full democratic political competition inside the USSR.[97] Yet in 1963, as in 1959 after Khrushchev visited America and in 1955 after the Geneva summit, many Soviets and Americans envisioned the possibility of ending the mutual demonization and the costly arms race of the Cold War. Now the question was whether others could build upon the fitful progress that had been made since Stalin's death.

15

DÉTENTE, 1964–1979

OVERVIEW

Despite the shock of President Kennedy's assassination in November 1963, Soviet and American leaders continued in the next decade to pursue their common interests in avoiding dangerous confrontations, controlling the spread of nuclear weapons, and limiting the cost of the arms race. Extending the momentum created by the partial test ban treaty of 1963, the Soviet Union and the United States reached an agreement to curb the proliferation of nuclear weapons in 1968. They then signed both a Strategic Arms Limitation Treaty (SALT I) and an Anti-Ballistic Missile (ABM) Treaty in 1972. By that point, the frosty hostility of the past seemed to have given way to an era of friendly collaboration, with expanding trade and widening cooperation in many other areas, from cultural exchanges to space exploration.

Yet, in the following years, friction, suspicion, and competition increasingly overshadowed cooperation. While Americans overwhelmingly approved of the relaxation of tensions called "détente" during the early 1970s, in the rest of the decade they increasingly associated the word with weakness and appeasement. Top Soviet leaders valued détente so highly in the first half of the decade that they hesitated to take steps that would jeopardize it, but by the fall of 1979 they felt there was little left to lose. Gravely weakened by 1976, détente was dead even before the Soviet Union invaded Afghanistan in December 1979.

How could détente appear so far-reaching yet be so fragile? How could the warming of relations lead to almost euphoric enthusiasm yet also provoke angry opposition?

At the time, conservative anticommunists such as former California Governor Ronald Reagan had a simple explanation: détente was a naïve policy that emboldened Soviet aggression all around the world until the West finally awoke to the Communist threat. In more sophisticated ways, many scholars have blamed the demise of détente on Soviet adventurism in the "Third World."[1]

Yet Soviet military interventions in Angola, Ethiopia, and Afghanistan were actually more hesitant, reactive and defensive than rampantly aggressive. In addition, US leaders also intervened across the planet, from Chile to Angola and the Horn of Africa.

Moreover, the geopolitical competition in such "Third World" countries was not the sole cause of the deterioration of US–Soviet relations. Internal dynamics in the United States and the Soviet Union also gravely undermined détente. In the USSR, General Secretary Leonid Brezhnev, who led the ouster of Khrushchev in October 1964, sold détente to his colleagues as a form of peace from strength. The dramatic growth of the Soviet military, particularly its nuclear arsenal, gave ammunition to critics of détente in America. As Brezhnev's health deteriorated after 1974, he lost the ability to check Soviet militarism and wisely manage relations with Washington. In the United States, presidents sought agreements with the Soviet Union to boost their popularity, yet also faced intense criticism from ambitious political rivals, whose rhetoric and maneuvers disrupted détente.[2]

In both countries, the producers of images of the other superpower – politicians, journalists, cartoonists, and filmmakers – shaped public opinion in ways that subordinated ideological differences in the first decade after the Cuban missile crisis yet fueled the inflammation of ideological hostility in the second half of the 1970s. As tensions relaxed in the first phase, the two nations came to be less central to each other's self-definition. While Americans turned increasing attention to a costly war in Vietnam, Russians grew more anxious about rising frictions with the People's Republic of China. For a time, Communist China seemed the most dangerous enemy to many both in the United States and in the USSR. Yet, as the devastating war in Vietnam ended in the mid-1970s, US–Soviet ideological antagonism revived, in part because many Americans yearned to recover a faith in their moral superiority.[3] By the end of the decade, the two nations had once again become the primary foils for the definitions of their respective national identities – intimate enemies.

This chapter presents a balanced and inclusive perspective on the rise and fall of détente. While giving due attention to developments in Asia, Africa, and Latin America, it emphasizes the roles of domestic politics both in the lessening and in the worsening of tensions. The demise of détente, it shows, was not simply an inevitable result of Soviet aggressiveness and the ideological differences between the two countries, but also a product of exaggerations of threats, mismanagement of politics, and unwise decisions by flawed human beings.

THE DEVELOPMENT OF DÉTENTE IN THE SHADOWS
OF THE BOMB AND THE VIETNAM WAR, 1964–1968

At the outset of his presidency, Lyndon Johnson worried that, if he made concessions to the Soviet Union, conservative Republicans would call him pro-Russian, and that would jeopardize his prospects in the 1964 presidential election. Yet he also thought it would tarnish Kennedy's memory and his own prestige if Congress rejected the sale of wheat to the USSR that JFK had authorized. Johnson and his aides therefore pushed the wheat sale through Congress in December 1963. Johnson disliked the appearance of being reactive to a Khrushchev peace offensive and prodded his aides for ideas to seize the initiative in a continuing propaganda struggle. Yet he shared Khrushchev's interests in averting dangerous confrontations and curbing military spending, and he wanted to present himself as a man of peace. Moreover, he believed that sober American and Soviet leaders had a common interest in containing hotheaded Communist China, including preventing Beijing from developing nuclear weapons.[4]

Johnson's conflicting concerns about his public image strongly influenced his campaign against Republican candidate Barry Goldwater. On the one hand, Johnson presented himself as a vigilant anticommunist who would "never forget that the men in the Kremlin remain dedicated dangerous Communists." On the other hand, Johnson's campaign depicted Goldwater as a reckless fanatic who would risk an atomic Armageddon. Johnson won by a landslide in an election widely regarded as a repudiation of simplistic, old-fashioned anticommunism.[5]

As the Johnson administration cautiously pursued "peaceful engagement" with the Soviet Union, American moviemakers repeatedly ridiculed Russophobic anticommunism and portrayed right-wing militants as more dangerous threats than Russian leaders. *Dr. Strangelove*, which opened in theaters in January 1964, lampooned anticommunist generals and scientists as lunatics who were eager for nuclear war against the Soviet Union. Critics hailed the movie's brilliant satire against nuclear brinksmanship and anti-Soviet paranoia. Subsequent movies widened the break with what one reviewer called a "catatonic cold war trance." The political thriller *Seven Days in May*, released soon after *Dr. Strangelove*, depicted a conspiracy by right-wing extremists, headed by the Chairman of the Joint Chiefs of Staff, to overthrow a president who had signed a nuclear disarmament treaty. *Fail Safe*, screened in the fall of 1964, dramatized nightmares of nuclear war with an accidental launching of a US attack on the Soviet Union and with a president effectively cooperating with Russian leaders to shoot down US bombers. Two years later, *The Russians Are Coming, the Russians Are Coming* again featured the danger of confrontation and the necessity of collaboration, but in the format of a farce. At the climax of the movie, an armed standoff between a Soviet submarine crew and New England townspeople gives way to Russian–American cooperation, first in the rescue of a child and then in the escorting of the submarine out of the harbor ahead of an attack by US planes.[6]

While American movies helped to create political space for better relations with the Soviet Union by marginalizing Russophobic reactionaries, they also contributed to a decline in the demonization of Russia through their humanization of Russian characters. *The Russians Are Coming* featured a romance between a pretty American girl and a brave, handsome Russian sailor, who – in contrast to the seduction and conversion stories of the past – did not defect to the United States but returned to his homeland. Despite the differences between their nations, the movie suggested, Russians and Americans both felt patriotic pride, love, and compassion. Several months earlier, *Doctor Zhivago* conveyed a similar message in a sweeping epic that took the Russian Revolution as the backdrop for a soulful love story. Loosely based on a novel by Boris Pasternak, the movie inspired great enthusiasm from reviewers, who believed it championed the priceless value of individuals beyond the claims of states. Like Americans, the movie suggested, Russians and Communists could be both ruthless and tender, bad and good.[7]

Public opinion surveys captured related shifts in popular attitudes toward Russia. Although a majority of Americans continued to have negative views of Russia, the number of those who held "highly unfavorable" views of Russia declined from 74 percent in 1957 to 48 percent in 1967. Most Americans came to see Russia as a lesser threat than "Red China," and by 1967 a strong plurality even viewed Russia as a likely ally in a war against Communist China (see Figure 15.1).[8]

In the context of declining public antipathy to Russia and an escalating war in Vietnam, the Johnson administration pursued an increasingly ambitious policy of "bridge building" toward the Soviet bloc. Many lower-level officials saw expanding trade and cultural exchanges with Eastern Europe and the USSR as ways to divide and weaken the Soviet empire. But Johnson and his top advisers saw "bridge building" more as a way to facilitate breakthroughs in arms control that would be the crowning achievements of his presidency. Offsetting the ugly images of an increasingly unpopular war in Vietnam, Johnson came by 1967 to speak in glowing terms about how Americans were "in the midst of a great transition . . . from the harsh spirit of

"I Say The U.S. And Russia Are On A Collusion Course!"

Figure 15.1 "I Say the U.S. and Russia Are on a Collusion Course!" *Washington Post*, August 15, 1965. Cartoonist Herbert Block contrasted a bellicose Mao to a businesslike Soviet. Herblock Cartoon, © The Herb Block Foundation.

the cold war to the hopeful spirit of common humanity." Johnson's meetings with Soviet Premier Aleksei Kosygin at Glassboro, New Jersey in June 1967 yielded no breakthroughs, but by July 1968 Johnson was able to sign an agreement with the USSR and more than fifty other countries to bar the spread of nuclear weapons. He eagerly anticipated a summit meeting in Moscow that fall that would be the greatest accomplishment of his administration.[9]

The most powerful Soviet leader was even more interested in moving beyond "Cold War" competition and confrontation. Leonid Brezhnev had a sincere desire for peace rooted in the suffering he saw as a political commissar in the war against Nazi Germany. Unlike Soviet ideologues, whom he scorned, Brezhnev did not view the struggle for peace as a clever way to outwit capitalist enemies while making gains at their expense. Instead, he genuinely sought an easing of tensions with the West to enhance Soviet security, expand trade, and consolidate his primacy in the Kremlin.[10]

Yet Brezhnev and Kosygin worried that embracing the United States as it expanded its military involvement in Vietnam would damage Soviet prestige in the world communist movement. In addition, Brezhnev had to deal with Soviet military leaders' stubborn opposition to any arms control agreement that would lock in US strategic superiority. Brezhnev responded by arguing that he was approaching US leaders from a position of strength, with quantitative superiority in weapons. At the same time, Brezhnev and other Soviet leaders feared that the expansion of American trade, tourism, and cultural influence in the Soviet bloc posed a serious threat to Communist power; they repeatedly decried the danger of economic penetration and ideological subversion.[11]

The fascination of Soviet youth with American music, dance, and fashion sometimes prompted light-hearted ridicule in Soviet films or cartoons.[12] Yet Communist officials' worries about the seductive allure of the American way of life also contributed to vehement and pervasive anti-American propaganda. Numerous cartoons in Soviet magazines, for example, depicted US involvement in Vietnam as wantonly cruel imperialist aggression, portrayed America as a land of racism and political violence, and warned about the deadly deceptions of Western advertising.[13] Although some Soviet films, television shows, and radio stations drew enormous mass audiences, most films could not compete with the higher production values of Hollywood movies and efforts to imitate the American-style combination of news and entertainment did not get listeners to stop tuning in to foreign radio broadcasts.[14] While elite Soviet youth who loved jazz or rock and roll did not necessarily see experimental music as incompatible with communist ideals, the strong appeal of Western popular culture to growing numbers of disaffected young people alarmed Soviet leaders, propagandists, and KGB officers.[15]

Soviet leaders' diffuse fears of Western economic penetration and cultural infiltration became much sharper in 1968, when liberalizing developments in Czechoslovakia seemed to pose an imminent threat of the restoration of capitalism, the ouster of all pro-Soviet Communists, and the withdrawal of the country from the Warsaw Pact. After the reformist Alexander Dubček became the head of the Czechoslovak Communist

Party in January 1968, the lifting of press censorship, formation of political "clubs," and calls for the reestablishment of non-Communist parties in Czechoslovakia sparked such ferment among Soviet students and intellectuals that Kremlin leaders feared the Prague Spring could have dangerous repercussions in the Soviet Union. Although Brezhnev was very reluctant to intervene, in August the Politburo decided to launch a massive military invasion of Czechoslovakia in order to avert the loss of Czechoslovakia from the camp of socialist countries. Since Czechoslovakian military leaders ordered soldiers not to resist, the invasion caused relatively few deaths, but the occupation was intensely unpopular and had a searing impact on reformist Soviet intellectuals and officials.[16]

To justify the invasion, Soviet leaders and propagandists emphasized threats from the West, particularly "ideological subversion."[17] Since the Soviet Union and the countries of Eastern Europe were interdependent, Brezhnev warned, internal and external threats to socialism in one country became problems for all of the socialist countries. In what came to be known as the "Brezhnev Doctrine," Soviet leaders declared that attempts to roll back socialism, break the links between socialist countries, or deviate from the principles of Marxism-Leninism would not be tolerated – statements that foreshadowed years of ideological rigidity.[18]

Many American journalists and politicians immediately denounced the invasion of Czechoslovakia. The *New York Times* called it an "act of bestial imperialism"; the *Wall Street Journal* labeled it a "savage military attack"; the *Washington Post* printed a cartoon showing a brutal Brezhnev with a smoking gun in his hand standing over the body of a woman labeled "FREEDOM."[19]

Yet the far more destructive and bloody US war in Vietnam constrained American indignation. As the frustrated editors of the *Wall Street Journal* noted, "a good many Americans" said the Soviet invasion was terrible but then pointed to "what we are doing in Vietnam." The *Journal* lamented the growing tendency "to view the two super-powers as equally cynical and callous." From a different angle, veteran columnist James Reston observed that Washington was in no position, after its interventions in Vietnam, Cuba, Guatemala (1954), and the Dominican Republic (1965), "to take the self-righteous position that it will not do business" with the Kremlin because of Czechoslovakia. Militant anticommunists sought to use the invasion of Czechoslovakia to reinforce images of the USSR as a dangerous enemy, yet the invasion did not have a deep, lasting impact on American attitudes toward the Soviet Union.[20]

Although Republican Senators delayed ratification of the nuclear non-proliferation treaty, the Johnson administration and leading newspaper editors remained convinced that the United States had to engage with the Kremlin to pursue arms control. When Soviet tanks rolled into Prague, a dejected Johnson declared at a Cabinet meeting that "The Cold War is not over," yet within weeks he reiterated his interest in traveling to Moscow to discuss a strategic arms limitation agreement. By November, Soviet leaders concluded that the benefits of détente could be regained quickly, though they decided to put off a summit meeting with Johnson upon learning that his Republican successor, Richard Nixon, disliked the idea.[21]

THE FLOURISHING OF DÉTENTE UNDER NIXON AND BREZHNEV, 1969–1974

Building upon foundations set earlier, between 1969 and 1972 the United States and the Soviet Union negotiated agreements to control the arms race, broaden trade, and expand cultural and intellectual exchanges. Nixon and Brezhnev consolidated their authority and enhanced their domestic popularity by presenting themselves as champions of peace who were moving their countries away from the confrontations of the Cold War.

Yet their achievement soon began to be shaken, and after 1974 superpower détente gradually fell apart. Despite the personal warmth between Brezhnev and Nixon, Soviet and American conceptions of détente diverged. Moreover, the ways in which US leaders sold détente domestically set up disillusionment. As a result, the five and a half years of Nixon's presidency marked a missed opportunity for a more sustained easing of tensions.

Upon narrowly defeating Democrat Hubert Humphrey in 1968, Nixon chose as his National Security Adviser Henry Kissinger, a Harvard professor of political science. Kissinger had a deep aversion to emotional, populist, and ideological approaches to foreign policy rooted in his traumatic early life as a Jew in Nazi Germany. Nixon and Kissinger both recognized the constraints on US power from the costly and unpopular war in Vietnam, a weakened US economy, and congressional pressure to cut military spending. They also agreed that the United States had little or no ability to engineer the internal transformation of the Soviet Union but that it could heighten Soviet interest in better relations with America by opening negotiations with Russia's adversary, Communist China. Together they devised a strategy to restrain Moscow through a combination of threats to use nuclear weapons, punishments for aggression, and incentives for cooperation – access to American grain, technology, and financing. In the short term, they sought to contain Soviet expansionism while retrenching from US overextension. In the longer term, they suggested, the Soviet Union might become so enmeshed in economic relations with America that it would recognize its stake in US prosperity and cease competing with the United States around the world.[22]

While some have praised Nixon for being "deftly sure-footed on the world stage," his approach to US–Soviet relations was shaky.[23] The deeply insecure and volatile Nixon sought to manipulate opinion through inspiring images and stirring speeches that were at odds with his cynical confidential comments. Believing that "the American people are suckers" who needed hope for peace, Nixon fostered public expectations of a dramatic shift to more cooperative relations with the Soviet Union while he privately continued to think of Soviet leaders as dangerous competitors. He persistently exaggerated Soviet aggressiveness, undervalued Soviet restraint, and relied heavily on an image of recklessness about using force to intimidate foreign leaders. Nixon's frequently simplistic and deceptive approach undermined sustained progress in Soviet–American relations.[24]

Kissinger has often been lauded as a brilliant strategist and clever tactician who engineered a realist reorientation of US policies.[25] He certainly deserves credit for having a farsighted vision of the potential evolution of world politics. Yet Kissinger's persistent duplicity and amorality sparked distrust, resentment, and a major backlash against détente.[26]

Since Nixon won the popular vote for the presidency by less than 1 percent and more Americans identified with the Democratic Party (55 percent) than with the Republican Party (34 percent), he had reason to be anxious about his prospects for re-election. Believing that Democrats had advantages in domestic policies, Nixon focused on foreign policies – especially ending the Vietnam War "with honor" and handling relations with the Communist powers – as keys to victory in 1972. Along with Kissinger, who dazzled many correspondents with his intellectual brilliance, Nixon succeeded in impressing many journalists and winning broad public approval for his foreign policy moves.[27]

Yet Nixon's high approval ratings obscured mistakes and failures that would undermine relations with Moscow. Although Democrats maintained strong majorities in both House and Senate, the president showed little interest in cultivating members of Congress, for whom he expressed contempt. Since the influence of the Republican Right declined significantly during his first four years in office and since most elected Republicans refrained from criticizing a president from their party, Nixon had reason to feel that he did not need to worry very much about right-wing criticism. Yet Nixon's embrace of Brezhnev and even more his opening to China alienated conservative activists, who spurred opposition to his policies, especially after the president was wounded by a scandal over his campaign team's break-in to Democratic headquarters at the Watergate office complex in Washington in 1972. Moreover, Nixon's concentration on the propagation of his personal image as a peacemaker contributed to his neglect of careful explanation of how agreements with the Soviet Union served US interests.[28]

In the first two years of Nixon's presidency, with Soviet officials divided between Communist ideologues who wanted to roll back the influence of a weakened United States and more pragmatic leaders who hoped for genuine collaboration with America, the Kremlin staunchly resisted US efforts to link arms control negotiations to Soviet restraint of North Vietnam. Consequently, the talks made little progress.

By the spring of 1971, however, Brezhnev had strengthened his authority enough to announce an ambitious foreign policy that prioritized relations with the United States and pursued peaceful coexistence with all capitalist countries. In a grand synthesis, Brezhnev offered something to each of several different constituencies. Keenly aware of persistent problems in Soviet industrial productivity and agricultural output, Brezhnev recognized the need to obtain capital, technology, expertise, and goods from the West in order to boost Soviet production and placate Soviet consumers. To control the effects of opening doors to the West, the Kremlin would intensify repression of public dissent, as orthodox Communists desired. Yielding to pressure from the Minister of Defense, Brezhnev vowed to continue meeting the demands of a vast military–industrial complex that underpinned Soviet claims to superpower status. In the dominant Soviet view, it was above all the increased power of the Soviet Union that made possible the *razriadka* (relaxation of tensions) of the 1970s, which promised both the avoidance of war between the great powers and the advance of socialism around the world.[29]

Since tensions eased with the United States and with West Germany (following the adoption of a policy of *Ostpolitik* by Social Democratic Chancellor Willy Brandt in 1969), the most worrisome threat to Soviet security came from Communist China. Soviet concern mounted in February 1972, when Nixon made a dramatic journey to Beijing. Yet US efforts to use the opening to China as leverage on Moscow did not work as Nixon and Kissinger hoped. Soviet leaders did urge North Vietnam to focus on diplomacy rather than waging war, but Hanoi disregarded that advice and launched a major offensive into South Vietnam on March 30.[30] Fearing that he might "lose" South Vietnam and as a result lose the presidential contest in November, Nixon ordered the massive bombing of North Vietnam and the mining of its major harbors even though he knew that risked causing Moscow to cancel a scheduled summit in May.

Angered by the bombing, Soviet citizens sent numerous letters to the Kremlin demanding a rejection of Nixon's visit – a reflection not only of Soviet propaganda about the brutal war in Vietnam, but also of popular antiwar sentiment. Politburo hard-liners also pressed for withdrawal of the invitation to Nixon, but Brezhnev, Kosygin, and Gromyko decided to go ahead with the summit that they believed would serve vital Soviet interests.[31]

Suspecting (wrongly) that Moscow had colluded with Hanoi's offensive and believing (wrongly) that the Kremlin could control its militantly independent client, Nixon insisted for weeks that the Soviet Union had to compel North Vietnam to be more restrained on the battlefield and more forthcoming at the negotiating table or else he would cancel the summit. Brezhnev responded firmly, criticizing America's "shameful war," defending Soviet support for a fellow socialist country, and explaining that it was up to Washington to extricate itself from the conflict through direct negotiations with the Vietnamese. Although Nixon concluded that the Russians "aren't going to help," he decided to proceed with the trip. A poll he ordered showed 60 percent of Americans wanted him to go ahead with the summit in spite of the North Vietnamese invasion. Nixon did not want to dash public hopes or give Democrats grounds to criticize his handling of superpower relations. Moreover, he relished the idea of "a hell of a summit" that would enhance his chances of being re-elected in November.[32]

When Nixon arrived in Moscow in May, Soviet leaders sternly condemned America's "very cruel military actions" in Vietnam, thereby creating a formal record of standing up against US "aggression" that they could send to their Communist allies. However, thereafter they treated Nixon much more cordially and they offered to be more active in conveying US positions to the North Vietnamese. While seeking to insulate themselves from criticism for welcoming the bloodstained US president to Moscow, Brezhnev and his allies in the Politburo thus demonstrated their eagerness to remove a major obstacle to the pursuit of Soviet political, economic, and strategic interests.[33]

Among the numerous agreements signed in Moscow, the most important were two deals concerning nuclear weapons. In the first, the superpowers restricted themselves to deploying two anti-ballistic missile (ABM) systems each – one to defend the capital and a second to defend an ICBM site. In the second deal, they agreed to complicated limits on the numbers of nuclear weapons they could deploy. Even before he signed the SALT

I treaty, Nixon worried about "a massive right-wing revolt" because hawks would object that the agreement allowed the Soviet Union a higher number of missiles (while giving the United States an edge in the number of warheads). Yet Nixon and his aides, with some overconfidence, believed right-wing Republicans would be compelled to support their party's president and that he therefore could weather the coming storm.[34]

Immediately upon returning to Washington, at the beginning of June, Nixon sought to shape American public understanding of the summit and of détente in general with a dramatic address to a joint session of Congress. Although he cautioned that Soviet leaders remained committed to an ideology hostile to American values and would continue to be competitors of the United States, he emphasized the potential to move beyond the era of rivalry. Reminding Americans of what they had seen in televised coverage of the summit, Nixon suggested that the American flag flying above the Kremlin was a symbol of how the two countries could build a new, cooperative relationship. Perhaps most importantly, Nixon declared that the United States and the Communist powers were "making progress toward a world in which leaders of nations will settle their differences by negotiation, not by force, and in which they learn to live with their differences so that their sons will not have to die for those differences." Thus, Nixon, the former vehement anticommunist, envisioned that the confrontations of the Cold War would end not with an American victory, but with mutual acceptance of peaceful coexistence.[35]

Even before Nixon's glowing speech, many American newspapers hailed the Moscow summit. Champions of arms control praised it as an important first step toward a safer future. Beyond the substantive agreements, liberal editors argued, the summit was important for its impact on Soviet and American popular attitudes. After years of bloody war in Vietnam, some were so eager to believe in the possibility of peace and the transcendence of ideological competition that they set aside their doubts.[36]

Enthusiasm was not universal. For example, right-wing evangelical Christians, who clung to their negative images of communist foes throughout Nixon's presidency, argued that arms control agreements were part of a Soviet strategy to weaken America's defenses.[37] Yet, among mainstream Americans, hopes soared high. Nationwide surveys after Nixon's trip to Moscow found that 61 percent approved of his handling of the presidency – a gain of 8 percentage points over his approval rating two months earlier and a stronger boost than he received from his earlier trip to China.[38]

The foundation for optimism was not as strong as Nixon suggested. In Moscow, American and Soviet leaders agreed on an idealistic set of basic principles to guide superpower relations, including renunciation of efforts to obtain unilateral advantages at the expense of the other, renunciation of the use or threat of force, and avoidance of confrontations. Soviet leaders had shown more interest in the adoption of the principles than Nixon and Kissinger had, yet both sides found it difficult to abide by the ideas. Despite Soviet objections, Nixon continued to use force against North Vietnam, which culminated in unprecedentedly intense bombing at Christmas 1972.[39] He also pushed the CIA to destabilize the democratically elected socialist government of Chile, which was overthrown in a bloody military coup in September 1973.[40] Soviet leaders hoped that the superpowers might cooperate against Communist China and probed the possibility of joint action against Chinese nuclear weapons facilities, yet Nixon and Kissinger played on Soviet fears that improved US–Chinese relations might lead to military cooperation between them.[41]

The greatest test of the basic principles came in the Middle East. Brezhnev and Gromyko warned repeatedly that Soviet-armed Arab nations might attack Israel if they saw no prospect of a negotiated settlement of territorial grievances and urged superpower cooperation to avert a war. After Egypt and Syria attacked in October 1973 and an Israeli counteroffensive threatened to eliminate Egyptian forces in the Sinai Peninsula, Brezhnev proposed to Nixon that both superpowers dispatch military units to enforce a ceasefire. But he also warned that Moscow might act unilaterally if the United States did not agree to act jointly. In response, Kissinger and other national security officials ordered a worldwide alert of US military forces, in an effort to send an intimidating signal to Moscow. The crisis soon ended, primarily because Kissinger put more pressure on Israel to stop attacking Egyptian troops, yet it led to mutual recriminations and resentment. Americans vented anger at the "irresponsible" conduct and "spoiling role" of the Kremlin. Soviets expressed bitterness at their exclusion from diplomacy in the region.[42]

While international tensions roiled détente, dynamics in American public opinion and US domestic politics played more important roles in undermining the new Soviet–American relationship. By the time Brezhnev came to America for a second summit meeting in June 1973, many Americans had come to have more positive views of the Soviet Union than in 1967. Yet a majority (57 percent) still held unfavorable opinions of Russia, and more Americans viewed Communist China favorably.[43] In addition, two trends in US opinion indicated potential trouble in the future. First, American journalists and politicians increasingly complained that the Soviet Union gained more than the United States did, especially a numerical advantage in ICBMs from the SALT agreement and the ability to purchase such massive amounts of grain that it drove up prices in US markets.[44] Second, and perhaps most important, Jewish leaders, intellectuals, and members of Congress criticized Soviet domestic policies, particularly restrictions on the emigration of Soviet Jews and punishment of dissident thinkers. Although aides warned as early as July 1972 that growing public and congressional pressure on the issue could generate a major political problem, Nixon was not alarmed, and Kissinger resolved to resist the pressure for what he saw as inappropriate interference in Soviet domestic affairs. They sought to keep American Jewish leaders quiet and told leaders of Congress that formal, public pressure would backfire, causing the Kremlin to close the door on Jewish emigration.[45]

Nixon and Kissinger assured Soviet leaders that they would contain the criticism. Kissinger vowed to Gromyko in December 1973 that the administration soon would "start a publicity campaign," but the Senate hearings that would have launched the campaign were postponed to the summer of 1974 and then they captured little media attention. Nixon boasted to Brezhnev in June 1974 that he was "in a unique position of being able to bring the American public along in support of détente." Yet revelations of Nixon's culpability in the Watergate scandal eroded his authority with members of Congress and destroyed his credibility with most of the American public.[46]

Soviet leaders complained about the passivity of Nixon and Kissinger. Brezhnev expressed indignation at the "anti-Soviet propaganda" in the United States and felt the White House should be able to direct the American press in the same way as he instructed Soviet publications. Dobrynin told Kissinger that Soviet leaders felt that he was "not aggressive enough" in promoting détente. Soviet officials feared that the shift to more cooperative relations could be reversed if attitudes in the United States did not change.[47]

Soviet representations of America became more complicated in the early 1970s. True, basic contrasts of exploitative US imperialism to a supposedly benign Soviet internationalism continued to buttress affirmations of the superiority of the USSR.[48] And after the Moscow summit in 1972, cartoonists still criticized US bombing of Vietnam and the massive spending on the greedy US military–industrial complex.[49] Yet the total number of anti-American cartoons declined dramatically. Films continued to warn Soviet citizens against being seduced by the projected paradise of the West, but they also depicted the United States in more complex ways than in previous decades. In one movie, *A Dear Boy* (1974), the son of a Soviet diplomat and the son of a US millionaire work together to escape from kidnappers. This unusual movie, based on a play by the famous writer Sergei Mikhalkov, expressed ambivalence about the violent, colorful, exciting American way of life at the same time as it gave Soviet establishment sanction to a vision of Soviet–American cooperation.[50]

Despite Soviet leaders' concern about the weakening of Nixon's authority and his administration's inaction in the face of a developing crusade against détente, the Politburo remained firmly committed to working with him. Brezhnev warmly welcomed Nixon to Moscow and the Crimea in June 1974. The two leaders signed several new agreements, including one that limited the number and power of underground nuclear explosions and one that reduced the number of ABM systems each superpower would deploy from two to one. Pleased by the development of realistic cooperation, Kremlin leaders increasingly downplayed the role of ideology in Soviet foreign relations.[51]

Nixon had hoped that the third summit would dramatize the indispensability of his international leadership, yet it did little to stem his political demise. As an African American newspaper that had glowed with hopes two years before observed, Nixon's report on his new trip to Moscow "stirred no ripple of enthusiasm." Détente, *Time* commented, had "lost some of its earlier magic." One reason détente went from enjoying nearly universal approval to being increasingly under attack was the belief that the United States was giving (particularly in trade) more than it was getting. Most importantly, with the United States freed from the embarrassment of its bloody war in Vietnam, a growing number of Americans became more inclined to express outrage at Soviet suppression of human rights and to demand changes in Soviet internal policies as a condition of détente.[52]

DÉTENTE IN DOUBT, 1974–1976

By the time Nixon resigned in August 1974, then, many Americans had begun to doubt the value of détente. During the next two years, the misgivings deepened and spread. Nixon's successor, Gerald Ford, a conservative former Congressman from Michigan, immediately assured Soviet leaders that he would continue Nixon's policies and retained Kissinger as Secretary of State. Yet, by the spring of 1976, when former California governor Ronald Reagan challenged Ford for the Republican nomination, Ford and his political advisors viewed "détente" as such a political liability that they decided to stop using the word and to reduce Kissinger's visibility. The Ford administration's shift in public posture in turn exacerbated Soviet leaders' doubts about the US commitment to improved relations.[53]

The disruption of relations stemmed above all from failures to manage perceptions and expectations. Whereas Nixon sought to steer American public images of superpower relations, Ford lacked the confidence and sophistication to guide media representations. While Kissinger continued to receive high approval ratings from the general public, critics increasingly charged him with being dishonest and un-American in his *Realpolitik* approach to foreign policy. As early as August 1975, the Policy Planning Staff (PPS) of the State Department cautioned Kissinger that "détente diplomacy is in trouble" and argued that "perceptions may be more critical than reality."[54]

Kissinger vowed to Soviet diplomats that he would make speeches that would quell criticism of détente, but he failed to make compelling public arguments for détente. In private, Kissinger repeatedly told journalists and government officials that the United States had gotten more from détente than the Soviet Union had – citing Soviet assistance in ending the Vietnam War, the reduced Soviet influence in the Middle East, Soviet concessions in arms control negotiations, and the failure of Washington to deliver the economic benefits promised in 1972. Yet Kissinger did not publicly make such a case.[55]

Despite the shortcomings of Kissinger and Ford, a majority of Americans continued to approve of détente. When pollsters asked Americans in 1974 whether they thought it possible for the United States and Russia to reach "a long-term agreement in the world," 69 percent – almost 15 percent more than in 1972 – said yes. Drawing on such opinion surveys and a review of editorials, State Department officials concluded in December 1974 that "détente with the Soviet Union enjoys broader national support today than at any time in the post-war period." A year later, pollsters still concurred that most Americans accepted détente, preferring it to more expensive and dangerous Cold War strategies.[56]

Yet the wide approval of détente was also shallow and vulnerable to challenges from aroused critics. While Nixon–Kissinger realists and many liberal internationalists accepted détente's foundation upon a rough strategic parity with the Soviet Union,[57] conservative nationalists and emerging neoconservatives rejected the idea that the United States was no longer number one in the world. Sensitive to criticism along that line, Ford and his aides emphasized their commitment to keeping the United States "second to none," but such statements alarmed Soviet leaders without satisfying American champions of military superiority.[58] Whereas Kissinger's European-style policies assumed that the United States was a nation like other nations, Reagan and other critics insisted that America was different from and morally superior to all other nations. America, liberal and conservative idealists agreed, could not merely pursue its interests in a cold-blooded way; it had to stand up for moral principles.

One principle to uphold was the right of free emigration. Senator Henry Jackson, who hoped to win the Democratic nomination for president in 1976 and had significant support from Jewish Americans, gained much attention for his championing of the cause of Soviet Jewry. Most Americans approved of the campaign, which appealed strongly to America's self-image as a nation of immigrants called to redeem other nations.[59]

The campaign brought significant problems of perception. Believing that the Soviet Union was "in deep economic trouble" and desperate for trade, credits, and technology from the United States, Jackson and his supporters thought Washington could compel Moscow to allow many more Jews to leave each year – perhaps as many as 100,000. After complex negotiations with Kissinger and Ford about how to attach emigration conditions to a US–Soviet trade agreement, Jackson claimed at a White House press conference on October 18, 1974 that he and Ford had agreed that Moscow would be required to issue a minimum of 60,000 visas per year. Soviet leaders had given private assurances that the number of exit visas would rise beyond the 35,000 issued in 1973, but they had refused to commit themselves to a specific number and they could not allow the public perception that they had capitulated to American pressure concerning Soviet internal affairs. Angered by Jackson's statement, they quickly repudiated the trade agreement. In the next year, Jewish emigration declined dramatically.

Jackson and his supporters had miscalculated badly. They overestimated the Soviets' need for credits from America at a time when they were gaining more revenue from oil exports and could obtain much larger credits from other nations (such as France and Japan). They also disregarded how intensely proud Soviet leaders resented what they perceived as efforts to humiliate and discriminate against the Soviet Union by attaching conditions to the extension of most favored nation status that were not applied to other countries. Soon some politicians who had collaborated with Jackson, including Representative Charles Vanik, backpedaled and pleaded with Soviet leaders to allow emigration to inch upward again in exchange for modification of congressional restrictions.[60]

American desires to stand tall for principles were evident also in two incidents in the summer of 1975. When Ford declined to meet with exiled Soviet writer Alexander Solzhenitsyn, editors and politicians decried an alleged cowering deference to the feelings of Kremlin rulers. Then, when

Ford traveled to Finland to meet with Brezhnev and sign the Helsinki Final Act, which stipulated that European borders could not be changed by force, critics charged that he had abandoned East European peoples who longed for freedom and condoned an oppressive Soviet sphere of influence.[61]

The Ford administration's handling of two other international developments in 1975 also contributed to the erosion of American public support for détente by fostering impressions of unrestrained Soviet adventurism and receding US global influence. In the first four months of the year, North Vietnamese victories caused the already low morale of South Vietnamese forces to disintegrate and the unpopular President Nguyen Van Thieu to panic. By the end of April, North Vietnamese soldiers rode Soviet-supplied tanks into Saigon. Although US officials privately recognized the fundamental weaknesses of the South Vietnamese military and government that caused the defeat, after the fall of Saigon Kissinger fueled alarm about Soviet expansionism. In a speech in St. Louis on May 12, for example, Kissinger declared, "The expansion of Soviet military power and its extension around the world is a serious concern to us." Even as he acknowledged that the Soviet opportunity to gain a new naval base in Vietnam was not primarily a result of Soviet action, Kissinger charged that Soviet willingness to exploit such strategic opportunities constituted "a heavy mortgage on détente." Such rhetoric handed ammunition to conservatives eager to discredit détente.[62]

As South Vietnam collapsed, a new problem for superpower relations flared up in southwestern Africa. While Angola, a former colony of Portugal, prepared for independence in 1975, three armed groups vied for power in a civil war greatly intensified by foreign meddling. Moscow provided aid to a Marxist movement (the MPLA), which had support across different ethnic groups. Beijing supported the rival FNLA. Meanwhile, Washington collaborated with Zaire and apartheid South Africa to covertly assist both the FNLA and UNITA, which was dominated by the Ovimbundu tribe. In August 1975, citing the massive foreign aid to the FNLA and UNITA, Fidel Castro asked Brezhnev to approve the dispatch of Cuban troops to support the MPLA. Worried about damaging détente, Brezhnev declined. Yet, after South African forces, encouraged by Kissinger, invaded Angola in October, Brezhnev agreed to transport thousands of Cuban soldiers to defend the MPLA. Following the Cuban defeat of the South African invaders, Congress barred further US funding of Angolan insurgents. Frustrated, Kissinger portrayed Soviet policy as a flagrant violation of détente and shaped a lasting misperception that the Soviet Union had been wantonly expansionist. While Brezhnev actually had been hesitant, the MPLA victory inspired optimism among Soviet officials that they could continue to assist the advance of socialism in the Global South.[63]

Kissinger and Ford decided to punish Moscow by deferring a visit by Brezhnev to the United States, postponing Cabinet-level delegations to the USSR, and delaying a meeting of a Soviet–American commercial commission. Upset, PepsiCo head Donald Kendall told Ford, "There was nothing wrong with the Soviets supporting their side – just like we do." However, Kissinger felt the administration should "keep clobbering" the Kremlin about Angola and disregarded Soviet protests that he was overreacting. Brezhnev suspected that Kissinger and Ford were cynically using developments in Angola as a pretext to pressure Moscow and increase military spending. Thus, while neither Washington nor Moscow had vital interests in Angola, the superpowers' interventions there severely damaged their relations.[64]

Kissinger's distortion of the Soviet role in Angola helped spur a turn in the Soviet press toward more negative depictions of the Ford administration. As National Security Adviser Brent Scowcroft reported in April 1976, Soviet media began to charge that, in order to improve its electoral prospects, the administration was siding at times with American opponents of détente. By the end of the year, the Soviet press passed negative judgments on the Ford administration, especially on account of its policy toward southern Africa, its heating of the arms race, and its assistance to the manufacture of an artificial image of a Soviet threat.[65]

On the whole, Soviet journalists in the 1970s depicted the United States with more subtlety than in previous decades. Sometimes, especially in the non-conformist writer Vassily Aksyonov's account of his travels through America in 1975, enthusiasm and excitement predominated. However, as historian Dina Fainberg has shown, the leading Soviet correspondents sent to the United States continued to emphasize the negative and pervasive influence of capitalist ideology on the American way of life. Genrikh Borovik, Melor Sturua, Stanislav Kondrashov, and others disagreed about whether racism, atomized individualism, consumerist selfishness, or wealthy elites' control of politics was the worst evil. Yet, in different ways, they all discredited America's claim to be a beacon to the world and implicitly showed the superiority of socialist ideals. Thus, the Soviet correspondents, moved by their genuine faith in socialism, affirmed Soviet identity in contrast to the United States.[66]

On the American side, the most influential correspondents sent to Russia in the mid-1970s affirmed the superiority of the American way of life, but also urged acceptance of Soviet differences from the United States.

In *Russia: The People and the Power* (1976), Robert Kaiser of the *Washington Post* argued that "Russians could not live like ... Americans even if they wanted to, which they do not." Kaiser urged that, instead of trying to Americanize Russia or imagining the USSR as a terrible menace that had to be confronted, Americans should pursue a policy of peaceful accommodation that eventually would undermine the Soviet autocracy. In *The Russians*, a more vivid volume that captured more attention, Hedrick Smith of the *New York Times* similarly emphasized the "enduring characteristics of the Russians as a people" and asserted that the leaders and the submissive people shared an authoritarian frame of mind. Although Smith's descriptions were often condescending and pessimistic, he did not summon Americans to condemn or contain Russia. Reviewers drew from *The Russians* the conclusions that the slovenly Soviets were less threatening than had been supposed, that Russians were hopelessly docile, and that Americans should put aside their own yardsticks in assessing them.[67]

Scholars put other spins on Soviet differences from America. Left-leaning writers, above all Stephen Cohen, emphasized differences *among* Soviet leaders and argued that reducing tensions with the USSR would allow Soviet reformers to make changes that would lead to a moderation of expansionism and to internal liberalization. In contrast, conservatives, most importantly Harvard historian Richard Pipes, stressed Russia's inherent differences *from* the West, including its deeply entrenched xenophobia and fanaticism, and linked those differences to its alleged aggressive menace. Anticommunists had more opportunities to influence US policy. Pipes, for example, served as an adviser to Senator Jackson and as principal author of a report in 1976 that asserted that US intelligence analysts underestimated the threat posed by the military build-up of the Soviet Union, which allegedly had gained strategic superiority. That message suited the interests of the military–industrial complex. It also catered to what historian and former diplomat George F. Kennan called the "addiction of the American political establishment to the cultivation of a Cold War image of the Soviet Union." Observing the presidential campaigns of 1976, Kennan despaired because both parties' nominees seemed "quite prepared to sacrifice our relations with the Soviet Union in order to play up to ethnic minorities among the voters."[68]

CARTER, BREZHNEV, AND THE DEMISE OF DÉTENTE, 1977–1979

As he campaigned in 1976, Democrat and former Georgia governor Jimmy Carter repeatedly criticized the immorality of US foreign policies in the Kissinger years. He also pounced on Ford's confused denial that the Soviet

Union dominated Eastern Europe in a debate in October and condemned the Soviet Union for violating the Helsinki agreement on human rights. Yet Carter did not totally repudiate détente. Instead, he hoped for dramatic improvements in relations with Moscow, though on new terms. Carter's dream of a world without nuclear weapons inclined him to be ambitious about arms negotiations with the Soviet Union. In addition, his vision of America regaining its moral stature entailed a shift away from the degrading influence of its past excessive fear of communism.[69]

Carter's statements about the Soviet Union angered Brezhnev, who found them insulting. However, US businessman Armand Hammer assured Brezhnev that Carter's remarks were merely designed to help him win the election. In January 1977, Brezhnev decided to make a "show of goodwill" to Carter. Firmly rejecting the "class war" approach of Soviet ideologists, Brezhnev extended an olive branch to the new president in a major speech just before Carter took office. Although speechwriter and international relations aide Anatoly Chernyaev was concerned that a continuing build-up of Soviet military capabilities would make it more difficult to convince the West of Moscow's peaceful intentions, he thought Brezhnev's address succeeded in dulling the edge of Western complaints about a Soviet threat. Hence, in both capitals there were grounds for optimism as Carter became president.[70]

Yet, from the outset of the Carter–Brezhnev era, Soviet–American relations were rocky. Carter quickly antagonized Soviet leaders by sending a supportive letter to dissident physicist Andrei Sakharov and welcoming exiled dissident Vladimir Bukovsky to the White House – steps the Kremlin resented as interference in Soviet internal affairs. Even worse, in the eyes of Politburo leaders, was Carter's decision to send Secretary of State Cyrus Vance to Moscow with sweeping arms control proposals that abandoned the framework established by Brezhnev and Ford at Vladivostok in late 1974. Angered by the setting aside of that accord and by being treated haughtily by Americans who seemingly thought they could impose a new agenda, Soviet leaders flatly rejected the new proposals. Having grown accustomed to being respected as equals by Nixon and Ford, Kremlin leaders deeply resented being treated like "some banana republic," as a key foreign policy adviser recalled. Disturbed by how dissidents like Sakharov and Bukovsky were being used as weapons against the Kremlin, Soviet leaders lashed back with propaganda about alleged human rights violations in capitalist countries.[71]

A new crisis in Africa further roiled Soviet–American relations. Ethiopia, the third most populous nation in Africa, had been a major recipient of US military aid since the 1950s, and the United States had established an important radar system there. Despite a bloody revolution in 1974, the United States dramatically increased its aid for the next two years, partly in response to an alliance between neighboring Somalia and the Soviet Union. When the ruthless Marxist leader of Ethiopia, Mengistu Haile Mariam, approached Moscow for more arms in 1976, Soviet leaders responded cautiously, not wanting to jeopardize their investment in Somalia. Knowing that Somali leader Siad Barre hoped to conquer the vast Ogaden region of Ethiopia, Soviet leaders tried to restrain him. However, in March 1977, when the Somali Ambassador to Washington asked for economic and military aid, Vice President Walter Mondale urged Carter to seize the opportunity to oust the Soviets from their port at Berbera, Somalia. Although the United States knew Siad Barre planned to invade the Ogaden, Carter directed his Cabinet to "move in every possible way to get Somalia to be our friend" in order to compensate for the loss of the US position in Ethiopia.[72]

By June, Somalia was waging war, at first through a "liberation front," then more directly. But the Carter administration nonetheless proceeded to arrange weapons shipments for Somalia through Saudi Arabia and other allies. As Carter told journalists, he wanted to "aggressively challenge" the Soviet Union for influence around the world, including in Somalia.[73]

Angered by the Somali clash with Ethiopia, in September Brezhnev demanded that Siad Barre withdraw from the Ogaden or face a cut-off of Soviet aid. After Somalia expelled Soviet advisers and revoked Soviet access to Berbera in November, Moscow sent 1,000 soldiers to oversee a successful counterattack by Ethiopia and 16,000 Cuban troops. As in Angola two years earlier, the Soviet military intervention was a defensive response to a foreign invasion, yet it undermined support for détente in America. Frustrated by the geopolitical setback in the Horn of Africa, National Security Adviser Zbigniew Brzezinski proposed sending an aircraft carrier to the region. However, Carter and Vance decided against such a bluff and the crisis gradually subsided.[74]

Carter was more receptive to Brzezinski's advice in other areas, including about how to shape attitudes toward Soviet–American relations through public statements. In two major addresses in 1977 and 1978, Carter succeeded in affirming American national identity by highlighting an idealistic US mission in the world. However, he failed to define a clear direction for US policy toward the Soviet Union, to overcome growing domestic doubts about his leadership, or to allay Kremlin perceptions of him as arrogantly unilateral.

At the University of Notre Dame in May 1977, Carter sought to move America beyond the Vietnam War, which had sapped worldwide faith in the United States. Instead of being driven by "that inordinate fear of communism" that led the United States to embrace dictators and wage war in Southeast Asia, Carter vowed, America's foreign policy henceforth would be founded on its commitment to human rights and confidence that "democracy's example will be compelling" to peoples around the world. Although he declared that he believed in détente as a path toward peace, he cast Moscow as an adversary, a "totalitarian" nation that persecuted dissidents and tried to "impose its system of society" on other countries. Carter showed no awareness of any tension between his use of the USSR as a foil for the reaffirmation of the virtues of the United States and his desire to "build a bridge of mutual confidence" with Soviet leaders. However, key figures in the foreign policy establishment sensed trouble. Veteran columnist David Broder, for example, worried that Brzezinski was fueling Carter's moralism so much that they would neglect more disciplined thinking about US interests.[75]

A year later, Carter sought to overcome perceptions of him as a weak, vacillating leader by writing and delivering an address at the US Naval Academy. More stridently than at Notre Dame, Carter stressed the economic and political superiority of the democratic United States over the Soviet Union, whose oppressive form of government was "becoming increasingly unattractive to other nations." Although he thus cast American–Soviet relations in classic Cold War terms as a global ideological rivalry, Carter still espoused détente as "central to world peace." Yet, rejecting the Soviet approach to détente as involving both cooperation and competition for influence around the world, he demanded that Moscow "choose either confrontation or cooperation."[76]

Carter's speech at Annapolis alarmed liberal advocates of arms control without satisfying militant anticommunists. The American Committee on East–West Accord, chaired by George F. Kennan and liberal economist John Kenneth Galbraith, sent a letter to Carter and met with Brzezinski to urge the administration to "moderate the tone of its discourse." Similarly worried that Carter's vehement criticism of Moscow would jeopardize passage of a SALT II treaty, Senator George McGovern (Democrat, South Dakota) told reporters he saw "no purpose in ginning the American people into a kind of anti-Soviet hysteria." On the other side, Senator Jackson welcomed Carter's "growing recognition that the Soviet Union is a repressive totalitarian state," but complained that his tougher words were contradicted by a still soft policy.[77]

Both Cold Warriors and advocates of détente recognized that words mattered. Soviet leaders understood that, too. A first blast from *Pravda* charged that the Carter administration was "working up anti-Soviet hysteria." A week later an unusually long 5,000 word article published in newspapers across the USSR warned that Carter's new line threatened to trigger a new cold war. What may have angered Soviet leaders most was the way Carter's disparaging words challenged their proud self-image as a superpower on a par with the United States. That was the intention of some members of Carter's team. A White House official who briefed reporters before the Annapolis speech explained that, if the Russians were going to poke their fingers into small nations around the globe, "then we're going to treat them as petty spoilers rather than the mature superpower they say they are."[78]

While Washington and Moscow sparred, filmmakers struggled to adapt to the ambivalent era of détente, when it was unclear to many whether the other superpower was a partner or an enemy. One of the most striking expressions of this uncertainty, *Telefon*, appeared in American theatres at the end of 1977. On the one hand, the movie seemed to revert to 1950s fears of Communist penetration and subversion: a Soviet intelligence operation had established a network of brainwashed agents inside the United States ready to respond to orders to destroy American targets. On the other hand, the movie featured successful collaboration between a KGB major and a CIA double agent to find a rogue Stalinist fanatic from the KGB before he could activate all the agents and trigger a third world war. In the end, the CIA agent, who has fallen in love with the KGB major, rejects orders to kill him, and the couple go off together, defying both of the superpower spy agencies. Neither a financial nor an artistic triumph, *Telefon* nonetheless reflected the complexity of American popular attitudes in the late 1970s, when many still held hopes for détente.[79]

Soviet films, which continued to require approval by Communist Party propaganda officials, tended to express more harshly negative views of the United States, yet they still embodied some ambivalence. *On the Islands of Grenada*, produced in late 1979 and early 1980, depicted a violent, American-engineered coup, yet it blamed the treacherous CIA rather than the oblivious US president and it showed an American kitchen with a full refrigerator. *Shooting Range*, a stylish animated short film, similarly nodded to the seductive appeal of American life with its jazzy score and its kaleido-scopic color, though it warned that being seduced made one a victim of soulless, exploitative capitalism.[80]

Many Americans at the time – including Ronald Reagan, the former governor of California who became a radio commentator and newspaper columnist – believed that glimpses of the American consumer paradise would turn Russians into admirers and even tacit allies of the United States. Some scholars, similarly, have suggested that the growing awareness of the American standard of living and the heightened cultural infiltration in the era of détente contributed significantly to the collapse of faith in communism. Seeing the abundance of goods in Western stores in contrast to the empty shelves in the USSR did indeed shake the confidence of some Soviet socialists – including Anatoly Chernyaev, a top adviser to the International Department of the Communist Party who frequently traveled abroad.[81]

However, as a 1976 survey of the Soviet population and post-Soviet interviews with "Soviet baby boomers" show, many Soviet citizens who knew of the comforts and conveniences in capitalist countries still believed in the advantages of the socialist system that gave them free education, subsidized housing, and generous paid vacations without requiring them to work very strenuously. Although formal ideological indoctrination failed to prevent many Soviet young people from becoming cynical about the increasingly corrupt system or apathetic about Marxism-Leninism, subtler forms of propaganda often succeeded in instilling negative views of American crime, violence, and unemployment, and buttressing faith in the (eventual) superiority of Soviet socialism.[82]

Among the most widely disseminated images of the United States were the cartoons in the humor magazine *Krokodil*. Almost six million copies of the magazine were published three times a month in the late 1970s. *Krokodil* persistently depicted the United States as a dark double of the bright USSR. It featured positive images of the Soviet Union (as a happy, modern, space-traveling, peace-loving country) on many front covers, while disseminating extremely negative images of the United States (as a decadent, aggressive, militaristic, war-mongering country) on most back covers. The most striking example of this contrast appeared on the sixtieth anniversary of the October 1917 revolution, when the front cover depicted the Soviet rise from the ruins of the First World War to urban modernity and the back cover showed the decline of American capitalism from global hegemon to decrepitude (Figures 15.2 and 15.3).

As Soviet and American image-makers battled, relations between the two governments deteriorated. In January 1979, when the United States and Communist China completed the normalization of their diplomatic relations, Carter and Brzezinski welcomed Chinese leader Deng Xiaoping to Washington and endorsed his vehement opposition to the Soviet Union, thereby angering Soviet leaders. As Washington and Beijing developed

Figure 15.2 "1917–1977." *Krokodil,* No. 31, November 1977. Courtesy of *Novaia Gazeta.*

a tacit strategic alliance against Moscow, American public images of Communist China changed. By early 1979, more Americans viewed China favorably (26 percent) than saw Russia positively (15 percent) and the number of Americans who had unfavorable feelings about China (24 percent) was much smaller than the number who had negative feelings about Russia (41 percent).[83]

The rising American hostility to Russia stemmed in part from misrepresentation of a development in which the Soviets played little role: the overthrow of an authoritarian client of the United States in the Middle East. In January 1979, the Shah of Iran, facing widespread opposition to his rule, flew to Egypt. Two weeks later the anti-American and anticommunist Ayatollah Ruhollah Khomeini returned to Tehran from exile in Paris, and his supporters completed the seizure of power. The Islamic revolution surprised the KGB: it had no high-level agents in Iran after September 1977, and its officers had little room to operate under the eyes of the Shah's secret police. Although the head of the KGB, Yuri Andropov, had ordered officers to try to destabilize the Shah's regime, he had been less hopeful about a left-leaning revolution than worried about the US use of Iran as a base for measures against the Muslim republics of the USSR. However, Brzezinski

Figure 15.3 "Old Age Is Not Happiness." *Krokodil*, No. 31, November 1977. Courtesy of *Novaia Gazeta.*

argued persistently in White House meetings that the Soviet Union had instigated the uprising. In addition, Brzezinski inspired a *Time* cover story that depicted Iran as part of a "crescent of crisis" along the shores of the Indian Ocean. *Time* asserted, citing the apocryphal "Will" of Peter the Great, that it was "beyond dispute" that the Soviet Union sought to "extend its influence throughout the crisis area." The accompanying cover graphically conveyed the nightmarish threat: a fearsome bear with its jaws gripping land near Iran stared menacingly at the oil-rich region centering on the Persian Gulf and Saudi Arabia.[84]

There was one major positive development in American–Soviet relations in 1979 – the long-awaited signing of the SALT II treaty by Carter and

Brezhnev in Vienna in June. Yet it did little to halt the worsening of tension between the two nations. Since the treaty's high limits to the number of launchers of nuclear weapons in each country's arsenal did not do much to slow the arms race, it won only tepid support from proponents of arms control. Although SALT II embodied Senator Jackson's demand for equal numerical limits, he nonetheless charged Carter with "appeasement" of the Soviets. In the wake of the Vienna summit, conservatives intensified their denunciations of the Soviet Union, with the *Wall Street Journal* shrilly indicting the Soviets for having "the most belligerently atheistic regime around."[85]

Even where the Soviet Union did nothing, Americans found cause for outrage. In the weeks after the Vienna summit, US intelligence officials leaked to congressional staffers and key senators communications and photographic evidence of a Soviet military unit in Cuba. Encouraged by hawks such as Paul Nitze, intelligence officials also passed the news to the press. As the story spread in the media in late August, Frank Church, chair of the Senate Foreign Relations Committee, decided to take a tough stand. Church (Democrat, Idaho) had favored the SALT II treaty, but, worried about being attacked from the right in the election of 1980, he demanded the withdrawal of Soviet troops from Cuba as a condition for ratification of SALT II. Secretary of State Vance noted at a press conference that the Soviet unit had been in Cuba for years, but unwisely committed the administration to changing the situation. Brzezinski seized upon Vance's mishandling of the incident to promote a tougher posture toward Moscow, telling Carter that "the increasingly pervasive perception here and abroad is that ... the Soviets are increasingly assertive and the US more acquiescent."[86]

Although the Soviet brigade had been in Cuba since 1962, the uproar in Washington, fueled in part by American politicians' concerns about their images, severely damaged prospects for the arms control treaty. It emboldened critics of SALT II to call for outright rejection of the treaty and made ratification by the Senate very problematic.[87] It also angered Soviet leaders, who resented being falsely accused and suspected that Carter and Brzezinski had manufactured an artificial crisis to justify backing out of the treaty and launching a military build-up.[88]

By the fall of 1979, then, Soviet–American relations had been seriously strained. While some Soviet officials feared sinister forces were maneuvering the United States toward confrontation with the Soviet Union, American conservatives warned that Moscow sought such military superiority that it would be able to dictate to Washington, turning the United States "into a big Finland," as the *Wall Street Journal* put it. In that context, Soviet leaders saw little left to be gained through détente, and American hard-liners saw much to be gained from further dramatizations of Soviet threats.[89]

Earlier, in March 1979, when Afghan Communist leaders pleaded for Soviet military intervention to rescue their unpopular neo-Stalinist regime, Brezhnev had rejected the appeal because he wanted to sign the SALT II treaty and preserve détente with Western Europe. However, in the fall, KGB chief Andropov and Defense Minister Dmitry Ustinov developed plans for an invasion that Brezhnev approved in December without consulting Soviet diplomatic experts. The elderly Kremlin trio's unwise decision stemmed in part from Brezhnev's anger at the assassination in October of a favored prime minister, Nur Muhammad Taraki, by his deputy Hafizullah Amin and suspicion that Amin (who had studied in New York) was an American agent. The decision also was spurred by worries about a growing CIA-supported Islamist insurgency. The Carter administration knew that providing substantial aid to the rebels could provoke Soviet military intervention, but it decided to risk sending limited assistance and gradually escalated the support in the second half of 1979. Soviet leaders feared that, if they did not prop up a reliable regime in Kabul, the United States could use Afghanistan as a base for destabilizing Soviet Central Asia. They also were alarmed by a NATO decision on December 12 to deploy new short-range missiles in Western Europe, which suggested that such missiles could be placed in Afghanistan as well if Moscow did not preserve a client state there. Although dogmatic ideology and a sense of mission to modernize a backward country also influenced some Soviet leaders, the invasion on December 24 was primarily a defensive move.[90]

Shocked, Carter declared that the invasion was the greatest threat to peace since the Second World War – an overreaction influenced by Brzezinski's nightmarish vision that Soviet forces would use landlocked Afghanistan as a base for threatening vital oil shipments in the Persian Gulf. In response, Carter put off submitting the SALT II treaty to consideration by the Senate, imposed an embargo on grain sales to the Soviet Union, and ordered a boycott of the summer Olympic Games in Moscow. The boycott, spurred by Carter's desire to appear tough in an election year, stemmed also from the belief that it would stun the Soviet people and shake the legitimacy of the Soviet state. In reality, the boycott failed to prevent more than 5,000 athletes from competing in Moscow, had little impact on Soviet popular views, and had no effect at all on the Soviet war in Afghanistan, which expanded instead of being quickly concluded, as Brezhnev had expected.[91]

The misguided Soviet invasion and Carter's reactions strongly affected American media images and popular attitudes, reviving a sense of US moral superiority.[92] At the winter Olympics in New York in February 1980, when a young US hockey team upset a heavily favored veteran Soviet team, it triggered a cathartic response across the United States, with millions singing "The Star Spangled Banner," honking horns, and waving the Stars and Stripes. The affirmation of America's youthful heroes in contrast to Soviet villains marked an end to the ambivalence about the USSR in the fifteen turbulent years of détente.[93]

CONCLUSION

While ideological differences between the superpowers generally had been set aside in the rise of détente, the resurgence of ideological passions figured significantly in the demise of détente. After 1974, politicians such as Reagan and Carter reasserted American exceptionalism and used Soviet totalitarian evil as a foil for the affirmation of American democratic virtue. Although Brezhnev said in the early 1970s that "we only use ideology on the domestic front," after the successful defense of Marxist forces in Angola in 1975, he and other Soviet leaders grew more enthusiastic about how the world seemed to be moving their way.[94] The revival of the influence of ideologies was not simply inevitable.[95] Instead, it hinged on a turn of events, particularly the ignominious end to the disastrous US war in Vietnam. As we have seen, the deterioration of relations also stemmed from a series of misperceptions, miscalculations, and mishandled crises. Those unforced errors had major consequences. For example, if an overconfident Senator Jackson had not disrupted negotiations over Jewish emigration, the US–Soviet trade agreement would not have been canceled, and if the Carter administration had not mismanaged the flap over a supposed Soviet combat brigade in Cuba, the Senate might have ratified the SALT II treaty. Such mistakes exacerbated frictions before the ill-conceived Soviet invasion of Afghanistan nailed shut the coffin of détente. In 1980, American–Soviet relations entered a new phase that would bring the most extreme demonization and dangerous tension since the Cuban missile crisis of 1962.

16

FROM ARMAGEDDON TO ACCOMMODATION, 1980–1989

OVERVIEW

Although relations between the United States and the Soviet Union were already severely strained by the beginning of 1980, in the next four years the superpowers' relationship deteriorated even further, to the point of acute confrontation. The top leaders of the two countries did not meet. Arms control negotiations deadlocked. Fears of nuclear war gripped many people in each country. Propagandistic vilification of the enemy escalated to a level not seen since the early 1950s.

Yet by the end of the decade American–Soviet relations improved so much that many declared the Cold War to be over. President Reagan and General Secretary Gorbachev met every year. They signed a treaty that for the first time actually led to the elimination of nuclear missiles. Fears of war between the two superpowers almost disappeared. Mutual demonization largely ended.

How did this astonishing transformation happen? Many different explanations have been offered, but almost all of them focus on the ideas and actions of top political leaders. Republican partisans have claimed that President Ronald Reagan won the Cold War and caused the collapse of the Soviet Union by pursuing a tough, uncompromising policy that featured a massive military build-up, economic warfare, covert support for anticommunist insurgencies around the world, and rhetorical denunciation of the "evil empire."[1] Democrats and their academic supporters have objected to giving Reagan so much credit, insisting that he had the good fortune to be in office when a strategy of containment, launched by Democrat Harry Truman forty years earlier, finally worked.[2] In stark contrast to such American triumphalist accounts, some US experts on the Soviet Union and leading Russian historians have argued that Mikhail Gorbachev, the dynamic leader of the Soviet Union from 1985 to 1991, took the initiatives that reshaped relations with the United States, not because of but in spite of US hard-line policies.[3] More balanced interpretations have recognized that both Reagan and Gorbachev deserve credit for the surprising turn in Soviet–American relations, and that changes on each side facilitated further steps on the other side. Yet even the best of these studies have concentrated on the great men at the summits of the two political systems rather than on the much broader changes in beliefs and emotions in the two countries.[4]

Reagan and Gorbachev did not by themselves cause the transformation of American–Soviet relations. Although Reagan had a vague sense of the directions in which he wanted to go, he did not recognize the contradictions between his desires to denounce Soviet leaders, undermine their power, alarm them, and negotiate arms reductions with them. Lacking the energy to coordinate a coherent policy and the specific knowledge to chart a clear course, he depended heavily on his advisers, who were deeply divided over relations with the Soviet Union for the first seven years of his presidency.[5] Some of Reagan's public statements had profound effects, but they were not the primary cause of the dramatic changes in American public perceptions of the Soviet Union.[6] A close follower of polls about public approval of him, Reagan modified his rhetoric and changed his approach to the Soviet Union in part as a response to public fears of nuclear war and to prodding from his wife, who realized that peace was becoming much more popular than fire-breathing anticommunism.[7] Gorbachev, similarly, adapted to his domestic political situation, tightening economic constraints, and the changing international environment more than he imposed his vision.[8] When he became General Secretary, he did not have a definite plan to reform the Soviet Union or transform Soviet relations with America.[9] Instead, his thinking evolved in response to waves of opinion that had been set in motion earlier in the decade, and he adopted ideas both from foreign interlocutors and from Soviet intellectuals.[10]

The people who first envisioned the possibility of overcoming the danger of nuclear war and ending Soviet–American enmity were not high government officials but peace activists in the United States and Europe.[11] In response to the Reagan administration's alarming rhetoric and the escalation of tensions between the superpowers in the early 1980s, American doctors, nurses, lawyers, business executives, and housewives formed new organizations dedicated to changing attitudes and policies. They then established direct contact with Soviet citizens by traveling to the Soviet Union and by inviting Soviets to come to the United States. Even at the peak of American–Soviet hostility in 1983, when leaders of the two superpowers demonized their counterparts as monsters or fascists, American and Soviet citizens began to see first-hand the humanity of the supposed enemy nation. Through such citizen diplomacy in the following years many thousands of Americans and Russians who had feared and distrusted the other nation came to know, trust, respect, and even love people in the other country. The extensive media coverage of the citizen diplomacy projects began to change broader public opinion even before Reagan and Gorbachev first met in November 1985.

Widening the historical lens to capture the ideas and actions of many people beyond top political leaders allows a more inclusive view of the transformation of American–Soviet relations in the 1980s. It also entails a broader perspective on movements for peace in the decade. An American movement for a "nuclear freeze" that arose between 1980 and 1984 has often been seen as a failure because the proposed halt to the testing and deployment of nuclear weapons was not adopted as US government policy.[12] In addition, it has frequently been asserted that the antinuclear movement, narrowly associated with the freeze campaign, declined in influence after 1984.[13] Yet the freeze campaign was part of a much wider movement against the nuclear arms race and for Soviet–American understanding that continued to grow after Reagan's landslide re-election in 1984. That movement sought not only to promote better relations between Washington and Moscow but also to influence how Americans and Russians thought and felt about each other. By shattering stereotypes and replacing antipathy with empathy, citizen activists contributed significantly to the warming of Soviet–American relations.[14]

Citizen diplomats participated in a broader contest in each country over images of the other that also involved filmmakers, cartoonists, journalists, and politicians. Focusing above all on that struggle over perceptions and beliefs illuminates how the Soviet Union and the United States moved from the brink of Armageddon to mutual accommodation in the most remarkable sea change in the entire history of American–Russian relations.

THE SOVIET INVASION OF AFGHANISTAN AND THE US PRESIDENTIAL CAMPAIGN OF 1980

The Soviet military intervention in Afghanistan at the end of 1979 triggered worldwide condemnation in the first months of 1980. Soviet foreign policy advisers, who had not been consulted by top Kremlin leaders before the assault on Kabul, were stung by the denunciations – which came even from normally friendly Communist parties. Some advisers struggled to justify the action. For example, Boris Ponomarev, head of the International Department of the Central Committee of the Communist Party of the Soviet Union, tried to argue that Moscow could not allow a potential turncoat to be in power on the border of the USSR. Yet even Ponomarev joined others – especially the leading expert on the United States, Georgy Arbatov – in urging a withdrawal of Soviet forces. However, the announcement in June 1980 of a partial withdrawal of some Soviet units from Afghanistan did little to diminish the intense anti-Soviet campaign in the West.[15]

In the United States, with a presidential campaign under way, the loudest voices not only castigated the brutal Soviet invasion but also demanded a massive US military build-up to contain Soviet aggression. The Soviet intervention in Afghanistan appeared to confirm the truth of militant Cold Warriors' claims about a grave communist threat. Hard-line organizations, well-funded by defense contractors and wealthy conservatives, produced alarmist pamphlets, advertisements, and documentaries asserting that the USSR had pulled ahead in the arms race, built missiles much larger than US missiles, and gained the ability to menace America with a nuclear first strike. Neoconservative intellectuals dissatisfied by Carter's belated responses to these alleged dangers defected from the Democratic Party, attacked timorous liberalism, and supported the vehemently anticommunist Republican Ronald Reagan.[16]

Yet there were also important countercurrents. In January, Senator Edward Kennedy (Democrat, Massachusetts) delivered a major speech in which he criticized President Carter's "exaggeration and hyperbole" about the Soviet invasion of Afghanistan and urged that the United States "not foreclose every opening to the Soviet Union." Kennedy thereby breathed new fire into his previously lackluster campaign for the Democratic presidential nomination.[17] On February 1, the *New York Times* featured a long op-ed by senior statesman George Kennan, who analyzed Soviet motives in Afghanistan as defensive, lamented the "militarization of thought and discourse" in Washington, and warned of the danger from "a breakdown of political communication." Kennan's essay and a subsequent appearance on the *60 Minutes* television show had a sensational effect, energizing likeminded Americans and prompting a surge in donations to the American Committee on East–West Accord.[18] Opponents of hysteria about a Soviet threat were active on local as well as national stages. For example, after a San Francisco television station broadcast a dramatization of Soviet submarines launching a first strike against US strategic forces that compelled the president to surrender, activists led by a Berkeley professor of journalism demanded and won the right to show a response, *First Strike: The Politics of Fear.*[19]

Recognizing how widespread popular concern about the exacerbation of tensions with the Soviet Union had become, even Carter turned to painting Reagan as a warmonger. By late October, Carter had closed the gap with his Republican opponent in opinion polls. Reagan ultimately prevailed in the election in part because he delivered a calm, moderate performance in a campaign-closing debate. While Carter repeatedly charged that Reagan's attitude toward the Soviet Union was dangerous and belligerent, Reagan emphasized his desires for peace and a mutual reduction of nuclear weapons. As the *New York Times* (which supported Carter) observed, "Reagan was impossible to tar as a war lover."[20]

Thus, although Reagan handily defeated Carter (by 51 percent to 41 percent of the popular vote), it would be misleading to remember the election of 1980 as a simple triumph for militant anticommunism. And, even though he lost the contest, Carter's prediction about the effect of Reagan's approach to the nuclear arms race would prove prescient: "the adversarial relationship between ourselves and the Soviet Union would undoubtedly deteriorate very rapidly."[21]

CONFRONTATION AND DEFIANCE, 1981–1982

The Reagan administration's initial statements and decisions were harsh and tough. At his first press conference on January 29, 1981, the new president denounced Soviet leaders for reserving to themselves "the right to commit any crime, to lie, to cheat," in order to attain their goal of a global Communist state. Believing that the weak Soviet economy could not withstand the strain of a new escalation of the arms race, Reagan approved a massive military build-up that he thought would force Moscow to make concessions in nuclear weapons negotiations. Reagan also authorized much more aggressive maneuvers by US air and sea forces near the borders of the USSR in order to rattle the nerves of Soviet leaders. Moreover, his director of the Central Intelligence Agency launched or expanded efforts to undermine Marxist governments in Nicaragua, Angola, Afghanistan, and Eastern Europe.[22]

Yet Reagan did not consistently take a hard line. In one of his first major decisions, he dismayed his more combative advisers by deciding to lift the embargo on grain sales to the Soviet Union, which he thought hurt American farmers (a politically important group) more than it hurt the Soviets.[23] Split between ideologues and pragmatists, the Reagan administration did not pursue relentless economic warfare against the faltering Soviet system.[24] While it imposed sanctions against the construction of a gas pipeline between the Soviet Union and Western Europe, it lifted those sanctions in late 1982 when European countries pledged to restrict the granting of credits to the USSR.[25] In private diary entries, Reagan angrily condemned Soviet leaders as "inhuman monsters" and in public speeches he repeatedly proclaimed that communism was doomed.[26] But he also often expressed interest in negotiating with Soviet leaders. After being shot and nearly killed at the end of March 1981, he handwrote a heartfelt letter to Leonid Brezhnev. Reagan pleaded that dissident Natan Shcharansky and a family of Pentecostal Christians be allowed to leave the Soviet Union. Such actions, he vowed, would facilitate negotiations. If the Kremlin made such gestures, Reagan told his Secretary of State the next year, he favored a summit meeting. At a National Security Council session in March 1982, Reagan even proposed (much as Eisenhower had in 1953) that Washington "confront the Russians and tell them all the things we could do for them if they'd quit their bad acting and join the civilized world."[27]

What were Soviet leaders to think of this peculiar mix of hostility, threats, offers, and overtures? At first, some Soviet officials hoped that Reagan might, like Nixon, set aside his anticommunist rhetoric and be a realist policymaker.[28] Such optimism quickly wilted. By 1982, intellectuals and advisers who sought to reform Soviet socialism and restore détente with the West faced accusations of being at best naïve and at worst traitors.[29] Increasingly alarmed by provocative US military maneuvers, angered by Reagan's vilification of them, and indignant at US efforts to dictate to them from a position of military superiority, Soviet leaders resolved to resist US pressure and, if necessary, counterbalance the US build-up with increased military expenditures. They also continued to aid Marxist guerrillas and governments in the Global South and declined a US offer for a massive grain sale in the fall of 1982.[30]

BIRTH OF THE FREEZE MOVEMENT, 1980–1982

Soviet leaders were not alone in being disturbed by the Reagan administration's words and actions. Troubled by the cost of the arms race and worried about the danger of nuclear war, many Americans joined a widespread movement that came to center on a proposal for a "nuclear freeze" – a bilateral, verifiable halt to the production and deployment of nuclear weapons by the United States and the Soviet Union. The proposal had been developed by former Massachusetts Institute of Technology graduate student Randall Forsberg in 1980 and endorsed by long-established peace organizations such as the American Friends Service Committee, the Fellowship of Reconciliation, and the Women's International League for Peace and Freedom. In the first two years of Reagan's presidency, the movement expanded far beyond such pacifist groups to involve numerous middle-class, middle-of-the-road citizens who had not been active in politics before. As US Senator and former astronaut John Glenn observed in

April 1982, the movement was "sweeping the country." On June 12, close to a million people participated in a massive demonstration in New York City, carrying banners urging: "Freeze the Arms Race!" and "Abolish Nuclear Weapons." In November, nuclear freeze initiatives passed in nine of the ten states where they were placed on the ballot.[31]

The size and passion of the movement forced the Reagan administration to respond.[32] Irritated, Reagan privately attacked antinuclear activists as "nuts" who supported communism (as his daughter Patti, who actively supported the movement, recalled). In public Reagan claimed that "many honest and sincere people" were being manipulated by sinister agents who sought to weaken America.[33] Although such smears of the peace movement have been echoed by some scholars, Soviet agents in reality exerted no significant influence on the authentic, homegrown movement.[34] Attacks on the movement as pro-Soviet actually helped it to garner more media attention and continue to grow. Already in April 1982, the Reagan administration felt serious pressure, with support for its arms build-up declining. In July, Reagan and his advisers decided to continue nuclear testing, but not to announce that "in the face of all the anti-nukes," as Reagan jotted in his diary.[35]

CONTESTATION IN POPULAR CULTURE, 1981–1982

The contest in the United States over the arms race and relations with the Soviet Union extended beyond politics to popular culture. Three films in the first years of the Reagan administration were especially revealing about the intense and conflicting attitudes toward the USSR: *Reds* (1981), *Firefox* (1982), and *E.T.* (1982).

At the end of 1981, the president hosted a screening of *Reds* in the White House Family Theater, with two of the movie's stars present. The film dramatized the story of the idealistic journalist John Reed, who enthusiastically witnessed the Bolshevik seizure of power in 1917 and helped found the Communist Labor Party of America in 1919. Reagan's anticommunism did not prevent him from enjoying the film. He considered it "a most imaginative job of film making" and thought "it should be a smash."[36] Yet more rigid anticommunists protested the film's alleged portrayal of the Communist system as benevolent and expressed consternation at Reagan's showing of the movie. Reed Irvine, chairman of the conservative watchdog Accuracy in Media, denounced *Reds* for making "a hero of one of the men who helped cultivate the cancer of communism in Russia" and pointed out that the Communist Party paper, *The Daily World*, had hailed the film for having "honestly depicted" the Great October Revolution. The grumbling was so widespread that William F. Buckley, Jr., conservative publisher of *The National Review*, and a longtime friend of Reagan, felt compelled to defend the president's screening of *Reds*, which he called "a fine movie."[37] Critics, who tended to be more liberal, raved about the "extraordinary" film and rejected the "narrow-minded" view of it as Communist propaganda.[38] The movie earned a healthy $40 million at the box office, was voted the best film of the year by the New York Film Critics Circle, and won left-leaning Warren Beatty an Academy Award for best director, thereby indicating that in the early 1980s American culture was not as dominated by right-wing anti-communist as many believed in subsequent decades. The controversy over the film was also significant for the way it foreshadowed Reagan's later divergence from more hard-line anti-Soviet figures.

On the other hand, in June 1982, Reagan noted being impressed by the work conservative actor and director Clint Eastwood had done on *Firefox*. Much like Reagan, the movie posited that the Soviets had gotten ahead of the United States in the arms race because of American softness during the era of détente. Most threateningly, the Soviets had built an amazing new fighter plane, so advanced that it could "change the shape of the world." Eastwood uses his Russian language ability (thanks to his Russian mother) to infiltrate the USSR. There he contacts a spy network of Jewish dissidents who are ready to die to help him because of their "resentment of the K.G.B." With their aid, Eastwood steals the plane, "Firefox," and flies it to the West. Several reviewers panned the movie as implausible and its fairly strong box office revenue ($47 million) may have stemmed more from dazzling special effects than from its political message. Yet it still reflected the ardent anti-communism of many Reagan supporters and it re-circulated old images of the Soviet Union as a dark prison with sinister Communist jailers.[39]

Critics expressed much greater enthusiasm in June 1982 for *E.T. the Extra-Terrestrial*, a top-grossing movie by liberal Hollywood director Steven Spielberg about a wise, gentle creature from outer space who is stranded near Los Angeles when his spaceship departs without him. E.T. is lovingly embraced by children, one of whom wears a "NO NUKES" T-shirt, but is treated much less kindly by domineering American adults and government security agents. A conservative critic slammed the "mawkish" movie, but a left-leaning commentator praised *E.T.* as a dramatization of the need for understanding between different nations.[40]

Filmmakers in the Soviet Union in the early 1980s had much less free-dom. Non-conformist directors who raised uncomfortable questions had difficulty getting their films shown.[41] Yet officially approved films still exerted powerful influence on Soviet moviegoers' attitudes. *Incident in Quadrant 36–80*, viewed by 33 million Soviet citizens after its release in December 1982, likely reinforced many viewers' pride in Soviet power and virtue as well as their suspicion or scorn for American armed forces. The movie portrayed Soviet sailors and naval aviators as brave, disciplined, skilled, and humane – even ready to sacrifice a Soviet crew to rescue endangered American submariners. Meanwhile, a US admiral and submarine captain were shown to be rash, undisciplined, panicky, and ruthless. By depicting an accidental launch of some of the US submarine's nuclear missiles at the USSR and the successful interception of the missiles by Soviet forces, the film dovetailed with the Kremlin's contrast of the menace of US militarism to the strength and peace-loving nature of the Soviet Union.[42]

MUTUAL DEMONIZATION AND THE PERIL OF ARMAGEDDON

With polls showing that roughly two-thirds of Americans supported the nuclear freeze idea and with Congress moving toward votes both on the freeze proposal and on Reagan's defense budget requests, the president had to do more to win support for his military build-up. In an effort to mobilize conservative Christians, on March 8, 1983 Reagan gave a major speech to the National Association of Evangelicals in Orlando, Florida. Attacking the freeze idea as "a very dangerous fraud" that would prevent his modernization of US forces, Reagan defended his approach of "peace through strength." Warning against the temptation to think of the arms race as a giant misunderstanding between morally equal superpowers, he urged evangelicals to take a stand in the righteous struggle against the "evil empire." Going further, Reagan recalled how, many years earlier, a young father had declared that he would rather see his little girls die than have them grow up under communism. That reiteration of the old "better dead than red" attitude may have contributed to the widespread revulsion at his speech, which was criticized not only by Protestant liberals and secular moderates, but even by Southern Baptists. While some scholars have claimed that the "evil empire" speech succeeded in undermining the Soviet system or pushing the Kremlin to negotiate, it actually led Soviet leaders to tighten ideological controls and be more pessimistic about negotiating with a primitively anticommunist president.[43]

Two weeks later, Reagan delivered a televised address to explain why his arms build-up was necessary and to call upon scientists to build a defensive system that would protect the United States from nuclear missiles. Although the Strategic Defense Initiative (SDI) sounded vaguely appealing to a slight majority of Americans (more to men than to women), it did not promise to end the danger of nuclear war anytime soon – even Reagan conceded that building the system might take twenty years or more.[44]

It also did not halt the momentum of the freeze movement. On the day of Reagan's "evil empire" speech, 5,000 freeze activists came to the Capitol to lobby Congress and the House Foreign Affairs Committee voted overwhelmingly (27–9) in favor of a freeze resolution. Six weeks after Reagan's SDI appeal, the House of Representatives passed the freeze proposal by a two-to-one margin (278–149).[45] Although SDI worried Soviet military leaders, Soviet scientists soon concluded that the proposal was impractical, and they ultimately convinced the Kremlin not to try to build a Soviet counterpart. In the short term, the most important impact of SDI was to exacerbate the suspicion of top Soviet leaders that Washington sought not only military superiority but also the ability to launch a first strike without fear of a devastating Soviet retaliation.[46]

Two incidents in the following months further inflamed Soviet–American tensions and heightened fears of nuclear war. In the early morning on September 1, 1983, a Korean Air Lines plane (KAL flight 007) headed from Alaska to Seoul veered far off course and intruded into sensitive Soviet airspace over military installations on the Kamchatka peninsula. Five months earlier, when the US Pacific Fleet had conducted massive, aggressive exercises near Kamchatka, six navy planes had violated Soviet borders. Now Soviet ground controllers thought KAL 007 might be a US Air Force reconnaissance plane that had flown near the Korean Air Lines plane that night. After KAL 007 did not respond to signals and warning shots, a Soviet fighter pilot shot it down, killing all 269 people on board (including 62 Americans). Disregarding US intelligence analysts' conclusion that Soviet military commanders confused the civilian airliner with a US spy plane, Reagan denounced the shoot-down as "an act of barbarism" that stemmed from the brutal nature of the Soviet system. American magazines followed the administration's lead, with *Newsweek* depicting the shoot-down as "murder in the air."[47]

Soviet leaders might have mitigated the damage if they had acknowledged their military's mistake, but instead they stubbornly defended their actions. Politburo members believed the incident was a deliberate US provocation. Even a young reformer, M. S. Gorbachev, stressed the need to take "an offensive position" in the propaganda battle. Soviet magazines of course reflected the official line, with a cartoon in *Ogonek* depicting the ghoulish CIA's provocation and Reagan's exploitation of it.[48]

Despite the superheated climate in the aftermath of the KAL 007 incident, on the night of September 26/27, a Soviet colonel at an early warning facility concluded that indications of US missile launches against the USSR were false alarms. Then, in the first week of November, NATO conducted a massive exercise (code-named Able Archer) to simulate a first strike against the Soviet Union. During the exercise Soviet intelligence reported an alert at US military bases that some leaders in Moscow interpreted as a sign of preparation for war. Fortunately, Soviet intelligence rightly concluded that Able Archer was only an exercise, and top Soviet military officers did not believe that a NATO nuclear strike was imminent.[49]

Although accidental nuclear war was avoided, fears of nuclear war rose to a fevered peak in the fall of 1983. The Soviet press regularly stressed the aggressive intentions of the United States and compared Reagan to Hitler. Especially for older Soviet citizens who remembered the Nazi invasion forty years earlier, the war scare was very real. Women in the countryside asked local Communist Party officials whether war was inevitable and their sons would have to die.[50]

In the United States, two movies powerfully dramatized the threat of nuclear war. *Testament*, released to theaters in early November, somberly focused on one California family's doomed struggle to keep going in the wake of nuclear war. The film may have been too grim for many Americans to watch: it grossed only $2 million. A movie for television, *The Day After*, much more graphically depicted the devastating consequences of a Soviet nuclear attack on Kansas. After Reagan watched an advance tape on October 10, he noted in his diary: "It's very effective and left me greatly depressed." When ABC broadcast the movie on November 20, 100 million Americans watched it. *The Day After* did not change the minds of many conservatives, who dismissed it as "propaganda" and insisted that the Reagan administration's bolstered deterrence was the way to avert nuclear war. But the film led to hundreds of media appearances by freeze activists and it moved many more Americans to become actively involved in the public debate over nuclear weapons and relations with the Soviet Union.[51]

REACHING OUT TO THE RUSSIANS, 1983–1984

One of the most prominent figures in the controversy was a vivacious schoolgirl in Maine, Samantha Smith, who expressed her fear of nuclear war in a letter to Soviet leader Yuri Andropov that *Pravda* published in April 1983. Invited to participate in a Soviet youth camp that summer, Smith became a celebrity in both countries. Conservative Americans complained that she became a pawn for misleading Soviet peace propaganda. However, her highly publicized visit led many Soviet citizens to be very fond of her and softened their views of America. It also helped to inspire many subsequent trips between the two countries by both children and adults.[52]

Among the Americans who became especially active in exchanges with the USSR in 1983 was a nurse and mother in northern California who had grown deeply concerned about securing a future for her four children. The patriotic daughter of an anticommunist Baptist father, Sharon Tennison hardly fit the conservative stereotype of a peace activist. In the early 1980s, she was one of thousands of mainstream Americans in communities across the United States who began meeting in small groups to talk about what could be done to avert a catastrophe from the superpowers' enmity and their nuclear arsenals. Like others, she had a hunch that the danger stemmed more from misunderstanding and fear than from diabolical intentions. Tennison decided "to go see the enemy." FBI agents warned her not to go. United States Information Agency officials urged her to leave diplomacy to professionals. But in September 1983 – two weeks after the shooting down of KAL 007 – Tennison led a group of twenty Americans to Moscow, Leningrad, and Tbilisi. At a time when the Soviet government persecuted unofficial Soviet peace activists who protested against the war in Afghanistan and the militarization of Soviet society, Tennison's delegation had to cooperate with leaders of the official Soviet Peace Committee, whose propagandistic rhetoric infuriated them. Yet the Americans also visited churches, schools, markets, and cemeteries, where they engaged Soviet citizens in personal conversations. They found that Soviets had a different worldview, but envied and admired Americans and were in important ways much like them.[53]

Inspired by the success of the first trip, in late 1983 Tennison founded the Center for US–USSR Initiatives (CUUI) in San Francisco. She then devoted herself to "full-time peace education," giving up to six presentations a day to Rotary clubs, colleges, churches, and professional groups. Starting in 1984, CUUI organized about twenty trips to the Soviet Union each year, with delegations composed of business owners, teachers, former military officers, retired missionaries, and many others. By arranging for more than 2,000 Americans of diverse backgrounds to travel to the Soviet Union and by organizing trips to the United States for a smaller number of Soviet citizens, Tennison and her staff of around 50 volunteers made a major contribution to countering the media demonization of the enemy in each country. In a newsletter she sent to hundreds of supporters, Tennison explained in July 1984: "It is significant when people meet each other and find that neither side grows horns and tails." By that point, she declared excitedly, the "sense of hopelessness and helplessness" that had prevailed earlier in the 1980s was "giving way to the most extraordinary actions" by "average people."[54]

Not far from Tennison's headquarters in San Francisco, another group concerned with the danger of nuclear war gathered a critical mass of members in the early 1980s. Strongly influenced by Jonathan Schell's description of the threat of nuclear war in *The Fate of the Earth* (1982), leaders of the Creative Initiative Foundation decided to focus on Soviet–American relations and adopted the name Beyond War. Guided by a spiritual belief that there was one earth and one humanity, Beyond War's members – including advertising executives, lawyers, Silicon Valley engineers, and housewives – dedicated themselves to averting Armageddon through educational campaigns in the United States and through outreach to the Soviet Union. With hundreds of members working full-time (many without pay), Beyond War rapidly expanded, establishing local groups in 400 California communities and in 66 cities in 25 other states. Soon 18,000 people subscribed to its newsletter. In 1984, Beyond War members used their technological sophistication to arrange a "spacebridge" in which Soviet and American audiences could see each other and interact via a satellite link. Televised on public stations across the United States in 1985, the spacebridge dramatized how Americans and Soviets could talk to each other in pursuit of the common goal of survival.[55] During the next three years, Beyond War leaders collaborated with prominent Soviet scientists and intellectuals on a book about the need for new thinking to overcome American–Soviet enmity. Extensive tours of the United States and USSR by contributors to the book had major impacts on attitudes in many cities in both countries.[56]

Like Tennison and the members of Beyond War, the granddaughter of President Dwight Eisenhower was shaken by fear of nuclear war. As she left home for work in Washington, D.C. one day in 1983, Susan Eisenhower "had an overwhelming flash ... that there was going to be some terrible nuclear disaster that day" and she would be unable to be with her three young daughters at the sudden end of their lives. The terrifying experience did not immediately lead her to activism. But, as she later confided, a person never "really gets over such a flash." In 1986, she left her public affairs company to become president of the Eisenhower World Affairs Institute and joined with the Chautauqua Institution to sponsor a major exchange in which 200 US government officials and opinion leaders traveled to the Soviet Union to meet and debate their Soviet counterparts. Unlike more combative members of the US delegation, Eisenhower hoped "to make a breakthrough beyond superpower point scoring and one-upmanship."[57]

The peak of Soviet–American tension in the fall of 1983 marked a turning point not only for Eisenhower and Tennison, but also for American art historian Suzanne Massie. A conservative Democrat who had criticized détente and demonstrated in support of Soviet dissidents, Massie had been denied a visa to the USSR since 1971. Finally allowed to visit Moscow again in September, 1983, she was disturbed by the intense fear and suspicion of the United States that she encountered. A deputy director of the influential Institute for the Study of the USA and Canada angrily told her: "Reagan is at war with us!" Another leader of the institute shook his fist and shouted: "You don't know how close war is!" Worried by the toxic relations between the superpowers, Massie decided to contact Reagan in order to try to prevent the two countries from destroying each other. She first met twice in November with the pragmatic new National Security Advisor Robert McFarlane (who had replaced anticommunist ideologue William Clark). Massie found McFarlane interested in developing a dialogue that could lead to a *modus vivendi* with the Soviet Union. Ten weeks later, at her first meeting with Reagan, Massie began a long process of educating the president about the Russian people, "humanizing them so that he no longer viewed them as faceless communists." She also urged "far broader contacts between ordinary people on both sides," pushed for the resumption of cultural exchanges, and served as a semi-official emissary between Reagan and Soviet officials. Thus, Massie's high-level efforts paralleled the grass-roots work of Tennison, Beyond War, and many others.[58]

Massie's reports to McFarlane on the need to defuse the tense situation resembled what McFarlane learned from other sources. In October, a veteran Soviet journalist told Jack Matlock, the top expert on the Soviet Union at the National Security Council, that Soviet leaders believed the Reagan administration was trying to overthrow the Soviet system and they had no choice but to fight back. After Foreign Minister Gromyko made similar comments to the US Ambassador in Moscow, a worried Matlock reported on Soviet fears to McFarlane on October 28.[59]

By the middle of November, Reagan, troubled by what he heard about Soviet anxieties, began to show a new empathy for Soviet leaders and a keener interest in establishing contacts with them. On November 18, he wrote in his diary: "I feel the Soviets are so defense minded, so paranoid about being attacked that . . . we ought to tell them no one here has any intention of doing anything like that." Little came from efforts by Secretary of State George Shultz to create what Reagan called "a back channel contact" with Soviet leaders, many of whom believed they could not negotiate with Reagan as equals and hoped he would not be re-elected.[60]

Yet Reagan had other reasons to at least sound more conciliatory. After meeting with speechwriters on January 6, 1984 about an address on relations with the Soviet Union, Reagan wryly noted that the speech was intended "to reassure the eggheads & our European friends I don't plan to blow up the world." With polls showing many Americans (especially women) fearful about superpower relations, and with White House political advisers counseling that Reagan's image as a hard-line Cold Warrior would be a political vulnerability in the 1984 campaign, Nancy Reagan urged her husband to soften his rhetoric. In the speech on January 16, which major newspapers interpreted as motivated by domestic politics, the president used the words "peace" and "peaceful" eighteen times, expressed his interest in dialogue with Soviet leaders, and acknowledged that "people want to raise their children in a world without fear and without war." In a passage Reagan himself added, he envisioned that, if ordinary American and Soviet parents met someday, then, instead of debating the merits of their two systems, they would talk about their desires for safe futures for their children.[61]

Soviet leaders did not respond to Reagan's address. Andropov, who had declared in September that there was no prospect of an evolution for the better in Reagan administration policy, was deathly ill. Gromyko, who disdained the "fascism" he saw in Washington, did not circulate the text of Reagan's speech to other Soviet officials.[62]

After the ailing Konstantin Chernenko replaced Andropov in February, Reagan (with encouragement from Massie) repeatedly expressed his genuine desire to meet with Chernenko. Yet, as former National Security Adviser Brent Scowcroft reported in April after a trip to Russia, the Soviets continued to give Reagan a cold shoulder, at least in part because they did not want to help him get re-elected.[63]

Nuclear freeze activists made major efforts to defeat Reagan in 1984, with many joining the campaign of his Democratic opponent, Walter Mondale. The most prominent activist, Australian American physician Helen Caldicott, made television ads and gave numerous speeches for the Democratic Party, in which she emphasized that American children would die in a nuclear war. While Caldicott succeeded in galvanizing many women, her assertion that the re-election of Reagan would lead to nuclear war seemed less convincing after he softened his rhetoric about the Russians. Accepting the Republican nomination in August, Reagan asked the Soviets, "for the sake of our children," to join him in reducing and eliminating "doomsday weapons." Speaking at the United Nations in September, Reagan once again vowed that he was "ready for constructive negotiations with the Soviet Union." Military contractors who supported Reagan vastly outspent nuclear freeze and peace organizations.

Mondale endorsed a nuclear freeze, but was a lackluster campaigner. With the economy having rebounded strongly from a recession in 1982, and with many Americans feeling a renewed patriotism, the genial Reagan handily defeated Mondale.[64]

Reagan's overwhelming electoral victory discouraged many nuclear freeze activists, and many scholars have argued that the freeze movement faded away after its political failure in 1984.[65] Yet the broader antinuclear and peace movement had already won important gains. Citizen diplomats had begun to reach out to Soviets before Reagan did, and they had helped create a political climate that led Reagan to change his rhetoric. After the 1984 election, membership in peace groups continued to grow and citizen diplomacy initiatives spread like wildfire. Hence, despite the success of Reagan's 1984 campaign, the stage was set for continued contestation over American–Soviet relations.[66]

INTENSIFIED CONFLICT, 1985–1986

Although Reagan did not campaign as an aggressive anticommunist in 1984, some Cold Warriors acted as if his re-election mandated a more vigorous anti-Soviet crusade. While the CIA had been content to provide Afghan *mujahideen* with enough support to wound but not kill the Russian bear in Afghanistan, key members of Congress now demanded that the United States help the Muslim "freedom fighters" win the war. The most colorful of the congressional champions, the cocaine-snorting, skirt-chasing Charlie Wilson (Democrat, Texas), found a new sense of purpose in a crusade against the Soviet military in Afghanistan. In March 1985, Reagan approved a change of objective from merely harassing Soviet forces to driving them out of Afghanistan. Reagan saw no contradiction between that anticommunist military campaign and his increasingly serious interest in diplomatic engagement with Moscow. Instead, he felt such support for anticommunist insurgents around the world would help press Soviet leaders to negotiate on American terms.[67]

The dramatic escalation of aid to the *mujahideen* and the US unwillingness to settle for a coalition government in Kabul made it more difficult for civilian leaders in the Kremlin to withdraw Soviet forces. Although top leaders in Moscow viewed the 1979 invasion as a mistake and doubted that the Red Army could defeat the Afghan guerrillas, they feared that a complete victory by the *mujahideen* would allow the United States to create military and espionage bases in Afghanistan. They also worried that it would shatter the Soviet Union's image as a staunch defender of "Third World" nations against American imperialism.[68]

Reagan and his hard-line advisers and supporters also remained determined to help the Nicaraguan *contras* overthrow the Sandinista government, to continue a military build-up, and to push forward with SDI. Although he faced strong resistance in each area from Congress, Reagan continued to believe that an arms race would compel Kremlin leaders to make concessions because they could not "squeeze their people any more to try & stay even with us."[69]

On the other hand, Reagan fully approved Secretary of State Shultz's desire to negotiate with Soviet leaders, and that increasingly disturbed conservatives who associated negotiation with appeasement. Republicans such as Senator Gordon Humphrey of New Hampshire and columnist George Will repeatedly sought meetings with the president to express their concern that US policy was softening.[70]

Hard-liners attacked moderates in the Soviet Union, too. Near the end of 1984, Kremlin leaders announced plans for a dramatic increase in military spending, and they seemed on the verge of a sweeping purge of reformist intellectuals. Much like American hawks, Soviet hawks believed that the only language their adversary understood was strength.[71]

Even key reform-minded Soviet officials saw no hope for taming the US anticommunist crusade. In 1984, Alexander Yakovlev, who had become director of the prestigious Institute of World Economy and International Relations (IMEMO) after serving as Ambassador to Canada, published a book about how the world was *On the Edge of an Abyss* because the American "ruling clique," like the Nazis in Germany, was propagating hysteria about a Soviet threat in order to justify a war for world supremacy. Yakovlev believed that American "chauvinism," spread by an "all-powerful propaganda machine," was "not evoking any notable moral protest by American public opinion." He was particularly disturbed by Reagan's August 1984 joke before a radio broadcast that he had outlawed the Soviet Union forever and the bombing would start in five minutes. That seemed to Yakovlev serious evidence of Reagan's "maniacal anti-Sovietism and hatred for the Soviet people."[72]

IMAGES OF COOPERATION, DEFECTION AND CONFLICT IN POPULAR CULTURE, 1984–1986

During a phase in US–Soviet relations when intense competition persisted but some glimpsed possibilities for cooperation, filmmakers produced an unusually large number of pictures about American–Russian interactions. While most Hollywood movies in this period featured stories of defections or violent conflicts, one dramatized and urged collaboration. In *2010*, released in December 1984, Soviet cosmonauts and American astronauts engage in a joint mission to Jupiter, while on earth a confrontation in Central America causes the hostile superpowers to veer toward nuclear war. Although officials on earth order the Soviet and American crews to separate, the dangers of space flight bring them together. The movie, which did well at the box office (earning $40 million), thus constituted an appeal for Americans and Russians to set aside their ideological differences and work together on common problems.[73]

Two other movies in the mid-1980s revisited the theme of Russians being drawn to defect to the West that had been dramatized in *Ninotchka* (1939) and *Silk Stockings* (1957). In the comedy *Moscow on the Hudson*, first screened in April 1984, a saxophonist from dreary Moscow decides to defect when his touring circus troupe makes a shopping pilgrimage to the consumer paradise of a Bloomingdale's store. Although the movie sought to balance American clichés about deprived Russians' longing for blue jeans with bows to Soviet clichés about American street crime and unemployment, it ultimately celebrated US diversity and freedom so much that critics tended to find it too cloyingly sweet.[74] While *Moscow on the Hudson* reaped a respectable $25 million, another movie released the next year grossed more money ($42 million) and contrasted the bleak Soviet Union more starkly to America. Despite a plot that critics called "ludicrous" or "preposterous," *White Nights* benefited from the dazzling dancing of Mikhail Baryshnikov, who had defected from the Kirov Ballet while in Toronto in 1974. When Baryshnikov escapes from the vicious KGB and the USSR in the movie, along with him comes a Black tap dancer who had defected to Russia years earlier because of US actions in Vietnam. *White Nights* thus did its bit to contribute to the Reagan era expunging of guilt over the Vietnam War as well as to the affirmation of American moral and artistic superiority.[75]

While stories of defectors scored some points in the Soviet–American rivalry, several movies that dramatized violent conflict cumulatively had more powerful impacts at the box office and in American minds. *Red Dawn*, released to theaters shortly before the Republican convention in August 1984, depicted an invasion of the United States by Soviet, Cuban, and Nicaraguan forces, heroically resisted by a small band of teenagers in Colorado. The movie thus reverted to the nightmarish visions of a Soviet menace in the early 1950s. Although critics generally derided *Red Dawn*, the film earned more than $38 million and reinforced right-wing Americans' hatred of brutal, barbarous Russians even after Reagan shifted away from his demonization of them.[76]

Rambo: First Blood Part II, screened less than a year later, in the spring of 1985, allowed many Americans the vicarious pleasure of seeing an extremely muscular Sylvester Stallone kill not only Vietnamese soldiers holding US POWs but also the sadistic Soviet advisers ultimately to blame for communist evil in Southeast Asia. While liberal critics denounced the movie for fostering mindless aggression, it was extremely popular (grossing $150 million in the United States). It also received an endorsement from Reagan, who declared that it showed him what to do to free US hostages in the Middle East.[77]

Before the end of 1985, Stallone again took the fight to the Soviets, this time as an earthy American boxer who battles a much bigger Russian product of the totalitarian system. Americans paid more than $127 million to watch the smashing of the cold, heartless Soviet fighting machine in *Rocky IV*. As the *Wall Street Journal* observed, a major reason for the wide appeal of *Rocky* and *Rambo* was the resonance of "the message that Soviet society is not at all like ours, and that the Soviet government deep in its shriveled little heart does not wish us well."[78]

Soviet cultural officials bitterly complained that *Rocky*, *Rambo*, and *Red Dawn* propagated a pathological "anti-Russian phobia." Yet Hollywood studios had not fired their last shot in the cultural Cold War. *Top Gun*, the box office champion of 1986 with $176 million in ticket sales, thrilled audiences by showing a rambunctious Navy pilot give the finger to a Soviet flier and then shoot down Soviet planes painted bad guy black. The *New York Times'* critic faulted the celebration of triumph in aerial combat as "awfully foolish" at a time when the superpowers possessed so many nuclear weapons.[79]

Yet Soviet movies in 1986 were hardly more restrained or sophisticated than American films. *Solo Voyage*, seen by 38 million Soviet citizens, started from the premise of a CIA plot to blow up an American ocean liner and blame it on the Soviet Union. When the plot fails, CIA commandos take over a nuclear base and prepare to launch missiles against a Soviet fleet. A third world war is averted when Soviet marines overpower the evil Americans just in time. As melodramatic as any Hollywood production, *Solo Voyage* contrasted humane Soviet officers to vicious American villains and the peace-loving USSR to the perfidious United States. *Interception* (*Perekhvat*), similarly, depicted a sinister US plot to infiltrate submarines near Vladivostok that is foiled when a brave Soviet border guard relentlessly pursues a CIA infiltrator and saboteur.[80]

Thus, in both countries in the mid-1980s, popular movies persisted in promoting basic us versus them demonological constructs. The main difference was that much bigger budgets enabled American movies to be more lavish productions with sophisticated special effects. *Rambo* and other movies appealed so strongly that Soviet citizens sold thousands of videocassettes on the black market.[81] As a result, belligerently nationalistic Hollywood films were knocking out the Soviet competition as well as outweighing American films that championed cooperation.

BREAKTHROUGHS: ENDINGS OF "THE COLD WAR"

In March 1985, amid the reignited conflict that followed Reagan's re-election, seventy-three-year-old Konstantin Chernenko, a conservative Communist functionary, died. The Politburo selected as his replacement the energetic fifty-four-year-old Mikhail Gorbachev. Since he had risen through the Communist Party in a backward region of southern Russia, served as the Kremlin's supervisor of agriculture, and seen the much greater efficiency of capitalist agriculture on a trip to Canada in 1983, Gorbachev knew the Soviet system was plagued by corruption, hypercentralization, and low morale. "We can't go on living like this," he confided to his wife and closest advisers upon taking power. The principal slogan for Gorbachev's first year in power, *uskorenie* (acceleration), reflected his drive to get the country growing more rapidly, in part through decreased vodka consumption and increased labor productivity. In order to focus on such internal reform, Gorbachev needed to reduce external tensions, so he launched a peace offensive. Hoping to mobilize peace movements in the West against the US and NATO build-ups, he proposed a freeze on the superpowers' nuclear arsenals in late March and announced a halt to the deployment of SS-20 missiles in April. Then in the summer, Soviet scientists, strongly influenced by their contacts in the West, especially with leaders of the International Physicians for the Prevention of Nuclear War (IPPNW), convinced him to proclaim a unilateral moratorium on Soviet tests of nuclear weapons. Gorbachev's advisers believed such steps, combined with Gorbachev's personal charm, began to dissipate Western fears and stereotypes about a Soviet threat.[82]

Of more lasting importance than the specific proposals of the peace offensive were two social and intellectual developments that accompanied Gorbachev's accession to power. First, innovative thinkers, who believed East–West hostility was not inevitable and whose voices had been subdued in previous years, gained greater influence on policymaking. "Inside dissidents" who had risen to top positions in academic institutes and the Central Committee of the Communist Party since the period of détente in the 1970s now had more freedom to express their ideas and be heard by top leaders. Second, in contrast to older leaders who had been born before the revolutions of 1917 and who had been deeply scarred by the German invasion of 1941, the new generation of leaders had traveled much more outside the USSR and grown less fearful of the West. As early as January 1986, Gorbachev believed that no one would attack the Soviet Union even if it disarmed.[83]

Although American hard-liners dismissed Gorbachev's peace offensive as a deceptive campaign to get the West to lower its guard, Reagan repeatedly expressed keen interest in meeting the new Soviet leader. Secretary of State Shultz and White House adviser Mike Deaver (a confidant of Nancy Reagan) spearheaded contacts with Gorbachev and new Soviet Foreign Minister Eduard Shevardnadze. The two sides agreed to meet at Geneva in November 1985. Lengthy discussions, including one-on-one talks between Reagan and Gorbachev, brought no progress on the conflicts in Afghanistan or Central America and no arms control agreement. However, the two leaders did agree to revive cultural exchanges and to issue a joint statement that "a nuclear war cannot be won and must never be fought." More importantly, meeting Gorbachev confirmed Reagan's hunch that he was a new kind of Soviet leader, a genuine human being with whom he could work. Reagan's inclination in favor of diplomatic engagement received strong positive reinforcement when a joint session of Congress clamorously applauded his report on the Geneva summit and polls showed that 81 percent of Americans approved of his handling of it. Although Gorbachev found Reagan to be ill-informed and like a political "dinosaur," the Geneva meeting strengthened his belief that he could win over US public opinion on arms race issues and thereby apply pressure to Reagan.[84]

In the following year, Gorbachev built on the positive momentum from Geneva with several important moves. At a Communist Party Congress in February 1986, he proclaimed for the first time the key principles of a "new political thinking," including the ideas that the world was interdependent; that security must be mutual; and that security hinged on political understanding rather than quests for military superiority. Although Gorbachev had not yet freed himself from some traditional Communist stereotypes, his embrace of the "new thinking" represented a major step away from the conventional Soviet emphasis on inherent conflict between the socialist and capitalist worlds. As his close adviser Anatoly Chernyaev observed, Gorbachev believed coexistence with the West was not a temporary tactic but a fundamental "law" that must govern Soviet foreign policy.[85]

Near the end of April, a massive explosion at the Chernobyl nuclear power plant, which spewed radiation across Ukraine, Belarus, and nearby countries, gave Gorbachev an opportunity to stress to the Politburo how devastating nuclear war would be. The disaster also helped him to press for greater openness, in contrast to the regime's withholding of information about the accident (which led to panic in the USSR and outrage in neighboring countries).[86]

Impatient for a breakthrough in relations with Washington, Gorbachev pushed for another meeting with Reagan, this time in Iceland in October. Meeting without their top national security officials, the two leaders agreed in principle on the desirability of dramatically reducing and even eliminating their strategic nuclear arsenals, though Reagan rejected Gorbachev's condition that SDI tests be confined to laboratories. Despite the disappointment of not concluding a disarmament agreement, the Reykjavík summit encouraged Gorbachev because it showed him that Reagan sincerely sought a world without nuclear weapons, did not intend to attack the Soviet Union, and was not a captive of the US military industrial complex.[87]

Six weeks after the meeting in Iceland, a scandal erupted in Washington that in the short term disrupted progress in relations with Moscow, but in the longer term gave Reagan a strong incentive for successful engagement with Gorbachev. The revelation that National Security Council staff had run a complex scheme to sell arms to pariah Iran and use surplus proceeds to fund Nicaraguan *contras* (circumventing a Congressional ban) sparked a furor and raised questions about whether Reagan was dishonest or mentally unfit for the presidency. Together with discoveries about Soviet espionage and bugging of the US Embassy in Moscow, the Iran–*contra* affair caused a delay of several months in following up on the Reykjavík discussions. As Reagan noted in his diary, the scandal also caused his approval ratings to fall precipitously, from more than 70 percent earlier in 1986 to as low as 44 percent in early March of 1987. By February, as Reagan's advisers tried to help him overcome the damage, they also sought to resume progress in relations with Gorbachev.[88]

Two key developments on the Soviet side facilitated movement toward an arms reduction treaty. First, the Soviet leadership began to take American public opinion more seriously, to develop a more complex understanding of it, and to realize how to influence overall opinion in a positive direction. Second, in February the Kremlin shifted from linking proposals for reductions in intermediate range and strategic nuclear forces to being willing to conclude separate agreements on the different types of missiles. The key proponent of untying the package of proposals, Alexander

Yakovlev, began to be vilified by Soviet hard-liners as an advocate of "complete capitulation to imperialism." But Gorbachev and Shevardnadze pushed forward in discussions with Shultz. In September, when Shultz and Shevardnadze signed an agreement at the White House for centers in each country to avert the danger of accidental war, Reagan observed that the meetings were "free of the hostility we used to see even if we were disagreeing on some things."[89]

By October 1987, American public opinion strongly preferred cooperation to confrontation. Two-thirds of Americans surveyed that month thought the United States should try harder to reduce tensions with the Russians, while only a quarter said the United States should get tougher. In addition, 58 percent disagreed with the idea that the Soviet Union was an "evil empire." Among those with college degrees (who were most likely to follow world news), the figure rose to over 70 percent.[90]

The culmination of progress in negotiations came in December, when Gorbachev traveled to Washington to sign a treaty for the withdrawal of intermediate range nuclear weapons from Europe (Soviet SS-20s and the Pershing and cruise missiles NATO had deployed in 1983). By the time Gorbachev arrived in the capital, he was so popular that journalists wrote of "Gorbymania." With an attractive, fashionably dressed wife accompanying him, the smiling Gorbachevs seemed completely unlike the dour Soviet leaders and their frumpy spouses that Americans had seen before. Benefiting from the association with Gorbachev as well as the achievement of the treaty, Reagan saw a dramatic rise in his approval rating in the afterglow of the summit. To some, including Shultz's top aide Charles Hill, it seemed the Cold War was already ending.[91]

The breakthrough intensely displeased conservative Republicans. A cartoon in the *Philadelphia Inquirer* on December 9 mocked their disgruntlement: the Far Right shouts "Bah! Humbug!" as Reagan and Gorbachev happily listen to children singing a Christmas carol (see Figure 16.1). Denouncing the Intermediate-Range Nuclear Forces (INF) Treaty, in January the Conservative Caucus published a newspaper ad that declared "APPEASEMENT IS AS UNWISE IN 1988 AS IN 1938," compared Gorbachev to Hitler, and likened Reagan to British Prime Minister Neville Chamberlain (who had negotiated the Munich Pact of 1938). Neoconservative members of the Reagan administration who resigned from their posts in 1987, including Assistant Secretary of Defense Richard Perle, also opposed ratification of the treaty.[92]

Neoconservatives and conservatives had been carried to power in 1980 on a wave of anti-Soviet nationalism, but now they were swept aside by a tide

Figure 16.1 "Bah! Humbug!" Cartoon by Tony Auth, December 9, 1987. From *The Philadelphia Inquirer.* © 1987 Philadelphia Inquirer, LLC. All rights reserved. Used under license.

of opinion in favor of improving relations with the reforming Soviet Union. Soviet foreign policy advisers observed that American democracy had become an effective check on Pentagon aggression. At the end of May 1988, as Reagan traveled to Moscow for another summit with Gorbachev, the Senate voted overwhelmingly (93–5) to ratify the INF Treaty. The discussions in Moscow yielded no progress toward a new agreement on reducing strategic weapons (START). But what mattered most was the fact that the crusading anticommunist president stood next to Gorbachev in Red Square and declared that he no longer considered the Soviet Union an "evil empire." Gorbachev's reforms – including permitting religious freedom, freer speech, a freer press, and small-scale private enterprise – had changed the Soviet Union so much, Reagan said, that they marked "a new era." After returning to Washington, Reagan noted with pleasure in his diary: "My approval rating is up to 60%. It is 80% regarding dealing with the Soviet U."[93]

Reagan's visit to Moscow also gave a needed boost to Gorbachev, who faced persistent ideological opposition from neo-Stalinists. Gorbachev had argued in April that a full withdrawal of Soviet troops from Afghanistan would be of great value for his overall effort to end the Western demonization of the Soviet Union and convince foreign nations that he meant what he said about adopting a new approach to resolving international problems. "Our enemies and opponents will have their strongest arguments knocked out of their hands," he assured the Politburo. With the fading of the far right in the United States, Gorbachev's most entrenched opponents were actually now in his own Communist Party. Reagan's embrace of Gorbachev in Moscow made it more difficult for hard-line Soviet officials to argue that the West posed such a threat that the Kremlin had to maintain tough discipline and postpone potentially destabilizing changes.[94]

Orthodox Communists, most notably Yegor Ligachev, were outmaneuvered by Gorbachev, Yakovlev, and Shevardnadze. In late July, Shevardnadze instructed Soviet diplomats at the Foreign Ministry that "the struggle between two opposing systems" was "no longer the decisive tendency of the present age." In a major address at the United Nations in December, Gorbachev went much further. Beyond enunciating to the world the principles of Soviet new political thinking, he announced a unilateral cut of half a million soldiers and the withdrawal of six tank divisions from Eastern Europe. Pledging Soviet respect for "freedom of choice" for all peoples to choose their own political systems, Gorbachev signaled that the Soviet Union would no longer try to maintain the domination of Eastern Europe that had spurred the deterioration of Soviet–American relations in the late 1940s. The bold speech increased the number of Americans who believed the Cold War was melting (though they were still a minority).[95]

Although Gorbachev's trips to America and Reagan's journey to Moscow garnered more national media attention, thousands of other American and Soviet citizens visited former enemy nations in the same years. Already in the summer of 1985, Gorbachev recognized the huge importance of such citizen encounters. After an international youth festival in Moscow and an American–Soviet peace cruise down the Volga River, Gorbachev explained to the Politburo that such contacts between American visitors and regular Soviet people did more to break stereotypes of a Soviet threat than all of the USSR's foreign propaganda.[96]

Citizen exchanges expanded rapidly in the following years, with energetic sponsorship by organizations like the New England-based Bridges for Peace, the Arkansas-based Peace Links, and the Committee of Soviet Women with its headquarters in Moscow.[97] In the most ambitious effort, in 1988 the Center for U.S.–U.S.S.R Initiatives (CUUI) brought 400 Soviet teachers, journalists, doctors, and other citizens to the United States – twice as many as the total number of Soviet visitors to the United States in the early 1980s. The Soviet citizens met Americans in 160 different communities, from Yorba Linda, California to Montague, Massachusetts. When four

Soviet visitors arrived in Mountain Home, Arkansas, journalists came from 100 miles away to cover the story. More than 1,000 newspaper articles about the Soviets, Meet Middle America! (SMMA) project featured stories about how Americans and Soviets discovered their common humanity.[98]

Upon returning to the USSR, the Soviet visitors were deluged with requests to speak and write about what they saw and experienced in America. One educator from the Perm region who participated in the SMMA tour gave more than 100 lectures in which he told his shocked fellow citizens about how well Americans lived (at a time when worsening shortages were eroding belief in socialism). A columnist for one of the most widely read newspapers reported that the way Soviet people had changed in the Gorbachev era, recovering their individual dignity and responsibility, enabled them to make such a positive impression on Americans, who then abandoned old prejudices. A historian from Moscow who visited Nashville, Tennessee as part of a Peace Links-sponsored tour wrote an article for a leading journal in which she described how the American middle class lived in nice, modern houses, how family life was more important to Americans than Soviets had thought, how face-to-face meetings were showing that both peoples wanted peace, and how Americans were slowly outgrowing their stereotypes of the USSR.[99] Such promotion of mutual understanding and trust led Alexander Yakovlev to consider the exchanges "very useful."[100]

For decades, Soviet–American enmity had been fueled by fear, suspicion, and ignorance. Now those feelings were being extinguished, not merely because top leaders of the two countries signed agreements, but also because Soviets and Americans were encountering each other and finding that their common humanity far outweighed their differences. Perhaps the most striking illustration of the developing bonds involved Susan Eisenhower and the prestigious, non-conformist Soviet physicist Roald Sagdeev. Raised by a strongly anticommunist family, Eisenhower had "absorbed much of the fear or suspicion of *anything* Soviet or Russian that was pervasive in American society." Yet her involvement in citizen diplomacy in the late 1980s and her collaboration with Sagdeev on a book led to their marriage in the fall of 1989. She saw the wedding as a bridge between the two countries, and American journalists treated it as a "Cold War is over" story.[101]

DISCARDING ENEMY IMAGES IN MASS MEDIA

While many thousands of Soviets and Americans saw first-hand that they were not irreconcilably different, image-makers worked to challenge preconceptions and adapt to improving superpower relations in a parallel way.

In May 1988, for example, when the *Seattle Post-Intelligencer* sponsored a USSR–USA Cartoon Exchange, Soviet artist Valentin Druzhinin and American cartoonist David Horsey pictured themselves with pins, poised to puncture popular misconceptions about each other's nations. Seven months earlier, the movie *Russkies* opened in theaters. Echoing *The Russians Are Coming* (1966), the comedy centered on a handsome Russian sailor stranded on an American shore, ridiculed the anti-Soviet hostility of some adults, and depicted the affectionate ties that develop between the sailor and local children. Although *Russkies* did poorly at the box office, it indicated how filmmakers were beginning to respond to the warming of US–Soviet relations. Shortly after Reagan returned from Moscow in June 1988, *Red Heat* depicted a tough, honest Soviet police officer coming to Chicago in pursuit of an evil drug smuggler. There he tersely expresses disgust at pornography on American television ("Capitalism!") but gruffly works together with a Chicago cop to find and kill the murderous bad guy. Unlike *Moscow on the Hudson* and earlier stories of consumerist seduction, *Red Heat* shows the stoic, clean-living Russian returning to his homeland.[102]

While the picture about American and Soviet police partners earned a modest profit and praise from prominent critics, the third installment of the anti-Soviet *Rambo* series lost money in the domestic market and received dismal reviews. *Rambo III* showed its muscular hero rescuing his former superior officer from being tortured by his Russian captors in Afghanistan. In a deliberate contrast to the Soviet talk of peace and disarmament, speeches in the movie charged the Soviets with systematically slaughtering two million Afghans and trying to wipe out an entire race of people. Released late in May 1988, after Gorbachev had announced the withdrawal of Soviet forces from Afghanistan and just before Reagan visited Moscow, *Rambo III* seemed to critics to be "out of date." The movie's star, Sylvester Stallone, complained that he took a lot of heat for the movie: people asked him why he was making the Russians look bad. The box office bomb reflected how rapidly many Americans had lost a taste for anticommunist melodramas since 1986.[103]

As late as the spring of 1987, Soviet propagandists regularly attacked American popular culture. In April 1987, for example, *Krokodil* printed a cartoon that depicted "American cultural exports" to Western Europe as a Wild West invasion of porno films, *Rambo*, and exaggerations of the Soviet threat. Yet, less than a year later, the Soviet government partnered with a nonprofit group based in San Francisco to host the first American film festival in Moscow since 1959. Among the thirty films shown in sold-out theaters was *King's Row* (1942) starring Ronald Reagan. A century earlier, American journalist James Buel had prophesied that Russian resistance to the

Figure 16.2 *Krokodil*, No. 3, January 1989. Zubin Mehta and Gennadii Rozhdestvenskii conducted their orchestras together in Moscow after Reagan and Gorbachev met there in June 1988. Courtesy of *Novaia Gazeta*.

eastward spread of "civilization" would be futile. After 1988, Russia stopped resisting the spread of American consumer culture. In January 1989, for example, *Krokodil* celebrated the growing cultural exchange and cooperation with a cartoon featuring top conductors from the United States and USSR in a joint concert.[104] (See Figure 16.2.)

CONCLUSION

The dramatic transformation of American–Soviet relations in the 1980s has often been seen as a result of the policies of top leaders. Yet, well before Reagan put his arm around Gorbachev in Red Square and said that the Soviet Union was no longer an "evil empire," many other Americans had visited Russia and seen for themselves that Russians were not monsters, but loving humans much like themselves. Similarly, many Soviets who encountered American visitors or traveled to the United States dropped their propaganda-instilled stereotypes of America as a violent, crime-plagued aggressor and embraced cooperation to shape a more peaceful world. In light of such changes, the shift of American–Soviet relations from nuclear terror to friendly accommodation cannot be satisfactorily understood as simply orchestrated "from above"; it must be seen as having emerged to a significant extent "from below." While Reagan and Gorbachev had agreed to dismantle only a small fraction of their countries' nuclear missiles, a broader social, cultural, and ideological transformation had been launched.

17

TRANSFORMATION AND REVERSION, 1989–1999

OVERVIEW

By early 1989 many people in the United States and in the Soviet Union believed that the Cold War was ending and a new era of peaceful cooperation was dawning. Yet the next decade actually brought turmoil instead of smooth sailing.

Under Reagan's successor, George H. W. Bush, the United States first stubbornly maintained that the Cold War had not ended, then belatedly recognized the need to move beyond the superpower conflict. Instead of responding magnanimously to the transformations of Eastern Europe and the Soviet Union, the Bush administration narrow-mindedly exploited Soviet economic desperation to push for the integration of a unified Germany in NATO, dismissed Soviet suggestions for a new pan-European security arrangement, and insisted on full repayment of Soviet debts.[1] Gorbachev's introduction of competitive elections in the spring of 1989 seemed to move the Soviet Union toward democracy, but in the next two years he vacillated, appointed hard-line officials who tried to overthrow him, and finally had to resign as his rival Boris Yeltsin dissolved the USSR. Anticommunists in both Russia and the United States who blamed communism for the Cold War expected that a democratic Russia naturally would have friendly relations with a democratic America, and most Americans at first idolized Yeltsin as a brave champion of freedom.[2] Yet he became increasingly autocratic, used military force against his political opponents, and launched a disastrous war in a secessionist southern republic. By the end of Yeltsin's reign in 1999, after US and Russian forces nearly clashed in the Balkans, American–Russian relations had reverted to being almost as acrimonious as they had been before the dramatic changes of the late 1980s.

Politicians, journalists, and scholars have presented a wide range of explanations for the turbulent course of Russian–American relations in the 1990s. Republican leaders in the United States asserted that America won the Cold War and helped to liberate Russians from communism, but that the Democratic administration of Bill Clinton then promoted the wrong, big government model of development in Russia and condoned Russia's regression to a corrupt authoritarianism.[3] Democratic officials and their supporters, by contrast, have argued that whereas the stingy Bush administration failed to provide sufficient support to post-Soviet Russia, the more enlightened Clinton administration genuinely sought to include Russia in its strategy for enlarging democracy and backed Yeltsin as the only Russian leader who could prevent a restoration of Communists to power. According to the Democratic narrative, on the whole Russia was moving in the right direction until a former KGB officer took control in 2000 and reversed much of the progress that had been made.[4] Prominent Russophile scholars in the United States, on the other hand, have faulted both the Clinton and the Bush administrations for a badly misguided crusade to remake Russia in America's image that caused much unnecessary suffering and destroyed prospects for more gradual and democratic reform.[5] Many Russian nationalists presented angrier indictments of US policies that, they claimed, caused the collapse of the Soviet Union and then propped up the corrupt Yeltsin regime that meekly accepted Western policies contrary to Russia's interests.[6]

Such divergent views have shared a tendency to apportion blame for what went wrong one-sidedly on specific individuals, parties, or nations. This chapter presents a more balanced and inclusive perspective by focusing not only on top leaders, but also on habits of thought, expectations, and values that shaped politics in America and Russia. Accounts that have riveted attention on presidents of the two countries have tended to defend the leaders' views or to exaggerate their impact on developments that often rushed past them.[7] By contrast, examining attitudes and assumptions that were widely shared in Russia and America illuminates how illusions and misconceptions sparked much of the tension and resentment that arose in the course of the decade. Contrary to the claims of conspiracy theorists and Russophobes, the deterioration of American–Russian relations in the 1990s did not stem mainly from sinister American plots to break Russia or from the malignant recidivism of Russian imperialism. Instead, as we will see, the degeneration of relations was driven to a great extent by American triumphalist mythology about how the Cold War ended, unrealistically high Russian expectations of American aid and respect, and domestic political dynamics in each country.

DEMOCRATIZATION, DISINTEGRATION, AND DIPLOMACY: 1989–1992

Having worked with President Reagan and Secretary of State Shultz to largely end the Soviet–American ideological rivalry and military confrontation by the end of 1988, Mikhail Gorbachev looked forward to further breakthroughs both at home and abroad at the start of 1989. Above all, he sought to transform the tightly centralized Communist dictatorship into a democratic socialist state. Building upon the policy of *glasnost'* that had freed the Soviet press and encouraged public discussion of the problems of the Soviet system in the preceding years, in the spring of 1989 Gorbachev pushed forward with competitive elections for many Soviet government positions, which some conservative Communists lost. Acutely aware of the inefficiency and waste in the militarized Soviet planned economy, Gorbachev sought to encourage small-scale private enterprise, allow greater autonomy for factory managers, attract foreign investment, and reduce outlays for the arms industries. Reviving economic productivity would, he hoped, make it attractive for the many Soviet republics to remain part of a voluntary union. Unwilling to continue bearing the burden of propping up neo-Stalinist dictatorships in the Soviet external empire, Gorbachev urged East European Communist leaders to reform their systems as he was transforming his.

Undertaking such far-reaching and potentially destabilizing changes required peaceful international relations. Gorbachev and Foreign Minister Eduard Shevardnadze pursued that goal by completing the withdrawal of Soviet forces from Afghanistan in February 1989 and by engaging in discussions with foreign leaders about the resolution of conflicts in other parts of the world, particularly southern Africa and Central America. They hoped to go far beyond reducing tensions, though. Ultimately, Gorbachev and Shevardnadze sought to integrate the previously isolated Soviet Union into the world. As a respected member of the international community, the USSR would maintain its prestige as a great power while obtaining the benefits of expanded economic relations with the flourishing capitalist states.

As he took office in January 1989, President Bush did not understand how Gorbachev looked at the world and what he wanted to achieve. A year earlier, when the popular Soviet leader came to Washington for a summit with Reagan, then Vice President Bush confided that his presidential campaign in 1988 would feature "hardline statements" about US–Soviet relations which Gorbachev should not take "too seriously."[8] Yet tough anticommunism was not merely a campaign tactic for Bush to win the support of conservative Republicans, who viewed him as at best a pragmatic moderate and at worst a "wimp." Bush and his advisers believed that Reagan and Shultz had gone too far in their engagement with Gorbachev and made unnecessary concessions to the weakening Soviet Union. Veterans of the Gerald Ford administration of the mid-1970s, Bush and his National Security Adviser, Brent Scowcroft, believed that the easing of tensions then had exposed Ford to criticism as being soft and had been followed by renewed Soviet aggressiveness in the world. Wary of being burned again, Bush and Scowcroft doubted the sincerity of Gorbachev's "new thinking" and suspected that it was merely part of an ongoing propaganda battle between the superpowers.[9]

Bush, Scowcroft, and their advisers remained captives of the competitive political culture of the Cold War. Disregarding the Soviet withdrawal from Afghanistan and Soviet reformers' interest in shifting from enmity to partnership, the Bush administration continued to view the Soviet Union as an adversary whose primary goals were to weaken NATO, split the United States from its allies, and make the USSR a stronger, more assertive military power. Early policy memos focused on seizing the initiative from Gorbachev and "getting ahead" of him. Scowcroft, a former Air Force general, fixated on Soviet military capabilities and thought the Cold War could end only with a US victory after Soviet forces were compelled to withdraw from East Germany and Eastern Europe. He worried that a diminished sense of a Soviet threat would make it difficult to justify massive military budgets and maintain the US preponderance of power.[10]

Instead of moving forward with the momentum generated by Reagan and Gorbachev, therefore, Bush and his advisers decided to pause and conduct a protracted review of Soviet–American relations. That review, finally completed in May 1989, called for a strategy of projecting confidence about American objectives, prioritizing relations with US allies, modernizing US nuclear forces, and exploiting the weakness of Soviet ties to Eastern Europe. In short, the strategy envisioned a continuation of the Cold War struggle. It completely disregarded recommendations from the astute US Ambassador to Russia, Jack Matlock, for close diplomatic engagement with Gorbachev, including an early summit meeting.[11]

The Bush administration's passivity and procrastination provoked widespread criticism from Reagan, George Kennan, and many others. Stung by the reproaches, Bush and his more forward-leaning Secretary of State James Baker decided to "get moving." Their public rhetoric changed, with Bush espousing the idea of going "beyond containment" in a speech on May 12. But newspapers criticized even that speech for lagging behind Gorbachev and failing to match his actions. And, in private, Bush continued to lack a vision of how meeting with Gorbachev could facilitate dramatic changes in the Soviet Union.[12] Some of his advisers, such as deputy national security adviser Robert M. Gates, whose sight was dimmed by memories of the past, were even more dubious about the prospect of significant reform in the Soviet system.[13]

While Reagan's embrace had enhanced Gorbachev's stature, Bush's distance undermined Gorbachev's confidence and exposed him to criticism from Soviet hard-liners. The KGB, for example, informed Gorbachev that reactionaries were driving US policies aimed at weakening the USSR.[14] Instead of seizing opportunities to exert positive influence toward the best possible outcomes, Bush and his advisers focused on avoiding mistakes and worried about worst-case scenarios, including the ouster of Gorbachev by an old-line Communist diehard. Instead of having a long-range vision of the benefits of a continuing partnership with the Soviet Union, the Bush administration concentrated on securing the gains it could get in the near term.[15]

By July 1989, prodded by East European and West European leaders, Bush finally realized Gorbachev's vital role in the earthshaking changes under way. With typically extreme personalization, he exclaimed to Scowcroft: "Look, this guy *is perestroika*."[16] Yet Bush did not meet the Soviet leader until a summit at Malta in December. In the meantime, Bush and his aides watched in amazement as revolutions swept through Central and Eastern Europe, from Berlin in early November to Prague, Budapest, and other capitals in the following weeks.

Bush's restraint during the tumultuous events was wise. His rejection of a proposal that he fly to Berlin to hail the demise of communism there avoided "sticking it in Gorbachev's eye."[17] His resolve not to show a "we won, you lost" attitude at Malta avoided alienating Gorbachev. Although the shipboard summit in the Mediterranean yielded no definite agreements, it finally led Bush to realize that Gorbachev did not see the world the way he imagined the Communist leader did. According to Scowcroft, it also "laid to rest the notion – for now – that the Administration is dragging its feet and is unwilling to engage the Soviets." That confidential statement marked how deeply public criticism had affected the Bush team.[18]

Most important to Gorbachev and his top aides was the simple fact that "the USSR and U.S. are no longer enemies," as foreign policy adviser Anatoly Chernyaev noted. Looking back on the preceding years, Gorbachev explained to Bush that "the methods of the Cold War were defeated" and that "the man in the street" had realized that earlier and more keenly than top leaders had. Hence, officials were "lagging behind our people, who want to become closer." Gorbachev recognized that some figures in both countries had not yet abandoned "the vestiges of images of an enemy." He may not have realized, though, that many of the citizen activists who had worked hardest to overcome American–Soviet enmity now felt that they had accomplished their mission. Their retirement from the campaign, combined with the persistence of old stereotypes in the minds of others, created the danger of a relapse in the future.[19]

At the time, however, the meeting in the Mediterranean eased Soviet anxieties and thereby emboldened Gorbachev to push ahead with the internal transformation of the USSR. As Chernyaev observed, "after Malta we were assured that the external conditions for an acceleration of perestroika had been secured. The external threat ... was now no more. Our hands were free."[20] The threats to Gorbachev's vision of a democratic, socialist Soviet Union now arose more from internal developments: mounting nationalist agitation for independence around the southern and western periphery; interethnic violence; increasing anticommunist sentiment among people impatient with the slow pace of change; hardening resistance to reforms from orthodox Communist officials; and an economic crisis worsened by Gorbachev's misguided decentralization policies. Instead of retreating in the face of those problems, Gorbachev took one of his boldest steps – in March he pushed the Congress of People's Deputies to revoke Article 6 of the Soviet Constitution, which designated the Communist Party as the "ruling party" of the USSR.[21]

Unlike Chinese Communist leaders, who prioritized economic reform and violently suppressed pro-democracy demonstrators in Beijing in June 1989, Gorbachev showed an aversion to the use of force and emphasized political transformation. By deliberately creating free political competition, he inadvertently allowed a strong rival for power to emerge.

Boris Yeltsin, the Communist Party boss of Sverdlovsk (in the Ural region), had been brought to Moscow in 1985. As head of the party in the capital, he gained a reputation as a populist with attacks on elite privileges and energetic banter with crowds. At a Central Committee meeting in October 1987, Yeltsin complained that the people had yet to get any benefits from *perestroika* and brashly criticized the development of a "cult of personality" around Gorbachev. The harsh reaction of party leaders to Yeltsin's attack nearly ended his political career. Yet, in the following years, Yeltsin made a comeback, winning election to the Congress of People's Deputies in 1989 and then becoming chairman of a new parliament for the Russian Republic in May 1990.

While Gorbachev most admired the social democracies of Western Europe, Yeltsin came to idealize the efficient, productive United States as the opposite of the backward, bungling Soviet Union. On his first trip to

America in September 1989, Yeltsin was amazed by the abundance of food in a Houston supermarket, which utterly convinced him that the standard of living of average American families was much, much higher than that of Soviet families. Thirty years after Nikita Khrushchev had been impressed by a modern Iowa farm, Yeltsin was awed by the advanced technology at an Indiana pig farm – not only the expensive harvesting machine, but also the computers on the farmer's desk. Yeltsin dreamed grandiosely of having American companies build a million apartments and grow soybeans on a million hectares of land in Russia.[22] (In later years, he would even want to take an oath of office on a Bible as US presidents did and purchase electric golf carts like the one he saw George Bush ride in at Camp David.)[23]

The rise of a power-hungry challenger to Gorbachev posed a problem for the Bush administration. Bush viewed the burly, emotional, hard-drinking Yeltsin as "a wild man."[24] When Yeltsin first visited the White House in September 1989, he threw a fit about not being granted a formal meeting with the president – only a more casual "drop by" chat in deference to Gorbachev's position as top leader of the USSR. After meeting the General Secretary at Malta, Bush preferred the more cerebral, moderate Gorbachev as a force for stability, one of Bush's highest values. Worried that the amiable Gorbachev might be overthrown by a tough military leader and that the nuclear-armed Soviet Union might disintegrate into warring republics, Bush and Baker tried to buttress Gorbachev's authority with prestige-enhancing meetings.

In contrast to the National Endowment for Democracy, which used funds from Congress to support independence activists in the republics, Bush and Baker sought to discourage nationalist separatism.[25] Most strikingly Bush delivered a speech on August 1, 1991, in Kiev (Kyiv), where he declared that "Americans will not support those who seek independence in order to replace a far-off tyranny with a local despotism." The address provoked a protest outside the White House by Ukrainian Americans and prompted withering criticism from columnist William Safire, who memorably dubbed it the "'Chicken Kiev' speech."[26]

Although Bush and Baker snubbed and slighted Yeltsin, his power grew as Gorbachev failed to pull the Soviet economy out of its tailspin. The fall in the world price of oil after 1985 and a drastic decline in Soviet revenue from vodka sales due to Gorbachev's anti-alcohol campaign caused a large budget deficit. The problem might have been manageable if Gorbachev had been able to cut spending on the military more deeply and reduce subsidies to inefficient collective farms and wasteful factories, but he faced determined resistance from the bureaucrats who managed the military–industrial and agro-industrial complexes. To counter the budget shortfall, the Kremlin therefore resorted to printing more money. That sparked inflation and made many producers more reluctant to put goods on the market for diminishing returns. Shelves in state stores became more barren. Lines for the many scarce items grew longer. People got angrier.[27]

In the summer of 1990, Gorbachev thought he had found a solution to the economic crisis: a plan for a transition to a market economy in 500 days, with broad privatization of state enterprises, freeing of prices from state control, and decentralization of much decision-making. Although Yeltsin agreed to support the plan, Soviet bureaucrats adamantly opposed it and advocated a much slower transition. Unable to arrange a compromise between reformers and conservative officials, Gorbachev dropped the plan by October 1990.[28]

Facing a stalemate at home, Gorbachev grew increasingly desperate for foreign aid. Yet, since the Soviet Union had not adopted a clear plan for economic reform, Bush and Scowcroft reasonably opposed large-scale financial assistance. That, Scowcroft later explained, would have been "putting money down a rat hole." Since Soviet officials were unable to explain the disappearance of extensive aid from Germany, such views were warranted.[29]

Bush and Scowcroft believed it was in the US interest to keep Gorbachev in power for as long as possible.[30] Against the wishes of Soviet military leaders, Gorbachev reluctantly accepted the reunification of Germany in the first months of 1990. Although German leaders repeatedly pledged that NATO would not expand to the east, US leaders backed away from a hypothetical offer by Baker that NATO would not move even one inch to the east. Gorbachev and Shevardnadze eventually accepted complicated language in an agreement that allowed NATO troops to be deployed temporarily in eastern Germany. Later, many Russians' belief that NATO expansion violated promises made in 1990 would provoke a deep sense of betrayal.[31]

After Iraq invaded Kuwait in August 1990, Gorbachev cooperated with Bush's multilateral effort to reverse the aggression, even though Iraq had been a major client of the Soviet Union in the preceding decades. When Bush brushed aside Gorbachev's efforts to arrange a peaceful withdrawal of Iraqi forces and launched a successful ground war, Gorbachev did not vehemently object, even though the war dashed his hopes for a peaceful, multipolar post-Cold War world.[32] On July 31, 1991, with Bush in Moscow, Gorbachev signed a long-negotiated Strategic Arms Reduction Treaty (START). No other Soviet leader could be expected to be so cooperative. "[Y]ou are my man," Bush assured Gorbachev that summer.[33]

Yet, when hardline Soviet officials launched a coup to prevent the dissolution of the Soviet Union in the middle of August and placed Gorbachev under house arrest, Bush and Scowcroft did not immediately and emphatically condemn the coup. Instead, thinking the coup might succeed and that Gorbachev might already be dead, Bush at first tried to preserve the possibility of relations with a new government and only mildly criticized the plotters for their "extra-constitutional" move. However, the poorly organized and half-hearted coup faltered, primarily because key figures such as Minister of Defense Dmitry Yazov did not want to shed the blood of fellow Russians.[34] Gorbachev refused to cooperate with the conspirators. Yeltsin mounted a tank outside the Russian parliament and read a defiant proclamation. Bush then issued a more unequivocal condemnation. The coup ended, Gorbachev returned to Moscow, and American newspapers lionized Yeltsin as a hero with an "unshakeable commitment to the constitutional rule of law."[35]

Many Americans viewed the defeat of the coup not solely as an achievement by courageous Soviet citizens, but also as a victory for American ideals and influence. "We have just had a tremendous triumph for our values and for our vital interests," Bush privately exulted.[36] Political cartoonists depicted Yeltsin raising high the torch of liberty or even as the Statue of Liberty itself.[37] Columnists and cartoonists suggested that Soviet citizens and soldiers resisted or defected from the coup attempt because they wanted to continue enjoying the hamburgers and fries of McDonald's (which had opened its first restaurant in Moscow in 1990).[38] Thus, as in the fall of 1905 and the spring of 1917, many in the United States exaggerated the impact of America on developments in Russia.

By envisioning the resistance to the coup as a virtually unanimous popular uprising against communism, many Americans also created a foundation for subsequent disillusionment and undue alarm at the later resurgence of the Communist Party in Russia. "[T]he people rose all across the country" to rally behind Yeltsin, one typical editorial declared, and as a result "communism breathed its last this week in the land of its birth."[39] Tens of thousands of people (by some accounts, over 100,000) did bravely demonstrate against the coup in Moscow, St. Petersburg, and Yeltsin's home town of Sverdlovsk (soon renamed Yekaterinburg), while much smaller crowds protested in a number of other cities.[40] In addition, there were strong demands for national independence in several regions, including the Baltic and Ukraine. Yet, across Russia, by far the largest republic in the USSR, many local and regional government officials (more than 70 percent according to one investigation) either supported the coup or sat on the fence.[41] Meanwhile, the majority of citizens went about their daily lives and waited to learn the outcome.[42] According to a poll on the first day of the coup, August 19, a quarter of Russians thought life would improve if the coup succeeded, another quarter felt life would change for the worse, and 42 percent had no definite opinion.[43] In other opinion surveys in 1991, most Russians continued to express support for socialism and the preservation of the Soviet Union.[44] Thus, popular attitudes were complex and divided, rather than united in enthusiasm about democracy and capitalism.

Yet, at the time, Yeltsin's actions seemed to confirm American assumptions. He banned the Communist Party in the aftermath of the coup. At the end of October, he announced a radical move to rapidly create a market economy, beginning with liberalization of prices in January 1992. Although he had only a vague notion about the economic changes, Yeltsin promised that they would bring pain for everyone for only six months and that by the fall of 1992 living standards would improve. In a campaign speech in June 1991, Yeltsin had denounced Communists for conducting a Marxist experiment on the Russian people. Now, five months later, he launched a free market experiment inspired by theories of Western economists and guided by American advisers who helped to design the plans for "shock therapy."[45] In December 1991, Yeltsin agreed with the leaders of Belarus and Ukraine to replace the Soviet Union with a much looser Commonwealth of Independent States. Having had the last planks of his power pulled out from under his feet, Gorbachev resigned on Christmas Day. The red hammer-and-sickle flag was hauled down over the Kremlin, and the Russian tricolor was raised in its place. While many Americans still had fond feelings for Gorbachev, almost all welcomed the burial of the Soviet Union.

Although Bush earlier had refrained from gloating, he now claimed credit for the "victory" over communism in televised remarks on Christmas evening and then in his State of the Union speech at the end of January. As he started his campaign for re-election, with the US economy troubled by high unemployment and slow growth, Bush decided to highlight the "changes of almost biblical proportions" in the outside world in the preceding year. Disregarding Gorbachev's vital role in ending the Soviet–American rivalry, Bush declared: "By the grace of God, America won the cold war."[46] Thus, domestic political needs overwhelmed both truthfulness and the wise restraint Bush had shown earlier.

The rhetorical gambit did not work. Most Americans had their eyes on the US economy and the future, not on the demise of Soviet communism in the past. Editors tended to ignore Bush's celebration of the Cold War triumph, commented that his speech did not stir the nation's imagination, and complained that he failed to restore confidence in the economy. Bush failed to win re-election in November – an outcome many attributed to the perception that he cared more about international relations than about domestic prosperity.[47]

Yet, in the following years, as Bush and his advisers reiterated their assertions in memoirs and as other Republican politicians sought to bask in the artificial glory, many Americans embraced a deeply misleading triumphalist view. By conflating the end of the Cold War (which a majority of Americans, including Bush himself, declared over by November 1990) and the collapse of the Soviet Union more than a year later, this view muddled popular memories.[48] It contributed to exaggerated notions of the ability of the United States to remake the world by overthrowing foreign governments. Moreover, it fed Russian ultranationalists' conspiracy theories that a CIA plot had caused the break-up of the Soviet Union.[49]

In June 1992, Yeltsin came to Washington to meet with Bush, hoping to forge a lasting partnership with the United States and procure massive assistance for Russia's difficult economic transformation. In an address to a joint session of Congress on June 17, Yeltsin made his pitch. While starkly blaming communism for past Soviet–American enmity and vowing that he would not let that "evil" arise again in Russia, he also warned that that "nightmare" could come back. "It was precisely in a devastated country with an economy in near paralysis that bolshevism succeeded in building a totalitarian regime," he recalled. To prevent that from happening again, Congress should pass legislation to support Russian reforms and encourage the private sector to invest in the Russian market. That was obviously in America's interest: if Russia's reforms failed, it would cost "hundreds of billions" to cope with the consequences.[50]

Yeltsin received thirteen standing ovations during his flattering speech, which praised America as "the great land of freedom" and extolled the prospect of fulfilling Woodrow Wilson's dream of a world made safe for democracy. He also convinced many newspaper editors that he deserved major financial support – not only to reciprocate his lopsided concessions on arms reductions and ease the pain his reforms were causing the Russian people, but also because it seemed unlikely that any other Russian leader would be as favorable to US interests. As the Baltimore *Sun* put it, "He may well be democracy's last, best hope in the land of our old Cold War enemy."[51]

Yet many members of Congress remained reluctant to appropriate funds for Russia. Some, particularly Senator John McCain (Republican, Arizona), seized on a Yeltsin vow to investigate thoroughly whether there were any American prisoners of war (POWs) in Russia as a reason to hold up any financial assistance until Russia completed the investigation. Others reflected the continuing power of Cold War habits of thought. Most notably,

Senator John Glenn (Democrat, Ohio), a former astronaut who had competed with Soviet cosmonauts in the space race, declared that the possibility that American POWs might be in Russia "shows the difference in attitudes, how we view the importance of each individual, while they view everything collectively."[52]

Ultimately Congress did pass a Freedom Support Act that allocated several hundred million dollars to meet humanitarian needs, support the creation of private businesses, promote educational reform, and assist other projects in the former Soviet Union. Yet that amounted to only a couple of dollars for each Russian man, woman, and child. Thus, Yeltsin failed to persuade Congress to think about "the longer term prospects of our relations" and make a suitable investment. The *Philadelphia Inquirer* was therefore prescient when it worried that Congress would "conclude that a toothless bear can just be ignored."[53]

Russia did gain some advantages from engagement with the Bush administration. Although Bush refused Yeltsin's request to refer to Russia as an ally in June 1992, Russia did informally join the elite group of industrialized nations (G7) that summer. Skillfully coordinating with other Western leaders, Bush and Baker applied effective pressure on Ukraine, Belarus, and Kazakhstan to transfer nuclear weapons to Russian territory. The START II treaty, which Yeltsin and Bush signed in January 1993, reduced the danger of nuclear war, in part by decreasing reliance on tactical nuclear weapons and taking US nuclear bombers off alert. Under a farsighted program designed by Senators Sam Nunn (Democrat, Georgia) and Richard Lugar (Republican, Indiana), the United States helped Russia secure its nuclear weapons and provided employment for Russian scientists (who otherwise might have been tempted to work for other countries).[54]

Yet, in comparison with Russian hopes for a full strategic partnership and generous financial assistance for an economic transformation, the results were deeply disappointing.[55] Yeltsin's idealistic Foreign Minister, Andrei Kozyrev, who had been so entranced by the presumed shared values of Russia and America that in the spring of 1992 he did not think much about Russia's distinct interests, conceded in October that the "honeymoon period" had ended.[56] The growing perception in Russia that the United States was exploiting Russia's weakness was a major political liability for Yeltsin and Kozyrev. Both inside and outside Yeltsin's circle of advisers, influential figures criticized Kozyrev's approach to foreign policy and urged that Russia should stand up more assertively for its interests, especially in neighboring former Soviet republics known as the "Near Abroad."[57] Thus, in Russia as well as in

America, domestic political dynamics began to undermine the prospects for a post-Cold War partnership between Russia and the United States.

BILL AND BORIS: 1993–1999

While the patrician Bush initially treated Yeltsin with reserve, the next US president embraced him much more warmly. During the 1992 presidential campaign, Arkansas governor Bill Clinton repeatedly criticized Bush for being too cautious about providing assistance to Russia.[58] After Clinton became president in January 1993, he stressed to aides the need to help Yeltsin "big-time" so the Russian economy would improve and Yeltsin could face down challengers in the Russian parliament. Clinton's key adviser on Russia, former *Time* magazine contributor Strobe Talbott, urged, in an implicit rebuke of Bush administration policy, that the United States should not only try "to prevent the worst but also to nurture the best that might happen in the former Soviet Union."[59] When Clinton and Yeltsin met throughout the decade, they not only shook hands; they hugged.[60]

Yet the Clinton team shared some of the Bush administration's core assumptions, objectives, and tactics. They believed that Russia was weak and would remain debilitated for the foreseeable future. In that near term, they sought to advance US interests and goals even when the policies posed problems for the pliable leader they liked in Moscow. Like Bush, they offered Russia symbolic gestures (such as formally becoming a member of the G-8) in return for substantive policy concessions.[61] Despite Talbott's profession of good intentions, in practice, the Clinton administration, like Bush and his advisers, focused less on shaping an ideal outcome in Russia and more on avoiding a disaster, with Russia "going bad." While earlier presidents had feared being attacked for losing Vietnam or another foreign country, the Clinton team worried about being accused of having "lost Russia."[62]

That approach led Clinton and his aides to concentrate on personal support for Yeltsin rather than on promoting political principles. Although Clinton knew that Yeltsin was an erratic alcoholic, he strongly believed that "Yeltsin drunk is better than most of the alternatives sober."[63] Instead of allowing Russians to determine political outcomes in their country, therefore, the Clinton administration repeatedly intervened to influence decisions and developments. In April 1993, three weeks before a referendum on Yeltsin's leadership and policies, Clinton met with Yeltsin and emphasized at a press conference "that a lot of money was coming" to Russia because of US support for Yeltsin and Russia's democracy.[64] In September, as tension between Yeltsin and the Russian parliament escalated and Yeltsin disbanded the parliament, Clinton wholeheartedly backed Yeltsin. After nationalists riled up by Yeltsin's vice president attacked the Ostankino television station on October 3, Yeltsin ordered the army to confront his opponents and tanks then fired on the parliament building. But that did not lead Clinton to waver in his support for Yeltsin.[65] At the end of 1994, Yeltsin launched a brutal war to suppress separatists in the southern republic of Chechnya, which alarmed East Europeans and heightened some US officials' belief in the need to expand NATO.[66] Instead of expressing reservations about the often indiscriminate use of force, Clinton publicly compared Yeltsin to President Abraham Lincoln, who had preserved the Union during the American Civil War.[67]

Owing to the horrific, unsuccessful war in Chechnya, the continuation of a deep economic depression, and an alarming increase in crime, by the end of 1995 less than 10 percent of Russians approved of Yeltsin, and a reorganized Communist Party had become the most popular force in Russian politics.[68] Fearing that he would lose in a presidential election scheduled for June 1996, in March Yeltsin approved a plan to postpone the election, ban the Communists, and shut down the Russian parliament again. But Yeltsin's daughter Tatyana and his aide Anatolii Chubais persuaded him of the need to go forward with the election – a point Clinton also pressed in a letter.[69]

Yeltsin's unpopularity and disdain for democratic processes did not deter the Clinton administration from redoubling its efforts to keep Yeltsin in power. In March 1996, with a campaign for the Russian presidency under way, the International Monetary Fund (IMF), prodded by Clinton, announced a $10 billion loan to the Russian government. In April, Clinton and the other leaders of the G-7 came to Moscow for a meeting in order "to give Yeltsin a pre-election boost," as Talbott candidly acknowledged. In May, the head of the World Bank traveled to Moscow to announce a $500 million project for the Russian coal industry. Drawing on foreign credits, Yeltsin bought votes with handouts to pensioners, students, and other groups. A trio of highly paid Republican consultants from California and a prominent American public relations firm provided advice about Yeltsin's campaign and advertising, which dwelled on the harshness of life in the Soviet past. After all those efforts, on June 16, Yeltsin won 36 percent of the votes, only slightly more than the 32 percent for the Communist candidate, Gennady Zyuganov.[70]

Some Americans expressed alarm about a possible Communist victory. Syndicated columnist William Safire warned that the smooth-talking Zyuganov would "be pushed aside by the hard-line Bolsheviks soon after the Communists gained power," the government would retake control of the media, and "the clock would be turned back" to the Soviet era. Former

Vice President Dan Quayle predicted that Zyuganov would "lead Russia back toward an aggressive and expansionist foreign policy." Cartoonists envisioned Russians resurrecting statues of Lenin.[71]

In reality, Zyuganov, who would be the undisputed leader of the Communist Party for many years, was more prepared than Yeltsin was to abide by the rules of a democratic polity. He recognized that there had been grave defects in the Soviet system, including state control of all property, and he assured foreign investors at Davos, Switzerland that he favored a mixed economy, with both public and private ownership. Although Zyuganov believed that Russia had a unique civilization and values that differentiated it from the West and the free market model, he did not want to return to the antipathy of the Cold War. Hence, as one American newspaper wisely commented, Americans should not have gotten "goose bumps of fear at the mention of Zyuganov."[72]

Thanks in part to a secret deal with Alexander Lebed, a general who finished third in the election and then threw his support to Yeltsin, the American-backed candidate defeated the Communist leader in a run-off in July. Russian voters did not know that Yeltsin had a heart attack (his fourth) after the first round. In the following years he would be almost as incapacitated as Leonid Brezhnev had been in the late 1970s.[73]

Yet, having helped secure the re-election of his buddy, "Ole Boris," Bill Clinton could now proceed with the eastward expansion of NATO. Three years earlier, Clinton had already decided to extend NATO protection to Eastern Europe, even though Yeltsin had bent over backward to demonstrate that Russia was no longer a threat. According to some scholars, Clinton was moved by moral considerations and emotional pleas from Czech and Polish leaders who had been anticommunist activists.[74] But Clinton's policy was more strongly influenced by domestic political considerations. Senator Robert Dole (Republican, Kansas), who had presidential ambitions, criticized Clinton for moving too slowly to expand NATO and for being too deferential to Russia. Republican gains in the November 1994 congressional elections tilted Clinton further toward NATO enlargement, which he knew would appeal to voters of East European descent in electorally crucial states.[75]

Yeltsin angrily objected to what he regarded as a betrayal by his friend. "There should no longer be enemies, winners or losers," in Europe, he argued. Clinton delayed the expansion to avoid undermining Yeltsin's electoral prospects in 1996, but then moved ahead. In March 1999, Poland, Hungary, and the Czech Republic formally joined the alliance.[76]

"TO THE BRINK": RUPTURE OVER KOSOVO

While the expansion of NATO into the former Soviet sphere of influence in the northern and central parts of Eastern Europe strained Russian–American relations, a NATO air war in the southern part of the region caused a worse diplomatic rupture. It also nearly led to a military clash and poisoned Russian popular views of the United States and NATO.

The conflict stemmed from worsening hostilities between Serbia and ethnic Albanians (Kosovars), who constituted around 80 percent of the population in the Serbian province of Kosovo. After Slobodan Milošević, the nationalist leader of Serbia, stripped Kosovo of its autonomous status in 1989, tensions escalated between the Muslim Kosovars and Orthodox Christian Serbs, who viewed Kosovo as a sacred historical site of the development of their culture, religion, and nation. Starting in 1996, Kosovo Liberation Army (KLA) guerrillas with bases in neighboring Albania attacked Serbian government officials and police stations. Serbian forces retaliated, sought to crush the KLA fighters, and expelled many ethnic Albanians from Kosovo. With hundreds of thousands of Kosovars living as refugees in Albania and Macedonia or hiding in the mountains of Kosovo, a major humanitarian crisis developed.

Since Russia had had close ties to Serbia for centuries, Russian leaders expected to play a central role in addressing the crisis. As Prime Minister Yevgeny Primakov told Secretary of State Madeleine Albright, "Russia has been present in the Balkans for two hundred years, maybe more."[77] In the nineteenth century, many Russians had embraced the mission of liberating their Slavic and Christian brethren in the Balkans from domination by the Ottoman Empire, and during the world wars of the twentieth century, Russians and Serbs had been allies. Believing that unwise Serbian policies and overreactions to KLA attacks contributed to the worsening situation, Russian leaders worked vigorously and effectively to moderate Serbian conduct. The Russian diplomatic effort included a meeting between Yeltsin and Milošević in Moscow in June 1998. Although tensions rose again in the first months of 1999, Primakov believed that the KLA, emboldened by US support, bore much of the blame and that a diplomatic resolution of the conflict remained possible.[78]

US officials viewed the conflict very differently. In the first half of the 1990s, Bosnian Serbs had committed appalling atrocities against Bosnian Muslims that ended only after NATO air and ground operations led to the Dayton Accords of 1995, under which both Russian and American troops participated in peacekeeping forces in Bosnia. Regretting that he had not intervened earlier in that case and had not intervened at all to halt a genocide in Rwanda in 1994, President Clinton resolved not to let Kosovo become another Bosnia – a horrific slaughter and the subject of a protracted political controversy in the United States. Although Clinton recognized that Milošević's "ethnic cleansing" in Kosovo was not the same as Hitler's extermination of the Jews, he and his aides repeatedly invoked the specter of the Holocaust in public explanations of his military intervention.[79]

Clinton and his advisers knew that many KLA leaders were unsavory figures.[80] The KLA got much of its funding from drug trafficking and other criminal activity.[81] A senior US diplomat had labeled the KLA a "terrorist group" in 1998. American journalists reported that the KLA had carried out "random kidnappings and executions."[82] A prosecutor appointed by the United Nations found that KLA forces used beatings and killings to drive Serb and Roma civilians out of western Kosovo in the spring of 1998.[83] When Russian and American pressure periodically succeeded in getting Milošević to restrain Serb forces, KLA fighters resumed attacks in the hope of provoking massacres that would lead to international military intervention.[84]

Yet, as the crisis worsened, US officials grew closer to KLA leaders. According to Albright, Washington considered arming the KLA, but decided not to do so, because it would alienate European leaders.[85] However, in a conversation with Vice President Al Gore, Primakov charged that the United States was sending weapons to the KLA.[86] Reports by journalists, drawing on CIA sources and European diplomats, indicated that US agents at a minimum provided tactical advice and communications equipment to the KLA, which received sniper rifles from Albanian American supporters in the United States.[87] Later accounts indicate that the CIA did help arm the KLA.[88] While the official US goal was to restore autonomy to Kosovo, not detach it from Serbia, Albright secretly encouraged KLA leaders "to delay, but not abandon, their aspirations for independence." Thus, US leaders increasingly sided with the KLA and defined Milošević alone as "the problem."[89]

If US representatives had taken more balanced and flexible negotiating positions, and if they had allowed Russia a greater role in shaping the terms of the final ultimatum presented to Milošević in March, they probably could have secured Serbian acceptance of their demands without having to go to war.[90] For example, if US officials had not demanded that NATO forces have access to all Yugoslav territory and if they had allowed some Serbian forces to remain in the northernmost part of Kosovo, where the ethnic Serb population was greatest, Milošević might have agreed to the terms.

But Albright, driven by a vision that Milošević had to be defeated in order to integrate the Balkans into a democratic Europe, opposed compromise as akin to appeasement.[91] Instead of recognizing that Russia had a special concern with the Balkans, many US officials viewed southeastern Europe as a *Western* sphere of influence.[92]

Believing that a couple of days of bombing would compel Milošević to submit to US terms, American diplomats underestimated the Russian reaction and downplayed the probable damage to Russian–American relations.[93] However, immediately after NATO planes began bombing Serbia, Yeltsin vehemently condemned "NATO's attempt to enter the twenty-first century as global policeman" and vowed: "Russia will never agree to it." Reminding Americans that Russia had nuclear weapons, Yeltsin warned early in April that the NATO air war could spark a world war.[94] Russian diplomats informed their US counterparts that Russian military units were eager to fight for Serbia and that political pressure was rising for Russia to form a military alliance with Yugoslavia and Belarus.[95]

Milošević did not buckle as the Americans expected. The bombing continued for seventy-nine days, killing hundreds of Serbian civilians. On May 7, a US plane bombed the Chinese Embassy in Belgrade, killing three Chinese citizens and wounding many more. The Serbian ethnic cleansing became much more aggressive, with Serbian fighters burning numerous villages and forcing hundreds of thousands of Kosovo Albanians to flee into Albania or Macedonia.[96]

Contrary to later assertions by Clinton and others, the air war did not by itself break Milošević's will and lead to a NATO victory.[97] Instead, Russian diplomatic involvement proved essential. Belatedly recognizing "Russia as the key to an acceptable outcome," Albright urged discussions with Russian leaders.[98] On April 3, Clinton sent a message to Moscow in which he expressed interest in a Yeltsin proposal for an emergency G-8 meeting on Kosovo and dangled an economic reward for Russian cooperation: he pledged that he would "work hard with partners to reschedule Russia's debt" once Russia reached an agreement on it with the IMF.[99] Three weeks later, Yeltsin called Clinton and stressed the need to bring the crisis to an end. He assigned former prime minister Viktor Chernomyrdin to work with Finnish leader Martti Ahtisaari and Strobe Talbott to formulate new peace terms and get Milošević to accept them. Yeltsin wanted a deal to be reached before a G-8 meeting scheduled for June 20 in Germany. On June 3, Milošević agreed to the terms.[100] In the following week, NATO bombing ended, Serbian forces withdrew from Kosovo, and refugees began returning to the province.

Yet, just as the crisis seemed to be resolved, a new incident threatened to spark a clash. Some Russian military leaders, unhappy with the way the conflict was ending, decided to try to establish an independent zone of occupation in northern Kosovo – something that had been discussed, but not clearly agreed to, with US and NATO leaders. On June 10, a small force of 200 to 300 Russian soldiers moved in armored personnel carriers from their peacekeeping positions in Bosnia to the airport at Pristina, the capital of Kosovo. US General Wesley Clark, supreme commander of NATO, ordered a British general to evict the Russians from the airport and to block the runways to prevent additional Russian forces or supplies from reaching the airport by air. Clark saw the issue in terms of establishing the superiority of NATO in the occupation of Kosovo and preventing Russia from unilaterally establishing a "coequal" position. The British general rejected the order as unnecessarily risking a confrontation with the Russian force. "It's not worth starting World War III," he told Clark. Instead, British soldiers gave the Russian troops food and water. The issue subsided and Russians were brought into the multinational peacekeeping force in Kosovo.[101]

On the same day that Russian soldiers drove to Pristina, Clinton declared in a televised speech to the American people that "we have achieved a victory for a safer world, for our democratic values, and for a stronger America." Although he acknowledged that the result had been "assisted by the diplomatic efforts of Russia," he indicated that NATO unity and resolve had been the main cause of success. In words that foreshadowed later American regime change campaigns, Clinton urged the Serbian people to overthrow Milošević, declaring that the United States would not aid the reconstruction of what NATO planes had destroyed as long as Milošević remained in power. Thus, Clinton reflected rising American ambitions to remove undesirable foreign leaders which would stoke future tensions with Russia.[102] The war did not bring a shining victory for human rights: in the aftermath 100,000 Serbs were displaced, some 2,000 Serbs and Albanians disappeared, and Kosovo Albanians reportedly killed scores of abducted persons in order to harvest and sell their organs. In the following years, Kosovo continued to suffer from ethnic violence, widespread unemployment, and rampant criminal activity.[103]

"Our cooperation came to the brink of collapse with Kosovo," Yeltsin told Clinton when they met in Germany on June 20. The two leaders' and countries' "friendship had reached its limits," Yeltsin warned, because of US unilateralism. Continued friendly relations would be possible "only if we act together." Seeking validation of Russia's global status despite its grave weaknesses, Yeltsin declared that "everything depends on these two powerful countries." Clinton did not respond fully to Yeltsin's desire for an equal and mutually respectful relationship – something previous Russian leaders also had sought but not achieved (except perhaps Brezhnev in the early 1970s). Although he said "yes" when Yeltsin asked whether he agreed with his statements, Clinton quickly turned the discussion away from general principles to specific issues, including getting the Duma to ratify START II despite US research on missile defense systems and "cutting missile technology going to Iran." Russia's reward for such strategic cooperation would be economic benefits, Clinton indicated. "After Kosovo, you could see renewed investment interest in Russia." Moreover, Clinton wanted to make the Jackson–Vanik amendment "go away," so Russia could gain most favored nation status for exports to the United States. But he could not persuade Congress to repeal the amendment unless Yeltsin suppressed anti-Semitic agitation by Russian nationalists and got the Duma to rescind a law on religion that restricted the activities of foreign and "non-traditional" religious groups.[104]

Yeltsin's ability to do any of the things Clinton wanted had been severely damaged by the NATO war against Serbia. Around 90 percent of Russians opposed the NATO bombing campaign and felt threatened by the alliance's actions. Communist leader Zyuganov compared "NATO ideology" to "Hitlerism." Political cartoons in *Sovetskaia Rossiia* (*Soviet Russia*, a paper affiliated with the Communist Party) depicted Clinton, Albright, and the secretary general of NATO fulfilling the earlier German drive to the east (*Drang nach Osten*). As liberal economist Yegor Gaidar told Strobe Talbott, the Kosovo war was "a disaster" for westernizers in Russia.[105]

State Department officials and Washington policy intellectuals believed that the Kosovo war would not have a significant long-term impact on relations between Russia and the West.[106] They were wrong. Although Yeltsin tried to resume cooperation, the war had a deep and lasting impact on Russian attitudes, planting fear and suspicion of US intentions that would influence Russian interpretations of later US actions. As one Russian political scientist observed, "The bombing of Yugoslavia became a turning point in the development of Russia's consciousness," leading both government officials and ordinary citizens to realize that the United States was ready to use military force to reshape the world as it wished and to intervene in regions where it had no vital national interest.[107] If Americans like Albright could portray a conflict inside Yugoslavia between ruthless Serbian nationalists and thuggish Kosovar guerrillas as part of a wider struggle "between autocracy and democracy,"[108] what would keep them from championing the cause of brutal insurgents inside Russia?

Reflection on such questions contributed to a heightened Russian interest in strong relations with the People's Republic of China. Already in 1995, in the midst of a war in Chechnya, Yeltsin had stated wishfully that leaning on China's shoulder would cause the West to treat Russia with respect. After the Kosovo war, many other Russian political figures urged an alliance with China against the United States, and within two years Russia and China concluded a friendship treaty.[109]

NEW BLOOD AND BAD BLOOD

During the Kosovo war and in its aftermath, Yeltsin made a series of moves to prepare for his retirement from Russian political life. On May 12, 1999, he dismissed the popular Prime Minister Primakov, whose friendly relations with the Communist Party made him unacceptable to Yeltsin as a possible replacement in the presidency. Three days later, Yeltsin survived several votes in the Duma on motions to impeach him because of the disastrous war in Chechnya, the violent clash with the parliament in 1993, and other issues. Then, on August 9, Yeltsin changed prime ministers again, this time appointing the little-known Vladimir Putin, who had headed the intelligence and security service (FSB) for the previous year. As Yeltsin explained in a memoir, he saw Putin as meeting Russia's need for a "new quality in the state, a steel backbone that would strengthen the political structure of authority." At the end of the year, Yeltsin surprised many by resigning the presidency six months before his term would end. After asking the Russian people to forgive him for his mistakes and failures, he named Putin as his heir, praising him as "a strong man" and a member of a new generation that would lead Russia in the next century.[110]

Noting Yeltsin's repeated references to strength, top US diplomats interpreted the move as an effort not only to consolidate Russian society around a more vigorous leader, but also to install a successor who would be capable of "standing up to pressure from outsiders." Yeltsin's anger at the United States in his last months as president supports that interpretation. At a meeting in Turkey in the middle of November, an irate Yeltsin accused Clinton of being to blame for the deterioration of American–Russian relations in the preceding years. He was still fuming about the US-led "aggression" against Serbia, which he felt left Clinton no right to give Russians sermons about a new war that had broken out with Islamist insurgents in Chechnya (discussed in the next chapter). A few weeks later, in China, Yeltsin reacted to American criticism of the Russian handling of Chechnya by complaining that Russia did not get the respect it deserved as a nation with "a full arsenal of nuclear weapons."[111]

CONCLUSION

Contrary to later American nostalgia about the Yeltsin era as a time of warm, cooperative relations between two democracies, the first post-Cold War decade actually saw a reversion to the kind of tensions and recriminations that had marked the Cold War. In America, mythological notions about how the Cold War ended fueled a haughty unilateralism that Russians increasingly resented. In Russia, a rising authoritarianism and devastating wars in Chechnya stoked American anxieties that Russia was returning to old and ugly traditions.

After Yeltsin left office, Putin would – like Yeltsin in 1992 – seek a full economic and strategic partnership with the United States. Yet, as we shall see, American–Russian relations in the twenty-first century would continue to be marred by many of the dynamics that roiled relations between the two countries at the end of the twentieth century, including American post-Cold War arrogance, Russian demands for respect of spheres of influence, and domestic political pressures for assertive policies in both countries.

18

FROM PARTNERS TO ARCHENEMIES, 2000–2020

OVERVIEW

During the first two decades of the twenty-first century, Russian–American relations degenerated from a friendly partnership to bitter enmity. The deterioration was not relentless; it came in two major phases.

After Islamist terrorists attacked New York and Washington on September 11, 2001, Presidents Vladimir V. Putin and George W. Bush took important steps toward a strategic and economic partnership. Russia provided extensive assistance to the US war against the terrorists and the Taliban regime that hosted their leaders in Afghanistan. Meanwhile, the White House and American corporations worked with the Kremlin and Russian companies to expand the export of Russia's most valuable resource, oil. Yet, by 2007, friction between Russia and Western countries, especially the United States, became so severe that journalists began to write about "The New Cold War."[1]

Relations then improved for a few years during the presidencies of Democrat Barack Obama and Dmitry Medvedev (though Putin, while Prime Minister, remained the most powerful figure in Moscow). In high-points of the "reset" of relations, Obama and Medvedev signed a new strategic arms reduction treaty in 2010 and the United States supported Russia's joining of the World Trade Organization in 2011. Yet, after that brief phase of warm cooperation, relations deteriorated even more sharply than during the preceding decade. By 2019, large majorities in each country came to believe that the other nation was treating their land as an enemy or rival.[2]

Two kinds of explanation for this drastic and dangerous deterioration of relations have been prevalent. One type has blamed Putin and Russian actions; the other has faulted US policies. Both approaches have some value, but neither provides a fully satisfactory explanation.

Many in the United States attributed the problems in American–Russian relations to the background, character, beliefs, and ambitions of one man. According to Bush's Vice President, Dick Cheney, and many others, the troubles stemmed from Putin's having been a KGB officer in the Soviet era, which spurred him to try "to reverse the trend" of the post-Cold War era.[3] Others who blamed Putin, including political scientist and diplomat Michael McFaul, stressed Putin's need for "perpetual conflict with external enemies" to maintain support for his rule. According to this line of interpretation, the main problem was Russian aggression abroad driven by a compulsion to shore up a corrupt and shaky autocracy.[4]

Such portrayals of Putin as the culprit are one-sided and misleading about the sources of American–Russian conflict. Characterizations of Putin as once and forever a KGB agent with a paranoid Cold War mentality and inveterate hostility to the West disregard dramatic changes in his views and policies.[5] After the Cold War ended, Putin resigned from the KGB, served as deputy to the reformist mayor of St. Petersburg, and even helped a young McFaul arrange a democracy-promotion workshop for the National Democratic Institute.[6] When he became president in 2000, he did not set out to reestablish the lost Soviet empire.[7] Instead, one of his first foreign policy moves was to close former Soviet bases overseas, including a listening post in Cuba – a step that shocked Russian military and intelligence officials.[8]

Depictions of Putin as being locked into a confrontational course by his desperate need for foreign enemies to overcome domestic political challenges ignore his repeated overtures for better relations, his cooperation with US leaders on issues such as removing chemical weapons from Syria and restraining Iran's nuclear program, and his persistently high approval ratings (above 60 percent).[9] Although the Kremlin used exaggerations of foreign threats to rally nationalist support, especially after facing massive domestic protests in 2011, Russian anti-American sentiment peaked in response to actual conflicts over Kosovo in 1999, Iraq in 2003, Georgia in 2008, and Ukraine in 2014.[10] Assertions that a more democratic leader than Putin would not have objected to NATO expansion or US military interventions[11] disregard how angry the supposedly democratic Boris Yeltsin became at NATO's enlargement and its bombing of Serbia in 1999.[12] Portrayals of Putin as a rabid chauvinist in this era are unfounded: his perceptions of Russian national interests were in the main stream of Russian nationalism, not among ultranationalist extremists.[13] Claims that Putin was "quite close" to radical Eurasianist philosopher Alexander Dugin[14] disregard Dugin's sharp criticisms of Putin and the differences between their worldviews (though Putin adopted elements of an older form of Eurasianism as relations with the West worsened, especially after 2011).[15]

Understanding Russia's part in the deterioration of Russian–American relations therefore requires moving beyond vilification of Putin to analysis of how his statements and actions both reflected and shaped the worldviews of many Russians. It also requires examination of how Russian mass media, increasingly under state control, stoked hostility to the United States with exaggerated or even invented depictions of American threats.

Putin repeatedly asserted that the rise in tensions between the United States and Russia stemmed from a series of American actions, including the expansion of NATO into the former Soviet Union, deployment of missile defense systems in Eastern Europe, incitement of revolutions in former Soviet states, and destructive interventions in countries from Iraq and Syria to Libya and Venezuela. Similarly, several prominent scholars have placed all (or almost all) of the blame on US policies, founded on Cold War triumphalism, a misguided pursuit of liberal global hegemony, and a shortsighted expectation that Russia would continue to be weak. According to this school of thought, Russian moves have been generally defensive or reactive, and no electable Russian leader would have passively accepted all of the US actions.[16]

As some US officials acknowledged, there is much truth in such criticisms of US policies.[17] However, it is important to recognize that there has been fault on both sides in the clashes of values, interests, and ambitions.[18]

When Putin first came to power in 1999–2000, he already had a vision for reviving Russia's economy through the development of its mineral resources and restoring its status as a respected great power.[19] Attaining those objectives did not require conflict with the United States. Instead, Putin initially hoped to pursue his goals through a partnership with America.[20] After US policies frustrated that hope, Putin's subsequent moves were often like those of a judo master grappling with a more powerful opponent.[21] Yet increasingly, over time, he shifted from reacting to US initiatives to aggressively pursuing Russian objectives, including by annexing Crimea in 2014, supporting separatists in eastern Ukraine, and intervening decisively in a civil war in Syria.

Furious at American scorn for Russia as a weak regional power, disregard for Russian interests, and rhetorical support for Russian critics of the Kremlin, Putin taunted America for having an obsolete liberal model, bragged about new Russian weapons that could threaten the United States, and depicted protesters against him as pawns of Washington. When his previously successful agenda of economic growth and political stabilization stalled by 2011, he began emphasizing the difference between Western liberalism and Russian traditional values to mobilize support from conservatives, including leaders of the Russian Orthodox Church.[22] He also relied more heavily on aides in the security services, who cracked down more harshly on opponents of the regime. Russian leaders thereby greatly inflamed American antipathy to Putin and Russia.

Hence, the collisions between the two countries are best seen not as inevitable products of the nefarious nature of Putin or the wolfish greed of US expansionism, but as conflicts unnecessarily provoked and exacerbated by individuals in each country. Often those actors – both in Washington and in Moscow – engaged in political theatrics that played well at home but antagonized foreign audiences.

Conflicts between American and Russian national identities also greatly complicated efforts to accommodate the divergent interests of the two countries. Yet the definitions of identities were not static, and the clashes between the dominant American and Russian exceptionalisms did not make conflict immutable.[23] Instead, as tensions rose and faded, then rose again, politicians and journalists with diverse ideological orientations in each country competed to shape policy agendas and images of the other nation.[24] Those contests are therefore at the center of the story of American–Russian relations in the first two decades of the twentieth century.

A BUDDING PARTNERSHIP, 2001–2002

On a sunny day in June 2001, when Presidents Bush and Putin first met, they immediately began to form a warm personal bond, based in part on their shared Christianity. At the summit meeting in Slovenia, Bush, a born-again Christian, mentioned that he had been struck by a story that Putin's mother had secretly baptized him and given him a cross, which Putin later had blessed in Israel. Putin responded by telling Bush that, when his *dacha* had burned to the ground five years earlier, the metal cross was the only thing he was able to recover from the ruins. After the meeting, when journalists asked Bush whether he trusted the Russian leader, he praised Putin as "an honest, straightforward man." Then he added: "I looked him in the eye" and "was able to get a sense of his soul."[25]

Years later, after US–Russian relations had deteriorated, American politicians and journalists regularly derided Bush for having been naïve about Putin, who, they implied, was innately incapable of having a sincere interest in good relations with the United States. In 2008, for example, Democratic presidential aspirant Hillary Clinton mockingly proclaimed that she could have told Bush that Putin "was a KGB agent. By definition he doesn't have a soul."[26]

Yet, in the first years of the twenty-first century, Putin showed a genuine desire to develop a strategic and economic partnership with the United States. From his first year as Russian President in 2000, when he felt he had generally cordial personal relations with President Bill Clinton, through

2002, Putin repeatedly expressed serious interest in the possibility of Russia joining NATO.[27] When terrorists attacked the United States in September 2001, Putin immediately called the White House to express his sympathy and offer Russia's full support. As the United States waged war in Afghanistan to eliminate the bases of the terrorists and overthrow the Taliban regime, Russia provided important help with intelligence, contacts, and logistics. Overriding vehement resistance from the Russian military, Putin opened Russian airspace to US military transport planes, urged the leaders of Uzbekistan and Tajikistan to allow the United States to establish bases in their countries, and directed veterans of the Soviet war in Afghanistan to share lessons from their experiences with US officers. In addition, Russia played a vital role in supporting American diplomats in the formation of a post-Taliban government for Afghanistan. As Russia cooperated with the United States in these ways, Putin hoped to persuade Americans to see Russia's war against Muslim separatists in Chechnya as part of what Americans called the "global war on terrorism."[28]

OF OIL AND AN OLIGARCH

In November 2001, at the height of American–Russian cooperation in Afghanistan, Bush invited his friend Putin to his ranch in Texas. "We are seeing a historic change in relationship between Russia and the United States," Bush declared in a toast. Russia was not an enemy but "a strong partner in the fight against terrorism." Hoping to broaden the nascent partnership, the two presidents issued a joint statement on the building of a new Russian–American economic relationship that would center on cooperation in the extraction and export of the vast energy resources of the former Soviet Union. In the following year, Russian companies were invited to participate in a pipeline from Baku through Georgia to Turkey, American oil companies and the Russian government cooperated in the creation of a pipeline consortium for the transport of oil from Kazakhstan to Novorossisk, and the Russian oil company Yukos began shipping oil to the United States.[29]

Yet American enthusiasts about the prospects for a major expansion of trade and investment sometimes neglected differences between American and Russian approaches to the relationship between government and business. In June 2002, for example, US Ambassador to Moscow Alexander Vershbow expressed his expectation that, in return for access to American markets and investment, Russia would "divorce politics from commerce." However, Putin believed strongly that, for Russia to recover from the weakness and confusion of the 1990s, when major state assets had been privatized at steeply discounted prices, it was vital to increase, not decrease, the Kremlin's role in managing the development of Russian resources, especially oil and natural gas, its most important sources of revenue. That did not mean there was a stark, irreconcilable difference between Russian mercantilism and American free market economics: in reality, the Kremlin took less control of Russian oil resources than the governments of most oil-exporting countries did, while the US government and giant corporations often worked closely together. But diverging ideas about the proper roles of governments and businesses did contribute to increasing friction. Putin, who had made a point of instructing Russian oligarchs to stay out of politics, was in no mood, for example, to be lectured by the arrogant head of ExxonMobil about arrangements for a purchase of Yukos.[30]

Tensions culminated in a sensational clash between Putin and the head of Yukos, Mikhail Khodorkovsky, that would have a deep impact on Russian–American relations. In the 1990s, Khodorkovsky, like other oligarchs, had utilized close ties to Kremlin officials to gain control of state assets for a fraction of their value. He also had used shady practices to cheat shareholders, including a major American investor. However, in the first years of the twenty-first century, Khodorkovsky sought to present Yukos as a model of a modern, Western-style corporation. Thinking that close ties to America would protect him from the Kremlin, Khodorkovsky repeatedly visited the United States, met with key US officials (including the Russophobic Vice President Cheney), made large donations to think tanks, and gave speeches about Russia's need to choose democracy instead of authoritarianism. Defying Putin, Khodorkovsky supported the illegal and devastating US war in Iraq in 2003, negotiated directly with China about the construction of a pipeline, used money to line up many supporters in the Duma, and proceeded with plans to sell a large stake in Yukos to ExxonMobil even after Putin told him he disapproved of the sale. Many Russian elites believed Khodorkovsky had overstepped limits respected by other oligarchs, and the overwhelming majority of Russians favored action against the tycoons. Finally, late in October 2003, masked agents of the Federal Security Service (FSB) stormed onto Khodorkovsky's plane in Siberia and arrested him. Convicted on grossly exaggerated charges of fraud, tax evasion, and embezzlement, Khodorkovsky was imprisoned until 2013.[31]

Many American politicians, journalists, and scholars denounced the show trial of Khodorkovsky as a travesty of justice and a setback to the cause of democracy. Thus, a complex case in which Putin had hesitated while Khodorkovsky repeatedly and provocatively challenged the president's authority became a simple morality play with the oligarch as hero and Putin as a tyrannical villain.[32] While Russia did not go as far as Saudi Arabia, Brazil, or Norway in state control of energy resources, Russia was stigmatized for rolling back privatization – a stigma that worsened as Putin's aides brazenly dismembered and swallowed Yukos.

Although Bush resisted pressure to toughen policy toward Putin, after 2003 American–Russian economic relations did not develop as the two leaders had hoped. In January 2004, Russia denied licenses to ExxonMobil and Chevron for offshore drilling near the island of Sakhalin. In 2005, after Secretary of Commerce Don Evans left Bush's cabinet, he declined an invitation from Putin to become chairman of the state-owned oil company Rosneft. Although Russian export of oil to the United States increased, American investment in Russia's energy sector did not. While total trade between Russia and the United States grew from around $10 billion in 2001 to near $35 billion in 2009, much of that increase stemmed from a dramatic rise in the price of oil.[33] One major consequence of the limited development of Russian–American economic relations was that it inhibited the emergence of strong lobbies for dialogue and cooperation between the two countries when conflicts erupted in other areas.[34]

BATTLING OVER THE BORDERLANDS

The most important cause of the deterioration of relations from partnership to hostility was increasing geopolitical rivalry on the periphery of Russia. Whereas in the early twentieth century the main battleground had been Manchuria and in the middle of the twentieth century the primary contested region had been Eastern Europe, in the early twenty-first century the struggle for influence focused above all on the southern and southwestern edges of Russia, from Chechnya and Georgia to Ukraine.

From the outset of Putin's leadership, he faced a challenge in the Caucasus. In August 1999, two days before President Yeltsin made Putin prime minister, the radical Chechen warlord Shamil Basaev and a Saudiborn al-Qaeda militant who used the name Abu Ibn al-Khattab led a raid into Dagestan that they hoped would ignite war against Russia throughout the northern Caucasus region. With more than 100 Arabs joining the fight, they sought to create a Muslim state between the Caspian and Black Seas. Fearing that Islamist rebellion in the Caucasus could spark the disintegration of the multinational Russian Federation, Putin resolved to crush the "bandits." In September, the bombing of apartment buildings in Moscow and Volgodonsk, widely blamed on Chechen terrorists, increased Russian support for war (in contrast to the first war in Chechnya, which had been extremely unpopular). Relying heavily on air power, Russia gained control of much of Chechnya in the fall, captured the flattened capital Grozny in February 2000, and then waged a protracted war against Chechen guerrillas, who retreated into the southern mountains.[35]

While President Clinton had condoned Yeltsin's brutal, unsuccessful war in Chechnya in the mid-1990s as necessary to hold Russia together, the Clinton administration condemned Russia's "indiscriminate killing" in the new war and urged Putin to negotiate a settlement with Chechen leaders (advice he disregarded). When Chechen terrorists seized a theater in Moscow in October 2002 and a school in southern Russia in May 2004, George W. Bush emphatically blamed the terrorists for the sieges, which led to the deaths of hundreds of adults and children. Insufficient training of the secret services and their disregard for the lives of the hostages contributed to numerous casualties during the storming of the buildings. Strikingly, many American journalists, intellectuals, and politicians not only criticized Russia's botched termination of the sieges, but also expressed sympathy with Chechen rebels – something Putin bitterly resented. During the US war in Iraq, journalists and neoconservative intellectuals blamed US soldiers' killing and torture of Iraqi civilians on mistakes and "bad apples," but they attributed Russian brutality in Chechnya to the fundamental ethos of its military and the callousness of its top political leaders. Thus, instead of strengthening American–Russian solidarity in a global struggle against Islamist terrorism, the war in Chechnya led to the blackening of American public images of Russia and Putin.[36]

As Russia struggled to pacify Chechnya, a new point of friction with America developed to the south, in Georgia. In the decade after the disintegration of the Soviet Union, Washington provided more than $1 billion in financial aid to Georgia under the leadership of former Soviet Foreign Minister Eduard Shevardnadze, who was fondly remembered for his role in the ending of the Cold War. Then widespread fraud in a November 2003 parliamentary election sparked peaceful demonstrations that led to the resignation of Shevardnadze and the election of Mikheil Saakashvili, who had earned a law degree at Columbia University.

Although the US Agency for International Development (USAID) and financier George Soros' Open Society Institute financially assisted the "Rose Revolution,"[37] it did not provoke immediate opposition from Russia. Instead, Moscow facilitated the return to Georgia of the breakaway region of Adjara and the exile of its corrupt ruler.

While ethnic Georgians predominated in Adjara, Ossetians and Abkhazians made up the majorities of the population in two other provinces that had fought bloody wars of independence against Georgia in the early 1990s. From the beginning of his presidency, Saakashvili vowed to recover the "lost territories." Georgian territorial claims triggered conflict with Russia, which had placed peacekeepers in South Ossetia and Abkhazia, and had promised to protect their autonomy. As tensions mounted, Russia barred imports of Georgian wine in 2006, upgraded relations with Abkhazia and South Ossetia in April 2008, and conducted military exercises in the Caucasus that looked to some observers like training for war against Georgia.[38]

The wise and experienced US Ambassador to Moscow, William Burns, emphatically warned in February 2008 that promoting NATO membership for Georgia would make a Russian–Georgian armed conflict likely and disrupt opportunities to work with Russia on other issues, particularly on restricting an Iranian nuclear program. But Vice President Cheney effectively championed Georgian entry into NATO as part of an effort to build a historic legacy for the outgoing Bush administration. Thus, domestic image-making and ideology trumped sober realism.[39] Although President Bush privately cautioned Saakashvili against military adventurism, he also pushed NATO to pledge in April 2008 that Georgia (along with Ukraine) would become a member of NATO, something Russia had adamantly stated it opposed. The impulsive and emotional Saakashvili also may have been emboldened by top US officials' public statements of general support for Georgia, by the enthusiasm of junior officials dazzled by his pro-American vision of democratization, by the fact that 2,000 US troops participated in a military exercise with Georgian forces in the summer of 2008, and by the presence of 130 US military advisers in the Georgian Ministry of Defense.[40]

On August 7, 2008, after artillery and mortar exchanges between Ossetian and Georgian forces, Saakashvili ordered an invasion of South Ossetia. Georgian rockets killed Russian peacekeepers, Georgian tanks rolled into the capital, Tskhinvali, and Georgian fighters shot hundreds of Ossetians. Early on August 8, Russian soldiers counterattacked and soon drove Georgian troops out of South Ossetia. With Putin determined to make Georgians pay, Russian forces drove toward Tbilisi. Putin considered overthrowing Saakashvili until French leader Nicolas Sarkozy dissuaded him.[41] Bush's advisors seriously considered military intervention, including bombing a tunnel between Russia and South Ossetia and providing Stinger anti-aircraft missiles to Georgia. Fortunately, cooler heads prevailed. Through telephone calls to the Russian chief of staff, the chairman of the

US Joint Chiefs of Staff helped to avert conflict between US and Russian forces and even secured Russian acquiescence as the United States airlifted 1,800 Georgian troops who had been serving in Iraq back to Georgia.[42]

Although Saakashvili started the war, American media overwhelmingly depicted it as a simple and blatant case of Russian aggression. Editors compared it to the invasions of Hungary, Czechoslovakia, and Afghanistan. Columnists likened Putin to Hitler. Cartoonists resurrected old symbols, especially the bloodthirsty bear, to stigmatize Russia. Thus, even as the United States was bogged down in much more devastating wars in Iraq and Afghanistan, many Americans cast Russia as a demonic Other.[43]

Ignoring the local origins of the war in a long-term conflict between Ossetians and Georgia, American commentators depicted it as a confrontation between Russia and the West, between barbarism and civilization, between evil and good. Saakashvili had cleverly established the foundations for this treatment by investing since 2004 in lobbying in Washington that promoted the notion that Georgia was "one of us." After launching the attack on South Ossetia, he had easy access to American television and newspapers, where he gave interviews and published columns that distorted the conflict and claimed it was about "American values."[44]

The short, five-day war had a lasting and poisonous impact on Russian–American relations. In the United States, former Clinton administration officials Strobe Talbott and Ronald Asmus promoted the idea that the real cause of the war had been imperialist Russia's drive to obstruct Georgia's laudable desire to join NATO.[45] Even after a report by the Council of the European Union unambiguously pinned responsibility for starting the war on Georgia, journalists habitually referred to it simply as a "Russian invasion." In Russia, the overwhelming majority of the public, including many pro-Western liberals, denounced Georgian aggression, while a significant minority (22 percent) blamed the United States for the war. Like Putin, many Russians also felt disgusted by how US officials and journalists could "swap good and bad, black and white."[46]

Films helped to entrench one-sided views of the conflict. *Olympus Inferno*, which premiered on Russian television in 2009, focused on Georgian atrocities witnessed by an American scientist. Later, *5 Days of War* (2011), a Hollywood production financed by Georgian businessmen, dramatized Russian atrocities and showed an American journalist struggling to reveal the truth about the Russian aggression.[47]

While Georgia was a small nation that did relatively little trade with Russia, Ukraine was much larger, had roughly ten times as many people, and had deep economic connections to Russia. Ukraine became an

American–Russian battleground when the 2004 presidential campaign there pitted Viktor Yanukovych, whose base of support was in the eastern and southeastern regions most closely intertwined with Russia, and Viktor Yushchenko, who had bases of support in western and central Ukraine and was married to a former US State Department official. Russia provided substantial financial support to the Yanukovych campaign, and Putin made personal appearances on behalf of Yanukovych (though he did not like him personally). In November 2004, Yanukovych reportedly garnered 49 percent of the votes while Yushchenko received 46 percent. Outraged by news of ballot stuffing and multiple voting, 200,000 protesters in Kiev demanded a new election. Many young activists had received training in social mobilization sponsored by Freedom House. Yushchenko's party benefited from training provided by the International Republican Institute and National Democratic Institute. Although Ukrainians were the primary actors, the US democracy promotion organizations claimed they played major roles in the developments, and one prominent analyst later concluded that the foreign assistance was "consequential in tipping the balance in favor of the democratic challengers."[48] When Yushchenko defeated Yanukovych by a margin of 8 percent, American politicians and journalists hailed a triumph for democracy and for Ukrainians' supposed desires to emulate the example of the United States.[49] Some US officials also excitedly believed that they now had "an opportunity to redraw the map of Europe and Eurasia" by bringing Ukraine into NATO much sooner than they had previously thought possible.[50]

Yet the aftermath of the so-called Orange Revolution proved disappointing to its American supporters. The Ukrainian parliament rejected a bill Yushchenko promoted to allow foreign troops to conduct training exercises in Ukraine, and most Ukrainians opposed joining NATO until 2014.[51] Under the increasingly unpopular Yushchenko, Ukraine's weak economy continued to be plagued by corruption. After Yanukovych's Party of the Regions won a plurality of the vote in fair elections in 2006, he returned to being prime minister, and then in 2010 he was elected president with 49 percent of the vote. Thus, the Orange Revolution did not bring a decisive victory for American-supported forces in Ukraine, which remained deeply divided, with pro-Russian and anti-NATO sentiment especially strong in the southeast and east.

Ukraine also became a site of contestation over memories of the past. In 2007 and 2010, Yushchenko pandered to nationalists in western Ukraine by awarding the title of Hero of Ukraine to Roman Shukhevych and Stepan Bandera, leaders of nationalist forces that massacred Jews and Poles during the Second World War. In the same years, Russia launched a propaganda campaign against the valorization of "fascists" during the Second World War.[52] This "memory war" would fuel an actual war later.

Conservative figures in Moscow worried that the Western-supported revolutions in Georgia and Ukraine were rehearsals for a regime change in Russia itself. They developed conspiracy theories about Western plots to use a fifth column to undermine Russia that mobilized support for the Kremlin and justified suppression of opposition.[53] Putin shared conservatives' fears. In January 2006, he asserted that "foreign secret services" were financing nongovernmental organizations (NGOs) in Russia, and the Kremlin then imposed new restrictions on NGOs. Although Western writers often asserted that such measures stemmed from Putin's peculiar personal "paranoia" about subversion, his distaste for revolution was shared by the majority of Russians, who valued the stability of his presidency and did not want to risk returning to the turmoil of the 1990s.[54]

Fears that Americans hoped to promote a revolution in Russia were not entirely unfounded: critics of Bush's embrace of Putin both inside and outside the administration did seek to alter Russia's government. One of the most prominent academic critics, Michael McFaul, persistently focused on the completion of a democratic revolution in Russia that had been left unfinished in the 1990s. In a 2005 paper on "regime change," McFaul urged "condemnation of Russia's antidemocratic policies" in order to embolden reformers inside Russia who were still fighting for democracy. McFaul's ideas, shared by other leading US experts on Russia, were welcomed by Vice President Cheney, who secretly met with a Russian opponent of Putin, Vladimir Ryzhkov. Then, in May 2006, Cheney flew to Lithuania to give a major speech to leaders of the Baltic states that had recently joined NATO and leaders of Black Sea countries that aspired to membership in NATO. Describing the Baltic region as "the very front lines of freedom," Cheney cast Russia as a land of unfreedom. Hailing the "brave leaders of color revolutions," Cheney forecast that what had happened in Tbilisi and Kiev would occur also in Moscow.[55] The provocative speech angered Putin, who called it "a relic of Cold War thinking."[56]

In the wake of the "color revolutions," Putin seemed to US leaders to become a different man than the partner against terrorism in 2001. In July 2006, Bush confided to the prime minister of Slovenia: "I think Putin is not a democrat anymore. He's a tsar. I think we've lost him."[57] Bolstered by Russia's increased revenue from high oil prices and worried about possible challenges to his power, Putin had in fact grown more assertive internationally and more authoritarian domestically.

Many observers saw a turning point in Putin's speech at the Munich Conference on Security Policy in February 2007. After years of restraining Russian responses to US policies, Putin now had the nerve to sharply criticize the United States, particularly for the horrific war in Iraq, which had been launched under false pretenses and without United Nations (UN) authorization. Although Russian forces had killed tens of thousands of civilians in Chechnya in the preceding years, Putin dwelled on how many people were dying because of "illegitimate actions" by the United States and its allies. Referring to those military operations, Putin chastised the United States for its "almost uncontained hyper use of force" and charged that the United States had "overstepped its national borders in every way." Although Putin criticized "Cold War bloc thinking," urged cooperation on security issues, and recalled how "the fall of the Berlin Wall was possible thanks to a historic choice" for freedom by Russians as well as other peoples, many Americans considered the speech the declaration of a second Cold War.[58] Senator John McCain, a champion of the war against Iraq, who attended the conference, responded to Putin by declaring that "Moscow must understand that it cannot enjoy a genuine partnership with the West so long as its actions, at home and abroad, conflict fundamentally with the core values of the Euro-Atlantic democracies."[59] That hypocritical statement, made after years when the United States flagrantly violated such values in its "global war on terror," together with Putin's audacious speech, reflected how American and Russian elites were returning to the finger-pointing and scapegoating that had marred American–Russian relations for much of the previous century.

While Putin had changed, so had Bush. In the 2000 presidential campaign, he had declared that "the only people who are going to reform Russia are Russians," yet in 2006 he approved Cheney's crusading speech on the edge of Russia. Bush disregarded how his administration's "Freedom Agenda," including war in Iraq, support for color revolutions, and sharp criticism of a rollback of democracy in Russia, had antagonized Putin and intensified his drive toward more authoritarian rule. During the Russian–Georgian war in 2008, alarmed that Russia might engineer a regime change in Tbilisi, Bush reverted to Cold War rhetoric about rallying "the free world" against Russian aggression.[60]

At a press conference near the end of his presidency, Bush said his relationship with Putin was "still friendly" and he emphasized that, despite the recent tensions, there was "common ground," especially on the issue of nuclear proliferation. Yet, as Bush left office he handed his successor a very mixed legacy, with an accumulation of negative emotions and images both in Russia and in the United States.[61]

THE OBAMA ADMINISTRATION AND THE FAILED "RESET" OF RELATIONS

Democrat Barack Obama, who observed the drastic deterioration of relations with Russia during his successful presidential campaign in 2008, decided to pursue a fresh start by downplaying ideology and focusing on pragmatic cooperation where the interests of the two countries converged. The "reset" policy achieved important results from 2009 to 2011. Obama worked closely with Dmitry Medvedev, a young, liberal-sounding lawyer who became president in May 2008 when Putin shifted to being prime minister. Through fourteen meetings and phone calls, Obama and Medvedev agreed on the terms of a new strategic arms reduction treaty (New START), signed in April 2010, that required both sides to reduce the number of deployed strategic nuclear warheads from 2,200 to 1,550 by 2018. Following a separate Obama–Medvedev agreement in July 2009, Russia allowed NATO to greatly expand its shipments of supplies across Russian territory to forces fighting Taliban insurgents in Afghanistan. That northern supply route proved especially important when Pakistan cut off the shipment of supplies across its territory to Afghanistan after a US raid in May 2011 killed Osama bin Laden at a compound in Pakistan.[62]

Following the achievements in strategic cooperation, the main area of future opportunity that Obama and Vice President Joe Biden saw was building stronger ties of trade and commerce. In a speech at Moscow State University in March 2011, Biden hailed large recent investments in Russia by corporations such as Pepsico, major deals by American oil companies with Russian partners, and the expansion of manufacturing in Russia by big companies such as General Electric. With US assistance, Russia joined the World Trade Organization in December 2011, an important step toward the expanded economic relationship Bush and Putin had envisioned but not achieved. That year total trade between the two countries reached a peak of $43 billion, including $35 billion worth of American imports from Russia.[63]

Yet, even as the reset seemed to be fulfilling its promise, US engagement with Russia stalled. After developing close ties with Medvedev, Obama withdrew from such intense involvement once the New START treaty had been signed. Some of the officials who then played more prominent roles had histories of tensions with the Kremlin. Secretary of State Hillary Clinton outraged Putin by criticizing fraud in a Russian election in December 2011. When the blatant fraud triggered massive protests in Moscow that seemed to some participants to have the spirit of a "revolution," Putin accused Clinton of sending a signal that instigated the demonstrations.[64] That episode gave Putin and his aides a pretext to develop an aggressive media campaign against opposition leaders, who were accused of being American agents.[65]

Michael McFaul, who had overseen the design of the reset policy as the top Russia expert at the National Security Council, believed that the United States could champion democratic opponents of Putin at the same time as it worked with the Russian government on important issues. After McFaul became Ambassador to Moscow at the end of 2011, he immediately angered the Kremlin by meeting with liberal Russian critics of Putin and vigorously expressing moral support for them. Such American words and gestures made it easier for the Kremlin to depict the anti-Putin activists (who were often young, Westernized professionals) as pro-American subversives. Putin's denunciations of alleged American meddling also may have helped him to win re-election in 2012 by mobilizing Russians outside the largest cities. According to McFaul, by supporting Russian advocates of universal values Americans "were a threat to Russia's increasingly autocratic regime," and Putin "genuinely believed that we were seeking to subvert his regime." After the election, the Kremlin clamped down harder on NGOs and drove American democracy promotion organizations (the National Democratic Institute and International Republican Institute) out of the country.[66]

US officials' exaggeration of their ability to influence Russian politics contributed to the rising friction. Obama and his top advisors had hoped that they could build up the diminutive Medvedev's authority at the expense of Putin, whom they distrusted and disliked. On the eve of a trip to Moscow in July 2009, Obama annoyed Putin by saying that, while Medvedev understood "that the old Cold War approach to US–Russia relations is outdated," Putin still had "one foot in the old ways of doing business." In June 2010, when an FBI plan to arrest Russian spies in America threatened to create a flap that would damage relations with Moscow, Secretary of Defense Robert Gates suggested that the administration should avoid embarrassing Medvedev by arresting the spies while he was visiting the United States and instead try "to flip this on Putin." In March 2011, Biden told prominent Russian opponents of Putin that he thought Putin should not run for a new term as president in 2012. Biden's brash remarks, Gates's unexecuted scheme, and Obama's condescending scorn reflected a serious misreading of the situation: Medvedev lacked an independent base of power, and Putin remained the dominant figure in Moscow.[67]

Even more than Biden and Obama, key members of Congress exaggerated Washington's potential to alter Russian conduct. In December 2012, Congress imposed travel bans and sanctions on Russian officials who had been involved in the prosecution, beating, and death while in custody of Sergei Magnitsky, a tax accountant who, it was claimed, had exposed schemes to steal assets of the most important American investor in Russia, Bill Browder. After Magnitsky's death in 2009, the pugnacious Browder launched a determined campaign to bring Magnitsky's killers to justice through publicity and lobbying Congress. Prodded by Browder, Senator Benjamin Cardin (Democrat, Maryland), an ardent crusader for human rights in Russia, introduced the Magnitsky Act in 2010 and pushed for its approval in spite of opposition from the Obama administration. Although he knew Russian oligarchs and political leaders, including Putin, tended to show no weakness and to escalate confrontations, Browder somehow expected the visa restrictions and sanctions to "send shock waves through the Russian elite" and "destroy the equilibrium of the Russian authorities." The Magnitsky Act, finally passed in 2012, repealed the Jackson–Vanik restrictions dating from 1974, yet imposed new sanctions at the same time. It succeeded in angering Putin, but, instead of backing down, he became more defiant. Accused officers received awards instead of punishment, and the Kremlin retaliated against the Magnitsky Act by cruelly imposing a ban on American adoptions of Russian children, many of whom had special needs that wealthy American adoptive parents could afford to address.[68]

Although Congress, the White House, and the American press lacked the ability to alter Russia's political course in a positive way, they could demonstrate their sympathy with Russians who seemed to embody American values. The most sensational opportunity for that appeared in February 2012, when, in the last weeks of the presidential campaign, members of a feminist group called Pussy Riot entered the Cathedral of Christ the Savior in Moscow, pulled colorful balaclavas over their faces, and shouted a profanity-laced "punk prayer" for the Mother of God to "chase Putin out." Putin's first reaction was only to mock the group for having earlier filmed themselves in a public sexual orgy. Yet the vulgar antics of Pussy Riot offended many Russians, especially those who considered themselves Orthodox, and it outraged Patriarch Kirill, whose support Putin increasingly needed.[69] The feminists' stunt also appalled many political opponents of Putin, who thought the tasteless provocation would benefit the Kremlin and mobilize its conservative supporters. Yet, when three members of Pussy Riot were sentenced to two years in prison, they became martyrs for the cause of freedom in the eyes of many Americans.[70]

Such international support for Pussy Riot was seized on by the Kremlin as new evidence of a Western plot to undermine Russia. The Putin regime used the case to expand a campaign portraying Russia as a stronghold of "traditional values" in contrast to the allegedly degenerate United States.[71]

Around the same time, the Obama administration demonstrated its sense of American moral superiority and its scorn for a Russian law that banned homosexual propaganda among minors by sending famous retired gay and lesbian athletes in a delegation to the Olympics in Sochi, in southern Russia – despite the objections of some US officials to provocatively politicizing a sporting event. Thus, although Obama initially had distanced himself from Bush's "Freedom Agenda," his administration's rhetoric and gestures toward Russia became increasingly moralistic and ideological as relations became more fraught with tension.[72] Putin's regime at the same time embraced a conservative agenda uniting domestic and foreign policy to place Russia as a champion of an anti-liberal and anti-American world.[73]

More important than media campaigns, congressional interference, and leaders' personal irritations in the deterioration of relations were a series of international developments, including US deployment of missile defense systems (MDSs) and civil wars in Libya and Syria. Earlier, in December 2001, when the Bush administration first informed Putin of its intention to withdraw from the 1972 Anti-Ballistic Missile Treaty, Putin called the decision "a big mistake," but then set the issue aside in order to focus on development of a partnership with the United States. As the Bush administration moved forward with plans to place missile defense interceptors in Poland and a related radar installation in the Czech Republic in 2006 and 2007, Russian military officials expressed concern that in the future the United States might give the system additional capabilities that would compromise Russia's deterrence of nuclear attacks. Yet Putin refrained from reacting emotionally to a plan he had been unable to alter. After tensions with the Obama administration began to rise, Russian officials' tone changed: in November 2011 Putin called the erection of an MDS "a danger to Russia" and Medvedev threatened to deploy short-range Iskander missiles in Kaliningrad, next to Poland. Despite US efforts to ease Russian concerns by modifying the phases of US deployments, friction increased. Although the United States insisted that the purpose of the MDS was to protect Europe from Iranian missiles, the United States went ahead with deployment of an MDS in Romania in 2016 after Russia helped the United States get a deal constraining Iranian nuclear development in 2015. Russian officials then denounced the MDS as a violation of the 1987 Intermediate-Range Nuclear Forces

(INF) Treaty amid ominous public discussion in Russia of a nuclear confrontation that would leave Romania in "smoking ruins."[74]

In the case of Libya, tacit cooperation soured into a sharp sense of betrayal among Russians. In March 2011, as dictator Muammar Qaddafi's forces advanced toward rebels in eastern Libya, Biden urged Medvedev to allow a UN resolution authorizing the use of force to prevent Qaddafi from crushing his foes in Benghazi. After stressing that the military mission must be a limited effort to avert a slaughter, Medvedev agreed not to veto the UN resolution. US, British, and French bombing of Libya then went far beyond humanitarian protection of the rebels to assisting their bloody overthrow of Qaddafi by October 2011. Already in May, Medvedev felt betrayed and expressed his anger at the US bait and switch in a meeting with Obama. Putin and most of the Russian foreign policy establishment felt that a naïve, weak Medvedev had been deceived into acquiescing in another American regime change campaign, one that led to years of fighting and turmoil in Libya. They were right. Although Obama had been ambivalent, his advisors, including Hillary Clinton and Ben Rhodes, had been eager to oust Qaddafi, and they had seen the UN resolution for bombing in defense of Benghazi as only the first step in the campaign. The episode had a deep and lasting impact on Putin's view of the United States.[75]

At the same time as the Libya campaign, in August 2011, Obama began calling for Syrian President Bashar al-Assad to step aside and approved modest aid to some of the groups fighting against his government. Since Syria had long been a client of Russia, which maintained an important naval base at Tartus, this marked yet another challenge to Russian interests. Putin, who knew that a rising number of Syrian rebels were radical Islamists, was appalled that, when he asked US officials who they envisioned would replace Assad, they said they did not know. Even though some of Obama's advisors suspected that US intervention could make conditions in Syria worse, they still felt that the United States had to do something in response to the violence and human suffering. In September 2013, after reports that the Syrian regime had used chemical weapons (which Obama said earlier would be crossing a red line), Obama came to the verge of ordering air strikes against Syria. However, Putin persuaded him instead to pursue a plan for the removal and destruction of Syria's chemical weapons.[76]

As that largely successful effort indicated, US–Russian cooperation remained possible. In a surprise to Obama, Russia also played a very helpful role in a long multilateral drive to halt Iran's nuclear program. By approving tougher economic sanctions, delaying a shipment of anti-aircraft missiles, and facilitating the success of negotiations, Russia contributed significantly to the reaching of a deal with Iran in 2015. Moreover, Russia showed serious, sustained interest in working with the United States for joint action against al-Qaeda and Islamic State terrorist groups in Syria. Unfortunately, opposition from the Pentagon blocked the implementation of an agreement reached by Foreign Minister Sergei Lavrov and Secretary of State John Kerry (who had replaced Clinton for Obama's second term).[77]

Yet the overall trajectory of Russian–American relations was a downward spiral after Putin returned to being Russia's president in 2012. In the summer of 2013, Edward Snowden, a contractor for the National Security Agency who had released to the press thousands of classified documents that showed pervasive US spying around the world, flew to Moscow. Kerry asked Russia to extradite Snowden for trial in the United States, but Putin refused. When Russia granted Snowden asylum in August, an embarrassed and angry Obama canceled plans to meet with Putin at a G20 summit in St. Petersburg.[78]

A few months later, a dangerous confrontation developed in Ukraine as a result of a tug-of-war between the European Union (EU) and Russia. In November 2013, Ukrainian president Viktor Yanukovych triggered a political crisis by deciding not to sign an Association Agreement with the EU that would have compelled potentially destabilizing economic reforms. Instead, he accepted a $15 billion loan and a deep discount on gas from Russia, which hoped to pull Ukraine into a Eurasian Economic Union. Protesters who wanted Ukraine to be integrated into modern, prosperous Europe became radicalized as Yanukovych's security forces brutally tried to disperse demonstrations. US Assistant Secretary of State Victoria Nuland, wife of the neoconservative champion of regime change Robert Kagan, focused on ensuring that a pro-Western technocrat she favored would become prime minister in a reorganized government.[79] In early February 2014, a recording of a crude conversation between Nuland and the US Ambassador in Kyiv, posted on YouTube, seemed to show that the United States was plotting behind the scenes as well as giving moral support to demonstrators.

For weeks, protesters hurled Molotov cocktails at truncheon-wielding riot police on the other side of barricades. Then, on February 20, according to some scholars, snipers fired on both sides, killing scores of protesters and police. (While some asserted that the government ordered snipers to fire, others claimed snipers worked for far-right Ukrainian forces.[80]) In a telephone conversation on February 21, Obama and Putin agreed to push for implementation of an agreement for formation of a national unity government and new elections in Kyiv. But the militant crowd rejected the compromise, and Yanukovich, fearing assassination, fled. American diplomats celebrated what they regarded as a great victory, and Obama stopped reaching out to Putin.[81]

Faced with the revolution in Kyiv, Putin quickly decided to secure control of Crimea, a strategic peninsula that Khrushchev had transferred to Ukraine in 1954, but that the overwhelming majority of Russians had considered theirs for centuries, ever since Russia seized it in war against the Ottoman Empire. At the end of February, Russian soldiers in green uniforms without insignia captured the Crimean parliament building and joined other Russian forces in surrounding Ukrainian bases. In a hastily organized referendum in March, more than 90 percent of Crimeans reportedly voted to secede from Ukraine (though many of the Tatar minority boycotted the referendum). Two days later, Putin signed a treaty for the annexation of Crimea and delivered a speech full of nationalist pride in Crimea's return "home" to Russia.[82]

Television documentaries that centered on interviews with Putin also sought to consolidate national sentiment around the idea of a Great Russia, in part by using the image of the United States as the hostile Other. In a conversation with Andrey Kondrashov, creator of the Russian television documentary *Crimea: The Way Home* (2015), Putin declared that Russians were moved to help Crimea's inhabitants by "an outburst of nationalism in Ukraine." He also proclaimed that Russia had prepared to use nuclear weapons if a third party (meaning the United States) intervened in the conflict in Ukraine – a statement that provoked international indignation. In Vladimir Soloviev's documentary *The President* (2015), Putin asserted that the Russian security services had traced direct contacts between guerrillas in the North Caucasus and US special services representatives, who, he claimed, helped the militants with transport.[83]

Putin and his propaganda aides claimed that he acted quickly during the crisis in Ukraine because of the imminent threat that neo-Nazi thugs from Kyiv would invade Crimea. In contrast, Western critics asserted that the Russian invasion was part of a long-planned drive to reconstruct much of the old Soviet empire. However, scholars have argued convincingly that Putin and his aides hurriedly put into motion an improvised operation primarily because they feared that Russia would lose access to the vital base for its Black Sea Fleet and that, if Ukraine were to join NATO, Crimea might even host NATO ships and troops.[84]

In March, a separatist movement that had deep local roots but was also fired up by alarmist Russian media reports emerged in eastern Ukraine.[85] Although 70 percent of the people in eastern Ukraine wanted to keep the country intact, in April separatists proclaimed the establishment of people's republics in the regions of Donetsk and Lugansk (Luhansk). When professional armed forces without identifying insignia occupied key buildings in the town of Slovyansk on April 12, it marked the beginning of a long struggle against Ukrainian paramilitary and regular military forces. Igor Girkin, a former colonel in the Russian security service (FSB) with passionate monarchist views, became the leader of the Donetsk armed forces. When Ukrainian forces seemed on the verge of defeating the insurgents in the summer of 2014, Russia escalated its support, including providing anti-aircraft missiles. In July, at the height of the fighting, a civilian airliner flying from Amsterdam to Malaysia was shot down, killing almost 300 on board the plane, most of them Dutch citizens. (Although Russia stubbornly denied responsibility, Dutch investigations later concluded that the plane had been downed by a Buk missile that had been transported from Russia to Ukraine.) American magazines immediately blamed Putin personally for the shoot-down. After insurgents, with support from Russian "volunteers," drove Ukrainian forces back in August, they signed a ceasefire in September. However, artillery shelling and skirmishes along the front lines continued in the following years.[86]

Despite loud calls from some American politicians for providing weapons to Ukrainian forces, Obama decided that doing so would provoke a further escalation of Russian backing of eastern separatists. Washington therefore supplied only non-lethal equipment to Ukrainian units. It imposed sanctions against some of Putin's closest aides in response to the annexation of Crimea and then a new round of sanctions in July 2014 in response to the intensified fighting in eastern Ukraine. The US and European Union sanctions provoked defiance from Russia, which imposed countersanctions against imports of European food.

Both Russian and American leaders made false statements about events in Ukraine that eroded what little trust remained between them and widened the divide between their nations' views. Putin lied about the role of Russian special forces in the seizure of Crimea. His aides exaggerated the real but localized menace from Ukrainian ultranationalist paramilitary groups and invented or distorted some incidents. On the other hand, Secretary of State Kerry falsely claimed in a speech in Kyiv in March 2014 that protesters against Yanukovych were "unarmed except with ideas" and that they had stood "peacefully against tyranny." (In reality, some protesters were armed with hunting rifles as well as Molotov cocktails.) Like Kerry, in a speech in Estonia in September 2014, Obama disregarded the prominent role of neo-fascist members of the Svoboda (Freedom) and Pravy Sektor

(Right Sector) groups in fighting in Kyiv, insisted that the protests in Ukraine "were not led by neo-Nazis and fascists," and denied that they aimed at an armed seizure of power.[87]

The dishonest rhetoric of politicians, together with media images of evil enemies, helped spur sharp increases in Russian and American popular antipathies to the opposing countries. After conflict erupted over Ukraine in 2014, the percentage of Russians with positive views of the United States and its policies declined to just 18 percent. Although the Kremlin actively promoted negative images of a hostile United States to encourage Russians to rally around it, anti-Americanism and authoritarianism were not simply manufactured artificially by elites, transmitted by television, and passively absorbed by brainwashed masses, as émigré Russian journalists claimed. Liberal-leaning Russians who protested the annexation of Crimea were ostracized by fellow citizens and they were increasingly perceived as an ally of the foreign adversary. Putin called them "national traitors" in his annexation speech, thus portraying all the domestic opposition as a part of Russia's American Other.[88] On the other side, the percentage of Americans who viewed Russia as the greatest enemy of the United States rose from only 2 percent in 2012 to 18 percent in 2015. Thus, Americans ranked Russia as a greater threat than even rocket-rattling North Korea, longtime foe Iran, and rapidly growing China. The shift from valuing Russia as a partner against terrorism to loathing Russia as America's archenemy would go even further in the following years.[89]

AMERICAN–RUSSIAN TENSION PEAKS: 2016–2020

During and after the US presidential election campaign of 2016, American–Russian tension rose to a frenzied intensity not seen since the confrontations of the early 1980s. The increasing American hostility toward Russia stemmed in part from Russian interference in the election. Yet the real grievances were greatly inflamed by American politicians and journalists, who were determined to depict Russia as a terrible menace to the United States and the entire world order. Some left-leaning writers attributed the threat inflation to the US military–industrial complex's need for foreign enemies, yet they presented little direct evidence of the influence of arms manufacturers.[90] A more convincing explanation centers on how American journalists and politicians sought to tarnish domestic foes by associating them with Russia, to deflect attention from problems inside the United States, and to affirm American moral superiority in spite of US conduct that raised doubts about American claims to exceptional virtue. Meanwhile, conservative and nationalist media in Russia, particularly state-controlled television stations, depicted American liberalism as an immoral and aggressively universalist force that undermined traditional family and spiritual values.[91] Thus, the problems in American–Russian relations stemmed not only from conflicts of vital interests, but also from the ways in which the two nations defined their identities in contrast to each other and used each other as scapegoats for their own failings.

As the United States entered the election year, American political and media elites expressed great exasperation at Russia's successful use of air power to attack US-supported rebels against President Bashar al-Assad of Syria. Putin had launched the military intervention in 2015 mainly to avert the loss of an ally, but also to enhance Russian influence in the Middle East and raise Russia's international status.[92] By the beginning of 2017, Russian bombing, combined with ground assaults by the Syrian Army and its Iranian and Lebanese allies, crushed the rebels in their stronghold of east Aleppo, where they had refused to distance themselves from their al-Qaeda-linked Islamist allies. Simmering frustration at Obama's refusal to order air strikes and America's seeming impotence while Putin acted decisively was like dry kindling waiting for a match.[93]

In the middle of the election campaign, in July 2016, a controversy erupted over alleged Russian hacking into the computers of the Democratic National Committee (DNC). Emails released by WikiLeaks showed that DNC officials had inappropriately sought to aid Hillary Clinton against her Democratic rival Bernie Sanders. Journalists who backed Clinton quickly tried to turn attention from the embarrassing emails to the idea of "a Kremlin conspiracy to aid Donald J. Trump," the Republican nominee.[94]

Russia continued to figure prominently in the presidential campaign in other ways. Trump and his running mate, Mike Pence, repeatedly asserted that Trump would be more effective in dealing with Putin and that Putin was a stronger leader than Obama – praise that Russian media used to bolster Putin's prestige. On the other side, Clinton and her supporters repeatedly called Trump "Putin's puppet," insinuating that Trump would do Russia's bidding at the expense of US interests.[95] That tactic resembled the way Putin branded his domestic opponents tools of the United States or the West.

The attacks on Trump did not deter many of his blue collar and middle-class white supporters from voting for him. Influenced by Trump's positive comments about Putin, Republican approval of the Russian leader rose to 37 percent during the campaign.[96]

In a stunning surprise, Trump won the electoral college vote even while losing the popular vote. As they overcame their shock, liberal journalists, with the collaboration of intelligence officials, revived the old accusations about Russian hacking, often claiming that Russian interference had caused Clinton's defeat. Although an official intelligence assessment delivered to President-elect Trump early in January presented very little concrete evidence, newspapers gave the report banner headlines on front pages. And, with the aid of anonymous leaks from intelligence sources, partisan journalists tirelessly promoted suspicions and circulated discredited or unverified information, thereby disillusioning veteran Russian journalists who previously had admired American media standards.[97] *Time* and other magazines repeatedly propagated the widely held theory of Russian control over Trump with sensational covers.[98]

In reality, Trump took many steps that were contrary to Russia's interests, including launching an air strike against Russia's ally Syria, abrogating the nuclear deal with Iran, sending advanced weapons to Ukraine, opposing completion of a gas pipeline from Russia to Germany, and promoting the overthrow of the government of Venezuela (which Russia supported). However, those actions did not shake many liberals' belief that Trump was Putin's marionette.[99]

A special counsel appointed by the Department of Justice, Robert Mueller, painstakingly investigated the accusations of collusion and election interference for two years. He found convincing evidence that Russians had interfered in the US election, in part by trying to exacerbate political polarization with Facebook ads or spurious electronic messages. But they were a very small share of social media communication and had little impact.[100] Mueller did not establish that there had been any collusion between the Trump campaign and the Russian government.[101]

As Mueller's findings became public knowledge, the demonization of Putin and Russia shifted. For example, *Time* switched its focus to "Russia's Other Plot." In April 2019, a neon red cover depicted Putin standing behind a globe, staring intently at his "growing empire of rogue states," from Iran and Syria to the southern part of Africa, Venezuela, Peru, Cuba, and Nicaragua – a diverse array of states where actual Russian influence ranged from substantial to negligible. Similarly, State Department officials and politicians claimed that Russia, with its "malign efforts" across the globe, was the locus of evil and autocracy in the post-Cold War world.[102]

American vilification of Putin also centered on allegations of heinous violence. Senator Marco Rubio (Republican, Florida) dramatically charged in January 2017 that Putin was "a war criminal" because of Russia's bombing of Aleppo, a Syrian city partially controlled by Islamist terrorists. No prominent figure asked whether by that standard George W. Bush and Barack

Obama were war criminals because of the US bombing of Iraqi cities and Afghan villages, which caused many times more civilian deaths. With even more fervor than Rubio, Senator John McCain (Republican, Arizona) repeatedly thundered that Putin was "a murderer and a thug." Like McCain, many Americans found Putin personally culpable for the deaths of Russians who criticized or opposed him.[103]

Strong evidence indicates that Russian intelligence agents did in fact poison two former FSB officers in England. Alexander Litvinenko, who died in 2006, had called Putin a pedophile and worked for an exiled tycoon who sought to undermine Putin's government. Sergei Skripal, who almost died in 2018, had been convicted for selling Russian secrets to Britain and released in a prisoner exchange, but had then continued working with foreign intelligence services against Russia. Since Putin awarded a medal to one of the men accused of poisoning Litvinenko and had repeatedly said that traitors must be punished, there was reason to believe that he had ordered the killing of both Litvinenko and Skripal.[104]

Little or no evidence implicated Putin directly in other murders (as even some of the most vehement accusers conceded).[105] The deaths of some Russians that Americans initially added to the list of Putin's victims, such as former government official Mikhail Lesin, were later determined to have been caused by accidents.[106]

Yet prominent journalists took it as an established fact that Putin was a serial "killer," as one television commentator complained to Trump. When Trump replied that there were a lot of killers and the United States was not so innocent, journalists and politicians heatedly condemned his suggestion of a moral equivalency between virtuous America and depraved Russia.[107]

The divergence of American views of Russia had grown wider than at any time since the early 1930s, when liberals had admired the state-driven Stalinist modernization and conservatives had deplored the bloody, atheist, Communist dictatorship. Now liberals, including Obama, categorized Russia as a threat on a par with Islamic State terrorists, while Trump and many of his conservative supporters viewed Russia as a strong proponent of traditional values and an ally against terrorism.[108]

Russian leaders often complained about American Russophobia and sometimes asserted that Russia did not similarly demonize America. For example, in a major address soon after the election of Trump in 2016, Putin called for the normalization of relations with the United States and declared that Russia did not seek foreign enemies.[109]

Yet Putin could not resist taunting Americans and contrasting the two countries. In a 2019 interview, for example, he declared that "the liberal idea has become obsolete" and contrasted the allegedly excessive gender pluralism in the West to Russia's "traditional family values."[110]

Both under Obama and under Trump, America continued to be Russia's principal "Other." After the US imposition of sanctions in response to the annexation of Crimea in 2014, anti-Americanism became a dominant theme both in Russia's state controlled media and in much public discussion. Vitalii Podvitskii, a cartoonist for the Russian Information Agency, frequently depicted Obama as a demonic figure and regularly contrasted an aggressive America to a defensive Russia. In one cartoon, for example, Podvitksii showed a wantonly interventionist Uncle Sam setting fires around the world, with only a big Russian bear ready to stop the arsonist at the door to Ukraine (see Figure 18.1). Thus, Podvitskii simultaneously demonized the United States and naturalized a Russian neo-imperial intervention in Ukraine.[111]

In other cartoons, Podvitskii depicted Obama in the Black Overlord's costume,[112] symbolizing his protection of LGBTQ+ in the United States. Usually, American cartoonists coopted images of Darth Vader or Jabba the Hutt in order to label Russia the Evil Empire. The Russian anti-American discourse, however, worked at reversing the roles, which resulted in Obama wearing the colors of Evil and Putin the colors of Good.[113]

Figure 18.1 "Hello Sam." Cartoon by Vitalii Podvitskii, March 5, 2014. Published with permission of the author.

After the election of Trump, the number of Russians with favorable views of the United States rose for a time from 15 to 41 percent, yet Russian mass media continued to present many stories of American conspiracies to undermine or even destroy Russia, both in the past and in the present.[114] Russian journalists repeatedly attacked notions of American exceptionalism and went so far as to compare it to Nazi Germany's ideas of Aryan racial supremacy.[115]

Russian films and television series also propagated anti-American themes more heatedly than before, even as they adapted Hollywood techniques.[116] Already at the start of the century, films such as Alexey Balabanov's *Brother 2* (*Brat 2,* 2000) and Pavel Lungin's *Tycoon* (*Oligarkh,* 2002) had expressed anti-American sentiment through images of "new Russians," or Russian nouveau riches, as American wolves in Russian sheep's clothing.[117] By 2017, the cinematic anti-Americanism was even more vehement. The television series *Sleepers* (*Spyashchie*), which aired on Russia's Channel 1 in October 2017, became particularly notorious for its propagandistic clichés and hostile images. The sleepers were foreign agents (politicians and journalists) who would be activated during an international crisis to organize a revolution in Russia. This "liberal fifth column" was shown to be working in cooperation with an American diplomat (a clear reference to Ambassador Michael McFaul), who aimed to destroy Russia. In this morally black-and-white series, Russian liberals are traitors to the nation, and the Russian liberal project is the American project. After the series was sharply criticized on social media and in independent mass media outlets, director Yuri Bykov had to apologize publicly to Russians fighting for the liberalization of their country.

Russian films and television shows also constructed the image of a hostile American Other by turning to the history of the Cold War. Filmmakers used stories of the USSR defeating the United States in sports, as in Anton Megerdichev's *Three Seconds* (*Dvizhenie vverkh,* 2017), which showed the Soviet basketball team defeating the Americans at the Munich Summer Olympics in 1972. Several films dramatized Soviet feats in space, including Dmitry Kiselev's *Spacewalk* (*Vremia pervykh,* 2017), which lionized a cosmonaut who was the first man to walk in space in 1965. Although such films generally emphasized the virtues of Russian heroes more than they vilified Americans, they emphasized competition and at times projected paranoia into the past. Thus, *Salyut-7* (2017) depicted imaginary US efforts to capture a damaged Soviet space station in 1985, though in the end American space shuttle pilots salute the bravery and skill of the cosmonauts who repaired the station. More ominously, filmmakers produced stories about the unmasking of American spies trying to steal Russian missile secrets, as in Yuri Moroz's TV series *Operation Satan* (*Operatsiia "Satana,"* 2018).

On the other side, American journalists and filmmakers overwhelmingly depicted Russia in ways that recycled old stereotypes and affirmed American or Western identities. Russian American journalist Masha Gessen won a prestigious National Book Award in 2017 for an account that blamed "Russia's reversion to type" on the alleged relapse of the Russian people to the passive, fearful, lobotomized traits of "homo sovieticus" – an interpretation that resuscitated the old "totalitarian" model.[118] Three years later Gessen's colleague at *The New Yorker*, Joshua Yaffa, redeployed the notion of "homo sovieticus" in another widely noted book that contrasted Russians' pathological dependence on the state to an idealized free, autonomous Western individual.[119] The movie *Atomic Blonde* (released in July 2017) used the old Cold War battleground of Berlin as a stage and gave viewers the pleasure of seeing a beautiful Western agent repeatedly thrash sinister KGB agents and brutal Communist thugs.[120] In the even bloodier *Red Sparrow* (March 2018), an austere Russian female spy trainer declares that the Cold War did not end and tells a beautiful injured ballerina that her body "belongs to the state." Beyond reviving the old contrast between Western individualist freedom and Russian collectivist totalitarianism, the movie highlighted the moral difference between unscrupulous, sadistic Russians and American agents who would never countenance the same actions.[121]

While both *Atomic Blonde* and *Red Sparrow* did well at the box office, grossing around $50 million each, *Creed II* (November 2018) sold more than twice as many tickets for its revisiting of the story of a Russian–American showdown in the boxing ring that had been featured in *Rocky IV* (1985). In a video the previous year, Hollywood director Rob Reiner and actor Morgan Freeman depicted Putin as perpetually obsessed with getting revenge on the United States for its victory over his Communist motherland in 1991. Similarly, *Creed II* portrayed a Russian trainer as so ruthlessly determined to get payback for his humiliating defeat in the 1980s that he shows no human sympathy for his boxer son – until a Black American boxer beats the bigger Russian to a pulp. Thus, the popular movie reflected the pervasive connection between Russian challenges to the United States and American demonization of Russia.[122]

While movies and television shows propagated negative stereotypes, public animosity was also inflamed by new allegations of Russian misdeeds, including interference in the 2020 election and electronic espionage. Most important were two sensational charges in the summer of 2020: that Russian agents had paid bounties for the killing of US soldiers in Afghanistan and poisoned a prominent critic of the Kremlin.

Day after day in June and July, the *New York Times* blasted from its front pages stories that "Russia Secretly Offered Afghan Militants Bounties to Kill U.S. Troops," as the first headline screamed.[123] The stunning articles in America's most influential newspaper provoked a furor in Washington. Senator Ben Sasse (Republican, Nebraska) demanded a plan for revenge killings of Russian intelligence officers. Congressional committees held multiple hearings to investigate why the Trump administration had not retaliated against Russia. Most Americans (60 percent) believed the stories.[124]

Soon Pentagon officials and military leaders expressed doubts. General Kenneth McKenzie, head of US Central Command, repeatedly explained that his intelligence experts had found no evidence to confirm the allegations. Citing McKenzie's statements, former chair of the Joint Chiefs of Staff Colin Powell called the media reports "almost hysterical."[125]

Yet, even months later, presidential candidate Joe Biden rebuked President Trump for being "unwilling to take on Putin when he's actually paying bounties to kill American soldiers in Afghanistan."[126] After Biden had defeated Trump and become president, though, a thorough review by the intelligence community found only "low to moderate confidence" in the claims about bounties that were based primarily on hearsay from criminals under interrogation. As a result, the Biden administration decided – as the Trump administration had – not to take any action on the basis of such dubious claims.[127] Thus, a major controversy that greatly exacerbated American hostility to Russia was based on extremely weak evidence that was hyped for domestic political purposes.

After the initial furor over the alleged bounties had subsided by August 2020, a shocking development in Siberia roiled Russian relations with the West again. Returning from a political organizing trip to Tomsk, activist Aleksei Navalny suddenly became dangerously ill. Navalny was flown to Berlin, where German experts determined that he had been poisoned with a form of Novichok (the same chemical as had been used earlier against Skripal). Once Navalny had recovered, he directly accused Putin of having ordered his assassination. In December, pretending to be a Russian intelligence official, Navalny appeared to get an FSB agent to describe how he had helped remove traces of poison from Navalny's clothing, thereby adding credibility to the accusation.[128]

When Navalny returned to Moscow in January 2021, the Russian authorities immediately arrested him for having failed to comply with the terms of his parole on an earlier conviction for embezzlement, and a judge eventually sentenced him to three years in prison. For the next two weeks, hundreds of thousands of people across Russia marched to demand freedom for Navalny and to protest conditions in Russia. American politicians and democracy promoters excitedly hailed the protests by "the Russian people" as a sign of impending revolution.[129] Yet only 22 percent of Russians supported the protests – a significant minority, but not a revolutionary wave.[130] The broader significance of the episode was the way it worsened the polarization between the United States and Russia, with many Americans viewing Navalny as akin to heroic dissidents in the Soviet era and with the Russian government branding Navalny's organization an "extremist" group and compelling it to shut down in April.[131]

CONCLUSION

Thus, at the start of the third decade of the twenty-first century, Russian–American relations were severely strained and often depicted in melodramatic terms. Both in the United States and in Russia, few public figures considered whether the deterioration of relations from the budding partnership in 2001 had been a tragedy, with possibilities for friendly cooperation repeatedly undermined by domestic political dynamics, media sensationalism, and yearnings to affirm national identities in contrast to the most intimate of enemies.

At the beginning of the century, Putin and many others had not believed that Russia's desires to be respected as a great power, to protect the rights of Russian speakers in neighboring countries, and to exert strong influence in the "Near Abroad" necessitated conflict with the United States. Yet those same ambitions would be sparks of a war in Ukraine that led Russia and America into one of the most dangerous confrontations in the history of their relations.

CONCLUSION

As a new US President took office in 2021, US–Russian relations veered between cooperation and confrontation. In February, Washington and Moscow agreed to extend the New Strategic Arms Reduction Treaty (which had been signed in 2010) for another five years. But in March, Joseph R. Biden called Vladimir Putin "a killer," souring relations between Russia and the United States and leading to a reduction in the number of staff members in both diplomatic missions. Just a month later, however, Biden proposed holding a bilateral summit, which finally took place in Geneva on June 16, 2021. This event planted the seeds of hope for an improvement in bilateral relations – albeit more among Russian observers than among their American counterparts. Biden's critics in the United States in fact saw this meeting as "appeasing" Putin, whom many American politicians, experts, and journalists had by that time represented as the epitome of evil.[1]

This summit was the last face-to-face meeting between the presidents of the two countries. By the fall of 2021, the Kremlin was amassing more troops on the border with Ukraine, while the United States signed a strategic partnership agreement with Ukraine that committed it to uphold Ukraine's territorial integrity, including Crimea.[2] In December, Russia sent NATO and the United States an ultimatum demanding security guarantees. These entailed signing an agreement and a treaty enshrining a commitment on the part of NATO not to admit Ukraine and Georgia as members; the United States' withdrawal of its nuclear weapons from the territories of those countries that had become members of NATO after May 27, 1997 (so called new members); and Washington's agreement not to engage in any military activities in Ukraine, Eastern Europe, the South Caucasus, and Central Asia.[3] The demands were more sweeping than before, and for the first time were presented as an ultimatum. The United States and NATO refused to comply, and on February 24, 2022, Russia commenced its full-scale invasion of Ukraine.

This naked aggression against a neighboring state prompted a heated wave of pro-Ukrainian feelings and anti-Putin hatred in American society, with the latter hatred frequently extended to Russia and Russians as a whole. For its part, amid growing US and Western aid to Ukraine and unprecedented sanctions, Russian propaganda described the war as a confrontation between Russia and the United States.[4] However, this is not the only reason why the war in Ukraine represents a turning point in bilateral relations. Rather, the shockingly deep crisis has highlighted and magnified specific features of these relations that have been developing for decades. It has once again foregrounded the images, fears, and hopes that have been accumulating since the first contacts between the two countries.

LONG-TERM POLITICAL AND IMAGOLOGICAL PATTERNS

As we have shown in this book, the history of Russian–American relations has long featured alternations between pragmatic cooperation and conflict rooted in divergent interests, values, and identities. Despite their different ideologies and political systems, the Russian Empire and the North American republic engaged in mutually beneficial and pragmatic cooperation for most of the nineteenth century. Both countries were keenly interested in trade and technological exchange. The trend toward a partnership was particularly obvious during European crises, because the interests of the two countries did not clash in Europe, and since Russia and the United States shared desires to counter the designs of Great Britain in the world in the era of Pax Britannica. The United States and Russia were also brought closer together by the fact that the European Other was equally important in shaping the American and Russian identities. Moreover, people in both countries saw territorial expansion as a part of their destinies, and both the United States and Russia had institutions of unfree labor – namely slavery and serfdom.

The late nineteenth and early twentieth centuries saw the first large-scale clash of values in US–Russia relations. Initially, it took place at the societal level, before rising to the level of interstate relations during the first crisis in bilateral relations. This development involved a collision between the two countries' respective messianic and geopolitical projects in the Far East and intensified competition on the world grain and oil markets. In that context, Russia and the United States became each other's constitutive Others. However, after the crisis of 1903–1905, tensions eased and gave way to a new pragmatic rapprochement during the First World War. Thus, between the 1880s and the First World War, bilateral relations went through a complete cycle: from pragmatic cooperation through confrontation and back to collaboration.

The Russian revolutions of 1917 set off another cycle in bilateral relations, which began with the dramatic warming of US–Russia ties after the overthrow of the autocracy in February, then spiraled downward to the October Revolution and the United States' interventions against the fledgling Soviet state. During this period, Americans pictured Russia as an object of their crusade for global reform on the basis of the principles of freedom and democracy proclaimed by President Woodrow Wilson. From that point on, the Russian Other became solidly integrated into Washington's foreign policy, and an ideological approach rooted in values and identities often shaped US policies toward Russia (both Soviet and post-Soviet). This vision reflected Americans' own messianic zeal, religious enthusiasm, and faith in being part of the struggle for Russian freedom.

Despite US and Allied support for anti-Bolshevik forces in the Russian Civil War, the Red Army defeated the Whites. The United States then refused to recognize the communist and atheist regime for a dozen years, even as economic relations between the two countries expanded dramatically. Mutual diplomatic recognition in 1933 began a new series of chills and thaws: from the cooling-off in the late 1930s against the backdrop of the Moscow trials and the Nazi–Soviet Pact to the comradeship-in-arms during the Second World War; from the confrontation during the early stages of the Cold War to the thaw of the late 1950s; from the Berlin crises and the Cuban missile crisis to the détente of 1963–1979; from the renewed hostility in the early 1980s to the end of the Cold War; from the honeymoon in bilateral relations in the 1990s to the disappointment of the mid-2000s; and from the "reset" of 2008–2012 to the crisis over Ukraine that started in 2014 and peaked after Russia's full-scale invasion.

The value-based approach moved to the fore during periods of confrontation. At these times, both sides sought to depict their own problems or failures as the result of the other side's nefarious activities, thereby helping to transform the latter into a "dark double" and scapegoat. Politicians and experts, journalists and cartoonists eagerly used the image of the Other for domestic political purposes. The conflicts in US–Russia relations also stemmed from a clash between two messianic projects, each of which made a claim to universality. The Soviet project carried a message of social justice and internationalism. After the collapse of the Soviet Union, in the 1990s the national messianic idea temporarily disappeared in the context of Russia's integration into the world market economy and adaptation of universal liberal values. However, in the twenty-first century, the Russian messianic project gradually revived, with a focus on protecting traditional values in domestic policies and an anti-hegemonic stance in international relations. The American project, meanwhile, envisaged advancing the universal values of freedom and democracy throughout the world. The image of the (American or Russian) Other frequently served to highlight the advantages of one's own messianic project.

Periods of strife and "cold spells" in US–Russia relations stemmed from both objective and subjective factors. Miscalculations, incorrect gauging of the other side's intentions, and mutual stereotypes became real hindrances to expanding pragmatic agendas and exacerbated tensions. These developments manifested themselves especially starkly during the Cold War, the time of a zero-sum game, and remain relevant for the United States' relations with post-Soviet Russia. For instance, from the end of the 1980s, Russian society and elites were searching for a new identity and were ready to absorb many of the universal values so important to Americans. However, political and military elites in the United States failed to seize the chance to integrate their former enemy into the Western security system.

During warmer periods, by contrast, bilateral relations were dominated by a pragmatic approach, the expansion of areas of cooperation, and a search for similarities between the development trajectories of the United States and Russia. As a result, each country played a different role in shaping the other's identity than during periods of confrontation, and the array of images expanded accordingly. This trend was foregrounded during economic modernization in the Russian Empire, in the USSR, and in post-Soviet Russia, when Americans taught Russians lessons in economic efficiency, capitalism, and advanced technology. That being said, since the nineteenth century, the two countries' technical and technological cooperation has been on different levels. It has usually been spearheaded by the government in Russia and by private business on the other side of the Atlantic. This was the case during the reigns of Nicholas I and Nicholas II; during Stalin's industrialization and the Second World War alliance, when the USSR received technical and technological assistance under the Lend–Lease program; and during the reforms of both Nikita Khrushchev in the twentieth century and Dmitry Medvedev in the twenty-first century.

A warming climate in US–Russia relations inevitably accompanied joint struggles by the two states against common threats, as during the world wars in the twentieth century and during the "war on terror" in the early twenty-first century. In these instances, Russians and Americans alike believed that international challenges could enable the two countries to overcome their ideological conflicts and foster pragmatic interactions based on equal partnership and mutual respect for national interests. However, these hopes frequently proved to be illusory. They were shattered by ideological conflicts between values and identities, as well as by the shortsightedness and national egoism of political and military elites. None of this eliminated the potential for pragmatic cooperation, but it did create real obstacles.

As this book has shown, Americans' views of Russia were fully formed by the late nineteenth century. In these representations, Russia had a variety of faces; the question was always which face would be presented at a specific moment in time – and with what goal.

The image of Russia that has been the most widespread, popular, and widely disseminated in the media is that of a country of despotism and abuse of power – a gigantic prison for all political dissenters. This regime has been seen as personified by rulers from Ivan the Terrible to Joseph Stalin to Vladimir Putin. Such an image of Russia has usually been constructed by opposing American values to perceived Russian ones: freedom vs. political slavery, democracy vs. authoritarianism/totalitarianism, Christian faith vs. atheism, energy vs. inertia, and individualism vs. collectivism. The generalized image of an American was typically contrasted with the Russian Other.

Proponents of this approach pointed to persistent authoritarian tendencies in tsarist, Soviet, and post-Soviet Russia, to police abusing power and the population's lack of civil rights and political liberties. They described Russia by reference to Western characteristics it did not possess, rather than those it had developed, thus making the country appear even more backward. American conservative pessimists – from nineteenth-century politicians such as Henry Cabot Lodge to twentieth-century historians like Richard Pipes – spread the image of an immutable Russia with despotic authorities and a society that, owing to its national character, was not ready to partake of the fruits of freedom and democracy. It was such conservatives who made the largest contribution to shaping the Orientalist discourse about Russia. Many of them spoke of its non-Western essence by comparing it to oriental despotic states, by likening it to the Ottoman Empire, and by describing the "Asiatic" essence of the rulers of the Russian Empire, the USSR, and post-Soviet Russia.[5]

For their part, universalist liberals – from the nineteenth-century American friends of Russian freedom such as Edmund Noble to the twentieth-century specialists in Russian studies like Martin Malia – distinguished Russia's xenophobic government from the Russian people, whom they saw as ready to change should their circumstances alter and as waiting for help from across the ocean to break the chains of their political slavery. They believed that a "Russian 1776" could come and that the United States had a role to play in Russia's makeover. This belief was rooted in Americans' own values and identities. Their idealism and messianic zeal regularly produced "crusades" for the liberation of tsarist, Soviet, and post-Soviet Russia. As a result, American society went through repeated cycles of hopes that Russia would change and disappointment in the outcomes achieved. This occurred during the first Russian revolution of 1905–1907; during the tenure of the Provisional Government between the February Revolution and the October Revolution in 1917; at the peak of hopes for the liberalization of Soviet society during the Second World War; and after the collapse of the USSR, when most of the American political and expert community believed that Yeltsin's Russia could transition rapidly to a market economy and democracy.

Each time, universalist-liberal faith in Russian liberals and Russian society during the cycle's peak gave way to disappointment and pessimism about an "immutable Russia" during the cycle's downturn. Each time, American experts, politicians, and public figures launched heated discussions about why the United States had once again "lost" Russia and whether American assistance to Russian liberals had been timely and sufficiently energetic. And, each time, Americans exaggerated their influence on events on the other side of the Atlantic.

As this book has demonstrated, from the nineteenth century onward, the range of Russian images of the United States was rich and diverse. However, the precise hierarchy of these images at any given time depended on events in Russia itself, on the climate of bilateral relations, and on the ideological creed of a given observer.

Russian revolutionaries and reformers envisioned the United States as a source of inspiration, from Alexander Radishchev in the 1780s, the Decembrists of 1825, and the Populists (*narodniki*) of the 1870s, to liberals at the time of the Russian revolutions, Soviet dissidents, and the 1990s reformers. All of them idealized the American political system as a model to be emulated. Defenders of the authoritarian regime and national conservative thinkers claimed that it was this temptation of the American Other as a model of liberty that made the United States a menace to Russia. As a result, those who were inspired by the American way of development were portrayed as traitors to the nation and a "fifth column." These issues, along with the actual US policies, are the roots of applied Americanophobia in Russia throughout time, from the tsarist era to the USSR to the post-Soviet period.

The image of the United States as a source of technological innovations was no less inspiring for all those who dreamed of modernizing Russia's economy. For over two centuries, American entrepreneurs exported new equipment and technologies to Russia, assisted in building industrial enterprises, and helped to bring about agrarian and transportation revolutions. The American model of economic efficiency inspired governmental reformers in tsarist Russia and, at the turn of the twentieth century, those liberal Western-leaning Russian professors who dwelled on "what America is teaching Russia." In 1918, Bolshevik leaders Lenin and Trotsky pondered the usefulness of the American development model for Soviet Russia. Stalin's industrialization was implemented under the banner of "Fordization" and American technological assistance. Nikita Khrushchev dreamed of overtaking the United States in meat and milk production and took lessons in "maize studies" from Iowa millionaire farmer Roswell Garst. Still, however much Soviet leaders were inspired by American technological development, they never forgot to condemn racism, materialism, and plutocracy in the United States as the antithesis of Soviet equality and idealism. The 1990s reformers in post-Soviet Russia likewise relied on help from across the Atlantic and on the miraculous power of American economic advice. And, during the "reset," Dmitry Medvedev dreamed of creating a Russian hi-tech center on the model of Silicon Valley in the United States.

For people in Russia, the image of the United States as an ally and an equal partner in the world wars or the "war on terror" was also very important. During the war against Nazi Germany, Soviet propaganda posters and cartoons frequently acclaimed America and Britain as vital allies. At the start of the twenty-first century, when President Putin sought to achieve an equal partnership with the United States, he often referred to Americans as partners. Despite increased tensions in bilateral relations after 2014, he still regularly mentioned Soviet and American troops meeting at the Elbe (the last time in May 2020). This was an enduring symbol of Russian hopes.

OLD TRENDS AND NEW TENDENCIES AFTER THE RUSSIAN INVASION OF UKRAINE

Russia's war with Ukraine has been the most serious blow to US–Russian relations since the end of the Cold War. For many experts and journalists in both countries, it appears that this war must be understood in the context of US–Russian relations, rather than simply as a Russian–Ukrainian conflict.

The outbreak of the war provoked an explosion of emotions and made the dominant assessments on both sides black and white, just as they had been during the Cold War. For US commentators, "that [was] a fight between good and evil. This [is] a fight between democracy and authoritarianism."[6] Russian propaganda, meanwhile, stated that Russia was waging a "war against the world Evil: the united misanthropic West and its Ukrainian accomplices, the Bandera Nazis."[7] The Kremlin kept the United States firmly as the focus of its explanation of the war. According to the government-controlled media, Russia was at war not against Ukraine, but against the United States, which was primarily responsible for the conflict and had promoted its escalation.[8] This helped to explain why the Russian army was not as successful as expected, as well as why Russia was fighting its closest neighbor in the first place. Some writers asserted that it was the United States that had made the two Slavic countries fight each other.[9]

Among many reasons for the war discussed in the two countries, each side chose some as the most important. American commentators often emphasized Putin's and the Russian elite's alleged desire to restore the USSR or even the Russian Empire.[10] Others saw in the war the Russian ruling group's desire to prevent the formation in Russia's neighborhood of a successful democratic country, which would threaten the stability of Russia's own authoritarian power.[11] Some strategists indicated that the aim of the war was to consolidate the earlier annexation of Crimea by creating a "land corridor" between the peninsula and the Russian mainland.[12] President Vladimir Putin, in his speech announcing the war, claimed that the goals of the "special military operation" were the fight against the spread of "Nazism" in Ukraine and the protection of the Russian-speaking inhabitants of that country. Eight months before the attack, he called for the preservation of a "united people," or a "single nation," clearly siding with the nationalistic view of the Ukrainians as a part of a large Russian nation.[13]

A widespread view in Russia, shared by some American and British analysts, was that the war was a response to American hegemonic ambitions and NATO's eastward expansion, which reached the point of promising Ukraine membership in the military–political bloc already in 2008, and which continued to be promoted in the following years. The advance of NATO (as well as the European Union) toward Russia's borders was widely perceived in Russia as a threat; the United States' and the West's deafness to Russia's diplomatic protests, according to this argument, left the Kremlin with no choice but war.[14] An opposite position attributed the war to the authoritarian Russian leadership's resistance to democracy-promotion efforts and considered it the duty of the United States to support a democratic Ukraine.[15]

American political elites and influential foreign policy experts diverged, with a minority urging pragmatic adjustment to Russian territorial gains while a majority insisted on the need for a clear victory over Russia. Former US Ambassador to the USSR Jack Matlock called for not making Russia a pariah state.[16] Another veteran of Cold War diplomacy, Henry Kissinger, also dared to depart from the morally charged discourse when he suggested that Ukraine may need to cede territories Russia occupied before the war (Crimea, Donetsk, and Luhansk) to stop the bloodshed and ensure its continued existence.[17] His discussion with the billionaire philanthropist George Soros at the annual World Economic Forum in Davos in May 2022 illustrated the polarization within the American political and intellectual establishments. Kissinger cautioned against turning the war into a battle "against Russia itself" rather than for "the freedom of Ukraine," while Soros warned that victory in the war against Putin's Russia was necessary to save civilization and urged the West to provide Ukraine with everything it needed to prevail.[18] The debate continued into the second year of the war. On one side, Anne Applebaum and Jeffrey Goldberg opined that "The future of the democratic world will be determined by whether the Ukrainian military can break a stalemate with Russia and drive the country backwards."[19] On the other hand, experts such as Samuel Charap and Carter Malkasian urged an armistice to halt the bloodshed.[20]

Another important dispute centered on the methods and approaches by which the United States should support Ukraine. The first US response to the outbreak of the war was to impose new sanctions on the Russian economy and Russian citizens; the number of bans increased as the war continued. The US government, however, was initially very cautious about Ukraine's demands for military aid and modern weaponry. To many observers, this meant risking a direct military clash and a third world war.[21] Former President and, at the time, Republican presidential contender Donald Trump insisted that "Joe Biden should not be dragging us further toward the Third World War by sending cluster munitions to Ukraine."[22] Such debates were fueled by Putin, who warned several times that nuclear weapons could be used in the conflict – leading observers to recall the 1962 Cuban Missile Crisis, when the superpowers came to the brink of war.[23]

The language used by propagandists and politicians alike to describe the other side drew from previous epochs. Both Russians and Americans used the labels "fascists" or "Nazis" to refer to their adversaries, just as had occurred during the Cold War, especially in its early stages. Russian propaganda employed these terms against the Ukrainians,[24] with any support for Ukraine coming from the United States or Europe depicted as "support for the Nazis." Russian propagandist discourse regularly compared the anti-Russian consolidation of the Western world to the German-led attack on the USSR in 1941. Leading Russian TV propagandist Vladimir Soloviev even used his Jewish origins as a pretext for decrying all his foes as Nazis and anti-Semites.[25] For its part, from the start of the invasion, media in the United States compared Putin to Hitler and Russia to Nazi Germany. Prominent historian Timothy Snyder called Russia "fascist" and supported the use of the term "Russism" or "Ruscism," coined in Ukraine as a combination of Russia and fascism, despite its ethnically targeted (and thus racist) connotations.[26] Snyder's main message was very clear. If Russia was fascist, then the threat it posed to the world could be eliminated by defeating it militarily, as happened with Nazi Germany. This vision provoked a heated response from some scholars of Russia in the United States. The prominent French American expert on Russian far-right groups Marlene Laruelle called it an example of a "shoddy, media-ready 'analysis' from public intellectuals that does its best to ignore any sociological knowledge about the country,"[27] while the leading US experts on European fascism likewise criticized use of the term.[28]

AMERICANS AND RUSSIANS LOOK AT EACH OTHER THROUGH THE LENS OF THE WAR

The outbreak of war sparked an important debate within the United States, which can be seen as a discussion on whether Russia remains a constitutive Other for American identity or whether it has vacated this place for China.[29] The discussion revolving around the extent to which Russian society supports the invasion of Ukraine has reignited enduring American discussions regarding Russia's destiny. Is it fated to remain authoritarian, or does it harbor the potential for reform in the future?

The debate centers on Russian public opinion-poll numbers and doubts as to whether these could reveal anything about an authoritarian society in wartime. Participants in these debates have included not only Americans and Russian émigré activists, but also anti-war Russians who have remained in Russia but have been able to participate in these exchanges in Zoom meetings, on social networks, and in publications. This argument deserves attention because it reveals the variety of American attitudes toward Russia and Russians and exposes historically rooted misconceptions.

The question around numbers of pro-war and antiwar Russians has quickly become one of the main bones of contention. Inside Russia, war-related propaganda and social–political pressures have rendered polling and public surveys dubious. Days after Putin's invasion of Ukraine, various leading Russian pollsters published studies showing high support for his "special military operation." On February 28, official state pollster VTsIOM announced that 68 percent of Russians supported the decision to start the operation, a figure that increased to 74 percent by March 23.[30] The independent Levada Center also demonstrated an abrupt rise in support for the president and the government over the first month of the war.[31] The government and pro-war politicians began to use these figures as a kind of political weapon.[32] These poll results also led many journalists and analysts to embrace the idea – spread by Kremlin propaganda – that the war against Ukraine was not just Putin's but Russia's.[33] Some analysts, however, pointed to the background fear caused by the state repressions of the Stalin era still haunting Russian society and predetermining compliance with the regime's war.[34]

Other Russian and some foreign experts drew attention to the fact that the opinion polls produced a picture that contrasted with witness accounts, which registered little enthusiasm for the war among Russians. Whereas the majority of Russians felt eagerness in March 2014 for the annexation of Crimea, the dominant mood in March 2022 was anxiety (as an FOM poll showed).[35] At the beginning, there was little support for the war; rather, there was visible fear of the authorities and a lack of inclination to join the army.

The mood in Russia was far from enthusiastic.[36] Indeed, tens of thousands of protesters took to the streets on the day of Russia's invasion, despite the threat of cruel prosecution. In fact, this was a rare case where, in the first days of a war, the state experienced not a patriotic "rallying around the flag," but mass protests. At least 15,000 activists were detained in the first 3 weeks of the war; human rights organizations reported police brutality and several cases of protesters being tortured in detention.[37] The state aimed to frighten people into silence. Thus, in July 2022, Alexey Gorinov, a member of the Krasnoselsky district council in Moscow, was sentenced to seven years in prison after making antiwar comments at a council meeting in March, including stating that Russia was waging a war of aggression against Ukraine.[38]

Diverse Russians, from democrats to intellectuals, sought to prove to their compatriots and the world that various poll results, particularly those asking specifically about public support for the war, should be interpreted carefully. It was Putin's war, they said, not Russia's, and the Russian people were victims of the ruling regime. Bearing this out, opposition anti-Putin and antiwar politicians Alexei Navalny and Ilya Yashin built wide coalitions.

Navalny was imprisoned before the war and published his antiwar theses from jail in February 2023.[39] He died in prison a year later, from a blood clot according to Russian media and the head of Ukrainian military intelligence, but opponents of Putin called his death a murder.[40] Yashin was sentenced to eight and a half years in prison for his antiwar position. There were other signs of the unpopularity of the war. A "partial mobilization" announced by Putin on September 21, 2022, caused hundreds of thousands of Russians to flee the country immediately, while a year later wives of those mobilized organized the most visible antiwar protest since the spring of 2022.[41]

According to the political scientist Maxim Alyukov, citizens who live in autocracies are often afraid of answering survey and poll questions, particularly when it comes to politics, where they "lie about their real preferences."[42] If we equate loyalty to the Putin regime with support for the war, then the level of support is indeed high: the president has consistently had high approval ratings. However, if we look only at those who "support the war," the numbers are significantly lower. Polls by the Chronicles research project, organized by Aleksei Miniailo, show that as few as 3 percent of Russians "wanted" war.[43] In addition, in-depth interviews with over thirty supporters of the war showed that few passionately justified it. More deferred to Putin's presumed greater knowledge and showed a desire to separate their everyday lives from politics.[44] This reveals a more nuanced landscape of Russians' attitude toward the war than the black-and-white picture that the media and politicians preferred to draw.

The battle over interpretations of the Russian people's attitudes toward Putin and the war reveals, first and foremost, the Kremlin's hegemony over messaging and propaganda. Pro-Putinists, anti-Putinists, and large parts of Western societies shared the idea that Russians are, for the most part, "Putinists." This attitude meshed well with the century-long tradition of American "Russophobes" or pessimists, who deemed the Russians unchangeable and hostile. Such an attitude was always linked to political pressure to isolate and contain Russia rather than attempting to change it.

During the war, US discussions of Russia came to be dominated by demonization of Russia and complete disappointment not only with the actions of its Putin-led authoritarian government, which started a war with Ukraine, but also with the passivity of Russian society. Just as has happened many times since the nineteenth century, the US debate on Russia again divided between conservatives and others who see Russia as an immutable country in which an authoritarian government lives in harmony with a paternalism-loving population, on the one hand, and liberals and others who are friends of those fighting for Russian freedom from an oppressive regime, on the other hand. However, some of the most prominent American liberals who hoped to reform Russia and differentiated between the people and the government developed doubts about whether ordinary Russians shared political elites' imperialist views.[45]

A different tradition, represented by "Russophiles" promoting Russian culture, also persisted. Calls by Ukrainians and Western friends of Ukraine to "cancel Russian culture" on the grounds that it allegedly represents an "imperial discourse" and has "promoted Russian aggression" became widespread in Europe and the United States, forcing defenders of Russian culture to take a stand. The heirs of the American Russophiles who gave American society a taste for Russian culture around the turn of the twentieth century and helped set up cultural exchanges during the Cold War condemned the ostracizing of Russian culture. Their ranks included both liberals and conservatives, who were united by their admiration for Russia's cultural legacy and saw it as not limited to the borders of the Russian state.[46]

After February 2022, the image of a demonic Russian Other became entrenched in American public and political discourse. In the past, the "Russia/Soviet card" was actively played in the inter-party struggle, particularly during presidential campaigns (the most recent prominent case of this was in 2016). As the 2024 presidential election campaign heated up, the initial bipartisan consensus on Russia's war against Ukraine started to erode, with a growing number of Republicans expressing opposition to spending so much money in support of Ukraine and a desire to focus more on threats in other parts of the world, including the border with Mexico and China.[47]

Russia, in turn, is dominated by ideological anti-Americanism intended to maintain the image of the United States as a threat to national stability and security. The authorities use state-controlled media to project this image, which reaches part of Russian society. The demonic American Other dominates the official Russian identity discourse. It is constructed through such oppositions as conservatism vs. liberalism, nationalism vs. universalism, protecting traditional values vs. spread of LGBTQ+ freedoms, and national sovereignty vs. hegemonism. All of this contrasts the generalized image of a Russian with the American Other, and the Russian development path with American liberalism.

As in the past, the Russian government emphasized negative features of US development, primarily racial discrimination against Black Americans, Latinos, and Native Americans. In that sense, post-Soviet anti-American propaganda continued the tradition of Soviet propaganda, which was in turn heir to tsarist propaganda.[48] Contemporary Russian promoters of anti-

American discourse were just as careful in recording manifestations of racial inequality in the United States as were those who created the image of the "lynching United States of America" during the Cold War.[49] This discourse often emphasized American double standards and the hypocrisy of Washington administrations advocating for freedom and democracy throughout the world while supporting dictatorships or absolute monarchies such as Saudi Arabia or doing nothing about racial and ethnic discrimination in their own country.

Contemporary Russian anti-Americanists were no less attentive to the image of the United States as "the country of the yellow devil" – a country that remains dominated by the power of money even as its economic system goes through periodic crises. Soviet propagandists embraced this image, popularized by Maxim Gorky, and turned it into a stereotype, which Russian propagandists revived in the twenty-first century.[50]

However, the propaganda did not convince everybody. An independent Levada Center poll demonstrated a surge in negative attitudes toward the United States between spring 2022 and spring 2023, peaking at 77 percent in May 2023, before a relative decline in negative responses to 61 percent in August of the same year. Yet the question about Russians' attitudes toward Americans as people painted a different picture: in 2022, almost 49 percent had a "positive" attitude (compared with 40 percent who had a "negative" one), whereas by August 2023, 55 percent had a "positive" attitude toward Americans and only 27 percent a "negative" one.[51] As they did during the Cold War, Russians condemned the United States as a state, but distinguished it from the American people.

Since the late nineteenth century, Russia and the United States have employed images of the Other to rally their respective societies by offering them a binary, black-and-white picture of the world. The reasons for this mutual portrayal have not stemmed from international politics alone, be it NATO's eastward expansion or Russia's aggression. They also have arisen from the problems of each country's domestic development. For the United States, these have been mounting internal cleavages (ethnic, social, regional, within and between the Democratic and Republican Parties, between megalopolises and the hinterland). As in the past, the domestic crisis activated the use of the Russian Other. For Russia, Putin's desire to preserve his regime and power at any cost led him to turn to increasingly negative depictions of the United States. The contemporary confrontation between the United States and post-Soviet Russia, the most severe and dangerous one since the end of the Cold War, thus foregrounded recurrent patterns described in this book.

Yet crises in the past, such as in 1903–1905, 1919–1921, 1939–1941, 1947–1953, 1961–1962, and 1979–1983, were followed by periods of reduced tensions. The many ups and downs in relations between the two countries over the preceding centuries suggest that intense mutual enmity may not be destined to last forever.

Notes

INTRODUCTION

1. Wandycz, *The United States and Poland*, 58–84; Wieczerzak, "American Reactions to the Polish Insurrection of 1863."

2. Wieczerzak, *A Polish Chapter in Civil War America*, chapter 7; Kroll, *"Friends in Peace and War"*; Saul, *Distant Friends*, 340–354.

3. For lack of a term that is more precise without being clumsy, we use the conventional "Russians" to refer to the many peoples who lived in the tsarist, Soviet, and post-Soviet empires.

4. Address by Putin, September 30, 2022, www.kremlin.ru; Maksimov, *Bol'shaia Lozh'*; Yablokov, *Fortress Russia*, 56–57.

5. Kotkin, "Russia's Perpetual Geopolitics," 8. See also a prominent Washington expert's view that cooperation "has been the exception rather than the rule" in the history of US–Russian relations: Stent, *Putin's World*, 357.

6. For example, Kotkin, "Russia's Perpetual Geopolitics," 8.

7. Osgood, "The American Construction of the Communist Threat"; Iriye, "Culture and International History," 245; Hinds and Windt, *The Cold War as Rhetoric*, 101; Hunt, "Ideology," 228, 238.

8. Krebs, *Narrative and the Making of U.S. National Security*, 1–4.

9. For further discussion of differences between realist, liberal, and constructivist approaches, see Krebs, *Narrative and the Making of U.S. National Security*, 16–24; Hopf, *Reconstructing the Cold War*, 17–20.

10. On the methodology of constructivist analysis, see, for example, Wendt, *Social Theory of International Politics*; Neumann, *Uses of the Other*; Hixson, *The Myth of American Diplomacy*. For a recent application of this approach, see Borozna, *The Sources of Russian Foreign Policy Assertiveness*. On Soviet leaders' need for recognition of their identities by others, especially US leaders, see Radchenko, *To Run the World*.

11. See Tsygankov, *The Dark Double*.

12. See, for example, Finlay, Holsti, and Fagen, *Enemies in Politics*, chapter 1, and Makari, *Of Fear and Strangers*, esp. 177–178.

13. For example, on the less enduringly important Vietnamese and American constructions of images of each other, see Bradley, *Imagining Vietnam and America*.

14. Gleason, *The Genesis of Russophobia in Great Britain*; Sergeev, *The Great Game, 1856–1907*.
15. Perkins, *The Great Rapprochement*; Anderson, *Race and Rapprochement*; Cortada, *Two Nations over Time*; Mitchell, *The Danger of Dreams*.
16. Moser, *Twisting the Lion's Tail*.
17. Carley, *Silent Conflict*; Haslam, *Spectre of War*.
18. Chang, *Fateful Ties*, 3–4, 248–257.
19. As Chang notes, "rarely did the Chinese link their own country's destiny with that of America." *Fateful Ties*, 8. The periodic surges of intense pro- and anti-American feeling among educated, young, urban Chinese were exceptions. See, for example, Zhang, *America Perceived*. On identity in Chinese–US relations, see also Qing, *From Allies to Enemies*.
20. Davis and Trani, *Distorted Mirrors*, esp. xxii, 11, 352–353.
21. Dulles, *The Road to Teheran* (1944). Pitirim Sorokin's *Russia and the United States* (1944), written in a similar spirit, was a sociological study more than a historical survey.
22. Dean, *The United States and Russia* (1947).
23. Bailey, *America Faces Russia* (1950).
24. Williams, *American–Russian Relations 1781–1947* (1952), 4, 107, 159; Buhle and Rice-Maximin, *William Appleman Williams*, 45–55.
25. Gaddis, *Russia, the Soviet Union, and the United States* (first edition completed by March 1977), ix.
26. Sivachev and Yakovlev, *Russia and the United States* (finished in 1976, though published in 1979), xiv, 264.
27. Daniels, *Russia: The Roots of Confrontation* (1985), ix, 327, 357–369.
28. See, for example, Gaddis, *We Now Know*, 282–283; Westad, "Introduction," in Westad, *Reviewing the Cold War*, 1, 3; Hughes and Dockrill, "Introduction: The Cold War as History," in Dockrill and Hughes, eds., *Palgrave Advances in Cold War History*, 1–18; Nuti and Zubok, "Ideology," in Dockrill and Hughes, eds., *Palgrave Advances in Cold War History*, 73–110, esp. 102–103; Leffler, *For the Soul of Mankind*, 3–4. An exception to the general neglect of long-term historical perspectives is Westad, *The Global Cold War*, chapters 1 and 2.
29. *Istoriia Kommunisticheskoi Partii Sovetskogo Soiuza, Izdanie sed'moye* (Moscow, 1984), cited in Nadzhafov, "The Beginning of the Cold War between East and West," 140–174; Strel'nikov, *Tysiacha mil v poiskakh dushi*.
30. Zubok and Pechatnov, "Otechestvennaia istoriografiia 'kholodnoi voiny,'" *Otechestvennaia istoriia*, No. 4 (2003), 143–150 and No. 5 (2003), 139–148.
31. Two exceptions are Kurilla, *Zakliatye Druz'ia* and Zhuravleva, *The Common Past of Russians and Americans*.
32. Dulles, *The Road to Teheran*, 1–8, 78–79, 260–261.
33. Bailey, *America Faces Russia*.
34. Williams, *American–Russian Relations, 1781–1947*, 4, 24–44; Sivachev and Yakovlev, *Russia and the United States*, 15, 14, 23, 264–269.

35. Gaddis, *Russia, the Soviet Union and the United States*, xv, 1, 26.
36. On the methodology of cartoon analysis, see Kemnitz, "The Cartoon as a Historical Source," 81–93, Miller; "A Primer for Using Historical Images in Research"; Zhuravleva and Foglesong, "Konstruirovanie obraza Rossii v amerikanskoi politcheskoi karikature XX veka," 187–193.
37. *Bulletin for Cartoonists*, No. 25, November 30, 1918; Hecht, ed., *The War in Cartoons*.
38. John S. Knight, "Newspaper Readers' Post War Thinking Is More Serious," *Detroit Free Press*, December 8, 1946.
39. Efimov, *Boris Efimov*, 14.
40. Foreword by Iriye, in Sivachev and Yakovlev, *Russia and the United States*, vii.
41. Sivachev and Yakovlev, *Russia and the United States*.
42. Bolkhovitinov, *Stanovlenie russko-amerikanskikh otnoshenii, 1775–1815*; Bolkhovitinov, *Russko-amerikanskie otnosheniia, 1815–1832*; Bolkhovitinov, *Rossiia i voina SShA za nezavisimost, 1775–1783*; Bolkhovitinov, *Russko-amerikanskie otnoshenia i prodazha Aliaski, 1834–1867*; Bolkhovitinov, *Rossiia otkryvaet Ameriku, 1732–1799*; Bolkhovitinov, *Russia and the United States*; Saul, *Distant Friends*; Saul, *Concord and Conflict*; Saul, *War and Revolution*; Saul, *Friends or Foes? The United States and Soviet Russia, 1921–1941*.

CHAPTER 1: FROM FIRST CONTACTS TO FLEDGLING DIPLOMATIC RELATIONS, 1607–1807

1. *The True Travels, Adventures and Observations of Captain John Smith*, 42–43.
2. Dvoichenko-Markova, "Dzhon Smit v Rossii," 160.
3. Etkind, *Internal Colonization*, 123; Bassin, "Turner, Solov'ev, and the 'Frontier Hypothesis,'" 473–511.
4. Recent scholarship rejects the earlier hypothesis of a personal meeting between Penn and Peter. See Isaev, *U istokov amerikanskoy istorii*, 293–299.
5. Romaniello, "Through the Filter of Tobacco"; Price, "The Tobacco Adventure to Russia."
6. See letter from Ezra Stiles to Mikhail V. Lomonosov, February [9] 20, 1765; letter from Benjamin Franklin to Franz Ulrich Theodor Aepinus, [May 26] June 6, 1766, in *The United States and Russia: The Beginning of Relations*, 4–8; 12.
7. *Moskovskie vedomosti*, 1783. 2 (13) September. No. 71.
8. Evans, "Carlo Bellini and His Russian Friend Fedor Karzhavin"; Saul, *Distant Friends*, 8–10.
9. A full list of such publications and its analysis can be found in Nikoliukin, *Literaturnye sviazi Rossii i SShA*, 26–36.
10. Lomonosov, *Izbrannye proizvedeniia*, 239; Sumarokov, "O Amerike," *Trudoliubivaia pchela* (November 1759), 704.

11. "Pis'mo Indeitsa o Nravakh Evropeitsev," *Pokoiasshchiisia Trudoliubets* (1784), Ch. 2, 162–163.
12. Krylov and Klushin, *Amerikantsy* (comic opera).
13. See Bolkhovitinov, "The Declaration of Independence: A View from Russia."
14. Prevo, *Istoria o stranstviakh voobshche po vsem kraiam zemnogo kruga*; de La Porte, *Vsemirnyi puteshestvovatel* (America was described in Vol. 8). Taube, *Istoriia o aglinskoi torgovle.*
15. Ladygin, *Izvestie v Amerike o seleniiakh aglitskikh, v tom chisle nyne pod nazvaniem Soedinennykh Provintsii.*
16. Snell, *Von den Handlungsvortheilen, welche aus der Unabhängigkeit der Vereinigten Staaten von Nord-Amerika für das Russische Reich entspringen.*
17. Geberlin, "O vliianii nezavisimosti Soedinennykh oblastei Severo-Amerikanskikh v politicheskoe sostoianie Evropy," *Pribavlenie k Moskovskim vedomostiam* (1784), 306.
18. "O obraze pravleniia u amerikantsev i o grazhdanskom ikh ustanovlenii," *Pribavlenie k Moskovskim Vedomostiam*, No. 65 (1784), 516.
19. Geberlin, "O vliianii nezavisimosti," 306–344; "Kratkoe opisanie zhizni i kharaktera generala Vasgingtona," 362–372.
20. "Kratkoe opisanie zhizni i kharaktera generala Vasgingtona," 372.
21. Laserson, "Alexander Radishchev – An Early Admirer of America." The Russian word "vol'nost'" was translated here as "freedom," but some scholars prefer to translate it as "liberty" (see, for example, Blakely, "American Influences on Russian Reformist Thought in the Era of the French Revolution," 451–471).
22. Translated in Laserson, *The American Impact on Russia*, 61.
23. Radishchev, *Polnoe sobranie sochinenii*, Vol. 1, 316–317.
24. Zorin, "Intellektualnye prikliucheniia russkogo antifederalista: Radishchev, Kondorse i amerikanskaia konstitutsiia," *Quaestio Rossica*, Vol. 9., No. 2 (2021), 679–701.
25. [Khrapovitsky], *Pamiatnia zapiska A. V. Khrapovitskago*, 227.
26. Griffiths, "American Commercial Diplomacy in Russia," 407.
27. James Duane to Robert R. Livingston, July 8, 1777, in *Letters of Delegates to Congress, 1774–1789*, Vol. 7, 321.
28. Filimonova. *Dikhotomia "Svoi/Chuzhoy" i ee reprezentatsiia v politicheskoi kulture Amerikanskoi revoliutsii*, 252–265. Filimonova's research is based on the *Letters of Delegates to Congress, 1774–1789.*
29. Matos Franco, "Adventure, Mutual Images and Orientalism: Joel R. Poinsett in Russia."
30. Letter from John Quincy Adams to Abigail Adams, September 10, 1783, in *The United States and Russia: The Beginning of Relations*, 210.
31. Warren, *History of the Rise, Progress, and Termination of the American Revolution*, 302–303.
32. From a Letter of the United States Joint Commissioner at Paris, Silas Deane, to Charles W. F. Dumas, June 7, 1777, in *The United States and Russia: The Beginning of Relations*, 44.

33. *The United States and Russia: The Beginning of Relations*, 385.

34. Grinev, "The First Russian Settlers in Alaska."

35. *Istoriia Russkoi Ameriki*, Vol. 1, 311–314.

36. Ledyard to Jefferson, July 29, 1787, in *John Ledyard's Journey through Russia and Siberia*, 127.

37. See Owens with Petrov, *Empire Maker*.

38. Catherine the Great to Madame Bielke, June 30, 1775. Translated in Laserson, *The American Impact on Russia*, 33.

39. Letter from Catherine II to King George III, [Moscow], September 23 [October 4], 1775, in *The United States and Russia: The Beginning of Relations*, 33–35.

40. William Henry Drayton's Notes of Proceedings. Monday, February 15, 1779, in *Letters of Delegates to Congress*, Vol. 12, 72.

41. See Griffiths, *No Collusion! Catherine the Great and American Independence*.

42. "England" was the widely used term in Russia at the time and applied to the whole of Great Britain.

43. See *Vsepoddanneyshee mnenie grafa N. I. Panina*, 243–244. See also Griffiths, "Nikita Panin," 5.

44. See Griffiths, "An American Contribution to the Armed Neutrality."

45. Order of the Empress to Panin, May 26, 1779, cited in Griffiths, "Nikita Panin," 7.

46. See Madariaga, *Britain, Russia, and the Armed Neutrality of 1780*, 172; Dull, *A Diplomatic History of the American Revolution*, 128–133.

47. John Adams to the President of Congress, Paris, April 26, 1780, in *The Diplomatic Correspondence of the American Revolution*, Vol. 5, 26.

48. Benjamin Franklin to Samuel Huntington, President of Congress, August 9, 1780, in *The Works of Benjamin Franklin*, Vol. 5, 63.

49. Marquis de Verac to Vergennes, October 11, 1780, cited in Griffiths, "Nikita Panin," 15.

50. Verac to Vergennes, January 22, 1781, cited in Griffiths, "Nikita Panin," 17. For an analysis of the Russian position, see also Bolkhovitinov, *Russia and the American Revolution*, chapter 3.

51. Instruction from the President of the Continental Congress, Samuel Huntington, to the United States Minister-Designate to Russia, Francis Dana, Philadelphia, December [7] 18, 1780, in *The United States and Russia: The Beginning of Relations*, 98–102.

52. Despatch from Francis Dana to the President of the Continental Congress, Thomas McKean, No. 14, St. Petersburg, September 4/15, 1781, in *The United States and Russia: The Beginning of Relations*, 126.

53. See Griffiths, "Nikita Panin."

54. Letter from John Paul Jones to Ivan A. Osterman, St. Petersburg, January 31 [February 11], 1789, in *The United States and Russia: The Beginning of Relations*, 265.

55. Saul, *Distant Friends*, 25.

56. Cited in Blakely, "American Influences . . .," 459.

57. [J. H. Stone to Joseph Priestly, September 1802?] in Hans, "Tsar Alexander I and Jefferson: Unpublished Correspondence," 216.

58. Jefferson to Thomas Cooper, November 29, 1802? in Hans, "Tsar Alexander I and Jefferson: Unpublished Correspondence," 217.

59. Jefferson to Joseph Priestly, November 29, 1802, in Hans, "Tsar Alexander I and Jefferson: Unpublished Correspondence," 217. See also *The United States and Russia: The Beginning of Relations*, 359.

60. Cogliano, *Emperor of Liberty: Thomas Jefferson's Foreign Policy*, 1.

61. *Vestnik Evropy*, 1803. Pt. 9, 137–140, translation in Blakely, "American Influences," 467.

62. Thomas Jefferson to Governor John Langdon Monticello, March 5, 1810, cited in Cogliano, *Emperor of Liberty: Thomas Jefferson's Foreign Policy*, 2.

63. Frederic Cesar de La Harpe to J. H. Stone, October 20, 1803, in Hans, "Tsar Alexander I and Jefferson: Unpublished Correspondence," 218.

64. Thomas Jefferson to Alexander I, Washington, June 3 [15], 1804, in *The United States and Russia: The Beginning of Relations*, 404.

65. Alexander I to Thomas Jefferson, St. Petersburg, November 7 [19], 1804, in *The United States and Russia: The Beginning of Relations*, 419.

66. Quoted in Stillé, "The Life and Services of Joel R. Poinsett," 142–143. The conversation took place during the winter of 1806–1807. A few months later, in July 1807, Russia was forced to sign the Tilsit treaty with France and join the Continental blockade of England, making American trade even more desirable to the empire.

67. Thomas Jefferson to William Duane, July [8] 20, 1807, in *The United States and Russia: The Beginning of Relations*, 478–479.

CHAPTER 2: DIPLOMACY AND REBELLIONS, 1807–1841

1. Dulles, *The Road to Teheran*; Saul, *Distant Friends*.

2. Saul, *Distant Friends*, 86.

3. Despatch from Nikolai Ia. Kozlov to Nikolai P. Rumiantsev, No. 1. January [2] 14, 1813, in *The United States and Russia: The Beginning of Relations*, 915. Pavel Svin'in published not only newspaper articles, but also a brochure intended to challenge the superficial image of his country: Svenin, *Sketches of Moscow and St.-Petersburg*.

4. Svenin, *Sketches of Moscow and St.-Petersburg*, 2.

5. Svin'in, *Opyt zhivopisnago puteshestmia po Severnoi Amerike*, 23.

6. [Bulgarin, Faddey], *Vospominaniia Faddeia Bulgarina*, 57–58.

7. English translation: *A Sketch of the Internal Condition of the United States and Their Political Relations with Europe*.

8. *Pis'ma V. A. Zhukovskogo k A. Ia. Bulgakovu*, 1453, 1466.

9. According to American newspapers and diplomatic correspondence, the celebrations took place on March 25, 1813, in Boston, and on June 5, 1813, in Georgetown.

10. See Shulim, "The United States Views Russia"; Kurilla, "Russian Celebrations."

11. "Federal Festival," *National Intelligencer*, March 22, 1813.

12. *Correspondence Respecting Russia*, 23.

13. "Russian Festival," *Raleigh Register*, April 30, 1813.

14. "The Friends of the Navy," *The Military Monitor*, 379.

15. "The Russian Celebration," *National Intelligencer*, April 23, 1813.

16. See Bolkhovitinov (ed.), *Istoriia Russkoi Ameriki*, Vol. 2, 157–180.

17. See Bolkhovitinov, *Russko-amerikanskie otnosheniia*, 191–197.

18. "Review: Message from the President of the United States," *North American Review*, October 1822, 371, 391.

19. Saul, *Distant Friends*, 115.

20. See Bolkhovitinov, *Russko-amerikanskie otnosheniia*; Bolkhovitinov, *Doktrina Monro*.

21. May, *The Making of the Monroe Doctrine*, 255.

22. Ford, "Some Original Documents," 378–380.

23. J. R. Poinsett to Daniel Webster, [1823?] in *Papers of Daniel Webster: Correspondence*, Vol. 1, 344.

24. [Webster, Daniel], *Mr. Webster's Speech on the Greek Revolution*, 32–49.

25. Entry for November 27, 1823, in *Memoirs of John Quincy Adams*, Vol. 6, 214.

26. Cited in Allen, *Russia Looks at America*, 22.

27. Cited in Saul, *Distant Friends*, 90.

28. See, for details, Bolkhovitinov, *Russko-amerikanskie otnosheniia*, 451–491.

29. *The National Intelligencer*, September 14, 1826, Vol. XV, No. 4257, 3.

30. Raeff, "An American View," 287.

31. In the arbitration, the tsar awarded slave owners indemnity on the American terms.

32. Cited in Berquist, "Henry Middleton and the Arbitrament," 21.

33. Mayers, *The Ambassadors . . .*, 25.

34. Tocqueville, Alexis de, *Democracy in America*, 1969 [c. 1835], 413.

35. "European Views of American Democracy," *United States Magazine and Democratic Review*, Vol. 1, 1838, 94.

36. See Ivanchenko, "Pozitsiia redaktsionnogo kruzhka," 216–235.

37. See Nikoliukin, *Literaturnye sviazi*, 167–179.

38. Knight, "Ethnicity, Nationality and the Masses," 54.

39. Dallas, *Diary of George Mifflin Dallas*, 13.

40. Turgenev, "XI. Parizh (Khronika russkogo)," *Sovremennik*, Vol. 1, 1836, 258–295.

41. See Isaev, *Aleksis Tokvil*.

42. Kennan, *The Marquise de Custine*, 131–132.

43. Malia, *Russia under Western Eyes*, 92–98.

44. James Buchanan to Edward Buchanan, July 15–27, 1832, in *The Works of James Buchanan*, Vol. 2, 217.

45. Buchanan to Jane Slaymaker, October 31, 1832, in *The Works of James Buchanan*, Vol. 2, 265.

46. Buchanan to Louis McLane, No. 22, August 7, 1833, in *The Works of James Buchanan*, Vol. 2, 380.

47. See Belohlavek, *"Let the Eagle Soar!"*

48. Nicholas I even announced his decision in the presence of the English ambassador in order to nettle British diplomacy, which had lobbied in vain for a similar treaty.

49. AVPRI. F. Kantseliaria, Op. 469, 1837, D. 247, L. 35–35 ob., 38–38 ob., 46–47 ob., 48 ob.–49 ob.

50. Entry of July 23, 1839, in Dallas, *Diary of George Mifflin Dallas*, 209.

51. Buchanan to Clayton, April 17, 1849, in *Works of James Buchanan*, Vol. 8, 361.

52. Smith-Peter, "The Russian Federalist Papers."

CHAPTER 3: BEGINNING OF A FRIENDSHIP: COOPERATION, CRISIS, AND TRANSFORMATION, 1841–1860

1. See, for instance, Gaddis, *Russia, the Soviet Union and the United States*, 1–25; Bolkhovitinov, *Russko-amerikanskie otnosheniia i prodazha Aliaski*, 91.

2. *S.-Peterburgskie vedomosti*, April 4, 1861. Cited in Ivanov, *Konfederativnye Shtaty Ameriki*, 72.

3. C[ambreleng], "New Notes on Russia, by a Recent Visiter," *United States Magazine and Democratic Review*, Vol. 11, No. 50 (August 1842), 151–160; [Motley], "Peter the Great"; Maxwell, *The Czar, His Court and People*; Griffin, *Memoir of Col. Chas. Todd.*

4. AVPRI. F. 133. Kantselariia, Op. 469, 1850, D. 138, L.77 ob.

5. See Shewmaker, "Neill S. Brown's Mission to Russia."

6. Neill Brown to Daniel Webster, Nos. 2, 6, 12, 15, in NARS. M.35. Diplomatic Despatches. Russia, Vol. 14, R. 14.

7. *Foreign Relations of the United States, 1933–1939*, 289–291.

8. See Kurilla, *Zaokeanskie partnery*, 123–141.

9. [Melnikov], "Opisanie v tekhnicheskom otnoshenii."

10. [Melnikov], "Opisanie v tekhnicheskom otnoshenii," Vol. 2, No. 1 (1842), 37, 46–47.

11. [Melnikov], "Nachalo zheleznodorozhnogo stroitelstva v Rossii"; Melnikov, "Svedeniia o russkikh zheleznykh dorogakh," 164–165.

12. Benkendorf to Toll, March 8, 1841, in *Krasnyi arkhiv*, Vol. 3, No. 76 (1936), 11.

13. See Toll to Nicholas I, in *Krasnyi arkhiv*, Vol. 3, No. 76 (1936), 11.

14. Donesenie Nikolayu I komissii po ustroistvu zheleznoi dorogi mezhdu Peterburgom i Moskvoi, September 15, 1841, in *Krasnyi arkhiv*, Vol. 3, No. 76 (1936), 141–142.

15. Haywood, *Russia Enters the Railway Age*, 29.
16. Tarsaidze, "American Pioneers," 292.
17. Whistler brought to Russia his teenage son, who took his first lessons in professional painting at the Russian Academy of Fine Arts. Thus, the Russian railroad contract gave America one of its finest artists, James McNeill Whistler.
18. [Melnikov], "K istorii razvitiia parokhodstva na Volge," 320–321.
19. Melnikov, "Svedeniia o russkikh zheleznykh dorogakh," 308.
20. See Todd to Buchanan, January 22/February 3, 1846. NARS. M.35. Diplomatic Despatches. Russia. Vol. 14, R.14.
21. *Nile's National Register*, April 22, 1843.
22. Maxwell, *The Czar, His Court and People*, 128.
23. See Adas, *Dominance by Design*.
24. Rotchev, "Vospominaniia russkogo turista," 65.
25. Cited in *Istoriia Russkoi Ameriki*, Vol. 3, 355–357.
26. Gurovskii, "Pis'ma iz Ameriki," *Vestnik promyshlennosti*, 1858, 1, July, Smes', 37–38.
27. Gurovskii, "Promyshlennost i torgovlia v Soedinennykh Shtatakh," *Vestnik promyshlennosti*, 1858, 1, July. Obozrenie promushlennosti i torgovli, 40.
28. G. M. Hutton, Vice-Consul, to Marcy, November 17/29, 1856, 14–15. NARS. RG 59. M.81. R. 5. December 31, 1847–December 30, 1857.
29. Hutton to Marcy, March 1, 1857. NARS. RG 59. M.81. R. 5. December 31, 1847–December 30, 1857.
30. White, *Autobiography of Andrew Dickson White*, Vol. 1, 454.
31. Dow and Wilson, "The Czar's Colts," 35.
32. Bradley, *Guns for the Tsar*, 58.
33. Besides Colt's inventions, the War Ministry also reported in 1857 the successful completion of a test of carbines by the American Merrill (see "Perechen zaniatii," 180–181). At the very end of the period, Russia introduced to its army a gun by another American, Hiram Berdan; it would become famous in Russia as the *berdanka*.
34. Seymour to Marcy, August 16, 1855. Library of Congress Manuscript Division. William Learned Marcy Papers. Cont. 63, No. 46896.
35. G. M. Hutton to Marcy, November 17/29, 1856, 15. NARS. RG 59. M.81. R. 5. December 31, 1847–December 30, 1857.
36. Taylor, *Travels in Greece and Russia*, 369–370.
37. Charles S. Todd to John C. Calhoun, No. 50, December 12/24 1844. NARS. M.35. Vol. 14. R.14.
38. Adams, *Memoirs of John Quincy Adams*, Vol. 12, 187.
39. Todd to Webster, No. 26. February 10/22, 1843. NARS. M.35. Vol. 14. R.14.
40. [Calhoun], *The Papers of John C. Calhoun*, Vol. 21, 153. Todd was evoking Calhoun's participation as a Secretary of War in the annexation of Florida to the United States in 1819.
41. Ditson, *Circassia*, x–xi, 311.

42. *The New York Herald,* May 22, 1848.

43. Donelson to James Buchanan, No. 64, March 28, 1848. Library of Congress Manuscript Division. Andrew J. Donelson Papers. R.7, Vol. 13.

44. Ingersoll to Donelson, March 29, 1848, Library of Congress Manuscript Division. Andrew J. Donelson Papers. R.7, Vol. 13.

45. Ingersoll to James K. Polk, private, April 19, 1848, James K. Polk Papers, Series 2, General Correspondence, R. 52, Library of Congress Manuscript Division, Washington, D.C.

46. *The Great Speeches and Orations of Daniel Webster,* 568.

47. Cited in Eugene Anschel, ed., *The American Image of Russia, 1775–1917,* 107.

48. See, for instance, May, *The Making of the Monroe Doctrine,* 50–51.

49. *The Writings and Speeches of Daniel Webster,* Vol. 4, 213; *The Papers of Daniel Webster: Diplomatic Papers,* Vol. 2, 64.

50. *New Englander and Yale Review,* Vol. 9, No. 33 (February 1851), 89, 107–108.

51. *United States Magazine and Democratic Review,* Vol. 31, No. 172 (October 1852),301–304.

52. Herzen, *My Past and Thoughts,* 478.

53. Davis, *The War of Ormuzd and Ahriman.* Davis later became a Congressman from the Know Nothing-influenced American Party and a Radical Republican during the Civil War.

54. "The Great Republic Tested by the Touch of Truth" (manuscript), New York Public Library. Manuscripts and Archives Division. Aleksyei Grigoryevich Yevstafiev papers, 1814–1852, 5–7. (Published as Evstaf'ev, *The Great Republic.*)

55. Gurowski, *Russia as It Is,* 261–262.

56. Golovin, *Stars and Stripes,* vii, 113.

57. *United States Magazine and Democratic Review,* Vol. 31, No. 173 (November– December 1852), 432.

58. Marcy to Buchanan, private, March 12, 1854. Papers of William L. Marcy. Cont. 80 (Letterbook), 65. Library of Congress Manuscript Division, Washington, D.C.

59. Marcy to Seymour, No. 6, April 14, 1854. NARS. M. 35. DI. Russia. R. 136. Vol. 14, 109.

60. Seymour to Marcy, No. 43, August 2, 1855. NARS. RG. 59. M. 35. DD. Russia. R. 16.

61. Edward Stoeckl to Karl Nesselrode, June 29/August 10, 1854. Cited in Ponomarev, *Krymskaia voina,* 53.

62. Seymour to Marcy, No. 1, March 31, 1854. NARS. RG. 59. M. 35. DD. Russia. R. 16.

63. *The Englishwoman in Russia,* 270–271.

64. See *Treaties.*

65. For more about the Convention, see Ponomarev, *Krymskaia voina.* 95–111.

66. See Kurilla, *Zaokeanskie partnery,* 107–112.

67. Marcy to Seymour, No. 20, October 1, 1855. NARS. M. 35. DI. Russia. R. 136. Vol. 14, 123–124.

68. See Bolkhovitinov and Ponomarev, "Amerikanskie vrachi," 63–69.

69. Whisenhunt, "In the Service of the Tsar," 61.

70. Francis Pickens to Lewis Cass, No. 41, July 5, 1859. NARS. M. 35. DD. Russia. Vol. 18. R. 18.
71. Kolchin, *Unfree Labor.*
72. [Fitzhugh] "Southern Thought," *De Bow's Review*, Vol. 23. No. 4 (October 1857), 343. In contrast, Fitzhugh called the Pope "a radical reformer" and Louis Napoleon and Victoria "half-way socialists."
73. Francis Pickens to Lewis Cass, No. 41, July 5, 1859. NARS. M. 35. DD. Russia. Vol. 18, R. 18.
74. American surgeon Isaac Draper described in his Sebastopol diary the interest his Russian friends showed in Beecher-Stowe's book. See entry on January 27, 1855, in "Notes of Travel from the Diary of the Late Issac Draper, Jr., M.D. Surgeon in the Service of His Majesty the Emperor of Russia at the Siege of Sebastopol. By His Brother Seth Draper." Library of Congress Manuscript Division. The Isaac Draper, Jr. Collection.
75. Kachenovsky, "Zhizn' i sochineniia Danelia Vebstera"; Katchenovsky, *Daniel Webster.*
76. Kovalevsky, "Moe nauchnoe i literaturnoe skitalchestvo," 64.
77. Zelenyi, "O poslednikh piati godakh," 88.
78. White, *Autobiography*, 80–81.

CHAPTER 4: THE NOONDAY OF FRIENDSHIP, 1861–1881

1. Malkin, *Grazhdanskaia voina*; Woldman, *Lincoln and the Russians*; Noskov, *Amerikanskie diplomaty.* See also Kuropiatnik, *Rossiia i SShA*; and the detailed monographs of Norman E. Saul, *Distant Friends* and *Concord and Conflict.*
2. See, for example, Okun, *Rossiisko-amerikanskaia kompaniia*; Fedorova, *Russkaia Amerika*; Grinev, *Aliaska pod krylom*; Petrov, *Rossisko-amerikanskaia kompaniia*; Bolkhovitinov, *Russko-amerikanskie otnosheniia i prodazha Aliaski*; *Istoriia Russkoi Ameriki*; Vinkovetsky, *Russian America*; Farrow, *Seward's Folly.*
3 Cited in Malkin, *Grazhdanskaia voina,* 38–39.
4 *Krasnyi Arkhiv,* Vol. 94 (1939), 115–116.
5 Gorchakov to Stoeckl, February 24/March 8, 1862, in *Kantsler A. M. Gorchakov,* 276–277.
6 Bliemaier, "Cassius Marcellus Clay," 287.
7. *Life and Letters of Bayard Taylor,* Vol. 1, 392.
8. *The Unpublished Letters of Bayard Taylor,* 56.
9. Ibid., 60.
10. Quoted in Kiniapina, "Russia and the U.S. Civil War," 98.
11. Order of the Head of the Navy Ministry (initial draft of the plan to send a squadron to America), in Efimov, "Posylka dvukh eskadr," 106.
12. Navy Ministry Instruction to Counter-Admiral Lesovskii, July 14, 1863, in Adamov, "Soedinennye Shtaty v epokhu Grazhdanskoi voiny," 159–160.

13. Bolkhovitinov, "Russkie eskadry s SShA v 1863–1864 gg.," *Novaia i Noveishaia Istoriia*, No. 5 (1996), 195–216.

14. See, for example, "Emancipation of Serfs in Russia," *Boston Daily Advertiser*, April 12, 1861; "The Emancipation of the Serfs – Imperial Decree," *The Christian Recorder*, April 13, 1861.

15. "A Virginian Howl of Indignation against the Emancipation of Serfdom in Russia," *Cincinnati Daily Press*, April 25, 1861.

16. "Emancipation in Russia," *Atlantic Monthly*, Vol. 8, No. 45 (July 1861), 44.

17. See, for example, "A Woman's View of It," *Anti-slavery Bugle*, March 2, 1861.

18. *Douglass' Monthly*, June 1861.

19. *Douglass' Monthly*, November 1861.

20. White, "Development and Overthrow of the Russian Serf-System," *Atlantic Monthly*, November 1862.

21. *White Cloud Kansas Chief*, January 1, 1863.

22. Abraham Lincoln to Taylor, December 25, 1863; Taylor to Lincoln, December 28, 1863, http://quod.lib.umich.edu/l/lincoln/lincoln7/1:167.

23. Saul, *Distant Friends*, 328.

24. Motovilov, "Dokladnaia zapiska imperatoru Aleksandru II," 433.

25. Ivanov and Levitas, "N. G. Chernyshevsky o rabstve negrov," 118–138; Rogger, "Russia and the Civil War," 177–256.

26. V. Z. [Vissarion Zaitsev], "*Edinstvo roda chelovecheskogo* Katrfazha," *Russkoe Slovo*, No. 8 (1864), 93–100. (This is a review of a Russian translation of Jean Louis Armand de Quatrefages de Bréau, *Unité de l'espèce humaine*, Paris: Librairie Hachette, 1861.)

27. Kolchin, *Emancipation*, 33–34, 307.

28. Lang, "Results of the Serf Emancipation in Russia," 4, 47.

29. Saul, *Distant Friends*, 396.

30. Farrow, *Seward's Folly*, 22–23.

31. Whymper, *Travel and Adventure in the Territory of Alaska*.

32. For details about this visit, see Taker, *His Imperial Highness the Grand Duke Alexis*; Saul, *Concord and Conflict*, 20–39, 54–73; Farrow, *Alexis in America*

33. Fish to Curtin, January 6, 1871. NARS, RG. 59, M 35, Reel 23.

34. Saul, *Concord and Conflict*, 73–75.

35. *Ukazatel' russkogo otdela mezhdunarodnoi vystavki 1876 goda*; Vladimirov, *Russkii sredi Amerikantsev*, 325–330; *Otechestvennye Zapiski*, Vol. 225 (May 1876), 667–689; Vol. 226 (June 1876), 421–452; Vol. 228 (September 1876), 91–120; Vol. 228 (October 1876), 549–66; Vol. 229 (December 1876), 349–384; Kuropyatnik, *Rossiia i SShA*, 304–314; Saul, *Concord and Conflict*, 141–143.

36. *Harper's Weekly* (October 21, 1876), 855.

37. See, for example, Mendeleev, *Neftianaia promyshlennost' v Severo-Amerikanskom shtate Pensil'vaniia i na Kavkaze*; Iossa, *O metalurgicheskom otdele na Filadel'fiyskoi vystavke 1876*; Sytenko, *Pnevmaticheskie i gidravlicheskie tormoza, upotrebliaemye na zheleznykh dorogakh v Amerike*.

38. See, for example, Atkinson to Evarts, April 16, June 4, 1877. NARS, RG. 59, M 35.
39. Fadeev, *Mnenie o vostochnom voprose*, 42; *Moskovskie vedomosti*, January 27, 1869.
40. Kuropyatnik, *Rossiia i SShA*, 258–273, 281–284.
41. *New York Times*, August 27, September 10, and December 29, 1876; *Delo*, Vol. 11 (1876), 395–400.
42. Schuyler's Report on Central Asia, *FRUS*, Vol. 31, 819, 823–824; MacGahan, *Campaign on the Oxus, and the Fall of Khiva*; Schuyler, *Turkistan: Notes of a Journey in Russian Turkistan, Khokand, Bukhara, and Kuldja*.
43. On MacGahan, see Walker, *Januarius MacGahan: The Life and Campaigns of an American War Correspondent*.
44. Green, *Sketches of Army Life in Russia*, 162–169, 177–179.
45. *Harper's Weekly* (May 26, 1877), 408–409.
46. *New York Times*, August 30, 1877; Green, *Sketches of Army Life in Russia*, 14–15, 26, 72.
47. Quoted in Saul, *Concord and Conflict*, 121.
48. Green to Evarts, October 29, 1877. NARS, RG. 59, M 35, Reel 31; *New York Times*, September 9 and 27, 1877.
49. *Obzor vneshnei torgovli Rossii po evropeiskoi i aziatskoi granitsam za 1878 god*, 371–411; Bradley, *Guns for the Tsar*, 115–116, 161–163.
50. Bogolubov, *Ekspeditsiia v Ameriku na parokhode "Cimbria" v 1878 godu*; *Istoricheskii Vestnik*, No. 3 (1883), 604–606, 612. For Barker's correspondence with Semechkin, see in Barker Papers, Box 1, Correspondence in LC, MD; Kuropiatnik, *Rossiia i SShA*, 318–322.
51. *Memoirs of Thomas O. Selfridge, Jr.*, 233.
52. Enclosure in Schuyler to Fish, September 29, 1872. NARS, RG. 59, M 35, Reel 24.
53. Moon, *The American Steppes*, 148–158; Saul, *Concord and Conflict*, 75–85.
54. AVPRI, fond 137 Otchety MID, 1875, L. 343; Gorchakov to Shishkin, August 5, 1875, fond 133, Kantseliariia, Delo 108.
55. Schuyler, *Peter the Great*.
56. Getmant, *Turgenev in England and America*, 39–59; Nikoliukin, *Vzaimosviazi literatur Rossii i SShA: Turgenev, Tolstoy, Dostoevskii i America*, 77–131.
57. *Muzykal'nyi svet*, No. 11 (1872), 81–82; Slavinskii, *Pis'ma ob Amerike i Russkikh pereselentsakh*, 210–213; Saul, *Concord and Conflict*, 53–54.
58. For a range of Americans' opinions of Russia selected from newspaper columns, see Saul, *Concord and Conflict*, 189–192.
59. See, for example, Browne, *The Land of Thor*, 30.
60. *Boston Globe*, March 16, 1872.
61. Knox, *Overland through Asia*, 1870; Kennan, *Tent Life in Siberia and Adventures among the Koraks and Other Tribes of Kamchatka and Eastern Siberia*.
62. *New York Times*, May 4, 1879.
63. Quoted in Saul, *Concord and Conflict*, 195.
64. *New York Times*, August 22, 1880.

65. Arustamova, *Russko-amerikanskii dialog XIX veka*, 306–325; Gleason, "Republic of Humbug: The Russian Nativist Critique of the United States, 1830–1930," 8–9; Banerjee, "'The American Revolver': An Essay on Dostoevsky's *The Devils*," 278–283.
66. See notes in Kuropiatnik, *Rossiia i SShA*, 88–89.
67. Debogorii-Mokrievich, *Vospominaniia*, 10–11. The author of the reminiscences, Vladimir, was Ivan's cousin.
68. Machtet, "Russkaia sem'ia v Kansase," *Nedelia*, Vol. 31 (1875).
69. Etkind, *Tolkovanie puteshestvii*, 79–83.
70. For more on Russian emigrants' communal experiments in the United States, see Kuropiatnik, *Rossiia i SShA*, 93–104; Saul, *Concord and Conflict*, 213–222.
71. Vladimirov, *Russkii sredi Amerikantsev*, 305. See also Kurbskii, A. S. "Russkii rabochii u amerikanskogo plantatora," *Vestnik Evropy*, No. 7 (1883), 21–22.
72. Slavinskii, *Pis'ma ob Amerike*, 225.
73. See, for instance, the essays by A. S. Kurbskii in *Vestnik Evropy*, No. 6–9 (1873), No. 10–11 (1874), and No. 7–9 (1875).
74. Tsimmermann, *Soedinennye Shtaty Severnoi Ameriki: Iz puteshestviy 1857–1858 i 1869–1870*, 109–110, 172, 181.
75. Tsimmerman, "Votchinnyi zakon v Amerike i nashi stepi," *Otechestvennye Zapiski*, No. 234 (September 1877), 109–166. See also Nikoliukin, ed. *A Russian Discovery of America*, 172.
76. Ogorodnikov, *Ot N'iu-Yorka do San-Frantsisko i obratno v Rossiiu*, 261, 349–350. Ogorodnikov's descriptions of the hardships faced by Russian emigrants affected Dostoevsky's perception of America.
77. This point of view was also presented by Kurbskii and Vladimirov in their books, as well as by Skal'kovskii, *V strane iga i svobody*, 283, 388, 400.
78. Along with Cooper, Washington Irving remained popular in Russia. In the 1870s, this list also included Edgar Allan Poe, Bret Harte, and Mark Twain.
79. *Otechestvennye Zapiski*, No. 205 (May 1872), 250–258.

CHAPTER 5: ROMANCE AND REVULSION, 1881–1901

1. Laserson, *The American Impact on Russia, 1784–1917*, 293, 344; Gaddis, *Russia, the Soviet Union, and the United States*, 31; Williams, *American–Russian Relations*, 25–32; LaFeber, "The Turn of Russian–American Relations," 280.
2. Foglesong, *The American Mission and the "Evil Empire*,*"* 7–34; Engerman, *Modernization from the Other Shore*, 17–69; Zhuravleva, *Ponimanie Rossii v SShA*, 53–406.
3. Saul, *Concord and Conflict*, 233–420.
4. Wortman, *Scenarios of Power: Myth and Ceremony in the Russian Monarchy*, 245.
5. Murav'ev to Cassini, January 29/February 10, 1898. AVPRI, fond Kantseliariia, D. 113, 1898, L. 241 ob.–242.

6. This article provided that the inhabitants of two states "shall be at liberty to sojourn and reside in all parts whatsoever of said territories, in order to attend to their affairs, and they shall enjoy, to that effect, the same security and protection as natives of the country wherein they reside, on condition of their submitting to the laws and ordinances there prevailing."

7. Klier and Lambroza, eds., *Pogroms: Anti-Jewish Violence in Modern Russian History*, 40–134.

8. Kuznets, "Immigration of Russian Jews to the United States: Background and Structure," 39.

9. AVPRI, fond Posol'stvo v Vashingtone, D. 27 "Naturalization. Prinyatie amerikanskogo grazhdanstva."

10. *FRUS*, Vol. 48, 739.

11. Adler and Margalith, eds., *With Firmness in the Right*, 259–260.

12. *New York World*, March 26, 1887.

13. "Zadachi vneshnei politiki Rossii po otnosheniiu k Turtsii, Persii, Afganistanu i na Dal'nem Vostoke," January 1900. AVPRI, fond Sekretnyi arkhiv ministra, D. 191/187, L. 24–26.

14. See, for example, William Hunt, *Condition of Public Affairs and Opinion in Russia and of the Jews in Empire*, in NARS, RG. 59, M. 35, Reel 37; *Report of the Commissioners of Immigration upon the Causes Which Incite Immigration to the United States*, 26–101.

15. Lears, *Rebirth of a Nation*, esp. chapter 3.

16. See, for example, debate between William Chandler, senator and nativist, and Simon Wolf, one of the US Jewish leaders: *Washington Post*, April 25, 26, and 27, 1893.

17 Higham, *Send These to Me*, 117–137, 144–157.

18 Govorchin, *From Russia to America with Love*, 22–63; Nitoburg, *Russkie v SShA: Istoriia i sud'by*, 18–76. Ethnic Russians made up only 4.2 percent of Russian emigration: *Abstracts of Reports of the Immigration Commission with Conclusions and Recommendations and Views of the Minority*, Vol. 1, 86–96.

19 See, for example, *New York Times*, February 2, 3, and 16, 1882; *New York Evening Post*, February 1, 1882; *Commercial Advertiser*, March 15, 1882; *Congressional Record*, 47th Congress, 1st Session, Vol. 13, Part 1, 645, 738; Part 2, 1240, 1258, 1326, 1367, 1628, 1647; Part 3, 2026, 2044, 2096, 2141; Part 7, 6691; *Autobiography of John B. Weber*, 113–125.

20. "The Outrages in Russia," *Century* (April 1882), 949; *New York Star*, August 9, 1890; Shankman "Brothers across the Sea," 114–121.

21. *Washington Chronicle*, January 18, 1885.

22. About George Kennan's creed and activity in the 1880s–1890s, see Travis, *George Kennan and American–Russian Relationship*, 153–315.

23. "What Was Said of It Six Years Ago," *Free Russia* (February 1893), 5–6.

24. Foulke, *Slav or Saxon*, 10, 13–14, 22, 33–36, 45, 61–63, 72, 141, 144.

25. *Free Russia* (July 1892), 15–16; (April 1893), 5–6, 11; (January 1894), 1, 5, 8; (February 1894), 4–5; (March 1894), 3; (April 1894), 1–2; Foglesong, *The American Mission and the "Evil Empire,"* 23–25.

26. Nechiporuk, *Vo imia Nigilisma,* 40–186.

27. Noble, *Russia and the Russians.*

28. See, for example, *Free Russia* (June 1892), 15; (June/July 1894), 2; Foglesong, *The American Mission and the "Evil Empire,"* 18–23.

29. Travis, *George Kennan and American–Russian Relationship,* 173–174; Arnaud, *In Defence of Russia and Its Government;* "Charity Traveling Abroad," *Kansas City Times,* April 21, 1890; "Worse Than Russia," *Atlanta Constitution,* May 10, 1890.

30. Hapgood, *Russian Rambles; L. N. Tolstoy i SShA,* 75, 77, 201, 223, 252–253; Foglesong, "Istoki pervogo amerikanskogo krestovogo pokhoda za 'svobodnuiu Rossiiu,'" 121–124; Engerman, *Modernization from the Other Shore,* 41–42.

31. Saul, *The Life and Times of Charles R. Crane,* 39–79.

32. Malia, *Russia under Western Eyes,* 206–207.

33. AVPRI, fond Kantseliariia, D. 105, 1882, L. 112–114, 137–137 ob.; D. 96, 1889, L. 56–58 ob.; D. 173, 1896, L. 164 ob.–166; D. 113, 1898, L 138–150 ob.; D. 110, 1899, L. 165 ob.–166, 200–201, 272–272 ob.

34. Irwin, *Making the World Safe,* 26–27.

35. Williams, *The Roots of the Modern American Empire,* 293–294, 342–343; Westad, *The Global Cold War,* chapter 1.

36. Melville, *White Jacket; or the World in a Man-of-War,* 181.

37. Edgar, *The Russian Famine of 1891 and 1892.*

38. Benjamin F. Tillinghast, "Final Report of the Russian Famine Relief Commission to the Governor of the State of Iowa, June 1, 1892," in *State Historical Society of Iowa,* RG. 043, Governors' Records, G. VIII, Box 37, 4–7.

39. Zhuravleva, "American Corn in Russia," 23–45.

40. Blankenburg, *Philadelphia and the Russian Famine of 1891 and 1892.*

41. *Christian Herald,* March 23, April 13 and 27, 1892.

42. *Congressional Record,* 52nd Congress, 1st Session, Vol. 23, Part 1, 110–111, 157–177.

43. Hoyt, *Report of the Russian Famine Relief Committee of the United States,* 1.

44. Saul, *Concord and Conflict,* 355; Zhuravleva, *Ponimanie Rossii v SShA,* 209–257.

45. Andrey A. Bobrinskii, "Amerikanskaia pomosch' v 1892 i 1893 godakh," *Russkii vestnik,* Vol. 39, No. 2 (1894), 252–264.

46. See March–July 1892 issues of *Moskovskie vedomosti, Rizhskii vestnik,* and *S.-Peterburgskie vedomosti.*

47. Edgar, "Russia's Land System: The Cause of the Famine," 576–580; Edgar, "Russia's Conflict with Hunger," *Review of Reviews,* Vol. 5 (July 1892), 691–700; *Northwestern Miller,* Vol. 33 (June 10, 1892), 896b; Vol. 34 (July 15, 1892), 81; Blankenburg, *Philadelphia and the Russian Famine,* 3, 29, 37, 39, 49; Reeves, *Russia Then and Now. 1892–1917,* 37–43, 98–99.

48. Edgar, "Russian Famine," 64; *Northwestern Miller,* Vol. 33, No. 19 (May 6, 1892), 680; Blankenburg, *Philadelphia and the Russian Famine,* 28–29, 50; Reeves, *Russia*

Then and Now, 26, 77–79, 82; lecture by T. De Witt Talmage "Russia and the Czar," in LC, MD, Thomas De Witt Talmage Papers, Box 31.

49. In 1901, Vereshchagin's second and also very popular exhibition was organized in the United States. Vereshchagin, *Moi puti-dorogi*, 87–112; *Cosmopolitan*, Vol. 6 (February 1889), 311–326; Stasov, "V. V. Vereshchagin v Amerike i Iaponii," 129–133; Vereshchagin, *Vospominaniia syna khudozhnika*, 21–22, 100–101, 165–166; Ivanian, *Kogda govoriat muzy*, 51–54.

50. Evgeniia Lineva received a brilliant musical education, but was forced to cut short her successful career as an opera singer and to follow her husband to the United States, to which he emigrated for political reasons. Upon arriving in New York, she organized a choir of Russian students and emigrants: *New York Sun*, December 13, 1892.

51. Glukhovskii, *Kolumbova vystavka v Chikago: Otchet general'nogo komissara russkogo otdela*, 135, 149, 154; Ivanian, *Kogda govoriat muzy*, 62–63.

52. Yoffe, *Tchaikovsky in America*; Sidel'nikov and Pribegina, *25 dnei v Amerike*.

53. Volkonsky, *Moi vospominaniia*, Vol. 1, 271, 278, 285–297.

54. AVPRI, fond Kantseliariia, D. 101, 1893, L. 37–55.

55. Saul, *Concord and Conflict*, 369–374.

56. Volkonsky, *Moi vospominaniia*, 273, 275; Ozerov, *Amerika idet na Evropu*, 1, 15, 40–47, 54–55; Popov, *V Amerike*, 289–291; Allen, *Russia Looks at America*, 196–209.

57. A. A. Isaev, "Rossiia i Amerika na khlebnom rynke," *Vestnik Evropy*, Vol. 2, No. 4 (April 1889), 557, 567, 573–574.

58. Popov, *V Amerike*, 156–178.

59. Ianzhul and Ianzhul, *Chasy dosuga*, 40–49, 227–374; Ianzhul, *Vospominaniia I. I. Ianzhula o perezhitom i vidennom v 1864–1909 godakh*, 379, 405–406, 440–451.

60. Tverskoi, *Ocherki Severo-Amerikanskikh Soedinennykh Shtatov*.

61. Zhuravleva, *Ponimanie Rossii v SShA*, 321–324, 331–337.

62. McCormick, "The Wilson–McCook Scheme of 1896–1897," 47–58; LaFeber, "The Turn of the Russian–American Relations," 283–285; E. J. Hill, "A Trip through Siberia," *The National Geographic Magazine*, Vol. 13 (February 1902), 38–54.

63. Alexander Ford, "Russia's Field for Anglo-Saxon Enterprise in Asia," *Engineering Magazine*, Vol. 19 (June 1900), 354–357, 360–368.

64. Vanderlip, *In Search of a Siberian Klondike*. The Russian government licensed American engineers and entrepreneurs to mine gold in the Okhotsk and Kamchatka regions; Russian participation, however, was a mandatory condition for granting a mining concession to foreign businesses.

65. Queen, "Wharton Barker and Concessions in Imperial Russia, 1878–1892," 202–214.

66. "American Opportunities in Russia," *World's Work*, Vol. 5 (February 1903), 3139–3140.

67. Edwin Grosvenor, "Siberia," *The National Geographic Magazine*, Vol. 12 (September 1901), 317–324.

68. *Engineering Magazine*, Vol. 21 (April 1901), 29–47; (July 1901), 493–507; *Harper's Weekly*, Vol. 46 (March 1902), 362; Carstensen, *American Enterprise in Foreign Markets*; Saul, *Concord and Conflict*, 409–420, 451.

69. Allen, *Russia Looks at America*, 124–148.

70. Saul, *Concord and Conflict*, 273–279.

71. Tower to Hay, June 3, 1901. NARS, RG 59, DUSMR, M. 35, R. 58.

72. Engerman, *Modernization from the Other Shore*, 28–66; Nikolukin, *Vzaimosviazi litera- tur Rossii i SShA*, 77, 95, 102, 285; Saul, *Concord and Conflict*, 180–185, 320–323.

73. Steiner, *Tolstoy: The Man*; Nikoliukin, *Vzaimosviazi literatur Rossii i SShA*, 132–237; *L. N. Tolstoy i SShA: Perepiska*.

74. On American literature in Russia, see Rubakin, *Etiudy o russkoi chitaiushchei publike*; Allen, *Russia Looks at America*, 73–108.

75. See also Korolenko, *Puteshestvie v Ameriku*.

76. See, for example, Henry Cabot Lodge, "Some Impressions of Russia," *Scribner's Magazine*, Vol. 30 (April 1902), 570–580; Adams, *Vospitanie Genri Adamsa*, 488, 490–496, 524, 527.

77. Vladimir Il'in [Lenin], *Razvitie kapitalizma v Rossii* (St. Petersburg: Tipo- litografiia A. Leiferta, 1899).

78. Noskov, "'Net, svoboda ne tam': slavianofil'skii obraz Ameriki," 251–271; Gleason, "Republic of Humbug," 3–7; E. Pravdin, "Novorozhdennyi messianizm strany dollarov i Staryi Svet," *Istoricheskii Vestnik*, Vol. 74 (November 1898), 704–721.

CHAPTER 6: COLLISION AND REVOLUTION, 1901–1905

1. Romanov, *Rossiia v Man'chzhurii (1892–1906)*; Dennett, *Roosevelt and the Russo- Japanese War*; Dennis, *Adventures in American Diplomacy*, 170–258, 346–388; Zabriskie, *American–Russian Rivalry in the Far East*, 45–100; Moore, *Defining and Defending the Open Door Policy*.

2. The following book is an exception: Thompson and Hart, *The Uncertain Crusade*, 477–527.

3. Saul, *Concord and Conflict*, 423–436.

4. Schimmelpenninck van der Oye, *Toward the Rising Sun*, 25–171.

5. Puleston, *The Life and Work of Captain Alfred Thayer Mahan*, 218–223, 232–238.

6. Adams Brooks, *America's Economic Supremacy*, 175–193; Adams Brooks, *The New Empire*, 186, 194–195, 203.

7. AVPRI, fond Kantseliariia, D. 105, 1901, L. 52; *Diary of Gifford Pinchot*, October 15, 1902, 159. LC, MD, Gifford Pinchot Papers, Box 715.

8. Reinsch, *World Politics at the End of the 19th Century*, 211–216, 219–222, 225, 229, 254–257, 315–317; Edwin Grosvenor, "The Growth of Russia," *National Geographic*, Vol. 11 (May 1900), 176–182; J. K. Mumford, "Russia's Conquest of Asia," *World's Work*, Vol. 2 (May 1901), 704–719.

9. See, for example, Roosevelt to Cecil Arthur Spring Rice, August 11, 1899, in *LTR*, Vol. 2, 1051–1052. See also Roosevelt to Frederic René Coudert, July 3, 1901, in *LTR*, Vol. 2, 106.

10. Hay to Roosevelt, April 25 and 28, 1903. LC. MD, *Papers of John Hay*, Reel 2; Thayer, *The Life and Letters of John Hay*, 368–370.

11. Dennis, *Adventures in American Diplomacy*, 379–380.

12. *Washington Post*, April 24, May 9, 1903; *New York Times*, April 26, May 5, 1903; *New York World*, April 26, May 9 and 11, 1903; *New York Sun*, April 25 and 29; May 9 and 10, 1903; *Puck*, May 13, August 12, 1903; January 20, 1904 (cover); *Judge*, September 5, 1903; *Atlanta Constitution*, July 27, October 15, 1903.

13. *Novoe Vremia*, November 18/December 1, 1903, 3; December 12/25, 1903, 4.

14. Adler and Margalith, eds., *With Firmness in the Right*, 261; Klier and Lambroza, eds., *Pogroms: Anti-Jewish Violence in Modern Russian History*, 195–212; Zipperstein, *Pogrom: Kishinev and the Tilt of History*, xiv.

15. On the US reaction to the Kishinev pogrom, see Stiles, *Out of Kishineff*; Cyrus, ed., *The Voice of America on Kishineff*; Synger, ed., *Russia at the Bar of the American People*; Schoenberg, "The American Reaction to the Kishinev Pogrom of 1903," 263–283; Stults, "Roosevelt, Russian Persecution of the Jews, and American Public Opinion," 13–22; Best, *To Free a People*, 64–90; Zhuravleva, *Ponimanie Rossii v SShA*, 468–491.

16. *Judge*, June 6, 1903, front cover; *New York World*, May 16 and 24, 1903; *Philadelphia Inquirer*, December 30, 1903.

17. *Nation* (May 21, 1903), 407; *Arena*, Vol. 30 (August 1903), 138.

18. *Russia at the Bar of the American People*, 38, 65; Pérez, *The War of 1898*; Pérez, *Cuba in the American Imagination*, 24–94.

19. *Rossiia i SShA: Dokumenty*, 283–288.

20. Hoffman, "Subversive Patriotism," 69–100.

21. Behringer, "Images of Empire," 286–296.

22. *Novoe Vremia. Illustrirovannoe prilozhenie*, June 12/25, 1903, 11. See also *Novoe Vremia*, June 30/July 13, 1903, 3; September 1/14, 1903, 4.

23. *Novoe Vremia*, June 13/26, 1903, 4.

24. Foglesong, *The American Mission and the "Evil Empire,"* 28–29.

25. Shankman, "Brothers across the Sea," 118–119; *Chicago Daily Tribune*, March 11, 1904.

26. *Brooklyn Daily Eagle*, July 2, 1903.

27. Adler, Margalith, eds., *With Firmness in the Right*, 268–270.

28. *Novoe Vremia*, January 9/22, 1904, 3.

29. Scholars are unanimous that the causes of the Russo-Japanese War lay in the imperialist policies and expansionist ambitions of both countries; they differ, however, on whose actions served as the catalyst. For the latest publications on the Russo-Japanese War and its causes, see Steinberg, Menning, Schimmelpenninck van der Oye, Wolff, and Yokote, eds., *The Russo-Japanese War in Global Perspective*.

30. The second had been issued by Secretary of State John Hay in July 1900 in connection with international intervention in China during the Boxer Rebellion.

31. *Rossiia i SShA: Dokumenty*, 52–57; *FRUS, 1904* (Washington, 1905), 722–726.

32. For diplomatic correspondence on the matter, see *Rossiia i SShA: Dokumenty*, 64; *FRUS, 1904* (Washington, 1905), 727–777; *FRUS, 1905* (Washington, 1906), 742–754.

33. *Rossiia i SShA: Dokumenty*, 61–62, 70–75; *FRUS, 1904* (Washington, 1905), 428–429; *FRUS, 1905* (Washington, 1906), 757–760, 785–794; Cassini to Lamzdorf, April 6/19, 1905. AVPRI, fond Kantseliariia, D. 121(1), L. 72.

34. On Japan's propaganda campaign in the United States, see Pavlov, *Russko-iaponskaia voina 1904–1905 gg.*, 325–334; Kulanov and Molodiakov, *Rossiia i Iaponiia: Imidzhevye voiny*, 85–89.

35. Roosevelt to Hay, July 26, 1904. LC, MD, Theodore Roosevelt Papers, Reel 416.

36. George Kennan, "Which Is the Civilized Power?" *Outlook*, Vol. 78 (October 1904), 515; George Kennan, "Kak velos' prosveshchenie russkikh soldat v Iaponii," *Katorga i ssylka*, Vol. 31, No. 2 (1927), 158–165; Travis, *George Kennan and the American–Russian Relationship*, 257–264, 292–294.

37. Through the four war loans, Schiff's banking syndicate gave Japan a total of $180 million: see Best, "Financing a Foreign War: Jacob H. Schiff and Japan, 1904–1905," 314–320; *Rossiia i SShA: Dokumenty*, 57–59, 68–69, 77–78.

38. Oscar S. Straus, "Russia's Attitude toward America," *New York Times*, February 14, 1904.

39. Oscar S. Straus, "The United States and Russia: Their Historical Relations," *North American Review*, Vol. 181 (August 1905), 237–250.

40. On the stance of proponents of Russian–American cooperation, see Saul, *Concord and Conflict*, 479–480, 482–483, 485–487; Zhuravleva, *Ponimanie Rossii v SShA*, 330, 334–336, 526–529.

41. Wharton Barker, "The Secret of Russia's Friendship," *Independent*, Vol. 56 (February 1904), 645–649. See also "New Testimony to Russia's Friendship," *The Literary Digest*, Vol. 28 (April 1904), 543–544; Charles Emory Smith, "Russia," *The National Geographic Magazine*, Vol. 16 (February 1905), 56–57.

42. Beveridge, *The Russian Advance*.

43. *The Literary Digest*, Vol. 28 (January 1904), 101; *Century*, Vol. 68 (September 1904), 816–817; *Gunton's Magazine*, Vol. 26 (May 1904), 441–445. See also Gulick, *The White Peril in the Far East*, 155–156, 161–162.

44. For more on the US "war of images" against Russia during the Russo-Japanese war, see Zhuravleva, *Ponimanie Rossii v SShA*, 544–568.

45. *Judge*, April 8, 1905; April 30, 1904; *Philadelphia Inquirer*, March 27, 1905.

46. Cartoons in *Philadelphia Inquirer*, February 23, 1904; *Life*, March 31, 1904, front cover; April 13, 1905, front cover.

47. Cartoons in *Atlanta Constitution*, June 1, 1905; *Chicago Daily Tribune*, May 30, 1905.

48. Cartoons in *Atlanta Constitution*, February 23, 1904; *Chicago Daily Tribune*, June 10, 1905.

49. See, for example, *Judge*, May 8, 1904.

50. McCormick, *The Tragedy of Russia in Pacific Asia*; Stone, *Fifty Years a Journalist*, 277–282; Greenwood, *The American Observers of the Russo-Japanese War (1904–1905)*.

51. See, for instance, *Independent*, Vol. 56 (March 1904), 602–605; *Forum*, Vol. 36 (October 1904), 190; (January 1905), 349; *New York World*, January 29, 1905.

52. "Soedinennye Shtaty i Rossiia," *Novoe Vremia*, February 13/26, 1904, 3. See also *Novoe Vremia*, February 8/21, 1904; April 5/18, 1905; *Journal de St. Petersburg*, June 18/July 2, June 19/July 3, 1904.

53. "Count Cassini on Russia's Position in the Far East," *Review of Reviews*, Vol. 29 (June 1904), 723; Comte Cassini, "Russia in the Far East," *North American Review* (May 1904), 681–689.

54. Pavlov, *Russko-iaponskaia voina 1904–1905 gg.*, 332.

55. Esper Ukhtomsky, "A Russian View of American Sympathy," *Harper's Weekly*, Vol. 48 (May 1904), 826.

56. "Russia and the United States," *World's Work*, Vol. 9 (March 1905), 5894; "War Cartoons and Songs That Stir the Patriotism of Russians," *Chicago Daily Tribune*, May 4, 1904.

57. On visualizing the image of the Japanese and their allies in Russia during the war, see Norris, *A War of Images*, 107–134; Mikhailova, "Images of Enemy and Self: Russian 'Popular Prints' of the Russo-Japanese War," 30–53.

58. "Iaponskii imperator i ego lukavye dobrozhelateli, 1904." GPIB, Otdel redkikh knig, Papka 5 "Russko-Iaponskaia Voina."

59. See the following *lubki*: "Ataka na Port-Mone," 1904; "V pogone za den'gami. (Pesnia iapontsev)," 1904; "Pomogite na voennye nuzhdy," 1904. GPIB, Otdel redkikh knig, Papka 5 "Russko-Iaponskaia Voina."

60. Laserson, *The American Impact on Russia*, 325–329; Shelokhaev, ed., *Liberal'noe dvizhenie v Rossii 1902–1905 gg.*, 510–513, 564.

61. Solov'ev, *Vospominaniia diplomata*, 113–114.

62. Thorson, "American Public Opinion and the Portsmouth Peace Conference," 439–448; "Dnevnik F. F. Martensa za 1905–1906 gg." AVPRI, fond 340, Lichnyi arkhiv F. F. Martensa, D. 6, L. 34–34 ob.; Ivan Yakovlevich Korostovets, "Mirnye peregovory v Portsmute v 1905 g.: Dnevnik I. Ia. Korostovtsa, sekretaria Grafa S. Iu. Vitte vo vremia Portsmutskoi konferentsii. Iiul'–oktyabr', 1905," *Byloe*, Vol. 29, No. 1 (1918), 198, 209.

63. On the course and contents of the Portsmouth talks, see *Sbornik diplomaticheskikh dokumentov, kasaiushchikhsia peregovorov mezhdu Rossiei i Iaponiei o zakluchenii mirnogo dogovora (24 maya–3 oktyabrya)*. St. Petersburg, 1906; *FRUS, 1905* (Washington, 1906), 807–820; Howe, *George von Lengerke Meyer*, 167–170, 181–183, 197–205.

64. Witte, *Vospominaniia*, Vol. 2, 374–416; Korostovets, "Mirnye peregovory v Portsmute," No. 1, 179, 193; No. 3, 64–65, 69, 71; *Dnevnik F. F. Martensa*, L. 31–61; Feodor de Martens, "The Portsmouth Peace Conference," *North American Review*, Vol. 181 (November 1905), 646–647; Rosen, *Forty Years of Diplomacy*, 1,

266–267. See also *Novoe Vremya*, July 22/August 4, 1905, 3; August 2/15, 1905, 2; August 8/21, 1905, 2; August 12/25, 1905, 3.

65. Dennett, *Roosevelt and the Russo-Japanese War*, 238–239, 248–249, 264; Zabriskie, *American–Russian Rivalry in the Far East*, 122–124, 128; Dennis, *Adventures in American Diplomacy*, 14, 410–411; Trani, *The Treaty of Portsmouth*, 36–37, 59–62, 80–83, 138–159; Saul, "The Kittery Peace," *The Russo-Japanese War in Global Perspective*, Vol. 1, 503, 507.

66. Romanov, *Ocherki diplomaticheskoi istorii russko-iaponskoi voiny*, 494–495.

67. See, for example, Brodsky, *Amerikanskaia ekspansiia v Severo-Vostochnom Kitae*, 153–166.

68. Zhuravleva, *Ponimanie Rossii v SShA*, 581–617.

69. George Kennan, "The Sword of Peace in Japan," *Outlook*, Vol. 81 (October 1905), 357–365; "Roosevelt as Russia's Helper," *Review of Reviews*, Vol. 32 (October 1905), 475.

70. Korostovets, "Mirnye peregovory v Portsmute," No. 3, 84; *The Literary Digest*, Vol. 31 (September 1905), 335; *Harper's Weekly*, Vol. 49 (September 1905), 1337; McCormick, *The Tragedy of Russia in Pacific Asia*, Vol. 2, 145–146; Bailey, *America Faces Russia*, 204; Laserson, *American Impact on Russia*, 329–332.

71. Miliukov, *Russia and Its Crisis*; Alice Stone Blackwell, "Welcome to a Russian Woman," *Woman's Journal*, Vol. 35 (December 1904), 401; "Sympathy for Russian People," *The Providence Journal*, February 23, 1905.

72. On SAFRF's activities before and during the revolution, see Nechiporuk, *Vo imia Nigilisma*, 186–212.

73. See cartoons in *Chicago Daily Tribune*, January 24, 1905; *San Francisco Examiner*, February 3, 1905.

74. Thompson, *The Uncertain Crusade*, 25, 30, 34, 100; *Outlook*, Vol. 70 (January 1905), 218; *Arena*, Vol. 33 (February 1905), 210–213.

75. *Puck*, February 8, 1905, front cover.

76. *Chicago Daily Tribune*, January 31, March 6, November 13, 1905; *New York World*, February 25, 1905; *Columbus Evening Dispatch*, November 1, 1905; *Philadelphia Inquirer*, July 4, 1905.

77. Edmund Noble, "America and the Russian Crisis," *Free Russia* (March 1905), 35; Foglesong, "Redeeming Russia? American Missionaries and Tsarist Russia," 356–357; Foglesong, *The American Mission and the "Evil Empire,"* 34–36.

78. Edmund Noble, "American Views of Russian Assassination," *Free Russia* (April 1905), 50–51.

79. Mark Twain, "The Czar's Soliloquy," *North American Review*, Vol. 180 (March 1905), 324.

80. Jack London, "Revolution," 12–14, 16–17.

81. *Independent*, Vol. 59 (August 1905), 509–511; *Outlook*, Vol. 81 (November 1905), 596–598; (December 1905), 859–860; *McClure's Magazine*, Vol. 26 (April 1906), 655–662. See cartoons in *Chicago Daily Tribune*, October 28, November 1, 1905; *New York World*, November 1, December 7, 1905; *Judge*, November 25, 1905.

82. Howe, *George von Lengerke Meyer*, 286, 306–307.
83. George Kennan, "The Attitude of the Russian People," *Outlook*, Vol. 84 (October 1906), 328–332.
84. Walling, *Russia's Message*; Arthur Bullard, *Russia's Revolution: 1905–1906*, in Princeton University, Mudd Library, Arthur Bullard Papers, Box 5; Durland, *The Red Reign.*
85. For a detailed description of the American perception, see Thompson and Hart, *The Uncertain Crusade*; Zhuravleva, *Ponimanie Rossii v SShA*, 626–764; Foglesong, *The American Mission and the "Evil Empire,"* 34–43.

CHAPTER 7: INTERACTIONS AND CONTRADICTIONS, 1906–1914

1. Minger, "William Howard Taft's Forgotten Visit to Russia," 149–156.
2. *Rossiia i SShA: Dokumenty*, 383–386.
3. See, for example, Zabriskie, *American–Russian Rivalry in the Far East*, 131–191; Esthus, *Theodore Roosevelt and the International Rivalries*, 136–150; Williams, *American–Russian Relations 1781–1947*, 50–74; Ignat'ev, *Vneshnia politika Rossii*, 65, 125–134, 181–184; Shatsillo, *Rossiia i SShA: Ot Portsmutskogo mira do padeniia tsarizma*, 14–117.
4. Saul, *Concord and Conflict*, 509–588; Zhuravleva, *Ponimanie Rossii v SShA*, 787–980.
5. Ignat'ev, *Vneshnia politika Rossii*, 64–65.
6. The 1907 Gentlemen's Agreement between the two governments banned the immigration of Japanese laborers, though it did allow the immigration of the spouses and children of those Japanese immigrants who were already in the United States.
7. *Rossiia i SShA: Dokumenty*, 126–134.
8. For more details about the dynamics of US–Japan relations between the Russo-Japanese War and the First World War, see LaFeber, *The Clash: U.S.–Japanese Relations throughout History*, 85–106.
9. *New York World*, December 31, 1911; *Philadelphia Inquirer*, January 15, 1912.
10. Bailey, *America Faces Russia*, 224.
11. For further discussion, see Crane and Breslin, *An Ordinary Relationship: American Opposition to Republican Revolution in China.* On the US policy toward China after the end of the Russo-Japanese War and on the racial dimension of America's perception of the Chinese, see also Hunt, *The Making of a Special Relationship: The United States and China to 1914.*
12. Gaddis, *Russia, the Soviet Union, and the United States*, 40.
13. Saul, "A Diplomatic Failure and an Ecological Disaster: The United States, Russia, and the North Pacific Fur Seals, 1867–1914," 255–266. For the diplomatic correspondence from the time of the Washington conference, see *Rossiia i SShA: Documenty*, 237–277.
14. "Russia's Message," *Outlook*, Vol. 89 (August 1908), 764.

15. Travis, *George Kennan and American–Russian Relationship*, 284–285.
16. See Kennan's articles in *Outlook*, Vol. 85 (March 107), 751–755; *McClure's Magazine* (May 1908), 74–80; *Century*, Vol. 80 (June 1910), 163–165, 176; (July 1910), 403–404; (October 1910), 926–931.
17. Foulke, *A Random Record of Travel during Fifty Years*, 96, 98, 101–107.
18. Tchaikovsky to Kennan, January 8, 1907, NYPL, MAD, George Kennan Papers, Box 1.
19. See letter dated March 10, 1907, in John Ryland's Library, Manchester University, MD, Alexis Aladin Papers, Box 10, Bundle 24.
20. Nechiporuk, *Vo imia Nigilizma*, 232–245.
21. *Novoe Vremia*, August 5/18, 1907.
22. For more on Americans' response to the tours of Tchaikovsky, Aladin, and Milyukov, see Christian, *Alexis Aladin: The Tragedy of Exile*, 67–72; Good, *Strangers in a Strange Land*, 136–137; Zhuravleva, *Ponimanie Rossii v SShA*, 853–873.
23. *Outlook*, Vol. 90 (September 1908), 2–3; *New York Times*, August 23, September 13 and 21, 1908; *The Nation*, Vol. 87 (November 1908), 509–510; AVPRI, fond Posol'stvo v Vashingtone, D. 636, 639; fond Vtoroi departament I-1, D. 148; *FRUS, 1909*, 513–523.
24. The history of the 1832 treaty's abrogation is well researched. See, for example, Engel', *"Evreiskii Vopros" v russko-amerikanskikh otnosheniiakh*, 52–123; Best, *To Free a People*,166–205; Schachner, *The Price of Liberty: A History of the American Jewish Committee*, 12–58; Cohen, "The Abrogation of the Russo-American Treaty of 1832," 3–41; Healy, "Tsarist Anti-Semitism and Russian–American Relations," 418–425. For an analysis of the movement's rhetoric, see Zhuravleva, *Ponimanie Rossii v SShA*, 879–913.
25. "Some Reasons Why the Executive Should Not Favor the Denunciation of the Treaty of 1832 with Russia," February 1911. NARS, RG. 59, PRRSU, M 333, Reel 5; "The Following Reasons Why It Would Not Be Advisable to Abrogate the Commercial Treaty of 1832 with Russia," April 11, 1911. NARS, RG. 59, PRRSU, M 333, Reel 6.
26. Address of Louis Marshall on "Russia and the American Passport" before Council of American Hebrew Congregation in New York, January 19, 1911, 7–8, 14–16.
27. Travis, *George Kennan and American–Russian Relationship*, 272–277.
28. *Termination of the Treaty of 1832 between the United States and Russia*, 16.
29. See cartoons in *The Literary Digest*, Vol. 43 (December 1911), 1142, 1184; Vol. 44 (January 1912), 1–2; *Los Angeles Times*, December 16, 1911; *New York Times*, December 24, 1911.
30. Congressional Record, 62nd Congress, 2nd Session, Vol. 48, Part 1, 311–353, 453–454, 473–507; Part 12 (Appendix), 17.
31. Egert, *The Conflict between the United States and Russia*.
32. *Otmena Soedinennymi Shtatami Severnoi Ameriki dogovora 1832 g.* (St. Petersburg, 1912).

33. *Golos Moskvy*, December 14 and 29, 1911; January 1, 1912.

34. Pavel Nikolaevich Miliukov, *Vneshnaia politika Rossii v 1911 g.* GARF, fond 579, D. 1444, L. 18–19.

35. For more on the stances of various political parties in Russia concerning the abrogation of the treaty, see Engel', *"Evreiskii Vopros" v russko-amerikanskikh otnosheniiakh*, 91–97; Laserson, *The American Impact on Russia*, 359–363, 366–369.

36. Memorandum for the Secretary Relative to the Adverse Influence of the Prospective Treaty Termination on American Commercial Interests in Russia, July 1912. NARS, RG. 59, PRRSU, M 333, Reel 6.

37. For more on the economic consequences of abrogating the treaty, see Engel', *"Evreiskii Vopros" v russko-amerikanskikh otnosheniiakh*, 83–85, 110–116; Saul, *Concord and Conflict*, 578–579.

38. Gaddis, *Russia, the Soviet Union, and the United States*, 42; Saul, *Concord and Conflict*, 577.

39. Laserson, *The American Impact on Russia*, 370; Engel', *"Evreiskii Vopros" v russko-amerikanskikh otnosheniiakh*, 126; Cohen, *The Abrogation of the Russo-American Treaty of 1832*, 41; Gaddis, *Russia, the Soviet Union, and the United States*, 46; Foglesong, *The American Mission and the "Evil Empire*,*"* 44.

40. Shuster, *The Strangling of Persia*. See anti-Russian cartoons in *Philadelphia Inquirer*, December 27 and 28, 1911; *The Literary Digest*, Vol. 44 (January 1911), 2.

41. Core US exports to Russia included cotton, agricultural equipment and machinery, copper, non-ferrous metals, machine tools, compressors, washing and sewing machines, the products of the Remington and Underwood Typewriter Companies, and cash registers: *Rossiia i SShA: Torgovo-ekonomicheskie otnosheniia*, 13–16, 71–74.

42. John V. Hogan, "Russian–American Commercial Relations," *Political Science Quarterly*, Vol. 27 (December 1912), 638, 645; Saul, *Concord and Conflict*, 531, 533–543.

43. Shpotov, *Genri Ford: Zhizn' i biznes*, 335–337.

44. Saul, *Concord and Conflict*, 548–551.

45. *Novoe Vremia*, November 27/December 10, 1910.

46. See articles in *Novoe Vremia*, November 30/December 13, 1910; *Russkoe Slovo*, January 26, 1911; *Birzhevye Vedomosti*, January 12/25, 1911; *Autobiography of John Hays Hammond Illustrated with Photographs*, Vol. 2, 469–473; *New York Times*, February 4, 1911.

47. Askew, "Efforts to Improve Russo-American Relations before the First World War: The John Hays Hammond Mission," 183–185.

48. Saul, *War and Revolution*, 5–8.

49. Koshma and Sokal'skii, *Ob uchrezhdenii russkoi sel'skohoziaistvennoi agentury v SShA*; Allen, *Russia Looks at America*, 139–147, 161–168, 170–177; Michael, *More Corn for Bessarabia*.

50. Saul, *Concord and Conflict*, 552–555; Moon, *The American Steppes: The Unexpected Russian Roots of Great Plains Agriculture*, 70–74, 95–96, 102–106, 167–187.

51. "Ustav Russko-amerikanskoi torgovoi palaty, 1913," in *Rossiia i SShA: Torgovo-economicheskie otnosheniia. 1900–1930*, 75–80.

52. *New York Times*, July 13, 1913.

53. Davis, *The Russian Immigrants*, 8; Borodin, *Severo-Amerikanskie Soedinennye Shtaty i Rossiia*, 300–301; Vil'chur, *Russkie v Amerike*, 57–61; Nitoburg, *Russkie v SShA*, 23–29, 38–43.

54. *Rech*, July 31/August 13, 1907; August 7/20, 1908; December 30, 1909/ January 12, 1910; January 5/18, December 18/31, 1911; August 9/22, 1913; *Russkie Vedomosti*, December 30, 1909; *Birzhevye Vedomosti*, October 22/ November 4, 1908; July 27/August 9, October 4/17, 1912.

55. *Moskovskii Ezhenedel'nik*, October 3, 1909; March 27, June 26, 1910; *Russkie Vedomosti*, October 22, 1909; *Utro Rossii*, September 1, December 7, 1910; March 24, June 9, 1911; December 7 and 19, 1912; March 13, 1913.

56. *Golos Moskvy*, July 10, August 8 and 26, September 12, 16, and 30, 1908; March 6, April 7, June 9, 1910; November 18, 1912; January 31, 1913.

57. Mizhuev, *Istoriia velikoi amerikanskoi demokratii*; Mizhuev, *Prava cheloveka i grazhdanina*; Mizhuev, *Glavnye federatsii sovremennogo mira*.

58. Kovalevsky, *Istoriia amerikanskikh uchrezhdenii*.

59. Ozerov, *America idet na Evropy*; Ozerov, *Chemu nas uchit America?*

60. On the development of American Studies in Russia in 1905–1914, see Zhuravleva, "Russian Studies in the United States and Amerikanistika in the Russian Empire," 48–58; Laserson, *The American Impact on Russia*, 372–396.

61. Babin, *Istoriia Severo-Amerikanskikh Soedinennykh Shtatov*, Vol. 1, 489; Vol. 2, 412, 426, 440–441.

62. *New York World*, April 12, 1906.

63. *New York Times*, April 11, 1906.

64. See, for example, *San Francisco Call*, April 14, 1906. Gorky's visit to the United States has been extensively described in scholarship and evaluated from various points of view. See, for instance, Ganelin, "M. Gor'kii i amerikanskoe obshchestvo v 1906 godu," 200–222; H'etso, *Maksim Gor'kii: Sud'ba pisatelia*, 111–128; Good, *Strangers in a Strange Land*, 175–241.

65. When it was first published in August 1906 in *Appleton's Magazine* as "The City of Mammon," this sketch had an optimistic ending that held nothing of the hopeless pessimism of the ending to "The City of the Yellow Devil."

66. *Rossiia i SShA: Dokumenty*, 306–307, 582.

67. See, for example, *Zemshchina*, December 10/23 and 13/26, 1911.

68. Brooks, *When Russia Learned to Read*, 93, 142–153; Chukovskii, *Nat Pinkerton i sovremennaia literatura*.

69. Alexandrov, *The Black Russian*, chapters 3–5.

70. Saul, *Concord and Conflict*, 562–563; Allen, *Russia Looks at America*, 107–110.

71. See, for example, Phelps, *Essays on Russian Novelists*.

72. *Review of Reviews*, Vol. 38 (October 1908), 443–448; *Current Literature*, Vol. 45 (October 1908), 403–404; *Outlook*, Vol. 88 (March 1908), 743–746; *L. N. Tolstoy i SShA*, 773, 778, 792, 794, 878.

73. *Review of Reviews*, Vol. 39 (January 1909), 49; *Outlook*, Vol. 92 (May 1909), 105–108, 336–337; *Living Age*, Vol. 25 (May 1908), 433–434; *North American Review*, Vol. 192 (December 1910), 738–745; *L. N. Tolstoy i SShA*, 741–744, 863–868, 898–904.

74. Roosevelt Theodore, "Tolstoy," *Outlook*, Vol. 92 (May 1909), 105. For more on the influence of Russian literature on the perception of Russia in the United States, see Zhuravleva, *Ponimanie Rossii v SShA*, 951–963.

75. Orlenev, *Zhizn' i tvorchestvo russkogo aktera Pavla Orleneva, opisannye im samim*, 272; *Current Literature*, Vol. 39 (July 1905), 76–77; *Century*, Vol. 71 (December 1905), 301; Lewton, *Alla Nazimova*.

76. Chaliapin, *Stranitsi iz moei zhizni*, 124–125; *Craftsman*, Vol. 27 (November 1914), 136; *McClure's Magazine*, Vol. 41, No. 5 (September 1913), 33–44; Ivanian, *Kogda govoriat muzy*, 83–84. In 1926, Mordkin moved to the United States, founding a ballet school in New York that would become the beginnings of the world-famous American Ballet Theater.

77. *Charles R. Crane Memoirs*, 70–72, 86–87, Folder 11 "Philanthropy." BA, The Crane Family Papers, Box 18; Ivanian, *Kogda govoriat muzy*, 75; Vil'chur, *In the American Crucible*, 129.

78. Saul, *Concord and Conflict*, 557–558.

79. Harper, *The Russia I Believe in*, 29–30, 52–53, 56, 61.

80. Coolidge, *The United States as a World Power*, 213, 216, 218–223; Byrnes, *A History of Russian and East European Studies in the United States*, 5–19, 173–197.

81. Dubie, *Frank A. Golder: An Adventure of a Historian in Quest of Russian History*; Patenaude and Emmons, eds., *War, Revolution, and Peace in Russia: The Passages of Frank Golder, 1914–1927*, xi–xxvi.

82. Parry, *America Learns Russian*, 53–62.

CHAPTER 8: WARTIME HONEYMOON, 1914–1917

1. The best of all is Norman Saul's fundamental book *War and Revolution: The United States and Russia, 1914–1921*.

2. The post-Soviet historiography continued to insist that areas of conflict predominated. See, for example, Kozenko, "Nesostoiavsheesia sblizhenie," 140–144; Shatsillo, *Rossiia i SShA: Ot Portsmutskogo mira do padeniia tsarisma*.

3. Ganelin, *Rossiia i SShA. 1914–1917: Ocherki istorii russko-amerikanskikh otnoshenii*; Lebedev, *Russko-amerikanskie ekonomicheskie otnosheniia. 1900–1917 gg.*; Rielage, *Russian Supply Efforts in America*.

4. Grayson, *Russian–American Relations in World War I*.

5. For one of the best comprehensive overviews, see Winter, ed., *The Cambridge History of the First World War*.

6. For different aspects of the historiographical debates, see Paddock and Troy, eds., *Contesting the Origins of the First World War: An Historiographical Argument*.

7. Among the most recent works on this topic, see Chubarian, ed., *Rossiia v sisteme mezhdunarodnykh otnoshenii nakanune i v gody Pervoi mirovoi voiny*, Vol. 2: *Rossiia i sojuzniki*.

8. Foglesong, *America's Secret War against Bolshevism*, 26–29; Zhuravleva, *Ponimanie Rossii v SShA*, 879–912.

9. *Novoe Vremia*, January 14/27, 1914.

10. *PWW*, Vol. 30, 432; Vol. 31, 316, 459; Vol. 41, 184; Gaddis, *Russia, the Soviet Union, and the United States*, 54; Neu, *Colonel House*, 133–154.

11. Marye, *Nearing the End in Imperial Russia*, 17–18; *FRUS, 1914*, Supplement "The World War," 26–27.

12. Saul, *War and Revolution*, 12–14.

13. *PWW*, Vol. 30, 393–394.

14. Neu, *Colonel House*, 155–182.

15. *Rossiia i SShA: Documenty*, 645; AVPRI, F. 133, Kantseliariia MID, Op. 470, D. 62, L. 2.

16. *Utro Rossii*, January 11, 1917.

17. *Rech'*, November 6/19, 1914; January 9/22, March 15, 1915; November 1, 1916; *Vestnik Evropy*, No. 7 (1915), 273; No. 8 (1915), 308; *Utro Rossii*, August 22, October 11, 1915; May 24, 1916; January 25, 1917.

18. See Zhuravleva, "Natsional'no-religioznyi vopros v rossiysko-amerikanskikh otnosheniiakh v period Pervoi mirovoi voiny," 215–243.

19. AVPRI, fond Osobyi politotdel, D. 364, L. 1–84.

20. Mamatey, *The United States and East Central Europe. 1914–1918*, 41, 49, 84; Unterberger, *The United States, Revolutionary Russia, and the Rise of Czechoslovakia*, 12, 17; Wolff, *Woodrow Wilson and the Reimagining of Eastern Europe*, 56–114.

21. Wandycz, *The United States and Poland*, 105–130.

22. *PWW*, Vol. 35, 367; Vol. 37, 404–406, 414, 421–422; Vol. 38, 29–30, 72, 79–81, 106, 368–371, 396–397; Vol. 42, 432–433.

23. Wolff, *Woodrow Wilson and the Reimagining of Eastern Europe*, 122–130.

24. *Rossiia i SShA: Documenty*, 648.

25. Ibid., 307–308.

26. *New York Sun*, February 4, 14, and 24, 1915.

27. Saul, *War and Revolution*, 10–11, 38–39.

28. Marye, *Nearing the End in Imperial Russia*, 40; Francis, *Dollars and Diplomacy*, 13–16, 18–19, 28–30, 49–50.

29. See Ganelin, *Rossiia i SShA*, 27–28; Saul, *War and Revolution*, 17, 64, 73; Grayson, *Russian–American Relations in World War I*, 48, 53–54, 78; Trani and Davis, *The First Cold War*, 22–27.

30. Ganelin, *Rossiia i SShA*, 10–15, 34–44, 50–80.

31. *Birzhevye vedomosti*, December 5/18, 1915; *Utro Rossii*, August 30, November 2, December 2, 1915; May 14, 30, 1916; *Golos Moskvy*, May 23, 1915.

32. Saul, *War and Revolution*, 14–15; *Washington Post*, March 15, 1915; *Boston Transcript*, March 19, 1915; *Journal of Commerce*, March 20, 1915.

33. Lebedev, *Russko-amerikanskie ekonomicheskie otnosheniia*, 160; Rielage, *Russian Supply Efforts in America*, 14–24.

34. Gayduk, *Materialy i fakty o zagotovitel'noi deiatel'nosti russkikh voennykh komissii v Amerike*, 29–36.

35. Zaliubovsky, *Snabzhenie russkoi armii v Velikuiu voinu*, 8–16, 24–27, 121–127; *Rossiia i SShA: Documenty*, 743–746; Lebedev, *Russko-amerikanskie ekonomicheskie otnosheniia*, 205–209.

36. Ganelin, *Rossiia i SShA*, 19–21, 148.

37. *PWW*, Vol. 32, 67, 442; Vol. 33, 511.

38. Saul, *War and Revolution*, 62–71.

39. *Rossiia i SShA: Documenty*, 218.

40. Ganelin, *Rossiia i SShA*, 99–106, 115–116, 127.

41. *Vestnik Russko-Amerikanskoi Torgovoi Palaty*, No. 12 (1916), 342; No. 8 (1916), 221.

42. Saul, *War and Revolution*, 20–26, 66, 74–75; Anatoly Zaliubovsky, *Snabzhenie russkoi armii*, 28–120; Lebedev, *Russko-amerikanskie ekonomicheskie otnosheniia*, 164–167, 174–202, 233–237.

43. Ganelin, *Rossiia i SShA*, 21–22.

44. Libbey, "The American–Russian Chamber of Commerce," 233–236.

45. *Vestnik Russko-Amerikanskoi Torgovoi Palaty*, No. 1 (1915), 3–5; *Russkoe Slovo*, May 25/June 7, 1916.

46. *Rossiia i SShA: Torgovo-ekonomicheskie otnosheniia*, 87, 90, 96–97.

47. Ibid., 124–134, 142–145, 150–159.

48. Ibid., 81–85.

49. Miller, *The American YMCA and Russian Culture*, 20–21, 43–47.

50. On different aspects of humanitarian cooperation, see detailed discussions in *Rossiia i SShA: Documenty*, 790–800; *FRUS, 1915*, Supplement "The World War," 1013, 1019–1023; Davis and Trani, *The First Cold War*, 55–56; Saul, *War and Revolution*, 36–47; Miller, *The American YMCA and Russian Culture*, 113–118.

51. Child, *Potential Russia*, 186–187.

52. *Rosiia i SShA: Documenty*, 613.

53. Ibid., 620.

54. Ibid., 632.

55. Foglesong, *The American Mission and the "Evil Empire,"* 49.

56. Saul, *The Life and Times of Charles R. Crane*, 128–135.

57. For details, see Shatsillo, *Rasschet i bezrassudstvo*, 231–275.

58. *The Literary Digest*, August 14, 1915, 250–251; June 24, 1916, 1833; July 1, 1916, 11; *Outlook*, February 3, 1915, 263; *North American Review* (April 1916), 431–436; *Review of Reviews* (October 1915), 437; (July 1916), 56–64.

59. For more on this, see Saul, *War and Revolution*, 48–52.

60. *Outlook* (October 1914), 377–380; (March 1915), 767–770. On Kennan's activity in 1914–1917, see Travis, *George Kennan and the American–Russian Relationship*, 316–348.

61. [Nicholas Butler], *Osnovy prochnogo mira: Stat'i Cosmos'a, poiavivshiesia v newyorkskom Times* (New York, unpublished translation by Russian information bureau, 1917), 48–53. For the same idea, see Austin Ogg, "The Vast Empire of the Czars," *Munsey's Magazine*, Vol. 54 (1915), 641–680.

62. "The Slav: His Splendor, His Misery, and His Place among the Nations of Tomorrow," *Craftsman*, Vol. 27, No. 2 (1914), 135.

63. Young, *Abused Russia*, 102–104.

64. Herlihy, *The Alcoholic Empire*, 4, 8, 67–68.

65. For more detail about images of Russia in the United States in 1914–1916, see Foglesong, *The American Mission and the "Evil Empire,"* 47–50; Saul, *War and Revolution*, 27–31; Zhuravleva, *Ponimanie Rossii v SShA*, 998, 1001–1002, 1007–1011.

66. *New York Times*, January 15, 1917; *The Literary Digest*, November 27, 1916, 1216; December 6, 1916, 1528; February 10, 1917, 330–331.

67. About this trip, see Zhuravleva, "Rethinking Russia in the United States during the First World War: Mr. Sigma's American Voyage," 143–160.

68. *Rossiia i SShA: Documenty*, 631.

69. *The Literary Digest*, August 5, 1916, 295–296; *Novoe Vremia*, September 24, 1916. This article titled "The Russia–U.S. Rapprochement" was written by Arthur Henderson, American commercial agent in Russia.

70. AVPRI, fond Posol'stvo v Vashingtone, D. 525, L. 33–36; Saul, *War and Revolution*, 112–115.

71. See Parry, *America Learns Russian*, 65–72; Saul, *War and Revolution*, 52–58; Zhuravleva, "Russian Studies in the United States and *Amerikanistika* in the Russian Empire," 45–76.

72. Wiener, *An Interpretation of the Russian People*, 10, 14–15, 17, 95, 99.

73. *New York Times*, March 25, 1915.

74. Saul, *The Life and Times of Charles R. Crane*, 128.

75. Golder, *Guide to Materials for American History in Russian Archives*.

76. Emmons and Patenaude, eds., *War, Revolution, and Peace in Russia*, 3–86.

77. AVPRI, fond Posol'stvo v Vashingtone, D. 408, L. 3–5 ob., 7–7 ob.

78. Fortunatov, *Istoriia Soedinennykh Shtatov*, Chast' 1: 44–45; Chast' 2: 226.

79. *Izvestiia Obshchestva sblizheniia mezhdu Rossiei i Amerikoi*, No. 1 (1915), 2–3.

80. Borodin, *Severo-Amerikanskie Soedinennye Shtaty i Rossiia*; Borodin, *Amerikantsy i amerikanskaia kul'tura*.

CHAPTER 9: REVOLUTION AND INTERVENTION, 1917–1920

1. Tuveson, *Redeemer Nation*.

2. Smith, *Russia in Revolution*, 101–104; Lyandres, *The Fall of Tsarism*.

3. Joshua Butler Wright Diary, entries for January 25, February 1, February 22, and February 14, 1917, Mudd Manuscript Library, Princeton University; Houghteling, *A Diary of the Russian Revolution*, 64, 170.

4. Foglesong, *America's Secret War against Bolshevism*, 49.

5. For example, "Into the Light," *New York World*, March 17, 1917; "Welcome," *New York World*, March 24, 1917; "Welcome, Russia!" *Life*, May 10, 1917.

6. *New York Evening World*, March 17, 1917, 2.

7. "The Revolution in Russia" (editorial), *Brooklyn Eagle*, March 16, 1917, 6; "Crumbling Thrones" (editorial), *Atlanta Constitution*, March 18, 1917, 4; "Democracy Spreading in Russia" (editorial), *Philadelphia Inquirer*, March 17, 1917; Lasch, *The American Liberals and the Russian Revolution*, 29; Travis, *George Kennan and the American–Russian Relationship, 1865–1924*, 328.

8. Figes and Kolonitskii, *Interpreting the Russian Revolution*, 169–189; Steinberg, *The Russian Revolution, 1905–1921*, 69, 73, 76.

9. See, for example, Houghteling, *A Diary of the Russian Revolution*, 156, and the discussion of statements by Paul Miliukov and Boris Bakhmeteff later in this chapter.

10. "Soviet Appeal to the Peoples of All the World," March 14/27, 1917, in Browder and Kerensky, eds., *The Russian Provisional Government, 1917: Documents*, Vol. II: 1077–1078.

11. See, for example, Lasch, *The American Liberals and the Russian Revolution*, 36; Travis, *George Kennan and the American–Russian Relationship*, 340.

12. Adress to Congress, April 2, 1917, in Baker and Dodd, eds., *The Public Papers of Woodrow Wilson*, Vol. I, 12–14.

13. Dulles, *The Road to Teheran*, 98–99.

14. Miliukov message to Russian diplomats, March 4/17, 1917 and Miliukov interview with *Rech'*, March 23/April 5, 1917, in Browder and Kerensky, eds., *The Russian Provisional Government*, Vol. II, 1042, 1044–1045.

15. Killen, "The Search for a Democratic Russia," 237–256; Foglesong, *America's Secret War against Bolshevism*, 52.

16. S. D. Maslovskii, "Wilson's Response," *Delo Naroda*, No. 61, May 30, 1917; *Izvestiia*, No. 78, May 30, 1917; Soviet appeal "To the Socialists of All Countries," May 20, 1917, in Browder and Kerensky, eds., *The Russian Provisional Government*, Vol. II, 1110, 1112, 1171–1173.

17. "First Steps in Self-Government" (cartoon), *New York World*, April 26, 1917; "Better Hold That Loan for a While, Uncle," June 13, 1917. Editorial Cartoons of J. N. "Ding" Darling, Digital Library, University of Iowa, http://digital.lib.ui owa.edu; "An Address to Two Democracies" (editorial), *Brooklyn Daily Eagle*, June 11, 1917; "New Russia Answers Germany" (editorial), *Brooklyn Daily Eagle*, June 18, 1917; "Getting Rid of the Smock" (cartoon) from *Philadelphia Public Ledger*, reprinted in *Chicago Tribune*, June 20, 1917.

18. Secretary of State Lansing to Ambassador Francis, April 8/21, 1917, in Browder and Kerensky, eds., *The Russian Provisional Government*, Vol. II, 1053; Foglesong, *America's Secret War against Bolshevism*, 55.

19. Saul, *War and Revolution*, 106–107, 128–134; McKillen, *Making the World Safe for Workers*, 128–135.

20. Russell, *Unchained Russia*, 24; Miraldi, *The Pen Is Mightier*, 251–252; Ackerman, *Trotsky in New York, 1917*.

21. Russell, *Unchained Russia*, 4, 28, 32–34, 38; Saul, *War and Revolution*, 130.

22. Davis and Trani, *The First Cold War*, esp. 35; Listikov, *SShA i revoliutsionnaia Rossiia v 1917 godu*.

23. Foglesong, *America's Secret War against Bolshevism*, 108–110.

24. Lasch, *The American Liberals and the Russian Revolution*, 33.

25. Sanborn, *Imperial Apocalypse*, 206–209; Stockdale, *Mobilizing the Russian Nation*, 224–241; Foglesong, *America's Secret War against Bolshevism*, 108–109.

26. Houghteling, *A Diary of the Russian Revolution*, 179, 184; Joshua Butler Wright Diary, May 5, May 14, June 25, August 2, 1917; Lasch, *The American Liberals and the Russian Revolution*, 35, 54.

27. Sanborn, *Imperial Apocalypse*, 220–221; Smith, *Russia in Revolution*, 146–148.

28. Smith, *Russia in Revolution*, 148–154; Swain, *The Origins of the Russian Civil War*.

29. "Decree on Peace," in Wade, ed., *Documents of Soviet History*, Vol. 1: *The Triumph of Bolshevism 1917–1919*, 6–7.

30. Address to the American Federation of Labor Convention, November 12, 1917, *The Public Papers of Woodrow Wilson*, Vol. I, 120; "Socialist Leaders" (editorial), *Salt Lake Tribune*, November 10, 1917, 6; "Another Revolution in Russia" (editorial), *Philadelphia Inquirer*, November 9, 1917, 2; "U.S. Millions for Democracy, But Not a Cent for Anarchy" (cartoon), *Philadelphia Inquirer*, November 12, 1917, 1; "Don't You Know Me, Sister?" (cartoon), *New York World*, November 28, 1917.

31. McMeekin, *The Russian Revolution*, xv, xvi, 257, 127, 132, 256.

32. Zeman, ed., *Germany and the Revolution in Russia, 1915–1918*; Baumgart, *Deutsche Ostpolitik 1918*.

33. For further discussion, see Foglesong, "Foreign Intervention"; Foglesong, "Revolutionary Russia in American Eyes."

34. Beatty, *The Red Heart of Russia*, 56, 140; Ross, *Russia in Upheaval*, 334–335.

35. Mayer, *Wilson vs. Lenin*.

36. Salvatore, *Eugene V. Debs*, 286–291.

37. Travis, *George Kennan and the American–Russian Relationship*, 340, 342; Lansing letters and proposed statement, December 1917, quoted in Foglesong, *America's Secret War against Bolshevism*, 36.

38. Fourteen Points speech, January 8, 1918, and "Message to the People of Russia," March 11, 1918, in *The Public Papers of Woodrow Wilson*, Vol. I, 155–158, 191.

39. Unterberger, "Woodrow Wilson and the Russian Revolution"; Engelstein, *Russia in Flames*, 389–390.

40. Maddox, *The Unknown War with Russia*; Foglesong, *America's Secret War against Bolshevism*, chapters 3 and 4.

41. Kennan, *Soviet–American Relations, 1917–1920*, Vol 1, 31, vol. 2, 133, 222–223.

42. Ball, *Imagining America*, 43; McKenna, *All the Views Fit to Print*, 3, 33.

43. Fourteen Points speech, January 8, 1918, and "Message to the People of Russia," March 11, 1918, in *The Public Papers of Woodrow Wilson*, Vol. I, 158, 191.

44. Salzman, *Reform and Revolution*, esp. 284; Foglesong, *America's Secret War against Bolshevism*, 273–275.

45. McAdams, *Vanguard of the Revolution*, 98–99; Foglesong, *America's Secret War against Bolshevism*, 37; Debo, *Revolution and Survival*; McFadden, *Alternative Paths*.

46. Foglesong, *America's Secret War against Bolshevism*, 200.

47. Wilson's draft of an *aide-mémoire*, July 16, 1918, quoted in Foglesong, *America's Secret War against Bolshevism*, 162.

48. Lenin "Letter to American Workers," August 20, 1918, quoted in Foglesong, *America's Secret War against Bolshevism*, 223.

49. Unterberger, *The United States, Revolutionary Russia, and the Rise of Czechoslovakia*; Bacino, *Reconstructing Russia*; Tooze, *The Deluge*, chapter 8.

50. Rhodes, *The Anglo-American Winter War with Russia*.

51. Foglesong, *America's Secret War against Bolshevism*, chapter 8; Irwin, *Making the World Safe*, 151–163.

52. Kennan, "American Troops in Russia," 36–42; Unterberger, *Intervention against Communism*.

53. Davis and Trani, *The First Cold War*; Willett, *Russian Sideshow*; Richard, *When the United States Invaded Russia*.

54. Somin, *Stillborn Crusade*.

55. Foglesong, *America's Secret War against Bolshevism*, 182–183, 225–229; Strakhovsky, *American Opinion about Russia, 1917–1920*, 105–106.

56. Foglesong, *America's Secret War against Bolshevism*, 40, 186, 291.

57. Chafee, "A Contemporary State Trial – The United States *versus* Jacob Abrams et al.," 747–750; Foglesong, *America's Secret War against Bolshevism*, 275–289.

58 McAdams, *Vanguard of the Revolution*, 106–120; Pons, *The Global Revolution*, 12–13.

59 Gaddis, *Russia, the Soviet Union, and the United States*, 94–95.

60 See Fitzpatrick, "The Civil War as a Formative Experience."

61 Figes and Kolonitskii, *Interpreting the Russian Revolution*, chapter 6; Steinberg, Menning, Schimmelpenninck van der Oye, Wolff, and Yokote, eds., *The Russo-Japanese War in Global Perspective*.

62. See, for example, "Vrag khochet zakhvatit' Tulu" and "Petrograda ne otdadim" in Hoover Institution Poster Collection; Lafont, *Soviet Posters*, 132; *Krokodil*, No. 30, 30 October 1958 (front cover).

63. "Antanta," in Lafont, *Soviet Posters*, 36; "Liga Natsii," discussed in McKenna, *All the Views Fit to Print*, 30–31 and reproduced on page 65.

64. *Krokodil*, No. 28, October 1937 (front cover); "Umestnoe Napominanie Podzhigateliam Voiny," *Krokodil*, November 10, 1949.

65. Speech on September 19, 1959, in *Khrushchev in America*, 111.
66. See, for example, David K. Shipler, "The View from America," *New York Times Magazine*, November 10, 1985, 48.
67. Coben, *A. Mitchell Palmer*, 211; Foglesong, *America's Secret War against Bolshevism*, 282.
68. Wilson address at Des Moines, September 6, 1919, in *The Public Papers of Woodrow Wilson*, Vol. II, 15.
69. "Poisoning the Mind of Youth" (editorial), *Philadelphia Inquirer*, June 3, 1919, 12; Delegard, *Battling Miss Bolsheviki*; Mickenberg, "Suffragettes and Soviets," 1021–1051.
70. For example: "Put Them Out and Keep Them Out," *Philadelphia Inquirer*, October 12, 1919; "Wash the Red Out of Him with a Good Dose of Stars and Stripes," *Philadelphia Inquirer*, October 17, 1919; "A Man Is Known by the Company He Keeps," *Life*, January 1, 1920.
71. Gage, *G-Man*, 70–74.

CHAPTER 10: FROM ESTRANGEMENT TO ENGAGEMENT, 1921–1933

1. Among the best of the traditional diplomatic histories are Browder, *The Origins of Soviet–American Diplomacy*; Sevost'ianov, *Moskva–Vashington: Na puti k priznaniiu 1918–1933*.
2. Kennan, *Russia and the West under Lenin and Stalin*, 143, 181–186; Malia, *The Soviet Tragedy*, chapter 5; Ninkovich, *The Global Republic*, 255. The myth of Soviet autarky is refuted by Sanchez-Sibony, *Red Globalization* and Link, *Forging Global Fordism*.
3. See Jacobson, *When the Soviet Union Entered World Politics*.
4. Patenaude, *The Big Show in Bololand*.
5. Foglesong, *The American Mission and the "Evil Empire,"* 64; Ruotsila, *John Spargo and American Socialism*.
6. Kennan, *Russia and the West under Lenin and Stalin*, 171.
7. Patenaude, *The Big Show in Bololand*, 502–504, 508–509, 598, 600–604, 629.
8. McFadden and Gorfinkel, *Constructive Spirit*; Dekel-Chen, "Philanthropists, Commissars, and American Statesmanship Meet in Soviet Crimea, 1922–37"; Dekel-Chen, *Farming the Red Land*. A Catholic relief effort fed more than 150,000 children, but clashes with Soviet leaders spurred the American director of the mission to become one of the most vehement critics of the USSR. See McNamara, *A Catholic Cold War*, 27–77.
9. Rhodes, *James P. Goodrich, Indiana's "Governor Strangelove"*; Campbell, *Russia: Market or Menace?*
10. Uldricks, "Russia and Europe"; Carley, *Silent Conflict*.

11. Gaddis, *Russia, the Soviet Union, and the United States*, 91–93; Kostornichenko, "Proekt kontsessi amerikanskogo predprinimatelia Vashingtona B. Vanderlipa i sovetskaia vneshnaia politika nachala 1920-x gg."

12. Shishkin, *Stanovlenie Vneshnei Politiki Poslerevoliutsionnoi Rossii (1917–1930 gody) i Kapitalisticheskii Mir*, 311–328.

13. Salzman, *Reform and Revolution*, 311; Perkins, *Charles Evans Hughes and American Democratic Statesmanship*, 126–127.

14. Fink, *The Genoa Conference*.

15. Rhodes, *James P. Goodrich*, 115–119; Sevost'ianov, *Moskva–Vashington: Na puti k priznaniiu 1918–1933*, 89, 96.

16. Sevost'ianov, *Moskva–Vashington: Na puti k priznaniiu 1918–1933*, 98.

17. Maddox, *William E. Borah and American Foreign Policy*, 191, 204–208; Salzman, *Reform and Revolution*, 314; Ellis, *Frank B. Kellogg and American Foreign Relations, 1925–1929*, 40, 70–71.

18. "Mr. Harding and Russia," *New York Times*, September 24, 1920; Salzman, *Reform and Revolution*, 311–313; Maddox, *William E. Borah and American Foreign Policy*, 184, 203; Sevost'ianov, *Moskva–Vashington: Politika i diplomatiia Kremlia 1921–1941*, Vol. I, 127–138.

19. "Closer Contact with Russia," *New York World*, July 6, 1929.

20. "Recognition of the Soviets," *New York Times*, March 30, 1926; "What Is 'Recognition' Worth?" *Wall Street Journal*, January 17, 1924; "No Pay, No Recognition," *Houston Post*, reprinted in *Washington Post*, April 15, 1924; "American Concessions in Russia," *New York Times*, June 15, 1925.

21. "Inherent Antagonism," *Chicago Tribune*, reprinted in *Washington Post*, March 12, 1931; "Soviet Recognition," *Washington Post*, August 10, 1932.

22. "American Sentiment and European Revolutions," *New York Times*, March 2, 1924.

23. "The Voice of Russia," *Washington Post*, August 15, 1924. See also Bailey, *America Faces Russia*, 251–252.

24. Johnson, *The Peace Progressives and American Foreign Relations*, 143–145.

25. Report of Dawes speech on September 11, 1924 in Kirby, *Highlights: A Cartoon History of the Nineteen Twenties*, 50. See also "The Voice of Russia," *Washington Post*, August 15, 1924; "Moscow Helps La Follette," *Washington Post*, September 27, 1924; Draper, *American Communism and Soviet Russia*, 118.

26. Unger, *Fighting Bob La Follette*; Drake, *The Education of an Anti-imperialist*, 393–394, 412.

27. Kirby cartoons in *New York World*, March 25 and 28, 1921, September 13, 1924, and October 16, 1924; "The Exclusion of Trotsky," *New York World*, July 13, 1929.

28. McKillen, *Chicago Labor and the Quest for a Democratic Diplomacy, 1914–1924*; Larson, "Opposition to AFL Foreign Policy"; Luff, *Commonsense Anticommunism*.

29. Luff, *Commonsense Anticommunism*, 130–131; Michels, *A Fire in Their Hearts*, 228–249.

30. Mickenberg, "Suffragettes and Soviets"; Mickenberg, *American Girls in Red Russia*; Delegard, *Battling Miss Bolsheviki*; Foster, *The Women and the Warriors*.
31. Pfeffer, *A. Philip Randolph, Pioneer of the Civil Rights Movement*; Arnesen, "No 'Graver Danger': Black Anticommunism, the Communist Party, and the Race Question," 13–52; Makalani, *In the Cause of Freedom*; McDuffie, *Sojourning for Freedom*.
32. Powers, *Not without Honor*, 93–99; Kelley, *Hammer and Hoe*.
33. Zumoff, *The Communist International and US Communism, 1919–1929*.
34. Tucker, *Stalin as Revolutionary*, chapter 10; Pons, *The Global Revolution*, chapter 2; "Russian Paradoxes," *New York Times*, November 17, 1927 (editorial); Mark, "October or Thermidor?"
35. Barghoorn, *The Soviet Image of the United States*; Brooks, "Official Xenophobia and Popular Cosmopolitanism in Early Soviet Russia"; Ball, *Imagining America*, x, xiii; Fedorova, *Yankees in Petrograd, Bolsheviks in New York*, 4, 53.
36. Velikanova, *Popular Perceptions of Soviet Politics in the 1920s*, 34, 117; Sutton, *Western Technology and Soviet Economic Development, 1917 to 1930*, 168; Foglesong, *The American Mission and the "Evil Empire,"* 60–76.
37. Brooks, "Official Xenophobia and Popular Cosmopolitanism," 1440, 1447; Brooks, "The Press and Its Message: Images of America in the 1920s and 1930s"; Rogger, "*Amerikanizm* and the Economic Development of Russia"; Bailes, "The American Connection: Ideology and the Transfer of American Technology to the Soviet Union, 1917–1941."
38. For further discussion, see Golubev, "Amerika v sovetskoi karikature 1920–1930-x godov"; Golubev, *"Podlinnyi lik zagranitsy": Obraz vneshnego mira v sovetskoi politichiskoi karikature, 1922–1941 gg.*, chapter 4.
39. *Krokodil*, No. 6, February 1926; No. 2, January 1925. See also McKenna, *All the Views Fit to Print*, 66.
40. *Krokodil*, No. 35, 16 September 1923; No. 19, May 1929.
41. *Krokodil*, No. 25, July 1929. See also *Krokodil*, No. 37, 1 October 1923.
42. Esenin, "An Iron Mirgorod."
43. Mayakovsky, "My Discovery of America"; Mayakovsky, "Brooklyn Bridge," in *My Discovery of America*, 123–128; Jangfeldt, *Mayakovsky*, 324–328.
44. "Red Poet Pictures US as Dollar Mad," *New York Times*, December 21, 1925. See also Louis Rich, "Fiery Russian Poet Scolds New York," *New York Times*, October 11, 1925.
45. Fedorova, *Yankees in Petrograd*, 76–83.
46. Gleason, "Republic of Humbug."
47. Levitina, *"Russian Americans" in Soviet Film*, 98–100.
48. Kotkin, *Stalin*, 541, 561, 643, 671, 700; Deutscher, *The Prophet Unarmed*, 215.
49. Levitina, *"Russian Americans" in Soviet Film*.
50. Kenez, *Cinema and Soviet Society from the Revolution to the Death of Stalin*, 34–37, 48–49, 64–65; Taylor, *The Politics of the Soviet Cinema, 1917–1929*, 136; Youngblood, *Soviet Cinema in the Silent Era, 1918–1935*, 32–33. Another 1924 film, *The Cigarette*

Girl from Mosselprom, had a similar thrust. See Levitina, *"Russian Americans" in Soviet Film,* 93–94.

51. Ross, *Working-Class Hollywood.*
52. Robinson, *Russians in Hollywood, Hollywood's Russians,* 21–39; review of *The Last Command* by Mordaunt Hall in *New York Times,* January 23, 1928.
53. Ross, *Working-Class Hollywood.*
54. Cf. Hollander, *Political Pilgrims.* David-Fox persuasively criticized Hollander's work in *Showcasing the Great Experiment,* 108–109.
55. For a contrasting view, see Bailey, *America Faces Russia,* 259.
56. Foglesong, *The American Mission and the "Evil Empire,"* 71–72.
57. Rev. Harry Earl Woolever, "Russian Communists March on Washington," *The Christian Advocate* (New York), December 17, 1931, 1556.
58. Dan B. Brummitt, "How to Balk Communism in America," *The Christian Advocate,* October 29, 1931; Dan B. Brummitt, "Russia Is a Riddle," *The Christian Advocate,* September 24, 1931; "A Russian Mirror for Us," *The Literary Digest,* November 14, 1931.
59. "Mrs. Grady Depicts Russia in Distress," *New York Times,* July 10, 1931; "Author and Critic Clash on Russia," *Philadelphia Inquirer,* March 30, 1932.
60. "Reds Shame Idle Back to Machines," *New York Times,* April 25, 1933; Margaret Bourke-White, "Silk Stockings in the Five-Year Plan," *New York Times,* February 14, 1932.
61. See especially Rodgers, *Atlantic Crossings,* particularly page 381.
62. Mally, "Hallie Flanagan and the Soviet Union."
63. R. L. Duffus, "Waldo Frank's Russian Journey," *New York Times,* July 31, 1932; Filene, *Americans and the Soviet Experiment, 1917–1933,* 187–209.
64. "Will Durant Sees Slavery in Russia," *New York Times,* July 17, 1933.
65. Shpotov, "Vzaimospriatie Amerikantsev i Russkikh v gody pervoi piatiletki (po materialam pressy i delovoi perepiski)"; Shpotov, *Amerikanskii biznes i Sovetskii Soiuz v 1920–1930-e gody.*
66. Brooks, "The Press and Its Message," 242–243; *Krokodil,* No. 19, 1932; No. 24, August 1932; No. 36, December 1932.
67. Powers, *Not without Honor: The History of American Anticommunism,* 81–91.
68. Libbey, *Alexander Gumberg and Soviet–American Relations, 1917–1933.* See also Shishkin, *Stanovlenie Vneshnei Politiki Poslerevoliutsionnoi Rossii,* 328–330.
69. Dulles, *The Road to Teheran,* 189; Wilson, "American Business and the Recognition of the Soviet Union."
70. "Russia's Problem," "Complicated Economics," and "Russian Trade Restrictions," *Chicago Tribune,* July 30, September 23, and December 16, 1930; Filene, *Americans and the Soviet Experiment,* 230–233; Libbey, *Russian–American Economic Relations, 1763–1999,* esp. 102.
71. Sanchez-Sibony, *Red Globalization,* 27, 37, 45–49.
72. Filene, *Americans and the Soviet Experiment,* 234–235.
73. Plokhy, *The Gates of Europe,* 252–253.

74. Morris, *Stalin's Famine and Roosevelt's Recognition of Russia*; Gamache, "Breaking Eggs for a Holodomor."

75. United Ukrainian Organizations of the United Sates to the President, n.d., 1933, Box 42, Folder 4, Alexander Granovsky Papers, Immigration History Research Center Archives, University of Minnesota, Minneapolis.

76. Morris, *Stalin's Famine*, 141.

77. Browder, *The Origins of Soviet–American Diplomacy*; Maddux, *Years of Estrangement*; Kimball, *The Juggler*.

78. Sevost'ianov, *Moskva–Vashington: Na puti k priznaniiu 1918–1933*, 375–376; *Krokodil*, No. 12, April 1933; No. 32, November 1933.

79. McNamara, *A Catholic Cold War*, 81–82.

80. Richman, *The United States and the Soviet Union*.

81. "Protest Parade Harried by Reds," *The Sun*, November 18, 1933; "Attack Parade Held in Protest against Soviet," *Chicago Tribune*, December 18, 1933.

CHAPTER 11: HOPES AND HORROR, 1934–1941

1. Kennan, *Russia and the West under Lenin and Stalin*, 294; Kennan comments in *The Cold War: Comrades*, CNN documentary, 1998.

2. Dunn, *Caught between Roosevelt and Stalin*, 6, 263. For similar views, see Marks, *Wind over Sand*; Mayers, *The Ambassadors and America's Soviet Policy*, 104–105; Sibley, *Red Spies in America*, 8.

3. Haslam, *The Spectre of War*, 4, 272, 297.

4. Gaddis, *Russia, the Soviet Union, and the United States*; Kimball, *The Juggler*; Mal'kov, *Put' k imperstvu*, 236–247.

5. Adler and Paterson, "Red Fascism."

6. Farnsworth, *William C. Bullitt and the Soviet Union*, 118; Etkind, *Roads Not Taken*, 118.

7. Carley, *Stalin's Gamble*, chapter 9.

8. Memorandum by Roosevelt and Litvinov, November 15, 1933, in Baer, ed., *A Question of Trust*, 343–344.

9. Stalin to Litvinov, 13 November 1933, in Sevost'ianov, *Moskva–Vashington*, Vol. 3: *1933–1941*, 58.

10. Cassella-Blackburn, *The Donkey, the Carrot, and the Club*, 129.

11. See Phillips, *Between the Revolution and the West*, 134.

12. Henderson dispatch, November 16, 1936, in Baer, ed., *A Question of Trust*, 465–468.

13. Kennan to Ferris, January 12, 1931, and Kennan to Skinner, August 19, 1932, quoted in Gaddis, *George F. Kennan*, 58, 68.

14. Kennan, *Memoirs, 1925–1950*, 70.

15. See, for example, Etkind, *Roads Not Taken*, xi–xiv, 172–173.

16. Bohlen interview in 1979, quoted in Gaddis, *George F. Kennan*, 119. On Kennan's emotionalism, see Costigliola, "Kennan Encounters Russia, 1933–1937."

17. See, for example, Kotkin, *Stalin: Waiting for Hitler*, 579.

18. Rieber, *Stalin and the Struggle for Supremacy in Eurasia*, 154–155; Carley, *Stalin's Gamble*; front cover of *Krokodil*, No. 19, July 1936.

19. Davies and Harris, *Stalin's World*.

20. Kotkin, *Stalin: Waiting for Hitler*, 287, 314; Sevost'ianov, *Moskva–Vashington*, Vol. 3: *1933–1941*; Maddux, *Years of Estrangement*, 81–85.

21. Brandenberger, *Propaganda State in Crisis*.

22. Maddux, *Years of Estrangement*, 35, 37, 46, 67; Ulam, *Expansion and Coexistence*, 248.

23. Sevost'ianov, *Moskva–Vashington*, Vol. 3: *1933–1941*, 360–361, 442–443, 459–460.

24. Alexander A. Troyanovsky, "The Foreign Policy of Soviet Russia," *Vital Speeches of the Day*, Vol. 1, August 12, 1935, 727–731; Saul, *Friends or Foes?*, 311.

25. Troyanovsky to Litvinov, 20 October 1936, in Sevost'ianov, *Moskva–Vashington*, Vol. 3: *1933–1941*, 355–359.

26. Troyanovsky to Stalin, 20 October 1936, 1 June 1937, and 2 March 1938, in Sevost'ianov, *Moskva–Vashington*, Vol. 3: *1933–1941*, 360–361, 459–460, 544–548; Myers, *The Prophet's Army*; Kelly, *James Burnham and the Struggle for the World*, 35–58.

27. Ezhov to Stalin, 17 August 1938 (on Maurice Hindus), Troyanovsky to Stalin, 7 October 1938 (on John Lewis), Troyanovsky to Stalin, 29 January 1939 (on Philip LaFollette), Litvinov to Stalin, 15 February 1939 (against Roy Howard), in Sevost'ianov, *Moskva–Vashington*, Vol. 3: *1933–1941*, 598, 606, 609–610, 611–612.

28. "A Radical American Organization Takes a Hand in the Spanish Muddle," *Arizona Republic*, August 23, 1936; "The Menace of Tugwellism" (editorial) and "Gulliver Wakes Up in the Collective-Mind Utopia" (cartoon), *Philadelphia Inquirer*, August 30, 1936.

29. "Sharpening the Spearhead" (cartoon), *Chicago Tribune*, August 3, 1936.

30. Procter, *William Randolph Hearst: The Later Years, 1911–1951*, 194–210, quotation on page 208.

31. "Russia Recognizes Roosevelt" (editorial), *Chicago Tribune*, August 12, 1936; "Orders from Moscow" (cartoon), *Chicago Tribune*, August 29, 1936.

32. Ryan, *Earl Browder*, 108–109.

33. Lippmann, *The Good Society*; Warren, *Liberals and Communism*; Ryan, *John Dewey and the High Tide of American Liberalism*, 306.

34. Warren, *Liberals and Communism*, 76–87, 144.

35. Ryan, *Earl Browder*; Barrett, *William Z. Foster and the Tragedy of American Radicalism*.

36. Tucker, *Stalin in Power*, 209–212; Kotkin, *Stalin*, 104–106, 371.

37. "Trotsky May Earn a Martyr's Meed by Going to Moscow after It," *Arizona Republic*, August 26, 1936; "The New Terror in Russia," *Chicago Tribune*, August 31, 1936. For further analysis of American views of Trotsky and Stalin, see Mark, "October or Thermidor?"

38. "Soviet Justice," *Louisville Courier-Journal*, August 21, 1936; "Trotsky Bobs Up Again," *Atlanta Constitution*, August 22, 1936.
39. Arthur M. Howe, "Now and Then," *Brooklyn Daily Eagle*, January 27, 1937; "Behind the Soviet Trial," *Washington Post*, August 22, 1936; "Moscow's Tragic Folly," *Louisville Courier-Journal*, March 3, 1938; "The Culminating Russian Purge," *Chicago Tribune*, March 4, 1938. See also Warren, *Liberals and Communism*, 169.
40. "The Stalin Purge," *New York Times*, August 26, 1936; "A Weird Phantasmagoria of Murder," *Philadelphia Inquirer*, March 9, 1938. For further discussion, see Evans and Welch, *Witnessing Stalin's Justice*.
41. O'Neill, *The Last Romantic*, 181.
42. Maddux, "Red Fascism, Brown Bolshevism"; Alpers, *Dictators, Democracy, and American Public Culture*, 144, 153.
43. Warren, *Liberals and Communism*, 163–170; Bucklin, "The Wilsonian Legacy in Political Science," 136; Schuman and Soule, *America Looks Abroad*, 11.
44. Kennan, *Memoirs, 1925–1950*, 82–83; Bohlen, *Witness to History 1929–1969*, 44; MacLean, *Joseph E. Davies*; Mayers, *The Ambassadors and America's Soviet Policy*, 4, 7, 119–122; Davies to Hull, 1 April 1938 (intercepted and read by Soviet leaders), in Sevost'ianov, *Moskva–Vashington*, Vol. 3: *1933–1941*, 556–565.
45. See, for example, *Krokodil*, No. 26, 1936, 3, 10; No. 27, 1936, 11; No. 29, 1936, 11; No. 32, 1936, 12; No. 33, 1936, front and back covers.
46. Efimenko et al., *RKKA i Grazhdanskaia voina v Ispanii 1936–1939 gg.*
47. Tucker, *Stalin in Power*, 350–352, Kotkin, *Stalin*, 313–318; Tierney, *FDR and the Spanish Civil War*.
48. Haslam, *The Spectre of War*, 213–240; Tucker, *Stalin in Power*, 352; Kotkin, *Stalin*, 320, 347; Chapman, *Arguing Americanism*, 18. The number killed by the NKVD has been disputed, with some claiming thousands and others citing tens. Dan Kaufman, "Soldiers of Solidarity," *The New York Review*, February 24, 2022, 42.
49. "Bad News" (cartoon), "Beginning to Bear Fruit" (cartoon), "Communists in Spain Cry for a 'Baby Russia,'" *Chicago Tribune*, August 7, 12, and 17, 1936; "Moscow Moves the Puppet" (cartoon), *San Francisco Examiner*, August 22, 1936; Chapman, *Arguing Americanism*, 25, 40; Hochschild, *Spain in Our Hearts*, 166–174.
50. Warren, *Liberals and Communism*, 132; Carroll, *The Odyssey of the Abraham Lincoln Brigade*; Kirschenbaum, *International Communism and the Spanish Civil War*, 10, 78; Seidman, *Transatlantic Antifascisms*.
51. Radosh, Habeck, and Sevostianov, eds., *Spain Betrayed*.
52. Ibid., xxii, 502. For an incisive critique, see Graham, "Spain Betrayed?"
53. Powers, *Not without Honor*, 129–132.
54. See, for example, Sibley, *Red Spies in America*, 2–5, 39, 79.
55. Olmsted, *Red Spy Queen*, 28, 55, 147.
56. Meier, *The Lost Spy*, 7–8, 35–37, 84, 152.
57. Hornblum, *The Invisible Harry Gold*.
58. Craig, *Treasonable Doubt*; Steil, *The Battle of Bretton Woods*, 17, 22, 35–39, 52.
59. Tanenhaus, *Whittaker Chambers*, 84–114.

60. Sibley, *Red Spies in America*, 61.
61. Muir, "American Warship Construction for Stalin's Navy Prior to World War II," 337–351.
62. Haslam, *The Spectre of War*, 198, 264, 303, 316, 322.
63. Maddux, *Years of Estrangement*, 52.
64. Carley, *1939*; Kotkin, *Stalin: Waiting for Hitler*, 601, 621, 659–667.
65. Gaddis, *Russia, the Soviet Union, and the United States*, 139.
66. "New Soviet Envoy," *Washington Post*, May 12, 1939; Westbrook Pegler, "Comrade Oumansky," *Washington Post*, December 14, 1939; "Mr. Oumansky's Dignity," *Washington Post*, November 14, 1939; Maddux, *Years of Estrangement*, 98–99; "The Reds Start West," *Washington Post*, December 1, 1939.
67. Heinrichs, *Threshold of War*, 54–55.
68. "All Dressed Up in His New Uniform," *Chicago Tribune*, January 6, 1939.
69. McKenna, *All the Views Fit to Print*, 48–50; *Krokodil*, No. 28, October 1937, front cover.
70. Wolf, ed., *Ilf and Petrov's American Road Trip*, 15, 18, 25–27, 89, 101, 127–128; Fedorova, *Yankees in Petrograd, Bolsheviks in New York*, 92–93. For the full Russian language text, see Il'f and Petrov, *Odnoetazhnaia Amerika*.
71. Kirschenbaum, *Soviet Adventures in the Land of the Capitalists*, 10, 274–287, 319–323.
72. See, for example, *Krokodil*, No. 3, 1936; No. 9, 1936; No. 26, 1936; No 2, 1939; No. 8, 1939.
73. "Vybory v Amerike," *Krokodil*, No. 37, 1937, 14. See also a comparison of canal building: "Istoricheskaia Spravka," *Krokodil*, No. 10, 1937, 3.
74. For example, *Krokodil*, No. 21, 1939; No. 11, 1940, No. 9, 1940; No. 15, 1940.
75. See especially *Krokodil*, No. 31, 1939, back cover; No. 34, 1939, 13; No. 4, 1940, 5.
76. *Krokodil*, No. 9, March 1939, front cover; No. 5, 1941, front cover.
77. Makalani, *In the Cause of Freedom*, 186–194; Baldwin, *Beyond the Color Line and the Iron Curtain*; Duberman, *Paul Robeson*.
78. Roman, *Opposing Jim Crow*, 146–150.
79. Kelley, *Hammer and Hoe*, 100.
80. "'Democracies,'" *The Chicago Defender*, July 15, 1939.
81. Roman, *Opposing Jim Crow*, 196–204.
82. Frank S. Nugent, "'Ninotchka,' an Impious Soviet Satire Directed by Lubitsch, Opens at the Music Hall," *New York Times*, November 10, 1939; M.F.L., "Pronounced Ni-Notch-Ka," *Wall Street Journal*, November 10, 1939.
83. Bosley Crowther, "The Screen in Review," *New York Times*, December 26, 1940; "Gable and Lamarr Have Comic Hit in 'Comrade X,'" *Washington Post*, December 31, 1940; "Palace," *Washington Post*, January 9, 1941.
84. "UR History Professor Tells City Group of His Experiences," *Democrat and Chronicle* (Rochester), November 5, 1939.
85. Fitzpatrick, *Everyday Stalinism*, 89–93.

CHAPTER 12: ALLIES, 1941–1945

1. Dulles, *The Road to Teheran*, 220–221, 260–261; Ralph McGill, "Russian Aid in Our Civil War," *Atlanta Constitution*, May 23, 1945, 4.

2. Bailey, *America Faces Russia*, 323; Tzouliadis, *The Forsaken*, 210, 218. See also Plokhy, *Forgotten Bastards of the Eastern Front.*

3. Johnston, *Being Soviet*, chapter 2; V. V. Putin speech, May 9, 2015, http://en.kr emlin.ru/events/president/transcripts/49438.

4. Carleton, *Russia: The Story of War*, chapter 3. Some Russian scholars have challenged narrow concentration on the Soviet war effort. See Suprun, *Lend-liz i Rossiia*, esp. 6.

5. For example, Berkhoff, *Motherland in Danger*, 6, 273–274.

6. O'Brien, *How the War Was Won.*

7. Jones, *The Roads to Russia*; Weeks, *Russia's Life-Saver.*

8. Herring, *Aid to Russia*; Overy, *Russia's War*; Hill, *The Red Army and the Second World War*; Bystrova, *Lend-liz dlia SSSR.*

9. See, for example, Ambrose, *D Day*. On American amnesia, see Carleton, *Russia*, 106; Smelser and Davies, *The Myth of the Eastern Front*, 1.

10. Iosif Stalin, "Unity against the Nazis," *Vital Speeches of the Day*, Vol. 7, No. 19 (July 15, 1941), 586–588.

11. G. Dimitrov to Stalin, 17 April 1941, in Banac, ed. *Dimitrov and Stalin 1934–1943*, 185–187.

12. Berkhoff, *Motherland in Danger*, 253–279, esp. 273–274.

13. See, for example, *Krokodil*, No. 22, June 1942 (front cover); No. 45, 1943, 5; No. 23–24, 1944 (front cover and back cover); No. 41, 1944 (front cover); Zegers and Druick, eds., *Windows on the War*, 176, 182–183, 214, 215, 240, 244, 273, 290, 297, 301, 311, 313, 361, 363, 365, 366, 370, 371, 373.

14. Watson, *Molotov*, 203; Ilya Ehrenburgh, "Nazis Strip West, Russian Declares," *New York Times*, July 30, 1942; Ilya Ehrenburgh, "Red Army Awaits Allies," *New York Times*, August 22, 1942.

15. Johnston, *Being Soviet*, viii, 47, 55, 92; Roberts, *Stalin's Wars*, 179–180; McKenna, *All the Views Fit to Print*, 54–56. For a different view, see Pozniakov, "Amerikanskaia gumanitarnaia pomoshch' sovetskomu narodu (1941–1945)."

16. Roberts, *Stalin's Wars*, 177–191; Zubok, *A Failed Empire*, 13–14, 51; Pechatnov, "The Big Three after World War II."

17. Miller, *The United States and Italy, 1940–1950*; Roberts, *Stalin's Wars*, 175.

18. For a contrasting view, see Dunn, *Caught between Roosevelt and Stalin*, 3, 263.

19. Dallek, *Franklin D. Roosevelt and American Foreign Policy*; Kimball, *The Juggler*; Costigliola, *Roosevelt's Lost Alliances.*

20. Clemens, *Yalta*; Gardner, *Spheres of Influence*, 229–231; 324; Plokhy, *Yalta*. Harbutt's assertion in *Yalta 1945*, xvi, that at Yalta Roosevelt revolted against the Anglo-Soviet spheres-of-influence agreement is unconvincing.

21. Weinstein and Vassiliev, *The Haunted Wood*; Hornblum, *The Invisible Harry Gold.*

22. Craig and Radchenko, *The Atomic Bomb and the Origins of the Cold War*; Pechatnov and Edmondson, "The Russian Perspective," 93–94.

23. For example, "Any Enemy of Germany!" *Atlanta Constitution*, June 23, 1941; "We Must Seize Upon a Priceless Chance," *Louisville Courier-Journal*, June 27, 1941.

24. See, for example, "Hitler's Attack on Russia Poses New Problem for U.S.," *Brooklyn Daily Eagle*, June 23, 1941; "Hitler's War with Soviet Russia," *Philadelphia Inquirer*, June 23, 1941; Kyle Palmer, "The Problem Has Not Changed," *Los Angeles Times*, June 29, 1941.

25. "America, Wake Up!" *San Francisco Examiner*, June 30, 1941; "A Better and Unexpected Aperture Made in the Hitler Timetable," *Arizona Republic*, June 24, 1941.

26. "Americans Must Not Relax Suspicion of Communists Here," *Brooklyn Daily Eagle*, June 28, 1941; "Policy toward Russia," *Washington Post*, June 28, 1941; "Tweedledum and Tweedledee," *Wall Street Journal*, June 25, 1941; "Thieves Quarrel over The Swag" (cartoon), *Arizona Republic*, June 23, 1941; "Two Many Aces" (cartoon), *San Francisco Examiner*, June 27, 1941; "The Time to Act Is Now," *New York Times*, June 24, 1941.

27. George Gallup, "Victory for Russia Favored in Survey," *New York Times*, July 13, 1941.

28. See, for example, "Go It, Husband! Go It, Bear!" (cartoon), *Chicago Tribune*, June 24, 1941, 12; "And May They Both Be Equally and Completely Successful," June 29, 1941 (syndicated cartoon), editorial cartoons of J. N. "Ding" Darling, University of Iowa digital collections; Louther S. Horne, "Central States Say 'Dog-Eat-Dog,'" *New York Times*, June 29, 1941; "Here We Can Be Practical," *Wall Street Journal*, June 28, 1941; *Congressional Record* Vol. 87, 3052, 3857, 6775, 7305; Levering, *American Opinion and the Russian Alliance, 1939–1945*, 46, 49.

29. Levering, *American Opinion and the Russian Alliance, 1939–1945*, 127, 194; Small, "How We Learned to Love the Russians."

30. George Gallup, "Sentiment for Military Pact with Russia Found Rising," *Washington Post*, April 18, 1945.

31. "For This Is the Law of the Jungle," *Philadelphia Inquirer*, June 23, 1941; "An Example for San Francisco," *Philadelphia Inquirer*, April 29, 1945.

32. "Russians Win Race to Berlin as Many Hoped They Would," *Arizona Republic*, April 24, 1945; "End of Hitler's Power a Fact Though Mystery Shrouds Fate," *Brooklyn Daily Eagle*, May 2, 1945; "Together Now – For Final Victory!" *Philadelphia Inquirer*, April 28, 1945.

33. Scott and Krasilshchik, *Yanks Meet Reds*; "'V Day' Design," *Louisville Courier-Journal*, April 29, 1945; "It Won't Be Long Now," *Atlanta Constitution*, April 24, 1945; "Shake," *Atlanta Constitution*, April 28, 1945.

34. Bailey, *America Faces Russia*, 293–294; Levering, *American Opinion and the Russian Alliance*, 145. For a contradictory discussion, see Gaddis, *The United States and the Origins of the Cold War, 1941–1947*, 46.

35. O'Neill, *A Better World*, 84; Sirgiovanni, *An Undercurrent of Suspicion*, 187.

36. Foglesong, *The American Mission and the "Evil Empire,"* chapter 4.

37. For his speculation on this point, see Levering, *American Opinion and the Russian Alliance*, 137, 187–188.

38. See, for example, Robert Quillen, "One Threat to Freedom," *Atlanta Constitution*, February 2, 1945, 8; "Not Freedom, but Slavery," *San Francisco Examiner*, April 26, 1945.

39. "They Think They Know a Quicker Way to Get the Sap," *Chicago Tribune*, February 27, 1945, 1; "Aristocratic Southern Gentleman Gets Job as Chauffeur," *Chicago Tribune*, February 26, 1945, 1; "No Curfew for Joe," *Chicago Tribune*, February 27, 1945, 10.

40. "Political Crises in Europe Inevitable" (editorial), *Atlanta Constitution*, February 16, 1945; Ralph McGill, "One Word More," *Atlanta Constitution*, December 1, 1942, quoted in Teel, *Ralph Emerson McGill*, 199.

41. See, for example, "Our Position If Russia Is Taken Out" (cartoon by Daniel Bishop), *St. Louis Star-Times*, reprinted in *New York Times*, October 4, 1942, E3; "Following Through" (cartoon), *Brooklyn Eagle*, January 19, 1945; "The End of the Trail" (cartoon), *Atlanta Constitution*, February 2, 1945; "Russia Faces Treaty Decision" (editorial), *Los Angeles Times*, February 11, 1945, 18.

42. Reston, *Prelude to Victory*, 134–135.

43. For example, "Hitler Revives the Red Bogy," *St. Louis Post-Dispatch*, February 2, 1943; "World Awaits Big 3 Decisions on Knotty Postwar Problems," *Brooklyn Eagle*, February 11, 1945, 20.

44. *Time* covers, January 1, 1940, and January 4, 1943.

45. For example, "Hammer Blow Pincers," *Louisville Courier-Journal*, November 29, 1942; "Ivan Petruska Skivar," *Nashville Tennesseean*, reprinted in *Louisville Courier-Journal*, December 1, 1942; "Unter den Sickles," *Los Angeles Times*, April 24, 1945.

46. "History Was Made at Stalingrad," *Philadelphia Inquirer*, February 4, 1943; "Defeat at Stalingrad Sounds Nazi Death-Knell in Russia," *Brooklyn Daly Eagle*, February 4, 1943; "On from Stalingrad," *New York Times*, February 4, 1943.

47. For an illustration, see "Emphatic!" (front-page cartoon), *Chicago Tribune*, November 6, 1942.

48. Ryan, *Earl Browder*, 203–235; Gerstle, *Working-Class Americanism*.

49. For example, Ralph McGill, "Analyzing Crimea Conference," *Atlanta Constitution*, February 15, 1945, 10; "Big Three Meeting Has Clarified World Political Muddle," *Arizona Republic*, February 15, 1945, 18; Thomas L. Stokes, "The Lift from Yalta," *Los Angeles Times*, February 15, 1945, 12; Walter Lippmann, "The Big Difference," *Los Angeles Times*, February 16, 1945, 12. See also Levering, *American Opinion and the Russian Alliance*, 186.

50. See, for example, Perlmutter, *FDR and Stalin*.

51. "Soviet Arrest of 16 Poles Mars Agreement at Frisco," *Brooklyn Daily Eagle*, May 7, 1945; "It Would Help If the Pole Cat Were Removed" (cartoon), *Arizona Republic*, April 25, 1945; "Strive for the One Main Objective," *Philadelphia*

Inquirer, April 25, 1945; "Molotov's Role at San Francisco," *Los Angeles Times*, April 28, 1945.

52. Gaddis, *The United States and the Origins of the Cold War, 1941–1947*, 42, 62.
53. George Gallup, "Confidence Rises That Russia Will Aid War against Japan," *Washington Post*, March 14, 1945.
54. See, for example, George Gallup, "Atrocities Make 8 in 10 Favor German Labor in Torn Russia," *Washington Post*, May 6, 1945.
55. Foglesong, *The American Mission and the "Evil Empire,"* 100–104.
56. Bystrova, *Potselui cherez okean*; Starr, *Red and Hot*, 195; Ball, *Imagining America*, 179; Johnston, *Being Soviet*, 86–88.
57. Johnston, *Being Soviet*, 98–99; Zhuk, *Nikolai Bolkhovitinov and American Studies in the USSR*, 52.
58. Ilya Ehrenburg, "Hold Out," *Krasnaia Zvezda*, October 12, 1941, quoted in Rubenstein, *Tangled Loyalties*, 192.
59. Goldman and Filtzer, *Fortress Dark and Stern*, 309, 318–319.
60. Johnston, *Being Soviet*, 71–78, 96–99.
61. Plokhy, *Forgotten Bastards of the Eastern Front*, 29–30, 66–68.
62. Ibid., viii, 195, 288.
63. Ibid., 107–131; Fredman, *The Tormented Alliance*.
64. Pechatnov, *Stalin, Ruzvel't, Trumen: SSSR i SShA v 1940-x gg.*, 640.
65. Johnston, *Being Soviet*, 48–49, 85.
66. Youngblood, *Russian War Films*, chapter 3; Youngblood, "A War Remembered."
67. Bennett, *One World, Big Screen*, chapter 5; reviews of *Days of Glory* in the *Washington Post*, June 23, 1944 and the *New York Times*, June 17, 1944. On the lopsided cultural exchange, with many American films shown in the USSR, but few Soviet films screened in the USA, see Ivanian, *Kogda govoriat muzy*, 224–231.
68. Bennett, *One World, Big Screen*, 200; review of *Song of Russia* by Bosley Crowther in *New York Times*, February 11, 1944.
69. Youngblood, *Russian War Films*, 62–63. Bosley Crowther gave *No Greater Love* an ambivalent review in the *New York Times*, February 25, 1944.
70. Erskine Caldwell, "Why Hitler Failed in Russia," *The Advocate-Messenger* (Danville, Kentucky), February 6, 1942, 1, 6; Caldwell, *All-Out on the Road to Smolensk*; Bourke-White, *Shooting the Russian War*; Miller, *Erskine Caldwell*, 291–293; Caldwell, *Erskine Caldwell, Margaret Bourke-White, and the Popular Front*; Goldberg, *Margaret Bourke-White*, 238–246; Foglesong, *The American Mission and the "Evil Empire,"* 87–89.
71. *Time*, December 27, 1943; Foglesong, *The American Mission and the "Evil Empire,"* 83–84.
72. White, *Report on the Russians*, 49, 61, 26, 86, 38–39, 28.
73. Gaddis, *The United States and the Origins of the Cold War*, 45; Sterling North, "Stevens Writes on Russia, W. L. White Describes Trip in Contrasting Reports," *Washington Post*, March 18, 1945; Stevens, *Russia Is No Riddle*; Lauterbach, *These Are the Russians*.

74. Smelser and Davies, *The Myth of the Eastern Front,* 47; *Washington Times-Herald* (editorial), March 31, 1942, quoted in Reston, *Prelude to Victory,* 136; Ambassadors Steinhardt and Standley, cited in Dunn, *Caught between Roosevelt and Stalin,* 106, 180; Bullitt, "The World from Rome," *Life,* September 4, 1944; Gaddis, *The United States and the Origins of the Cold War,* 54–55.
75. Smelser and Davies, *The Myth of the Eastern Front,* 26, 30, 25; Willkie, *One World,* 84, 55, 79–80, 73, 54.
76. George Gallup, "Public Confidence in Soviet Intentions Shows Sharp Drop," *Washington Post,* June 6, 1945, 9.
77. Dallek, *Franklin D. Roosevelt and American Foreign Policy,* 527; Roosevelt to Stalin, April 11, 1945, Pechatnov and Magadeev, *Perepiska I. V. Stalina s F. Ruzvel'tom i Y. Cherchillem v gody Velikoi Otechestvennoi voiny,* Vol. 2, 501.
78. Zubok, *A Failed Empire,* 13–14.
79. Ehrenburg, *The War 1941–1945,* 176–177; Rubenstein, *Tangled Loyalties,* 222–223.
80. Zubkova, *Russia after the War,* 31–32; Bordiugov, "The Popular Mood in the Unoccupied Soviet Union," 65.
81. For example, Ryan, *Earl Browder,* 243; Craig, "The Nuclear Revolution," 362.

CHAPTER 13: FROM ALLIANCE TO ENMITY, 1945–1953

1. See, for example, Pechatnov, "'The Allies Are Pressing on You to Break Your Will . . .,'" esp. 5, 12, 24; Leffler, *For the Soul of Mankind,* 51, 75, 81.
2. Offner, *Another Such Victory.*
3. Costigliola, "After Roosevelt's Death": Costigliola, *Roosevelt's Lost Alliances.*
4. Naimark, *Stalin and the Fate of Europe,* esp. 12, 75.
5. See Tucker, *Political Culture and Leadership in Soviet Russia;* Fousek, *To Lead the Free World.*
6. Leffler, *For the Soul of Mankind,* esp. 57–82, 452–454.
7. See Zubok and Pechatnov, "Otechestvennaia istoriografiia 'kholodnoi voiny,'" 148.
8. Filitov, *"Kholodnaia voina,"* 6.
9. For example, Schlesinger, "The Origins of the Cold War," 47, 52; Gaddis, *We Now Know.*
10. The chapter thus builds on Masuda, *Cold War Crucible.*
11. C. L. Sulzberger, "Moscow Goes Wild over Joyful News," *New York Times,* May 10, 1945; Kennan, *Memoirs 1925–1950,* 253–255.
12. Zubkova, *Russia after the War,* 61–62, 95, 32, 74; Merridale, *Ivan's War,* 336–340; Zubok, *A Failed Empire,* 3; Burds, "The Early Cold War in Soviet West Ukraine, 1944–1948"; Plokhy, *Forgotten Bastards of the Eastern Front,* 72–73; Ehrenburg, *The War,* 189.
13. Naimark, *Stalin and the Fate of Europe,* 6, 11, 14–15, 268–270; Pechatnov, "The Big Three after World War II," 5–6, 10, 19; Roberts, *Stalin's Wars,* 269–271.

14. Zegers and Druick, eds., *Windows on the War*, 363, 366, 370, 374; cartoons in *Krokodil*, No. 25, 30 July 1945 (cover); No. 28, 30 August 1945; No. 29, 10 September 1945.
15. "Time for Straight Talk," *Chicago Tribune*, May 12, 1945.
16. Markowitz, *The Rise and Fall of the People's Century*; White and Maze, *Henry A. Wallace*; Fousek, *To Lead the Free World*, 78, 105.
17. Gallup, "Public Confidence in Russia Shows Sharp Recent Rise," *Washington Post*, September 5, 1945. See also Holsti, *Public Opinion and American Foreign Policy*, 74.
18. Sirgiovanni, *An Undercurrent of Suspicion*; Bill Hayden, "Twisted Reports on Russia" (letter), *St. Louis Post-Dispatch*, May 2, 1945; "A U.S.–Russian War?" *Collier's*, July 28, 1945 (editorial and cartoon).
19. A *Pravda* correspondent denounced the campaign. "Russ Charge Anti-Red Bias," *San Francisco Examiner*, May 29, 1945.
20. For background, see Storrs, *The Second Red Scare and the Unmaking of the New Deal Left*, 51–71. For examples of editorials and columns in the *San Francisco Examiner*, see "A Strategic Blunder," July 25, 1945; William Henry Chamberlin, "The Polish Tragedy," May 28, 1945; "Comrade Quisling," August 27, 1945. For wider discussion, see Adler and Paterson, "Red Fascism."
21 Inboden, *Religion and American Foreign Policy, 1945–1960*, chapter 1; Preston, "Peripheral Visions."
22 Trachtenberg, "The United States and Eastern Europe in 1945," esp. 98; Hamby, *Man of the People*, 316–321.
23. Holloway, *Stalin and the Bomb*, 116; Offner, *Another Such Victory*, 72, 75, 91. For a contrasting emphasis on Western concessions, see McCullough, *Truman*, 450.
24. Rotter, *Hiroshima*, 244.
25. Ibid., 232.
26. Pechatnov, "'The Allies Are Pressing on You to Break Your Will . . .,'" esp. 6, 14; Chubariyan and Pechatnov, "Molotov 'the Liberal.'"
27. Rotter, *Hiroshima*, 249; Offner, *Another Such Victory*, 108, 110, 113, 116, 117.
28. Offner, *Another Such Victory*, 105, 109; Trachtenberg, "The United States and Eastern Europe in 1945."
29. "A Present for Harry," *Chicago Tribune*, October 25, 1945 (cartoon); "Stop Onrush of Anarchy," *San Francisco Examiner*, October 10, 1945 (editorial).
30. "Land of Perpetual Darkness," *Chicago Tribune*, November 5, 1945 (cartoon); "New Graves in Europe," *Chicago Tribune*, October 19, 1945 (cartoon); "The Bear Went over the Mountain" (cartoon) and "Communism in Bavaria" (editorial), *San Francisco Examiner*, October 11, 1945; "Our Diplomatic Feebleness" (editorial), *San Francisco Examiner*, October 11, 1945.
31. Pechatnov, "Exercise in Frustration."
32. "Na aerodrome vremeni," *Krokodil*, No. 40, 30 December 1945; *Krokodil*, No. 6, 28 February 1946 (front cover); "Khamov Kovcheg," No. 7, March 1946, 3.

33. "Sekretnoe vospitaniu," *Krokodil*, No. 37, 30 November 1945 (cover); "Ni voiny, ni raboty," *Krokodil*, No. 34, 30 October 1945.

34. Offner, *Another Such Victory*, 122–126. For a different view, see Hamby, *Man of the People*, 345.

35. George Gallup, "Truman Popularity Shrinks But Majority Still Backs Him," *Washington Post*, February 1, 1946; Offner, *Another Such Victory*, 123.

36. Iosif Stalin, "New Five-Year Plan for Russia," *Vital Speeches of the Day*, Vol. 12, No. 10 (March 1, 1946), 300–304; Offner, *Another Such Victory*, 128; Costigliola, "The Creation of Memory and Myth."

37. Offner, *Another Such Victory*, 133; Kennan, *Memoirs*, 547–559.

38. Kennan, *Memoirs*, 547–559.

39. Offner, *Another Such Victory*, 134, 142, 152; Messer, *The End of an Alliance*, 188–189.

40. Yegorova, "The 'Iran Crisis' of 1945–46." See also Hasanli, *At the Dawn of the Cold War*; Zubok, "Stalin, Soviet Intelligence, and the Struggle for Iran, 1945–53."

41. "Russian Bear" (editorial), *Washington Post*, March 14, 1946, 8; "Red Herring" (editorial), *Washington Post*, April 10, 1946; "A Crucial Decision" (editorial), *New York Times*, March 28, 1946.

42. See, for example, "Mr. Byrnes' Role" (editorial), *Washington Post*, March 30, 1946; Joseph Alsop and Stewart Alsop, "Firmness and Patience Pay Off," *Washington Post*, April 7, 1946; "This Was the Purpose" (editorial), *New York Times*, April 5, 1946.

43. Yegorova, "The 'Iran Crisis' of 1945–46," 17.

44. "Red Herring," *Washington Post*, April 10, 1946; Markowitz, *Rise and Fall of the People's Century*, 171–172; "A Crucial UNO Meeting," *New York Times*, March 25, 1946.

45. George Gallup, "77 Per Cent of U.S. Voters Decry Red Policy in Iran," *Washington Post*, March 31, 1946.

46. Gaddis, *The United States and the Origins of the Cold War, 1941–1947*, 312.

47. "Secretary Byrnes' Speech," *Atlanta Constitution*, March 3, 1946; "America Moves Closer to the Brink of Decision," *Louisville Courier-Journal*, March 9, 1946; "Churchill at Fulton," *Minneapolis Star-Journal*, March 6, 1946; "No Contribution to Harmony" (cartoon against "Russia Haters"), *Minneapolis Star-Journal*, March 12, 1946.

48. "Wars and Rumors of Wars," *Atlanta Constitution*, March 7, 1946; Ralph McGill, "'So, the Russ Is on Us – Even Now!'" *Atlanta Constitution*, March 11, 1946; "Ironing Out the Differences" (cartoon), *Louisville Courier-Journal*, March 26, 1946; "A Big Three Meeting?" *St. Louis Post-Dispatch*, March 8, 1946.

49. "The Loan Would Serve the Purpose Ideally," *Louisville Courier-Journal*, March 7, 1946; Charles Shepard, "No Appeasement" (letter), *Atlanta Constitution*, March 20, 1946.

50. "Russians and Americans Hurl Words across a Wall," *Louisville Courier-Journal*, March 12, 1946; Samuel Grafton, "Mr. Churchill's Speech Will Call Forth More Russian Expansionism," *Louisville Courier-Journal*, March 8, 1946. See also "Talk Is Not Enough," *St. Louis Post-Dispatch*, March 21, 1946.

51. "Behind the Iron Curtain," *San Francisco Examiner*, August 23, 1945; "The Churchill Speech," *San Francisco Examiner*, March 8, 1946.
52. See David-Fox, "The Iron Curtain as Semipermeable Membrane."
53. Gaddis, *The United States and the Origins of the Cold War*, 309.
54. See, for example, Barnet Nover, "Winston Churchill's Plea," *Washington Post*, March 7, 1946; Walter Lippmann, "U.S.S. Missouri," *Washington Post*, March 9, 1946; Walter Lippmann, "Black Week," *Washington Post*, March 12, 1946; "Name Calling" (editorial), *Washington Post*, March 15, 1946.
55. Ralph McGill, "'So, the Russ Is on Us – Even Now!'" *Atlanta Constitution*, March 11, 1946; "What Churchill Wants," *Chicago Defender*, March 16, 1946; "The Answer Is 'No,' Mr. Churchill," *Atlanta Constitution*, March 6, 1946; Samuel Grafton, "Mr. Churchill's Speech Will Call Forth More Russian Expansionism," *Louisville Courier-Journal*, March 8, 1946.
56. Offner, *Another Such Victory*, 136–137; Roberts, *Stalin's Wars*, 307–308.
57. Burds, "The Early Cold War in Soviet West Ukraine, 1944–1948," 29.
58. Ehrenburgh, *Post-war Years*, 60, 79–80; "Visiting Russian Sums Up His Trip," *New York Times*, 26 June 1946; Walter Lippmann, "Right to Admit Faults Divides U.S., Russia," *Minneapolis Star Tribune*, July 6, 1946; "Reply to Ehrenburg," *Rochester Democrat and Chronicle*, July 8, 1946; "It Is Good to Be Free," *San Francisco Examiner*, August 29, 1946.
59. Burds, "The Early Cold War in Soviet West Ukraine, 1944–1948," 29, 22, 33; N. Novikov to Soviet leadership, September 27, 1946, *Mezhdunarodnaia Zhizn'*, No. 11, 1990, 148–154; "POPURRI 'NOVAIA VOINA' V ISPOLNENII SHUMOVOGO orXERSTra," Krokodil, No. 28, 1946 (back cover); Magnúsdóttir, *Enemy Number One*, 9, 11, 19.
60. Pechatnov, "Exercise in Frustration," 18–19; Pechatnov, *Stalin, Ruzvel't, Trumen*; Nadzhafov, "The Beginning of the Cold War between East and West"; Magnúsdóttir, *Enemy Number One*, 40.
61 Markowitz, *Rise and Fall of the People's Century*, 181–192; Offner, *Another Such Victory*, 175–178.
62 Eisenberg, *Drawing the Line*, 223–224, 84, 89; Roberts, *Stalin's Wars*, 352; James F. Byrnes, "A Self-Governing Germany," *Vital Speeches of the Day*, Vol. 12, No. 23 (September 15, 1946), 706–709.
63. Zubok, *A Failed Empire*, 89, 63–64, 71; Roberts, *Stalin's Wars*, 302; Eisenberg, *Drawing the Line*, 260–268.
64. Truman's address to a joint session of Congress, March 12, 1947, printed as Appendix A in Steil, *The Marshall Plan*, 433–439.
65. Fousek, *To Lead the Free World*, 132–133; Johnson, *Congress and the Cold War*, 14–21.
66. Barnet Nover, "It's Up to Us," and Herblock, "I'm Here to Stay, Too," *Washington Post*, March 13, 1947; "Warning to Russia," *New York Times*, March 13, 1947.
67. Hoopes and Brinkley, *Driven Patriot*, 250–257, 278–279.

68. "X" [George F. Kennan], "The Sources of Soviet Conduct," esp. 570, 574, 575–6, 582, 577, 579; Steel, *Walter Lippmann and the American Century*, chapter 34.

69. "X" [George F. Kennan], "The Sources of Soviet Conduct," 582, 580.

70. Lippmann, *The Cold War*.

71. George Gallup, "Term 'Cold War' Unknown to 46%," *Washington Post*, December 3, 1948.

72. For example, Hal Boyle, "Cold War Bath of Words and Dollars, Boyle Says," AP dispatch in *Town Talk* (Alexandria, Louisiana), November 18, 1947; "America's Thanksgiving Prayer," *Miami News*, November 25, 1948.

73. Gabler, *Winchell*, 354–355; 378–384.

74. George Sokolsky, "Guilty Reds Blame U.S. for Cold War," *Philadelphia Inquirer*, May 26, 1948.

75. For example, Peter Edson, "Cold War Is Poker Game Now – U.S. Needs Courage to Stay In," *Kokomo Tribune* (Indiana), March 26, 1948; "Come Back When You're Washed Up, Joe!" (cartoon), *Poughkeepsie Journal*, May 26, 1948; "The 'Cold War,'" *Brookville American* (Pennsylvania), June 17, 1948.

76. DeWitt MacKenzie, "'Cold War' between Russia, U.S. to Take Its Place in History of Warfare," AP column in *Hope Star* (Arkansas), November 13, 1947; R. O. Zollinger, "Weapons for Reds," *Austin American-Statesman*, November 20, 1947; Mark Sullivan, "Russia to Continue Making War Short of Pulling Trigger," *Cumberland News* (Maryland), March 9, 1948.

77. *Krokodil*, 30 April 1947, 10 June 1947. See also *Krokodil*, 30 July 1947.

78. *Krokodil*, 20 February 1947, 10 January 1947, 30 October 1947. See also Magnúsdóttir, *Enemy Number One*, 66.

79. Krokodil, 20 June 1947; Caute, *The Dancer Defects*, chapter 4.

80. *Russkii vopros*, directed by Mikhail Romm (1948).

81. Roberts, *Stalin's Wars*, 315–316; Narinsky, "Soviet Foreign Policy and the Origins of the Cold War."

82. Brogi, *Confronting America*; Naimark, *Stalin and the Fate of Europe*, 123–146; "A Rough Romeo," *Detroit News*, April 17, 1948; "The Egg Rolling on the Kremlin Lawn," *Los Angeles Times*, March 29, 1948; "Don't Tread on Me," *Boston Herald*, March 21, 1948; "Quick Lady, the Whip!" *Chicago Tribune*, April 11, 1948.

83. Shaw and Youngblood, *Cinematic Cold War*, 19, 40.

84. Ibid., 19–24, 82–95; Caute, *The Dancer Defects*, chapter 6; Fried, *The Russians Are Coming! The Russians Are Coming!*

85. Shaw and Youngblood, *Cinematic Cold War*, 40–47, 67–77; Caute, *The Dancer Defects*, chapter 5.

86. Kapterev, "Illusionary Spoils"; Report to G. M. Malenkov, 29 November 1950, Russian State Archive of Socio-Political History (RGASPI), f. 17, op. 132, D. 429, L. 50–54.

87. McKenna, *All the Views Fit to Print*, 79; V. Kruzhkov to M. A. Suslov, August 19, 1949 and September 3, 1949, RGASPI, f. 17, op. 132, D. 133, L. 48, 52.

88. Lafont, *Soviet Posters*, 128. For other examples, see "Nesokrushimaia stena" ("Indestructible Wall"), 1949, in Efimov, *Boris Efimov*, 201; McKenna, *All the Views Fit to Print*, 85–90.

89. Zubkova, *Russia after the War*, 82–86, 126; Lel'chuk and Pivovar, "Mentalitet Sovetskogo Obshchestva i 'Kholodnaia Voina.'" See also Zubok, *A Failed Empire*, 6.

90. Foglesong, *The American Mission and the "Evil Empire*," chapter 5; Tromly, *Cold War Exiles and the CIA*; Kennan Diary, October 4, 1949, Box 231, Kennan Papers, Princeton.

91. Belmonte, *Selling the American Way*, 35–36; Mikkonen, "Stealing the Monopoly of Knowledge?"

92. Belmonte, *Selling the American Way*, esp. 14; Engerman, *Know Your Enemy*, 48–60.

93. Goncharov, Lewis, and Litai, *Uncertain Partners*; Zubok and Pleshakov, *Inside the Kremlin's Cold War*, 62–63, 150.

94. Offner, *Another Such Victory*, 348, 367–369; "Hot Spot in the Cold War," *Louisville Courier-Journal*, June 27, 1950; "Sole Responsibility," *Los Angeles Times*, June 27, 1950; "Russia Has No Hand in Korea – Malik," *Los Angeles Times*, August 12, 1950.

95. Casey, *Selling the Korean War*, 97, 177, 358.

96. Offner, *Another Such Victory*, 371, 379; Adler and Paterson, "Red Fascism"; "Stalin," *Detroit Free Press*, January 23, 1948; "The Family Album," *Atlanta Constitution*, January 26, 1948; "Brushing Up," *St. Louis Post-Dispatch*, November 30, 1952.

97. Costigliola, ed., *The Kennan Diaries*, 310–324; Gaddis, *George F. Kennan*, 466–469.

98. Harrison Salisbury, "Stalin Is Prepared to Settle Issues, Soviet Press Says," *New York Times*, December 27, 1952; Volkogonov, *Stalin*, 568–571.

99. Mastny, *The Cold War and Soviet Insecurity*, 195.

100. Edmund Stevens, "Exit of a Reporter: Suspicion Closes In," *Christian Science Monitor*, October 18, 1949, reprinted in Hecker, *An Accidental Journalist*, 267–270.

CHAPTER 14: CRISES AND COEXISTENCE, 1953–1963

1. Leffler, *For the Soul of Mankind*, chapter II; Jervis, "Identity and the Cold War."

2. Hopf, *Reconstructing the Cold War*.

3. Brooks, "When the Cold War Did Not End."

4. Zubok and Pleshakov, *Inside the Kremlin's Cold War*, 86; Hopf, *Reconstructing the Cold War*, 148; Mastny, "The Elusive Détente."

5. "The Stilled Stalin," *Washington Post*, March 5, 1953 ; "Joseph Stalin," *New York Times*, March 6, 1953.

6. "Malenkov – The New Boss," *Washington Post*, March 7, 1953; Joseph Alsop and Stewart Alsop, "Will Stalin's Successor Be a Caligula?" *Washington Post*, March 6, 1953; James Reston, "Russia: The Challenge for the U.S.," *New York Times*,

March 8, 1953; "A Great Opportunity," *Christian Science Monitor,* March 7, 1953. For a partially contrasting view, see Brooks, "Stalin's Ghost."

7. Burnham, *Containment or Liberation?*; Chamberlin, *Beyond Containment;* Lyons, *Our Secret Allies.* For discussion, see Foglesong, *The American Mission and the "Evil Empire,"* chapter 5.

8. Harrison Salisbury, "Russia's Mood Is Grim as Her Dictator Dies," *New York Times,* March 8, 1953; Zubkova, *Russia after the War;* Gorbachev, *Memoirs,* 47; "Sunset of a God," *Washington Post,* March 5, 1953; Gilmore, *Me and My Russian Wife,* 291; Gilmore, *After the Cossacks Burned Down the "Y,"* 11.

9. Zubok, *A Failed Empire,* 165; Zubok, *Zhivago's Children,* 41, 44.

10. Hatzivassiliou, "Images of the Adversary," 91; Osgood, *Total Cold War,* 58–61.

11. Dwight D. Eisenhower, "Peace in the World," *Vital Speeches of the Day,* Vol. 19, No. 14 (May 1, 1953), 418–421.

12. Brooks, "Stalin's Ghost," 127–129; Mastny, "The Elusive Détente," 7.

13. Roberts, *Molotov,* 135–136; Zubok, *A Failed Empire,* 89; Mastny, "The Elusive Détente," 11; *Krokodil,* No. 21, July 30, 1953, front cover; Hixson, *Parting the Curtain,* 73–77; Mitrovich, *Undermining the Kremlin,* 133–134; Ostermann, *Between Containment and Rollback.*

14. "Sprouting of the Seed," *Wall Street Journal,* June 19, 1953, 6; "Ferment in Soviet Europe," *New York Times,* July 8, 1953, 26; George Gallup, "Overwhelming Majority Feel Russia Aims at World Rule," *Washington Post,* August 21, 1953, 3.

15. Duberman, *Paul Robeson;* Dudziak, *Cold War Civil Rights.*

16. *Krokodil,* July 20, 1953, back cover; November 20, 1953, 9; January 20, 1954, 8; Taubman, *Khrushchev,* 260–266.

17. Preston, *Sword of the Spirit, Shield of Faith,* 441–447, Herzog, *The Spiritual–Industrial Complex;* Peter Mark, "Kardinal ot Uoll-strita," *Ogonek,* December 6, 1953, in Ball, *Liberty's Tears,* 276–281.

18. Salisbury, *American in Russia;* Murray Seeger, *Discovering Russia;* Fainberg, "A Portrait of a Journalist as a Cold War Expert."

19. Frederick C. Barghoorn, "Assignment to the Heart of Russia," *New York Times Book Review,* February 13, 1955, 1, 20; George Gallup, "Informed U.S. Public Favors Co-existence," *Washington Post,* January 7, 1955, 19; Gallup, "Public Thinks Reds Still in Government," *Washington Post,* January 28, 1955, 21.

20. Fainberg, *Cold War Correspondents,* 78–84.

21. Zubok, "Soviet Policy Aims at the Geneva Conference, 1955."

22. Osgood, *Total Cold War,* 189–194.

23. For example, "President Eisenhower at the 'Summit,'" *Chicago Tribune,* July 18, 1955; William Randolph Hearst, Jr., "Russians' Smiles Seek to Lull West," *San Francisco Examiner,* July 19, 1955.

24. "Treaty with Russia Could Be Empty, Warns Lawrence," *Louisville Courier-Journal,* July 25, 1955. Cartoonists also expressed hopes for "liberation": see "Breakthrough" by Carmack in *Christian Science Monitor,* reprinted in *New York*

Times, July 31, 1955, "All the Way?" by Loring in *The Providence Journal,* reprinted n *New York Times,* August 7, 1955.

25. "Those Talking Conferences" (cartoon), *Chicago Tribune,* July 27, 1955; "It's Good to Keep Them Talking," *Courier* (Waterloo, Iowa), July 25, 1955.

26. 'Geneva Meeting Is Only the Beginning," *Atlanta Constitution,* July 21, 1955; 'Eisenhower Seizes 'Peace' Initiative," *Atlanta Constitution,* July 22, 1955; "Geneva Weather Report" (cartoon), *St. Louis Post-Dispatch,* July 24, 1955.

27. "What Benefits from the Soviet Visit," *Des Moines Register,* July 25, 1955; Harry Schwartz, "News Comes to Pravda and Truth to Izvestia," *New York Times,* July 31, 1955; Brown, "Diplomatic Farmers."

28. "A Stupendous Initiative," *Christian Science Monitor,* July 23, 1955; "Erasing It?" cartoon by Carmack, *Christian Science Monitor,* July 28, 1955; "East and West Linked by New Civility," *Christian Science Monitor,* July 23, 1955; George Gallup, "Majority Sees Better Relations with Soviet Union after Geneva," *Washington Post,* August 3, 1955, 12.

29. Huxtable, *News from Moscow,* "Soviet Press Says Talks Herald New Relations," *Washington Post,* July 25, 1955; *Krokodil,* No. 22, August 10, 1955, 11; No. 23, August 20, 1955, back cover; No. 24, August 30, 1955, back cover; Harry Schwartz, "Soviet Press Damps Down the Spirit of Geneva Now," *New York Times,* October 23, 1955.

30. Memorandum of Conversation, July 20, 1955, *Foreign Relations of the United States, 1955–1957,* Vol. V, 409; Fursenko and Naftali, *Khrushchev's Cold War,* 44.

31. "Excerpts from Speech by Khrushchev to 20th Congress of Soviet Communist Party," *New York Times,* February 15, 1956, 10; "The Communist Key," *Wall Street Journal,* February 17, 1956, 6; "Khrushchev Tells the World," *Christian Science Monitor,* February 16, 1956; "Left Hand, Right Hand," *Washington Post,* February 17, 1956; Stewart Alsop, "Different Tactics, Same Objective," *Washington Post,* March 25, 1956.

32. Dulles' remarks at NSC meeting, May 17, 1956; Editorial Note on May 17 OCB meeting; J. F. Dulles in telephone call, June 28, 1956, *Foreign Relations, 1955–1957,* Vol. XXV, 165–166; 167; 181.

33. Khrushchev remark to Danish prime minister, 5 March 1956, quoted in Zubok, "Soviet Policy Aims at the Geneva Conference," 64; Fursenko and Naftali, *Khrushchev's Cold War,* 87, 118–137.

34. Text of Stevenson speech to Polish veterans in Detroit, *New York Times,* September 4, 1956, 16; Foster Dulles to Eisenhower, September 5, 1956; Eisenhower address, October 23, 1956; Dulles address on October 27, 1956, *Foreign Relations, 1955–1957,* Vol. XXV, 243; 265; 317–318.

35. Taubman, *Khrushchev,* 358; Fursenko and Naftali, *Khrushchev's Cold War,* 123; *Foreign Relations, 1955–1957,* Vol. XXV, 195, 273, 348.

36 Allen Dulles to Eisenhower, November 20, 1956, *Foreign Relations, 1955–1957,* Vol. XXV, 473–475; Gati, *Failed Illusions.*

37 *Foreign Relations, 1955–1957,* Vol. XXV, 392, 394, 418–421, 438.

38. *Foreign Relations, 1955–1957,* Vol. XXV, 365, 397, 418, 421.

39. "For Freedom's Defenders," *New York Times,* October 29, 1956; "We Accuse," *New York Times,* November 5, 1956; "This Is My Meat!" cartoon in *Los Angeles Times,* November 10, 1956; Herblock cartoon in *Washington Post,* November 6, 1956.

40. "Let These People Go," *Washington Post,* October 27, 1956; Clare Booth Luce telegram, November 4, 1956, *Foreign Relations, 1955–1957,* Vol. XXV, 390; Gallup polls reported in *Washington Post,* July 13, 1955, 6; June 29, 1957, D11; May 6, 1956, E5; August 6, 1959, A17.

41. Khrushchev, *Nikita Khrushchev and the Creation of a Superpower,* 207–211; Hahn, *The United States, Great Britain, and Egypt, 1945–1956,* 234–235; Fursenko and Naftali, *Khrushchev's Cold War,* 159–182.

42. "The Coup in Iraq Spells Out Our Greatest Cold-War Defeat," *Louisville Courier-Journal,* July 15, 1958; "Banner with a Strange Device," *Detroit Free Press,* July 17, 1958; "What Move with the Red Checker?" *Los Angeles Times,* July 17, 1958.

43. Yaqub, *Containing Arab Nationalism*; Makdisi, *Faith Misplaced,* 220, 224, 250.

44. Namikas, *Battleground Africa*; Mazov, *A Distant Front in the Cold War.*

45. Gorsuch, *All This Is Your World,* 10.

46. Gunther, *Inside Russia Today,* 504–505; *Reader's Digest,* Vol. 71 (December 1957), 164–168; *Time,* April 14, 1958.

47. "Tass Assails Gunther," *New York Times,* April 11, 1958.

48. Gunther, *Inside Russia Today,* xviii, xix, 75, 397–398, 501–502.

49. Levine, *Main Street, U.S.S.R.,* 24, 26–27, 398–399, 400; review by William Hogan in *San Francisco Chronicle,* January 27, 1959, 29; review by W. H. Chamberlin in *Chicago Sunday Tribune,* February 1, 1959, 4; review by Marvin Kalb, *New York Times Book Review,* February 1, 1959, 3; *Time,* February 9, 1959; Averell Harriman, *Peace with Russia?*; review by Harrison Salisbury in *New York Times Book Review,* December 6, 1959; praise by Merle Fainsod in *New York Herald Tribune,* November 15, 1959.

50. *Foreign Relations of the United States, 1958–1960,* Vol. X, Part 2, 13, 50; Lyons, "The Soviet Regime and the Russian People," May 20, 1958, *Vital Speeches of the Day,* Vol. 24, No. 18, 556–560.

51. Tsipursky, *Socialist Fun*; cartoons in *Krokodil,* esp. No. 12, April 30, 1957, 16, and No. 24, August 30, 1957, 16; Taubman, *Khrushchev,* 383; Zubok, *Zhivago's Children,* 103–111.

52. Cf. Richmond, *Cultural Exchange and the Cold War,* 11–12.

53. Gilburd, "The Revival of Soviet Internationalism in the Mid to Late 1950s."

54. Tsipursky, *Socialist Fun*; Kulavig, *Dissent in the Years of Khrushchev,* 24; Zubok, *Zhivago's Children,* 80.

55. For example, *Krokodil,* No. 11, April 20, 1956, back cover; No. 26, September 20, 1956, back cover; No. 28, October 10, 1957, 12.

56. Dudziak, *Cold War Civil Rights,* esp. 12, 250; Rosenberg, *How Far the Promised Land?*

57. Isacoff, *When the World Stopped to Listen*, esp. 153–155; Tomoff, *Virtuosi Abroad*, 99–102.

58. Robinson, *Russians in Hollywood, Hollywood's Russians*, 169–174; Shaw, *Hollywood's Cold War*, 28–33.

59. Hixson, *Parting the Curtain*; Reid, "Who Will Beat Whom?"; Carbone, "Staging the Kitchen Debate."

60. Gorsuch, *All This Is Your World*, 13, 18; Pipes, *Alexander Yakovlev*, 14–15; Kalugin, *The First Directorate*, 24–32; Gilburd, "The Revival of Soviet Internationalism in the Mid to Late 1950s," 374; Gilburd, *To See Paris and Die*, 304–315.

61. Searcy, *Ballet in the Cold War*.

62. Richmond, *Cultural Exchange and the Cold War*, 123; Prevots, *Dance for Export*, 71–74; John Martin, "The Dance: A La Moiseyev," *New York Times*, April 20, 1958, X19; Hallinan, "The 1958 Tour of the Moiseyev Dance Company"; *Krokodil*, May 10, 1958, front cover; January 10, 1959, 9; February 20, 1959, 9; "Dancers' Success Hailed in Moscow," *New York Times*, April 17, 1958, p. 36. On the global reception of multiracial troupes of American dancers, see Phillips, *Martha Graham's Cold War*.

63. *Krokodil*, No. 23, August 20, 1959; "Good News," cover of *Krokodil*, No. 26, September 20, 1959; Magnúsdóttir, "'Be Careful in America, Premier Khrushchev!'"; Taubman, *Khrushchev*, 416–441.

64. Richard Pipes, "Now It's the Babbits Have Crush on Soviet," *Washington Post*, September 13, 1959, E1; George Gallup, "52 Pct. Call Mr. K's Visit Good Thing," *Washington Post*, September 28, 1959, A5; Gallup, "US Public Skeptical of K.'s Disarmament Plan," *Washington Post*, September 30, 1959, A8; Harrison Salisbury, "Khrushchev Visit: Impact in U.S.," *New York Times*, September 20, 1959, E5; "The Melting Ice," *Washington Post*, September 29, 1959, A16.

65. Speech by H. S. Khrushchev, September 28, 1959, in *Khrushchev in America*, 217–231; Thompson and Thompson, *The Kremlinologist*, 202.

66. *Krokodil*, No. 36, December 30, 1959, 3. For other illustrations in the Soviet campaign against "the Cold War," see *Krokodil*, No. 28, October 10, 1959 (front cover and back cover), No. 32, November 20, 1959 (front cover), No. 2, January 20, 1960, 11; No. 3, January 30, 1960 (front cover).

67. Taubman, *Khrushchev*, 441; *Krokodil*, No. 27, September 30, 1959, front cover; No. 11, April 20, 1959, 2–3; McKenna, *All the Views Fit to Print*, 105; Jenks, *The Cosmonaut Who Couldn't Stop Smiling*, 7, 26.

68. Wittner, *Resisting the Bomb*, 35; Evangelista, *Unarmed Forces*, 32.

69. Sherry, *In the Shadow of War*, 214–217; McDougall, *The Heavens and the Earth*, 171.

70. Evangelista, *Unarmed Forces*, 53–57; Memorandum of Conference with President Eisenhower, March 24, 1958; Memorandum of Conversation, April 8, 1958; Dulles to Eisenhower, April 30, 1958; Memorandum of Conversation on Nuclear Test Negotiations, May 5, 1959, *Foreign Relations, 1958–1960*, Vol. III, 567–570; 595; 605; 738.

71. Khrushchev, *Nikita Khrushchev and the Creation of a Superpower*, 301–302, 347.
72. Taubman, *Khrushchev*, 448–450; *Krokodil*, No. 12, April 30, 1960, back cover; Grose, *Gentleman Spy*, 488; Khrushchev, *Nikita Khrushchev and the Creation of a Superpower*, 351–352.
73. Ambrose, *Eisenhower*, Vol. II, 563–567; Geelhoed, *Diplomacy Shot Down*, x, 181–185, 244.
74. Taubman, *Khrushchev*, 442–468; Fursenko and Naftali, *Khrushchev's Cold War*, 262–290.
75. *Krokodil*, No. 14, May 20, 1960 (front cover); No. 15, May 30, 1960 (front cover and page 2); "Red Rallies Decry Spy Flight: Press, Radio Whip Up Indignation," *Chicago Tribune*, May 18, 1960.
76. "The Way of Self-Righteousness," *Wall Street Journal*, May 10, 1960, 16; Arthur Krock column, *New York Times*, May 13, 1960; Norman Cousins advert, "Time for Common Sense," *St. Louis Post-Dispatch*, May 13, 1960; "U-2 Shadow Falls over Many Fields," *Atlanta Constitution*, May 13, 1960.
77. Taubman, *Khrushchev*, esp. 534.
78. Kempe, *Berlin 1961*, 6, 9; Fursenko and Naftali, *"One Hell of a Gamble,"* 80.
79. Fursenko and Naftali, *"One Hell of a Gamble,"* 101–106; Schlesinger, *Robert Kennedy*, 419; Kempe, *Berlin 1961*, 139.
80. Fursenko and Naftali, *"One Hell of a Gamble,"* 88; Dobbs, *One Minute to Midnight*, 7; cartoon by Efimov in *Krokodil*, April 10, 1961; cartoon by Ganf in *Krokodil*, May 20, 1961; Taubman, *Khrushchev*, 490–493.
81. Taubman, *Khrushchev*, 495–502; Kempe, *Berlin 1961*, 226–251.
82. Kempe, *Berlin 1961*, 279–309.
83. Ibid., 379; Trachtenberg, *A Constructed Peace*.
84. Kempe, *Berlin 1961*, 444–446; Fursenko and Naftali, *Khrushchev's Cold War*, 409–411.
85. Taubman, *Khrushchev*, 531–556; Fursenko and Naftali, *"One Hell of a Gamble,"* 182–196.
86. Plokhy, *Nuclear Folly*.
87. Wittner, *Confronting the Bomb*, 92–97, 104; Swerdlow, *Women Strike for Peace*.
88. Robinson, *Russians in Hollywood*, 185–188; "Cinema: Summer's Fair Fare," *Time*, June 23, 1961.
89. Shaw and Youngblood, *Cinematic Cold War*, 127–154.
90. Text of Kennedy's speech in *Chicago Tribune*, July 27, 1963, 4.
91. Schlesinger, *A Thousand Days*, 911; "Invitation to Disaster," *Indianapolis Star*, July 27, 1963; "The Test Ban Treaty," *Chicago Tribune*, July 27, 1963.
92. For example, "The Senate and the Treaty," *New York Times*, July 27, 1963; "Shackling the Djinn," *Boston Globe*, July 27, 1963; "The Test Ban – Cause for Hope," *San Francisco Examiner*, July 27, 1963; "Setting the Stage," *St. Louis Post-Dispatch*, July 28, 1963.

93. "Nuclear Test Ban Is a Breakthrough," *Atlanta Constitution*, July 27, 1963; Lauren Soth, "What Does Test-Ban Treaty Mean?" *Des Moines Register*, July 28, 1963.
94. Schlesinger, *A Thousand Days*, 913; Leffler, *For the Soul of Mankind*, 165–189; Clarke, *JFK's Last Hundred Days*, 194–199; Taubman, *Khrushchev*, 582–604; Wittner, *Confronting the Bomb*, 107–110; Khrushchev, *Nikita Khrushchev*, 695.
95. Leffler, *For the Soul of Mankind*, 194; Taubman, *Khrushchev*, 604–605.
96. For the contrary view, see Stephanson, "The Cold War Considered as a US Project."
97. Schlesinger, *A Thousand Days*, 923.

CHAPTER 15: DÉTENTE, 1964–1979

1. For example, Leffler, *For the Soul of Mankind*, 259, 334; Savranskaya and Taubman, "Soviet Foreign Policy, 1962–1975," 135, 140–141; Friedman, *Shadow Cold War*, 218.
2. Caldwell, "US Domestic Politics and the Demise of Détente"; Zelizer, "Detente and Domestic Politics."
3. Foglesong, *The American Mission and the "Evil Empire,"* chapter 7; Keys, *Reclaiming American Virtue.*
4. Beschloss, ed., *Taking Charge*, 37, 112–114, 119–120, 137, 144–145, 293; Brands, "Progress Unseen," 263.
5. Johnson address, October 18, 1964, *Current Notes on International Affairs*, Vol. 35, No. 10 (1964), 34–37.
6. Shaw and Youngblood, *Cinematic Cold War*, 142–157; W. H. Von Dreele, "Satirist with Astigmatism," *National Review*, March 10, 1964, 203–204; review of *Dr. Strangelove* by Stanley Kaufmann in *The New Republic*, February 1, 1964, 28; "Cinema: Political Thriller," *Time*, February 21, 1964; Roswell L. Gilpatric, "'Strangelove'? 'Seven Days'? Not Likely," *New York Times*, May 17, 1964; review of *Fail Safe* by Bosley Crowther in *The New York Times*, September 16, 1964.
7. Robert Alden, "Screen: 'The Russians Are Coming,'" *New York Times*, May 26, 1966; Robinson, *Russians in Hollywood*, 215, 220–222; Bosley Crowther, "Adaptation of Pasternak Novel at the Capitol," *New York Times*, December 23, 1965; Stanley Kauffmann, "Doctoring Zhivago," *New Republic*, January 15, 1966, 34, 36; "The Doctor's Dilemma," *Newsweek*, January 3, 1966; "Movies: Oscar-Bound," *Time*, December 24, 1965; "Cinema: To Russia with Love," *Time*, December 31, 1965.
8. George Galllup, "Red China, Not Soviets, Seen Top Threat to U.S.," *Washington Post*, March 28, 1965; George Gallup, "Americans See Russia as Ally in China War," *Washington Post*, March 8, 1967.
9. Lerner, "'Trying to Find the Guy Who Invited Them'"; Johnson, "A Time of Testing and Transition," State of the Union address, January 10, 1967, *Vital*

Speeches of the Day, Vol. XXXIII, No. 8, February 1, 1967, 230–231; Hulsey, *Everett Dirksen and His Presidents*, 231–240; Dallek, *Flawed Giant*, 432–438, 554.

10. The Diary of Anatoly S. Chernyaev (www.nsarchive.org), entries for August 23, 1975, January 1, 1976, January 3, 1976, October 23, 1976, January 15, 1977, and January 17, 1977; Edemskiy, "Dealing with Bonn," esp. 16 and 21; Schattenberg, *Brezhnev*, 268, 284.

11. Kornienko, *Kholodnaia Voina*, 251; Haslam, *Russia's Cold War*, 218, 239; Schattenberg, *Brezhnev*, 286, 299; Lerner, "'Trying to Find the Guy Who Invited Them,'" 93–99.

12. For example, the popular comedy, *Kavkazskaia plennitsa* (1967).

13. Among the most vivid images: *Krokodil*, No. 11, April 1968 (front cover, on the murder of Martin Luther King); "Shooting Advertisements," No. 21, July 1968; and "Two-Party Policy in Vietnam," No. 28, October 1968.

14. Roth-Ey, *Moscow Prime Time*.

15. Yurchak, *Everything Was Forever, Until It Was No More*; Zhuk, *Rock and Roll in the Rocket City*.

16. Kramer, "The Czechoslovak Crisis and the Brezhnev Doctrine"; Chernyaev Diary, Epilogue for 1976 and entry for March 9, 1975.

17. Iu. Cherepanov cartoon, "Ot vorot – povorot," *Krokodil*, No. 28, October 1968, 3; Boris Yefimov cartoon, "Dve taktiki kontrrevoliutsii," *Krokodil*, No. 30, October 1968, 16.

18. Kramer, "The Czechoslovak Crisis and the Brezhnev Doctrine," 167–168.

19. "Russians, Go Home!" *New York Times*, August 22, 1968; "The Crushing of Czechoslovakia, *Wall Street Journal*, August 22, 1968; Herblock cartoon, "She Might Have Invaded Russia," *Washington Post*, September 3, 1968.

20. "Varieties of Intervention, *Wall Street Journal*, August 23, 1968; James Reston, "Washington: Czechoslovakia and Disarmament," *New York Times*, August 25, 1968; Joseph Alsop, "Complete Falsity of McCarthy's Views Spotlighted by Invasion," *Washington Post*, August 26, 1968; Senator Henry M. Jackson, "Does the Leopard Change His Spots?" *Vital Speeches of the Day*, Vol. XXXV, No. 4, December 1, 1968, 98–100.

21. "Reacting to Czechoslovakia," *New York Times*, September 8, 1968; "The Treaty Should Be Ratified," *Washington Post*," September 9, 1968; Lerner, "'Trying to Find the Guy Who Invited Them,'" 81, 103; Dallek, *Flawed Giant*, 595–596; Kramer, "The Czechoslovak Crisis," 166; Kornienko, *Kholodnaia Voina*, 259–260.

22. Ambrose, *Nixon: Ruin and Recovery, 1973–1990*; Isaacson, *Kissinger*; Hanhimaki, *The Flawed Architect*.

23. Logevall and Preston, "Introduction," in Logevall and Preston, ed., *Nixon in the World*, 4; Gavin, "Nuclear Nixon," in Logevall and Preston, ed., *Nixon in the World*, 141.

24. *Foreign Relations of the United States, 1969–1976*, Vol. XIV, 123–124, 270, 277, 437, 736, 901.

25. For example, Kalb and Kalb, *Kissinger*.

26. Schulzinger, *Henry Kissinger*; Hanhimaki, *The Flawed Architect*.

27. Sandbrook, "Salesmanship and Substance"; Greenberg, *Nixon's Shadow*, 276–281; Mason, "Foreign Policy and the Republican Quest for a New Majority"; Nelson, "Détente over Thirty Years."

28. Sandbrook, "Salesmanship and Substance," 86–95; Scanlon, "Building Consensus," 428–435.

29. Nelson, *The Making of Détente*, 127–135; Thompson, *The Hawk and the Dove*, 261; Ershova, *Dvizhenie za mir, protiv militarizma i voiny v SShA (1965–1978 gg.)*, esp. 3, 7.

30. Nguyen, *Hanoi's War*, 232–246.

31. Anatoly S. Chernyaev Diary, April 21 and 25, 1972, National Security Archive Electronic Briefing Book No. 379; Nelson, *The Making of Détente*, 140; Nguyen, *Hanoi's War*, 252–253; Hedrick Smith, "For Many Russians, Nixon's TV Address Hit Home," *New York Times*, May 29, 1972, 3.

32. *Foreign Relations of the United States, 1969–1976*, Vol. XIV, 322, 328, 445, 449, 513; 655–656, 684, 709, 725, 775, 776.

33. *Foreign Relations of the United States, 1969–1976*, Vol. XIV, 1051–1064, 1170, 1219–1220.

34. Memo from Nixon to Haig, May 20, 1972; Editorial Note citing Haldeman Diary, May 24, 1972; and message from Haig to Kissinger, May 25, 1972, *Foreign Relations of the United States, 1969–1976*, Vol. XIV, 965; 1022; 1113.

35. Transcript of Nixon's Address to Congress, *New York Times*, June 2, 1972, 12.

36. "The Moscow Summit," *New York Times*, May 28, 1972; "Rules for Coexistence," *New York Times*, May 30, 1972; "Moscow (III): A Summing Up," *Washington Post*, May 29, 1972; "Mission to Moscow," *Chicago Daily Defender*, May 30, 1972.

37. Turek, "A New Strategy for Peace?" M.A. Thesis, University of Virginia, 2009.

38. George Gallup, "Nixon Popularity Hits 2-Year Peak on Soviet Trip," *Washington Post*, June 4, 1972; "Poll Shows Nixon Retaining Approval," *New York Times*, June 25, 1972.

39. *Foreign Relations of the United States, 1969–1976*, Vol. XV, 13, 147, 206, 687.

40. Hersh, *The Price of Power*; Harmer, *Allende's Chile and the Inter-American Cold War*.

41. Chernyaev Diary, January 2, 1976; *Foreign Relations of the United States, 1969–1976*, Vol. XV, 17n, 458.

42. *Foreign Relations of the United States, 1969–1976*, Vol. XV, 5, 419, 607–609, 612–630, 794, 826, 1020; Bundy, *A Tangled Web*, 428–444; Hanhimaki, *The Flawed Architect*, 302–317; Daigle, *The Limits of Détente*.

43. George Gallup, "American Opinion of U.S.S.R. Rises," *Washington Post*, June 19, 1973, A12; Jespersen, *American Images of China, 1931–1949*, 182.

44. For an early example, see "Summing Up," *Wall Street Journal*, June 1, 1972.

45. *Foreign Relations of the United States, 1969–1976*, Vol. XV, 34, 72–73, 212, 293, 207, 309; Beckerman, *When They Come for Us, We'll Be Gone*, chapters 6–8; Barnett, *The Star and the Stripes*, chapter 5.

46. *Foreign Relations of the United States, 1969–1976*, Vol. XV, 665, 917, 645. See also Dobrynin, *In Confidence*, 303–304.

47. *Foreign Relations of the United States, 1969–1976*, Vol. XV, 100–104, 392, 876; Dobrynin, *In Confidence*, 316.
48. Rupprecht, *Soviet Internationalism after Stalin*, esp. 286.
49. For example, "Voenno-promyshlennyi brudershaft" by A. Semenov, *Krokodil*, No. 29, October 1972.
50. McKenna, *All the Views Fit to Print*, 117–119; Dobrynin, "The Silver Curtain," 863, 869.
51. Dobrynin, *In Confidence*, 307, 313, 314; Chernyaev Diary, May 13, July 6, and July 13, 1974.
52. "Failure of a Mission," *Chicago Defender*, July 9, 1974; "The Third Summit: A Time of Testing," *Time*, July 1, 1974; "Summits and Human Rights," *Washington Post*, July 8, 1974, A22; Keys, *Reclaiming American Virtue*, esp. 127–177.
53. "Dump Détente?" (editorial), *Charlotte Observer*, March 3, 1976; "Same Policy, Different Name," *Lincoln Star* (Nebraska), March 3, 1976; "Soviets Stunned – 'Détente' Inoperative," *Miami Herald*, March 3, 1976.
54. Memoranda from PPS to Kissinger, August 8, 1975 and December 10, 1975, *Foreign Relations of the United States, 1969–1976*, Vol. XVI, 722–723, 871–872.
55. Conversation between Kissinger and Reston, April 9, 1976, in *Foreign Relations of the United States, 1969–1976*, Vol. XVI, 1035.
56. Memorandum from Assistant Secretary of State for Public Affairs to Kissinger, December 9, 1974, in *Foreign Relations of the United States, 1969–1976*, Vol. XVI, 378–380; Murray Marder, "Public Called Wary on Foreign Policy," *Washington Post*, September 11, 1975.
57. For example, "Moscow (III): A Summing Up," *Washington Post*, May 29, 1972.
58. Chernyaev Diary, July 4, 1975.
59. Kachavi, "Insights Abandoned, Flexibility Lost," 524–526.
60. Orelick, *The Soviet Jewish-Americans*, 56; *Foreign Relations of the United States, 1969–1976*, Vol. XVI, 9–10, 41, 95, 165, 174, 180, 187, 404, 624, 673, 1104.
61. Schulzinger, *Henry Kissinger: Doctor of Diplomacy*, 213–239; Hanhimaki, *The Flawed Architect*, 435–452; Morgan, *The Final Act*.
62. Hanhimaki, *The Flawed Architect*, 382–398; "New Asian Danger Is Seen by Kissinger," *New York Times*, May 13, 1975; Memo from Sonnenfeldt and Hyland to Kissinger, April 16, 1975, *Foreign Relations of the United States, 1969–1976*, Vol. XVI, 548–551.
63. Gleijeses, *Conflicting Missions*, chapters 11–15; Westad, *The Global Cold War*, chapter 6; Kornienko, *Kholodnaia Voina*, 327–331; David Binder, "Kissinger Warns Soviet and Cuba on Aid to Angola," *New York Times*, November 25, 1975; "Kissinger Remarks on Angola," *New York Times*, December 24, 1975; *Foreign Relations of the United States, 1969–1976*, Vol. XVI, 899–900. 907; cartoon by Tony Auth, *Philadelphia Inquirer*, December 1, 1975.
64. Memorandum from Sonnenfeldt to Kissinger, January 9, 1976, in *FRUS, 1969–1976*, Vol. XVI, 895–896; Memorandum of Conversation between Ford and Kendall, April 8, 1976, in *FRUS, 1969–1976*, Vol. XVI, 1032; Memoranda of

Conversations between Ford and Kissinger, March 18, 1976 and October 3, 1976, in *FRUS, 1969–1976*, Vol. XVI, 1025, 1095; "Soviet Declares Kissinger Twists Its Angola Policy," *New York Times*, February 2, 1976; Chernyaev Diary, January 2, 1976.

65. Memo from Scowcroft to Ford, April 12, 1976, in *FRUS, 1969–1976*, Vol. XVI, 1037–1038; Memo from Sonnenfeldt to Kissinger, January 3, 1977, in *FRUS, 1969–1976*, Vol. XVI, 1106–1107. On Soviet officials' anger at US "slander," see Chernyaev Diary, May 22, 1976.

66. Aksyonov, *Non-stop around the Clock*; Fainberg, *Cold War Correspondents*, chapter 5.

67. Kaiser, *Russia*, xii; 453–479; Smith, *The Russians*, ix, 250, 499–507; Ivan Sanders, "Scrutinizing the Inscrutable," *Commonweal*, 18 June 1976, 406–408; Priscilla Buckley, "Getting to Know Them," *National Review*, February 20, 1976, 164–165; review by Allen Kassof in *New Republic*, May 1, 1976, 28–30; George Feifer, "Translations from the Russian," *Harper's Magazine*, Vol. 252, March 1976, 112, 116–117.

68. Engerman, *Know Your Enemy*, chapters 10 and 11; Cahn, *Killing Détente*; Costigliola, ed. *The Kennan Diaries*, 495–497 (entries for May [no date] and October 8, 1976).

69. Smith, *Morality, Reason, and Power*.

70. Chernyaev Diary, October 23, 1976, January 9, 1977, January 17, 1977, and January 21, 1977; Schattenberg, *Brezhnev*, 317; Christopher S, Wren, "Brezhnev Appeals to Carter on Arms," *New York Times*, January 18, 1977.

71. Blight and Lang, "FORUM: When Empathy Failed"; Chernyaev Diary, March 12, 1977.

72. Mitchell, *Jimmy Carter in Africa*, 177–254, quotation on page 199.

73. Ibid., 262.

74. Chernyaev Diary, May 22, 1977; Mitchell, *Jimmy Carter in Africa*, 287; Westad, *Global Cold War*, chapter 7; Mitchell, "The Cold War and Jimmy Carter," 79–80; Woodruff, *"Buried in the Sands of the Ogaden,"* esp. 70; Vaisse, *Zbigniew Brzezinski*, 304.

75. Carter's address at University of Notre Dame, May 22, 1977, published under the title "A Democratic Foreign Policy," *Vital Speeches of the Day*, Vol. 43, No. 17 (June 15, 1977), 514–517; James Chace, "How 'Moral' Can We Get?" *New York Times*, May 22, 1977; David S. Broder, "Carter's 'International Morality,'" *Washington Post*, May 29, 1977; Murray Marder, "Test of Carter's 'Feel Good' Foreign Policy Is Workability," *Washington Post*, May 24, 1977; "A 'New' Foreign Policy: Cash or Charge," *New York Times*, May 30, 1977.

76. Transcript of Carter's speech at Annapolis, *New York Times*, June 8, 1978.

77. "Soviet Intensifies Its Attacks on U.S. over Carter Speech," *New York Times*, June 12, 1978; Terence Smith, "McGovern and Church Chide Carter on His Speech," *New York Times*, June 9, 1978; Henry Jackson, "Tough Talk, Weak Acts," *Washington Post*, July 1, 1978.

78. "Soviet Intensifies Its Attacks on U.S. over Carter Speech," *New York Times*, June 12, 1978; "Soviet Says That Carter May Start New Cold War," *New York*

Times, June 17, 1978; Excerpts from Pravda commentary, *New York Times,* June 18, 1978; Kenneth H. Bacon, "Message to Moscow," *Wall Street Journal,* June 7, 1978.

79. *Telefon,* released 16 December 1977; Richard Schickel, "Wrong Number," *Time,* December 26, 1977.

80. Kozovoi, "'This Film Is Harmful': Resizing America for the Soviet Screen," 147–148; *Shooting Range,* directed by V. Tarasov (1979), in *Animated Soviet Propaganda: From the October Revolution to Perestroika* (DVD, 2006).

81. Reagan quoted in Foglesong, *The American Mission and the "Evil Empire,"* 167; Hixson, *Parting the Curtain*; Chernyaev Diary, December 5, 1974; July 2, 1977; December 4, 1977; November 20, 1979. See also Rosenberg, "Consumer Capitalism and the End of the Cold War."

82. Raleigh, *Soviet Baby Boomers,* 218–267.

83. Smith, *Morality, Reason, and Power,* 86–93; Steven V. Roberts, "Americans Provide Many Reasons for Partiality to China over Soviet," *New York Times,* February 4, 1979.

84. Andrew and Mitrokhin, *The World Was Going Our Way,* 178–183; Glad, *An Outsider in the White House,* 168–173; "Iran: The Crescent of Crisis," *Time,* January 15, 1979.

85. Smith, *Morality, Reason, and Power,* 78–79; "Down from the Summit Clouds," *New York Times,* June 19, 1979; "Down from the Summit," *Washington Post,* June 20, 1979; "Fear of Rejection" and "Umbrellas and God," *Wall Street Journal,* June 19, 1979.

86. Garthoff, *Détente and Confrontation,* 828–839; Smith, *Morality, Reason, and Power,* 214–215; Ashby and Gramer, *Fighting the Odds,* 591–596; Thompson, *The Hawk and the Dove,* 273–274; Newsom, *The Soviet Brigade in Cuba*; "Exploding Cigar," *Wall Street Journal,* September 7, 1979.

87. Carter, *White House Diary,* 354 (though see also page 359); oral history interview with Marshall D. Shulman, 689–697.

88. "Reject SALT Now," *Wall Street Journal,* September 11, 1979; Garthoff, *Détente and Confrontation,* 840–847; Duffy, "Crisis Politics."

89. "Reject SALT Now," *Wall Street Journal,* September 11, 1979.

90. Zubok, *A Failed Empire,* 260–264; Braithwaite, *Afgantsy,* 7, 71–94; Chernyaev Diary, December 30, 1979; Tobin, "The Myth of the 'Afghan Trap'"; Borovik, *The Hidden War,* 5–13.

91. Sarantakes, *Dropping the Torch*; Kalinovsky, *A Long Goodbye,* 62.

92. See, for example, editorials in the *New York Times* on January 1, 6, and 9, 1980: "Deeper and Dirtier in Afghanistan," "Counterpunching on Afghanistan," and "What Lies Broken in Afghanistan."

93. "Those Non-political Olympians," *New York Times,* February 26, 1980; "The Winning Spirit," *Wall Street Journal,* February 26, 1980; Mitchell, "The Cold War and Jimmy Carter," 84–85.

94. Schattenberg, *Brezhnev,* 304; Westad, *Global Cold War,* 241.

95. Cf. Brands, *The Twilight Struggle,* 144–145.

CHAPTER 16: FROM ARMAGEDDON TO ACCOMMODATION, 1980–1989

1. Schweizer, *Victory*; Schweizer, *Reagan's War*. More sophisticated studies that emphasize Reagan's role include Gaddis, *The Cold War: A New History*, esp. 222–228; Morgan, *Reagan*; Inboden, *The Peacemaker*.

2. Wilentz, *The Age of Reagan*, esp. 151.

3. Garthoff, *The Great Transition*; Zubok, *A Failed Empire*; Grachev, *Gorbachev's Gamble*. See also Kremeniuk, *Uroki kholodnoi voiny*.

4. Leffler, *For the Soul of Mankind*, esp. 452; Wilson, *The Triumph of Improvisation*, 2; Brown, *The Human Factor*.

5. Garthoff, *The Great Transition*, 758; Wilson, *The Triumph of Improvisation*, 2; Service, *The End of the Cold War*, 22. For a contrary claim that Reagan had a grand strategy, see Miles, *Engaging the Evil Empire*.

6. For a contrasting view, see Leffler, *For the Soul of Mankind*, 462–464.

7. Benze, *Nancy Reagan on the White House Stage*, 130–132; Massie, *Trust But Verify*, 246; Tumulty, *The Triumph of Nancy Reagan*, 433–439; Taubman, *In the Nation's Service*, 179–187.

8 The impact of Soviet economic problems on Gorbachev's "new thinking" in foreign policy is emphasized and at times exaggerated by Bartel, *The Triumph of Broken Promises*, esp. 17, 171, 180.

9 Zubok, *Collapse*, 23, 27, 62.

10. English, *Russia and the Idea of the West*; Evangelista, *Unarmed Forces*; Snyder, *Human Rights Activism and the End of the Cold War*.

11. See Nehring, "The Last Battle of the Cold War," esp. 317.

12. Waller, *Congress and the Nuclear Freeze*; Meyer, *A Winter of Discontent*; Hogan, *The Nuclear Freeze Campaign*; Martin, *The Other Eighties*.

13. Maar, *Freeze!*; Freeman, *Dreams for a Decade*; Eames, *A Voice in Their Own Destiny*.

14. Cortright, *Peace Works*; Foglesong, "When the Russians Really Were Coming"; Foglesong, "How American and Soviet Women Transcended the Cold War."

15. Anatoly Chernyaev Diary, entries for January 28, February 5, April 4, June 21, and June 22, 1980; Dobrynin, *In Confidence*, 448; Braithwaite, *Afgantsy*, 108–111.

16. Craig and Logevall, *America's Cold War*, 304–307; Zelizer, *Arsenal of Democracy*, 291–292; Vaisse, *Neoconservatism*, 180–186.

17. "Transcript of Kennedy's Speech at Georgetown University on Campaign Issues," *New York Times*, January 29, 1980, A12; Anthony Lewis, "A Happier Warrior," *New York Times*, January 31, 1980; Kennedy, *True Compass*, 375–376; Donaghy, *The Second Cold War*, 102.

18. "George F. Kennan, on Washington's Reaction to the Afghan Crisis," *New York Times*, February 1, 1980, A27; Costigliola, ed., *Kennan Diaries*, 523–524. See also Charles Mohr, "George Kennan Says U.S. Magnifies Soviet Threat," *New York Times*, February 28, 1980.

19. KRON-TV, "First Strike" (1979–1980); personal recollection of David Foglesong, who participated in the production of the response, organized by Professor Andrew Stern.

20. Zelizer, *Arsenal of Democracy*, 297; Schlesinger, *Journals, 1952–2000*, 441; "October 28, 1980 Debate Transcript," www.debates.org/voter-education/deb ate-transcripts/october-28-1980-debate-transcript; Hedrick Smith, "Carter and Reagan Voicing Confidence on Debate Showing," *New York Times*, October 30, 1980; "Words, and Music, in the Debate" (editorial), *New York Times*, October 30, 1980; Troy, *Morning in America*, 25, 47–48.

21. "October 28, 1980 Debate Transcript," www.debates.org/voter-education/deb ate-transcripts/october-28-1980-debate-transcript.

22. Garthoff, *The Great Transition*, 8–12; Hoffman, *The Dead Hand*, 63–65.

23. Brinkley, ed., *The Reagan Diaries*, 2, 10; Garthoff, *The Great Transition*, 44; Donaghy, *The Second Cold War*, 131–132.

24. Dobson, "The Reagan Administration, Economic Warfare, and Starting to Close Down the Cold War."

25. *The Reagan Diaries*, 89, 106, 109–112.

26. *The Reagan Diaries*, 21, 89; Reagan addresses at University of Notre Dame, May 17, 1981 and Westminster, June 8, 1982.

27. *The Reagan Diaries*, 14–15, 102, 75.

28. English, *Russia and the Idea of the West*, 161; Zubok, *A Failed Empire*, 272; Radchenko, *To Run the World*, 519–521.

29. English, *Russia and the Idea of the West*, 160–170.

30. Garthoff, *The Great Transition*, 11, 130–137; Zubok, *A Failed Empire*, 274; Arbatov, "What Lessons Learned?" 56–57.

31. Forsberg, *Toward a Theory of Peace*; Waller, *Congress and the Nuclear Freeze*, quote on page 86; Wittner, *Toward Nuclear Abolition*, 169–178.

32. Knopf, *Domestic Society and International Cooperation*, chapter 7; Knoblauch, *Nuclear Freeze in a Cold War*.

33. Davis, *The Way I See It*, 278–279, 297; Waller, *Congress and the Nuclear Freeze*, 79.

34. For echoes of the smears, see Service, *The End of the Cold War*, 31, 99–101, 262. For refutation, see Wittner, *Toward Nuclear Abolition*, 258, 263, 271.

35. Waller, *Congress and the Nuclear Freeze*, 92; *The Reagan Diaries*, 93.

36. *The Reagan Diaries Unabridged*, Vol. 1, entry for December 5, 1981.

37. "Mindszenty Group Seeks to Halt 'Reds,'" *New York Times*, January 1, 1982; Reed Irvine, "Movie Pleases Reds," *Beatrice Daily Sun* (Nebraska), January 7, 1982; William F. Buckley, Jr., "Seeing 'Reds,' with Open Eyes," *New York Daily News*, January 14, 1982. Irvine rebuked Buckley in a letter: "Seeing 'Reds,'" *Washington Post*, January 24, 1982.

38. See the reviews on December 4, 1981 in the *Washington Post*, *Wall Street Journal*, and *New York Times*. Coincidentally, Soviet director Sergei Bondarchuk also made a two-part film about John Reed and his wife Louise Bryant, titled *Red*

Bells (*Krasnye kolokola*). See John F. Burns, "John Reed a Soviet Screen Hero, Too," *New York Times*, February 8, 1982.

39. *The Reagan Diaries*, 89; Richard Schickel, "Fast Flight," *Time*, June 21, 1982; Vincent Canby, "Stealing 'Firefox,'" *New York Times*, June 18, 1982; Rita Kempley, "A Fizzled 'Firefox,'" Washington Post, June 18, 1982; Richard Grenier, "Summertime Visions," *Commentary*, August 1, 1982; Eliot, *American Rebel: The Life of Clint Eastwood*, 203–204.

40. Grenier, "Summertime Visions"; Palmer, *The Films of the Eighties*, 209, 232.

41. The Georgian director Tengiz Abuladze's anti-Stalinist *Repentance*, for example, though finished in 1984, could not be shown until 1986.

42. Shaw and Youngblood, *Cinematic Cold War*, 189–199.

43. Foglesong, *The American Mission and the "Evil Empire,"* 182–184.

44. Bjork, *The Strategic Defense Initiative*; Donaghy, *The Second Cold War*, 174–181.

45. Holsti, *Public Opinion and American Foreign Policy*, 212; *The Reagan Diaries*, 139–140; Waller, *Congress and the Nuclear Freeze*, 192, 201.

46. Haslam, *Russia's Cold War*, 341; English, *Russia and the Idea of the West*, 179; Sagdeev, *The Making of a Soviet Scientist*, esp. 273; Service, *The End of the Cold War*, 193–194; Garthoff, *The Great Transition*, 111–112; Grinevsky, "The Crisis That Didn't Erupt," 69–71; Westwick, "'Space-Strike Weapons' and the Soviet Response to SDI."

47. Hoffman, *The Dead Hand*, 64–65, 74–86; Garthoff, *The Great Transition*, 118–127; *Newsweek*, September 12, 1983; *Time* (cover), September 12, 1983.

48. Mikhail Puchkovskii, "Provokatsiia," *Ogonek*, No. 32, September 10, 1983; cartoon by Boris Yefimov, *Ogonek*, No. 39, September 24, 1983.

49. Hoffman, *The Dead Hand*, 6–11, 95; Holloway, "The Dynamics of the Euromissile Crisis, 1977–1983"; Adamsky, "'Not Crying Wolf': Soviet Intelligence and the 1983 War Scare"; Grinevsky, "The Crisis That Didn't Erupt," 74–75.

50 Hoffman, *The Dead Hand*, 89–90; Garthoff, *The Great Transition*, 135n; cartoons in *Krokodil*, No. 20 (July 1983), No. 21 (July 1983), and No. 25 (September 1983), 9.

51 Palmer, *The Films of the Eighties*, 192–194; *The Reagan Diaries*, 185–186; Overpeck, "'Remember! It's Only a Movie.' Expectations and Receptions of *The Day After* (1983)"; Hanni, "A Chance for a Propaganda Coup?"

52. Neumann, "Children Diplomacy during the Late Cold War"; Peacock, "Samantha Smith in the Land of the Bolsheviks"; Turygin, Kupriianov, and Talalaev, "Politicheskaia sotsializatsiia sovestkikh shkolnikov v prostranstve detskoi publichnoi diplomatii (na primere mezdunarodnykh vizitov)."

53. Tennison, *The Power of Impossible Ideas*; interview with Tennison by David Foglesong, December 22, 2015; Warner and Shuman, *Citizen Diplomats*, 131–151; Warner, *Invisible Threads*, esp. 66–69; Gordeeva, "'Fighting for Peace Is Everyone's Job.'"

54. *The Citizen Diplomat*, July 20, 1984.

55. Later spacebridges hosted by television personalities reached huge audiences and had sensational impacts, especially in the Soviet Union. See Pozner with Kahn, *Parting with Illusions*, esp. 252–269.

56. Foglesong, "When the Russians Really Were Coming"; Gromyko and Hellman, eds., *Breakthrough/Proryv*; Gelber and Cook, *Saving the Earth*.

57. Eisenhower, *Breaking Free*, 32, 12, 16, 203, 221, 22; Mackenzie, *When Stars and Stripes Met Hammer and Sickle*.

58. Massie, *Trust But Verify*, 17–19, 68–74, 87, 99–100.

59. Hoffman, *The Dead Hand*, 91–93

60. *The Reagan Diaries*, 199, 203.

61. *The Reagan Diaries*, 210; Benze, *Nancy Reagan on the White House Stage*, 130–132; Wittner, *Toward Nuclear Abolition*, 267, 319; "The Peace Issue," *Wall Street Journal*, January 17, 1984; "Evil Empire ... Come In, Evil Empire," *New York Times*, January 17, 1984; "Mr. Reagan and Arms Control," *Washington Post*, January 17, 1984; Matlock, *Reagan and Gorbachev*, 82–83.

62. Garthoff, *The Great Transition*, 130; Grachev, *Gorbachev's Gamble*, 21, 41.

63. *The Reagan Diaries*, 220–223, 231.

64. Waller, *Congress and the Nuclear Freeze*, 293–296; Caldicott, *A Desperate Passion*, 299–309; Meyer, *A Winter of Discontent*, 259; Reagan's remarks at Republican Convention, August 23, 1984, www.reaganlibrary.gov/archives/audio/remarks-president-reagan-during-acceptance-address-1984-republican-national; Rossinow, *The Reagan Era*, 167–176.

65. Waller, *Congress and the Nuclear Freeze*, 293–300; Hogan, *The Nuclear Freeze Campaign*; Meyer, *A Winter of Discontent*, xiv–xvii, 253.

66. Cortright, *Peace Works*; Warner and Shuman, *Citizen Diplomats*.

67. Crile, *Charlie Wilson's War*, esp. 250; Garthoff, *The Great Transition*, 712.

68. Kalinovsky, *A Long Goodbye*.

69. October 27, 1986 entry in *The Reagan Diaries*, 447. See also *Foreign Relations of the United States, 1981–1988*, Vol. VI, 21–22.

70. *The Reagan Diaries*, 288, 440; Service, *The End of the Cold War*, 115.

71. English, *Russia and the Idea of the West*, 186–190; Brown, *Seven Years That Changed the World*, 245; Chernyaev Diary, December 8, 1985 (on the views of B. N. Ponomarev).

72. Yakovlev, *On the Edge of an Abyss*, 11–14, 394–399.

73. Robinson, *Russians in Hollywood*, 240–241; Vincent Canby, "Movies: '2010' Pursues the Mystery of '2001,'" *New York Times*, December 7, 1984; William J. Broad, "Science Facts Help Propel Science Fiction in the Film '2010,'" *New York Times*, December 2, 1984; David Ansen, "Lost in the Cosmos," *Newsweek*, December 10, 1984, 94.

74. John Simon, "Between Two Nonworlds," *National Review*, June 1, 1984, 49; Richard Schickel and Richard Corliss, "Cinema: The Greening of the Box Office," *Time*, April 23, 1984; Vincent Canby, "Paul Mazursky's 'Moscow on the Hudson,'" *New York Times*, April 6, 1984.

75. David Ansen, "Hoofing It to Freedom," *Newsweek*, November 18, 1985; Vincent Canby, "Baryshnikov in 'White Nights,' Tale of Two Defectors," *New York Times*, November 22, 1985; Richard Corliss, "Cinema: Dancing Down the Steppes," *Time*, November 25, 1985.

76. Shaw, *Hollywood's Cold War*, 272–276; Stephen Prince, ed., *American Cinema of the 1980s* (New Brunswick, NJ: Rutgers University Press, 2007), 114–116; Vincent Canby, "Cockeyed at 'Red Dawn,'" *New York Times*, September 16, 1984 (quoted); Janet Maslin, "'Red Dawn,' on World War III," *New York Times*, August 10, 1984.

77. Youngblood and Shaw, *Cinematic Cold War*, 201–211; Richard Schickel, "Danger: Live Moral Issues," *Time*, May 27, 1985.

78. "Get 'Em, Rocky," *Wall Street Journal*, January 7, 1986.

79. Prince, ed., *American Cinema of the 1980s*, 145–149; Palmer, *The Films of the Eighties*, 208; Vincent Canby, "Vintage Plotting Propels Mach II Planes in 'Top Gun,'" *New York Times*, June 8, 1986.

80. Youngblood and Shaw, *Cinematic Cold War*, 199–201.

81. Ibid., 209–210, 212.

82. Gorbachev, *Memoirs*, 46–59; Grachev, *Gorbachev's Gamble*, 55–57; Evangelista, *Unarmed Forces*, 271–275; Chernyaev Diary, December 28, 1985, May 20, 1985, and September 21, 1985.

83. Primakov, *Russian Crossroads*, esp. 16; English, *Russia and the Idea of the West*, esp. 181–184; Chernyaev Diary, January 18, 1986.

84. Matlock, *Reagan and Gorbachev*, 149–169; *The Reagan Diaries*, 371; Service, *The End of the Cold War*, 163.

85. Chernyaev Diary, October 15, 1985, November 16, 1985, and December 8, 1985.

86. Brown, *Manual for Survival*.

87. Garthoff, *The Great Transition*, 754; Zubok, *A Failed Empire*, 287–289; English, *Russia and the Idea of the West*, 215–217; Grachev, *Gorbachev's Gamble*, 86, 95.

88. Matlock, *Reagan and Gorbachev*, 246–247; *The Reagan Diaries*, 452, 478, 480.

89. Primakov, *Russian Crossroads*, 31; Wilson, *Triumph of Improvisation*, 123; Pipes, *Alexander Yakovlev*, 50, 62; Chernyaev Diary, June 6, 1987; *The Reagan Diaries*, 530.

90. "A Survey of American Voters: Attitudes Concerning National Security Issues," by Marttila & Kiley, October 1987, Robert Teeter Collection, Box 41, George H. W. Bush Library, College Station, Texas.

91. *The Reagan Diaries*, 557; Service, *The End of the Cold War*, 578, note 32.

92. Cartoon by Tony Auth in *Philadelphia Inquirer*, December 9, 1987; advertisement in Washington *Times*, January 25, 1988; Vaïsse, *Neoconservatism*, 194, 200.

93. Jackson, "Soviet Reassessments of Ronald Reagan," 639–642; Matlock, *Reagan and Gorbachev*, 296–302; *The Reagan Diaries*, 619.

94. Kalinovsky, *A Long Goodbye*, 143.

95. Matlock, *Reagan and Gorbachev*, 304–305; Haslam, *Russia's Cold War*, 364–365; Grachev, *Gorbachev's Gamble*, 163–168; cartoon by Auth in *Philadelphia Inquirer*,

December 11, 1988; Richman, "Changing American Attitudes toward the Soviet Union."

96. Chernyaev Diary, August 27, 1985.

97. On the founder of Bridges for Peace, see Gardner, *D-Day and Beyond*. On the founder of Peace Links, see Eblen and Eblen, eds., *Betty Bumpers*. On the Committee of Soviet Women, see Galkina, *Komitet sovetskikh zhenshchin*, 319–323.

98. *Soviets, Meet Middle America!* documentary produced by Hartworks and CUUI, 1988; Kristin Turrilll, "Soviet Citizens Are Welcomed," *Baxter Bulletin* (Mountain Home, Arkansas), June 8, 1988; Tennison, *The Power of Impossible Ideas*, 67–73.

99. Victor Alexeev to David Foglesong, December 11, 2018; Pavel Voshchanov, "Mir spaset dobrota" ["The World Is Saved by Kindness"], *Komsomol'skaia Pravda*, undated 1989 clipping in possession of David Foglesong; N. A. Shvedova, "Two Weeks in Nashville," *SShA*, 1989.

100. Conversation between Alexander Yakovlev and George Frost Kennan, October 5, 1990, Moscow, National Security Archive, https://nsarchive.gwu.edu/sites/default/files/documents/20490193/1990-10-05-yakovlev-kennan-memcon-en.pdf.

101. Eisenhower, *Breaking Free*, 12, 196, 224; Donnie Radcliffe, "Ike Kin to Marry Soviet," *Washington Post*, January 6, 1990.

102. Alan Boyle, "Local Diplomats Put Faith in People Power – Amateurs Work to Build Bridges to Soviet Citizens," *Seattle Post-Intelligencer*, May 15, 1988; Vincent Canby, "'Russkies,' a Comedy Adventure," *New York Times*, November 6, 1987; Shaw, *Hollywood's Cold War*, 286–290; Richard Corliss, "Arnold Wry RED HEAT," *Time*, June 20, 1988; Vincent Canby, "U.S.–Soviet Buddy Movie with a Chicago Backdrop: Détente Comes to Chicago," *New York Times*, June 17, 1988.

103. David Denby, "On the Warpath," *New York*, June 6, 1988; David Ansen, "A Macho for All Seasons," *Newsweek*, May 30, 1988; Vincent Canby, "Will Summitry Sideline Rambo?" *New York Times*, June 19, 1988; Palmer, *The Films of the Eighties*, 210.

104. *Krokodil*, No. 10, April 1987; Esther B. Fein, "U.S. Film Stars Delight Muscovites," *New York Times*, February 28, 1988; Palmer, *The Films of the Eighties*, 209; Foglesong, *The American Mission and the "Evil Empire,"* 2; *Krokodil*, No. 3, January 1989, 15.

CHAPTER 17: TRANSFORMATION AND REVERSION, 1989–1999

1. Sarotte, *Not One Inch*; Zubok, *Collapse*, 8, 93; Hill, *No Place for Russia*.

2. For example, Kozyrev, "The Lagging Partnership," 59; Malia, *Russia under Western Eyes*, 412–413, 420, 425; McFaul, *From Cold War to Hot Peace*, 3, 20.

3. Transcript of George H. W. Bush's State of the Union address, *New York Times*, January 29, 1992; US Congress, Speaker's Advisory Group on Russia, *Russia's Road to Corruption*.

4. Talbott, *The Russia Hand*; Clinton, *My Life*.

5. Cohen, *Failed Crusade*; Reddaway and Glinski, *The Tragedy of Russia's Reforms*.

6. See, for example, cartoons from *Sovetskaia Rossiia* reproduced in Black, *Russia Faces NATO Expansion,* between pages 138 and 139.
7. Engel, *When the World Seemed New,* 290–291, 8, 473; Brands, *Making the Unipolar Moment,* 328, 288; Aron, *Yeltsin.*
8. Engel, *When the World Seemed New,* 2.
9. Bush and Scowcroft, *A World Transformed,* 14, 135, 143, 180; Beschloss and Talbott, *At the Highest Levels*; Engel, *When the World Seemed New,* 477.
10. Edward Rowny memo to Scowcroft, "Wresting the Initiative," January 31, 1989; Peter Rodman memo, "Getting Ahead of Gorbachev," February 9, 1989; Scowcroft memo for Bush, "Getting Ahead of Gorbachev," March 1, 1989; Bush to Gorbachev, May 7, 1989; Scowcroft memo for Bush, "A Strategic Choice: Do We Give Aid to the Soviet Union?" undated, c. early 1990; all in Condoleezza Rice Files, Bush Library, College Station, Texas. For a defense of Scowcroft, see Sparrow, *The Strategist,* esp. chapter 18.
11. Taubman, *Gorbachev,* 469–472.
12. Beschloss and Talbott, *At the Highest Levels,* 41–55; Bush's remarks in Texas on May 12, 1989, Condoleezza Rice Files, Bush Library; "One-upmanship," *Fort Worth Star-Telegram,* May 13, 1989; "Soviet Deeds, American Words," *New York Times,* May 14, 1989; Matlock, *Autopsy on an Empire,* esp. 539.
13. For example, Gates' speech, "Gorbachev and Critical Change in the Soviet Union," April 1, 1989, Rice Files, Bush Library; Gates, *From the Shadows,* 457–465.
14. Chernyaev, *My Six Years with Gorbachev,* 233; Zubok, *Collapse,* 165–168.
15. Goldgeier and McFaul, *Power and Purpose*; Zubok, *Collapse,* 249, 345. For a contrasting view, see Brands, *Making the Unipolar Moment,* 275.
16. Beschloss and Talbott, *At the Highest Levels,* 94.
17. Meacham, *Destiny and Power,* 382.
18. Engel, *When the World Seemed New,* 294; Scowcroft memo, December 5, 1989, Rice Files, Bush Library.
19. Diary of Anatoly S. Chernyaev, January 2, 1990; Memorandum of Conversation on the *Maxim Gorky* in Malta, December 2, 1989, 10:00–11:55 a.m., Rice Files, Bush Library, College Station, Texas; Foglesong, "When the Russians Really Were Coming," 14. Some citizen activists, on the other hand, continued and even expanded their efforts. See Tennison, *The Power of Impossible Ideas,* Part II; Ramseur, *Melting the Ice Curtain.*
20. Chernyaev, *My Six Years with Gorbachev,* 234–235.
21. Taubman, *Gorbachev,* 503–511; Zubok, *Collapse,* 42, 79.
22. Aron, *Yeltsin,* 324–329; Minaev, *Boris Yeltsin,* 151–153; Zubok, *Collapse,* 102, 195.
23. Colton, *Yeltsin,* 194, 264.
24. Beschloss and Talbott, *At the Highest Levels,* 349.
25. Geoghegan, "A Policy in Tension."
26. Plokhy, *The Last Empire,* 63–65; Zubok, *Collapse,* 262.
27. Miller, *The Struggle to Save the Soviet Economy,* 9, 62–67; Chernyaev Diary, May 13, 1989, May 28, 1989, and September 1, 1990; Zubok, *Collapse,* 24–25, 397.

28. Taubman, *Gorbachev*, 521–530.
29. Engel, *When the World Seemed New*, 446–450; Zubok, *Collapse*, 236. 339.
30. Engel, *When the World Seemed New*, 441.
31. Sarotte, *1989*, 110–115; Sarotte, *Not One Inch*, 48–68, 102–104; Short, *Putin*, 235–239. For another view, see Kramer, "The Myth of a No NATO Enlargement Pledge to Russia."
32. Chernyaev Diary, February 22 and March 2, 1991; Zubok, *Collapse*, 197.
33. Engel, *When the World Seemed New*, 450.
34. Beschloss and Talbott, *At the Highest Levels*, 422–429; Engel, *When the World Seemed New*, 458–470; Plokhy, *The Last Empire*, 112–118; Zubok, *Collapse*, 272–303.
35. Taubman, *Gorbachev*, 607–614; Aron, *Yeltsin*, 445; "Three Days That Shook the World: A Leader Is Restored, a Hero Created, and Freedom Won," *Atlanta Constitution*, August 22, 1991; "At Last the People Prevail," *Chicago Tribune*, August 22, 1991.
36. Bush's remark to British Prime Minister John Major, quoted in Engel, *When the World Seemed New*, 472.
37. "Cutting Torch," by Engelhardt, *St. Louis Post-Dispatch*, August 22. 1991; untitled cartoon by Mike Luckovich in *Atlanta Constitution*, August 23, 1991.
38. Clarence Page, "Coups in the Age of Big Macs and Fax Machines," *Chicago Tribune*, August 21, 1991; Danziger cartoon in *Christian Science Monitor*, reprinted in *Atlanta Constitution*, August 25, 1991. For further discussion, see Foglesong, *The American Mission and the "Evil Empire,"* 203–204.
39. "Communism's Last Gasp," *Arizona Republic*, August 22, 1991.
40. Bonnell, Cooper, and Freidin, *Russia at the Barricades*; Balzer, "Ordinary Russians?" For a contrasting view, see Kramer, Introduction to "Special Issue: The Collapse of the Soviet Union," 9.
41. Dunlop, *The Rise of Russia and the Fall of the Soviet Empire*, 199–201, 237.
42. Braithwaite, *Across the Moscow River*, 242; Zubok, *Collapse*, 280, 283, 289.
43. Dunlop, *The Rise of Russia and the Fall of the Soviet Empire*, 201–202.
44. Cohen, *Soviet Fates and Lost Alternatives*, 90–91; Foglesong, *The American Mission and the "Evil Empire,"* 203–204.
45. Colton, *Yeltsin*, 187–188, 193, 208, 229; Gaidar, *Days of Defeat and Victory*; Reddaway and Glinski, *The Tragedy of Russia's Reforms*.
46. Plokhy, *The Last Empire*, xiii–xiv; transcript of State of the Union address, *New York Times*, January 29, 1992.
47. "Bush Targets 'Hard Times,'" *Arizona Republic*, January 29, 1992, 1; "The Speech and the Vision," *Los Angeles Times*, January 29, 1992; "Prudence Not the Answer," *Atlanta Constitution*, January 29, 1992; Plokhy, *The Last Empire*, 391; Engel, *When the World Seemed New*, 476.
48. Richman, "Changing American Attitudes toward the Soviet Union," 138; "Bush Says Cold War Over as Summit Ends," *Los Angeles Times*, November 22, 1990.
49. Plokhy, *The Last Empire*, xvi, 391, 408; Schrecker, *Cold War Triumphalism*.

50. Address to Congress, June 17, 1992, www.c-span.org/program/joint-session-of-congress/boris-yeltsin-address-to-congress/173494.

51. "Beating Nukes into Plowshares," *Chicago Tribune*, June 19, 1992; "Yeltsin's Bear Hug," *Philadelphia Inquirer*, June 18, 1992; "Boris Yeltsin's Gamble," *Washington Post*, reprinted in *Bridgewater Courier-News*, June 22, 1992; "Yeltsin at the Summit," *Baltimore Sun*, June 16, 1992.

52. "The Cold War Is Hard to Shake," *Des Moines Register*, June 19, 1992; "Yeltsin and America's POWs," *Chicago Tribune*, June 19, 1992; Mary McGrory, "Yeltsin Got Applause, but Will He Get Dollars?" *Ithaca Journal*, June 24, 1992. On Glenn's distrust of the Soviets, see Glenn, *John Glenn: A Memoir*, 342.

53. Freedom Support Act (S.2532), which became law on October 24, 1992, www.congress.gov/bill/102nd-congress/senate-bill/2532/text; Colton, *Yeltsin*, 268; Yeltsin's address, June 17, 1992; "Yeltsin's Bear Hug," *Philadelphia Inquirer*, June 18, 1992.

54. Colton, *Yeltsin*, 268; Matlock, *Superpower Illusions*, 104–105.

55. For a broader discussion, see Sokolov, Inglehart, Ponarin, Vartanova, and Zimmerman, "Disillusionment and Anti-Americanism in Russia."

56. Kozyrev's remarks to Richard Nixon quoted in Simes, *After the Collapse*, 19; Tsygankov, *Russia's Foreign Policy*, 71.

57. Tsygankov, *Russia's Foreign Policy*, 70.

58. Talbott, *The Russia Hand*, 31; Christopher, *In the Stream of History*, 36.

59. Clinton, *My Life*, 504–505; Talbott, *The Russia Hand*, 47, 52.

60. Memorandum of Conversation between Yeltsin and Clinton, June 20, 1999, Clinton Digital Library.

61. Brands, *From Berlin to Baghdad*, 208; Brands, *Making the Unipolar Moment*, 276, 352, 304, 354.

62. Talbott, *The Russia Hand*, 41–43, 56, 58.

63. Ibid., 185; Colton, *Yeltsin*, 8, 226, 310, 311, 383.

64. Clinton, *My Life*, 508.

65. "Clinton Declares Full Support for Yeltsin," *Atlanta Constitution*, October 4, 1993; Clinton, *My Life*, 549; Colton, *Yeltsin*, 276–279.

66. Sarotte, *Not One Inch*, 220; Hill, *No Place for Russia*, 102–109.

67. Talbott, *The Russia Hand*, 204. See also ibid., 150–151.

68. Raleigh, *Soviet Baby Boomers*, 312, 326; Oushakine, *The Patriotism of Despair*.

69. Colton, *Yeltsin*, 349–357.

70. Sarotte, *Not One Inch*, 247; Talbott, *The Russia Hand*, 202; Colton, *Yeltsin*, 362–371.

71. William Safire, "Zyuganov Talks Sweet Reason but Carries a Communist Stick," *Lincoln Journal Star*, February 6, 1996; Dan Quayle, "The Positive Thinkers in Russia," *Indianapolis Star*, April 20, 1996; MacNelly cartoon, *Chicago Tribune*, June 16, 1996.

72. McFaul, *From Cold War to Hot Peace*, 40; Medish, ed., *My Russia: The Political Autobiography of Gennady Zyuganov*, xi, 94, 98, 101; "Russian Presidency," Minneapolis *Star Tribune*, June 3, 1996.
73. Colton, *Yeltsin*, 360, 371–372, 380–382.
74. Brands, *From Berlin to Baghdad*, 174.
75. Sarotte, *Not One Inch*, 5, 217, 227, 262.
76. Talbott, *The Russia Hand*, 139–153; Brands, *From Berlin to Baghdad*, 175–176, 180; Colton, *Yeltsin*, 363.
77. Primakov, *Russian Crossroads*, 182–183.
78. Ibid., 179–183, 265–272.
79. Clinton, *My Life*, 849; Clinton's speech to Veterans of Foreign Wars, May 13, 1999, https://edition.cnn.com/ALLPOLITICS/stories/1999/05/13/clinton.kosovo/transcript.html; Paris, "Kosovo and the Metaphor War.'
80. Albright, *Madam Secretary*, 386.
81. Andrew Higgins and Valeria Hopkins, "Kosovo's War Ended, but the Shooting Didn't," *New York Times*, April 3, 2018. Top leader Hashim Thaci was later indicted for war crimes. Isabella Kwai, "Kosovo President Resigns to Face War Crimes Case in the Netherlands," *New York Times*, November 5, 2020.
82. Chris Hedges, "Victims Not Quite Innocent," *New York Times*, March 28, 1999; Del Ponte, *Madame Prosecutor*, 276, 285–286; Hedges, *War Is a Force That Gives Us Meaning*, 105–106.
83. Del Ponte, *Madame Prosecutor*, 292.
84. Albright, *Madam Secretary*, 385–386.
85. Ibid., 411, 403.
86. Primakov, *Russian Crossroads*, 276.
87. Tom Walker and Aidan Laverty, "CIA Aided Kosovo Guerrilla Army All Along," *Sunday Times* (London), March 12, 2000.
88. Immerman, *The Hidden Hand*, 153; Prados, *The Ghosts of Langley*, 302.
89. Albright, *Madam Secretary*, 399, 402, 392; Clinton, *My Life*, 848–850.
90. Daalder and O'Hanlon, *Winning Ugly*, 12, 14, 15.
91. Albright, *Madam Secretary*, 380, 382.
92. Daalder and O'Hanlon, *Winning Ugly*, 13; Hill, *No Place for Russia*, chapter 5.
93. Goldgeier and McFaul, *Power and Purpose*, 251.
94. Daalder and O'Hanlon, *Winning Ugly*, 127; Goldgeier and McFaul, *Power and Purpose*, 255–256.
95. Albright, *Madam Secretary*, 413; Tsygankov, *Russia's Foreign Policy*, 112.
96. Del Ponte, *Madame Prosecutor*, 273, 275.
97. Clinton, *My Life*, 858–859; British historian John Keegan quoted in Albright, *Madam Secretary*, 421.
98. Albright, *Madam Secretary*, 413.
99. White House to US Embassy in Moscow, April 3, 1999, Clinton Library digital archive.

100. Goldgeier and McFaul, *Power and Purpose*, 256–260; Daalder and O'Hanlon, *Winning Ugly*, 166–174.
101. Goldgeier and McFaul, *Power and Purpose*, 260–264; "More Russian Troops Head for Pristina," *The Guardian*, June 15, 1999; Elizabeth Becker, "U.S. General Was Overruled in Kosovo," *New York Times*, September 10, 1999.
102. Transcript of Clinton's address, June 10, 1999, Miller Center, University of Virginia, online archive. Clinton later asked Yeltsin's successor, Vladimir Putin, "to get Milošević to leave." Memorandum of Telephone Conversation, September 30, 2000, Clinton Digital Library.
103. Daalder and O'Hanlon, *Winning Ugly*, 16; Del Ponte, *Madame Prosecutor*, 276–277, 291; Mulchinock, *NATO and the Western Balkans*, 196–198; Andrew Higgins and Valeria Hopkins, "Kosovo's War Ended, but the Shooting Didn't," *New York Times*, April 3, 2018. See also a Council of Europe report: Dick Marty, "Inhuman Treatment of People and Illicit Trafficking in Human Organs in Kosovo," January 7, 2011, https://assembly.coe.int/nw/xml/XRef/Xref-XM L2HTML-en.asp?fileid=12608&lang=en.
104. Memorandum of Conversation between Yeltsin and Clinton, June 20, 1999, Clinton Presidential Library (declassified document on website).
105. Raleigh, *Soviet Baby Boomers*, 332; Tsygankov, *Russia's Foreign Policy*, 112; Goldgeier and McFaul, *Power and Purpose*, 248; cartoons reproduced in Black, *Russia Faces NATO Expansion*, between pages 138 and 139; Talbott, *The Russia Hand*, 307.
106. Goldgeier and McFaul, *Power and Purpose*, 251; Daalder and O'Hanlon, *Winning Ugly*, 13–14, 198.
107. Alexander Lukin quoted in Tsygankov, *Russia's Foreign Policy*, 113. President Vladimir Putin complained to Clinton on September 6, 2000 that it was "not fair" that Russia was not consulted about the bombing of Yugoslavia and the detachment of Kosovo from Serbia. Memorandum of Conversation in New York City, Clinton Digital Library.
108. Albright, *Madam Secretary*, 406.
109. Yeltsin's remarks from July 1995 quoted in Lukin, *China and Russia: The New Rapprochement*, 77; Goldgeier and McFaul, *Power and Purpose*, 266.
110. Colton, *Yeltsin*, 428–432.
111. Talbott, *The Russia Hand*, 372, 362–364. See also Sarotte, *Not One Inch*, 331–332.

CHAPTER 18: FROM PARTNERS TO ARCHENEMIES, 2000–2020

1. MacKinnon, *The New Cold War*; Lucas, *The New Cold War*.
2. Hale and Kamenchuk, *Don't Call It a Cold War*, 12.
3. Cheney, *In My Time*, 513–514. See also Hill and Gaddy, *Mr. Putin*; Stent, *Putin's World*, 345, 348.

4. Stoner and McFaul, "Who Lost Russia (This Time)?" 181; Kathryn Stoner, "The U.S. Tried Working with Putin. It Didn't Work," *New York Times*, October 25, 2016; Stoner, *Russia Resurrected*; Lilia Shevtsova, "Ukraine Is Only One Small Part of Putin's Plans," *New York Times*, January 7, 2022.

5. Baker, *Days of Fire*, 200; Myers, *The New Tsar*, esp. 462–473; Benjamin Nathans, "The Real Power of Putin," *New York Review*, September 29, 2016, 88–92; Belton, *Putin's People*, esp. 15–16.

6. Myers, *The New Tsar*, 67; McFaul, *From Cold War to Hot Peace*, 17–18.

7. For the opposite view, see Van Herpen, *Putin's Wars*.

8. Zygar, *All the Kremlin's Men*, 19; Short, *Putin*, 379.

9. Frye, Gehlbach, Marquardt, and Reuter, "Is Putin's Popularity Real?"; Frye, *Weak Strongman*, esp. 53–57.

10. "US and Russia: Insecurity and Mistrust Shape Mutual Perceptions," November 4, 2016, https://globalaffairs.org/research/public-opinion-survey/us-and-russia-insecurity-and-mistrust-shape-mutual-perceptions#:~:text=New%20polling%20data%20from%20the%202016%20Chicago%20Council,at%20levels%20not%20seen%20since%20the%20Cold%20War.

11. Stoner, *Russia Resurrected*, 262–263.

12. See https://nsarchive.gwu.edu/briefing-book/nato-75-russia-programs/2021-11-24/nato-expansion-budapest-blow-1994; Sarotte, *Not One Inch*, esp. 316.

13. Matthew Rojansky, "Diplomatic Isolation of Russia Is Counterproductive," *New York Times*, October 25, 2016; Greene, *Putin v. the People*, esp. 226–227. For a contrary view, see Clover, *Black Wind, White Snow*.

14. Koposov, *Memory Laws, Memory Wars*, 251; Khapaeva, "Triumphant Memory of the Perpetrators."

15. Laruelle, ed., *Eurasianism and the European Far Right*, xiii; Laruelle, *Russian Nationalism*, 119–121; Robinson, *Russian Conservatism*, 211–212; Bassin and Pozo, eds., *The Politics of Eurasianism*.

16. Cohen, *Soviet Fates and Lost Alternatives*, 162–198; Cohen, *War with Russia?*; Walt, *The Hell of Good Intentions*, esp. 14; Mearsheimer, *The Great Delusion*, 171–179; Tsygankov, *Russia and America*; Sakwa, *The Putin Paradox*, 15, 153, 163, 215.

17. For example, Gates, *Duty*, 157–159.

18. Balanced analyses include Charap and Colton, *Everyone Loses*; Stent, *The Limits of Partnership*; Legvold, *Return to Cold War*.

19. Tsygankov, *The Strong State in Russia*, esp. 105–107; Sakwa, *The Putin Paradox*, 5, 16, 148, 230.

20. Short, *Putin*, 369–373.

21. Stent, *Putin's World*, 4, 361; Galeotti, *We Need to Talk about Putin*, 15, 20, 25.

22. Gel'man, *Authoritarian Russia*, 98; Short, *Putin*, 549–551. See also Matovski, "The Logic of Vladimir Putin's Popular Appeal," 231.

23. Cf. Nalbandov, *Not by Bread Alone*, 180–181.

24. On identity narratives in Russia, see Mankoff, *Russian Foreign Policy*; Tsygankov, *Russia's Foreign Policy*.

25. Bush, *Decision Points*, 195–196; Myers, *The New Tsar*, 102–103, 205–206; Baker, *Days of Fire*, 106–107.

26. "Hillary Clinton, Campaigning, Ponders Putin's Soul," Reuters, January 7, 2008. For a later example, see Landler, *Alter Egos*, 277.

27. Memoranda of Conversations between Putin and Clinton, March 27, June 9, and December 27, 2000, Clinton Digital Library; Charap and Colton, *Everyone Loses*, 68; Stent, *Putin's World*, 125.

28. Bush, *Decision Points*, 196; Myers, *The New Tsar*, 206–207; Short, *Putin*, 373–375; Tsygankov, *The Dark Double*, 19; Dobbins, *After the Taliban*, 41.

29. *Public Papers of the Presidents of the United States: George W. Bush, 2001*, 1400–1411 (hereafter cited as *PPPUS: GWB*); Baker, *Days of Fire*, 177; Tsygankov, *Russophobia*, 140–141.

30. Coll, *Private Empire*, 253–254, 273–274. For a broader discussion, see Miller, *Putinomics*.

31. Goldman, *Petrostate*; Yergin, *The Quest*; Sakwa, *Putin and the Oligarch*; Belton, *Putin's People*, 235–238; Miller, *Putinomics*, 41–46; Khodorkovsky, *The Russia Conundrum*, chapter 7.

32. Tsygankov, *Russophobia*, 148–149.

33. See https://www2.census.gov/programs-surveys/trade/balance/c4621.html; www.statista.com/chart/10398/us-merchandise-trade-with-russia.

34. Coll, *Private Empire*, 276–278.

35. Hahn, *Russia's Islamic Threat*; Myers, *The New Tsar*, 181–182; Short, *Putin*, 279, 374–375.

36. Tsygankov, *Russophobia*, 26, 69–91; Baker and Glasser, *Kremlin Rising*, esp. 117–119.

37. Mitchell, *The Color Revolutions*, 83–86.

38. Hill, *No Place for Russia*, 265; Toal, *Near Abroad*, 157.

39. Burns, *The Back Channel*, 230–234.

40. Mitchell, *The Color Revolutions*; Stent, *The Limits of Partnership*, 109, 164–170; Toal, *Near Abroad*, 157.

41 Toal, *Near Abroad*, 179–184; Myers, *The New Tsar*, 348–352.

42 Gates, *Duty*, 167–170; Baker, *Days of Fire*, 602–604.

43 Zbigniew Brzezinski, "Staring Down the Russians," *Time*, August 14, 2008; David Rivkin, "The Kremlin's 'Protection' Racket," *Wall Street Journal*, August 15, 2008; www.creators.com/read/michael-ramirez/08/08/67372.

44 "Stuck in Georgia," *New York Times*, August 27, 2008; Toal, *Near Abroad*, quotations on pages 124 and 176.

45 Asmus, *A Little War That Shook the World*, with preface by Talbott.

46 *Moscow Times*, August 13, 2008; Olga Ivanova in *Washington Post*, August 15, 2008; Lukyanov in *Moscow Times*, August 21, 2008; Markov in *Los Angeles Times*, August 25, 2008; Toal, *Near Abroad*, 184.

47. Eric Pape, "Seeking Drama in a Conflict That's Still Raw," *New York Times*, August 12, 2011; Stephen Holden, "More Than One Kind of Deadline," *New York Times*, August 18, 2011.
48. Mitchell, *The Color Revolutions*, 85–86; Polese, "Ukraine 2004," 267–268; McFaul, "Ukraine Imports Democracy," 81.
49. Foglesong, *The American Mission and the "Evil Empire,"* 224–225.
50. Ronald Asmus quoted in Charap and Colton, *Everyone Loses*, 82–83.
51. D'Anieri, *Ukraine and Russia*, 161; Plokhy, *The Gates of Europe*, 365.
52. Koposov, *Memory Laws, Memory Wars*, 182–183; Kasianov, "How a War for the Past Becomes a War in the Present," 152–154.
53. Yablokov, *Fortress Russia*, 80–81.
54. Mankoff, *Russian Foreign Policy*, 123, 141; Myers, *The New Tsar*, 278; Steven Lee Myers, "Putin Says Foreigners Use Private Groups to Meddle in Russia," *New York Times*, January 26, 2006; "Of Power and Paranoia," *Washington Post*, July 3, 2015; Treisman, *The Return*, esp. 384.
55. McFaul, *Russia's Unfinished Revolution*; McFaul, "American Efforts at Promoting Regime Change in the Soviet Union and Then Russia," 42–43; Baker, *Days of Fire*, 470; Cheney's speech in Lithuania, *New York Times*, May 4, 2006.
56. Short, *Putin*, 411.
57. Rice, *No Higher Honor*, 366; Baker, *Days of Fire*, 471.
58. Vladimir Putin, Speech and the Following Discussion at the Munich Conference on Security Policy, February 10, 2007, http://en.kremlin.ru/events/president/transcripts/24034; Gates, *Duty*, 156.
59. Thom Shanker and Mark Landler. "Putin Says U.S. Is Undermining Global Stability," *New York Times*, February 11, 2007, www.nytimes.com/2007/02/11/world/europe/11munich.html.
60. Bush's statement in October 2000 debate, quoted in Foglesong, *The American Mission and the "Evil Empire,"* 218; Bush's Remarks on the Situation in Georgia, August 13, 2008, *PPPUS: GWB, 2008–2009*, 1140; Bush's Statement on the Situation in Georgia, September 3, 2008, *PPPUS: GWB, 2008–2009*, 1173; Bush's Message to Congress, September 8, 2008, *PPPUS: GWB, 2008–2009*, 1182.
61. Remarks by DeMuth and Bush, December 18, 2008, *PPPUS: GWB, 2008–2009*, 1488.
62. Chollet, *The Long Game*, 64–65; Stent, *The Limits of Partnership*, chapter 9; McFaul, *From Cold War to Hot Peace*, 200.
63. Biden's remarks in Moscow, March 10, 2011, https://obamawhitehouse.archives.gov/the-press-office/2011/03/10/vice-president-bidens-remarks-moscow-state-university; www.census.gov/foreign-trade/balance/c4621.html.
64. Landler, *Alter Egos*, esp. 261–262, 270; "Clinton Cites 'Serious Concerns' about Russian Election," https://edition.cnn.com/2011/12/06/world/europe/russia-elections-clinton/index.html.
65. Gel'man. *Authoritarian Russia*, 121; Yablokov, *Fortress Russia*, 154–160.

66. Gessen, *Words Will Break Cement*, 97–98; Ellen Barry, "New U.S. Envoy Steps Into Glare of a Russia Eager to Find Fault," *New York Times*, January 23, 2012; Stent, *The Limits of Partnership*, 253; McFaul, *From Cold War to Hot Peace*, 263, 259. For further discussion of McFaul's ideas and impact, see Foglesong, "The Perils of Prophecy," 291–296.

67. Adrian Bloomfield, "Vladimir Putin Rejects Barack Obama's Claim He Has One Foot in the Past," London *Telegraph*, July 3, 2009; Gates, *Duty*, 410–411; "Biden 'Opposes' 3rd Putin Term," *Moscow Times*, March 11, 2011.

68. Browder, *Red Notice*, 125, 359, 291, 327.

69. Short, *Putin*, 541–542; "Russians Have No Respect for Pussy Riot, Poll Says," *Moscow Times*, September 13, 2013; Levada Center, "Pussy Riot Trial," in *Russian Public Opinion 2012–2013*, 121–123.

70. Myers, *The New Tsar*, 401–409; Garrels, *Putin Country*, 121; "A Spotlight on Mr. Putin's Russia," *New York Times*, February 6, 2014; Gessen, *Words Will Break Cement*; Sperling, *Sex, Politics, and Putin*.

71. Yablokov, *Fortress Russia*, 105.

72. McFaul, *From Cold War to Hot Peace*, 390.

73. Laruelle, "Making Sense of Russia's Illiberalism," 124.

74. Short, *Putin*, 366–376; DeYoung, *Soldier*, 362; Gates, *Duty*, 158–167; Stent, *The Limits of Partnership*, 228; Andrew Kramer, "Russia Calls New U.S. Missile Defense System a 'Direct Threat,'" *New York Times*, May 12, 2016.

75. Myers, *The New Tsar*, 382–385; McFaul, *From Cold War to Hot Peace*, 222–227; Jo Becker and Scott Shane, "Hillary Clinton, 'Smart Power' and a Dictator's Fall," *New York Times*, February 27, 2016; Rhodes, *The World as It Is*, 111–121, 151–152; Gordon, *Losing the Long Game*, 8–9, 184–185. US officials unconvincingly denied that Russia was "snookered": see Rice, *Tough Love*, 285–291. See also Power, *Education of an Idealist*, 303.

76. Myers, *The New Tsar*, 442–444; Rhodes, *The World as It Is*, 198, 25–27; Rice, *Tough Love*, 365.

77. Burns, *The Back Channel*, 220, 457; McFaul, *From Cold War to Hot Peace*, 173, 195; Kerry, *Every Day Is Extra*, 439; Roland Oliphant, "Barack Obama Praises Putin for Help Clinching Iran Deal," London *Telegraph*, 15 July, 2015; Helene Cooper and David Sanger, "Details of Syria Pact Widen Rift between John Kerry and Pentagon," *New York Times*, September 13, 2016.

78. Myers, *The New Tsar*, 439–442; Clapper, *Facts and Fears*, 234–235; Rice, *Tough Love*, 361.

79. One of Nuland's aides denied that Americans thought they could pick new leaders. Smith, *Ukraine's Revolt, Russia's Revenge*, 185.

80. Arel and Driscoll, *Ukraine's Unnamed War*, 86–89; Sakwa, *Frontline Ukraine*, 87–88; Ivan Katchanovski, "The Far Right, the Euromaidan, and the Maidan Massacre in Ukraine," *Labor and Society*, Vol. 23, No. 5 (2020), 5–29; Gabriel Whitehouse, "The Untold Story of the Maidan Massacre," BBC News Magazine, 11 February 2015; "Doubts about Reports of Maidan Snipers," German TV

ARD, April 2014; Marples, *Ukraine's Euromaidan*, 13–14; Clover, *Black Wind, White Snow*, 320–322.

81. Charap and Colton, *Everyone Loses*, 124–126; D'Anieri, *Ukraine and Russia*, 212–220.

82. Myers, *The New Tsar*, 460–464; Pleshakov, *The Crimean Nexus*; D'Anieri, *Ukraine and Russia*, 228–229.

83. US officials did meet Chechen separatist leaders, and one was granted asylum in 2004. However, a careful study found no publicly available evidence for Putin's claims of US governmental assistance to Chechen fighters, which he reiterated in Oliver Stone's documentary, *The Putin Interviews* (2017). "Claim (in 2004, 2015, and 2017): The U.S. Government Supported Chechen Separatism," Russia Matters, Belfer Center for Science and International Affairs, Harvard Kennedy School, www.russiamatters.org/node/20317.

84. Andrei Kondrashov, *Crimea: The Way Home* (Russian television documentary, 2015); Daniel Treisman, "Why Putin Took Crimea," *Foreign Affairs*, April 18, 2016; Soldatov and Rochlitz, "The *Siloviki* in Russian Politics," 10⁻.

85. Arel and Driscoll, *Ukraine's Unnamed War*, 2–8.

86. Sakwa, *Frontline Ukraine*; D'Anieri, *Ukraine and Russia*, 244; *The Week*, August 1, 2014; *Time*, August 4, 2014.

87. Myers, *The New Tsar*, 462, 468; Remarks by Kerry in Kyiv, March 4, 2014, https://2009-2017.state.gov/secretary/remarks/2014/03/222882.htm; Arel and Driscoll, *Ukraine's Unnamed War*, 74–86; Remarks by Obama in Estonia, September 3, 2014, obamawhitehouse.archives.gov. See also Kerry, *Every Day Is Extra*, 434–436; Black, "Setting the Tone," 182.

88. S. Pavlova, "Natsional-predateli Putina," *Svoboda*, March 19, 2014, www.svoboda.org/a/25302687.html.

89. Kurilla and Zhuravleva, "Russia's View on Obama's Presidency"; Ostrovsky, *The Invention of Russia*; Jeffrey M. Jones 2015. "Americans Increasingly See Russia as Threat, Top U.S. Enemy," *Gallup Poll Briefing*, February 1, 2015, https://research-ebsco-com.proxy.libraries.rutgers.edu/linkprocessor/plink?id=b95b2276-70b7-37cf-84cd-60110b061669.

90. Andrew Cockburn, "The New Red Scare," *Harper's*, December 2016; Kuzmarov and Marciano, *The Russians Are Coming, Again*.

91. Tsygankov, *The Dark Double*, esp. 71, 99.

92. Phillips, *The Battle for Syria*; Borshchevskaya, *Putin's War in Syria*; Geukjian, *The Russian Military Intervention in Syria*.

93. Robert D. Kaplan, "Eurasia's Coming Anarchy," *Foreign Affairs* (March/April 2016), 41; Andrew Higgins, "Putin, Admired by Donald Trump, Emphasizes Strength as Virtue," *New York Times*, September 10, 2016.

94. David Sanger and Nicole Perlroth, "As Democrats Gather, a Russian Subplot Raises Intrigue," *New York Times*, July 24, 2016; Nicholas Kristof, "Did Putin Try to Steal an American Election?" *New York Times*, July 28, 2016; *Time*, October 10, 2016.

95. For example, Jonathan Martin and Amy Chozick, "Donald Trump's Campaign Stands by Embrace of Putin," *New York Times*, September 8, 2016; "Clinton Calls Trump a 'Puppet' for Russia's Putin," *Wall Street Journal*, October 20, 2016; Bogoslaw, *Russians on Trump*, 159.

96. Campbell Robertson and Mitch Smith, "'What's the Big Deal?' Ask Trump Voters on Russia Hacking Report," *New York Times*, January 7, 2017; Nick Bayer, "Vladimir Putin's Popularity Is Skyrocketing among Republicans," *Huffington Post*, December 14, 2016.

97. Joe Klein, "Beware the Tricks and Traps of Donald Trump, News Manipulator in Chief," *Time*, December 26, 2016–January 2, 2017, 34; Robby Mook, "Russia's D.N.C. Hack Was Only the Start," *New York Times*, January 10, 2017; Nadezhda Azhgikhina, "The Abyss between Russian and US Media Just Got Wider," *The Nation*, December 22, 2017.

98. *Time*, May 29, 2017 and July 30, 2018; *Mother Jones*, October 2018; Foglesong, "The Face of the Enemy."

99. For example, Michelle Goldberg, "Putin Would Hate President Bernie Sanders," *New York Times*, February 24, 2020. The top expert on Russia at the National Security Council did not share the belief, see Hill, *There Is Nothing For You Here*, 200, 226.

100. Bail, Guay, Maloney et al., "Assessing the Russian Internet Research Agency's Impact on the Political Attitudes and Behaviors of American Twitter Users in Late 2017."

101. For a thoughtful discussion, see Kotkin, "American Hustle."

102. *Time*, April 15, 2019; Christopher T. Robinson, Deputy Assistant Secretary of State for European and Eurasian Affairs, testimony to Senate Foreign Relations Committee about Libya, February 12, 2020; Sanders, *Where We Go from Here*, 97–98, 104–105; Elizabeth Warren, "A Foreign Policy for All," *Foreign Affairs*, Vol. 98, No. 1 (January/February 2019).

103. Matt Flegenheimer, David E. Sanger, and Emmarie Huetteman, "Marco Rubio Won't Commit to Voting for Rex Tillerson," *New York Times*, January 10, 2017; McCain quoted in David Sanger, Maggie Haberman, and Clifford Krauss, "Rex Tillerson, Exxon Chief, Is Expected to Be Pick for Secretary of State," *New York Times*, December 10, 2016.

104. Myers, *The New Tsar*, 304–314, 478; Sir Robert Owen, "The Litvinenko Inquiry" (January 2016), www.litvinenkoinquiry.org; Putin Interview with *The Financial Times*, June 27, 2019, http://en.kremlin.ru/events/president/news/60836.

105. Knight, *Orders to Kill*, 6. On the murder of Boris Nemtsov, see Zygar, *All the Kremlin's Men*, 313–317; Sakwa, *The Putin Paradox*, 216–217; Short, *Putin*, 612–615, 641.

106. Steven Lee Myers, "Mikhail Lesin's Strange Death in U.S. Follows a Fall from Russia's Elite," *New York Times*, April 2, 2016; Steven Lee Myers, "Putin Ally Died in U.S. after Drunken Fall, Not Foul Play, Prosecutors Say," *New York Times*, October 28, 2016.

107. Foglesong, "Killer Putin and American Exceptionalism."
108. Obama's Farewell Address, January 10, 2017, https://obamawhitehouse.arch ives.gov/node/360231.
109. Deputy Foreign Minister Sergei Ryabkov, "Russia–US Relations after the Election," *International Affairs*, No. 5, 2016, reprinted in Bogoslaw, ed., *Russians on Trump*, 66–70; Presidential Address to the Federal Assembly, December 1, 2016, http://www.en.kremlin.ru/events/president/news/53379.
110. Putin Interview with *The Financial Times*, June 27, 2019, http://en.kremlin.ru/events/president/news/60836.
111. Zhuravleva, "Images of the United States in Putin's Russia, from Obama to Trump."
112. The Black Overlord is an internet meme of a tough-looking African American dressed in gay-style clothes who tirelessly fights evil in all its manifestations.
113. Vitaly Podvitsky, "Chernyi vlastelin," www.facebook.com/photo/?fbi d=1431928203743314&set=a.1400528000216668 and www.facebook.com/ph oto/?fbid=1400534290216039&set=a.1400528000216668; Vitaly Podvitsky, "Na vsiakuiu temnuiu storonu sily naidetsia svoi Dzhedai," https://polit.react or.cc/search/North+Memphis/29.
114. Borenstein, *Plots against Russia*.
115. Valerii Garbuzov criticized such propaganda in "Amerikanskaia iskliuchitel'-nost," *Nezavisimaia gazeta*, 16 June 2020.
116. Norris, *Blockbuster History*.
117. Goscilo and Goscilo, *Fade From Red*, chapter 4.
118. Gessen, *The Future Is History*.
119. Yaffa, *Between Two Fires*. For a critique and alternative perspective, see Sharafutdinova, *The Red Mirror*.
120. Stephanie Zacharek, "Full of Feral Grace, *Atomic Blonde* Kicks You Where It Hurts," *Time*, July 26, 2017; Sara Stewart, "'Atomic Blonde' is Sexy, Ass-Kicking Fun," *New York Post*, July 27, 2017.
121. Ward, "'Your Body Belongs to the State.'"
122. Reiner video: www.youtube.com/watch?v=V2av__s-598; A. O. Scott, "'Creed II' Review: A Poignant Boxing Movie Blends Old and New," *New York Times*, November 20, 2018; David Fear, "'Creed II' Review: Michael B. Jordan Gets Back in the Ring," *Rolling Stone*, November 16, 2018.
123. *New York Times*, June 26, 2020.
124. Alexander Bolton, "GOP Senator: Russia Should Be Labeled State Sponsor of Terror If Intelligence Is Accurate," *The Hill*, June 30, 2020; "Most Americans Believe Russia Targeted U.S. Soldiers, Want Sanctions in Response, Reuters/Ipsos Poll Shows," Reuters, July 8, 2020.
125. Luis Martinez, "Top General Has Doubts Russian Bounty Program Killed US Troops in Afghanistan," July 7, 2020, https://abcnews.go.com/Politics/top-gen eral-doubts-russian-bounty-program-killed-us/story?id=71653874; Sam Dorman, "Colin Powell Suggests Media Had 'Hysterical' Reaction to Russian Bounty

Reports," July 9, 2020, https://nypost.com/2020/07/09/colin-powell-suggests-media-had-hysterical-reaction-to-russian-bounty-reports.

126. "Debate Transcript," *USA Today*, October 23, 2020.

127. Background Press Call by Senior Administration Officials on Russia, April 15, 2021, https://nypost.com/2020/07/09/colin-powell-suggests-media-had-hysterical-reaction-to-russian-bounty-reports.

128. Short, *Putin*, 638–643; Anton Troianovski, "Navalny Says Russian Agent Confessed to Plot to Poison Him," *New York Times*, December 21, 2020.

129. Gordon Humphrey and Joe Lieberman, "A Vision for Russia," *The Hill*, January 20, 2021; Janusz Bugajski, "Biden Must Prepare for an Imploding Russia," *Washington Examiner*, January 25, 2021; Stephen Nix and Joshua Solomon, "Support for the Russian People Is Support for Our National Security," *The Hill*, February 3, 2021.

130. "January Protests," October 2, 2021, https://www.levada.ru/en/2021/02/11/january-protests.

131. "The Extraordinary Courage of Aleksei Navalny," *New York Times*, January 17, 2021; Anton Troianovski and Andrew Kramer, "Navalny's Group Is Shutting All Its Offices in Russia," *New York Times*, April 29, 2021.

CONCLUSION

1. News conference following Russia–US Talks, June 16, 2021, http://en.kremlin.ru/events/president/transcripts/65870; Remarks by President Biden in Press Conference, June 16, 2021, https://ru.usembassy.gov/remarks-by-president-biden-in-press-geneva; Anton Troianovski, "Moscow Commentators Celebrate That Biden Sees Russia as a Great Power," *New York Times*, June 17, 2021; "Vybor prezidentov," *Izvestiia*, June 17, 2021; "Russian Media Generally Pleased with Putin–Biden Summit," BBC Monitoring, June 17, 2021; Samuel Chamberlain, "Graham Accuses Biden of Putin 'Appeasement' ahead of Geneva Summit," *New York Post*, June 15, 2021, https://nypost.com/2021/06/15/graham-accuses-biden-of-putin-appeasement-ahead-of-geneva-summit; Masha Gessen, "The High Cost of Biden's Meeting with Putin," *The New Yorker*, June 17, 2021.

2. U.S.–Ukraine Charter on Strategic Partnership, United States Department of State, November 10, 2021.

3. "Agreement on Measures to Ensure the Security of the Russian Federation and Member States of the North Atlantic Treaty Organization," 17 December 2021, MID RF, https://mid.ru/ru/detail-material-page/1790803/?lang=en; "Treaty between the United States of America and the Russian Federation on Security Guarantees," 17 December 2021, MID RF, https://mid.ru/ru/detail-material-page/1790818/?lang=en.

4. See, for example, Vyacheslav Zilanov, "SShA i Britaniia vtiagivaiut Evropu v ukrainskii konflikt," *IA Realist,* June 6, 2022, https://realtribune.ru/ssha-i-bri taniya-vtyagivajut-evropu-v-ukrainskij-konflikt.

5. On Lodge's views, discussed in Chapter 5, see Zhuravleva, *Ponimanie Rossii v SShA,* esp. 375–376. On Pipes' ideas, mentioned in Chapter 15, see Pipes, "Russia's Past, Russia's Future"; Engerman, *Know Your Enemy,* 266, 283–285; Nowak, "A 'Polish Connection.'" On American views of "Asiatic despotism" in Imperial Russia and the Soviet Union, see Foglesong, *The American Mission and the "Evil Empire,"* 14, 79, 95.

6. A lexander Vindman, "Why It's the 'Beginning of the End' for Putin, Transcript," *New York Times.* March 1, 2022, www.nytimes.com/2022/03/01/o pinion/alexander-vindman-ukraine-russia-war.html?showTranscript=1.

7. Nikolay Filippov, "Trevozhny aprel' 2022-go," *Krymskaia Pravda,* April 16, 2022, https://c-pravda.ru/news/2022-04-16/trevozhnyjj-aprel-2022-go. See also Vyacheslav Dvornikov, "'Kholodilnuk protiv televizora – v sovremennoi Rossii ne rabotaet': Aleksei Levinson o tom, kak izmenilos' rossiiskoe obshchestvo za polgoda voiny," *The Bell,* August 25, 2022, https://thebell.io/kholodilnik-protiv-televizora–v-sovremennoy-rossii-ne-rabotaet-kak-izmenilos-rossiyskoe-obshchest vo-za-polgoda-voyny.

8. See, for example, Vyacheslav Zilanov, "SShA i Britaniia vtiagivaiut Evropu v ukrainskii konflikt," *IA Realist,* June 6, 2022, https://realtribune.ru/ssha-i-bri taniya-vtyagivajut-evropu-v-ukrainskij-konflikt.

9. Shura Burtin, "Voiti vo mrak i nashchupat' v nem liudei," *Meduza,* April 24, 2022, https://meduza.io/feature/2022/04/24/voyti-vo-mrak-i-naschupat-v-nem-lyudey.

10. John Warren, "Putin's Dark Designs: Restore the Pre-1917 Russian Empire (Interview with Paul D'Anieri)," *UC Riverside News,* March 1, 2022, https://new s.ucr.edu/articles/2022/03/01/putins-dark-designs-restore-pre-1917-russian-e mpire; Nathan Hodge, "Restoration of Empire is the Endgame for Russia's Vladimir Putin," *CNN,* June 11, 2022, www.cnn.com/2022/06/10/europe/rus sia-putin-empire-restoration-endgame-intl-cmd/index.html; Plokhy, *The Russo-Ukrainian War: The Return of History.*

11. Lucian Kim, "Why Isn't Russia a Democracy?" *Foreign Policy,* October 30, 2022, https://foreignpolicy.com/2022/10/30/russia-democracy-putin-soviet-union-cold-war.

12. Anchal Vohra, "Is Ukraine's Endgame a Russian Land Bridge?" *Foreign Policy,* April 20, 2022, https://foreignpolicy.com/2022/04/20/is-ukraines-endgame-a-russian-land-bridge.

13. Vladimir Putin, "Address by the President of the Russian Federation," February 24, 2022, http://en.kremlin.ru/events/president/news/67843; Vladimir Putin "On the Historical Unity of Russians and Ukrainians," July 12, 2021, http://en.kremlin.ru/events/president/news/66181.

14. Tatiana Stanovaya, "What the West (Still) Gets Wrong about Putin," *Foreign Policy*, June 1, 2022, https://foreignpolicy.com/2022/06/01/putin-war-ukrain e-west-misconceptions; Dmitri Trenin, "Six Months into the Conflict, What Exactly Does Russia Hope to Achieve in Ukraine?" *The Transnational*, September 21, 2022, https://transnational.live/2022/09/21/dmitry-trenin-si x-months-into-the-conflict-what-exactly-does-russia-hope-to-achieve-in-ukraine; "Ukraine, Russia, and the New World Order: Interview with Fyodor A. Lukyanov," *Institut Montaigne*, 13 October, 2022, www.institutmontaigne.or g/en/expressions/ukraine-russia-and-new-world-order; "John Mearsheimer on Why the West Is Principally Responsible for the Ukrainian Crisis," *The Economist*, March 19, 2022, www.economist.com/by-invitation/2022/03/11/john-mear sheimer-on-why-the-west-is-principally-responsible-for-the-ukrainian-crisis; Sakwa, *The Lost Peace: How the West Failed to Prevent a Second Cold War*.

15. Laura Thornton, "How Democracies Can Respond to the Invasion of Ukraine," *Lawfare*, March 30, 2022, www.lawfaremedia.org/article/how-democracies-can-respond-invasion-ukraine.

16. Natalie Colarossi, "Cold War Ambassador Fears World Where Russia Is a 'Pariah,'" *Newsweek*, April 5, 2022, www.newsweek.com/cold-war-ambassador-fears-world-where-russia-pariah-1695174.

17. Timothy Bella, "Kissinger Says Ukraine Should Cede Territory to Russia to End War," *Washington Post*, May 24, 2022, www.washingtonpost.com/world/2022/0 5/24/henry-kissinger-ukraine-russia-territory-davos.

18. "Debate: Kissinger vs. Soros on Russia's War in Ukraine," *Russia Matters*, June 9, 2022, www.russiamatters.org/node/27728.

19. Anne Applebaum and Jeffrey Goldberg, "The Counteroffensive," *The Atlantic*, June 2023, www.theatlantic.com/magazine/archive/2023/06/counteroffen sive-ukraine-zelensky-crimea/673781. Similar views were expressed by Andrea Kendall-Taylor and Erika Frantz, "The Treacherous Path to a Better Russia: Ukraine's Future and Putin's Fate," *Foreign Affairs*, Vol. 102, No. 4 (2023), 8–21, as well as by Garry Kasparov and Mikhail Khodorkovsky, "Don't Fear Putin's Demise: Victory for Ukraine, Democracy for Russia," *Foreign Affairs* (online), January 20, 2023.

20. Samuel Charap, "An Unwinnable War: Washington Needs an Endgame in Ukraine," *Foreign Affairs*, Vol. 102, No. 4 (2023), 22–35; Carter Malkasian, "The Korea Model: Why an Armistice Offers the Best Hope for Peace in Ukraine," *Foreign Affairs*, Vol. 102, No. 4 (2023), 36–51. See also George Beebe and Anatol Lieven, "The Diplomatic Path to a Secure Ukraine," Quincy Institute Paper No. 13, February 2024.

21 Bryan Frederick, Mark Cozad, and Alexandra Stark, *Understanding the Risk of Escalation in the War in Ukraine*, RAND Corporation, 2023, www.rand.org/pubs/ research_briefs/RBA2807-1.html.

22 Rebecca Shabad, "Trump Denounces Biden's Decision to Send Cluster Munitions to Ukraine," *NBC news*, July 11, 2023, www.nbcnews.com/politics/d

onald-trump/trump-denounces-bidens-decision-send-ukraine-cluster-muni
tions-rcna93704.

23. Lawrence Wittner, "What Cuban Missile Crisis Teaches Us about Ukraine," *The Riverdale Press*, February 28, 2022, www.riverdalepress.com/stories/what-cuban-missile-crisis-teaches-us-about-ukraine,77815; Griff Witte, "In Putin's Ukraine Quagmire, Echoes of Soviet Failure in Afghanistan," *Washington Post*, April 2, 2022, www.washingtonpost.com/world/2022/04/02/ukraine-afghanistan-rus sia-parallels-quagmire.

24. Address by the President of the Russian Federation, February 24, 2022, http:// en.kremlin.ru/events/president/news/67843.

25. Sam Sokol, "Putin's Favorite TV Host Mixes Nuclear Threats, Jewish Roots and Antisemitic Quotes," *Haaretz*, April 26, 2022, www.haaretz.com/world-news/eur ope/2022-04-26/ty-article/.premium/putins-favorite-tv-host-mixes-nuclear-thr eats-jewish-roots-and-antisemitic-quotes/00000180-66d0-d5b7-a3e3-f7d9191b0000.

26. Timothy Snyder, "We Should Say It. Russia Is Fascist," *New York Times*, May 19, 2022, www.nytimes.com/2022/05/19/opinion/russia-fascism-ukraine-putin .html.

27. Marlene Laruelle, "Is Russia Fascist?" *Postsocialism*, May 24, 2022, https://post socialism.org/2022/05/24/is-russia-fascist; Laruelle, *Is Russia Fascist? Unraveling Propaganda East and West*.

28. Robert Coalson, "Nasty, Repressive, Aggressive – Yes. But Is Russia Fascist? Experts Say 'No,'" *Radio Free Europe – Radio Liberty*, April 9, 2022, www.rferl.or g/a/russia-repressive-aggressive-not-fascist/31794918.html.

29. A Pew research center poll in July 2023 revealed that 50 percent of Americans named China as the country they saw as the greatest threat to the United States – "almost three times the share who name Russia (17%)." Nam Lam and Laura Silver, "Americans Name China as the Country Posing the Greatest Threat to the U.S.," *Pew Research Center*, July 27, 2023, www.pewresearch.org/sh ort-reads/2023/07/27/americans-name-china-as-the-country-posing-the-great est-threat-to-the-us; Willnat, Tang, Shi, and Zhan, "Media Use and National Image: How Americans and Chinese Perceive the U.S.–China Trade War."

30. "Spetsial'naia voennaia operatsiia v Ukraine: Otnoshenie i tseli," *VTsIOM*, 28 February 2022, https://wciom.ru/analytical-reviews/analiticheskii-obzor/s pecialnaja-voennaja-operacija-v-ukraine-otnoshenie-i-celi.

31. "Odobrenie institutov, reitingi partii i politikov," *Levada-Tsentr*, March 30, 2022. www.levada.ru/2022/03/30/odobrenie-institutov-rejtingi-partij-i-politikov.

32. Maksim Alyukov, "Oprosy obshchestvennogo mneniia kak politicheskoe oruz-hie," *Open Democracy*, March 9, 2022, www.opendemocracy.net/ru/oprosy-obsc hestvennogo-mneniya-kak-politicheskoe-oruzhie-alyukov.

33. Ivan Nechiporenko, "Faced with Foreign Pressure, Russians Rally around Putin, Poll Shows," *New York Times*, March 31, 2022, www.nytimes.com/2022/03/31/ world/europe/putin-approval-rating-russia.html.

34. Andrei Kolesnikov, "How Russians Learned to Stop Worrying and Love the War: The Pliant Majority Sustaining Putin's Rule," *Foreign Affairs*, February 1, 2023.

35. "Sotsial'nye nastroeniia: Kratkosrochnaia i dolgosrochnaia perspektiva," *FOM* (Fond Obshchestvennoe mnenie), March 29, 2022, https://fom.ru/Nastroeni va/14708.

36. Vitaliy Shevchenko, "Ukraine War: Protester Exposes Cracks in Kremlin's War Message," *BBC*, March 15, 2022, www.bbc.com/news/world-europe-60749064.

37. "More Than 15,000 Russians Have Been Arrested in Anti-war Protests," *The Economist*, March 22, 2022, www.economist.com/graphic-detail/2022/03/22/ more-than-15000-russians-have-been-arrested-in-anti-war-protests; "Russia: Brutal Arrests and Torture, Ill-Treatment of Anti-war Protesters," *ReliefWeb*, March 9, 2022, https://reliefweb.int/report/russian-federation/russia-brutal-arrests-and-torture-ill-treatment-anti-war-protesters.

38. "Moscow City Councillor Gets Seven Years' Jail for Anti-war Comment," *Reuters*, July 8, 2022, www.reuters.com/world/europe/moscow-city-councillor-gets-seve n-years-jail-anti-war-comment-2022-07-08.

39. "15 punktov grazhdanina Rossii, zhelaiushchego blaga svoei strane," *Naval'nyi*, February 20, 2023, https://navalny.com/p/6634.

40. Anatoly Kurmanaev, "Here's What We Know about the Cause of Navalny's Reported Death," *New York Times*, February 16, 2024; "HUR Chief Budanov Says Seems Navalny Died of Detached Blood Clot," *Kyiv Post*, February 26, 2024.

41. "Russian Men Leave Country, Fearing Call to Fight in Ukraine," PBS, September 23, 2022, www.pbs.org/newshour/world/russian-men-leave-coun try-fearing-call-to-fight-in-ukraine; Ben Noble and Nikolai Petrov, "Putin Faces Growing Threat from the Wives and Mothers of Mobilized Soldiers," Chatham House, December 8, 2023, www.chathamhouse.org/2023/12/putin-faces-grow ing-threat-wives-and-mothers-mobilized-soldiers.

42. Darragh Roche, "Putin's Approval Ratings Suffer First Fall since Start of Ukraine War," *Newsweek*, September 30, 2022, www.newsweek.com/putin-approval-rat ings-suffer-first-fall-since-start-ukraine-war-russia-1747743; Maksim Alyukov, "Oprosy obshchestvennogo mneniia kak politicheskoe oruzhie," *Open Democracy*, March 9, 2022, www.opendemocracy.net/ru/oprosy-obschestven nogo-mneniya-kak-politicheskoe-oruzhie-alyukov.

43. "'Voennaia operatsiia otrazhaet interesy 3%': Bol'shinstvu rossiian okazalas' ne nuzhna pobeda nad Ukrainoi," *Kapital strany*, July 22, 2022, https://web.arch ive.org/web/20220727065907/https://kapital-rus.ru/news/388801-voen naya_operaciya_otrajaet_interesy_3_bolshinstvu_rossiyan_okazalas/? ysclid=l5kq614w11594525257.

44. Ishchenko and Zhuravlev, "Imperialist Ideology or Depoliticization? Why Russian Citizens Support the Invasion of Ukraine."

45. McFaul, "Are Russians Imperialists?"

46. Pesenti, "Cancelling Russian Culture Is Today's Moral Imperative"; Kevin M. F. Platt, "The Profound Irony of Canceling Everything Russian," *New York*

Times, April 22, 2022; Cathy Young, "Efforts to Cancel Russian Culture Are Misguided," *Newsday*, June 15, 2023.

47. See, for example, a speech by Senator Josh Hawley (Republican, Missouri) on February 16, 2023, www.hawley.senate.gov/hawley-delivers-national-security-speech-china-and-ukraine-time-truth.

48. See Valerii Garbuzov, "Direktor Instituta SShA i Kanady Valerii Garbuzov ob utrachennykh illuziiakh ukhodiashchei epokhi," *Nezavisimaia gazeta*, August 29, 2023, www.ng.ru/ideas/2023-08-29/7_8812_illusions.html. For the publication of this article revealing the return of Russian anti-American propaganda to the worst Soviet patterns, Garbuzov was immediately fired from the position of director of the major Russian think tank studying the United States, the Institute for USA and Canada Studies.

49. For one instance, see "Professor NIU VShE upal v obmorok v efire 'Vechera s Vladimirom Solov'evym,'" RTVi News, March 22, 2023, https://rtvi.com/news/professor-niu-vshe-upal-v-obmorok-v-efire-vechera-s-vladimirom-solovevym.

50. "Kollaps uzhe ne otmenit': Khazin predrek ekonomicheskii krakh SShA," *Rambler-Finansy*, October 27, 2023, https://finance.rambler.ru/economics/51667397.

51. "Velikie Strany, otnoshenie k SShA, ES, Kitaiu i Ukraine, grazhdanam etikh stran," *Levada-Tsentr*, September 12, 2023, www.levada.ru/2023/09/12/velikie-strany-otnoshenie-k-ssha-es-kitayu-i-ukraine-grazhdanam-etih-stran.

Bibliography

PRIMARY SOURCES

Archival Collections

College Park, MD
National Archives and Record Service (NARS)
Record Group (RG) 59. Department of State

- Dispatches from the United States Ministers to Russia (DUSMR), M 35;
- Diplomatic Instructions of the Department of State (DIDS), Russia, M 77;
- Decimal Files, 1910–1929. Records Relating to the Political Relations with Russia and the Soviet Union (PRRSU), M 316, 333.

College Station, TX
George H. W. Bush Presidential Library

- Condoleezza Rice Files
- Robert Teeter Collection

Des Moines, IA
State Historical Society of Iowa.

- RG. 043. Governors' Records

Little Rock, AR
Clinton Presidential Library

- Memoranda of Telephone Conversations (Digital Library)

Manchester (Great Britain)
John Ryland's Library, Manchester University
Manuscript Division

- Alexis Aladin Papers

Moscow (Russia)
The Foreign Policy Archive of Imperial Russia (AVPRI)

- Fond 133, Kantseliariia
- Fond 134, Arkhiv "Voina"
- Fond 135, Osobyi politotdel
- Fond 137, Otchety MID
- Fond 155, Vtoroi departament (I-1)
- Fond 170, Posol'stvo v Vashingtone
- Fond 340, Lichnyi arkhiv F. F. Martensa

The Russian State Archive of Socio-political History (RGASPI)

- Fond 17

The State Archive of the Russian Federation (GARF)

- Fond 579, Pavel Nikolaevich Miliukov

The State Public Historical Library (GPIB)

- Otdel redkikh knig

New York, NY
Bakhmeteff Archive of Russian and East European History and Culture (BA),
    Columbia University

- The Crane Family Papers

The New York Public Library (NYPL)
Manuscripts and Archives Division (MAD)

- George Kennan Papers
- Aleksyei Grigoryevich Yevstafiev Papers

Princeton, NJ
Seeley G. Mudd Manuscript Library, Princeton University

- Arthur Bullard Papers
- George F. Kennan Papers
- Joshua Butler Wright Diary

Stanford, CA
Hoover Institution Archives

- Poster Collection

Washington, D.C.
Library of Congress (LC)
Manuscript Division (MD)

- Andrew J. Donelson Papers

- Gifford Pinchot Papers
- The Isaac Draper, Jr. Collection
- James K. Polk Papers
- John Hay Papers
- Theodore Roosevelt Papers
- Thomas De Witt Talmage Papers
- Wharton Barker Papers
- William L. Marcy Papers

PUBLISHED DOCUMENTS

Abraham Lincoln to Taylor, December 25, 1863; Taylor to Lincoln, December 28, 1863, http://quod.lib.umich.edu/l/lincoln/lincoln7/1:167.

Abstracts of Reports of the Immigration Commission with Conclusions and Recommendations and Views of the Minority, Vol. 1. Washington: Government Printing Office, 1911.

Adamov E. A. "Soedinennye Shtaty v epokhu Grazhdanskoi voiny i Rossiia," *Krasnyi arkhiv*. 1930, Vol. 1 (38), pp. 159–160.

Address of Louis Marshall on "Russia and the American Passport" before Council of American Hebrew Congregation in New York, January 19, 1911. New York, 1911.

Adler, Cyrus, ed. *The Voice of America on Kishineff*. Philadelphia: Jewish Publication Society of America, 1904.

Adler, Cyrus and Aaron M. Margalith, eds. *With Firmness in the Right: American Diplomatic Action Affecting Jews, 1840–1945*. New York: American Jewish Committee, 1946.

Baker, Ray Stannard and William E. Dodd, eds. *The Public Papers of Woodrow Wilson*, 2 vols. New York: Harper, 1927.

Banac, Ivo, ed. *Dimitrov and Stalin 1934–1943: Letters from the Soviet Archives*. New Haven: Yale University Press, 2000.

Bashkina, Nina N., Nikolai N. Bolkhivitinov, and John H. Brown, eds. *The United States and Russia: The Beginning of Relations, 1765–1815*. Washington: US Government Printing Office, 1980.

Beschloss, Michael R., ed. *Taking Charge: The Johnson White House Tapes, 1963–1964*. New York: Simon & Schuster, 1997.

Browder, Robert Paul and Alexander F. Kerensky, ed. *The Russian Provisional Government, 1917: Documents*, 3 vols. Stanford: Stanford University Press, 1961.

Congressional Record. Washington: Government publications: 47th Congress, 1st Session, Vol. 13, 1882; 52nd Congress, 1st Session, Vol. 23, 1892; 62nd Congress, 2nd Session, Vol. 48, 1912.

The Diplomatic Correspondence of the American Revolution. Ed. Jared Sparks. Boston, 1829.

Efimenko, A. R. et al. *RKKA i Grazhdanskaia voina v Ispanii 1936–1939 gg.*, 8 vols. Moscow: Rosspen, 2019.

Efimov A. V. "Posylka dvukh eskadr v Severnuiu Ameriku (dokumenty)," *Istorik-Marxist.* 1936, Vol. 3, No. 55.

Efimov, Boris. *Boris Efimov: Uroki istorii XX veka v karikaturakh.* Moscow: Izdatel'stvo Skanrus, 2007.

Executive Documents Printed by Order of The House of Representatives. 1863–1864.

Foreign Relations of the United States, 1873–1874, Vol. 31. Washington: US Government Printing Office, 1874.

Foreign Relations of the United States, 1892, Vol. 48. Washington: US Government Printing Office, 1892.

Foreign Relations of the United States, 1904. Washington: US Government Printing Office, 1905.

Foreign Relations of the United States, 1905. Washington: US Government Printing Office, 1906.

Foreign Relations of the United States, 1909. Washington: US Government Printing Office, 1910.

Foreign Relations of the United States, 1933–1939: Diplomatic Papers: The Soviet Union, 1933–1939. Washington: US Government Printing Office, 1952.

Foreign Relations of the United States, 1955–1957, Vol. XXV: *Eastern Europe.* Washington: US Government Printing Office, 1990.

Foreign Relations of the United States, 1958–1960, Vol. III: *National Security Policy, Arms Control and Disarmament.* Washington: US Government Printing Office, 1996.

Foreign Relations of the United States, 1958–1960, Vol. X, Part 1: *Eastern Europe Region; Soviet Union; Cyprus.* Washington: US Government Printing Office, 1993.

Foreign Relations of the United States, 1969–1976, Vol. XIV: *Soviet Union October 1971–May 1972.* Washington: US Government Printing Office, 2006.

Foreign Relations of the United States, 1969–1976, Vol. XV: *Soviet Union June 1972–August 1974.* Washington: US Government Printing Office, 2011.

Foreign Relations of the United States, 1969–1976, Vol. XVI: *Soviet Union, August 1974–December 1976.* Washington: US Government Printing Office, 2012.

Foreign Relations of the United States, 1981–1988, Vol. VI: *Soviet Union, October 1986–January 1989.* Washington: US Government Printing Office, 2016.

Hans, N. "Tsar Alexander I and Jefferson: Unpublished Correspondence," *The Slavonic and East European Review,* Vol. 32, No. 78 (December 1953).

Lafont, Maria. *Soviet Posters: The Sergo Grigorian Collection.* Munich: Prest, 2007.

Letters of Delegates to Congress, 1774–1789, 26 vols. Ed. P. H. Smith. Washington: Library of Congress, 1976–2000.

Levada Analytical Center, Russian Public Opinion 2012–2013. Moscow: Levada Center, 2013.

Link, Arthur S., ed. *The Papers of Woodrow Wilson (PWW).* Princeton: Princeton University Press. Vol. 7 (1970); Vol. 10 (1971); Vol. 30 (1979); Vol. 31

(1980); Vol. 32 (1980); Vol. 33 (1980); Vol. 35 (1981); Vol. 37 (1982); Vol. 38 (1982); Vol. 41 (1983); Vol. 42 (1983).

Morison Elting Elmore, ed. *The Letters of Theodore Roosevelt*, Vols. 2–7. Cambridge: Harvard University Press, 1952–1954.

Obzor vneshnei torgovli Rossii po evropeiskoi i aziatskoi granitsam za 1878 god. St Petersburg: Tipografia V. Kirshbauma, 1879.

Otchety starshego agenta Ekaterinoslavskogo zemstva v Soedinennykh Shtatakh I. B. Rosena. Ekaterinoslav, 1908, 1909.

Otmena Soedinennymi Shtatami Severnoi Ameriki dogovora 1832 g. St. Petersburg, 1912.

The Papers of John C. Calhoun. Ed. Robert L. Meriwether et al., Vol. 21. Columbia, 1993.

Pechatnov, V. O. and I. E. Magadeev, *Perepiska I. V. Stalina s F. Ruzvel'tom i Y. Cherchillem v gody Velikoi Otechestvennoi voiny*, 2 vols. Moscow: OLMA, 2015.

Pis'ma V. A. Zhukovskogo k A. Ia. Bulgakovu, Russkii Arkhiv. 1868. No. 9.

Public Papers of the Presidents of the United States: George W. Bush, 2001. Washington: US Government Printing Office, 2003.

Radosh, Ronald, Mary R. Habeck, and Grigory Sevostianov, eds. *Spain Betrayed: The Soviet Union in the Spanish Civil War.* New Haven: Yale University Press, 2001.

Report of the Commissioners of Immigration upon the Causes Which Incite Immigration to the United States, 52nd Congress, 1st Session, House of Representatives, Ex. Doc. 235, Part 1. Washington, 1892.

Sbornik diplomaticheskikh dokumentov, kasajushchikhsia peregovorov mezhdu Rossiei i Iaponiei o zakluchenii mirnogo dogovora (24 maia–3 oktiabria). St. Petersburg: MID, 1906.

Sevost'ianov, Grigory N., ed. *Moskva–Vashington: Politika i diplomatiia Kremlia 1921– 1941*, 3 vols. Moscow: Nauka, 2009.

Sevost'ianov, Grigory N., ed. *Rossiia i SShA: Torgovo-economicheskie otnosheniia. 1900– 1930. Sbornik documentov.* Moscow: Nauka, 1996.

Synger, Isidor, ed., *Russia at the Bar of the American People.* New York: Funk & Wagnalls, 1904.

Taker, William W. *His Imperial Highness the Grand Duke Alexis in the United States of America during the Winter of 1871–1872.* Riverside Press, 1872.

Termination of the Treaty of 1832 between the United States and Russia. Washington: US Government Printing Office, 1911.

Ukazatel' russkogo otdela mezhdunarodnoi vystavki 1876 goda. St. Petersburg, 1876.

United States Congress, Speaker's Advisory Group on Russia, *Russia's Road to Corruption: How the Clinton Administration Exported Government Instead of Free Enterprise and Failed the Russian People.* Washington, September 2000.

United States Senate Committee on Foreign Relations, Minority Staff Report, *Putin's Asymmetric Assault on Democracy in Russia and Europe: Implications for U.S. National Security.* Washington: US Government Publishing Office, January 10, 2018.

The Unpublished Letters of Bayard Taylor in the Huntington Library. Ed. J. R. Schultz. San Marino, CA, 1937.

Vsepoddanneyshee mnenie grafa N. I. Panina, Sbornik Imperatorskogo Russkogo Istoricheskogo Obshchestva, Vol. 145.

Wade, Rex A., ed. *Documents of Soviet History,* Vol. 1: *The Triumph of Bolshevism 1917–1919.* Gulf Breeze, FL: Academic International Press, 1991.

The Works of Benjamin Franklin. Philadelphia, 1809.

The Works of James Buchanan. Ed. John Bassett Moore. Philadelphia and London, 1908, Vol. 2.

Webster, D. *The Works of Daniel Webster.* Boston, 1854.

Webster, Daniel. *Papers of Daniel Webster: Correspondence.* Hanover, NH, 1976.

Webster, Daniel. *The Writings and Speeches of Daniel Webster.* National Edition, 18 vols. Ed. J. W. McIntire. Boston: Little, Brown & Co. 1903.

Webster, Daniel. *The Great Speeches and Orations of Daniel Webster.* Boston, 1889.

Worthington, C. Ford. "Some Original Documents on the Genesis of the Monroe Doctrine," *Proceedings of the Massachusetts Historical Society,* 2nd ser. Vol. 15 (1901–1902), 378–380.

Treaties and Other International Agreements of the United States of America, 1776–1949, 12 vols. Ed. Ch. I. Bevans. Washington, 1968–1976.

Zeman, Z. A. B., ed. *Germany and the Revolution in Russia, 1915–1918.* London: Oxford University Press, 1958.

PUBLISHED DIARIES, MEMOIRS, AND CONTEMPORARY WRITINGS

A Sketch of the Internal Condition of the United States and Their Political Relations with Europe, by a Russian. Translated from the French by an American. Baltimore: E. J. Coale, 1826.

Adams, Brooks. *America's Economic Supremacy.* New York: Harper & Bros., 1947.

Adams, Brooks. *The New Empire.* New York: The Macmillan Company, 1902.

Adams, Henry. *Vospitanie Genri Adamsa.* Moscow: Progress, 1988.

Adams, John Q. *Memoirs of John Quincy Adams. Comprising Portions of His Diary from 1795 to 1848,* 12 vols. Ed. Charles Francis Adams. Freeport, NY: Books for Libraries Press, 1969 (repr.; 1st publ. 1874–1877).

Aksyonov, Vassily. *Non-stop around the Clock.* Translated by Stephanie Sides. Monterey: Monterey Institute of International Studies, 1983.

Albright, Madeleine. *Madam Secretary.* New York: Miramax Books, 2003.

Arnaud, Charles de. *In Defence of Russia and Its Government: An Answer to Mr. George Kennan's Articles on Siberia in the Century.* New York: Anson D. F. Randolph, 1888.

Autobiography of John B. Weber. Buffalo, NY: J. W. Clement Co., 1924.

Autobiography of John Hays Hammond Illustrated with Photographs, 2 vols. New York: Farrar & Rinehart, Murray Hill, 1935.

Babin, Aleksey V. *Istoriya Severo-Amerikanskikh Soedinennykh Shtatov.* St. Petersburg: Tipografia Trynke i Fusno, 1912, Vols. 1–2.

Baer, George W. ed. *A Question of Trust: The Origins of U.S.–Soviet Relations: The Memoirs of Loy W. Henderson.* Stanford: Hoover Institution Press, 1986.

Beatty, Bessie. *The Red Heart of Russia.* New York: Century, 1918.

Beveridge, Albert J. *The Russian Advance.* New York and London: Harper & Brothers Publishers, 1904.

Blankenburg, Rudolf. *Philadelphia and the Russian Famine of 1891 and 1892.* Philadelphia: Russian Famine Relief Committee, 1892.

Bogolubov, N. F. *Ekspeditsiia v Ameriku na parokhode "Cimbria" v 1878 godu.* Kronshtadt, 1898.

Bohlen, Charles E. *Witness to History 1929–1969.* New York: W. W. Norton, 1973.

Borodin, Nikolai A. *Amerikantsy i amerikanskaia kul'tura.* Petrograd: Obschestvennaia pol'za, 1915.

Borodin, Nikolai A. *Severo-Amerikanskie Soedinennye Shtaty i Rossiia.* Petrograd: Knizhnoe Izdatel'stvo "Ogni," 1915.

Bourke-White, Margaret. *Shooting the Russian War.* New York: Simon & Schuster, 1942.

Brinkley, Douglas, ed. *The Reagan Diaries.* New York: HarperCollins, 2007.

Browder, Bill. *Red Notice: A True Story of High Finance, Murder, and One Man's Fight for Justice.* New York: Simon & Schuster, 2015.

Browne, John Ross. *The Land of Thor.* New York: Harper and Brothers, 1870.

Bulgarin, Faddey. *Vospominaniia Faddeya Bulgarina.* St. Petersburg: Tipografia Karla Kraia, 1849.

Burnham, James. *Containment or Liberation?* New York, 1953.

Burns, William J. *The Back Channel: A Memoir of American Diplomacy and the Case for Its Renewal.* New York: Random House, 2019.

Bush, George and Brent Scowcroft, *A World Transformed.* New York: Knopf, 1998.

Bush, George W. *Decision Points.* New York: Crown, 2010.

Caldicott, Helen Broinowski. *A Desperate Passion: An Autobiography.* New York: W. W. Norton, 1996.

Caldwell, Erskine. *All-Out on the Road to Smolensk.* New York: Duell, Sloan and Pearce, 1942.

Campbell, Thomas. *Russia: Market or Menace?* London: Longmans, 1932.

Carter, Jimmy. *White House Diary.* New York: Farrar, Straus and Giroux, 2010.

Chafee, Zechariah. "A Contemporary State Trial – The United States *versus* Jacob Abrams et al.," *Harvard Law Review,* Vol. XXXIII, No. 6 (April 1920), 747–750.

Chaliapin, Feodor. *Stranitsi iz moei zhizni.* Perm': Knizhoe izdatel'stvo, 1961.

Chamberlin, William Henry. *Beyond Containment.* Chicago: Henry Regnery Co., 1953.

Cheney, Dick with Liz Cheney. *In My Time: A Personal and Political Memoir.* New York: Simon & Schuster, 2011.

Chernyaev, Anatoly S. *My Six Years with Gorbachev.* University Park: Pennsylvania State University Press, 2000.

Chernyaev, Anatoly S. *The Diary of Anatoly S. Chernyaev*. Published by the National Security Archive. https://nsarchive.gwu.edu/anatoly-chernyaev-diary.

Child, Richard W. *Potential Russia*. New York: E. P. Dutton and Company, 1916.

Christopher, Warren. *In the Stream of History: Shaping Foreign Policy for a New Era*. Stanford: Stanford University Press, 1998.

Chukovskii, Korney. *Nat Pinkerton i sovremennaia literatura*. Moscow: Sovremennoe tvorchestvo, 1910.

Clapper, James. *Facts and Fears: Hard Truths from a Life in Intelligence*. New York: Viking, 2018.

Clinton, Bill. *My Life*. New York: Alfred A. Knopf, 2004.

Coolidge, Archibald Cary. *The United States as a World Power*. New York: The Macmillan Company, 1908.

Correspondence Respecting Russia, between Robert Goodloe Harper, Esq., and Robert Walsh, Jr., Together with the Speech of Mr. Harper, Commemorative of the Russian Victories, Delivered at Georgetown, Columbia, June 5th, 1813, and An Essay on the Future State of Europe. Philadelphia, 1813.

Costigliola, Frank, ed. *The Kennan Diaries*. New York: W. W. Norton, 2014.

Dallas, G. M. *Diary of George Mifflin Dallas, While United States Minister to Russia 1837 to 1839, and to England 1856 to 1861*. Ed. Susan Dallas. Philadelphia, 1892.

Darling, J. N. *Ding Goes to Russia*. New York: Whittesley House, 1932.

Davis, Henry W. *The War of Ormuzd and Ahriman in the Nineteenth Century*. Baltimore: James S. Waters, 1852.

Davis, Patti. *The Way I See It*. New York: Putnam, 1992.

de La Porte, Joseph. *Vsemirnyi puteshestvovatel, ili Poznanie Starago i Novogo Sveta*. St. Petersburg: Veitbrekht i Shnor, 1778–1794.

Debogorii-Mokrievich, Vladimir Karpovich. *Vospominaniia*, issues 1–2. Paris: Imprimerie J. Allemane, 1894–1895.

Del Ponte, Carla with Chuck Sudetic. *Madame Prosecutor: Confrontations with Humanity's Worst Criminals and the Culture of Impunity*. New York: Other Press, 2008.

Ditson G. L. *Circassia; or a Tour to the Caucasus*. New York and London, 1850.

Dobrynin, Anatoly. *In Confidence: Moscow's Ambassador to America's Six Cold War Presidents*. New York: Random House, 1995.

Durland, Kellogg. *The Red Reign: The True Story of an Adventurous Year in Russia*. New York: The Century Co., 1907.

Edgar, William C. *The Russian Famine of 1891 and 1892: Some Particulars of the Relief Sent to the Destitute Peasants by the Millers of America in the Steamship Missouri*. Minneapolis: Millers & Manufacturers Insurance Co., 1893.

Efimov, Boris. *Boris Efimov: Uroki istorii XX veka v karikaturakh*. Izdatel'stvo Skanrus, 2007.

Evstaf'ev, Aleksei. *The Great Republic Tested by the Touch of Truth*. Ed. Susan Smith-Peter. Bloomington: Slavica, 2022.

Egert, Vasily P. *The Conflict between the United States and Russia*. St. Petersburg, 1912.

Ehrenburg, Ilya. *Men, Years – Life*, Vol. V: *The War 1941–1945*. London: Macgibbon & Kee, 1964.

Ehrenburgh, Ilya. *Post-war Years 1945–1954*. Cleveland: World Publishing Company, 1967.

Eisenhower, Susan. *Breaking Free: A Memoir of Love and Revolution*. New York: FSG, 1995.

Emmons, Terence and Bertrand M. Patenaude, eds. *War, Revolution, and Peace in Russia: The Passages of Frank Golder, 1914–1927*. Stanford, CA: Hoover Institution Press, 1992.

Esenin, Sergei. "An Iron Mirgorod," in Olga Peters Hasty and Susanne Fusso, eds. *America through Russian Eyes, 1874–1926*. New Haven: Yale University Press, 1988, 145–158.

Fadeev Rostislav Andreevich, *Mnenie o vostochnom voprose*. St. Petersburg: Tipografia Gogenfel'dena, 1870.

Fortunatov, Stepan F. *Istoriia Soedinennykh Shtatov: Kurs, chitannyi v 1915–1916 gg. po zapiskam slushatel'nits*. Moscow: Ob-vo pri istoriko-filosofskom fakul'tete Moskovskikh vysshikh zhenskikh kursov, 1916.

Foulke, William Dudley. *A Random Record of Travel during Fifty Years*. New York: Oxford University Press, 1925.

Foulke, William Dudley. *Slav or Saxon: A Study of the Growth and Tendencies of Russian Civilization*. New York: Putnam's, 1887.

Francis, David R. *Dollars and Diplomacy: Ambassador David Rowland Francis and the Fall of Tsarism, 1916–1917*. Durham: Duke University Press, 1981.

Fukuyama, Francis. "The End of History," *The National Interest*, No. 16 (Summer 1989), 3–18.

Gaidar, Yegor. *Days of Defeat and Victory*. Seattle: University of Washington Press, 1999.

Gardner, Clinton C. *D-Day and Beyond: A Memoir of War, Russia, and Discovery*. Bloomington: Xlibris, 2004.

Gates, Robert M. *Duty: Memoirs of a Secretary at War*. New York: Knopf, 2014.

Gayduk, Moisei. *"Utiug": Materialy i fakty o zagotovitel'noi deyatel'nosti russkikh voennykh komissii v Amerike*. New York, 1918.

Gilmore, Eddy. *After the Cossacks Burned Down the "Y"*. New York: Farrar, Straus and Giroux, 1964.

Gilmore, Eddy. *Me and My Russian Wife*. Garden City, NY: Doubleday, 1954.

Glenn, John. *John Glenn: A Memoir*. New York: Bantam, 1999.

Glukhovskii, P. I. *Kolumbova vystavka v Chikago: Otchet general'nogo komissara russkogo otdela*. St. Petersburg: Tipografia Kirshbauma, 1895.

Golder, Frank. *Guide to Materials for American History in Russian Archives*. Washington: Carnegie Institution of Washington, 1917.

Golovin, Ivan. *Stars and Stripes, or American Impressions*. London and New York, 1856.

Gorbachev, Mikhail. *Memoirs*. New York: Doubleday, 1995.

Graham, Thomas. *Getting Russia Right*. New York: Polity Press, 2023.

Green, Francis. *Sketches of Army Life in Russia*. New York: Charles Scribner's Sons, 1880.

Griffin, G. W. *Memoir of Col. Chas. Todd*. Philadelphia: Claxton, Remsen & Haffelfinger, 1873.

Gromyko, Anatoly and Martin Hellman, eds. *Breakthrough/Proryv: Emerging New Thinking. Soviet and Western Scholars Issue a Challenge to Build a World beyond War*. New York: Walker and Company, 1989.

Gulick, Sidney Lewis. *The White Peril in the Far East: An Interpretation of the Significance of the Russo-Japanese War*. New York: F. H. Revell, 1905.

Gunther, John. *Inside Russia Today*. New York: Harper, 1958.

Gurowski, Adam. *Russia as It Is*. New York, 1854.

Hapgood, Isabel. *Russian Rambles*. Boston and New York: Houghton, Mifflin and Company, 1895.

Harding, Luke. *A Very Expensive Poison: The Assassination of Alexander Litvinenko and Putin's War with the West*. New York: Vintage, 2017.

Harper, Paul V. *The Russia I Believe In: The Memoirs of Samuel N. Harper. 1902–1941*. Chicago: University of Chicago Press, 1945.

Harriman, Averell. *Peace with Russia?* New York: Simon & Schuster, 1959.

Hecht, George J., ed. *The War in Cartoons*. New York: E. P. Dutton, 1919.

Herzen, A. *My Past and Thoughts*. Berkeley: University of California Press, 1982.

Hill, Fiona. *There Is Nothing for You Here: Finding Opportunity in the Twenty-First Century*. Boston: Mariner Books, 2021.

Houghteling, James L. *A Diary of the Russian Revolution*. New York: Dodd, Mead, 1918.

Howe, M. A. DeWolfe. *George von Lengerke Meyer: His Life and Public Services*. New York: Dodd, Mead, 1920.

Hoyt, John W. *Report of the Russian Famine Relief Committee of the United States*. Washington: Rufus Darby, 1893.

Ianzhul, Ivan. *Vospominaniia I. I. Ianzhula o perezhitom i vidennom v 1864–1909 godakh*, 2nd ed. St. Petersburg: Tipografia tovarishchestva N. Ia. Stoikovoi, 1911.

Ianzhul, Ivan and Ekaterina Ianzhul. *Chasy dosuga: Ocherki i kartinki po ekonomicheskim, obschestvennym i literaturnym voprosam*. Moscow: Tipografia A. I. Mamontova, 1896.

Il'f, Ilya and Evgenii Petrov. *Odnoetazhnaia Amerika*. Moscow: Tekst, 2007.

Iossa, Nikolay. *O metalurgicheskom otdele na Filadel'fiyskoy vystavke 1876*. St. Petersburg, 1877.

John Ledyard's Journey through Russia and Siberia, 1787–1788: The Journal and Selected Letters. Ed. Stephen D. Watrous. Madison: University of Wisconsin Press, 2011 (1st ed. c. 1966).

Kachenovsky, D. I. "Zhizn' i sochineniia Danelia Vebstera," *Russkii vestnik*. 1856. Vol. 3, June, No. 1, pp. 385–416; Vol. 4, July, No. 2, pp. 239–278.

Kaiser, Robert G. *Russia: The People and the Power*. New York: Atheneum, 1976.

Kalugin, Oleg. *The First Directorate*. New York: St. Martin's Press, 1994.

Kennan, George. "Kak velos' prosveshchenie russkikh soldat v Iaponii," *Katorga i ssylka*, Vol. 31, No. 2 (1927), 158–165.

Kennan, George. *Tent Life in Siberia and Adventures among the Koraks and Other Tribes of Kamchatka and Eastern Siberia.* New York: G. P. Putnam's Sons, 1881.

Kennan, George F. "Contemporary Perspectives," in Ivo J. Lederer, ed. *Russian Foreign Policy: Essays in Historical Perspective.* New Haven: Yale University Press, 1962, 595–601.

Kennan, George F. *Memoirs, 1925–1950.* Boston: Little, Brown, 1967.

Kennan, George F. *On Dealing with the Communist World.* New York, 1964.

Kennedy, Edward M. *True Compass: A Memoir.* New York: Hachette, 2009.

Kerry, John. *Every Day Is Extra.* New York: Simon & Schuster, 2018.

Khodorkovsky, Mikhail. *The Russia Conundrum.* New York: St. Martin's Press, 2022.

Khrapovitsky, A. V. *Pamiatnia zapiska A. V. Khrapovitskogo, stats-sekretaria imperatriitsy Ekateriny vtoroi.* Moscow: Universitetskaia tipografiia, 1862.

Khrushchev in America. New York: Crosscurrents Press, 1960.

Kirby, Rollin. *Highlights: A Cartoon History of the Nineteen Twenties.* New York: W. F. Payson, 1931.

Knox, Thomas W. *Overland through Asia: Pictures of Siberian, Chinese, and Tartar Life.* Chicago: F. S. Gilman & Co., 1870.

Kornienko, Georgii. *Kholodnaia Voina: Svidel'stvo ee uchastnika.* Moscow: Olma-Press, 2001.

Korolenko, Vladimir Galakyionovich. *Puteshestvie v Ameriku: Nabliudeniia, razmyshleniia, nezakonchennye rasskazy.* Moscow: Zadruga, 1923.

Korostovets, Ivan Yakovlevich. "Mirnye peregovory v Portsmute v 1905 g.: Dnevnik I. Ia. Korostovtsa, sekretaria grafa S. Iu. Vitte vo vremia Portsmutskoi konferentsii. Iiul'–oktyabr', 1905," *Byloe*, Vol. 29, No. 1 (1918), 177–220; Vol. 30, No. 2 (1918), 110–146; Vol. 31, No. 3 (1918), 58–86.

Koshma, A. G. and L. P. Sokal'skii. *Ob uchrezhdenii russkoi sel'skohoziaistvennoi agentury v SShA.* Odessa, 1906.

Kovalevsky, M. M. "Moe nauchnoe i literaturnoe skitalchestvo," *Russkaia mysl.* 1895, Vol. 1.

Kovalevsky, Maxim Maximovich, *Istoriia amerikanskikh uchrezhdenii.* St. Petersburg: Litografia lektsii, 1908.

Kozyrev, Andrei. "The Lagging Partnership," *Foreign Affairs*, Vol. 73, No. 3 (May 1994), 59–71.

"Kratkoe opisanie zhizni i kharaktera generala Vasgingtona," *Pribavlenie k Moskovskim vedomostiam*, No. 46–47, 362–372.

Krylov, I. and A. Klushin. *Amerikantsy* (comic opera in two acts), www.operalib.eu/americani/rid.html.

L. N. Tolstoy i SShA. Perepiska. Moscow: IMLI RAN, 2004.

Ladygin, D. *Izvestie v Amerike o seleniiakh aglitskikh, v tom chisle nyne pod nazvaniem Soedinennykh Provintsii.* St. Petersburg: Tipografia Morskogo kadetskogo korpusa, 1783.

Lang, J. *Results of the Serf Emancipation in Russia.* Loyal Publication Society, 1864.

Lauterbach, Richard E. *These Are the Russians.* New York: Harper, 1945.

Levine, Irving R. *Main Street, U.S.S.R.* Garden City, NY: Doubleday, 1959.

Lippmann, Walter. *The Cold War: A Study in U.S. Foreign Policy.* New York: Harper, 1947.

Lippmann, Walter. *The Good Society.* Boston: Little, Brown, 1937.

Lomonosov, M. *Izbrannye proizvedeniia.* Leningrad: Sovetskii pisatel, 1986.

London, Jack. "Revolution," in *Revolution and Other Essays.* New York: The Macmillan Company, 1910.

Lyons, Eugene. *Our Secret Allies: The Peoples of Russia.* New York: Duell, Sloan & Pearce, 1953.

MacGahan, Januaris, *Campaign on the Oxus, and the Fall of Khiva.* New York: Harper and Bros., 1874.

Maksimov, Anatolii. *Bol'shaia Lozh': 1000-letniaia popytka Zapada likvidirovat' Rossiskuiu Gosudarstvennost'.* Moscow: Izdatel'stvo Algoritm, 2014.

Marye, George T. *Nearing the End in Imperial Russia.* Philadelphia: Dorrance & Co, 1929.

Massie, Suzanne. *Trust But Verify: Reagan, Russia and Me.* Rockland, ME: Maine Authors Publishing, 2013.

Matlock, Jack F., Jr. *Autopsy on an Empire: The American Ambassador's Account of the Collapse of the Soviet Union.* New York: Random House, 1995.

Maxwell, J. S. *The Czar, His Court and People, Including a Tour in Norway and Sweden.* New York: Baker and Scribner, c. 1848.

Mayakovsky, Vladimir. "My Discovery of America," in Olga Peters Hasty and Susanne Fusso, eds. *America through Russian Eyes, 1874–1926.* New Haven: Yale University Press, 1988, 159–220.

Mayakovsky, Vladimir. *My Discovery of America.* Translated by Neil Cornwell. London: Hesperus Press, 2005.

McCormick, Frederick. *The Tragedy of Russia in Pacific Asia,* 2 vols. New York: The Outing Publishing Company, 1905.

McFaul, Michael. *From Cold War to Hot Peace: An American Ambassador in Putin's Russia.* Boston: Houghton Mifflin Harcourt, 2018.

Medish, Vadim. ed. *My Russia: The Political Autobiography of Gennady Zyuganov.* Armonk, NY: M. E. Sharpe, 1997.

Melnikov, P. P. "K istorii razvitiia parokhodstva na Volge," *Krasnyi arkhiv.* 1938, Vols. 89–90.

Melnikov, P. P. "Svedeniia o russkikh zheleznykh dorogakh." Published by M. Krutikov, *Krasnyi arkhiv,* Vol. 99, 1940.

Melnikov, P. P. "Opisanie v tekhnicheskom otnoshenii zheleznykh dorog Severo-amerikanskikh shtatov," *Zhurnal putei soobshcheniia.* (1842), Vol. 2, No. 1, 15–85; No. 2, 95–197; No. 3, 209–265; No. 4, 285–374; Vol. 3, No. 1, 1–70; No. 2, 85–156.

Melnikov, P. P. "Nachalo zheleznodorozhnogo stroitelstva v Rossii," *Krasnyi arkhiv*, 1940, Vol. 99, 127–179.

Melville, George W. *In the Lena Delta: A Narrative of the Search for Lieut.-Commander De Long and His Companions*. Boston: Houghton Mifflin, 1885.

Melville, Herman. *White Jacket; or the World in a Man-of-War*. New York: Harper & Brothers Publishers, 1855.

Memoirs of Thomas O. Selfrudge, Jr. New York: G. P. Putnam's Sons, 1924.

Mendeleev, Dmitry, *Neftianaia promyshlennost' v Severo-Amerikanskom shtate Pensil'vaniia i na Kavkaze*. St. Petersburg: Tipografia tovarishchestva obshchestvennaia pol'za, 1877.

Michael, Louis G. *More Corn for Bessarabia: Russian Experience 1910–1917*. East Lansing: Michigan State University Press, 1983.

Milukov, Pavel. *Russia and Its Crisis*. Chicago: University of Chicago Press, 1905.

Mizhuev, Pavel Grigorievich. *Glavnye federatsii sovremennogo mira*. St. Petersburg: G. F. Lvovich, 1907.

Mizhuev, Pavel Grigorievich. *Istoriia velikoi amerikanskoi demokratii*. St. Petersburg: Brokgauz i Efron, 1906.

Mizhuev, Pavel Grigorievich. *Prava cheloveka i grazhdanina*. St. Petersburg: Tipografia Al'tshulera, 1906.

Motley, J. L. "Peter the Great," *North American Review*, Vol. 61, No. 129 (October 1845), 269–319.

Motovilov, N.A. "Dokladnaia zapiska imperatoru Aleksandru II," in Aleksandr Strizhev, ed. *Serafimo-Diveevskie predaniia*. Moscow: Palomnik, 2006, 431–440.

Noble, Edmund. *Russia and the Russians*. Boston: Houghton, Mifflin and Co., 1900.

Nuland, Victoria. "Pinning Down Putin: How a Confident America Should Deal with Russia," *Foreign Affairs*, Vol. 99, No. 4 (July/August 2020), 93–106.

Ogorodnikov, Pavel Ivanovich. *Ot N'iu-Yorka do San-Frantsisko i obratno v Rossiiu*. St. Petersburg: Izdanie knigoprodavtsev O. Kolesova i F. Minina, 1872.

Orlenev, Pavel Nikolaevich. *Zhizn' i tvorchestvo russkogo aktera Pavla Orleneva, opisannye im samim*. Leningrad and Moscow: Iskusstvo, 1961.

Ozerov, Ivan Khristoforovich. *America idet na Evropy*. St. Petersburg: Tipografia V. Kirshbauma, 1903.

Ozerov, Ivan Khristoforovich. *Chemu nas uchit America?* Moscow: Pol'za, 1908.

Pennell, Joseph. *The Jew at Home: Impressions of a Summer and Autumn Spent with Him*. New York: Appleton, 1892.

Phelps, William Lyon. *Essays on Russian Novelists*. New York: The Macmillan Company, 1911.

Popov, Petr Ivanovich. *V Amerike: Ocherki amerikanskoi zhizni po lichnym nabludeniiam avtora, prozhivshego v Amerike bezvyezdno 23 goda (1872–1895)*. St. Peterburg: Tipografia Stasulevicha, 1906.

Pozner, Vladimir with Brian Kahn. *Parting with Illusions*. New York: Atlantic Monthly Press, 1990.

Prevo. *Istoria o stranstviakh voobshche po vsem kraiam zemnogo kruga,* in 22 parts. Moscow: Universitetskaia tipografia, 1784.

Primakov, Yevgeny. *Russian Crossroads: Toward the New Millennium.* New Haven: Yale University Press, 2004.

Radishchev, A. N. *Polnoe sobranie sochinenii.* Moscow and Leningrad: Izdatel'stvo Akademii nauk, 1938–1954, Vol. 1.

Ramsay, David. *Universal History Americanised,* 12 vols. Philadelphia: M. Carey, 1819.

Reagan, Ronald. *The Reagan Diaries Unabridged,* 2 vols. New York: Harper, 2009.

Reeves, Francis B. *Russia Then and Now. 1892–1917.* New York: G. P. Putnam's Sons, 1917.

Reinsch, Paul S., *World Politics at the End of the 19th Century, as Influenced by the Oriental Situation.* New York: Macmillan Co., 1900.

Reston, James. *Prelude to Victory.* New York: Knopf, 1942.

Rhodes, Ben. *The World as It Is: A Memoir of the Obama White House.* New York: Random House, 2018.

Rice, Susan. *Tough Love: My Story of the Things Worth Fighting For.* New York: Simon & Schuster, 2019.

Rosen, Roman Romanovich. *Forty Years of Diplomacy,* Vols. 1–2. New York: Alfred A. Knopf. 1922.

Ross, Edward Allsworth. *Russia in Upheaval.* New York: Century, 1918.

Rotchev, A. G. "Vospominaniya russkogo turista. Iz puteshestvii A. G. Rotcheva," *Panteon. Zhurnal literaturno-khudozhestvennyi, izdavaemyi Fedorom Koni.* December 1853, Vol. 12, issue 12.

Rubakin, Nikolay Alexandrovich. *Etiudy o russkoi chitaiushchei publike: Fakty, tsifry i nabludeniia.* St. Petersburg: Izdanie N. P. Karabasnikova, 1895.

Russell, Charles Edward. *Unchained Russia.* New York: D. Appleton and Company, 1918.

Sagdeev, Roald Z. *The Making of a Soviet Scientist.* New York: Wiley, 1994.

Salisbury, Harrison E. *American in Russia.* New York: Harper, 1955.

Sanders, Bernie. *Where We Go from Here.* New York: Thomas Dunne Books, 2018.

Schlesinger, Arthur M. *Journals, 1952–2000.* New York: Penguin, 2007.

Schuman, Frederick L. and George Soule. *America Looks Abroad.* Foreign Policy Association pamphlet, August 1938.

Schuyler, Eugene. *Turkistan: Notes of a Journey in Russian Turkistan, Khokand, Bukhara, and Kuldja,* 2 vols. New York: Scribner, Armstrong & Co, 1876–1877.

Schuyler, Eugene. *Peter the Great, Emperor of Russia: A Study of Historical Biography,* 2 vols. New York: Charles Scribner's Sons, 1884.

Scott, Mark and Semyon Krasilshchik, eds. *Yanks Meet Reds: Recollections of U.S. and Soviet Vets from the Linkup in World War II.* Santa Barbara: CAPRA Press, 1988.

Shulman, Marshall D. Oral history interviews at Columbia University, 1993–1995.

Shuster, Morgan W. *The Strangling of Persia: A Story of the European Diplomacy and Oriental Intrigue That Resulted in the Denationalization of Twelve Million Mohammedans, a Personal Narrative.* New York: The Century Co., 1912.

Skal'kovskii, Konstantin A. *V strane iga i svobody: Putevye vpechatleniia.* St. Petersburg: Tipografia tovarishchestva pol'za, 1878.

Slavinskii, Nikolai. *Pis'ma ob Amerike i Russkikh pereselentsakh.* St. Petersburg: Tipografia P. P. Merkul'eva, 1873.

Smith, Christopher M. *Ukraine's Revolt, Russia's Revenge.* Washington: Brookings Institution Press, 2022.

Smith, Hedrick. *The Russians.* New York: Quadrangle, 1976.

Snell, Karl F. M. *Von den Handlungsvortheilen, welche aus der Unabhängigkeit der Vereinigten Staaten von Nord-Amerika für das Russische Reich entspringen: Ein Versuch.* Riga, 1783.

Solcv'ev, Jury Jakovlevich. *Vospominaniia diplomata, 1893–1922.* Minsk: Harvest, 2003.

Stasov, Vladimir Vasil'evich. "V. V. Vereshchagin v Amerike i Iaponii," in *Stat'i i zametki,* Vol. 1. Moscow: Izdatel'stvo Akademii khudozhestv SSSR, 1952, 128–143.

Steiner, Edward A. *Tolstoi: The Man.* New York: Kessinger Publishing, 1903.

Stevens, Edmund. *Russia Is No Riddle.* New York: Greenberg, 1945.

Stiles, William Curtis. *Out of Kishineff: The Duty of American People to the Russian Jew.* New York: G. W. Dillingham Company, 1903.

Stone, Melville E. *Fifty Years a Journalist.* Garden City, NY: Doubleday, Page and Company, 1921.

Strel'nikov, Boris G. *Tysiacha mil v poiskakh dushi.* Moscow: Pravda, 1979.

Svenin, P. *Sketches of Moscow and St.-Petersburg.* Philadelphia, 1813.

Svin'in, P. P. *Opyt zhivopisnago puteshestmia po Severnoi Amerike Pavla Svin'ina.* St. Petersburg: Tipografia Kraia, 1818.

Sytenko, I. A. *Pnevmaticheskie i gidravlicheskie tormoza, upotrebliaemye na zheleznykh dorogakh v Amerike.* Moscow, 1877.

Taker, William W. *His Imperial Highness the Grand Duke Alexis in the United States of America during the Winter of 1871–1872.* Cambridge, MA: Riverside Press, 1872.

Talbott, Strobe. *The Russia Hand: A Memoir of Presidential Diplomacy.* New York: Random House, 2002.

Taube, F. W. *Istoriia o aglinskoi torgovle, manifakturakh, seleniiakh i moreplavanii v drevnie, srednie i neoveishie vremen, do 1778 goda.* Moscow: Universitetskaia tipografiia, 1783.

Taylor, B. *Travels in Greece and Russia, with an Excursion to Crete.* New York, 1859, 369–370.

Taylor, Bayard. *Life and Letters of Bayard Taylor,* 2 vols. Ed. Marie Hansen-Taylor and Horace E. Scudder. Boston, 1884.

Tennison, Sharon. *The Power of Impossible Ideas: Ordinary Citizens' Extraordinary Efforts to Avert International Crisis.* Temple, TX: Odenwald Press, 2012.

Thayer, William A. *The Life and Letters of John Hay.* Boston and New York: Houghton Mifflin Company, 1915.

The Englishwoman in Russia: Impressions of the Society and Manners of the Russians. By a Lady, Ten Years Resident in That Country. New York, 1855.

The True Travels, Adventures and Observations of Captaine John Smith, in Europe, Africe, and America, beginning about the yeere 1598, and continued to this present 1629, Vol. 1. Richmond, 1819.

Tocqueville, Alexis de, *Democracy in America,* ed. J. P. Mayer and translated by George Lawrence. Garden City, NY: Anchor Books, 1969 (1st ed. c. 1835).

Tsimmermann, Eduard R. *Soedinennye Shtaty Severnoi Ameriki: Iz puteshestvii 1857–1858 i 1869–1870.* Moscow: Izdanie K. T. Soldatenkova, 1873.

Tverskoi, Petr. *Ocherki Severo-Amerikanskikh Soedinennykh Shtatov.* St. Petersburg: Tipografia I. N. Skorokhodova, 1895.

Vanderlip, Washington. *In Search of a Siberian Klondike.* New York: The Century Co., 1903.

Vil'chur, Mark Efimovich. *V Amerikanskom gornile: Putevye zametki. Prikliucheniia i mytarstva russkogo immigranta.* New York, 1914.

Vil'chur, Mark Efimovich. *Russkie v Amerike.* New York, 1918.

Vladimirov, Mikhail M. *Russkii sredi Amerikantsev. 1872–1876. Moi lichnye vpechatlenia kak tokoria, chernorabochego, plotnika i puteshestvennika.* S:. Petersburg: Tipografia tovarishchestva obshchestvennaia pol'za, 1877.

Volkonsky, Sergey. *Moi vospominaniia,* Vol. 1. Moscow: Zakharov, 2004.

Vospominaniia I. I. Ianzhula o perezhitom i vidennom v 1864–1909. Moscow: Gosudarstvennaia publichnaia istoricheskaia biblioteka Rossii, 2006.

Walling, William English, *Russia's Message: The True World Import of the Revolution.* New York: Doubleday, Page & Co., 1908.

Warren, Mercy Otis. *History of the Rise, Progress, and Termination of the American Revolution,* Vol. 2. Boston: Larkin, 1805.

Webster, Daniel. *Mr. Webster's Speech on the Greek Revolution.* Washington, 1824.

White A. D. *Autobiography of Andrew Dickson White, with Portraits,* 2 vols. New York: Century, 1922 (1st ed. 1905).

White, W. L. *Report on the Russians.* New York: Harcourt, Brace, 1945.

Whymper, Frederick. *Travel and Adventure in the Territory of Alaska, Formerly Russian America – Now Ceded to the United States – and in Various Other Parts of the North Pacific.* Harpers, 1869.

Wiener, Leo. *An Interpretation of the Russian People.* New York: McBride, Nast & Company, 1915.

Willkie, Wendell L. *One World.* New York: Simon & Schuster, 1943.

Witte, Sergey Jul'evich. *Vospominaniia,* Vols. 1–2. Tallin and Moscow: Skif Aleks, 1994.

Wolf, Erika. ed. *Ilf and Petrov's American Road Trip: The 1935 Travelogue of Two Soviet Writers.* New York: Princeton Architectural Press, 2007.

"X" [George F. Kennan], "The Sources of Soviet Conduct," *Foreign Affairs,* Vol. 25, No. 4 (July 1947), 566–582.

Yakovlev, Alexander. *On the Edge of an Abyss: From Truman to Reagan. The Doctrines and Realities of the Nuclear Age.* Moscow: Progress Publishers, 1985.

Young, Charles C. *Abused Russia.* New York: Devin-Adair, 1915.

Zaliubovsky, Anatoly. *Snabzhenie russkoi armii v Velikuiu voinu vintovkami, pulemetami, revol'verami i patronami k nim.* Belgrade: Izdanie Tsentral'nogo praveniia Obshchestva russkikh ofitserov-artilleristov za rubezhom, 1936.

Zelenyi P. A. "O poslednikh piati godakh krepostnogo sostoyaniia," in *Velikaya reforma*, Vol. 4. Moscow, 1911.

Newspapers and Magazines

Anti-slavery Bugle
Arena
Artilleriiskii zhurnal
Atlanta Constitution
Atlantic Monthly
Birzhevye vedomosti
Boston Daily Advertiser
Boston Globe
Boston Transcript
Brooklyn Daily Eagle
Century
Chicago Daily Tribune
Chicago Defender
Christian Herald
Christian Recorder
Cincinnati Daily Press
Columbus Evening Dispatch
Commercial Advertiser
Commonweal
Cosmopolitan
Craftsman
Current Literature
De Bow's Review
Delo
Delo Naroda
Douglass' Monthly
Engineering Magazine
Foreign Policy
Forum
Free Russia (New York)
Golos Moskvy
Gunton's Magazine
Haaretz
Harper's Magazine
Harper's Weekly

Independent
Istoricheskii Vestnik
Izvestiia
Izvestiia Obshchestva sblizheniia mezhdu Rossiei i Amerikoi
Journal de St. Petersburg
Journal of Commerce
Judge
Kansas City Times
Krasnyi arkhiv
Krokodil
Life
Living Age
Los Angeles Times
McClure's Magazine
Moskovskie vedomosti
Moskovskii Ezhenedel'nik
Munsey's Magazine
Muzykal'nyi svet
National Intelligencer
National Review
Nedelia
New Englander and Yale Review
New Republic
New York Evening Post
New York Herald
New York Sun
New York Times
New York World
Newsday
Newsweek
Nile's National Register
North American Review
Northwestern Miller
Novoe Vremia
Oteshestvennye Zapiski
Outlook
Panteon
Philadelphia Inquirer
Pokoiashchiisia Trudoliubets
Political Science Quarterly
Pribavlenie k Moskovskim vedomostiam
Puck
Raleigh Register

Rech'
Review of Reviews
Rizhskii Vestnik
Russkaia mysl
Russkie vedomosti
Russkii Arkhiv
Russkoe slovo
S.-Peterburgskie vedomosti
Salt Lake Tribune
San Francisco Call
San Francisco Examiner
Scribner's Magazine
Sovremennik
The Christian Advocate
The Economist
The Literary Digest
The Military Monitor, and American Register
The Nation
The National Geographic Magazine
The Providence Journal
The Riverdale Press
Trudoliubivaia pchela
UC Riverside News
United States Magazine and Democratic Review
Utro Rossii
Vestnik Evropy
Vestnik promyshlennosti
Vestnik Russko-Amerikanskoi Torgovoi Palaty
Vital Speeches of the Day
Wall Street Journal
Washington Post
Woman's Journal
World's Work
Zemshchina
Zhurnal putey soobshcheniia

WEB SITES (GOVERNMENT, NGO, MEDIA)

BBC, www.bbc.com
CNN, www.cnn.com
IA Realist, https://realtribune.ru
Index on Censorship, www.indexoncensorship.org
Lawfare, www.lawfaremedia.org

NBC news, www.nbcnews.com

Official Internet Resources of the President of Russia, http://kremlin.ru

OpenDemocracy, www.opendemocracy.net

Postsocialism, https://postsocialism.org

Radio Free Europe – Radio Liberty, www.rferl.org

RAND Corporation, www.rand.org

Reliefweb, https://reliefweb.int

Reuters, www.reuters.com

Russia Matters, www.russiamatters.org

The Ministry of Foreign Affairs of the Russian Federation, https://mid.ru

The White House, www.whitehouse.gov

SECONDARY SOURCES

Ackerman, Kenneth D. *Trotsky in New York, 1917: A Radical on the Eve of Revolution.* New York: Counterpoint, 2016.

Adamsky, Dmitry. "'Not Crying Wolf': Soviet Intelligence and the 1983 War Scare," in Leopoldo Nuti, Frederic Bozo, Marie-Pierre Rey, and Bernd Rother, eds. *The Euromissile Crisis and the End of the Cold War.* Washington: Woodrow Wilson Center Press, 2015, 49–65.

Adas, Michael. *Dominance by Design: Technological Imperatives and America's Civilizing Mission.* Cambridge, MA: Belknap Press, 2006.

Adler, Les K. and Thomas G. Paterson, "Red Fascism: The Merger of Nazi Germany and Soviet Russia in the American Image of Totalitarianism, 1930's–1950's," *American Historical Review*, Vol. 70, No. 4 (April 1970), 1046–1064.

Alexandrov, Vladimir. *The Black Russian.* New York: Atlantic Monthly Press, 2013.

Allen, Robert V. *Russia Looks at America: The View to 1917.* Washington: Library of Congress, 1988.

Alpers, Benjamin L. *Dictators, Democracy, and American Public Culture: Envisioning the Totalitarian Enemy, 1920s–1950s.* Chapel Hill: University of North Carolina Press, 2003.

Ambrose, Stephen E. *D Day: June 6, 1944. The Climactic Battle of World War II.* New York: Simon & Schuster, 1995.

Ambrose, Stephen E. *Eisenhower,* Vol. II. New York: Simon & Schuster, 1984.

Ambrose, Stephen E. *Nixon: Ruin and Recovery, 1973–1990.* New York: Simon & Schuster, 1991.

Anderson, Stuart. *Race and Rapprochement: Anglo-Saxonism and Anglo-American Relations, 1895–1904.* Rutherford, NJ: Fairleigh Dickinson University, 1981.

Andrew, Christopher and Vasili Mitrokhin, *The World Was Going Our Way: The KGB and the Battle for the Third World.* New York: Basic Books, 2005.

Anschel, Eugene, ed. *The American Image of Russia, 1775–1917.* New York: Frederick Ungar, 1974.

Arel, Dominque and Jesse Driscoll. *Ukraine's Unnamed War: Before the Russian Invasion of 2022.* Cambridge: Cambridge University Press, 2023.

Arbatov, Alexei. "What Lessons Learned?" in Kiron Skinner, ed. *Turning Points in Ending the Cold War.* Stanford: Hoover Institution Press, 2008, 40–62.

Arnesen, Eric. "No 'Graver Danger': Black Anticommunism, the Communist Party, and the Race Question," *Labor: Studies in Working-Class History of the Americas,* Vol. 3, No. 4 (Winter 2006), 13–52.

Aron, Leon. *Yeltsin: A Revolutionary Life.* New York: St. Martin's Press, 2000.

Arustamova, Anna A. *Russko-amerikanskii dialog XIX veka: Istoriko-literaturnyi aspekt.* Perm': Permskii gosudarstvennyi universitet, 2008.

Ashby, LeRoy and Rod Gramer, *Fighting the Odds: The Life of Senator Frank Church.* Pullman, WA: Washington State University Press, 1994.

Askew, William C. "Efforts to Improve Russo-American Relations before the First World War: The John Hays Hammond Mission," *Slavonic and East European Studies,* Vol. 31 (December 1952), 179–185.

Asmus, Ronald D. *A Little War That Shook the World: Georgia, Russia, and the Future of the West.* New York: Palgrave Macmillan, 2010.

Bacino, Leo J. *Reconstructing Russia: U.S. Policy in Revolutionary Russia, 1917–1922.* Kent, OH: Kent State University Press, 1999.

Bail, Christopher A., Brian Guay, Emily Maloney et al. "Assessing the Russian Internet Research Agency's Impact on the Political Attitudes and Behaviors of American Twitter Users in Late 2017," *Proceedings of the National Academy of Sciences,* Vol. 117, No. 1 (January 7, 2020), 243–250.

Bailes, Kendall. "The American Connection: Ideology and the Transfer of American Technology to the Soviet Union, 1917–1941," *Comparative Studies in Society and History,* Vol. 23, No. 3 (July 1981), 421–448.

Bailey, Thomas A. *America Faces Russia: Russian–American Relations from Early Times to Our Day.* Ithaca, NY: Cornell University Press, 1950.

Baker, Peter and Susan Glasser. *Kremlin Rising: Vladimir Putin's Russia and the End of Revolution.* New York: Scribner, 2005.

Baker, Peter. *Days of Fire: Bush and Cheney in the White House.* New York: Doubleday, 2013.

Baldwin, Kate A. *Beyond the Color Line and the Iron Curtain: Reading Encounters between Black and Red, 1922–1963.* Durham, NC: Duke University Press, 2002.

Baldwin, Kate A. *The Racial Imaginary of the Cold War Kitchen: From Sokol'niki Park to Chicago's South Side.* Hanover, NH: Dartmouth College Press, 2016.

Ball, Alan M. *Imagining America: Influence and Images in Twentieth-Century Russia.* Lanham, MD: Rowman & Littlefield, 2003.

Ball, Alan M. *Liberty's Tears: Soviet Portraits of the "American Way of Life" during the Cold War.* New York: Oxford University Press, 2016.

Banerjee, Maria. "'The American Revolver': An Essay on Dostoevsky's *The Devils,*" *Modern Fiction Studies,* Vol. 27, No. 2 (1981), 278–283.

Barghoorn, Frederick C. *The Soviet Image of the United States: A Study in Distortion.* New York: Harcourt Brace, 1950.

Barnett, Michael N. *The Star and the Stripes: A History of the Foreign Policies of American Jews.* Princeton: Princeton University Press, 2016.

Barrett, James R. *William Z. Foster and the Tragedy of American Radicalism.* Urbana: University of Illinois Press, 1999.

Bartel, Fritz. *The Triumph of Broken Promises: The End of the Cold War and the Rise of Neoliberalism.* Cambridge, MA: Harvard University Press, 2022.

Bassin, Mark. "Turner, Solov'ev, and the 'Frontier Hypothesis': The Nationalist Signification of Open Spaces," *The Journal of Modern History,* Vol. 65, No. 3 (September 1993), 473–511.

Bassin, Mark and Gonzalo Pozo, eds. *The Politics of Eurasianism: Identity, Popular Culture and Russia's Foreign Policy.* Lanham, MD: Rowman & Littlefield, 2017.

Baumgart, Winfried. *Deutsche Ostpolitik 1918.* Vienna and Munich: Oldenbourg, 1966.

Beckerman, Gal. *When They Come for Us, We'll Be Gone: The Epic Struggle to Save Soviet Jewry.* Boston: Houghton Mifflin, 2010.

Behringer, Paul J. Welch. "Images of Empire: Depictions of America in Late Imperial Russian Editorial Cartoons," *Russian History,* Vol. 45, No. 4 (2018), 279–318.

Belmonte, Laura A. *Selling the American Way: U.S. Propaganda and the Cold War.* Philadelphia: University of Pennsylvania Press, 2008.

Belohlavek J. M. *"Let the Eagle Soar!": The Foreign Policy of Andrew Jackson.* Lincoln, NE and London: University of Nebraska Press, 1985.

Belton, Catherine. *Putin's People: How the KGB Took Back Russia and Then Took on the West.* New York: Farrar, Straus and Giroux, 2020.

Bennett, M. Todd. *One World, Big Screen: Hollywood, the Allies, and World War II.* Chapel Hill: University of North Carolina Press, 2012.

Benze, James G., Jr. *Nancy Reagan on the White House Stage.* Lawrence, KS: University Press of Kansas, 2005.

Berkhoff, Karel C. *Motherland in Danger: Soviet Propaganda during World War II.* Cambridge, MA: Harvard University Press, 2012.

Berquist, Harold E., Jr. "Henry Middleton and the Arbitrament of the Anglo-American Slave Controversy by Tsar Alexander I," *The South Carolina Historical Magazine,* Vol. 82, No. 1 (January 1981), 20–31.

Beschloss, Michael R. and Strobe Talbott. *At the Highest Levels: The Inside Story of the End of the Cold War.* Boston: Little, Brown, 1993.

Best, Gary D. "Financing a Foreign War: Jacob H. Schiff and Japan, 1904–05," *American Jewish Historical Quarterly,* Vol. 61, No. 4 (June 1972), 313–324.

Best, Gary D. *To Free a People: American Jewish Leaders and the Jewish Problem in Eastern Europe, 1890–1914.* Westport, CT: Greenwood Press, 1982.

Bjork, Rebecca S. *The Strategic Defense Initiative: Symbolic Containment of the Nuclear Threat.* Albany, NY: State University of New York Press, 1992.

Black, J. L. "Setting the Tone: Misinformation and Disinformation from Kyiv, Moscow, Washington and Brussels in 2014," in J. L. Black and Michael Johns, eds. *The Return of the Cold War: Ukraine, the West and Russia.* London: Routledge, 2016, 163–189.

Black, J. L. *Russia Faces NATO Expansion: Bearing Gifts or Bearing Arms?* Lanham, MD: Rowman & Littlefield, 2000.

Blakely, Allison, "American Influences on Russian Reformist Thought in the Era of the French Revolution," *Russian Review*, Vol. 52, No. 4 (October 1993), 451–471.

Bliemaier, J. K. "Cassius Marcellus Clay in St. Petersburg," *The Register of the Kentucky Historical Society*, Vol.73, No. 3 (1975), 263–287.

Blight, James G. and Janet M. Lang, "FORUM: When Empathy Failed: Using Critical Oral History to Reassess the Collapse of U.S.–Soviet Détente in the Carter–Brezhnev Years," with commentaries, *Journal of Cold War Studies*, Vol. 12, No. 2 (Spring 2010), 29–109.

Boehling, Rebecca L. *A Question of Priorities: Democratic Reforms and Economic Recovery in Postwar Germany.* Providence: Berghahn Books, 1996.

Bogoslaw, Laurence. *Russians on Trump: Press Coverage and Commentary.* Minneapolis: East View Press, 2018.

Bolkhovinov, N. N. *Doktrina Monro: Proiskhozhdenie i kharakter.* Moscow: Izdatel'stvo Instituta mezhdunarodnykh otnoshenii, 1959.

Bolkhovitinov, N. N., ed. *Istoriia Russkoi Ameriki*, 3 vols. Moscow: Mezhdunarodnye otnosheniia, 1997–1999.

Bolkhovitinov, N. N. *Russia and the American Revolution.* Tallahassee, FL: Diplomatic Press, 1976.

Bolkhovitinov, N. N. *Russko-amerikanskie otnosheniia i prodazha Aliaski: 1834–1867.* Moscow: Nauka, 1990.

Bolkhovitinov, N. N. *Russko-amerikanskie otnosheniia, 1815–1832.* Moscow: Nauka, 1975.

Bolkhovitinov, Nikolai N. "The Declaration of Independence: A View from Russia," *The Journal of American History*, Vol. 85, No. 4 (March 1999), 1389–1398.

Bolkhovitinov, N. N. and V. N. Ponomarev. "Amerikanskie vrachi v Krymskoi voine," *SShA: Ekonomika. Politika. Ideologia*, No. 6 (1980), 63–69.

Bonnell, Victoria, Ann Cooper, and Gregory Freidin. *Russia at the Barricades: Eyewitness Accounts of the August 1991 Coup.* Armonk, NY: M. E. Sharpe, 1994.

Bordiugov, Gennadi. "The Popular Mood in the Unoccupied Soviet Union: Continuity and Change during the War," in Robert W. Thurston and Bern Bonwetsch, eds. *The People's War: Responses to World War II in the Soviet Union.* Urbana: University of Illinois Press, 2000.

Borenstein, Eliot. *Plots against Russia: Conspiracy and Fantasy after Socialism.* Ithaca, NY: Cornell University Press, 2019.

Borovik, Artyom. *The Hidden War.* New York: Grove Press, 1990.

Borozna, Angela. *The Sources of Russian Foreign Policy Assertiveness*. Cham: Springer International Publishing, 2022.

Borshchevskaya, Anna. *Putin's War in Syria: Russian Foreign Policy and the Price of America's Absence*. London: I.B. Tauris, 2021.

Bradley, Joseph. *Guns for the Tsar: American Technology and the Small Arms Industry in Nineteenth-Century Russia*. DeKalb: Northern Illinois University Press, 1990.

Bradley, Mark. *Imagining Vietnam and America: The Making of Postcolonial Vietnam, 1919–1950*. Chapel Hill: University of North Carolina Press, 2000.

Braithwaite, Rodric. *Afgantsy: The Russians in Afghanistan, 1979–89*. New York: Oxford University Press, 2011.

Brandenberger, David. *Propaganda State in Crisis: Soviet Ideology, Indoctrination, and Terror under Stalin, 1927–1941*. New Haven: Yale University Press, 2011.

Brands, Hal. "Progress Unseen: U.S. Arms Control Policy and the Origins of Détente, 1963–1968," *Diplomatic History*, Vol. 30, No. 2 (April 2006), 253–285.

Brands, Hal. *From Berlin to Baghdad: America's Search for Purpose in the Post-Cold War World*. Lexington: University Press of Kentucky, 2008.

Brands, Hal. *Making the Unipolar Moment: U.S. Foreign Policy and the Rise of the Post-Cold War Order*. Ithaca, NY: Cornell University Press, 2015.

Brodsky, Roman Mikhailovich. *Amerikanskaia ekspansiia v Severo-Vostochnom Kitae. 1898–1905*. L'vov: Izdatel'stvo L'vovskogo Universiteta, 1905.

Brogi, Alessandro. *Confronting America: The Cold War between the United States and the Communists in France and Italy*. Chapel Hill: University of North Carolina Press, 2011.

Brooks, Jeffrey. "Official Xenophobia and Popular Cosmopolitanism in Early Soviet Russia," *American Historical Review*, Vol. 97, No. 5 (December 1992), 1431–1448.

Brooks, Jeffrey. "The Press and Its Message: Images of America in the 1920s and 1930s," in Sheila Fitzpatrick, Alexander Rabinowitch, and Richard Stites, eds. *Russia in the Era of NEP: Explorations in Soviet Society and Culture*. Bloomington: Indian University Press, 1991, 231–252.

Brooks, Jeffrey. "Stalin's Ghost: Cold War Culture and U.S.–Soviet Relations," in Klaus Larres and Kenneth Osgood, eds. *The Cold War after Stalin's Death: A Missed Opportunity for Peace?* Lanham, MD: Rowman & Littlefield, 2006, 115–134.

Brooks, Jeffrey. "When the Cold War Did Not End: The Soviet Peace Offensive of 1953 and the American Response," Kennan Institute Occasional Paper No. 278, Washington: Woodrow Wilson International Center for Scholars, 2000, 1–19.

Brooks, Jeffrey. *When Russia Learned to Read: Literacy and Popular Literature, 1861–1917*. Princeton: Princeton University Press, 1985.

Browder, Robert Paul. *The Origins of Soviet–American Diplomacy*. Princeton: Princeton University Press, 1953.

Brown, Archie. *Seven Years That Changed the World: Perestroika in Perspective*. New York: Oxford University Press, 2007

Brown, Archie. *The Human Factor: Gorbachev, Reagan, and Thatcher, and the End of the Cold War*. New York: Oxford University Press, 2020.

Brown, Kate. *Manual for Survival: A Chernobyl Guide to the Future*. New York: W. W. Norton, 2019.

Brown, Peggy Ann. "Diplomatic Farmers: Iowans and the 1955 Agricultural Delegation to the Soviet Union," *The Annals of Iowa*, Vol. 72, No. 1 (Winter 2013), 31–62.

Buhle, Paul M. and Edward Rice-Maximin. *William Appleman Williams: The Tragedy of Empire*. New York: Routledge, 2011.

Bucklin, Steven J. "The Wilsonian Legacy in Political Science: Denna F. Fleming, Frederick L. Schuman, and Quincy Wright," Ph.D. thesis, University of Iowa, 1993.

Bundy, William. *A Tangled Web: The Making of Foreign Policy in the Nixon Presidency*. New York: Hill and Wang, 1998.

Burds, Jeffrey. "The Early Cold War in Soviet West Ukraine, 1944–1948," Carl Beck Papers in Russian and East European Studies, Number 1505, 2001.

Byrnes, Robert Francis. *A History of Russian and East European Studies in the United States*. Lanham, Maryland: University Press of America, 1994.

Bystrova, I. V. *Lend-liz dlia SSSR: Ekonomika, tekhnika, liudi (1941–1945)*. Moscow: Izdatel'stvo "Kuchkovo pole," 2019.

Bystrova, I. V. *Potselui cherez okean: "Bol'shaia troika" v svete lichnykh kontaktov (1941–1945 gg.)*. Moscow: Rosspen, 2011.

Cahn, Anne Hessing. *Killing Détente: The Right Attacks the CIA*. University Park, PA: Pennsylvania State University Press, 1998.

Caldwell, Dan. "US Domestic Politics and the Demise of Détente," in Odd Arne Westad, ed. *The Fall of Détente: Soviet–American Relations during the Carter Years*. Oslo: Scandinavian University Press, 1997, 95–117.

Caldwell, Jay E. *Erskine Caldwell, Margaret Bourke-White, and the Popular Front: Photojournalism in Russia*. Athens, GA: University of Georgia Press, 2016.

Carbone, Cristina. "Staging the Kitchen Debate: How Splitnik Got Normalized in the United States," in Ruth Oldenziel and Karin Zachmann, eds. *Cold War Kitchen: Americanization, Technology, and European Users*. Cambridge, MA: MIT Press, 2009, 59–82.

Carleton, Gregory. *Russia: The Story of War*. Cambridge, MA: Harvard University Press, 2007.

Carley, Michael Jabara. *1939: The Alliance That Never Was and the Coming of World War II*. Chicago: Ivan Dee, 1999.

Carley, Michael Jabara. *Silent Conflict: A Hidden History of Early Soviet–Western Relations*. Lanham, MD: Rowman & Littlefield, 2014.

Carley, Michael Jabara. *Stalin's Gamble: The Search for Allies against Hitler, 1930–1936*. Toronto: University of Toronto Press, 2023.

Carroll, Peter N. *The Odyssey of the Abraham Lincoln Brigade: Americans in the Spanish Civil War*. Stanford: Stanford University Press, 1994.

Carstensen, Fred V. *American Enterprise in Foreign Markets: Singer and International Harvester in Imperial Russia*. Chapel Hill: University of North Carolina Press, 1984.

Casey, Steven. *Selling the Korean War: Propaganda, Politics, and Public Opinion*. New York: Oxford University Press, 2008.

Cassella-Blackburn, Michael. *The Donkey, the Carrot, and the Club: William C. Bullitt and Soviet–American Relations, 1917–1948*. Westport, CT: Praeger, 2004.

Caute, David. *The Dancer Defects: The Struggle for Cultural Supremacy during the Cold War*. Oxford: Oxford University Press, 2003.

Chang, Gordon H. *Fateful Ties: A History of America's Preoccupation with China*. Cambridge, MA: Harvard University Press, 2015.

Chapman, Michael E. *Arguing Americanism: Franco Lobbyists, Roosevelt's Foreign Policy, and the Spanish Civil War*. Kent, OH: Kent State University Press, 2011.

Charap, Samuel and Timothy J. Colton. *Everyone Loses: The Ukraine Crisis and the Ruinous Contest for Post-Soviet Eurasia*. New York: Routledge, 2017.

Chollet, Derek. *The Long Game: How Obama Defied Washington and Redefined America's Role in the World*. New York: Public Affairs, 2016.

Christian, Reginald Frank. *Alexis Aladin: The Tragedy of Exile*. New York: Legas, 1999.

Chubarian, Alexandr Oganovich, ed. *Rossiia v sisteme mezhdunarodnykh otnoshenii nakanune i v gody Pervoi mirovoi voiny*, Vol. 2: *Rossiia i sojuzniki*. Moscow, Mezhdunarodye otnosheniia, 2020.

Chubariyan, A. O. and V. O. Pechatnov, "Molotov 'the Liberal': Stalin's 1945 Criticism of his Deputy," *Cold War History*, Vol. 1, No. 1 (August 2000), 129–140.

Clarke, Thurston. *JFK's Last Hundred Days: The Transformation of a Man and the Emergence of a Great President*. New York: Penguin, 2013.

Clemens, Diane Shaver. *Yalta*. New York: Oxford University Press, 1970.

Clover, Charles. *Black Wind, White Snow: The Rise of Russia's New Nationalism*. New Haven: Yale University Press, 2016.

Coben, Stanley. *A. Mitchell Palmer: Politician*. New York: Columbia University Press, 1963.

Cogliano, Francis D. *Emperor of Liberty: Thomas Jefferson's Foreign Policy*. New Haven: Yale University Press, 2014.

Cohen, Naomi W. "The Abrogation of the Russo-American Treaty of 1832," *Jewish Social Studies*, Vol. 25, No. 1 (January 1963), 3–41

Cohen, Stephen F. *Failed Crusade: America and the Tragedy of Post-communist Russia*. New York: W. W. Norton, 2000.

Cohen, Stephen F. *Soviet Fates and Lost Alternatives: From Stalinism to the New Cold War*. New York: Columbia University Press, 2011.

Cohen, Stephen F. *War with Russia? From Putin and Ukraine to Trump and Russiagate*. New York: Hot Books, 2019.

Coll, Steve. *Private Empire: Exxonmobil and American Power.* New York: Penguin, 2012.

Colton, Timothy J. *Yeltsin: A Life.* New York: Basic Books, 2008.

Corkin, Paul K. *Big Daddy from the Pedernales: Lyndon Baines Johnson.* Boston: Twayne, 1986.

Cortada, James W. *Two Nations over Time: Spain and the United States, 1776–1977.* Westport, CT: Greenwood Press, 1978.

Cortright, David. *Peace Works: The Citizen's Role in Ending the Cold War.* Boulder: Westview Press, 1993.

Costigliola, Frank. "After Roosevelt's Death: Dangerous Emotions, Divisive Discourses, and the Abandoned Alliance," *Diplomatic History,* Vol. 34, No. 1 (January 2010), 1–23.

Costigliola, Frank. "The Creation of Memory and Myth: Stalin's 1946 Election Speech and the Soviet Threat," in Martin J. Medhurst and H. W. Brands, eds. *Critical Reflections on the Cold War: Linking Rhetoric and History.* College Station: Texas A&M University Press, 2000, 38–54.

Costigliola, Frank. "'I Had Come as a Friend': Emotion, Culture, and Ambiguity in the Formation of the Cold War, 1943–45," *Cold War History,* Vol. 1, No. 1 (August 2000), 103–128.

Costigliola, Frank. *Kennan: A Life between Worlds.* Princeton: Princeton University Press, 2023.

Costigliola, Frank. "Kennan Encounters Russia, 1933–1937," in Choi Chatterjee and Beth Holmgren, eds. *Americans Experience Russia: Encountering the Enigma, 1917 to the Present* (New York: Routledge, 2013), 50–66.

Costigliola, Frank. *Roosevelt's Lost Alliances: How Personal Politics Helped Start the Cold War.* Princeton: Princeton University Press, 2012.

Craig, Campbell and Sergey Radchenko, *The Atomic Bomb and the Origins of the Cold War.* New Haven: Yale University Press, 2008.

Craig, Campbell. "The Nuclear Revolution: A Product of the Cold War, or Something More?" in Richard Immerman and Petra Goedde, eds. *The Oxford Handbook of the Cold War.* Oxford: Oxford University Press, 2013.

Craig, R. Bruce. *Treasonable Doubt: The Harry Dexter White Spy Case.* Lawrence, KS: University Press of Kansas, 2004.

Crane, Daniel M. and Thomas A. Breslin. *An Ordinary Relationship: American Opposition to Republican Revolution in China.* Miami: Florida International University Press, 1986.

Crile, George. *Charlie Wilson's War.* New York: Grove Press, 2003.

Daniels, Robert V. *Russia: The Roots of Confrontation.* Cambridge, MA: Harvard University Press, 1985.

D'Anieri, Paul. *Ukraine and Russia: From Civilized Divorce to Uncivil War.* Cambridge: Cambridge University Press, 2019.

Daalder, Ivo H. and Michael E. O'Hanlon, *Winning Ugly: NATO's War to Save Kosovo.* Washington: Brookings Institution Press, 1999.

Daigle, Craig. *The Limits of Détente: The United States, the Soviet Union, and the Arab–Israeli Conflict, 1969–1973*. New Haven: Yale University Press, 2012.

Dallek, Robert. *Flawed Giant: Lyndon Johnson and His Times*. New York: Oxford University Press, 1998.

Dallek, Robert. *Franklin D. Roosevelt and American Foreign Policy, 1932–1945*. New York: Oxford University Press, 1979.

David-Fox, Michael. "The Iron Curtain as Semipermeable Membrane," in Patryk Babiracki and Kenyon Zimmer, eds. *Cold War Crossings: International Travel and Exchange across the Soviet Bloc, 1940s–1960s* (College Station: Texas A&M University Press, 2014), 14–39.

David-Fox, Michael. *Showcasing the Great Experiment: Cultural Diplomacy and Western Visitors to the Soviet Union, 1921–1941*. New York: Oxford University Press, 2012.

Davies, Sarah and James Harris. *Stalin's World: Dictating the Soviet Order*. New Haven: Yale University Press, 2014.

Davis, Donald E. and Eugene P. Trani. *Distorted Mirrors: Americans and Their Relations with Russia and China in the Twentieth Century*. Columbia: University of Missouri Press, 2002.

Davis, Donald E. and Eugene P. Trani. *The First Cold War: The Legacy of Woodrow Wilson in U.S.–Soviet Relations*. Columbia: University of Missouri Press, 2002.

Davis, Jerome. *The Russian Immigrants*. New York: Macmillan Co., 1922.

Dean, Vera Micheles. *The United States and Russia*. Cambridge, MA: Harvard University Press, 1947.

Debo, Richard K. *Revolution and Survival: The Foreign Policy of Soviet Russia, 1917–1918*. Toronto: University of Toronto Press, 1979.

Dekel-Chen, Jonathan. "Philanthropists, Commissars, and American Statesmanship Meet in Soviet Crimea, 1922–37," *Diplomatic History*, Vol. 27, No. 3 (June 2003), 353–376

Dekel-Chen, Jonathan. *Farming the Red Land: Jewish Agricultural Colonization and Local Soviet Power, 1924–1941*. New Haven: Yale University Press, 2005.

Delegard, Kirsten Marie. *Battling Miss Bolsheviki: The Origins of Female Conservatism in the United States*. Philadelphia: University of Pennsylvania Press, 2012.

Dennett, Tyler. *Roosevelt and the Russo-Japanese War*. New York: Doubleday, Page & Co., 1925.

Dennis, Alfred L. P. *Adventures in American Diplomacy, 1896–1906*. New York: E. P. Dutton & Co., 1928.

Deutscher, Isaac. *The Prophet Unarmed: Trotsky: 1921–1929*. New York: Oxford University Press, 1970.

DeYoung, Karen. *Soldier: The Life of Colin Powell*. New York: Knopf, 2006.

Dobbins, James F. *After the Taliban: Nation-Building in Afghanistan*. Washington: Potomac Books, 2008.

Dobbs, Michael. *One Minute to Midnight: Kennedy, Khrushchev, and Castro on the Brink of Nuclear War*. New York: Knopf, 2008.

Dobrynin, Sergei. "The Silver Curtain: Representations of the West in the Soviet Cold War Films," *History Compass*, Vol. 7, No. 3 (2009), 862–878.

Dobson, Alan P. "The Reagan Administration, Economic Warfare, and Starting to Close Down the Cold War," *Diplomatic History*, Vol. 29, No. 3 (June 2005), 531–556.

Donaghy, Aaron. *The Second Cold War: Carter, Reagan, and the Politics of Foreign Policy.* Cambridge: Cambridge University Press, 2021.

Dow, R. A. and R. L. Wilson. "The Czar's Colts," *Nineteenth Century*, Vol. 6, No. 4 (1980), 34–37.

Drake, Richard. *The Education of an Anti-imperialist: Robert La Follette and U.S. Expansion.* Madison: University of Wisconsin Press, 2013.

Draper, Theodore. *American Communism and Soviet Russia.* New York: Vintage, 1986 (1st ed. 1960).

Duberman, Martin Bauml. *Paul Robeson.* New York: Knopf, 1988.

Dubie, Alain. *Frank A. Golder: An Adventure of a Historian in Quest of Russian History.* Boulder: East European Monographs, 1989.

Dudziak, Mary. *Cold War Civil Rights: Race and the Image of American Democracy.* Princeton: Princeton University Press, 2000.

Duffy, Gloria Charmian. "Crisis Politics: The Carter Administration and Soviet Troops in Cuba, 1979," Ph.D. thesis, Columbia University, 1991.

Dull, Jonathan R. *A Diplomatic History of the American Revolution.* New Haven: Yale University Press, 1987, 128–133.

Dulles, Foster Rhea. *The Road to Teheran: The Story of Russia and America, 1781–1943.* Princeton: Princeton University Press, 1944.

Dumbrell, John. *President Lyndon Johnson and Soviet Communism.* New York: Manchester University Press, 2004.

Dunn, Dennis J. *Caught between Roosevelt and Stalin: America's Ambassadors to Moscow.* Lexington: The University Press of Kentucky, 1998.

Dvoichenko-Markova, Eufrosina. "Dzhon Smit v Rossii," *Novaia i noveishaia istoriia*, No. 3 (1976), 158–160.

Eames, Anthony M. *A Voice in Their Own Destiny: Reagan, Thatcher, and Public Diplomacy in the Nuclear 1980s.* Amherst: University of Massachusetts Press, 2023.

Eblen, Anna L. and Martha Jane Eblen, eds. *Betty Bumpers: Champion of Childhood Immunization and Peace.* Lanham, MD: Rowman & Littlefield, 2013.

Edemskiy, Andrey. "Dealing with Bonn: Leonid Brezhnev and the Soviet Response to West German Ostpolitik," in Carole Fink and Bernd Schaefer, eds. *Ostpolitik, 1969–1974: European and Global Responses.* Cambridge: Cambridge University Press, 2008, 15–38.

Eisenberg, Carolyn Woods. *Drawing the Line: The American Decision to Divide Germany, 1944–1949.* Cambridge: Cambridge University Press, 1996.

Eliot, Marc. *American Rebel: The Life of Clint Eastwood.* New York: Harmony Books, 2009.

Ellis, L. Ethan. *Frank B. Kellogg and American Foreign Relations, 1925–1929*. New Brunswick: Rutgers University Press, 1961.

Engel, Jeffrey A. *When the World Seemed New: George H. W. Bush and the End of the Cold War*. Boston: Houghton Mifflin Harcourt, 2017.

Engel', Valerii Viktorovich. *"Evreiskii Vopros" v russko-amerikanskikh otnosheniiakh: Na primere "pasportnogo" voprosa 1864–1913*. Moscow: Nauka, 1998.

Engelstein, Laura. *Russia in Flames: War, Revolution, Civil War, 1914–1921*. New York: Oxford University Press, 2017.

Engerman, David C. *Know Your Enemy: The Rise and Fall of America's Soviet Experts*. New York: Oxford University Press, 2009.

Engerman, David C. *Modernization from the Other Shore: American Intellectuals and the Romance of Russian Development*. Cambridge, MA: Harvard University Press, 2003.

English, Robert D. *Russia and the Idea of the West: Gorbachev, Intellectuals, and the End of the Cold War*. New York: Columbia University Press, 2000.

Ershova, E. N. *Dvizhenie za mir, protiv militarizma i voiny v SShA (1965–1978 gg.)*. Moscow: Nauka, 1980.

Esthus, Raymond A. *Theodore Roosevelt and the International Rivalries*. Waltham: Ginn-Blaisdell, 1970.

Etkind, Alexander. *Internal Colonization: Russia's Imperial Experience*. Cambridge: Polity Press, 2011.

Etkind, Alexander. *Roads Not Taken: An Intellectual Biography of William C. Bullitt*. Pittsburgh: University of Pittsburgh Press, 2017.

Etkind, Aleksander. *Tolkovanie puteshestvii: Rossiia i SShA v travelogakh i intertekstakh*. Moskva: Novoe literaturnoe obozrenie, 2001.

Evangelista, Matthew. *Unarmed Forces: The Transnational Movement to End the Cold War*. Ithaca, NY: Cornell University Press, 1999.

Evans, Frank B. "Carlo Bellini and His Russian Friend Fedor Karzhavin," *The Virginia Magazine of History and Biography*, Vol. 88, No. 3 (July 1980), 338–354.

Evans, Kelly J. and Jeanie M. Welch. *Witnessing Stalin's Justice: The United States and the Moscow Show Trials*. New York: Bloomsbury, 2023.

Fainberg, Dina. "A Portrait of a Journalist as a Cold War Expert," *Journalism History*, Vol. 41, No. 3 (Fall 2015), 153–164.

Fainberg, Dina. *Cold War Correspondents: Soviet and American Reporters on the Ideological Frontlines*. Baltimore: Johns Hopkins University Press, 2020.

Farnsworth, Beatrice. *William C. Bullitt and the Soviet Union*. Bloomington: Indiana University Press, 1967.

Farrow, Lee A. *Alexis in America: A Russian Grand Duke's Tour, 1871–1872*. Baton Rouge: Louisiana State University Press, 2014.

Farrow, Lee A. *Alexis in America: A Russian Grand Duke's Tour, 1871–1872*. Baton Rouge: Louisiana State University Press, 2014.

Farrow, Lee A. *Seward's Folly: A New Look at the Alaska Purchase*. Fairbanks: University of Alaska Press, 2016.

Fedorova, Milla. *Yankees in Petrograd, Bolsheviks in New York: America and Americans in Russian Literary Perception.* DeKalb: Northern Illinois University Press, 2013.

Fedorova, Svetlana. *Russkaia Amerika: Ot pervykh poselenii do prodazhi Aliaski. Konets XVIII veka–1867 god.* Moscow: Lomonosov, 2011.

Figes, Orlando and Boris Kolonitskii. *Interpreting the Russian Revolution: The Language and Symbols of 1917.* New Haven: Yale University Press, 1999.

Filene, Peter G. *Americans and the Soviet Experiment, 1917–1933.* Cambridge, MA: Harvard University Press, 1967.

Filimonova, Maria. *Dikhotomia "Svoi/Chuzhoi" i ee reprezentatsiia v politicheskoi kul'ture Amerikanskoi revolyutsii.* St. Petersburg: Aleteia, 2019.

Filitov, A. M. *"Kholodnaia voina": Istoriograficheskie diskussii na Zapade.* Moscow: Nauka, 1991.

Fink, Carole. *The Genoa Conference: European Diplomacy, 1921–1922.* Syracuse, NY: Syracuse University Press, 1993.

Finlay, David J., Ole R. Holsti, and Richard R. Fagen, *Enemies in Politics.* Chicago: Rand McNally & Company, 1967.

Fitzpatrick, Sheila, "The Civil War as a Formative Experience," in Abbot Gleason, Peter Kenez, and Richard Stites, eds. *Bolshevik Culture: Experiment and Order in the Russian Revolution.* Bloomington: Indiana University Press, 1985.

Fitzpatrick, Sheila. *Everyday Stalinism: Ordinary Life in Extraordinary Times: Soviet Russia in the 1930s.* New York: Oxford University Press, 1999.

Foglesong, David S. *America's Secret War against Bolshevism: U.S. Intervention in the Russian Civil War, 1917–1920.* Chapel Hill: University of North Carolina Press, 1995.

Foglesong, David S. *The American Mission and the "Evil Empire": The Crusade for a "Free Russia" since 1881.* Cambridge: Cambridge University Press, 2007.

Foglesong, David S. "Foreign Intervention," in Edward Acton, Vladimir Cherniaev, and William G. Rosenberg, eds. *Critical Companion to the Russian Revolution, 1914–1921.* London: Arnold, 1997.

Foglesong, David S. "How American and Soviet Women Transcended the Cold War," *Diplomatic History,* Vol. 46, No. 3 (June 2022), 527–548.

Foglesong, David S. "Istoki pervogo amerikanskogo krestovogo pokhoda za 'svobodnuiu Rossiiu,'" *Rossiia,* Vol. 21, No. 5 (2002), 104–118.

Foglesong, David S. "Redeeming Russia? American Missionaries and Tsarist Russia, 1886–1917," *Religion, State and Society,* Vol. 25, No. 4 (1997), 353–368.

Foglesong, David S. "Revolutionary Russia in American Eyes," *Vestnik Sankt Peterburgskogo universiteta,* Vol. 63, No. 3 (2018), 957–974.

Foglesong, David S. "The Face of the Enemy," *Raritan,* Vol. 39, No. 2 (2019), 161–174.

Foglesong, David S. "The Perils of Prophecy: American Predictions about Russia's Future since 1881," in V. V. Noskov and W. G. Rosenberg, eds. *Russia and the*

United States: Perceiving Each Other. St. Petersburg: Nestor-Istoriia, 2015, 282–298.

Foglesong, David S. "When the Russians Really Were Coming: Citizen Diplomacy and the End of Cold War Enmity in America," *Cold War History*, Vol. 20, No. 4 (2020), 419–440.

Forsberg, Randall Caroline Watson. *Toward a Theory of Peace: The Role of Moral Beliefs*. Ed. Matthew Evangelista and Neta C. Crawford. Ithaca, NY: Cornell University Press, 2020.

Fosler-Lussier, Danielle. *Music in America's Cold War Diplomacy*. Berkeley: University of California Press, 2015.

Foster, Carrie A. *The Women and the Warriors: The U.S. Section of the Women's International League for Peace and Freedom, 1915–1946*. Syracuse, NY: Syracuse University Press, 1995.

Fousek, John. *To Lead the Free World: American Nationalism and the Cultural Roots of the Cold War*. Chapel Hill: University of North Carolina Press, 2000.

Fredman, Zach. *The Tormented Alliance: American Servicemen and the Occupation of China, 1941–1949*. Chapel Hill: University of North Carolina Press, 2022.

Freeman, Stephanie L. *Dreams for a Decade: International Nuclear Abolitionism and the End of the Cold War*. Philadelphia: University of Pennsylvania Press, 2023.

Fried, Richard. *The Russians Are Coming! The Russians Are Coming! Pageantry and Patriotism in Cold-War America*. New York: Oxford University Press, 1999.

Friedman, Jeremy. *Shadow Cold War: The Sino-Soviet Competition for the Third World*. Chapel Hill: University of North Carolina Press, 2015.

Frye, Timothy. *Weak Strongman: The Limits of Power in Putin's Russia*. Princeton: Princeton University Press, 2021.

Frye, Timothy, Scott Gehlbach, Kyle Marquardt, and Ora Reuter. "Is Putin's Popularity Real?" *Post-Soviet Affairs*, Vol. 33, No. 1 (2016), 1–15.

Fursenko, Aleksandr and Timothy Naftali, *"One Hell of a Gamble: Khrushchev, Castro, and Kennedy 1958–1964*. New York: W. W. Norton, 1997.

Fursenko, Aleksandr and Timothy Naftali. *Khrushchev's Cold War*. New York: W. W. Norton, 2006.

Gabler, Neal. *Winchell: Gossip, Power and the Culture of Celebrity*. New York: Knopf, 1994.

Gaddis, John Lewis. *George F. Kennan: An American Life*. New York: Penguin, 2011.

Gaddis, John Lewis. *Russia, the Soviet Union, and the United States: An Interpretive History*, 2nd ed. New York: McGraw-Hill, 1990.

Gaddis, John Lewis. *The Cold War: A New History*. New York: Penguin, 2005.

Gaddis, John Lewis. *The United States and the Origins of the Cold War, 1941–1947*. New York: Columbia University Press, 1972.

Gaddis, John Lewis. *We Now Know: Rethinking Cold War History*. New York: Oxford University Press, 1997.

Gage, Beverly. *G-Man: J. Edgar Hoover and the Making of the American Century*. New York: Viking, 2022.

Galeotti, Mark. *We Need to Talk about Putin: How the West Gets Him Wrong.* London: Penguin, 2019.

Galkina, G. N. *Komitet sovetskikh zhenshchin: Stranitsy istorii (1941–1992).* Moscow: Izdatel'skii dom TONChU, 2013.

Gamache, Ray. "Breaking Eggs for a Holodomor: Walter Duranty, the *New York Times*, and the Denigration of Gareth Jones," *Journalism History*, Vol. 39, No. 4 (Winter 2014), 208–218.

Ganelin, Rafail Sh. "M. Gor'kii i amerikanskoe obshshestvo v 1906 godu," *Russkaia literatura*, No. 1 (1985), 200–222.

Ganelin, Rafail Sh. *Rossiia i SShA. 1914–1917: Ocherki istorii russko-amerikanskikh otnoshenii.* Leningrad: Nauka, 1969

Gardner, Lloyd. *Spheres of Influence: The Great Powers Partition Europe, from Munich to Yalta.* Chicago: Ivan Dee, 1993.

Garrels, Anne. *Putin Country: A Journey into the Real Russia.* New York: Farrar, Straus and Giroux, 2016.

Garthoff, Raymond L. *Détente and Confrontation: American–Soviet Relations from Nixon to Reagan.* Washington: Brookings Institution Press, 1985.

Garthoff, Raymond L. *The Great Transition: American–Soviet Relations and the End of the Cold War.* Washington: Brookings Institution Press, 1994.

Gati, Charles. *Failed Illusions: Moscow, Washington, Budapest, and the 1956 Hungarian Revolt.* Stanford: Stanford University Press, 2006.

Gavin, Francis J. "Nuclear Nixon: Ironies, Puzzles, and the Triumph of Realpolitik," in F. Logevall and A. Preston, eds. *Nixon in the World: American Foreign Relations, 1969–1977.* New York: Oxford University Press, 2008.

Geelhoed, E. Bruce. *Diplomacy Shot Down: The U-2 Crisis and Eisenhower's Aborted Mission to Moscow, 1959–1960.* Norman: University of Oklahoma Press, 2020.

Geist, Edward M. *Armageddon Insurance: Civil Defense in the United States and Soviet Union, 1945–1991.* Chapel Hill: University of North Carolina Press, 2019.

Gelber, Steven M. and Martin L. Cook, *Saving the Earth: The History of a Middle-Class Millenarian Movement.* Berkeley: University of California Press, 1990.

Gel'man, Vladimir. *Authoritarian Russia: Analyzing Post-Soviet Regime Changes.* Pittsburgh: University of Pittsburgh Press, 2015.

Geoghegan, Kate. "A Policy in Tension: The National Endowment for Democracy and the U.S. Response to the Collapse of the Soviet Union," *Diplomatic History*, Vol. 42, No. 5 (2018), 772–801.

Gerstle, Gary. *Working-Class Americanism: The Politics of Labor in a Textile City, 1914–1960.* Princeton: Princeton University Press, 1989.

Gessen, Masha. *Words Will Break Cement: The Passion of Pussy Riot.* New York: Penguin, 2014.

Getmant, Royal. *Turgenev in England and America.* Urbana: University of Illinois Press, 1941.

Geukjian, Ohannes. *The Russian Military Intervention in Syria.* Montreal: McGill-Queen's University Press, 2022.

Gilburd, Eleonory. "The Revival of Soviet Internationalism in the Mid to Late 1950s," in Denis Kozlov and Eleonory Gilburd, eds. *The Thaw: Soviet Society and Culture during the 1950s and 1960s.* Toronto: University of Toronto Press, 2013, 362–401.

Gilburd, Eleonory. *To See Paris and Die: The Soviet Lives of Western Culture.* Cambridge, MA: Harvard University Press, 2018.

Gimbel, John. *The American Occupation of Germany: Politics and the Military, 1945–1949.* Stanford: Stanford University Press, 1968.

Glad, Betty. *An Outsider in the White House: Jimmy Carter, His Advisers, and the Making of American Foreign Policy.* Ithaca, NY: Cornell University Press, 2009.

Gleason, Abbott. "Republic of Humbug: The Russian Nativist Critique of the United States, 1830–1930," *American Quarterly,* Vol. 44, No. 1 (March 1992), 1–23.

Gleason, John Howes. *The Genesis of Russophobia in Great Britain: A Study of the Interaction of Policy and Opinion.* Cambridge, MA: Harvard University Press, 1950.

Goldberg, Vicki. *Margaret Bourke-White: A Biography.* New York: Harper & Row, 1986.

Goldgeier, James M. and Michael McFaul. *Power and Purpose: U.S. Policy toward Russia after the Cold War.* Washington: Brookings Institution Press, 2003.

Goldman, Marshall I. *Petrostate: Putin, Power, and the New Russia.* New York: Oxford University Press, 2008.

Goldman, Wendy Z. and Donald Filtzer. *Fortress Dark and Stern: The Soviet Home Front during World War II.* New York: Oxford University Press, 2021.

Golubev, A. V. "Amerika v sovetskoi karikature 1920–1930-x godov," in *Rossiia i mir glazami drug druga: Iz istorii vzaimovospriatiia,* No. 4. Moscow, 2007.

Golubev, A. V. *"Podlinnyi lik zagranitsy": Obraz vneshnego mira v sovetskoi politichiskoi karikature, 1922–1941 gg.* Moscow: Tsentr gumanitarnykh initsiativ, 2018.

Goncharov, Sergei, John W. Lewis, and Xue Litai, *Uncertain Partners: Stalin, Mao, and the Korean War.* Stanford: Stanford University Press, 1993.

Good, Jane Elizabeth. "Strangers in a Strange Land: Five Russian Radicals Visit the United States 1890–1908," Ph.D. thesis, Washington, The American University, 1979.

Gordeeva, Irina. "'Fighting for Peace Is Everyone's Job': The Independent Peace Movement in the USSR and the Soviet View of Public Diplomacy in the 1980s," in Óscar J. Martín García and Rósa Magnúsdóttir, eds. *Machineries of Persuasion: European Soft Power and Public Diplomacy during the Cold War.* Berlin: Walter de Gruyter, 2019.

Gordon, Philip H. *Losing the Long Game: The False Promise of Regime Change in the Middle East.* New York: St. Martin's Press, 2020.

Gorsuch, Anne E. *All This Is Your World: Soviet Tourism at Home and Abroad after Stalin.* New York: Oxford University Press, 2011.

Goscilo, Helena and Margaret B. Goscilo. *Fade from Red. The Cold War Ex-enemy in Russian and American Film 1990–2005.* Washington: New Academic Publishing, 2014.

Govorchin, Gerald Gilbert. *From Russia to America with Love: A Study of the Russian Immigrants in the United States.* Pittsburgh: Dorrance Publishing Company, 1993.

Grachev, Andrei. *Gorbachev's Gamble: Soviet Foreign Policy and the End of the Cold War.* Cambridge: Polity Press, 2008.

Graham, Helen. "Spain Betrayed? The New Historical McCarthyism," *Science & Society*, Vol. 68, No. 3 (Fall 2004), 364–369.

Grayson, Benson L. *Russian–American Relations in World War I.* New York: Ungar, 1979.

Greenberg, David. *Nixon's Shadow: The History of an Image.* New York: W. W. Norton, 2003.

Greene, Samuel A. and Graeme B. Robertson. *Putin v. the People: The Perilous Politics of a Divided Russia.* New Haven: Yale University Press, 2019.

Greenwood, John T. "The American Observers of the Russo-Japanese War (1904–1905)," Ph.D. thesis, Kansas State University, 1971.

Griffiths, David M. "American Commercial Diplomacy in Russia, 1780 to 1783," *The William and Mary Quarterly*, Vol. 27. No. 3 (July 1970), 379–410.

Griffiths, David M. "An American Contribution to the Armed Neutrality of 1780," *The Russian Review*, Vol. 30. No. 2 (April 1971), 164–172.

Griffiths, David M. "Nikita Panin, Russian Diplomacy, and the American Revolution," *Slavic Review*, Vol. 28. No. 1 (March 1969), 1–24.

Griffiths, David M. *No Collusion! Catherine the Great and American Independence.* Ed. George E. Munro. Bloomington: Slavica, 2020.

Grinev, A. V. *Aliaska pod krylom dvuglavogo orla.* Moscow: Academia, 2018.

Grinev, Andrei V. "The First Russian Settlers in Alaska," *The Historian*, Vol. 75, No. 3 (Fall 2013), 443–474.

Grinevsky, Oleg. "The Crisis That Didn't Erupt: The Soviet–American Relationship, 1980–1983," in Kiron Skinner, ed. *Turning Points in Ending the Cold War.* Stanford: Hoover Institution Press, 2008, 63–92.

Grose, Peter. *Gentleman Spy: The Life of Allen Dulles.* Boston: Houghton Mifflin, 1994.

H'etso, Geyr. *Maksim Gor'kii: Sud'ba pisatelia.* Moscow: Nasledie, 1997.

Hahn, Gordon M. *Russia's Islamic Threat.* New Haven: Yale University Press, 2007.

Hahn, Peter L. *The United States, Great Britain, and Egypt, 1945–1956: Strategy and Diplomacy in the Early Cold War.* Chapel Hill: University of North Carolina Press, 1991.

Hale, Henry E. and Olga Kamenchuk, "Don't Call It a Cold War: Findings from the Russian–American Relations Survey 2019." Working Group Paper 10, July 2020. Cambridge, MA: Working Group on the Future of U.S.–Russia Relations.

Hallinan, Victoria. "The 1958 Tour of the Moiseyev Dance Company: A Window into American Perception," *Journal of History and Cultures*, No. 1 (2012), 51–64.

Hamby, Alonzo. *Man of the People: A Life of Harry S. Truman.* New York: Oxford University Press, 1995.

Hanhimäki, Jussi. *The Flawed Architect: Henry Kissinger and American Foreign Policy.* New York: Oxford University Press, 2004.

Hanni, Adrian. "'A Chance for a Propaganda Coup?' The Reagan Administration and *The Day After* (1983)," *Historical Journal of Film, Radio, and Television,* Vol. 36, No. 3 (2016), 415–435.

Harbutt, Fraser J. *Yalta 1945: Europe and America at the Crossroads.* Cambridge: Cambridge University Press, 2010.

Harmer, Tanya. *Allende's Chile and the Inter-American Cold War.* Chapel Hill: University of North Carolina Press, 2011.

Hasanli, Jamil. *At the Dawn of the Cold War: The Soviet–American Crisis over Iranian Azerbaijan, 1941–1946.* Lanham, MD: Rowman & Littlefield, 2006.

Haslam, Jonathan. *Russia's Cold War: From the October Revolution to the Fall of the Wall.* New Haven: Yale University Press, 2011.

Haslam, Jonathan. *The Spectre of War: International Communism and the Origins of World War II.* Princeton: Princeton University Press, 2021.

Hatzivassiliou, Evanthis. "Images of the Adversary: NATO Assessments of the Soviet Union, 1953–1964," *Journal of Cold War Studies,* Vol. 11, No. 2 (Spring 2009), 89–116.

Haywood, R. M. *Russia Enters the Railway Age, 1842–1855.* Boulder: East European Monographs, 1998.

Healy, Ann E. "Tsarist Anti-Semitism and Russian–American Relations," *Slavic Review,* Vol. 42, No. 3 (Fall 1983), 418–425.

Hecker, Cheryl. *An Accidental Journalist: The Adventures of Edmund Stevens, 1934–1945.* Columbia: University of Missouri Press, 2007.

Hedges, Chris. *War Is a Force That Gives Us Meaning.* New York: Public Affairs, 2002.

Heinrichs, Waldo. *Threshold of War: Franklin D. Roosevelt and American Entry into World War II.* New York: Oxford University Press, 1988.

Herlihy, Patricia. *The Alcoholic Empire: Vodka and Politics in Late Imperial Russia.* New York: Oxford University Press, 2002.

Herring, George. *Aid to Russia, 1941–1946: Strategy, Diplomacy, the Origins of the Cold War.* New York: Columbia University Press, 1973.

Hersh, Seymour. *The Price of Power: Kissinger in the Nixon White House.* New York: Simon & Schuster, 1983.

Herzog, Jonathan P. *The Spiritual–Industrial Complex: America's Religious Battle against Communism in the Early Cold War.* New York: Oxford University Press, 2011.

Higham, John. *Send These to Me: Jews and Other Immigrants in Urban America.* New York: Atheneum, 1975.

Hill, Alexander. *The Red Army and the Second World War.* Cambridge: Cambridge University Press, 2017.

Hill, Fiona and Clifford G. Gaddy. *Mr. Putin: Operative in the Kremlin.* Washington: Brookings Institution Press, 2013.

Hill, William H. *No Place for Russia: European Security Institutions since 1989.* New York: Columbia University Press, 2018.

Hinds, Lynn Boyd and Theodore Otto Windt, Jr. *The Cold War as Rhetoric: The Beginnings, 1945–1950.* Westport, CT: Praeger, 1991.

Hixson, Walter L. *The Myth of American Diplomacy: National Identity and U.S. Foreign Policy.* New Haven: Yale University Press, 2008.

Hixson, Walter L. *Parting the Curtain: Propaganda, Culture, and the Cold War, 1945–1961.* New York: St. Martin's Press, 1997.

Hochschild, Adam. *Spain in Our Hearts: Americans in the Spanish Civil War, 1936–1939.* Boston: Houghton Mifflin, 2016.

Hoffman, David E. *The Dead Hand: The Untold Story of the Cold War Arms Race and Its Dangerous Legacy.* New York: Doubleday, 2009.

Hoffman, Zachary. "Subversive Patriotism: Aleksei Suvorin, Novoe Vremia, and Right-Wing Nationalism during the Russo-Japanese War," *Ab Imperio,* No. 1 (2018), 69–100.

Hogan, J. Michael. *The Nuclear Freeze Campaign: Rhetoric and Foreign Policy in the Telepolitical Age.* East Lansing, MI: Michigan State University Press, 1994.

Hollander, Paul. *Political Pilgrims: Travels of Western Intellectuals to the Soviet Union, China, and Cuba, 1928–1978.* New York: Oxford University Press, 1981.

Holloway, David. "The Dynamics of the Euromissile Crisis, 1977–1983," in Leopoldo Nuti, Frederic Bozo, Marie-Pierre Rey, and Bernd Rother, eds. *The Euromissile Crisis and the End of the Cold War.* Washington: Woodrow Wilson Center Press, 2015, 11–28.

Holloway, David. *Stalin and the Bomb.* New Haven: Yale University Press, 1994.

Holsti, Ole. *Public Opinion and American Foreign Policy.* Ann Arbor: University of Michigan Press, 2004.

Hoopes, Townsend and Douglas Brinkley, *Driven Patriot: The Life and Times of James Forrestal.* New York: Alfred A. Knopf, 1992.

Hopf, Ted. *Reconstructing the Cold War: The Early Years, 1945–1958.* New York: Oxford University Press, 2012.

Hopf, Ted. *Social Construction of International Politics: Identities and Foreign Policies, Moscow, 1955 and 1999.* Ithaca, NY: Cornell University Press, 2002.

Hornblum, Allen M. *The Invisible Harry Gold: The Man Who Gave the Soviets the Atom Bomb.* New Haven: Yale University Press, 2010.

House, John M. *Wolfhounds and Polar Bears: The American Expeditionary Force in Siberia, 1918–1920.* Tuscaloosa: University of Alabama Press, 2016.

Hughes, Geraint and Saki Ruth Dockrill. "Introduction: The Cold War as History," in Saki Ruth Dockrill and Geraint Hughes, eds. *Palgrave Advances in Cold War History.* New York: Palgrave, 2006.

Hulsey, Byron C. *Everett Dirksen and His Presidents.* Lawrence, KS: University Press of Kansas, 2000.

Hunt, Michael H. "Ideology," in Michael J. Hogan and Thomas G. Paterson, eds. *Explaining the History of American Foreign Relations,* 2nd ed. Cambridge: Cambridge University Press, 2004, 221–240.

Hunt, Michael H. *The Making of a Special Relationship: The United States and China to 1914.* New York: Columbia University Press, 1983.

Huxtable, Simon. *News from Moscow.* New York: Oxford University Press, 2022.

Ignat'ev, Anatolii Venediktovich. *Vneshniaia politika Rossii, 1907–1914: Tendentsii, liudi, sobytiia.* Moscow: Nauka, 2000.

Immerman, Richard H. *The Hidden Hand: A Brief History of the CIA.* Hoboken, NY: Wiley Blackwell, 2014.

Inboden, William. *The Peacemaker: Ronald Reagan, the Cold War, and the World on the Brink.* New York: Dutton, 2022.

Inboden, William. *Religion and American Foreign Policy, 1945–1960: The Soul of Containment.* New York: Cambridge University Press, 2008.

Iriye, Akira. "Culture and International History," in Michael J. Hogan and Thomas G. Paterson, eds. *Explaining the History of American Foreign Relations,* 2nd ed. Cambridge: Cambridge University Press, 2004, 241–256.

Irwin, Julia F. *Making the World Safe: The American Red Cross and a Nation's Humanitarian Awakening.* New York: Oxford University Press, 2013.

Isaacson, Walter. *Kissinger: A Biography.* New York: Simon & Schuster, 1992.

Isacoff, Stuart. *When the World Stopped to Listen: Van Cliburn's Cold War Triumph and Its Aftermath.* New York: Knopf, 2017.

Isaev S. "Tokvil v russkoi dorevolutsionnoi publitsistike," in S. A. Isaev. *Aleksis Tokvil i Amerika ego vremeni.* St. Petersburg: Nauka, 1993.

Isaev, Sergey. *U istokov amerikanskoi istorii: Kvakerstvo, Uiliam Penn i osnovanie kolonii Pensilvaniia.* St. Petersburg: Nestor-istoria, 2018.

Ishchenko, Volodymyr and Oleg Zhuravlev. "Imperialist Ideology or Depoliticization? Why Russian Citizens Support the Invasion of Ukraine," *HAU Journal of Ethnographic Theory,* Vol. 12, No. 3 (2022), 668–676.

Ivanchenko, Yaroslav. "Pozitsiia redaktsionnogo kruzhka 'Moskovskogo telegrafa' v otnoshenii Soedinennykh Shtatov," in *Amerikanskii ezhegodnik, 1980.* Moscow: Nauka, 1981, 216–235.

Ivanian, Eduard Alexandrovich. *Kogda govoriat muzy: Istoriia rossiisko-amerikanskikh kul'turnykh sviazei.* Moscow: Mezhdunarodnye otnosheniia, 2007.

Ivanov, R. F. *Konfederativnye Shtaty Ameriki (1861–1865 gg.).* Moscow: Institut vseobshchei istorii RAN, 2002.

Ivanov, R.F. and I. Ia. Levitas "N. G. Chernyshevskii o rabstve negrov v SShA i probleme grazhdanskikh svobod," in *Amerikanskii ezhegodnik, 1980.* Moscow: Nauka, 1981, 118–138.

Jackson, William D. "Soviet Reassessment of Ronald Reagan, 1985–1988," *Political Science Quarterly,* Vol. 113, No. 4 (1998–1999), 617–644.

Jacobson, Jon. *When the Soviet Union Entered World Politics.* Berkeley: University of California Press, 1994.

Jangfeldt, Bengt. *Mayakovsky: A Biography.* Chicago: University of Chicago Press, 2014.

Jenks, Andrew L. *The Cosmonaut Who Couldn't Stop Smiling: The Life and Legend of Yuri Gagarin*. DeKalb: Northern Illinois University Press, 2014.

Jespersen, T. Christopher. *American Images of China, 1931–1949*. Stanford: Stanford University Press, 1996.

Johnson, Robert David. *Congress and the Cold War*. Cambridge: Cambridge University Press, 2006.

Johnson, Robert David. *The Peace Progressives and American Foreign Relations*. Cambridge: Harvard University Press, 1995.

Johnston, Timothy. *Being Soviet: Identity, Rumour, and Everyday Life under Stalin 1939–1953*. New York: Oxford University Press, 2011.

Jones, Robert Huhn. *The Roads to Russia: United States Lend-Lease to the Soviet Union*. Norman: University of Oklahoma Press, 1969.

Kachavi, Noam. "Insights Abandoned, Flexibility Lost: Kissinger, Soviet Jewish Emigration, and the Demise of Détente," *Diplomatic History*, Vol. 29, No. 3 (June 2005), 503–530.

Kalb, Bernard and Marvin Kalb, *Kissinger*. Boston: Little, Brown, 1974.

Kalinovsky, Artemy. *A Long Goodbye: The Soviet Withdrawal from Afghanistan*. Cambridge, MA: Harvard University Press, 2011.

Kantsler, A. M. *Gorchakov: 200 let so dnia rozhdeniia*. Moscow: Mezhdunarodnye otnosheniia, 1998.

Kasianov, Georgiy. "How a War for the Past Becomes a War in the Present," *Kritika*, Vol. 16, No. 1 (Winter 2015), 149–155.

Kapterev, Sergei. "Illusionary Spoils: Soviet Attitudes toward American Cinema during the Early Cold War," *Kritika*, Vol. 10, No. 4 (Fall 2009), 779–807.

Katchenovsky, D. *Daniel Webster: Étude biographique*. Brussels and Ostend, 1858.

Kelley, Robin D. G. *Hammer and Hoe: Alabama Communists during the Great Depression*. Chapel Hill: University of North Carolina Press, 1990.

Kelly, Daniel. *James Burnham and the Struggle for the World: A Life*. Wilmington, DE: ISI Books, 2002.

Kemnitz, Thomas M. "The Cartoon as a Historical Source," *Journal of Interdisciplinary History*, Vol. 4, No. 1 (Summer 1973), 81–93.

Kempe, Frederick. *Berlin 1961: Kennedy, Khrushchev, and the Most Dangerous Place on Earth*. New York: Putnam, 2011.

Kenez, Peter. *Cinema and Soviet Society from the Revolution to the Death of Stalin*. London: I.B. Tauris, 2001.

Kennan, George F. "American Troops in Russia: The True Record," *Atlantic Monthly*, No. 203 (January 1959), 36–42.

Kennan, George F. *Russia and the West under Lenin and Stalin*. New York: New American Library, 1961.

Kennan, George F. *Soviet–American Relations, 1917–1920*, 2 vols. Princeton: Princeton University Press, 1956–1958.

Kennan, George F. *The Marquise de Custine and His Russia in 1839*. Princeton: Princeton University Press, 1971.

Keys, Barbara J. *Reclaiming American Virtue: The Human Rights Revolution of the 1970s.* Cambridge, MA: Harvard University Press, 2014.

Khapaeva, Dina. "Triumphant Memory of the Perpetrators: Putin's Politics of Re-Stalinization," *Communist and Post-Communist Studies,* Vol. 49, No. 1 (February 2016), 61–73.

Khrushchev, Sergei N. *Nikita Khrushchev and the Creation of a Superpower.* University Park: Pennsylvania State University Press, 2000.

Killen, Linda. "The Search for a Democratic Russia: Bakhmetev and the United States," *Diplomatic History,* Vol. 2, No. 3 (Summer 1978), 237–256.

Kimball, Warren. *The Juggler: Franklin Roosevelt as Wartime Statesman.* Princeton: Princeton University Press, 1991.

Kiniapina, N. S. "Russia and the U.S. Civil War," in Norman E. Saul and Richard D. McKinzie, eds. *Russian–American Dialogue on Cultural Relations, 1776–1914.* Columbia: University of Missouri Press, 1996.

Kirschenbaum, Lisa A. *International Communism and the Spanish Civil War.* Cambridge: Cambridge University Press, 2015.

Kirschenbaum, Lisa A. *Soviet Adventures in the Land of the Capitalists: Ilf and Petrov's American Road Trip.* Cambridge: Cambridge University Press, 2024.

Klehr, Harvey, John Earl Haynes, and Fridrikh Igorevich Firsov. *The Secret World of American Communism.* New Haven: Yale University Press, 1995.

Klier, John and Shlomo Lambroza, eds. *Pogroms: Anti-Jewish Violence in Modern Russian History.* New York: Cambridge University Press 1992.

Knight, Amy. *Orders to Kill: The Putin Regime and Political Murder.* New York: St. Martin's Press, 2017.

Knight, Nathaniel. "Ethnicity, Nationality and the Masses: Narodnost' and Modernity in Imperial Russia," in David L. Hoffmann and Yanni Kotsonis, eds. *Russian Modernity: Politics, Knowledge, Practices.* New York: Macmillan, 2000.

Knoblauch, William M. *Nuclear Freeze in a Cold War: The Reagan Administration, Cultural Activism, and the End of the Arms Race.* Amherst: University of Massachusetts Press, 2017.

Knopf, Jeffrey W. *Domestic Society and International Cooperation: The Impact of Protest on US Arms Control Policy.* Cambridge: Cambridge University Press, 1998.

Kolchin, Peter. *Emancipation: The Abolition and Aftermath of American Slavery and Russian Serfdom.* New Haven: Yale University Press, 2024.

Kolchin, Peter. *Unfree Labor: American Slavery and Russian Serfdom.* Cambridge, MA: Belknap Press, 1987.

Koposov, Nikolay. *Memory Laws, Memory Wars: The Politics of the Past in Europe and Russia.* Cambridge: Cambridge University Press, 2018.

Kostornichenko, V. N. "Proekt kontsessi amerikanskogo predprinimatelia Vashingtona B. Vanderlipa i sovetskaia vneshnaia politika nachala 1920-x gg.," *Amerikana,* No. 4 (2000), 79–88.

Kotkin, Stephen. "American Hustle: What Mueller Found – and Didn't Find – about Trump and Russia," *Foreign Affairs,* Vol. 98, No. 4 (July/August 2019), 62–78.

Kotkin, Stephen. "Russia's Perpetual Geopolitics: Putin Returns to the Historical Pattern," *Foreign Affairs*, Vol. 95, No. 3 (May/June 2016), 2–9.

Kotkin, Stephen. *Stalin: Paradoxes of Power, 1878–1928*. New York: Penguin, 2014.

Kotkin, Stephen. *Stalin: Waiting for Hitler, 1929–1941*. New York: Penguin, 2017.

Kozenko, Boris D. "Nesostoiavsheesia sblizhenie: Rossiia i SShA v 1914–1917 godakh," in V. L. Mal'kov, ed. *Pervaia mirovaia voina: Prolog XX veka*. Moscow: Nauka, 1998.

Kozovoi, Andrei. "'This Film Is Harmful': Resizing America for the Soviet Screen," in Sari K. Autio-Sarasmo and Brendan Humphreys, eds. *Winter Kept Us Warm: Cold War Interactions Reconsidered*. Helsinki: Aleksanteri Institute, 2010.

Kramer, Mark. "The Czechoslovak Crisis and the Brezhnev Doctrine," in Carole Fink, Philip Gassert, and Detlef Junker, eds. *1968: The World Transformed*. Cambridge: Cambridge University Press, 1998, 111–172.

Kramer, Mark. "Introduction to Special Issue: The Collapse of the Soviet Union (Part 2)," *Journal of Cold War Studies*, Vol. 5, No. 4 (Fall 2003), 3–42.

Kramer, Mark. "The Myth of a No NATO Enlargement Pledge to Russia," *Washington Quarterly*, Vol. 32, No. 2 (2009), 39–61.

Krebs, Ronald R. *Narrative and the Making of U.S. National Security*. New York: Cambridge University Press, 2015.

Kremeniuk, V. A. *Uroki kholodnoi voiny*. Moscow: Aspekt Press, 2015.

Kroll, C. Douglas. *"Friends in Peace and War": The Russian Navy's Landmark Visit to Civil War San Francisco*. Washington: Potomac Books, 2007.

Kulanov, Alexander and Vasily, Molodiakov. *Rossiia i Iaponiia: Imidzhevye voiny*. Moscow: AST, 2007.

Kulavig, Erik. *Dissent in the Years of Khrushchev: Nine Stories about Disobedient Russians*. New York: Palgrave, 2003.

Kurilla, Ivan. "'Russian Celebrations' and American Debates about Russia in 1813," *Nationalities Papers: The Journal of Nationalism and Ethnicity*, Vol. 44, No. 1 (2016), 114–123.

Kurilla, Ivan. "Abolition of Serfdom in Russia and American Newspaper and Journal Opinion," in William Benton Whisenhunt and Norman E. Saul, eds. *New Perspectives on Russian–American Relations*. New York: Routledge, 2016, 64–73.

Kurilla, Ivan. *Zakliatye Druz'ia: Istoriia mnenii, fantazii, kontaktov, vzaimo (ne) ponimaniia Rossii i SShA*. Moscow: Novoe literaturnoe obozrenie, 2018.

Kurilla, Ivan. *Zaokeanskie partnery: Amerika i Rossiia v 1830–1850-e gody*. Volgograd: Izdatel'stvo Volgogradskogo universiteta, 2005.

Kurilla, Ivan and Victoria I. Zhuravleva. "Russia's View on Obama's Presidency: From Hopes to Disappointments," in Matthias Maass, ed. *The World Views of the Obama Era*. New York: Palgrave Macmillan, 2018, 113–140.

Kuropyatnik, G. P. *Rossiia i SShA: Ekonomicheskie, kul'turnye i diplomaticheskie sviazi, 1867–1881*. Moscow: Nauka, 1981.

Kuzmarov, Jeremy and John Marciano. *The Russians Are Coming, Again: The First Cold War as Tragedy, the Second as Farce*. New York: Monthly Review Press, 2018.

Kuznets, Simon. "Immigration of Russian Jews to the United States: Background and Structure," in Jeffrey S. Gurock, ed. *East European Jews in America, 1880–1920: Immigration and Adaptation*, 3 vols. New York: Routledge, 1998.

LaFeber, Walter. "The Turn of the Russian–American Relations, 1889–1905," in *Russkoe otkrytie Ameriki: Sbornik statei, posviashchennyi 70-letiiu akademika N. N. Bolkhovitinova*. Moscow: Rosspen, 2002, 280–291.

LaFeber, Walter. *The Clash: U.S.–Japanese Relations throughout History*. New York: W. W. Norton, 1997.

Landler, Mark. *Alter Egos: Hillary Clinton, Barack Obama, and the Twilight Struggle over American Power*. New York: Random House, 2016.

Larson, Simeon. "Opposition to AFL Foreign Policy: A Labor Mission to Russia, 1927," *Historian*, Vol. 43, No. 3 (Summer 1981), 345–364.

Laruelle, Marlene. "Introduction," in Marlene Laruelle, ed. *Eurasianism and the European Far Right*. Lanham, MD: Lexington Books, 2015.

Laruelle, Marlene. *Is Russia Fascist? Unraveling Propaganda East and West*. Ithaca, NY: Cornell University Press, 2021.

Laruelle, Marlene. "Making Sense of Russia's Illiberalism," *Journal of Democracy*, Vol. 31, No. 3 (July 2020), 115–129.

Laruelle, Marlene. *Russian Nationalism: Imaginaries, Doctrines, and Political Battlefields*. London: Routledge, 2019.

Lasch, Christopher. *The American Liberals and the Russian Revolution*. New York: Columbia University Press, 1962.

Laserson, Max M. "Alexander Radishchev – An Early Admirer of America," *The Russian Review*, Vol. 9, No. 3 (July 1950), 179–186.

Laserson, Max M. *The American Impact on Russia – Diplomatic and Ideological*. New York: Macmillan, 1950.

Laserson, Max M. *The American Impact on Russia: Diplomatic and Ideological, 1784–1917*. New York: Macmillan, 1950.

Lears, Jackson. *Rebirth of a Nation: The Making of Modern America, 1877–1920*. New York: HarperCollins, 2009.

Leffler, Melvyn P. *For the Soul of Mankind: The United States, the Soviet Union, and the Cold War*. New York: Hill and Wang, 2007.

Legvold, Robert. *Return to Cold War*. Malden, MA: Polity Press, 2016.

Lel'chuk, V. S. and E. I. Pivovar. "Mentalitet Sovetskogo Obshchestva i 'Kholodnaia Voina,'" *Otechestvennaia Istoriia*, No. 6 (1993), 63–78.

Lerner, Mitchell. "'Trying to Find the Guy Who Invited Them': Lyndon Johnson, Bridge Building, and the End of the Prague Spring," *Diplomatic History*, Vol. 32, No. 1 (January 2008), 77–103.

Levering, Ralph B. *American Opinion and the Russian Alliance, 1939–1945*. Chapel Hill: University of North Carolina Press, 1976.

Levitina, Marina L. *"Russian Americans" in Soviet Film: Cinematic Dialogues between the US and the USSR*. London: I.B. Tauris, 2015.

Lewton, Lusy Olga. *Alla Nazimova, My Aunt: A Personal Memoir*. Ventura: Minuteman Press, 1988.

Libbey, James K. *Alexander Gumberg and Soviet–American Relations, 1917–1933*. Lexington: University Press of Kentucky, 1977.

Libbey, James K. "The American–Russian Chamber of Commerce," *Diplomatic History*, Vol. 9, No. 3 (1985), 233–248.

Libbey, James K. *Russian–American Economic Relations, 1763–1999*. Gulf Breeze, FL: Academic International Press, 1999.

Link, Stefan J. *Forging Global Fordism: Nazi Germany, Soviet Russia, and the Contest over the Industrial Order*. Princeton: Princeton University Press, 2020.

Listikov, S. V. *SShA i revoliutsionnaia Rossiia v 1917 godu*. Moscow: Nauka, 2006.

Listikov, S. V. *Voina, revoliutsiia, mir: Rossiia v mezhdunarodnykh otnosheniiakh. 1915–1925*. Moscow: Aspekt Press, 2019.

Logevall, Frederik and Andrew Preston, eds. *Nixon in the World: American Foreign Relations, 1969–1977*. New York: Oxford University Press, 2008.

Lucas, Edward. *The New Cold War: Putin's Russia and the Threat to the West*. New York: Palgrave Macmillan, 2008.

Luff, Jennifer. *Commonsense Anticommunism: Labor and Civil Liberties between the World Wars*. Chapel Hill: University of North Carolina Press, 2012.

Lukin, Alexander. *China and Russia: The New Rapprochement*. Cambridge: Polity, 2018.

Lyandres, Semion. *The Fall of Tsarism: Untold Stories of the February 1917 Revolution*. New York: Oxford University Press, 2013.

Maar, Henry Richard. *Freeze! The Grassroots Movement to Halt the Arms Race and End the Cold War*. Ithaca, NY: Cornell University Press, 2021.

Mackenzie, Ross. *When Stars and Stripes Met Hammer and Sickle: The Chautauqua Conferences on U.S.–Soviet Relations, 1985–1989*. Columbia: University of South Carolina Press, 2006.

MacKinnon, Mark. *The New Cold War: Revolutions, Rigged Elections, and Pipeline Politics in the Former Soviet Union*. New York: Carroll & Graf, 2007.

MacLean, Elizabeth Kimball. *Joseph E. Davies: Envoy to the Soviets*. Westport, CT: Greenwood Press, 1992.

Madariaga, Isabel de. *Britain, Russia, and the Armed Neutrality of 1780*. New Haven: Yale University Press, 1962.

Maddox, Robert J. *The Unknown War with Russia: Wilson's Siberian Intervention*. San Rafael, CA: Presidio Press, 1977.

Maddox, Robert James. *William E. Borah and American Foreign Policy*. Baton Rouge: Louisiana State University Press, 1969.

Maddux, Thomas R. "Red Fascism, Brown Bolshevism: The American Image of Totalitarianism in the 1930s," *Historian*, Vol. 40, No. 1 (November 1977), 85–103.

Maddux, Thomas R. *Years of Estrangement: American Relations with the Soviet Union, 1933–1941*. Tallahassee: University Presses of Florida, 1980.

Magnúsdóttir, Rósa. "'Be Careful in America, Premier Khrushchev!': Soviet Perceptions of peaceful coexistence with the United States in 1959," *Cahiers du monde russe*, Vol. 47, No. 1–2 (2006), 109–130.

Magnúsdóttir, Rósa. *Enemy Number One: The United States of America in Soviet Ideology and Propaganda, 1945–1959.* New York: Oxford University Press, 2019.

Makalani, Minkah. *In the Cause of Freedom: Radical Black Internationalism from Harlem to London, 1917–1939.* Chapel Hill: University of North Carolina Press, 2011.

Makari, George. *Of Fear and Strangers: A History of Xenophobia.* New York: W. W. Norton, 2021.

Makdisi, Ussama. *Faith Misplaced: The Broken Promise of U.S.–Arab Relations: 1820–2001.* New York: Public Affairs, 2010.

Malia, Martin. *Russia under Western Eyes: From the Bronze Horseman to the Lenin Mausoleum.* Cambridge, MA: Harvard University Press, 1999.

Malia, Martin. *The Soviet Tragedy: A History of Socialism in Russia, 1917–1991.* New York: Free Press, 1994.

Malkin M. M. *Grazhdanskaia voina v SShA i tsarskaia Rossiia.* Moscow and Leningrad: OGIZ, 1939.

Mal'kov, V. L. *Put' k imperstvu: Amerika v pervoi polovine XX veka.* Moscow: Nauka, 2004.

Mally, Lynn. "Hallie Flanagan and the Soviet Union: New Heaven, New Earth, New Theater," in Choi Chatterjee and Beth Holmgren, eds. *Americans Experience Russia: Encountering the Enigma, 1917 to the Present.* New York: Routledge, 2013, 31–49.

Mamatey, Victor S. *The United States and East Central Europe. 1914–1918: A Study in Wilsonian Diplomacy and Propaganda.* Princeton: Princeton University Press, 1957.

Mankoff, Jeffrey. *Russian Foreign Policy: The Return of Great Power Politics* Lanham, MD: Rowman & Littlefield, 2009.

Mark, Eduard. "October or Thermidor? Interpretations of Stalinism and the Perception of Soviet Foreign Policy in the United States, 1927–1947," *American Historical Review*, Vol. 94, No. 4 (October 1989), 937–962.

Markowitz, Norman D. *The Rise and Fall of the People's Century: Henry A. Wallace and American Liberalism, 1941–1948.* New York: Free Press, 1973.

Marks, Frederick W. *Wind over Sand: The Diplomacy of Franklin Roosevelt.* Athens, GA: University of Georgia Press, 1988.

Marples, David. *Ukraine's Euromaidan: Analyses of a Civil Revolution.* Stuttgart: Ibidem-Verlag, 2015.

Martin, Bradford. *The Other Eighties: A Secret History of America in the Age of Reagan.* New York: Hill and Wang, 2011.

Mason, Robert. "Foreign Policy and the Republican Quest for a New Majority," in Robert Mason and Iwan Morgan, eds. *Seeking a New Majority: The Republican Party and American Politics, 1960–1980.* Nashville: Vanderbilt University Press, 2013, 160–176.

Mastny, Vojtech. "The Elusive Détente: Stalin's Successors and the West," in Klaus Larres and Kenneth Osgood, eds. *The Cold War after Stalin's Death: A Missed Opportunity for Peace?* Lanham, MD: Rowman & Littlefield, 2006, 3–26.

Mastny, Vojtech. *The Cold War and Soviet Insecurity: The Stalin Years.* New York: Oxford University Press, 1996.

Masuda, Hajimu. *Cold War Crucible: The Korean Conflict and the Postwar World.* Cambridge, MA: Harvard University Press, 2015.

Matlock, Jack F. *Superpower Illusions: How Myths and False Ideologies Led America Astray – and How to Return to Reality.* New Haven: Yale University Press, 2010.

Matlock, Jack. *Reagan and Gorbachev: How the Cold War Ended.* New York: Random House, 2004.

Matos Franco, Rainer. "Adventure, Mutual Images and Orientalism: Joel R. Poinsett in Russia, 1806–1808," in *Americana*, Vol. 15. St. Petersburg and Volgograd: Volgograd State University Press, 2017, 206–238.

Matovski, Aleksandar. "The Logic of Vladimir Putin's Popular Appeal," in Karrie Koesel, Valerie Bunce, and Jessica Weiss, eds. *Citizens and the State in Authoritarian Regimes: Comparing China and Russia.* New York: Oxford University Press, 2020.

May, Ernest R. *The Making of the Monroe Doctrine.* Cambridge, MA: Belknap Press, 1975.

Mayer, Arno J. *Wilson vs. Lenin: Political Origins of the New Diplomacy, 1917–1918.* Cleveland: Meridian Books, 1964.

Mayers, David. *The Ambassadors and America's Soviet Policy.* New York: Oxford University Press, 1995.

Mazov, Sergey. *A Distant Front in the Cold War: The USSR in West Africa and the Congo, 1956–1964.* Washington: Woodrow Wilson Center Press, 2010.

McAdams, A. James. *Vanguard of the Revolution: The Global Idea of the Communist Party.* Princeton: Princeton University Press, 2017.

McCormick, Thomas, "The Wilson–McCook Scheme of 1896–1897," *Pacific Historical Review,* Vol. 36, No. 1 (February 1967), 47–58.

McCullough, David. *Truman.* New York: Simon & Schuster, 1992.

McDougall, Walter A. . . . *the Heavens and the Earth: A Political History of the Space Age.* New York: Basic Books, 1985.

McDuffie, Erik S. *Sojourning for Freedom: Black Women, American Communism, and the Making of Black Left Feminism.* Durham, NC: Duke University Press, 2011.

McFadden, David and Claire Gorfinkel. *Constructive Spirit: Quakers in Revolutionary Russia.* Pasadena: Intentional Productions, 2004.

McFadden, David W. *Alternative Paths: Soviets and Americans, 1917–1920.* New York: Oxford University Press, 1993.

McFaul, Michael. "American Efforts at Promoting Regime Change in the Soviet Union and Then Russia: Lessons Learned," CDDRL Working Paper Number 44, September 2005.

Michael, Michael. "Are Russians Imperialists?" *Demokratizatsiya: The Journal of Post-Soviet Democratization*, Vol. 30, No. 4 (Fall 2022), 421–432.

McFaul, Michael. *Russia's Unfinished Revolution*. Ithaca, NY: Cornell University Press, 2001.

McFaul, Michael. "Ukraine Imports Democracy: External Influences on the Orange Revolution," *International Security*, Vol. 32, No. 2 (Fall 2007), 45–83.

McKenna, Kevin J. *All the Views Fit to Print: Changing Images of the U.S. in Pravda Political Cartoons, 1917–1991*. New York: Peter Lang, 2001.

McKillen, Elizabeth. *Chicago Labor and the Quest for a Democratic Diplomacy, 1914–1924*. Ithaca, NY: Cornell University Press, 1995.

McKillen, Elizabeth. *Making the World Safe for Workers: Labor, the Left, and Wilsonian Internationalism*. Urbana: University of Illinois Press, 2013.

McMeekin, Sean. *The Russian Revolution: A New History*. New York: Basic Books, 2017.

McNamara, Patrick. *A Catholic Cold War: Edmund A. Walsh, S.J., and the Politics of Anticommunism*. New York: Fordham University Press, 2005.

Meacham, Jon. *Destiny and Power: The American Odyssey of George Herbert Walker Bush*. New York: Random House, 2015.

Mearsheimer, John J. *The Great Delusion: Liberal Dreams and International Realities*. New Haven: Yale University Press, 2018.

Meier, Andrew. *The Lost Spy: An American in Stalin's Secret Service*. New York: W. W. Norton, 2008.

Melton, Carol Willcox. *Between War and Peace: Woodrow Wilson and the American Expeditionary Force in Siberia, 1918–1921*. Macon, GA: Mercer University Press, 2001.

Merridale, Catherine. *Ivan's War: Life and Death in the Red Army, 1939–1945*. New York: Henry Holt, 2006.

Messer, Robert L. *The End of an Alliance: James F. Byrnes, Roosevelt, Truman, and the Origins of the Cold War*. Chapel Hill: University of North Carolina Press, 1982.

Meyer, David S. *A Winter of Discontent: The Nuclear Freeze and American Politics*. New York: Praeger, 1990.

Michels, Tony. *A Fire in Their Hearts: Yiddish Socialists in New York*. Cambridge, MA: Harvard University Press, 2005.

Mickenberg, Julia L. *American Girls in Red Russia: Chasing the Soviet Dream*. Chicago: University of Chicago Press, 2017.

Mickenberg, Julia. "Suffragettes and Soviets: American Feminists and the Specter of Revolutionary Russia," *Journal of American History*, Vol. 100, No. 4 (March 2014), 1021–1051.

Mikhailova, Yulia, "Images of Enemy and Self: Russian 'Popular Prints' of the Russo-Japanese War," *Acta Slavica Iaponica*, Vol. 16 (1998), 30–53.

Mikkonen, Simo. "Stealing the Monopoly of Knowledge? Soviet Reactions to U.S. Cold War Broadcasting," *Kritika*, Vol. 11, No. 4 (Fall 2010), 771–805.

Miles, Simon. *Engaging the Evil Empire: Washington, Moscow, and the Beginning of the End of the Cold War*. Ithaca, NY: Cornell University Press, 2020.

Miller, Bonnie M. "A Primer for Using Historical Images in Research," *American Periodicals*, Vol. 27, No. 1 (April 2017), 73–94.

Miller, Chris. *Putinomics: Power and Money in Resurgent Russia.* Chapel Hill: University of North Carolina Press, 2018.

Miller, Chris. *The Struggle to Save the Soviet Economy: Mikhail Gorbachev and the Collapse of the USSR.* Chapel Hill: University of North Carolina Press, 2016.

Miller, Dan B. *Erskine Caldwell: The Journey from Tobacco Road.* New York: Knopf, 1995.

Miller, James Edward. *The United States and Italy, 1940–1950: The Politics and Diplomacy of Stabilization.* Chapel Hill: University of North Carolina Press, 1986.

Miller, Matthew L. *The American YMCA and Russian Culture: The Preservation and Expansion of Orthodox Christianity, 1900–1940.* Lanham, MD: Lexington Books, 2015.

Minaev, Boris. *Boris Yeltsin: The Decade That Shook the World.* London: Glagoslav Publications, 2015.

Minger, Ralph E. "William Howard Taft's Forgotten Visit to Russia," *Russian Review*, Vol. 22, No. 2 (April 1963), 149–156.

Miraldi, Robert. *The Pen Is Mightier: The Muckraking Life of Charles Edward Russell.* New York: Palgrave Macmillan, 2003.

Mitchell, Lincoln A. *The Color Revolutions.* Philadelphia: University of Pennsylvania Press, 2012.

Mitchell, Nancy. "The Cold War and Jimmy Carter," in M. Leffler and O. A. Westad, eds. *The Cambridge History of the Cold War*, Vol. III: *Endings.* Cambridge: Cambridge University Press, 2010, 66–88.

Mitchell, Nancy. *The Danger of Dreams: German and American Imperialism in Latin America.* Chapel Hill: University of North Carolina Press, 1999.

Mitchell, Nancy. *Jimmy Carter in Africa: Race and the Cold War.* Stanford: Stanford University Press, 2016.

Mitrovich, Gregory. *Undermining the Kremlin: America's Strategy to Subvert the Soviet Bloc, 1947–1956.* Ithaca, NY: Cornell University Press, 2000.

Moon, David. *The American Steppes: The Unexpected Russian Roots of Great Plains Agriculture, 1870s–1930s.* Cambridge: Cambridge University Press, 2020.

Moore, Gregory. *Defining and Defending the Open Door Policy: Theodore Roosevelt and China, 1901–1909.* Lanham, MD, Lexington Books, 2015.

Morgan, Iwan. *Reagan: American Icon.* London: I.B. Tauris, 2016.

Morgan, Michael Cotey. *The Final Act: The Helsinki Accords and the Transformation of the Cold War.* Princeton: Princeton University Press, 2018.

Morris, M. Wayne. *Stalin's Famine and Roosevelt's Recognition of Russia.* Lanham, MD: University Press of America, 1994.

Moser, John E. *Twisting the Lion's Tail: American Anglophobia between the World Wars.* New York: New York University Press, 1999.

Muir, Malcolm. "American Warship Construction for Stalin's Navy Prior to World War II: A Study in Paralysis of Policy," *Diplomatic History*, Vol. 5, No. 4 (1981), 337–351.

Mulchinock, Niall. *NATO and the Western Balkans: From Neutral Spectator to Proactive Peacemaker.* New York: Palgrave Macmillan, 2007.

Myers, Constance Ashton. *The Prophet's Army: Trotskyists in America, 1928–1941.* Westport, CT: Greenwood Press, 1977.

Myers, Steven Lee. *The New Tsar: The Rise and Reign of Vladimir Putin.* New York: Knopf, 2015.

Nadzhafov, Dzhahangir G. "The Beginning of the Cold War between East and West: The Aggravation of Ideological Confrontation," *Cold War History,* Vol. 4, No. 2 (January 2004), 140–174.

Naimark, Norman. *Stalin and the Fate of Europe: The Postwar Struggle for Sovereignty.* Cambridge, MA: Harvard University Press, 2019.

Nalbandov, Robert. *Not by Bread Alone: Russian Foreign Policy under Putin.* Lincoln, NE: Potomac Books, 2016.

Namikas, Lise. *Battleground Africa: Cold War in the Congo, 1960–1965.* Stanford: Stanford University Press, 2013.

Narinsky, Mikhail. "Soviet Foreign Policy and the Origins of the Cold War," in Gabriel Gorodetsky, ed. *Soviet Foreign Policy, 1917–1911: A Retrospective.* London: Frank Cass, 1994, 105–110.

Nechiporuk, Dmitry Mikhailovich. *Vo imia nigilisma: Amerikanskoe obshchestvo druzei russkoi svobody i russkaia revolutsionnaia emigratsia.* Moscow: Nestor Istoriya, 2018.

Nehring, Holger. "The Last Battle of the Cold War: Peace Movements and German Politics in the 1980s," in Leopoldo Nuti, Frederic Bozo, Marie-Pierre Rey, and Bernd Rother, eds. *The Euromissile Crisis and the End of the Cold War.* Stanford: Stanford University Press, 2015, 309–330.

Nelson, Keith L. "Détente over Thirty Years," in Robert D. Schulzinger, ed. *A Companion to American Foreign Relations.* Malden, MA: Blackwell, 2003, 422–431.

Nelson, Keith L. *The Making of Détente: Soviet–American Relations in the Shadow of Vietnam.* Baltimore: Johns Hopkins University Press, 1995.

Neu, Charles E. *Colonel House: A Biography of Woodrow Wilson's Silent Partner.* New York: Oxford University Press, 2015.

Neumann, Iver B. *Uses of the Other: "The East" in European Identity Formation.* Minneapolis: University of Minnesota Press, 1999.

Neumann, Matthias. "Children Diplomacy during the Late Cold War: Samantha Smith's Visit of the 'Evil Empire,'" *History,* Vol. 104, No. 360 (2019), 275–308.

Newsom, David D. *The Soviet Brigade in Cuba: A Study in Political Diplomacy.* Bloomington: Indiana University Press, 1987.

Nguyen, Lien-Hang T. *Hanoi's War: An International History of the War for Peace in Vietnam.* Chapel Hill: University of North Carolina Press, 2012.

Nikoliukin, Aleksander Nikolaevich. *Vzaimosviazi literatur Rossii i SShA: Turgenev, Tolstoy, Dostoevskii i America.* Moscow: Nauka, 1987.

Nikoliukin, Aleksander Nikolaevich, ed. *A Russian Discovery of America.* Moscow: Nauka, 1986.

Nikoliukin, Aleksandr. *Literaturnye sviazi Rossii i SShA.* Moscow: Nauka, 1981.

Ninkovich, Frank. *The Global Republic: America's Inadvertent Rise to World Power.* Chicago: University of Chicago Press, 2014.

Nitoburg, Eduard L'vovich. *Russkie v SshA: Istoriia i sud'by. 1870–1970. Etnoistorichesky ocherk.* Moscow: Nauka, 2005.

Norris, Stephen M. *A War of Images: Russian Popular Prints, Wartime Culture, and National Identity, 1812–1945.* DeKalb: Northern Illinois University Press, 2006.

Norris, Stephen M. *Blockbuster History in the New Russia: Movies, Memory, and Patriotism.* Bloomington: Indiana University Press, 2012.

Noskov, V. V. *Amerikanskie diplomaty v Sankt-Peterburge v epokhu velikikh reform.* St. Petersburg, 2018.

Noskov, Vladimir Vital'evich, "'Net, svoboda ne tam': Slavianofil'skii obraz Ameriki," in *Amerikanskii ezhegodnik, 2003.* Moscow: Nauka, 2005, 251–271.

Nowak, Andrzej. "A 'Polish Connection' in American Sovietology, or The Old Homeland Enmities in the New Host Country Humanities," *Ab Imperio*, No. 4 (2007), 237–259.

O'Brien, Phillips Payson. *How the War Was Won: Air–Sea Power and Allied Victory in World War II.* Cambridge: Cambridge University Press, 2015.

O'Neill, William L. *A Better World. The Great Schism: Stalinism and the American Intellectuals.* New York: Simon & Schuster, 1982.

O'Neill, William L. *The Last Romantic: A Life of Max Eastman.* New York: Oxford University Press, 1978.

Offner, Arnold A. *Another Such Victory: President Truman and the Cold War.* Stanford: Stanford University Press, 2002.

Okun, S. B. *Rossiisko-amerikanskaia kompaniya.* Moscow and Leningrad: Sotsekiz, 1939.

Olmsted, Kathryn S. *Red Spy Queen: A Biography of Elizabeth Bentley.* Chapel Hill: University of North Carolina Press, 2002.

Orelick, Annelise. *The Soviet Jewish-Americans.* Westport, CT: Greenwood Press, 1999.

Osgood, Kenneth. "The American Construction of the Communist Threat," in David C. Engerman, Max Paul Friedman, and Melani McAlister, eds. *The Cambridge History of America and the World*, Vol. IV: *1945 to the Present.* Cambridge: Cambridge University Press, 2021, 124–147.

Ostermann, Christian. *Between Containment and Rollback: The United States and the Cold War in Germany.* Stanford: Stanford University Press, 2021.

Ostrovsky, Arkady. *The Invention of Russia: From Gorbachev's Freedom to Putin's War.* New York: Viking, 2015.

Oushakine, Serguei Alex. *The Patriotism of Despair: Nation, War, and Loss in Russia.* Ithaca, NY: Cornell University Press, 2009.

Overpeck, Deron. "'Remember! It's Only a Movie': Expectations and Receptions of *The Day After* (1983)," *Historical Journal of Film, Radio and Television*, Vol. 32, No. 2 (June 2012), 267–292.

Overy, Richard. *Russia's War: A History of the Soviet War Effort: 1941–1945*. New York: Penguin, 1997.

Owens, Kenneth N. with Alexander Yu. Petrov. *Empire Maker: Alexandr Baranov and Russian Colonial Expansion into Alaska and Northern California*. Seattle, WA: University of Washington Press, 2015.

Paddock, Troy, ed. *Contesting the Origins of the First World War*. New York: Routledge, 2020.

Palmer, William J. *The Films of the Eighties: A Social History*. Carbondale, IL: Southern Illinois University Press, 1993.

Paris, Roland. "Kosovo and the Metaphor War," *Political Science Quarterly*, Vol. 117, No. 3 (Fall 2002), 423–450.

Parry, Albert. *America Learns Russian: A History of the Teaching of the Russian Language in the United States*. Syracuse, NY: Syracuse University Press, 1967.

Patenaude, Bertrand M. *The Big Show in Bololand: The American Relief Expedition to Soviet Russia in the Famine of 1921*. Stanford: Stanford University Press, 2002.

Paterson, Thomas G. *On Every Front: The Making of the Cold War*. New York: W. W. Norton, 1979.

Pavlov, Dmitry Borisovich. *Russko-iaponskaia voina 1904–1905 gg.: Sekretnye operatsii na sushe i na more*. Moscow: Materik, 2004.

Peacock, Margaret. "Samantha Smith in the Land of the Bolsheviks: Peace and the Politics of Childhood in the Late Cold War," *Diplomatic History*, Vol. 43, No. 3 (June 2019), 418–444.

Pechatnov, V. O. "'The Allies Are Pressing on You to Break Your Will . . .' Foreign Policy Correspondence between Stalin and Molotov and Other Politburo Members, September 1945–December 1946," Cold War International History Project Working Paper No. 26, Washington, September 1999.

Pechatnov, V. O. "The Big Three after World War II: New Documents on Soviet Thinking about Post War Relations with the United States and Great Britain," Cold War International History Project Working Paper No. 13, Washington, 1995.

Pechatnov, V. O. "Exercise in Frustration: Soviet Foreign Propaganda in the Early Cold War, 1945–47," *Cold War History*, Vol. 1, No. 2 (January 2001), 1–27.

Pechatnov, V. O. *Stalin, Ruzvel't, Trumen: SSSR i SShA v 1940-x gg*. Moscow: Terra, 2006.

Pechatnov, V. O. and C. Carl Edmondson. "The Russian Perspective," in Ralph B. Levering, Vladimir O. Pechatnov, Verena Botzenhart-Viehe, and C. Earl Edmonson, *Debating the Origins of the Cold War: American and Russian Perspectives*. Lanham, MD: Rowman & Littlefield, 2002.

Pérez, Louis A. *Cuba in the American Imagination: Metaphor and the Imperial Ethos*. Chapel Hill: University of North Carolina Press, 2008.

Pérez, Louis A., Jr. *The War of 1898: The United States and Cuba in History and Historiography.* Chapel Hill: University of North Carolina Press, 1998.

Perkins, Bradford. *The Great Rapprochement: England and the United States, 1895–1914.* New York: Atheneum, 1968.

Perkins, Dexter. *Charles Evans Hughes and American Democratic Statesmanship.* Boston: Little, Brown, 1956.

Perlmutter, Amos. *FDR and Stalin: A Not So Grand Alliance, 1943–1945.* Columbia: University of Missouri Press, 1993.

Pesenti, M. "Cancelling Russian Culture Is Today's Moral Imperative," *Index on Censorship*, Vol. 51, No. 2 (2022), 74–75.

Petrov, A. Iu. *Rossiisko-amerikanskaia kompaniia: Deiatel'nost' na otechestvennom i zarubezhnom rynkakh (1799–1867).* Moscow: Institut vseobshchei istorii RAN, 2006.

Pfeffer, Paula F. *A. Philip Randolph, Pioneer of the Civil Rights Movement.* Baton Rouge: Louisiana State University Press, 1996.

Phillips, Christopher. *The Battle for Syria: International Rivalry in the New Middle East.* New Haven: Yale University Press, 2016.

Phillips, Hugh D. *Between the Revolution and the West: A Political Biography of Maxim M. Litvinov.* Boulder: Westview Press, 1992.

Phillips, Victoria. *Martha Graham's Cold War: The Dance of American Diplomacy.* New York: Oxford University Press, 2020.

Piero Gleijeses, *Conflicting Missions: Havana, Washington, and Africa, 1959–1976.* Chapel Hill: University of North Carolina Press, 2002.

Pipes, Richard. *Alexander Yakovlev: The Man Whose Ideas Delivered Russia from Communism.* DeKalb: Northern Illinois University Press, 2015.

Pipes, Richard. "Russia's Past, Russia's Future," *Commentary*, Vol. 101, No. 6 (June 1996), 30–38.

Pleshakov, Constantine. *The Crimean Nexus: Putin's War and the Clash of Civilizations.* New Haven: Yale University Press, 2017.

Plokhy, Serhii. *Forgotten Bastards of the Eastern Front: American Airmen behind the Soviet Lines and the Collapse of the Grand Alliance.* New York: Oxford University Press, 2019.

Plokhy, Serhii. *The Gates of Europe: A History of Ukraine.* New York: Basic Books, 2021.

Plokhy, Serhii. *The Last Empire: The Final Days of the Soviet Union.* New York: Basic Books, 2014.

Plokhy, Serhii. *Nuclear Folly: A History of the Cuban Missile Crisis.* New York: W. W. Norton, 2021.

Plokhy, Serhii. *The Russo-Ukrainian War: The Return of History.* New York: W. W. Norton, 2023.

Plokhy, S. M. *Yalta: The Price of Peace.* New York: Viking, 2010.

Polese, Abel. "Ukraine 2004: Informal Networks, Transformation of Social Capital and Coloured Revolutions," *Journal of Communist Studies and Transition Politics*, Vol. 25, Nos. 2–3 (June–September 2009), 255–277.

Ponomarev, V. N. *Krymskaia voina i russko-amerikanskie otnosheniia.* Moscow: Institut vseobshchei istorii RAN, 1993.

Pons, Silvio. *The Global Revolution: A History of International Communism, 1917–1991.* New York: Oxford University Press, 2014.

Power, Samantha. *The Education of an Idealist: A Memoir.* New York: William Morrow, 2019.

Powers, Richard Gid. *Not without Honor: The History of American Anticommunism.* New York: Free Press, 1995.

Pozniakov, V. V. "Amerikanskaia gumanitarnaia pomoshch' sovetskomu narodu (1941–1945)," in *Amerikanskii ezhegodnik, 1990,* Moscow: Nauka, 1991, 38–56.

Prados, John. *The Ghosts of Langley: Into the CIA's Heart of Darkness.* New York: New Press, 2017.

Preston, Andrew. "Peripheral Visions: American Mainline Protestants and the Global Cold War," *Cold War History,* Vol. 13, No. 1 (2013), 109–130.

Preston, Andrew. *Sword of the Spirit, Shield of Faith: Religion in American War and Diplomacy.* New York: Knopf, 2012.

Prevots, Naima. *Dance for Export: Cultural Diplomacy and the Cold War.* Middletown, CT: Wesleyan University Press, 1998.

Price, Jacob M. "The Tobacco Adventure to Russia: Enterprise, Politics, and Diplomacy in the Quest for a Northern Market for English Colonial Tobacco, 1676–1722," *Transactions of the American Philosophical Society,* New Series, Vol. 51, No. 1 1961), pp. 1–120.

Procter, Ben. *William Randolph Hearst: The Later Years, 1911–1951.* New York: Oxford University Press, 2007.

Puleston, William. *The Life and Work of Captain Alfred Thayer Mahan, U.S.N.* New Haven: Yale University Press, 1939.

Queen, G. S. "Wharton Barker and Concessions in Imperial Russia, 1878–1892," *Journal of Modern History,* Vol. 17, No. 3 (1945), 202–214.

Qing, Simei. *From Allies to Enemies: Visions of Modernity, Identity, and U.S.–China Diplomacy, 1945–1960.* Cambridge, MA: Harvard University Press, 2007.

Radchenko, Sergey. *To Run the World: The Kremlin's Cold War Bid for Global Power.* Cambridge: Cambridge University Press, 2024.

Raeff, Marc. "An American View of the Decembrist Revolt," *The Journal of Modern History,* Vol. 25, No. 3 (September 1953), 286–293.

Raleigh, Donald J. *Soviet Baby Boomers: An Oral History of Russia's Cold War Generation.* New York: Oxford University Press, 2012.

Ramseur, David. *Melting the Ice Curtain: The Extraordinary Story of Citizen Diplomacy on the Russia–Alaska Frontier.* Fairbanks: University of Alaska Press, 2017.

Reddaway, Peter and Dmitri Glinski. *The Tragedy of Russia's Reforms: Market Bolshevism against Democracy.* Washington: United States Institute of Peace Press, 2001.

Reid, Susan E. "Who Will Beat Whom? Soviet Popular Reception of the American National Exhibition in Moscow, 1959," *Kritika,* Vol. 9, No. 4 (Fall 2008), 855–904.

Rhodes, Benjamin D. *James P. Goodrich, Indiana's "Governor Strangelove": A Republican's Infatuation with Soviet Russia.* Selinsgrove: Susquehanna University Press, 1996.

Rhodes, Benjamin D. *The Anglo-American Winter War with Russia.* New York: Greenwood Press, 1988.

Riccardi-Swartz, Sarah. *Between Heaven and Russia: Religious Conversion and Political Apostasy in Appalachia.* New York: Fordham University Press, 2022.

Richard, Carl J. *When the United States Invaded Russia: Woodrow Wilson's Siberian Disaster.* Lanham, MD: Rowman & Littlefield, 2012.

Richman, Alvin. "Changing American Attitudes toward the Soviet Union," *Public Opinion Quarterly*, Vol. 55, No. 1 (1991), 135–148.

Richman, John. *The United States and the Soviet Union: The Decision to Recognize.* Raleigh: Camberleigh and Hall, 1980.

Richmond, Yale. *Cultural Exchange and the Cold War: Raising the Iron Curtain.* University Park: Pennsylvania State University Press, 2003.

Rieber, Alfred J. *Stalin and the Struggle for Supremacy in Eurasia.* Cambridge: Cambridge University Press, 2015.

Rielage, Dale C. *Russian Supply Efforts in America during the First World War.* Jefferson, NC: McFarland, 2002.

Robert Jervis, "Identity and the Cold War," in Melvyn Leffler and Odd Arne Westad, eds. *The Cambridge History of the Cold War*, Vol. II. Cambridge: Cambridge University Press, 2010, 22–43.

Roberts, Geoffrey. *Molotov: Stalin's Cold Warrior.* Washington: Potomac Books, 2012.

Roberts, Geoffrey. *Stalin's Wars: From World War to Cold War, 1939–1953.* New Haven: Yale University Press, 2006.

Robinson, Harlow. *Russians in Hollywood, Hollywood's Russians: Biography of an Image.* Boston: Northeastern University Press, 2007.

Robinson, Paul. *Russian Conservatism.* DeKalb: Northern Illinois University Press, 2019.

Rodgers, Daniel T. *Atlantic Crossings: Social Politics in a Progressive Age.* Cambridge, MA: Harvard University Press, 1998.

Rogger, Hans. "America in the Russian Mind, or Discoveries of America," *Pacific Historical Review*, Vol. 47, No. 1 (February 1978), 27–51.

Rogger, Hans. "*Amerikanizm* and the Economic Development of Russia," *Comparative Studies in Society and History*, Vol. 23, No. 3 (July 1981), 382–420.

Rogger, Hans. "Russia and the Civil War," in Harold Hyman, ed. *Heard round the World: The Impact Abroad of the Civil War.* New York: Knopf, 1969, 177–256.

Roman, Meredith L. *Opposing Jim Crow: African Americans and the Soviet Indictment of U.S. Racism, 1928–1937.* Lincoln, NE: University of Nebraska Press, 2012.

Romaniello, Matthew P. "Through the Filter of Tobacco: The Limits of Global Trade in the Early Modern World," *Comparative Studies in Society and History*, Vol. 49, No. 4 (October 2007), 914–937.

Romanov, Boris Alexandrovich. *Ocherki diplomaticheskoi istorii Russko-iaponskoi voiny, 1895–1907.* Moscow and Leningrad: Nauka, 1955.

Rosenberg, Emily. "Consumer Capitalism and the End of the Cold War," in Melvyn Leffler and Odd Arne Westad, eds. *The Cambridge History of the Cold War*, Vol. III: *Endings*. Cambridge: Cambridge University Press, 2010, 489–512.

Rosenberg, Jonathan. *How Far the Promised Land? World Affairs and the American Civil Rights Movement from the First World War to Vietnam*. Princeton: Princeton University Press, 2006.

Ross, Steven J. *Working-Class Hollywood: Silent Film and the Shaping of Class in America*. Princeton: Princeton University Press, 1998.

Rossinow, Doug. *The Reagan Era: A History of the 1980s*. New York: Columbia University Press, 2015.

Roth-Ey, Kristin. *Moscow Prime Time: How The Soviet Union Built the Media Empire That Lost the Cultural Cold War*. Ithaca, NY: Cornell University Press, 2011.

Rotter, Andrew J. *Hiroshima: The World's Bomb*. New York: Oxford University Press, 2008.

Rubenstein, Joshua. *Tangled Loyalties: The Life and Times of Ilya Ehrenburg*. New York: Basic Books, 1996.

Ruotsila, Markku. *John Spargo and American Socialism*. New York: Palgrave, 2006.

Rupprecht, Tobias. *Soviet Internationalism after Stalin: Interaction and Exchange between the USSR and Latin America during the Cold War*. Cambridge: Cambridge University Press, 2015.

Ryan, Alan. *John Dewey and the High Tide of American Liberalism*. New York: W. W. Norton, 1995.

Ryan, James G. *Earl Browder: The Failure of American Communism*. Tuscaloosa: University of Alabama Press, 1997.

Sakwa, Richard. *Frontline Ukraine: Crisis in the Borderlands*. London: I.B. Tauris, 2015.

Sakwa, Richard. *Putin and the Oligarch: The Khodorkovsky–Yukos Affair*. London: I.B. Tauris, 2014.

Sakwa, Richard. *The Lost Peace: How the West Failed to Prevent a Second Cold War*. New Haven: Yale University Press, 2023.

Sakwa, Richard. *The Putin Paradox*. London: I.B. Tauris, 2020.

Salvatore, Nick. *Eugene V. Debs: Citizen and Socialist*. Urbana: University of Illinois Press, 1982.

Salzman, Neil V. *Reform and Revolution: The Life and Times of Raymond Robins*. Kent, OH: Kent State University Press, 1991.

Sanborn, Joshua A. *Imperial Apocalypse: The Great War and the Destruction of the Russian Empire*. New York: Oxford University Press, 2014.

Sanchez-Sibony, Oscar. *Red Globalization: The Political Economy of the Soviet Cold War from Stalin to Khrushchev*. Cambridge: Cambridge University Press, 2014.

Sandbrook, Dominic. "Salesmanship and Substance: The Influence of Domestic Policy and Watergate," in Frederik Logevall and Andrew Preston, eds. *Nixon in the World: American Foreign Relations, 1969–1977*. New York: Oxford University Press, 2008, 85–103.

Sarantakes, Nicholas Evan. *Dropping the Torch: Jimmy Carter, the Olympic Boycott, and the Cold War*. New York: Cambridge University Press, 2011.

Sarotte, Mary Elise. *Not One Inch: America, Russia, and the Making of Post-Cold War Stalemate*. New Haven: Yale University Press, 2021.

Sarotte, Mary Elise. *1989: The Struggle to Create Post-Cold War Europe*. Princeton: Princeton University Press, 2009.

Saul, Norman E. *Concord and Conflict: The United States and Russia, 1867–1914*. Lawrence, KS: University Press of Kansas, 1996.

Saul, Norman E. *Distant Friends: The United States and Russia, 1763–1867*. Lawrence, KS: University Press of Kansas, 1991.

Saul, Norman E., "A Diplomatic Failure and an Ecological Disaster: The United States, Russia, and the North Pacific Fur Seals, 1867–1914," in *Russkoe otkrytie Ameriki: Sbornik statei, posviashchennyi 70-letiiu akademika N. N. Bolkhovitinova*. Moscow: Rosspen, 2002, 255–256.

Saul, Norman E. *Friends or Foes? The United States and Russia, 1921–1941*. Lawrence, KS: University Press of Kansas, 2006.

Saul, Norman E. *The Life and Times of Charles R. Crane, 1858–1939: American Businessman, Philanthropist, and the Founder of Russian Studies in America*. Lanham, MD: Lexington Books, 2013.

Saul, Norman E. *War and Revolution: The United States and Russia, 1914–1921*. Lawrence, KS: University Press of Kansas, 2001.

Savranskaya, Svetlana and William Taubman, "Soviet foreign policy, 1962–1975," in M. Leffler and O. A. Westad, eds. *The Cambridge History of the Cold War*, Vol. II: *Crises and Détente*. Cambridge: Cambridge University Press, 2010, 134–157.

Scanlon, Sandra. "'Building Consensus': The Republican Right and Foreign Policy, 1960–1980," in Robert Mason and Iwan Morgan, eds. *Seeking a New Majority: The Republican Party and American Politics, 1960–1980*. Nashville: Vanderbilt University Press, 2013, 143–159.

Schachner, Nathan. *The Price of Liberty: A History of the American Jewish Committee*. New York: American Jewish Committee, 1948.

Schattenberg, Susanne. *Brezhnev: The Making of a Statesman*. London: I.B. Tauris, 2022.

Schimmelpenninck, David van der Oye. *Toward the Rising Sun: Russian Ideologies of Empire and the Path to War with Japan*. DeKalb: Northern Illinois University Press, 2001.

Schlesinger, Arthur M., Jr. "The Origins of the Cold War," *Foreign Affairs*, Vol. 46, No. 1 (October 1967), 22–52.

Schlesinger, Arthur M., Jr. *A Thousand Days: John F. Kennedy in the White House*. Boston: Houghton Mifflin, 1965.

Schlesinger, Arthur M., Jr. *Robert Kennedy and His Times*. Boston: Houghton Mifflin, 1978.

Schoenberg, Philip E. "The American Reaction to the Kishinev Pogrom of 1903," *American Jewish Historical Quarterly*, Vol. 63, No. 3 (1947), 263–283.

Schrecker, Ellen. ed. *Cold War Triumphalism.* New York: New Press, 2004.

Schulzinger, Robert D. *Henry Kissinger: Doctor of Diplomacy.* New York: Columbia University Press, 1989.

Schweizer, Peter. *Reagan's War: The Epic Story of His Forty-Year Struggle and Final Triumph over Communism.* New York: Doubleday, 2002.

Schweizer, Peter. *Victory: The Reagan Administration's Secret Strategy That Hastened the Collapse of the Soviet Union.* New York: Atlantic Monthly Press, 1994.

Scott, Mark and Semyon Krasilshchik, *Yanks Meet Reds: Recollections of U.S. and Soviet Vets from the Linkup in World War II.* Santa Barbara: Capra Press, 1988.

Searcy, Anne. *Ballet in the Cold War.* New York: Oxford University Press, 2020.

Seeger, Murray. *Discovering Russia: 200 Years of American Journalism.* Bloomington: Authorhouse, 2005.

Seidman, Michael. *Transatlantic Antifascisms: From the Spanish Civil War to the End of World War II.* Cambridge: Cambridge University Press, 2018.

Sergeev, Evgeny. *The Great Game, 1856–1907: Russo-British Relations in Central and East Asia.* Baltimore: Johns Hopkins University Press, 2013.

Service, Robert. *The End of the Cold War, 1985–1991.* New York: Public Affairs, 2015.

Sevost'ianov, G. N. *Moskva–Vashington: Na puti k priznaniiu 1918–1933.* Moscow: Nauka, 2004.

Shankman Arnold, "Brothers across the Sea. Afro-Americans on the Persecution of Russian Jews, 1881–1917," *Jewish Social Studies,* Vol. 27, No. 2 (1974), 114–121.

Sharafutdinova, Gulnaz. *The Red Mirror: Putin's Leadership and Russia's Insecure Identity.* New York: Oxford University Press, 2020.

Shatsillo, Vyacheslav K. *Rasschet i bezrassudstvo: Germano-amerikanskie otnosheniia 1898–1917.* Moscow: Institut vseobshchei istorii RAN, 1998.

Shatsillo, Vyacheslav K. *Rossiia i SShA: Ot Portsmutskogo mira do padeniia tsarisma.* Moscow: Tovarishchestvo nauchnykh izdanii KMK, 2019.

Shaw, Tony and Denise J. Youngblood, *Cinematic Cold War: The American and Soviet Struggle for Hearts and Minds.* Lawrence, KS: University Press of Kansas, 2010.

Shaw, Tony. *Hollywood's Cold War.* Amherst: University of Massachusetts Press, 2007.

Shekhovtsov, Anton. "Aleksandr Dugin's Neo-Eurasianism and the Russian–Ukrainian War," in Mark Bassin and Gonzalo Pozo, eds. *The Politics of Eurasianism: Identity, Popular Culture and Russia's Foreign Policy.* Lanham, MD: Rowman & Littlefield, 2017, 181–200.

Shelokhaev, Valentin Valentinovich, ed. *Liberal'noe dvizhenie v Rossii 1902–1905 gg.* Moscow: Rosspen, 2001.

Sherry, Michael S. *In the Shadow of War: The United States since the 1930s.* New Haven: Yale University Press, 1995.

Shewmaker, Kenneth E., "Neill S. Brown's Mission to Russia, 1850–53," *Diplomacy and Statecraft,* Vol. 12, No. 4 (December 2001), 81–98.

Shishkin, V. A. *Stanovlenie vneshnei politiki poslerevoliutsionnoi Rossii (1917–1930 gody) i kapitalisticheskii mir: Ot revoliutsionnogo "zapadnichestva" k "natsional-bol'shevizmu": Ocherk istorii.* St. Petersburg: Dmitrii Bulanin, 2002.

Short, Philip. *Putin.* New York: Henry Holt and Company, 2022.

Shpotov, Boris Mikhailovich. "Vzaimospriatie amerikantsev i russkikh v gody pervoi piatiletki (po materialam pressy i delovoi perepiski)," *Otechestvennaia Istoriia,* No. 4 (2007), 135–140.

Shpotov, Boris Mikhailovich. *Amerikanskii biznes i Sovetskii Soiuz v 1920–1930-e gody: Labirinty ekonomicheskogo sotrudnichestva.* Moscow: Librokom, 2013.

Shpotov, Boris Mikhailovich. *Genri Ford: Zhizn' i biznes.* Moscow: Knizhyi dom UNIVERSITET, 2003.

Shulim, J. I. "The United States Views Russia in the Napoleonic Age," *Proceedings of the American Philosophical Society,* Vol. 102, No. 2 (April 1958), 148–159.

Sibley, Katherine A. S. *Red Spies in America: Stolen Secrets and the Dawn of the Cold War.* Lawrence, KS: University Press of Kansas, 2004.

Sidel'nikov, Leonid Sergeevich and Galina Alexeevna, Pribegina. *25 dnei v Amerike.* Moscow: Muzyka, 1991.

Simes, Dimitri K. *After the Collapse: Russia Seeks Its Place as a Great Power.* New York: Simon & Schuster, 1999.

Sirgiovanni, George. *An Undercurrent of Suspicion: Anti-communism in America during World War II.* New Brunswick: Transaction Publishers, 1990.

Sivachev, N. V. and N. N. Yakovlev, *Russia and the United States: U.S.–Soviet Relations from the Soviet Point of View.* Chicago: University of Chicago Press, 1979.

Small, Melvin. "How We Learned to Love the Russians: American Media and the Soviet Union during World War II," *Historian,* Vol. 36, No. 3 (May 1974), 455–478.

Smelser, Ronald and Edward J. Davies II, *The Myth of the Eastern Front: The Nazi–Soviet War in American Popular Culture.* Cambridge: Cambridge University Press, 2008.

Smith, Gaddis. *Morality, Reason, and Power: American Diplomacy in the Carter Years.* New York: Hill and Wang, 1986.

Smith, S.A. *Russia in Revolution: An Empire in Crisis, 1890–1928.* New York: Oxford University Press, 2017.

Smith-Peter, Susan. "The Russian Federalist Papers: Alexei Evstaf'ev, the War of 1812, and Russian–American Relations," in William Benton Whisenhunt and Norman E. Saul, eds. *New Perspectives on Russian–American Relations.* New York: Routledge, 2016, 20–35.

Snyder, Sarah B. *Human Rights Activism and the End of the Cold War: A Transnational History of the Helsinki Network.* New York: Cambridge University Press, 2011.

Sokolov, Boris, Ronald F. Inglehart, Eduard Ponarin, Irina Vartanova, and William Zimmerman. "Disillusionment and Anti-Americanism in Russia: From Pro-American to Anti-American Attitudes, 1993–2009," *International Studies Quarterly,* Vol. 62, No. 3 (2018), 534–547.

Soldatov, Andrei and Michael Rochlitz. "The *Siloviki* in Russian Politics," in Daniel Treisman, ed. *The New Autocracy: Information, Politics, and Policy in Putin's Russia.* Washington: Brookings Institution Press, 2018, 83–108.

Somin, Ilya. *Stillborn Crusade: The Tragic Failure of Allied Intervention in the Russian Civil War*. New Brunswick: Transaction Publishers, 1996.

Sparrow, Bartholomew. *The Strategist: Brent Scowcroft and the Call of National Security*. New York: Public Affairs, 2015.

Sperling, Valerie. *Sex, Politics, and Putin: Political Legitimacy in Russia*. New York: Oxford University Press, 2015.

Starr, S. Frederick. *Red and Hot: The Fate of Jazz in the Soviet Union*. New York: Oxford University Press, 1985.

Steel, Ronald. *Walter Lippmann and the American Century*. Boston: Little, Brown and Company, 1980.

Steil, Benn. *The Battle of Bretton Woods: John Maynard Keynes, Harry Dexter White, and the Making of a New World Order*. Princeton: Princeton University Press, 2013.

Steil, Benn. *The Marshall Plan: Dawn of the Cold War*. New York: Oxford University Press, 2021.

Steinberg, John W., Bruce W. Menning, David Schimmelpenninck van der Oye, David Wolff, and Shinji Yokote, eds. *The Russo-Japanese War in Global Perspective: World War Zero*. Leiden: Brill, 2007.

Steinberg, Mark D. *The Russian Revolution, 1905–1921*. New York: Oxford University Press, 2017.

Stent, Angela E. *Putin's World: Russia against the West and with the Rest*. New York: Twelve, 2019.

Stent, Angela. *The Limits of Partnership: U.S.–Russian Relations in the Twenty-First Century*. Princeton: Princeton University Press, 2014.

Stephanson, Anders. "The Cold War Considered as a US Project," in Silvio Pons and Federico Romero, eds. *Reinterpreting the End of the Cold War*. London: Frank Cass, 2005, 52–67.

Stillé, Charles J. "The Life and Services of Joel R. Poinsett," *The Pennsylvania Magazine of History and Biography*, Vol. 12, No. 2 (July 1888).

Stockdale, Melissa Kirschke. *Mobilizing the Russian Nation: Patriotism and Citizenship in the First World War*. Cambridge: Cambridge University Press, 2016.

Stoner, Kathryn and Michael McFaul. "Who Lost Russia (This Time)? Vladimir Putin," *Washington Quarterly*, Vol. 38, No. 2 (Summer 2015), 167–187.

Stoner, Kathryn. *Russia Resurrected: Its Power and Purpose in a New Global Order*. New York: Oxford University Press, 2021.

Storrs, Landon R. Y. *The Second Red Scare and the Unmaking of the New Deal Left*. Princeton: Princeton University Press, 2013.

Strakhovsky, Leonid. *American Opinion about Russia, 1917–1920* Toronto: University of Toronto Press, 1961.

Stults, Taylor. "Roosevelt, Russian Persecution of Jews, and American Public Opinion," *Jewish Social Studies*, Vol. 33, No. 1 (January 1971), 13–22

Suprun, M. N., ed. *Lend-liz i Rossiia*. Arkhangel'sk: OAO "IPP 'Pravda Severa'," 2006.

Sutton, Antony C. *Western Technology and Soviet Economic Development, 1917 to 1930*. Stanford: Hoover Institution Press, 1968.

Swain, Geoffrey. *The Origins of the Russian Civil War*. London: Longman, 1996.

Swerdlow, Amy. *Women Strike for Peace: Traditional Motherhood and Radical Politics in the 1960s*. Chicago: University of Chicago Press, 1993.

Tanenhaus, Sam. *Whittaker Chambers: A Biography*. New York: Random House, 1997.

Tarsaidze Alexandre. "American Pioneers in Russian Railroad Building," *Russian Review*, Vol. 9, No. 4 (October 1950), 286–295.

Taubman, Philip. *In the Nation's Service: The Life and Times of George P. Shultz*. Stanford: Stanford University Press, 2023.

Taubman, William. *Gorbachev: His Life and Times*. New York: W. W. Norton, 2017.

Taubman, William. *Khrushchev: The Man and His Era*. New York: W. W. Norton, 2003.

Taubman, William. *Stalin's American Policy: From Entente to Détente to Cold War*. New York: W. W. Norton, 1982.

Taylor, Richard. *The Politics of the Soviet Cinema, 1917–1929*. Cambridge: Cambridge University Press, 1979.

Teel, Leonard Ray. *Ralph Emerson McGill: Voice of the Southern Conscience*. Knoxville: University of Tennessee Press, 2001.

Thompson, Arthur W. and Robert A. Hart. *The Uncertain Crusade: America and the Russian Revolution of 1905*. Amherst: University of Massachusetts, 1970.

Thompson, Jenny and Sherry Thompson. *The Kremlinologists: Llewellyn E. Thompson. America's Man in Cold War Moscow*. Baltimore: Johns Hopkins University Press, 2018.

Thorson, Winston B. "American Public Opinion and the Portsmouth Peace Conference," *American Historical Review*, Vol. 53, No. 3 (April 1948), 439–448.

Tierney, Dominic. *FDR and the Spanish Civil War: Neutrality and Commitment in the Struggle That Divided America*. Durham, NC: Duke University Press, 2007.

Toal, Gerard. *Near Abroad: Putin, the West, and the Contest over Ukraine and the Caucasus*. New York: Oxford University Press, 2017.

Tobin, Conor. "The Myth of the 'Afghan Trap': Zbigniew Brzezinski and Afghanistan, 1978–1979," *Diplomatic History*, Vol. 44, No. 2 (April 2020), 237–264.

Tomoff, Kiril. *Virtuosi Abroad: Soviet Music and Imperial Competition during the Early Cold War, 1945–1958*. Ithaca, NY: Cornell University Press, 2015.

Tooze, Adam. *The Deluge: The Great War, America and the Remaking of the Global Order, 1916–1931*. New York: Viking, 2014.

Trachtenberg, Marc. "The United States and Eastern Europe in 1945," *Journal of Cold War Studies*, Vol. 10, No. 4 (Fall 2008), 94–132.

Trachtenberg, Marc. *A Constructed Peace: The Making of the European Settlement*. Princeton: Princeton University Press, 1999.

Trani, Eugene P. *The Treaty of Portsmouth: An Adventure in American Diplomacy*. Lexington: University of Kentucky Press, 1969.

Trani, Eugene P. and Donald E. Davis. *The First Cold War: The Legacy of Woodrow Wilson in U.S.–Soviet Relations*. Columbia: University of Missouri Press, 2002.

Travis, Frederick F. *George Kennan and the American–Russian Relationship, 1865–1924.* Athens, OH: Ohio University Press, 1990.

Treisman, Daniel. *The Return: Russia's Journey from Gorbachev to Medvedev.* New York: Free Press, 2011.

Tremlett, Giles. *The International Brigades: Fascism, Freedom and the Spanish Civil War.* London: Bloomsbury Publishing, 2020.

Tromly, Benjamin. *Cold War Exiles and the CIA: Plotting to Free Russia.* New York: Oxford University Press, 2019.

Troy, Gil. *Morning in America: How Ronald Reagan Invented the 1980s.* Princeton: Princeton University Press, 2005.

Tsipursky, Gleb. *Socialist Fun: Youth, Consumption, and State-Sponsored Popular Culture in the Soviet Union, 1945–1970.* Pittsburgh: University of Pittsburgh Press, 2016.

Tsygankov, Andrei. *The Dark Double: US Media, Russia, and the Politics of Values.* New York: Oxford University Press, 2019.

Tsygankov, Andrei P. *Russia and America: The Asymmetric Rivalry.* Cambridge: Polity, 2019.

Tsygankov, Andrei P. *Russia's Foreign Policy: Change and Continuity in National Identity,* 4th ed. Lanham, MD: Rowman & Littlefield, Fourth Edition, 2016.

Tsygankov, Andrei P. *Russophobia: The Anti-Russian Lobby and American Foreign Policy.* New York: Palgrave Macmillan 2009.

Tsygankov, Andrei P. *The Strong State in Russia: Development and Crisis.* New York: Oxford University Press, 2014.

Tucker, Robert C. *Political Culture and Leadership in Soviet Russia: From Lenin to Gorbachev.* New York: W. W. Norton, 1988.

Tucker, Robert C. *Stalin as Revolutionary, 1879–1929.* New York: W. W. Norton, 1973.

Tucker, Robert C. *Stalin in Power: The Revolution from Above, 1928–1941.* New York: W. W. Norton, 1990.

Tumulty, Karen. *The Triumph of Nancy Reagan.* New York: Simon & Schuster, 2021.

Turek, Lauren Frances. "A New Strategy for Peace? Public Opposition to Détente during Nixon's Era of Negotiation," M.A. thesis, University of Virginia, 2009.

Turygin, Aleksandr A., Boris V. Kupriianov, and Artem A. Talalaev. "Politicheskaia sotsializatsiia sovestkikh shkolnikov v prostranstve detskoi publichnoi diplomatii (na primere mezdunarodnykh vizitov)," *Sib Skript,* Vol. 25, No. 3 (2023), 332–342.

Tuveson, Ernest Lee. *Redeemer Nation: The Idea of America's Millennial Role.* Chicago: University of Chicago Press, 1968.

Tzouliadis, Tim. *The Forsaken: An American Tragedy in Stalin's Russia.* New York: Penguin, 2008.

Uldricks, Teddy J. "Russia and Europe: Diplomacy, Revolution, and Economic Development in the 1920s," *International History Review,* Vol. 1, No. 1 (January 1979), 55–83.

Unger, Nancy C. *Fighting Bob La Follette.* Madison: Wisconsin Historical Society Press, 2008.

Unterberger, Betty M. "Woodrow Wilson and the Russian Revolution," in Arthur Link, ed. *Woodrow Wilson and a Revolutionary World.* Chapel Hill: University of North Carolina Press, 1982.

Unterberger, Betty M. *Intervention against Communism: Did the United States Try to Overthrow the Soviet Government, 1918–1920?* College Station: Texas A&M Press, 1987.

Unterberger, Betty M. *The United States, Revolutionary Russia, and the Rise of Czechoslovakia.* Chapel Hill: University of North Carolina Press, 1989.

Vaisse, Justin. *Neoconservatism: The Biography of a Movement.* Cambridge, MA: Harvard University Press, 2010.

Vaisse, Justin. *Zbigniew Brzezinski: America's Grand Strategist.* Cambridge, MA: Harvard University Press, 2018.

Van Herpen, Marcel. *Putin's Wars: The Rise of Russia's New Imperialism.* Lanham, MD: Rowman & Littlefield, 2014.

Velikanova, Olga. *Popular Perceptions of Soviet Politics in the 1920s: Disenchantment of the Dreamers.* New York: Palgrave Macmillan, 2013.

Vereshchagin, Vasily Vasil'evich. *Moi puti-dorogi.* Moscow: Koktebel', 2018.

Vereshchagin, Vasily Vasilievich. *Vospominaniia syna khudozhnika.* Leningrad: Khudozhnik RSFSR, 1978.

Vinkovetsky Ilya. *Russian America: An Overseas Colony of a Continental Empire, 1804–1867.* Oxford: Oxford University Press, 2011.

Volkogonov, Dmitri. *Stalin: Triumph and Tragedy.* New York: Grove Weidenfeld, 1991.

Walker, Dale L., *Januarius MacGahan: The Life and Campaigns of an American War Correspondent.* Athens, OH: Ohio University Press, 1988.

Waller, Douglas C. *Congress and the Nuclear Freeze: An Inside Look at the Politics of a Mass Movement.* Amherst: University of Massachusetts Press, 1987.

Walt, Stephen M. *The Hell of Good Intentions: America's Foreign Policy Elite and the Decline of U.S. Primacy.* New York: Farrar, Straus and Giroux, 2018.

Wandycz, Piotr S. *The United States and Poland.* Cambridge, MA: Harvard University Press, 1980.

Ward, Dan. "'Your Body Belongs to the State': The Mobilization of the Action Heroine in Service of the State in Red Sparrow and Atomic Blonde," in Tatiana Prorokova-Konrad, ed. *Cold War II: Hollywood's Renewed Obsession with Russia.* Jackson: University Press of Mississippi, 2020, 112–128.

Warner, Gale. *The Invisible Threads: Independent Soviets Working for Global Awareness and Social Transformation.* Washington: Seven Locks Press, 1991.

Warner, Gale and Michael Shuman. *Citizen Diplomats: Pathfinders in Soviet–American Relations and How You Can Join Them.* New York: Continuum, 1987.

Warren, Frank A. *Liberals and Communism: The "Red Decade" Revisited.* New York: Columbia University Press, 1993 (1st ed. 1966).

Watson, Derek. *Molotov: A Biography.* Basingstoke: Palgrave Macmillan, 2005.

Weeks, Albert L. *Russia's Life-Saver: Lend-Lease Aid to the U.S.S.R. in World War II.* Lanham, MD: Rowman & Littlefield, 2004.

Weinstein, Allen and Alexander Vassiliev. *The Haunted Wood: Soviet Espionage in America – the Stalin Era.* New York: Random House, 1999.

Wendt, Alexander. *Social Theory of International Politics.* New York: Cambridge University Press, 2004.

Westad, Odd Arne. *The Global Cold War: Third World Interventions and the Making of Our Times.* Cambridge: Cambridge University Press, 2005.

Westad, Odd Arne. *Reviewing the Cold War: Approaches, Interpretations, Theory.* London: Frank Cass, 2000.

Westwick, Peter J. "'Space-Strike Weapons' and the Soviet Response to SDI," *Diplomatic History,* Vol. 32, No. 5 (November 2008), 955–979.

Whisenhunt, William Benton. "In the Service of the Tsar: American Surgeons in the Crimean War, 1853–1856," in William Benton Whisenhunt and Norman E. Saul, eds. *New Perspectives on Russian–American Relations.* New York: Routledge, 2016.

White, Graham and John Maze. *Henry A. Wallace: His Search for a New World Order.* Chapel Hill: University of North Carolina Press, 1995.

Wieczerzak, Joseph. "American Reactions to the Polish Insurrection of 1863," *Polish American Studies,* Vol. 22, No. 2 (1965), 90–98.

Wieczerzak, Joseph W. *A Polish Chapter in Civil War America: The Effects of the January Insurrection on American Opinion and Diplomacy.* New York: Twayne, 1967.

Wilentz, Sean. *The Age of Reagan: A History, 1974–2008.* New York: Harper Collins, 2008.

Willett, Robert L. *Russian Sideshow: America's Undeclared War, 1918–1920.* Washington: Brassey's, 2003.

Williams, William Appleman. *American–Russian Relations, 1781–1947.* New York and Toronto: Rinehart & Co., 1952.

Williams, William Appleman. *The Roots of the Modern American Empire: A Study of the Growth and Shaping of Social Consciousness in a Marketplace Society.* New York: Random House, 1969.

Willnat, Lars, Shuo Tang, Jian Shi, and Ning Zhan. "Media Use and National Image: How Americans and Chinese Perceive the U.S.–China Trade War," *International Communication Gazette,* Vol. 84, No. 7–8 (2022), 633–654.

Wilson, James Graham. *The Triumph of Improvisation: Gorbachev's Adaptability, Reagan's Engagement, and the End of the Cold War.* Ithaca, NY: Cornell University Press, 2014.

Wilson, Joan Hoff. "American Business and the Recognition of the Soviet Union," *Social Science Quarterly,* Vol. 52, No. 2 (September 1971), 349–368.

Wilson, Joan Hoff. *Ideology and Economics: U.S. Relations with the Soviet Union, 1918–1933.* Columbia: University of Missouri Press, 1974.

Winter, Jay, ed. *The Cambridge History of the First World War,* 3 vols. Cambridge: Cambridge University Press, 2014.

Wittner, Lawrence. *Resisting the Bomb: A History of the World Nuclear Disarmament Movement, 1954–1970.* Stanford: Stanford University Press, 1997.

Woldman, Albert A. *Lincoln and the Russians.* Cleveland, NY: World Publishing Company, 1952.

Wolff, Larry. *Woodrow Wilson and the Reimagining of Eastern Europe.* Stanford: Stanford University Press, 2020.

Woodruff, Louise. *"Buried in the Sands of the Ogaden": The United States, the Horn of Africa, and the Demise of Détente.* Kent, OH: Kent State University Press, 2013.

Wortman, Richard S. *Scenarious of Power: Myth and Ceremony in Russian Monarchy. From Peter the Great to the Abdication of Nicholas II.* Princeton: Princeton University Press, 2006.

Yablokov, Ilya. *Fortress Russia: Conspiracy Theories in Post-Soviet Russia.* Cambridge: Polity Press, 2018.

Yaqub, Salim. *Containing Arab Nationalism: The Eisenhower Doctrine and the Middle East.* Chapel Hill: University of North Carolina Press, 2004.

Yegorova, Natalia I. "The 'Iran Crisis' of 1945–46: A View from the Russian Archives," Cold War International History Project Working Paper No. 15, Washington, 1996.

Yergin, Daniel. *The Quest: Energy, Security, and the Remaking of the Modern World.* New York: Penguin, 2011.

Yoffe, Elkhonon. *Tchaikovsky in America: The Composer's Visit in 1891.* New York: Oxford University Press, 1986.

Youngblood, Denise J. "A War Remembered: Soviet Films of the Great Patriotic War," *American Historical Review,* Vol. 106, No. 3 (June 2001), 839–856.

Youngblood, Denise J. *Russian War Films: On the Cinema Front, 1914–2005.* Lawrence, KS: University Press of Kansas, 2007.

Youngblood, Denise J. *Soviet Cinema in the Silent Era, 1918–1935.* Ann Arbor: UMI Research Press, 1985.

Yurchak, Alexei. *Everything Was Forever, Until It Was No More: The Last Soviet Generation.* Princeton: Princeton University Press, 2005.

Zabriskie, Edward. *American–Russian Rivalry in the Far East.* Philadelphia: University of Pennsylvania Press, 1946.

Zegers, Peter Kort and Douglas Druick, eds. *Windows on the War: Soviet TASS Posters at Home and Abroad, 1941–1945.* New Haven: Yale University Press, 2011.

Zelizer, Julian E. *Arsenal of Democracy: The Politics of National Security – From World War II to the War on Terrorism.* New York: Basic Books, 2010.

Zelizer, Julian E. "Detente and Domestic Politics," *Diplomatic History,* Vol. 33, No. 4 (September 2009), 653–670.

Zhang, Hong. *America Perceived: The Making of Chinese Images of the United States, 1945–1953.* Westport, CT: Praeger, 2002.

Zhuk, Sergei I. *Nikolai Bolkhovitinov and American Studies in the USSR: People's Diplomacy in the Cold War.* Lanham, MD: Lexington Books, 2017.

Zhuk, Sergei I. *Rock and Roll in the Rocket City: The West, Identity, and Ideology in Soviet Dniepropetrovsk, 1960–1985.* Washington: Woodrow Wilson Center Press, 2010.

Zhuravleva, Victoria I. "American Corn in Russia: Lessons of the People-to-People Diplomacy and Capitalism," *Journal of Russian American Studies*, Vol. 1, No. 1 (May 2017), 23–45.

Zhuravleva, Victoria I. *The Common Past of Russians and Americans.* Moscow: Russian State University for the Humanities, 2021.

Zhuravleva, Victoria I. "Images of the United States in Putin's Russia, from Obama to Trump," *Journal of Soviet and Post-Soviet Politics and Society*, Vol. 4, No. 1 (2018), 145–181.

Zhuravleva, Victoria I. "Natsional'no-religioznyi vopros v rossiysko-amerikanskikh otnosheniiakh v period Pervoi mirovoi voiny," in *Amerikanskii ezhegodnik, 2002.* Moscow: Nauka, 2004, 215–243.

Zhuravleva, Victoria I. "Rethinking Russia in the United States during the First World War: Mr. Sigma's American Voyage," in William Benton Whisenhunt and Norman E. Saul, eds. *New Perspectives on Russian–American Relations.* New York: Routledge, 2016, 143–160.

Zhuravleva, Victoria I. "Russian Studies in the United States and *Amerikanistika* in the Russian Empire: Imagination and Study of the Other in the Context of Peace and World War," in Ivan Kurilla and Victoria I. Zhuravleva, eds. *Russian/Soviet Studies in the United States, Amerikanistika in Russia: Mutual Representations in Academic Projects.* New York: Lexington Books, 2016, 45–76.

Zhuravleva, Victoria I. *Ponimanie Rossii v SShA: Obrazy i mify. 1881–1914.* Moscow: Russian State University for the Humanities, 2012.

Zhuravleva, Victoria I. and David Foglesong, "Konstruirovanie obraza Rossii v amerikanskoi politicheskoi karikature XX veka," in Vadim A. Koleneko, ed. *Mify i realii amerikanskoi istorii v periodike XVIII–XX vv.*, Vol. 1. Moscow: Institut vseobshchei istorii RAN, 2008, 187–193.

Zipperstein, Steven J. *Pogrom: Kishinev and the Tilt of History.* New York: Liveright, 2018.

Zorin A. "Intellektualnye prikliucheniia russkogo antifederalista: Radishchev, Kondorse i amerikanskaia konstitutsiia," *Quaestio Rossica.* Vol. 9, No. 2 (2021), 679–701.

Zubkova, Elena. *Russia after the War: Hopes, Illusions, and Disappointments, 1945–1957*, translated and edited by Hugh Ragsdale. Armonk, NY: M. E. Sharpe, 1998.

Zubok, Vladislav M. *Collapse: The Fall of the Soviet Union.* New Haven: Yale University Press, 2021.

Zubok, Vladislav. *A Failed Empire: The Soviet Union in the Cold War from Stalin to Gorbachev.* Chapel Hill: University of North Carolina Press, 2008.

Zubok, Vladislav and Constantine Pleshakov, *Inside the Kremlin's Cold War: From Stalin to Khrushchev.* Cambridge, MA: Harvard University Press, 1996.

Zubok, V. M. and V. O. Pechatnov, "Otechestvennaia istoriografiia 'kholodnoi voiny,'" *Otechestvennaia istoriia*, No. 4 (2003), 143–150 and No. 5 (2003), 139–148.

Zubok, Vladislav M. "Soviet Policy Aims at the Geneva Conference, 1955," in Gunter Bischof and Saki Dockrill, eds. *Cold War Respite: The Geneva Summit of 1955*. Baton Rouge: Louisiana State University Press, 2000.

Zubok, Vladislav M. "Stalin, Soviet Intelligence, and the Struggle for Iran, 1945–53," *Diplomatic History*, Vol. 44, No. 1 (2020), 22–46.

Zubok, Vladislav M. *Zhivago's Children: The Last Russian Intelligentsia*. Cambridge, MA: Harvard University Press, 2009.

Zumoff, Jacob A. *The Communist International and US Communism, 1919–1929*. Chicago: Haymarket Books, 2015.

Zygar, Mikhail. *All the Kremlin's Men: Inside the Court of Vladimir Putin*. New York: Public Affairs, 2016.

Index